Dutch Contributions 1998
Linguistics

STUDIES IN
SLAVIC AND GENERAL
LINGUISTICS

VOLUME 24

edited by

A.A. Barentsen
B.M. Groen
J. Schaeken
R. Sprenger

Amsterdam - Atlanta, GA 1998

Dutch Contributions
to the Twelfth International
Congress of Slavists

Cracow

August 26 - September 3, 1998

Linguistics

edited by

A.A. Barentsen
B.M. Groen
J. Schaeken
R. Sprenger

♾ The paper on which this book is printed meets the requirements of "ISO 9706:1994, Information and documentation - Paper for documents - Requirements for permanence".

ISBN: 90-420-0702-8
©Editions Rodopi B.V., Amsterdam - Atlanta, GA 1998
Printed in the Netherlands

CONTENTS

Dutch Contributions to the Twelfth International Congress of Slavists, Cracow, Linguistics (= Studies in Slavic and General Linguistics Vol 24), 1–42. RODOPI, Amsterdam – Atlanta, GA 1998.

ОБ ИЗЪЯСНИТЕЛЬНЫХ ПРИДАТОЧНЫХ ПРЕДЛОЖЕНИЯХ ПРИ ГЛАГОЛАХ ОЖИДАНИЯ
(С НЕКОТОРЫМИ РЕЗУЛЬТАТАМИ ИССЛЕДОВАНИЯ КОМПЬЮТЕРНЫХ КОРПУСОВ РУССКИХ ТЕКСТОВ 19-ГО И 20-ГО ВВ.)*

АДРИАН БАРЕНТСЕН

1. Некоторые особенности русских глаголов ожидания

На основе сходных семантических признаков и общих особенностей синтаксического поведения принято выделять различные группы глаголов: "глаголы движения", "перформативные глаголы" и т.д. В русском языке к подобным группам можно отнести и "глаголы ожидания": *ждать, ожидать, дождаться-дожидаться, подождать* и некоторые другие.

В семантическом плане эти глаголы отличаются определенной двойственностью. Они сочетают признаки, характерные для глаголов физической деятельности и местонахождения, с признаками, характерными для глаголов умственной деятельности (ср. *ждал/стоял на углу (ждал долго* и т.д.) и *ждал/узнавал, придет ли Иван*). В нашей ранней статье мы выразили эту двойственность в следующей формулировке:

аспект А:	*пребывать в каком-то состоянии* (СОСТ),
аспект Б:	*считая возможным и вероятным, что произойдет какое-то событие* (СОБ) (Барентсен 1980б: 24)

В этой формулировке деепричастный оборот символизирует присутствие определенной связи между двумя названными аспектами значения глаголов ожидания: пребывание субъекта в состоянии СОСТ мотивировано именно тем, что у него есть представление о будущем событии СОБ.

Данная семантическая структура также хорошо отражается в удачном общем толковании глаголов ожидания, которое дается в замечательном новом лексикографическом труде *Новый объяснительный словарь синонимов русского языка* (Апресян и др. 1997):

'зная или считая, что должно или может произойти некое событие, нужное субъекту или касающееся его, быть в состоянии готовности к нему, обычно находясь в том месте, где оно произойдет' (Апресян 1997: 112).

В синтаксическом плане особенности глаголов ожидания проявляются прежде всего при выборе падежной формы объекта. Как известно, в роли объекта ожидания определенные существительные приобретают форму винительного падежа (*ждал* **маму**), другие — форму родительного падежа (*ждал* **восхода** *солнца*), а в ряде случаев возможны обе формы: *ждал поезд/поезда* (Зализняк 1967: 49; Барентсен 1980а).[1]

Однако, вариативность в управлении глаголов ожидания наблюдается не только у именных объектов, но в гораздо большем масштабе и в рамках сложного предложения. Рассмотрение этого явления — центральная тема нашей статьи.

Как и у многих других глаголов, вместо именной группы в качестве объекта при глаголах ожидания могут выступать придаточные предложения (объектно-)изъяснительного типа. Это и логично, поскольку именно предложение как основная предикативная структура наиболее полно может передавать представление о событии СОБ.

С формальной точки зрения самый простой случай представляют собой предложения с бессоюзным подчинением (более характерные для непринужденной речи):

(1)   Я потом часто бывала в этом доме и почти всегда ловила себя на том, что **жду** – *вот сейчас откроется дверь*, и войдет Прокофьев. (Вишневская)

Однако в большинстве случаев связь между изъясняемым словом и придаточной частью предложения производится посредством того или иного союза (или союзного слова). Выбор используемого союзного средства является самой естественной основой для классификации структур с изъяснительной придаточной частью. В АГ-80 (1980: 473) данные союзы делятся на три группы:

1) союзы, принадлежащие сфере повествования: *что* [...];
2) союзы, принадлежащие сфере волеизъявления: *чтобы* [...];
3) союзы, принадлежащие сфере вопроса: *ли* [...].

Возможность использовать союзное слово связывается с третьей группой: "Изъяснительная связь при вопросе может быть оформлена также средствами местоименных вопросительных слов *кто, что, какой, сколько, когда, где* и др." (1980: 479).

Нетрудно заметить, что выбор союза в большой степени предопределяется семантикой изъясняемого слова. При определенном глаголе обычно встречаются только союзы одной, реже двух, из названных групп. (ср. *предполагать, <u>что</u>*; *хотеть, <u>чтобы</u>*; *спросить, придет <u>ли</u>*; *знать, <u>что</u>*, но и *знать, <u>почему</u>* и т.д.)

Своеобразие русских глаголов ожидания проявляется ярче всего в том, что круг используемых союзов здесь особенно велик. Во-первых, при них встречаются союзы **всех трех** названных групп. Во-вторых, определенные союзы другого (временного) типа (напр. *пока*) приобретают здесь объектно-изъяснительный оттенок (АГ-60: 308; Формановская 1978: 71).

Некоторое представление о широте этих возможностей могут дать следующие примеры из романа Л. Толстого "Анна Каренина". Чтобы показать, что в данном отношении русские глаголы ожидания довольно сильно отличаются от соответвующих глаголов других языков, приводим также их английские параллели (перевод К. Гарнетт):[2]

(2) Он **ждал**, *что* она *возразит*; но она молчала, глядя перед собою.
     He **waited** *for* her *to retort*, but she was silent, looking straight before her.

(3) И вдруг ему вспомнилось, как они детьми вместе ложились спать и **ждали** только того, *чтобы* Федор Богданыч *вышел* за дверь, чтобы кидать друг в друга подушками и хохотать, хохотать неудержимо [...]
     And suddenly he recalled how they used to go to bed together as children, and how they only **waited** *till* Fiodor Bogdanich *was out* of the room to fling pillows at each other and laugh, laugh irrepressibly [...]

(4) Алексей Александрович, готовый к своей речи, стоял, пожимая свои скрещенные пальцы и **ожидая**, *не треснет ли* еще где.
     Alexei Alexandrovich, ready for his speech, stood squeezing his crossed fingers, **waiting** *for* their crack *to come* again.

(5) Левин не слушал больше и **ждал**, *когда уедет* профессор.
     Levin listened no more, and simply **waited** *for* the professor *to go*.

(6) Левин сел в **ожидании**, *когда уедет* профессор [...]
     Levin sat down to **wait** *till* the professor *should go* [...]

(7) Она слышала его шаги и голос и **ждала** за дверью, *пока уйдет* mademoiselle Linon.

She had heard his steps and voice, and **had waited** at the door·
for Mademoiselle Linon *to go.*

2. Сравнение с конструкциями в других языках

Многобразию русских конструкций, представленных в приведенных
примерах, в английском языке соответствуют всего две конструкции:
to wait **till (until)** *Y* ((3) и (6)) и *to wait* **for** *X* **to** *do Y* ((2), (4), (5) и
(7)). И даже между этими конструкциями различия иногда весьма
незначительны (ср. (5) и (6)). Все же в них можно увидеть определенную связь с двойственностью в семантике ожидания, выраженной
в приведенных выше толкованиях. Конструкция *to wait* **for** *X* **to** *do Y*
подчеркивает "проспективную" часть толкования: представление о
будущем событии. Событие Y здесь больше всего имеет статус
объекта ожидания (в нашей формулировке: СОБ). Это связано еще
и с тем, что первая часть конструкции совершенно идентична с конструкцией, содержащей только именной объект (ср. *He waited* **for**
his mother 'Он ждал **маму**').

В конструкции *to wait* **till** *Y*, однако, событие Y представляется
всего лишь как **конец состояния** ожидания (в нашей формулировке:
СОСТ) (ср. *He waited* **till** *five o'clock* 'Он ждал **до пяти часов**').

Данное различие характерно не только для английского языка.
И в немецком языке существует возможность подчеркивать тот или
иной аспект ожидания. Различие здесь выражается выбором между
союзами *daß* и *bis.* Ср. следующие соответствия:

(5')a He **waited** *for* the professor *to go.*

  б Er **wartete** (darauf) *daß* der Professor *wegfahren würde.*

(6')a He **waited** *till* the professor *should go.*

  б Er **wartete** *bis* der Professor *wegfahren würde.*[3]

Интересно отметить, что при союзах *till* и *bis*· оба языка имеют
возможность влиять на смысл выказывания посредством выбора
глагольной формы. В примерах (6')a и (6')б глагольная форма указывает на то, что событие Y рассматривается прежде всего с позиции
ожидающего. Из этого вытекает, что здесь, в принципе, не ясно,
произошло ли это действие на самом деле. Если же мы хотим представить событие Y как реальное событие, выбирается скорее "нор-
мальная" форма прошедшего времени:

(6")a He **waited** *till* the professor *went away.*

  б Er **wartete** *bis* der Professor *wegfuhr.*

Подобный смысл в русском языке яснее всего передается конструкцией с союзом *пока не* и формой прошедшего времени.

(6")в Он *ждал, пока* профессор *не уехал.*

Следует отметить, что на практике выбор между первыми названными выше возможностями рассмотрения события Y (как СОБ или как конец СОСТ) часто не имеет большого значения. Это несомненно связано с тем, что оба аспекта события Y сильно взаимосвязаны: самым естественным окончанием состояния СОСТ является именно осуществление события СОБ. Поэтому и не удивительно, что данное противопоставление выражается не во всех языках. Отсутствие различия между двумя типами конструкций характерно для нидерландского языка. Здесь встречаются только конструкция с союзом *(tot)dat*, соответствующим английскому *till* и немецкому *bis*. Это значит, что примеры (5') и (6') переводятся на нидерландский язык одинаково:

(5', 6')г Hij **wachtte** *tot* de professor *weg zou gaan.*

Однако для различения разных степеней реальности события Y в нидерландском, так же, как и в английском и немецком языках, можно использовать различие между "прямыми" временными формами и формами с определенной "дополнительной ориентацией". Во фразе (5', 6')г использована форма "будущего в прошедшем", которая оставляет открытым вопрос, реализовалось данное событие или нет. Когда это событие воспринимается как реальное завершение ожидания, как в примере (6")в, и в нидерландском языке используется простая форма прошедшего времени:

(6")г Hij **wachtte** *tot* de professor weg *ging.*[4]

К языкам, в которых может "нейтрализоваться" противопоставление между представлением события Y как СОСТ или как конец СОБ, с определенными оговорками вероятности, можно отнести и французский язык. Как и в нидерландском языке, здесь встречается обычно одна конструкция: *attendre* **que** (+ форма сослагательного наклонения).[5] Сравните следующие два примера из романа "Мадам Бовари" Флобера с их английскими и русскими переводами:

(8) [Charles] marchait de long en large, **attendan**t *qu'Emma fût habillée.*
     [Charles] kept pacing up and down the room, **waiting** *for* Emma *to finish.*

[Шарль] расхаживал по комнате и **ждал**, *пока* Эмма *кончит* одеваться.

(9) [...] Charles, les mains vides, **attendait** *qu'*elle *eût fini*.

[...] Charles stood sheepishly by, **waiting** *till* she *had finished*.

[...] Шарль, опустив руки, **дожидался**, *пока* она *покончит* с этим делом.

Русский перевод иллюстрирует тот факт, что глаголы *ждать* и *дожидаться* в подобных случаях могут выступать как близкие синонимы.

В обоих случаях использована конструкция с союзом *пока*, представленная выше в примере (7). Бросается в глаза, что в отличие от примера (6") (с союзом *пока не*), в примерах (7) - (9) в придаточной части наблюдается так называемое "относительное время": в качестве "точки отсчета" при интерпретации временной формы здесь служит не момент речи, а действие главной части предложения.

На основе данных примеров могло бы сложиться впечатление, что выбор между *пока* и *пока не* в большой степени связан с выбором между "относительным" и "абсолютным" употреблением временной формы придаточной части. Как было показано в статье (Барентсен 1980б), такая связь действительно существует, но на самом деле взаимные отношения между выбором союза и временной формой являются более сложными: при союзе *пока* абсолютное время не исключается, а при союзе *пока не* изредка встречается также и относительное употребление временной формы. См. следующие два примера перевода конструкций с английским союзом *till(until)*:

(10) Still Dori did not let Bilbo down. He **waited** *till* he *had clambered* off his shoulders into the branches, and then he jumped for the branches himself. (Tolkien: The Hobbit)

И всё-таки Дори не бросил хоббита в беде: он **дождался**, *пока* тот *перелез* с его плеч на дерево, и только тогда подпрыгнул и ухватился за нижнюю ветку. (Перевод Н. Рахмановой)

(11) This time Alice **waited** patiently *until* [the Caterpillar] *chose* to speak again. (Caroll: Alice in Wonderland)

Алиса терпеливо **ждала**, *пока* Гусеница *не соблаговолит* снова обратить на нее внимание. (Перевод Н. Демуровой)[6]

Пример (10) иллюстрирует еще один важный факт, отличающий русский язык от ряда других европейских языков — наличие в группе глаголов ожидания форм совершенного вида *дождаться* и *выждать*, лексическое значение которых включает информацию об осуществлении ожидаемого события (СОБ).

В заключение нашего краткого обзора обращаем внимание на другое важное различие, связанное с лексическим составом данной группы в разных языках. Дело в том, что у разных глаголов удельный вес аспектов А и Б (см. пар. 1) может сильно колебаться. Существуют глаголы, значение которых сводится почти исключительно к "проспективному" аспекту ожидания (аспекту Б). В ряде случаев эти глаголы являются производными (префиксальными) образованиями от основного глагола ожидания, такие как немецкое *erwarten* и нидерландское *verwachten*. Однако в английском языке подобное значение имеет глагол *to expect*, формально не связанное с глаголом *to wait*. Глагол *to expect* часто переводится на русский язык глаголом *ожидать*, напр.:

(12)   He had not **expected** the Old Man *to fall* on his shoulders sobbing his gratitude and begging forgiveness for all the years of misery and loneliness [...] (W. Smith: The Diamond Hunters)
Он не **ожидал**, *что* Старик *упадет* ему на грудь, зарыдает и попросит прощения за все эти годы страданий и одиночества [...]

(13)   I had not **expected** *to see* him here [...] (G. Green: The Comedians)
Я не **ожидал** *встретить* его здесь.

В подобных случаях в русском языке характерно употребление союза *что*. Как демонстрирует приведенный выше пример (2), в русском языке этот союз встречается не только при глаголе *ожидать*, но и при глаголе *ждать*, т.е. при основном глаголе ожидания. В таком случае и этот глагол легко переводится английским *to expect*:

(14)   Она **ждала**, *что* он *пригласит* ее на вальс, но он не пригласил, и она удивлённо взглянула на него. (Л. Толстой: Анна Каренина)
She **expected** him *to ask* her for a waltz, but he did not, and she glanced wonderingly at him.

Как известно, для придаточных предложений с союзом *что* характерно выражение содержания мыслей, сообщений и т.д. В нидерландском языке союзу *что* соответствует союз *dat*. Однако, в отличие от русского языка, в нидерландском придаточные предложения с этим союзом сочетаются не с основным глаголом ожидания (*wachten*), а только с приставочным глаголом *verwachten*.[7] И в немецком языке соответствующий союз *daß* сочетается прежде всего с приставочным глаголом.[8]

На основе вышесказанного можно сделать вывод, что в ряде случаев у русских глаголов ожидания различие типа *to wait - to expect*, *warten - erwarten* выражено менее сильно, чем в ряде других языков.[9] Хотя удельный вес мыслительного компонента значения у русского глагола *ожидать* в основном выше, чем у глагола *ждать*, последний также свободно сочетается с союзом *что*, в то время как определенные формы глагола *ожидать* нередко используются в случаях, где довольно сильно представлен "физический" аспект ожидания.-[10]

Рассмотренные нами примеры показывают, что для русских глаголов ожидания характерен необычайно богатый выбор между разными конструкциями изъяснительного типа. Поэтому, в принципе, подробный анализ этих конструкций может способствовать лучшему пониманию функционирования данных союзных средств, т.е. лучшему пониманию того, как управление функционирует в рамках сложного предложения. Однако на данном этапе изучения русского языка фактически невозможно получить ясную картину функционирования изъяснительных конструкций при глаголах ожидания. В словарях и справочниках представлены не все возможности и дается слишком мало информации об их различительных признаках.[11]

Недостаток информации прежде всего ощущается при одном вопросе, который может волновать особенно нерусских исследователей и студентов русского языка: функционирование союза *пока*. Как показывают приведенные выше примеры, в позиции после глагола ожидания в русском языке обычно употребляется союз *пока* вместо союза *пока не*, который ожидался бы по аналогии с употреблением соответствующих союзов *till, bis, tot(dat)* и т.д. в других языках.

Последнему вопросу посвящена одна из наших прежних статей (Барентсен 1980б), в которой обсуждается также связь между данными вариантами и выбором временной формы в придаточной части. Однако пока осталось невыясненным, как конструкции с союзами *пока* и *пока не* при глаголах ожидания соотносятся с другими конструкциями при этих же глаголах. Прежде всего это относится к союзу (союзному слову?) *когда*, который довольно часто встречается при глаголах ожидания. (См. примеры (5) и (6).) Различие между этими конструкциями трудно уловимо и нелегко ответить на вопрос, какая из них является самой "нормальной".

Неясен также статус конструкций с союзом *чтобы* (ср. (3) и примечание 6). Тот факт, что в современном языке эта конструкция встречается редко, в то время как в произведениях Пушкина она, казалось бы, вполне обычна, наводит на мысль о возможных изменениях в употреблении данных конструкций в течение последних двух столетий.

Решение подобных вопросов требует наличия большого фактического материала. Ввиду уже упомянутой низкой частотности данных конструкций собрать достаточный материал "вручную" является почти невозможной задачей. Однако такая работа с недавнего времени стала осуществимой благодаря появлению все больших собраний русских текстов в виде компьютерных файлов, из которых при помощи компьютерного поиска легко извлекаются все нужные примеры.

Ниже мы хотим показать, какая складывается картина интересующих нас явлений на основе имеющихся в нашем распоряжении компьютерных корпусов.

В следующем параграфе дается краткий обзор этого материала. Далее в статье приводится таблица с количественными данными о распределении разных конструкций при глаголах данной группы. Значительная часть этих конструкций иллюстрируется примерами и сопровождаются комментарием об их самых характерных чертах.

3. Использованный материал

Наш основной материал состоит из подлинных русских прозаических текстов литературного характера: романов, повестей и рассказов, мемуаров и нескольких пьес, а также нескольких больших стихотворных текстов Пушкина.

Были составлены два корпуса примерно одинаковой величины. Корпус XIX охватывает 19-е столетие (от Пушкина до Чехова), а корпус XX – 20-е столетие (от Бунина до современной фантастики).

Каждый из этих корпусов содержит около 5 миллионов словоупотреблений. Если исходить из того, что стандартная книжная страница содержит примерно 290 словоупотреблений, то эти два корпуса соответствуют более чем 34 тыс. страниц книгопечатного текста.[12]

Поскольку наличие компьютерного варианта текста – явление пока до определенной степени случайное, наши корпуса имеют гораздо менее "уравновешенный" характер, чем известный "Уппсальский корпус" (см. Леннгрен 1993), в котором равномерно представлены разные жанры и писатели.

В наших корпусах некоторые писатели представлены гораздо бо́льшим количеством материала, чем другие. В ряде случаев это, конечно, связано и с объемом творчества того или иного автора (Корпус XIX содержит фактически всю прозу Лермонтова и Достоевского, но объем последнего материала почти в 20 раз больше первого). Некоторые авторы представлены отдельными произведениями.

Неравномерно представлены и разные периоды: в обоих корпусах вторая половина данного столетия представлена значительно бо́льшим количеством текстов, чем первая.

Несмотря на эти недостатки, материал, собранный в этих корпусах, как нам кажется, достаточно представителен для данных двух столетий, чтобы на его основе можно было сделать какие-то выводы об изменениях в использовании определенных структур.

Список авторов и произведений, представленных в корпусах дается в Приложении. Там же указан и объем различных частей (в тысячах словоупотреблений).[13]

4. Количественные данные о распределении конструкций

Схема 1 представляет количество разных конструкций при основных глаголах ожидания. В центральных клетках схемы указана частотность каждого типа сочетания при определенном глаголе в обоих корпусах (XX и XIX).

Условные сокращения:

чт - союз *что* (см. пример (2)),

чб - союз *чтобы* (см. пример (3)),

иф - конструкция с инфинитивом (см. пример (13)),

ли - союз *ли* (или *не ... ли*) (см. пример (4)),

сс - конструкция с союзным словом (*как, кто* и т.д.),[14] напр.:

(15) Майор не проронил ни слова, с любопытством **ожидая**, *чем кончится* этот поединок. (Белов)

вк - конструкция, состоящая из существительного — указания момента или периода времени, определяемого придаточным предложением содержащим слово *когда*, напр.:

(16) С тоской, как смерти, **ждала** Маша *того часа, когда* Гусев уйдет. (А. Толстой)

кд - остальные примеры со словом *когда* (см. пример (5) и (6)),

пк - союз *пока* (см. пример (7)),

пн - союз *пока не* (см. примеры (6")в и (11)).

Схема 1. Распределение конструкций при разных глаголов

	чт	чб	иф	ли	сс	вк	кд	пк	пн	
ждать										
XX	87	11	1	8	30	9	106	65	9	**326**
XIX	54	23	10	14	33	4	35	24	1	**198**
ожидать										
XX	65	3	40	2	6	1	15	8		**140**
XIX	98	24	44	11	32	4	4	9	1	**227**
ожидание										
XX	3			1			10	5	1	**20**
XIX	3		3		3		3	5		**17**
подождать										
XX		(2)	1	2	1		10	37	2	**55**
XIX			14	3	1		2	21	1	**42**
дожидаться										
XX	1	1			1	4	12	11	1	**31**
XIX		6		1	2	1	3	2		**15**
дождаться										
XX	3	3				8	23	22		**59**
XIX	1	1		1	1		2	8		**14**
выжидать										
XX					2		1	2		**5**
XIX	1	1	1	3	6	2	3	1		**18**
выждать										
XX		1			1		4	3	1	**10**
XIX		1	1			1	3	3		**9**
пережидать										
XX							1	2		**3**
XIX								1		**1**
переждать										
XX							1	2	1	**4**
XIX							1	2		**3**
поджидать										
XX							1	1		**2**
XIX	1			3			1			**5**
итого	317	77	115	49	120	34	240	234	18	**1204**
XX	159	21	42	13	42	22	183	158	15	**655**
XIX	158	56	73	36	78	12	57	76	3	**549**

12

Кроме глаголов мы включили в схему и отглагольное существительное *ожидание*, поскольку оно, в основном, сочетается с такими же изъяснительными конструкциями, как данные глаголы.

В схеме не представлены глаголы *прождать* и *пождать*, с очень низкой частотностью, и случаи с бессоюзным подчинением, которые в нашей статье особо не рассматриваются (см. пример (11)).[15]

Данные, представленные в Схеме 1, позволяют сделать **некоторые общие выводы:**

Цифры в правом нижнем углу указывают на то, что общее количество данных конструкций в литературных текстах нашего столетия (672) заметно выше, чем в текстах прошлого столетия (566). Бросаются в глаза также заметные изменения в частотности употребления определенных конструкций (цифры в нижней части схемы): в то время, как союз *что* в обоих корпусах встречается одинаково часто, заметно снизилась частотность союза *чтобы* и конструкций, относящихся к сфере вопроса (*ли* и союзные слова). С другой стороны, частотность временных союзов (*когда* и *пока* (*не*)) сильно возросла — на них приходится "львиная доля" общего роста изъяснительных конструкций при глаголах ожидания.

Крайний правый столбец схемы отображает частотность разных глаголов в изъяснительных конструкциях. Заметно увеличилось употребление "центрального" глагола *ждать*, частично, как нам кажется, за счет глагола *ожидать*. Интересно отметить, что более детальный анализ примеров показывает, что без изменения осталась частотность деепричастной формы *ожидая*: в Корпусе XIX она встречается 67 раз, в XX — 66. Это несомненно связано с тем, что деепричастие *ожидая* фактически "обслуживает" оба глагола, т.е. втягивается и в парадигму глагола *ждать*.

Определенное повышение частотности наблюдается у глаголов *дождаться* и *дожидаться*. Первый глагол в настоящее время является самым нейтральным "результативным" партнером глагола *ждать*. Рост частотности глагола *дожидаться* прежде всего связан с употреблением деепричастной формы (в XIX - 6, в XX - 19). (Интересно отметить, что в половине этих случаев, деепричастие *дожидаясь* сочетается с отрицанием.)

Остальные глаголы встречаются значительно реже, и поэтому цифры не дают достаточного основания, чтобы говорить об изменениях в их употреблении.

В следующих параграфах первая половина из представленных в Схеме 1 конструкций будет рассмотрена более детально. Будет уделено внимание не только общей характеристике конструкции, но и возможным историческим изменениям в их употреблении. О союзах *пока* и *пока не* см.: Барентсен 1980б. К вопросу о соотношении этих союзов с союзом *когда* мы намерены вернуться в отдельной статье.

5. Союз *что*

5.1 Глаголы *ждать* и *ожидать* (без отрицания)

Придаточные предложения с союзом *что* обычно выражают содержание чьих-нибудь мыслей, слов и т.д. При глаголах ожидания такие придаточные предложения сосредоточивают внимание почти исключительно на Аспекте Б (см. пар. 1). В связи с этим глаголы несовершенного вида этой группы обретают здесь вариант значения, очень близкий к значению глаголов *думать*, *предполагать* и т.д. Сильнее всего это представлено у глагола *ожидать*. Однако, как было отмечено в пар. 2, для русского языка характерно, что подобное значение, связанное в ряде языков с особыми глаголами (*to expect, erwarten, verwachten*), может выражаться и центральным, основным глаголом – *ждать*. Количественные данные, представленные в Схеме 1, показывают, что подобное употребление глагола *ждать* характерно уже для языка XIX века, но что в современном языке оно еще возросло, так что теперь оно встречается даже чаще, чем у глагола *ожидать*.

Во многих случаях этого типа глаголы *ждать* и *ожидать* почти не различаются в значении:

(15) Я **ждал**, *что* заросли *вскипят* разом и еще с десяток Гришиных родственников *кинутся*, пригибаясь, врассыпную от ограды. (Лукины)

(16) Он **ожидал**, *что* тот сейчас *превратится* во что-то совсем невообразимо мерзкое, ужасное, многоголовое, пышущее пламенем и источающее ядовитую слизь. (Легостаев)

(17) У меня не было сил подняться, я **ждал**, *что* черная громадина сейчас *развернется* и... Но из «Волги» выскочил молодой парень и бросился меня поднимать. (Незнанский)

(18) Он **ожидал**, *что* она ему *ответит*, но она не произносила ни слова. (Тургенев)

Однако при рассмотрении большого количества примеров обнаруживается, что все же чаще всего есть определенное семантическое различие между этими глаголами. Глагол *ожидать* совершенно нейтрально указывает на наличие у субъекта представления о будущем событии, в то время как у глагола *ждать* наличие такого представления сильнее связывается с другими аспектами поведения субъекта. В последней черте можно было бы увидеть остаток влияния Аспекта А. Этот аспект у глагола *ждать* теряется не до такой степени, как у глагола *ожидать*.

Следующий пример демонстрирует, что *ожидать* можно употреблять, когда субъект почти не осознает присутствие данного представления:

(19)   Я <u>подсознательно</u> **ожидал**, *что появится* знаменитый кожаный рыжий портфель, доставшийся Тарантулу еще от отца [...] (Лазарчук)

Для примеров с глаголом *ждать* характерно более заметное присутствие данного представления, которое может сопровождаться еще и различными чувствами субъекта.

Этот глагол, к примеру, легко сочетается с указателями продолжительности периода:

(20)   И <u>уже много лет</u> эта волшебная Барби **ждала**, *что* ее *найдет* мама. (Петрушевская)

(21)   Я <u>все</u> **ждал**, *что* он *спросит*: "Куда двинемся?" (Крапивин)

В примере (20) можно уловить еще и оттенок надежды. Подобные оттенки надежды и страха присутствуют и в следующих примерах:

(22)   Иван Григорьевич **ждал**, *что* Сталин *пригласит* его сесть *и прекратит* неловкость. (Рыбаков)

(23)   Они ждали. Каждый **ждал**, *что* другой *совершит* малейшую, но непоправимую ошибку. (Легостаев) [Речь здесь идет о поединке!]

(24)   Родионов упорно не смотрел на второго секретаря. Смотрел на телефон — **ждал**, *что* кто-нибудь *позвонит, спасет*. Было очень тяжело. (Шукшин)

(25)   Я <u>в ужасе</u> **ждал**, *что* Рита сейчас *повернется и скажет* что-нибудь насмешливое ... (Незнанский)

(26)   Он все время *ждал*, *что* вот *приедет* какая-нибудь инспекция и ревизия, и тогда он получит за все и сполна. (Войнович)

Различия между данными глаголами нейтрализуются в формах *ожидая* и *ожидание*. Поэтому эти формы могут сочетаться с обстоятельствами, которые при личных формах глагола характерны только для глагола *ждать*:

(27) Пять дней жил после того Город, <u>в ужасе</u> **ожидая**, *что потекут* с Лысой Горы ядовитые газы. (Булгаков)

(28) Рад он этому чувству <u>напряженного</u>, смертельного **ожидания**, *что* вот-вот *раскроется* какой-то немыслимый свет? (А. Толстой)

Следующий пример из произведений Гоголя, очевидно, следует интерпретировать как указание на определенное историческое изменение в значении глагола *ожидать*:

(29) <u>С занявшимся от страха дыханьем</u> он **ожидал**, *что* вот-вот *глянет* к нему за ширмы старик. (Гоголь)

В заключение этого параграфа обращаем внимание на то, что в специальной литературе и в языке периодической печати довольно часто встречаются формы *ожидалось* и *ожидается*:

(30) **Ожидалось**, *что* модные ГАПы и роботы помогут ликвидировать дефицит рабочей силы [...] (Уппсальский корпус 1)

(31) **Ожидается**, *что* этот спорный вопрос будет урегулирован в ближайшиие дни. (ИТАР-ТАСС-Экспресс)

5.2 Замечания о видо-временных формах в придаточной части

Ситуация, описываемая в придаточной части предложения данного типа, представляется не как часть объективной действительности, а как часть мыслей субъектного актанта глагола ожидания. В русском языке для подобных случаев характерно относительное употребление временной формы придаточной части. За точку отсчета здесь принимается не момент речи, а время существования ожидания. Поскольку СОБ по отношению к ожиданию является будущим событием, то в придаточной части естественно употребление формы будущего времени. Приведенные выше примеры показывают, что здесь чаще всего встречаются формы совершенного вида — простого будущего, которые лучше всего могут передавать событийный характер ожидаемого явления. Встречаются также сочетания краткой формы страдательного причастия с элементом *буд-*, которые имеют здесь также явно событийный характер:

(32) Герцог Берангер **ожидал**, *что* его энергия *будет востребована* ... (Легостаев)

У формы будущего несовершенного событийный характер СОБ приводит к тому, что данная форма интерпретируется прежде всего как обозначение <u>возникновения</u> описываемой ситуации:

(33)   Поставили гроб на скамьи у могилы. Стало тихо. Долго стояли так. На Ивлева начали посматривать – *ждали*, *что он будет говорить*. (Шукшин)

(34)   Варгези молчал. Павлыш **ожидал**, *что он будет разглагольствовать*, но тот молчал. (Булычев)

В следующем примере также можно увидеть направленность внимания на возникновение ситуации:

(35)   Пусть захлопнет здесь книгу тот читатель, кто **ждет**, *что она будет политическим обличением*. (Солженицын)

Однако в примерах такого типа это событие имеет несколько иной характер, чем в предыдущих: здесь речь идет не о возникновении описываемой ситуации как таковой, но о возникновении **восприятия** данной ситуации у субъекта главной части. Здесь как будто пропущено промежуточное "**окажется, что…**"

5.3   Отрицательные формы глаголов *ждать* и *ожидать*

Различия между глаголами *ждать* и *ожидать* намного ярче проявляются при отрицании. В сочетании с придаточными с союзом *что* глагол *ждать* при отрицании встречается редко. У глагола *ожидать* отрицание присутствует более чем в 30 % случаев. Характер последнего типа хорошо выражают следующие примеры:

(36)   Она сказала это по-английски, и все удивились, потому что никто **не ожидал**, *что новенькая станет отвечать*. (Булычев)

(37)   СВЕТЛАНА. Нет, **не ожидала** я от вас, *что вы меня в такую тюрьму заманите*. (Петрушевская)

(38)   Она очень огорчилась вашим отказом, – прибавил я, – она никак **не ожидала**, что *вы не захотите* к ней приехать. (Тургенев)

(39)   Подходя к перекрестку Гороховой и Садовой, он сам удивился своему необыкновенному волнению; он и **не ожидал**, *что* у него с такою болью *будет биться* сердце. (Достоевский)

Эти примеры следует интерпретировать как указание на то, что действие, названное в придаточной части, совершилось, вызвав удивление субъекта главной части. Употребляя данную конструкцию, говорящий подчеркивает, что в более ранний период у него не было никакого основания предполагать возможность совершения данного события. Это значит, что здесь налицо "ретроспективное" употребление формы прошедшего времени.[16] Такое ретроспективное употребление для отрицательных форм прошедшего времени глагола *ожидать* очень характерно. Менее ясно, по нашему мнению, следует ли примеры с глаголом *ждать* интерпретировать таким же образом:

(40) Ивлев приготовился спорить. Только он **не ждал**, наверно, *что* спор этот *произойдет* тотчас после собрания. (Шукшин)

(41) Я никак **не ждал**, *что* эта нищая дура *усадит* на поминки все деньги, которые получила от этого другого дурака... (Достоевский)

Возможность интерпретации как ретроспективность предполагает, что в данных случаях глагол *ждать* легко может заменяться на *ожидать*.

Ретроспективная интерпретация форм типа *не ожидал* имеет интересные последствия для выбора временных форм в придаточной части. Это проявляется в тех случаях, когда СОБ состоит не из "обычного" возникновения определенной ситуации, но из возникновения восприятия уже существующей ситуации субъектом главной части. (Ср. сказанное выше по поводу примера (35).) В таких случаях описываемая ситуация чаще всего еще существует в момент, с которого производится ретроспекция. Это значит, что данная ситуация описывается типично формой несовершенного вида. Довольно часто отправной точкой ретроспекции является момент речи. Описываемая ситуация в подобном случае вполне естественно выражается формой настоящего несовершенного:

(42) Я никогда **не ожидал**, *что* метеорологическая служба *работает* с такой точностью. (Незнанский)

(43) И тут произошло нечто из ряда вон выходящее: по коридору вели заключенного: видно, никак **не ожидали**, *что* в этом святилище *может оказаться* посторонний. (Н. Мандельштам)

(44) Да, я никак **не ожидала**, *что* это так *волнует*, — сказала Анна, краснея. (Л. Толстой)

(45) Ей хотелось сказать: я **не ожидала**, *что* вы *человек образованный*, но она не сказала, зато я знал, что она это подумала [...] (Достоевский)

Как показывают эти примеры, в придаточной части таких предложений обычно речь идет о "расширенном настоящем" – описывается какое-то общее свойство.

Изредка в подобных предложениях встречается форма прошедшего несовершенного:

(46) Базаров встал и толкнул окно. Оно разом со стуком распахнулось... Он **не ожидал,** *что* оно так легко *отворялось*; притом его руки дрожали. (Тургенев)

Форма прошедшего несовершенного указывает на то, что ретроспекция производится не с момента речи, но с определенного момента прошлого. (В данном примере это момент, следующий непосредственно за открытием окна.) Важно еще и то, что речь здесь идет не о свойстве с определенным "вневременным" характером (как в примере (44)), а о более "локализованном" свойстве, связанном с существованием данного окна в данном состоянии.

Кроме форм несовершенного вида можно встретить здесь еще и формы совершенного вида прошедшего времени с т.н. "перфектным значением". В наших единственных примерах ретроспекиция явно совершается с момента в прошлом:

(47) [Пассажиры из поезда] **не ждали,** *что* в арбатовское захолустье уже *проникла* идея автопроката. (Ильф и Петров)[17]

(48) Никто **не ожидал,** *что* пароход так скоро *подошел* к островку. (Писемский)[18]

Хотя оттенок ретроспективности при отрицания ожидания и очень характерен, это не единственно возможный случай. Подобный смысл, по естественным причинам, может возникнуть только при формах прошедшего времени. Ср. приведенные выше примеры со следующими примерами с формами деепричастия и настоящего времени:

(49) Освобожденный от тягомотины вежливости, он взглядывал круто, говорил неоспоримо, даже **не ожидая,** *что могут быть* возражения. (Солженицын)

(50) Он **не ожидает,** *что* мы так рано *выедем,* – говорил он, – но все-таки надо спешить. (Чехов)

5.4 Остальные глаголы

Очень характерно отсутствие придаточных изъяснительных с союзом *что* при глаголах *подождать* и *прождать.* У этих глаголов удельный вес Аспекта А – пребывание в состоянии ожидания – очень велик, поскольку они "ставят в фокус внимания в р е м я ожидания" (Апресян 1997: 115).

Как показывают следующие примеры, глаголы несовершенного вида *дожидаться, выжидать* и *поджидать* сочетаются с данными придаточными предложениями:[19]

(51) Она помолчала, словно **дожидаясь**, *что* Сол *отменит* свой приказ. (Резник)

(52) Она семенила на месте и беспрерывно приседала, с нетерпением **выжидая**, *что*, наконец-то, и ей *позволят* ввернуть своё слово, и дождалась. (Достоевский)

(53) Я посидел на террасе, **поджидая**, *что* вот-вот за цветником на площадке или на одной из аллей *покажется* Женя или донесется ее голос из комнат [...] (Чехов)

Интересно отметить, что все примеры этой группы, найденные в наших корпусах, содержат форму деепричастия. По сравнению с формой *ожидая*, в данных формах присутствует более сильный элемент направленности на осуществление ожидаемого события. (О дальнейших различительных признаках этих глаголов см.: Апресян (1997: 114-116).) Однако, как демонстрируют следующие примеры из других источников, в принципе, не исключается и возможность употребления данных глаголов и в других формах:

(54) Как мы пришли к Анне Ивановне, то меня провели в кабинет, сняли штаны, и пока я **дожидался**, *что зашьют*, сидел я один около двух часов в шлафроке. (Тургенев)[20]

(55) И жадно **выжидают** очи, *Что* жизнью *облекутся* сны. (Вяземский; **Карт.**)

(56) Она еще долго стояла за воротами, все **поджидала**, *что* вот-вот *появятся* ее "молодые". (Сартаков; **Карт.**)

Нами не было найдено примеров подобного употребления глагола *пережидать*. Поскольку этот глагол подчеркивает, что ожидание направлено на **окончание** определенной ситуации, он вообще употребляется довольно редко. Принципиальных причин отсутствия таких примеров мы пока не видим.

Из соответствующих глаголов <u>совершенного вида</u> в нашем материале представлен только глагол *дождаться*:

(57) **Дождался** Шухов, *что* все опять своё *заговорили* [...], наклонился к латышу [...] (Солженицын)

(58) Мужчины за окном, словно **дождавшись**, *что* их единственный зритель *успокоился*, приступили к действиям. (Резник)

(59) **Дождешься** еще, *что* она тебе *будет* в рожу *плевать*, как мне...
(Стругацкие)
(60) Есть счастье, а что с него толку, если оно в земле зарыто? [...]
Дождутся люди, *что* его паны *выроют* или казна отберет.
(Чехов)

Из результативного значения этого глагола вытекает, что событие, описываемое в придаточной части, является осуществленным событием Интересно отметить, что это отражается на способе употребления временных форм в придаточной части. Во всех примерах, имеющихся в нашем распроряжении, при главной части, относящейся к прошлому, в придаточной части используется форма прошедшего времени совершенного вида. Это значит, что в отличие от относительного употребления временных форм, характерного для конструкций с глаголами ожидания несовершенного вида, при совершенном виде мы встречаем абсолютное употребление временных форм. Таким образом описываемое событие рассматривается не с точки зрения субъекта ожидания, но с точки зрения рассказчика, который представляет данное событие как часть действительности. Таким образом в этих предложениях союз *что* употребляется в несколько ином значении: не для указания содержания мыслей, но для указания факта.

Примеры с формой непрошедшего времени имеют определенную семантическую специализацию: в таких предложениях, по-видимому, выражаются только события, неприятные для субъекта (см. (59)-(60)). Такое употребление менее характерно для прошедшего времени. В большинстве наших примеров с такой формой данный оттенок отсутствует. Однако в Словаре Ушакова это употребление глагола *дождаться* приводится отдельно ("Своим поведением довести себя до чего-то неприятного") и иллюстрируется именно формой прошедшего времени:

(61) **Дождался**-таки, *что* его *уличили*.

5.5 Употребление местоимения *того*

Тот факт, что глаголы ожидания управляют родительным падежом, иногда находит отражение и в сложных предложениях. В таких случаях придаточная часть представлена в главной части формой *того*:

(62) [Она] стояла, **ждала** несбыточного, – того, *что сойдет* с балкона барчук, *пойдет* по аллее, *увидит* ее и, внезапно свернув, *приблизится* к ней быстрыми шагами [...] (Бунин)

(63) **Не ожидал** он <u>и того</u>, *что* так *будут ныть* ноги от беспрерыв-
ного стояния, и что так будет ныть лицо от механической
приветливости. (Набоков)

(64) Он видел скачущих выжлятников в красных шапках по краям
поросшего оврага, видел даже собак и всякую секунду **ждал**
<u>того</u>, *что* на той стороне, на зеленях, *покажется* лисица.
(Толстой)

(65) Но конь, притупленной подковой / Неверный зацепляя лед, /
<u>Того</u> и **жди**, *что упадет*. (Пушкин)

Подобные случаи встречаются довольно редко. Употребление
местоимения *того* может быть мотивировано определенным парал-
лелизмом (см. (62) с параллельным именным объектом *несбыточного*)
или усилительным словом (см. *и* в (63)).

Подобное употребление соотносительного слова очень характерно
для языка Л. Толстого (см. (64)). Интересно отметить, что у этого
автора данное употребление сравнительно часто встречается и при
других конструкциях: при союзе *чтобы* (см. (3)) и при союзных словах,
как в следующем примере:

(66) Я чувствовал, что все смотрели на меня и **ожидали** <u>того</u>, *что*
я *скажу* [...] (Л. Толстой)

Сочетание *того и жди, (что)*, представленное в (65) стало фактически идиоматическим выражением для указания весьма возможного
события.

6. Союз *чтобы*

6.1 Разделение на две группы

Сложные предложения с изъяснительной придаточной частью с
союзом *чтобы* можно разделить на две группы, в зависимости от того,
чем употребление этого союза мотивировано:

Группа А - главная часть связывается с элементом волеизъявления
Группа Б - реальность содержания придаточной части отрицается
         или ставится под сомнение

Группа А является наиболее значительной. Случаи типа Б встречаются в русском языке XX века намного реже, чем в прошлом
столетии (см. Гард 1963: 273-274).

Изменения при глаголах ожидания особенно сильно сказываются во второй группе. Цифровые данные в Схеме 1 показывают, что употребление союза *чтобы* при глаголах ожидания в нашем столетии значительно сократилось. Оказывается, что значительная доля произошедших изменений связана с группой Б: в Корпусе XIX к этой группе относится больше четверти примеров (16), в то время как в Корпусе XX не встречается ни одного примера такого типа. Однако и по отношению к группе А, по-видимому, произошли определенные, менее заметные исторические изменения. Ниже мы рассмотрим обе группы отдельно.

6.2   Группа А: волеизъявление

В грамматической литературе обычно отличаются случаи, где волеизъявление или необходимость выражены самой семантикой изъясняемых слов (*хотеть, необходимо* и т.д.), от случаев, где изъясняемое слово само по себе не выражает этого значения (*сказать, важно*). В последних случаях вместо союза *чтобы* можно употреблять и другие союзы. Значение волеизъявления/необходимости при этом вносится в предложение исключительно самим фактом выбора союза *чтобы*.

Совершенно ясно, что рассматриваемые случаи употребления союза *чтобы* относятся к последнему типу. В АГ-80 об этой возможности говорится следующее: "Желательность может передаваться лексикой, называющей состояния размышления и ожидания" (478). Единственный пример с глаголом ожидания, который там приводится, содержит глагол *поджидать* (как раз отсутствующий в наших корпусах):

(67)   К окну приникнув головой, Я **поджидал** с тоскою нежной, *Чтоб* ты *явилась* – и с тобой Помчаться по равнине снежной. (Фет)

Следующие примеры из Корпуса XX иллюстрируют данное употребление союза *чтобы* при глаголе *ждать*. Они легко допускают указанную выше интерпретацию, что ожидание здесь сопровождается оттенком желательности, т.е. что субъект глагола *ждать* не только считает осуществление события СОБ возможным, но и хочет, чтобы оно осуществилось:

(68)   [Он] **ждал** <u>с нетерпением</u>, *чтобы оборвалась* поскорей угольная чернота, грохотавшая вдоль окон. (Набоков)

(69) Он останавливался несколько боком к тебе и, по-волчьи выставив плечо, туго повернув шею, скашивал в твою сторону свои кофейные глаза и молил тебя, **ждал**, *чтобы* ты ласково *взглянул* на него. (Уппсальский корпус 2)

(70) — Вы запретили ему все заграничные поездки, гноите его в провинциальной глуши и хладнокровно **ждете**, *чтобы* этот блестящий артист *превратился* в ничтожество. (Вишневская)

(71) Ну, если днём ещё убёг — другое дело, а если схоронился и **ждёт**, *чтобы* с вышек охрану *сняли*, не дождётся. (Солженицын)

Так как элемент желательности предполагает определенное внимание к общему состоянию субъекта, личные формы глагола *ожидать* отсутствуют (см 5.1). Как уже было сказано выше, подобные ограничения не относятся к форме *ожидая*:

(72) Эта чуткая тишина обнимала всё видимое, как бы **ожидая**, даже требуя, *чтоб сказано было* нечто особенно значительное. (Горький)[21]

Несколько примеров из Корпуса XIX (ср. и (3)):

(73) [...] Он говорил ей, что она похожа на собачку, которая **ждет**, *чтоб* ей *бросили* кусочек ветчины. (Чехов)

(74) Со жгучим, судорожным нетерпением **ждал** он, *чтоб* они поскорее *ушли*, чтобы тотчас же без них и приняться за дело. (Достоевский)[22]

(75) Растопчин, **ожидая** того, *чтоб* он *остановился* на указанном месте, хмурясь, потирал рукою лицо. (Толстой)[23]

Кроме глагола *поджидать* (см. (67)) встречаются и другие приставочные образования несовершенного вида. (Только глагол *пережидать* в нашем материале не представлен ни одним примером.) Оттенок желательности хорошо сочетается с присущим им оттенком целенаправленности:

(76) — Станция! — повторила телефонистка таким тоном, словно на своем коммутаторе только и **дожидалась**, *чтобы* ей *позвонили* из Красного. (Войнович)

(77) Я сажусь где-нибудь, слушаю эту музыку или чтение и **дожидаюсь** того, *чтобы* мне *можно было* самому сесть за фортепьяно. (Толстой)

(78)   Ганя был удивлен, но осторожно молчал и глядел на мать, **выжидая**, *чтоб* она *высказалась* яснее. (Достоевский)

Интересно отметить, что союз *чтобы* сочетается также с соответствующими глаголами совершенного вида:

(79)   После четырех суток моего поединка со следователем, **дождавшись**, *чтоб* я в своем ослепительном электрическом боксе *лег* по отбою, надзиратель стал отпирать мою дверь. (Солженицын)
(80)   Дали, значит, выпить ему кружечку. Когда вышел, **выждали**, *чтобы* все путем, никого, значит, рядышком *не было* и... придушили, в общем, петлей. (Незнанский)
(81)   [...] Непременно надо было **выждать**, *чтобы* девочка все *забыла* [...] (Достоевский)

Как было уже отмечено выше (5.4), данные глаголы указывают на осуществленность ожидаемого события, в результате чего придаточная часть приобретает сильный элемент фактичности. Поэтому появление союза *чтобы* в ней менее естественно. По всей вероятности, определенную роль здесь играет аналогия с другими конструкциями. Данные предложения характеризуются своеобразной "смесью" фактичности и желательности: они указывает на то, что осуществилось желаемое событие.

На основе того, что было сказано в начале пар. 5.4, следовало бы ожидать отсутствия примеров предложений с союзом *чтобы* при глаголе *подождать*. Однако в нашем материале есть два примера, которые, на первый взгляд, опровергают это предположение:

(82)   Кофе не утоляло жажды, она тщетно дула на него – и потом решила, что так как накрапывает дождь, нужно **подождать**, *чтобы* дождь *разбавил* кофе. (Набоков)
(83)   На пашню вышли не спеша, решили **подождать**, *чтобы* землю *обветрило*. (Айтматов)

Однако мы предполагаем, что эти примеры следует анализировать по-другому: придаточная часть в них относится к другому типу – к придаточным цели (ср. второй союз *чтобы* в примере (74)). Т.е., по нашему мнению, здесь присутствует определенные причинно-следственные отношения ("если подождать, дождь разбавит кофе").

Изредка встречаются примеры с отрицательной главной частью, которые по своей семантике нельзя отнести к группе Б и поэтому рассматриваются нами здесь. Поскольку в этих примерах оттенок желательности иногда очень трудно улавливается, их следует рассматривать скорее всего как переферийные случаи группы А.

(84)   Смущенный мастер Амати, извиняясь, скупал все игрушки подряд и садился в свой хрустальный лифт тут же около прилавка, даже **не ожидая,** *чтобы* продавщица *отвернулась.* (Петрушевская)

(85)   – Да что ж?.. За что же? Ведь я ей ничего такого не сделала.
– Добрые люди и **не ждут,** *чтоб* им прежде *делали,* Нелли. (Достоевский)

(86)   Долохов, уже переодетый в солдатскую серую шинель, **не дожидался,** *чтоб* его *вызвали.* (Толстой)

(87)   Постояв несколько времени в воротах,
Петя, **не дождавшись** того, *чтобы* все экипажи *проехали,* прежде других хотел тронуться дальше и начал решительно работать локтями [...] (Толстой)

Приведенные выше примеры демонстрируют, что при глаголах ожидания конструкция с союзом *чтобы,* в которой подчеркивается желательность ожидаемого события, является вполне "нормальной" в русском языке последних двух столетий. Данную конструкцию скорее всего нужно рассматривать как маркированный вариант конструкции с союзом *что.* Различие в значении данных двух вариантов часто едва ощутимо. Как нам кажется, подобная маркированность может отражаться в индивидуальном стиле определенных авторов. Характерно, что примеры употребления конструкции с союзом *чтобы* очень неравномерно распределены по авторам. Из 21 примера Корпуса XX одна треть относится к Набокову, а у авторов XIX века такие примеры чаще всего встречаются у Толстого (16) и Достоевского (11).

В заключение данного раздела приводим еще несколько замечаний, касающихся исторического развития.

И у самых ранних частей Корпуса XIX, у Пушкина и Лермонтова, встречаются примеры с данной конструкцией, которые фактически не ·отличаются от современных примеров:

26

(88) Они поют, и с небреженьем / Внимая звонкий голос их, / **Ждала** Татьяна <u>с нетерпеньем</u> / *Чтоб* трепет сердца в ней *затих*, / *Чтобы прошло* ланит пыланье. (Пушкин)

(89) Сюжет ее очень прост, – сказал Печорин, **не дожидаясь,** *чтобы* его *просили* […] (Лермонтов)

Однако некоторые примеры из произведений этого периода производят определенное впечатление устарелости:

(90) Сначала соседи смеялись между собою над высокомерием Троекурова и каждый день **ожидали,** *чтоб* незваные гости *посетили* Покровское, где было им чем поживиться […] (Пушкин)

(91) Вадим стоял перед ней, как Мефистофель перед погибшей Маргаритой, с язвительным выражением очей, как раскаяние перед душою грешника; сложа руки, он **ожидал,** *чтоб* она к нему *обернулась*, но она осталась в прежнем положении […] (Лермонтов)

Здесь не только употребляются личные формы глагола *ожидать*, но, по-видимому, и отсутствует оттенок желательности. Не исключено, что для авторов начала XIX века конструкция с союзом *чтобы* являлась не маркированным вариантом конструкции с союзом *что*, но одним из основных средств выражения объекта ожидания. Интересно отметить формальное сходство данной конструкции с конструкцией во французском языке (см. (8) и (9)).[24] Однако проверка гипотезы о другом статусе данной конструкции в период становления современного русского языка требует намного большего количества фактического материала.

6.2 Группа Б: отрицание или сомнение

Отрицание того или иного ментального образа передвигает этот образ в сферу ирреальности. В русском языке это может привести к замене союза *что* (с формой изъявительного наклонения) союзом *чтобы*, содержащим элемент *бы*, который является составной частью сослагательного наклонения (в сочетании с глагольными формами на -*л-*). Ср.: *Я думаю, что Иван это сделал* - *Я не думаю, чтобы Иван это сделал.*

В русском языке прошлого столетия это явление имело более широкое распространение, чем в наши дни. В Корпусе XIX встречается 15 примеров подобного типа с отрицательной формой глагола *ожидать*. Приведем некоторые из них:

(92) Как ни сильно желала Анна свиданья с сыном, как ни давно думала о том и готовилась к тому, она никак **не ожидала,** *чтоб* это свидание так сильно *подействовало* на нее. (Толстой)

(93) **Не ожидала** я, *чтоб* ты *была такая* злая, – сказала Любочка [...] (Толстой)

(94) Я никак **не ожидал,** *чтобы* вы меня даже *встретили.* (Лесков)

(95) При таких условиях **невозможно ожидать,** *чтобы* обыватели *оказали* какие-нибудь подвиги по части благоустройства и благочиния или особенно *успели* по части наук и искусств. (Салтыков-Щедрин)

К этой же сфере можно отнести и случаи с риторическим вопросом. Этот тип представлен следующим примером:

(96) [...] **Ждал ли** он, *чтобы* такой конец *был* пана Данила. (Гоголь)

По своему значению эти примеры не отличаются от случаев типа *не ожидал, что,* которые были рассмотрены в пар. 5.3 ((42)-(48)). Полное отсутствие подобных примеров в Копрусе XX говорит о том, что конструкция с союзом *чтобы* вышла из употребления. Мы предполагаем, что это связано с тем, что оттенок ретроспективности, характерный для этих предложений, приводит к тому, что субъект глагола главной части ощущает определенный сдвиг в сторону реальности: в какой-то момент представление о возможном будущем событии совершенно отсутствует, но в более поздний момент обнаруживается, что это событие произошло. Это значит, что в момент рассмотрения событие, описываемое в придаточной части, является вполне реальным. В языке наших дней этого, очевидно, достаточно, чтобы исключить возможность употребления конструкции с союзом *чтобы.* Таким образом, исчезновение этого типа употребления союза *чтобы* при глаголах ожидания хорошо объясняется семантическими факторами. Было бы очень интересно сравнить этот процесс с изменениями в других сочетаниях.

7. Инфинитив

7.1 Глаголы *ждать* и *ожидать* - XX в.

Как известно, в ряде случаев изъяснительное придаточное предложение заменяется инфинитивом, если субъекты обоих предикатов идентичны. Ср.: *Мы думаем, что он уедет рано - Мы думаем уехать рано* и *Я хочу, чтобы ты ушел - Я хочу уйти.*

Следующий пример демонстрирует, что такая конструкция встречается и у глаголов ожидания (см. также (13)):

(97)   Наверное, я **ожидал** *увидеть* нечто невыразимое [...]
       (Лазарчук)

Глаголы, допускающие такую инфинитивную конструкцию, различаются по тому, насколько "трансформация" придаточного предложения в инфинитив (при идентичном субъекте) является обязательной. Ср. невозможное *Я *хочу, чтобы я ушел* при возможном *Мы думаем, что уедем рано.* Глаголы ожидания относятся к тем, которые, в принципе, допускают обе возможности. Сравните:

(98)а   **Не ожидал,** *что* когда-нибудь вновь *увижу* тебя. (Легостаев)
(98)б   **Не ожидал** когда-нибудь вновь *увидеть* тебя.

Следует, однако, отметить, что на практике редко встречаются случаи, где данные конструкции взаимозаменяемы. В современном русском языке для обеих конструкций существуют факторы, препятствующие такой замене.

Прежде всего бросается в глаза, что инфинитивы, встречающиеся в таких предложениях, относятся к очень ограниченному кругу лексики. В Корпусе XX из 40 примеров с инфинитивом при глаголе *ожидать* 24 содержат глагол *увидеть.* Сравнительно часто, (по 6 раз каждый) встречаются еще и *услышать* и *встретить.* По одному разу представлены глаголы *поймать (взгляд), узнать, найти* и *получить.* По нашему мнению, данные глаголы связывает то, что они все каким-то образом обозначают появление объекта в сфере субъектного актанта (который здесь и является субъектом ожидания).

По-видимому, в современном русском языке данная конструкция при глаголах ожидания возможна только когда ожидаемое событие состоит в том, что ожидающий приходит в контакт с кем-нибудь или чем-нибудь, и когда основное внимание направлено на характер этого человека/предмета или его состояния.

Когда ожидаемое событие носит другой характер, замена изъяснительного предложения на инфинитив оказывается невозможной, даже при идентичном субъекте.

Кроме примера (98)а в Корпусе XX имеются еще два примера с идентичными субъектами. В обоих случаях замена на инфинитив невозможна поскольку главное внимание в них направлено на сам характер ожидаемого события (которое не состоит из появления кого-/чего-нибудь в сфере ожидающего):

(99) Видно, Николай Николаевич **не ожидал**, *что заболеет* [...]
      (Булычев)

(100) **Не ожидал**, *что буду пить* водку в Афганистане в таких усло-
      виях. (Незнанский)

Семантические факторы, по-видимому, не препятствуют замене
на параллельную конструкцию. Она, например, вполне возможна в
следующем предложении:

(101)а В магазинах Авессалом Владимирович производил такой сум-
        бур, так быстро появлялся и исчезал на глазах пораженных
        приказчиков, так экспансивно покупал коробку шоколада, что
        кассирша **ожидала** *получить* с него, по крайней мере, рублей
        тридцать. (Ильф и Петров)

(110)б [...] Кассирша **ожидала**, *что получит* с него, по крайней мере,
        рублей тридцать.

Факторы, затрудняющие замену инфинитива на придаточное предложение, имеют другой характер. Как было уже отмечено, сочетание
ожидал увидеть встречается очень часто. Это одно из наиболее общих
и удобных выражений для обозначения появления кого-/чего-нибудь
перед глазами субъекта. Оно имеет явное преимущество краткости,
экономности средств выражения. Поэтому инфинитив часто предпо-
читается "обычной" конструкции, особенно в тех случаях, где он не
"отягощен" разными обстоятельствами (ср. (97) и (98). Компактный
характер инфинитивной конструкции способствует ее употреблению
и в следующих примерах:

(111) Растерялась она, как подумал Марк Александрович, оттого,
      что никого **не ожидала** *встретить* в пустом коридоре. (Рыбаков)
      (Объектом инфинитива является отрицательное местоимение.)

(112) За дверью оказались не сени, которые **ожидал** *увидеть* Чон-
      кин [...] (Войнович)
      (Данная конструкция входит в состав определительного прида-
      точного предложения.)

(113) Коля даже **ожидал** *увидеть*, как из стены полезут зеленые
      веточки, но ничего подобного не случилось. (Булучев)
      (Здесь избегается скопление изъяснительных придаточных предло-
      жений.)[25]

Как демонстрируют приведенные выше примеры, данная конструкция очень сильно связана с глаголом *ожидать*. В Корпусе XX имеется всего лишь один пример с глаголом *ждать* (на 40 примеров с глаголом *ожидать*):

(114) Я **ждал** *встретить* карателя солдафона или революционного маниака-душителя, и не нашел ни того, ни другого. (Пастернак)

В этом примере глагол *ждать* легко заменяется на *ожидать*. Можно сделать вывод, что в современном языке данная конструкция почти целиком закреплена за глаголом *ожидать*. Это легко объясняется тем, что для данной конструкции характерна полная концентрация на определенных элементах СОБ.

7.2 Глаголы *ждать*, *ожидать* и *выжидать* - XIX в.

Во многих отношениях употребление инфинитивной конструкции в XIX веке похоже на то, что находим в более современном языке. Основное различие состоит в том, что в прошлом столетии конструкция имела несколько большее распространение. Она встречается чаще и не так сильно связана с глаголом *ожидать*; в 20 % случаев встречается глагол *ждать*. Вот несколько примеров:

(115) [...] Князь Андрей, встречаясь с новым лицом, особенно с таким, как Сперанский, которого знал по репутации, всегда **ждал** *найти* в нем полное совершенство человеческих достоинств. (Толстой)

(116) Я **ждал** *встретить* какого-нибудь грязного оборванца, испитого от разврата и отдающего водкой. (Достоевский)

Этот факт указывает на то, что в языке прошлого столетия данная конструкция была возможна и при более напряженном ожидании (см. также пример (120)). На это указывает и (единственный) пример с глаголом *выжидать*:

(117) А она мне ни с того ни с сего, знать, **выжидала** свое *ввернуть*, ехидная такая [...] (Достоевский)

В примерах в основном встречается инфинитив тех же глаголов, что и в современных текстах. Интересно отметить, что кроме глаголов совершенного вида, названных в предыдущем разделе, в текстах XIX-го столетия вместо глагола *увидеть* намного чаще используется глагол несовершенного вида *видеть*.[26]

(118) Пьер не заметил Наташи, потому что он никак **не ожидал**
       видеть ее тут [...] (Толстой)

Только у Достоевского и Чернышевского находим несколько
глаголов другого характера. См. (117) и следующие примеры:

(119) Я вот **ждал** вас *спросить*, - прибавил он, видя, что я не отве-
       чаю [...] (Достоевский)
(120) Вот пример, хоть бы этот самый Пселдонимов: он приехал
       давеча от венца в волнении, в надежде, **ожидая** *вкусить*...
       (Достоевский)
(121) По субботам он ходил под конвоем в свою городскую молель-
       ную (что дозволяется законами) и жил совершенно припеваючи,
       с нетерпением, впрочем, **ожидая** *выжить* свой двенадцатилетний
       срок, чтоб "зениться". (Достоевский)
(122) Быть может, он и прибодрился бы, подходя к скамье, но, за-
       стигнутый врасплох, раньше чем **ждал** *показать* ей свою фигуру,
       он был застигнут с пасмурным лицом. (Чернышевский)[27]

Приведенные примеры показывают, что хотя бы у этих авторов
данная конструкция в семантическом плане имеет другой, более
широкий, характер, чем то, что характерно для языка наших дней.

7.3   Глаголы *подождать* и *выждать*

Для языка XIX-го столетия довольно характерно еще и употребление сочетания инфинитива с глаголом *подождать*. В Корпусе XIX
имеется 14 примеров этого типа. По своей семантике они сильно
отличаются от конструкций, рассмотренных в двух предыдущих раз-
делах. Это связано с особым характером данного глагола. Как уже
было отмечено при обсуждении конструкций с союзами *что* и *чтобы*,
глагол *подождать* очень сильно концентрирует внимание на состоянии
ожидающего. По этой причине он и не сочетается с данными союзами,
связанными именно с представлением об ожидаемом событии.

Поэтому не удивительно, что и инфинитив при глаголе *подождать*
не обозначает ожидаемого события (как в конструкциях, рассмотренных в пар. 7.1-7.2), но связан именно с состоянием субъекта. Он
обозначает действие, которое уже началось или еще только наме-
чается, но от которого временно следует воздержаться, которое нужно
отложить:

(123) **Подождите** *говорить*, Степан Трофимович, подождите немного, пока отдохнете. (Достоевский)

(124) Стой, старина! **подожди** *пить*, дай прежде слово сказать!.. (Достоевский)

(125) Очень сожалею.
— **Подождите** *жалеть*. (Лесков)

Характерно, что в главной части обычно употребляется форма императива. Формы будущего простого здесь также часто имеют оттенок побуждения:

(126) «В эти три, много четыре дня [письмо] должно прийти; **подожду** *ехать* к Ольге», — решил он, тем более что она едва ли знает, что мосты наведены... (Гончаров)

(127) Вот иду я да и думаю: нет, этого христопродавца **подожду** еще *осуждать*. Бог ведь знает, что в этих пьяных и слабых сердцах заключается. (Достоевский)

Однако, как демонстрирует следующий пример, в принципе, не исключается и форма прошедшего времени:

(128) Павел Павлович несколько **подождал** *отвечать* [...] (Достоевский)

Глагол *выждать* встречается всего один раз в сочетании с инфинитивом. Он относится к тому же типу, что и примеры с глаголом *подождать*:

(129) Она... здесь, — медленно проговорил Рогожин, как бы капельку **выждав** *ответить*. (Достоевский)

Согласно цифровым данным, предствваленным в Схеме 1, данное сочетание в прошлом столетии было намного употребительнее, чем сейчас. В Корпусе XX имеется всего один пример этого типа (относящийся также к сфере побуждения):

(130) Решение бюро пока **подождем** *посылать*. Посмотрим... (Шукшин)

В данном значении глагол *подождать* сближается с глаголами *погодить* и *повременить*:

(131) — А-а, Трофимович. Трофимович был, — сказал Дудник, закрывая глаза и снова подставляя руку под подбородок.
— **Погоди** ты *спать*. (Войнович)

(132)   Если возможно, **повремените** *отдавать* мою рукопись в печать
   до утра среды. (Гл. Успенский; БАС)

В нашем распоряжении пока нет данных о частотности употребления этих глаголов, и мы не можем определить, имеют ли они
какое-либо влияние на низкую частотность сочетания глагола *подождать* с инфинитивом в текстах нашего столетия.

8.   Союз *ли* и союзные слова

Как было показано в предыдущих параграфах, при помощи союзов
что и *чтобы* и инфинитива можно непосредственно обозначать
ожидаемое событие.

При помощи средств из сферы вопроса (союз *ли* и союзные слова)
это событие обозначается менее непосредственно и с бóльшей неуверенностью. Этими средствами как бы передаются "внутренние"
вопросы, которые занимают человека и таким образом заставляют его
пребывать в состоянии ожидания. Интересно отметить, что тот факт,
что данные вопросы по-другому связаны с ожиданием, иногда отражается на знаках препинания. Вместо запятой используется тире или
двоеточие и в конце предложение ставится вопросительный знак:

(133)   Вернее **ждал** – *придется ли* работать? (Булычев)
(134)   И опять наступило тягостное, отупляющее **ожидание:** *изменится*
   погода *или нет*? (Айтматов)
(135)   Судорожно барабаня пальцами по медной пряжке ремня своего,
   он **ожидал:** *что еще скажет* она? (Горький)

Однако гораздо чаще данные предложения оформляются как
обычные сложные предложения, в которых изъясняемое слово относится к сфере вопроса:

(136)а И **ждали,** *что будет.* (Булычев)
(136)б И **спросили,** *что будет.*

Это указывает на то, что и у глаголов ожидания данный тип придаточного предложения в основном рассматривается как обозначение
объекта ожидания. В следующем примере придаточные с союзом *ли*
и союзным словом *что* выступают параллельно с придаточным с
союзом *когда* и даже с именными дополнениями:

(137)   Я положил трубку. Теперь мне оставалось только ждать.
   Ждать, *когда* Барон *найдет* эту Айну, **ждать,** *что* там, в Котласе,

узнает Светлов об этом боксере Акееве, **ждать** *сообщений* из Баку, **ждать** *завтрашнего прибытия* в Москву поезда № 37 Ташкент — Москва с бригадиром Германом Долго-Сабуровым, и **ждать,** *не найдет ли* бригада Пшеничного на Курской дороге какого-нибудь свидетеля убийства [...] (Незнанский и Тополь)

Тот факт, что вопросительные предложения менее непосредственно обозначают ожидаемое событие и воспринимаются до какой-то степени как обозначение душевного состояния ожидающего, хорошо объясняет довольно сильные изменения в употреблении этих придаточных предложений при разных глаголах. В то время, как в XIX веке они примерно одинаково часто сочетаются с глаголами *ждать* и *ожидать*, в нашем столетии такое употребление при глаголе *ожидать* очень резко упало (с 45 случаев до 8; см. Схему 1). Кроме того, почти все примеры из современных текстов содержат форму деепричастия, нейтрального по отношению к семантическому различию между этими глаголами:

(138) Помолчали. Майор не проронил ни слова, с любопытством **ожидая,** *чем кончится* этот поединок. (Белов)

Единственный наш пример с личной формой глагола *ожидать* был найден в произведениях Горького, т.е. относится к началу столетия:

(139) Судорожно барабаня пальцами по медной пряжке ремня своего, он **ожидал:** *что еще скажет* она? (Горький)

Однако в текстах прошлого столетия личные формы глагола *ожидать* встречаются примерно в половине случаев. Вот несколько примеров из произведений разных авторов:

(140) Чарский с беспокойством **ожидал,** *какое впечатление произведет* первая минута, но он заметил, что наряд, который показался ему так неприличен, не произвел того же действия на публику. (Пушкин)

(141) Он рассердился, приготовился даже задать что-то вроде потасовки приятелю нашему Селифану и **ожидал** только с нетерпением, *какую* тот с своей стороны *приведет* причину в оправдание. (Гоголь)

(142) Я со страхом **ожидала,** *что будет,* дрожала всеми членами. (Достоевский)

(143) Я чувствовал, что все смотрели на меня и **ожидали** того, *что я скажу* [...] (Толстой)

(144) Экс-гусар подошел к ней, вежливо поклонился и **ожидал**, *что она скажет.* (Лесков)

(145) Рассудив таким образом, глуповцы стали **ждать**, *не сделаются ли* все кредиторы разумными? (Салтыков-Щедрин)[28]

На основе предлагаемой выше характеристики данной конструкции можно ожидать и возможность сочетания подобных придаточных предложений с остальными глаголами ожидания несовершенного вида. (Глагол *пережидать* здесь снова не представлен.) Употребление этих глаголов можно проиллюстрировать следующими примерами:

(146) Она пошла дальше, **не дожидаясь**, *к какому придут решению.* (Пастернак)

(147) Обломов с любопытством смотрел на него и **дожидался**, *что он скажет.* (Гончаров)

(148) Фельдшер имел измученный вид. Он, видимо, с досадой **дожидался**, *скоро ли уйдет* заболтавшийся доктор. (Толстой)

(149) **Выжидаю** только, *как бы поумней* дело это *сделать.* (Бунин)

(150) С Филиппом Филипповичем что-то сделалось, вследствие чего его лицо нежно побагровело, и он не произнес ни одного звука, **выжидая**, *что будет* дальше. (Булгаков)

(151) По временам [он] садился у открытого окна и **поджидал**, *не проедет ли* кто. (Салтыков-Щедрин)

Как было отмечено в предыдущих параграфах, глагол *подождать* отличается тем, что он фактически не сочетается с непосредственным обозначением ожидаемого события. Тот факт, что при этом глаголе встречаются придаточные вопросительного типа, поддерживает наше утверждение, что этот тип концентрирует внимание прежде всего на состоянии ожидающего:

(152) **Подождем**, *чем* там *кончится* у Геры — может, эта штука оторвет ему яйца. (Лазарчук)

(153) Только вот **подожду**, *какое* это средство, про которое он говорит. (Чернышевский)

(154) К чести Аннушки надо сказать, что она была любознательна и решила еще **подождать**, *не будет ли* каких новых чудес. (Булгаков)

(155) Он **подождал**, *не ответит ли* что корнет. (Л. Толстой)

9. Заключение

Русские глаголы ожидания составляют весьма интересную группу
глаголов, которые по своему составу, внутренним связям и синтаксическому поведению заметно отличается от соответствующих глаголов
в западно-европейских языках. Детальный анализ поведения этих
глаголов может способствовать расширению наших знаний о функционировании синтаксических средств в рамках сложного предложения
и об их возможной семантической обусловленности. При этом, как
показывает наша статья, для создания более ясной картины работа
с корпусом компьютерных текстов фактически необходима.

Хотя корпусы, на которых основано наше исследование являются
довольно значительными по объему, мы все же считаем, что в ближайшем будущем следовало бы увеличить количество текстов и сделать
корпусы более уравновешенными.

Тот факт, что в наших корпусах представлены два последних
столетия, дал нам возможность обнаружить определенные изменения
в употреблении глаголов ожидания с придаточными изъяснительными.
Было бы интересно проверить, насколько материал компьютерных
корпусов применим для исследования других изменений в развитии
языка.

Что касается синхронных исследований, то значение наличия
компьютерных текстов для изучения языка прошлого столетия совершенно очевидно, поскольку тут нашими единственными источниками
являются именно тексты. Конечно же, при изучении современного
языка можно и нужно использовать и другие методы, такие как опрос
информантов при языковых экспериментах, интроспекция (если
исследователь изучает родной язык). Мы уверены в том, что, применяя эти методы для проверки гипотез и расширения знаний о
предмете, мы придем к более глубокому пониманию описанных
в нашей статье явлений. Поэтому к ряду вопросов надо будет обязательно вернуться.

Из-за недостатка места и времени некоторые из наиболее важных
типов конструкций при глаголах ожидания (конструкции с временными союзами) остались в нашей работе без внимания. Мы надеемся
вернуться к ним в отдельной статье. Прежде всего внимание должно
быть уделено слову *когда*. Что касается *пока (не)*, то наш новый
материал, как нам кажется, в главных чертах подтверждает то, о чем
было написано в работе (Барентсен 1980б).

Амстердамский университет

ПРИМЕЧАНИЯ

*   Приношу благодарность Валентине Барентсен-Орлянской за неоценимую помощь в редактировании статьи.

1   Именная группа в позиции объекта глагола ожидания определенным образом представляет ожидаемое событие (СОБ). Отглагольные существительные, такие как *восход, окончание* и т.д. обозначают непосредственно само это событие. Однако гораздо чаще данное событие обозначается косвенно, указанием главного его актанта. Данное событие в таком случае заключается в появлении этого актанта в сфере субъекта ожидания (ср. *ждал Ивана - ждал, пока придет* Иван).

Выбор падежной формы в большой степени мотивирован семантическими факторами, связанными с этим различием. Форма винительного падежа указывает на то, что объект представляет собой актант события СОБ и имеет достаточно ясный самостоятельный статус, т.е. представляется как "нечто, уже существующее" (Барентсен 1980а: 349).

По отношению к управлению глагола *ждать* и Апресян указывает на подобное смысловое противопоставление (по линии (не)известности/(не)определенности объекта ожидания (1997: 117).

2   Этот перевод входит в собрание англоязычных текстов на CD-rom'е "Library of the Future".

3   Выражаю благодарность моему коллеге Гунтеру Спису за его помощь при обсуждении данных немецких конструкций.

4   В принципе даже эта форма все же оставляет некоторую возможность для сомнения в реальности совершения данного события. Однако вместо простой формы прошедшего времени в придаточной части таких предложений встречается еще и форма плюсквамперфекта. При помощи этой формы подчеркивается завершение действия и, как нам кажется, таким образом увеличивается и степень его реальности:

(6'')д *Hij* **wachtte** *tot* de professor *weg was gegaan*.

Как иллюстрируют примеры (9) и (10), подобная возможность существует и в английском языке.

5   В принципе, однако, существует еще и конструкция *s'attendre à ce que*, которая могла бы больше соответствовать русской конструкции с союзом *что*. В доступном нам материале мы, однако, не нашли примеров с этой конструкцией.

6   Интересно отметить, что в переводе этого текста, сделанном Сириным (= Набоковым) использован другой союз (ср. пример (2)):

Аня терпеливо **ждала**, *чтобы* она вновь *заговорила*.

7   Примеры (2) и (14) переводятся на нидерландский язык соответственно:

(2)а *Hij* **verwachtte** *dat* zij tegenwerpingen *zou maken*

(14)а *Zij* **verwachtte** *dat* hij haar *zou uitnodigen* voor de wals.

[8] Ср. следующие соответствия, приведенные в статье немецкого слависта Обста (1990: 158):

(а) **erwarteten** alle, *daß* Hugo zum Aufzug ... *flitzen würde*. (H. Böll)

все они **ждали**, *что* Гуго стремглав *кинется* к лифту

(б) Filat [...] **erwartete**, *daß* er weiß der Teufel was *erzählen würde*.

Флилат **ожидал** [...], *что* он сейчас *расскажет* бог знает что. (Платонов)

[9] О различиях между парами *ждать/ожидать* и *warten/erwarten* см. статью, упомянутую в предыдущем примечании (Обст 1990).

[10] Здесь играют некоторую роль и факторы морфологического характера. Поскольку форма деепричастия несовершенного вида от глагола *ждать* избегается, вместо нее используется соответствующая форма от глагола *ожидать*: *ожидая*. У этой формы семантическое различие между данными глаголами фактически снято. Подобную же "нейтрализацию" находим и у отглагольного существительного *ожидание*.

[11] Приобретение такой информации на практике затрудняется тем, что многие из данных конструкций имеют довольно низкую частотность. Хотя основной глагол (*ждать*) и относится к словам с высокой частотностью, этот глагол сочетается с придаточным предложением сравнительно редко (менее, чем в 4% всех случаев употребления). Эти количественные данные мы основываем на материале "Уппсальского корпуса", послужившего основой для нового частотного словаря русского языка (Леннгрен 1993).

[12] Для сравнения указываем на то, что современные частотные словари русского языка (Засорина и др. 1977, Леннгрен 1993) основываются на корпусах содержащих по одному миллиону словоупотреблений.

[13] В нашем комментарии мы используем прежде всего примеры из этих корпусов. При рассмотрении более редких случаев, используем также примеры, собранные нами "вручную", или встречающиеся в компьютерных текстах информативного характера. К последним относятся тексты из раздела "специальная литература" Уппсальского корпуса, ряд выпусков интернетовской газеты "ИТАР-ТАСС-Экспресс" и т.д. Некоторые примеры сравнительно редких случаев были найдены в картотеке словарного кабинета АН СССР. Они снабжены пометой **Карт**.

[14] Придаточные предложения со словом *когда* рассматриваются отдельно. См. следующие два раздела (**вк** и **кг**).

[15] Такие случаи довольно редки, и в нашем материале они встречаются в основном у глагола *ждать* (изредка у глагола *ожидать*). Следующие примеры дают определенное представление об их характере:

Я **ждал** *он спросит*: на что намекаете? (Войнович)

Я все **ждала**, *переселимся* в Москву, там мне *встретится* мой настоящий, я мечтала о нем, любила... (Чехов)

Я **ожидал**, *ты скажешь* [...] (Снегов)

[16] Интересно отметить, что в нидерландском языке в подобных случаях употребляется не простая форма прошедшего времени (*ik verwachtte niet*), но форма плюсквамперфекта: *ik had niet verwacht*).

17 Как и в примерах (40) и (41), глагол *ждать* здесь легко заменяется на *ожидать*.

18 Не вполне ясно, относится ли этот пример на самом деле к данному типу. Приводим здесь более расширенный контекст:

— *Задний ход! — раздался голос капитана.*
Никто не ожидал, что пароход так скоро подошел к островку.
Все засуетились и пошли.

Как нам кажется, элемент сосредоточенности на результативном состоянии, характерный для перфектного значения, здесь едва различим. Нормальнее было бы употребить форму *подойдет*. За недостатком материала трудно решить, представлен ли здесь устарелый вариант.

19 Этот факт не находит отражения в описании Апресяна, где утверждается, что "Только синоним **ждать** управляет придаточным предложением, вводимым союзом *что*" (1997: 117).

20 Здесь выбор союза *что* вместо более употребительного союза *пока* может быть мотивирован тем, что последний уже один раз представлен в этом предложении.

21 Этот пример интересен еще тем, что субъектом ожидания не является лицо. "Тишина" здесь явно персонифицируется, ей приписываются чувства.

22 Второе придаточное предложение в этом примере относится к совершенно другому типу — к придаточным цели.

23 Обратите внимание на местоименный элемент *того*, употребление которого очень характерно для Толстого (см. 5.5). См. также примеры (3), (77) и (143).

24 Как известно, данные авторы часто пользовались французским языком.

25 Собственно говоря, речь здесь идет не о появлении кого-/чего-нибудь, но о восприятии события другого характера. По-видимому, стилистические факторы в этом случае действуют сильнее, чем семантические.

26 Как было уже отмечено Ю.С. Масловым, глаголы *видеть* и *слышать* имеют особый аспектуальный характер "непосредственного, непрерывного эффекта" (1984: 62). В ряде случаев это сильно сближает их по значению с глаголами совершенного вида.

27 У Чернышевского находим еще и следующие два примера, которые, по-видимому, относятся к другому типу. Прямым объектом глагола ожидания здесь является личное местоимение, а инфинитив имеет здесь скорее обстоятельственное значение. (Употребление сочетания "кого-л. ждут обедать" возможно и в современном языке, хотя в нашем корпусе оно не представлено примерами.)

Меня, я думаю, дома ждут обедать, — сказала Верочка: — пора.
"Маша, вы не ждите меня обедать: я не буду ныне обедать дома".

28 Обратите внимание и на обстоятельства *с беспокойством* (140), *с нетерпением* (141), которые в языке наших дней обычно не сочетаются с личными формами глагола *ожидать*, и на местоимение *того* (143), типичного для языка Толстого.

40

ЛИТЕРАТУРА

АГ-60
1960   *Грамматика русского языка. Том 2, часть вторая.* Москва.
АГ-80
1980   *Русская грамматика. Том II: Синтаксис.* Москва: Наука.
Апресян, Ю.Д.
1997   "*ЖДАТЬ 1.1*", Апресян и др., 112-120
Апресян и др.
1997   *Новый объяснительный словарь синонимов русского языка.*
            Первый выпуск. Москва: Школа «Языки русской культуры».
Барентсен, А.А.
1980а   "Объектные падежи при глаголе *ждать*", *Возьми на радость*, То
            Honour Jeanne van de Eng-Liemeier, 343-350. Amsterdam.
1980б   "Об особенностях употребления союза *пока* при глаголах ожи-
            дания", *Studies in Slavic and General Linguistics* 1. Amsterdam:
            Rodopi.
Гард (Garde, P.)
1963   *L'emploi du conditionnel et de la particule* by *en russe.* Aix-en-
            Provence.
Зализняк, А.А.
1967   *Русское именно склонение.* Москва.
Засорина, Л.Н. и др.
1977   *Частотный словарь русского языка.* Москва: Русский язык.
Леннгрен, Л.
1993   *Частотный словарь современного русского языка.* (Acta Universi-
            tatis Upsaliensis. Studia Slavica Upsaliensia 32). Uppsala.
Маслов, Ю.С.
1984(48)   "Вид и лексическое значение глагола в современном русском
            литературном языке", *Очерки по аспектологии*, 48-65. Ленинград.
            (Ранее опубликовано в *Известиях АН СССР, Отд. лит. и яз.*, 1948,
            т. 7, вып. 4, 303-316.)
Обст (Obst, U.)
1990   "Zur Semantik von russisch *ždat'/ožidat'* und deutsch *warten/er-*
            warten", »Tgolí chole Mêstro«, Gedenkschrift Für Reinhold Olesch
            (= Slawistische Forschungen 60), 153-172.
Формановская, Н.И.
1978   *Стилистика сложного предложения.* Москва: Русский язык.

ПРИЛОЖЕНИЕ:

СОДЕРЖАНИЕ ИСПОЛЬЗОВАННЫХ КОРПУСОВ

(Цифры обозначают объем данной части в тысячах словоупотреблений)

Корпус XIX:

(Место автора в списке определяется по возможности хронологически — по дате появления первого представленного в корпусе произведения.)

А.С. Пушкин: *Прозаические произведения*; *Евгений Онегин*; *Руслан и Людмила*; *Моцарт и Сальери*	(158)
Н.В. Гоголь: *Мертвые души*; *Сборники рассказов*; *Пьесы*	(437)
М.Ю. Лермонтов: *Герой нашего времени* и остальные прозаические произведения	(96)
Ф.М. Достоевский: Вся художественная проза	(1811)
И.С. Тургенев: Рассказы и романы	(326)
Л.Н. Толстой: *Автобиографическая трилогия*; *Анна Каренина*; *Война и мир*	(825)
И.А. Гончаров: *Обломов*	(147)
Н.Г. Чернышевский: *Что делать?*	(138)
А.Ф. Писемский: *Взбаламученное море*	(120)
Н.С. Лесков: *Некуда*; *На ножах*; *Соборяне*	(527)
М.Е. Салтыков-Щедрин: *История одного города*; *Господа Головлевы*	(136)
А.П. Чехов: Рассказы и Пьесы	(825)

	Итого:	**4945**

Корпус XX:

Первая половина столетия (1113):

М.А. Булгаков: *Белая гвардия*; *Театральный роман*; *Мастер и Маргарита*; *Багровый остров*; *Собачье сердце*; *Роковые яйца*; *Записки юного врача*; *Похождения Чичикова*	(307)
И. Бунин: Рассказы	(159)
М. Горький: *Жизнь Клима Самгина* (I)	(142)
И. Ильф и Е. Петров: *12 стульев*; *Золотой теленок*	(166)
В. Набоков: *Машенька*; *Король, дама, валет*; *Камера обскура*; *Другие берега*; *Незавершенный роман*; *Рассказы*	(264)
А. Платонов: *Котлован*	(35)
А.Н. Толстой: *Аэлита*	(40)

Вторая половина столетия (3839):

I Литературная часть "Уппсальского корпуса" (Подробное описание см. в работе Леннгрен 1993)	(500)

42

II Другие тексты:

Dutch Contributions to the Twelfth International Congress of Slavists, Cracow, Linguistics (= Studies in Slavic and General Linguistics Vol 24), 41–92. RODOPI, Amsterdam – Atlanta, GA 1998.

L'ASPECT DU VERBE ET LA GENÈSE DE LA NOMENCLATURE GRAMMATICALE RUSSE

ANDRIES BREUNIS

Après l'ère du tohu-bohu

L'analyse d'une langue s'opère généralement sur la base de ce qu'il y a, dans cette langue, de régulier. L'irrégulier, cela va de soi, y est subordonné, c'est accessoire, donc, c'est de moindre importance. C'est un fait évident aux yeux de tous, et même les linguistes le jugent indiscutable. Mais ce principe n'est pas si certain comme il en a l'air. Il n'existe pas de tout temps et, en tout cas, il n'a pas été depuis toujours inattaquable. A l'antiquité grecque, il y a eu des penseurs qui croyaient que l'irrégularité est toute naturelle, puisque elle découle de l'usage et de l'habitude, elle coule de source. Il faut s'incliner devant elle, parce que c'est justement l'irrégularité qui fait le charme du langage.

D'autres ont dit que la régularité est la norme. S'il y a de l'irrégularité, elle n'est qu'apparente; elle disparaît quand on change de point de vue. La controverse qui s'en est écoulée, entre anomalistes et analogistes, sur le domaine de la grammaire, était donc une dispute de méthode. Cette controverse-là avait été engagée par Cratès de Mallos, anomaliste par conviction, contre le savant alexandrin Aristarque de Samothrace. Mais quant à la pratique, comme la composition d'un véritable manuel de grammaire, on ignore, malheureusement, si les anomalistes ont su s'y prendre et comment ils se seraient tirés d'affaire.

Dionysius Thrax, grammairien à Alexandrie, disciple d'Aristarque, au temps, environ, du grand-père de Cléopâtre, a tranché la dispute d'une façon propre à un analogiste, du moins, pour autant qu'on puisse le conclure de ce qui reste de son oeuvre: un petit manuel de grammaire grecque. Un très petit livre, certes, inimaginable que ce serait l'oeuvre de vie d'un savant alexandrin, mais il est très consistant. Le livre présente tous les premiers éléments de la langue grecque. Denys de Thrace avait rassemblé des conceptions grammaticales, courantes à l'époque, pour en faire un système de description cohérent. Au fond, le système de Denys n'a jamais été amélioré. Dans la section qui contient ce qu'on appellerait aujourd'hui phonologie, il est vrai, on rencontre des idées primitives qui se basent sur l'écriture. Par exemple, les diphthongues (écrit ici avec *ph* et aussi avec *th*, parce que le mot vient de φθόγγος, "son") sont lettres, qui, dans la conception moderne, ne représentent qu'un seul son (comme en français *au, ai,* etc.). A d'autres endroits, il est question de *lettres* au lieu de *sons,* mais c'est une procédure qui a longtemps persisté. L'inventeur de la loi de la grande *Lautverschiebung* germanique, encore au début du dix-neuvième siècle, parlait en général de lettres, où la linguistique de nos jours emploie le nom de phonème. Il est clair pourtant ce qu'il a voulu dire, et le dernier mot n'a pas encore été dit là-dessus. Beaucoup de linguistes ne l'ont pas compris et font usage de l'expression de *mutation* pour *Verschiebung,* traduction qu'on ferait mieux de remplacer par *substitution.*

Reste à savoir, soit dit en passant, si la phonologie moderne elle-même, par son attitude envers le langage écrit, s'est suffisamment libérée de préjugés dûs à l'influence de l'écriture. En tout cas, je ne crois pas qu'elle ait réussi à y échapper et qu'elle ait pu corriger, dans la grammaire de Denys, tout ce qui est faux d'un point de vu scientifique.

Quant à la phonologie, si dans la grammaire antique les sons sont désignés par lettres, ce n'est pas que les anciens ont vraiment confondu le fond et la forme, tant qu'ils ont pu faire une distinction entre la main et les oreilles. Qui mieux est, si la linguistique de nos temps en venait à corriger les principes de la grammaire alexandrine (abstraction faite des doctrines phonologiques primitives), elle ébranlerait ses propres fondements. C'est que, la *grammaire* de Denys de Thrace, elle n'est pas qu'un manuel de l'apprentissage de la lecture et de l'écriture, elle est aussi l'art d'en parler, l'art de "parler langue". C'est l'abécédaire des recherches linguistiques et la source de tous ses babélismes.

Quoi qu'il en soit, ce qui est plus important, dans le système de Denys, que de prendre les désignations de *son* à la lettre, c'est la conception de grammaire qui comporte les notions des parties de discours et les autres notions grammaticales qui sont restées fondamentales jusqu'à présent. Ce n'est pas un hasard si l'on trouve dans une grammaire moderne, d'une autre langue que le vieux grec, des distinctions et notions qui sont semblables à celles de la grammaire grecque. Ce ne sont pas *universalia,* ce sont faits de la langue grecque selon la grammaire dionysienne, imposés à d'autres langues. Ce n'est pas la faute de Denys, sa grammaire n'est jamais, tout simplement, qu'une méthode, qui, probablement, aurait bien pu être une autre. C'est une méthode pour relever certains faits; et chaque méthode insiste sur certains faits, au détriment des autres. De ce point de vue, quand même, la grammaire de Denys, dans ce qui reste de la version qui lui est attribuée, est comme un programme politique réduit: moins il y a d'idées et de propositions, plus d'électeurs s'y retrouvent. Je le dis sans mauvaise intention, c'est pour expliquer qu'on dirait que Denys de Thrace, en effet, a évité le problème de l'analogie et de l'anomalie, en commençant par les notions les plus fondamentales. De la sorte, qu'on pourrait tout aussi bien maintenir que sa méthode a été projetée, à l'origine pour une description des rudiments de la langue grecque, mais aussi pour d'autres langues. Il a évité toutes les irrégularités apparentes. C'est exactement cela qui fait que sa grammaire s'applique facilement à d'autre langues.

Il est question, chez Denys, d'une "exposition de régularité" (ἀναλογίας ἐκλογισμός, Uhlig 1883: 6, 2), mais, en effet, on n'en retrouve rien dans les textes qui peuvent lui être attribués. Tous les cas du nom s'appellent "cas", y compris le nominatif (ὀνομαστική), quoique Denys y ajoute que le cas s'appelle aussi ὀρθή ou εὐθῦα, "casus rectus", "le cas direct". On croirait "direct", face aux cas obliques qui, par conséquent, seraient fondés sur le nominatif, mais le texte de Denys ne le dit pas. Une forme verbale qui s'appelle dérivée ou composée, est, apparemment, à en juger d'après le nom, censée être formée d'une forme non-dérivée ou non-composée, ou, du moins, de l'avoir été jadis. Mais la nature de la cohérence des phénomènes, c'est-à-dire, la direction de la dérivation, est indiquée rarement et seulement par la terminologie.

C'est Varron, polygraphe et grammairien romain, analogiste "convaincu" comme on dirait aujourd'hui, un des amis de Cicéron, qui a fait un pas plus loin que Denys de Thrace. Chez celui-ci les temps verbaux sont divisés en trois: l'heure qu'il est, donc le temps présent, le temps qu'on a devant soi, le futur, et le temps que l'on a déjà vécu, le temps passé, dont il y a quatre sortes: imparfait, parfait, plus-que-parfait et aoriste. Il y a des *parentés*: du présent avec l'imparfait, du temps parfait avec le plus-que-parfait et de l'aoriste avec le futur (Uhlig 1883: 53). On pourrait supposer qu'il est question ici de rapports de dérivation, mais il n'est pas clair. La parenté de l'aoriste avec le futur ne se révèle que par le *sigma* (λύσω, "je délierai"; ἔλυσα, "je déliai"). Le grammairien est en tout cas libre de choisir la parenté qu'il voudra.

Varron, par contre, a inventé un véritable système temporel pour le latin. Dans son *de lingua latina*, il avait exposé les deux doctrines, anomaliste et analogiste (on aurait dit, exposé selon leur interprétation la plus extrême, pour en choisir ce qui était pour lui le juste milieu, mais il a présenté un débat réel: Dahlmann 1932). Ainsi, il en a déduit la méthode à proportions et il l'a introduite dans la grammaire latine. Appliquée au système verbal, il a pu attribuer un imparfait et un futur au présent aussi bien qu'au parfait. Par analogie avec la subordination, au présent, de l'imparfait et du futur simple, il a admis la même relation au passé: un plus-que-parfait et un futur antérieur, subordonnés à (ou fondés sur) la forme du parfait.

Varron avait réfléchi sur l'origine du langage. En considérant que sa propre langue se compose de milliers de formes apparentées les unes aux autres par la déclinaison en diverses directions (*altus*, de là, le génitif, etc.: *alti*, etc., à partir de *altus* dans un autre sens: le féminin: *alta, altae*, etc., et, dans un autre sens encore, aussi *altitudo, altitudinis*, etc. etc.) il avait conclu qu'une langue s'est développée à partir d'un noyau, qui en est la source, un noyau de mots simples, un nombre limité de noms, imposés, jadis, aux choses. Il ne craignait pas l'effort des étymologies qui sont, pour le moins, audacieuses, en réduisant ainsi considérablement le nombre de mots primitifs. (Livres VI et VII). En même temps néanmoins, sa théorie historique contient des éléments dignes de notre attention. L'existence de liens flexionnels et dérivatifs est évidente. Si ses réflexions sur l'origine d'une langue nous mènent trop loin, Varron a posé à juste titre le problème des dérivations. Il s'explique au début du livre VIII. Comment pourrait-on retenir la masse de mots qui sont ainsi dérivés des noms de choses, sans les liens étymologiques qui sont clairs et transparents? Pour Varron, la méthode analogiste était une méthode qui coule de source.

C'était une méthode descriptive qui aurait pu ajouter explicitement la notion de subordination à la grammaire de Denys, d'une façon plus nuancée que la constatation que les mots motivés remontent aux mots immotivés. En plus, si Varron n'avait pas vraiment pu trancher la controverse entre les anomalistes et les analogistes, il aurait pu en finir avec la croyance, si celle-ci existait à l'époque, que les hommes, quand ils parlent, construisent des phrases en joignant les éléments de leur langue et en collant les morphèmes aux thèmes selon les règles, prétendument, règles de la langue, mais, en vérité, règles établies par les grammairiens. En appliquant sa méthode proportionnelle, Varron n'emploie que de formes complètes qui, éventuellement, sont fondées, selon les proportions, sur d'autre formations. Seulement, qui saurait dire quelles formations sont subordonnées à (ou fondées sur) quelles autres formations?

Beaucoup plus tard (nous sautons de l'antiquité au XVIII-ème siècle), des grammairiens russes ont supposé que *написать* aurait été dérivé de *написывать* qui (ils le disent eux-mêmes) n'existe pas (et qui ne peut exister à cause du sens, spécifique à la combinaison du préfixe *на-* et le verbe *писать*). Ils ont supposé que le passé a été formé du présent (ce qui implique la proportion *связываю* > *связывал* = *связываю* > *связал* = *вяжу - связал*), mais ils ont imaginé *написывать* et l'ont déduit selon la proportion *связать* > *связывать* = *написать* > x = *написать* > *написывать* (s'ils ne l'ont pas emprunté au vieux slave d'église).

Ainsi, on peut croire que les compositions ont été formées à partir des membres simples. Mais pour les formations nouvelles ou occasionnelles, on pourrait tout aussi bien faire naître des formes simples sur la base des compositions. Au lieu de former *innombrable* par analogie avec *croyable, nombrable* > *incroyable, innombrable*, on pourrait imaginer une proportion *incroyable* > *croyable* = *innombrable* > x = *innombrable* > *"nombrable"*.

Notre siècle a vu le retour de la notion de proportion dans la méthode linguistique de Kuryłowicz, qui l'a reprise, en fait, à Saussure. Celui-ci, à son tour, a peut-être songé à Varron. La méthode présuppose, pour les relations dérivatives, une forme de fondation et une forme fondée et des structures hiérarchiques: l'emploi d'une forme fondée réfère à la forme de fondation. C'est-à-dire, l'emploi, par exemple, de *beauté* nous rappelle *beau*, mais l'emploi de *beau* n'évoque pas forcément les dérivations qu'on pourrait en faire. En théorie, entre deux formes qui ont un lien dérivatif, l'une forme qui a une sphère d'emploi plus grande que celle de l'autre, peut être considérée comme forme de fondation.

Il y a, par conséquent, deux sortes de systèmes de formation de mots. L'un d'un ordre pratique: le locuteur peut former des mots nouveaux qui sont impliqués dans les liens de formation qu'il reconnaît. L'autre d'un ordre théorique, qui, bien évidemment, repose sur le système pratique, mais qui sert à déceler des règles qui président à la dérivation et la composition, c'est-à-dire, qui sert à découvrir des hiérarchies réelles qui surpassent la conscience du locuteur. C'est la quête de la structure.

La théorie peut être mise à l'épreuve, quand on la confronte aux faits fournis par l'histoire d'une langue. Elle peut être considérée comme valable, jusqu'à preuve du contraire. Ainsi, il s'est avéré que la forme de fondation n'est pas toujours une forme simple qui aurait produit ou influencé une forme composée.[1]

Quand on discerne certaines régularités dans une langue, il faut se rendre compte que les faits qu'on croit apercevoir, s'écoulent de la méthode, non pas des propriétés d'une langue, comme des vérités

48

mathématiques. Les propriétés elle-mêmes, quelques propriétés qu'on croie discerner, sont la méthode. La grammaire est toujours une méthode, c'est elle qui impose une structure à la langue. Et c'est la langue qui est l'objet de l'analyse, non pas la grammaire, qui, en conséquence, n'en est que le résultat toujours provisoire. Ce ne signifie pas que les recherches linguistiques sont illusoires. Le tout est de ne pas confondre des méthodes différentes.

L'examen d'une langue c'est l'examen de nos propres connaissances. C'est l'investigation de tout ce qu'on doit savoir pour avoir le droit de dire qu'on connaît cette langue. Une personne qui maîtrise une langue du point de vue matériel (elle connaît les faits) et social (elle peut se faire entendre et les autres le confirment d'une façon ou d'une autre), une personne qui la possède, autrement dit, tout simplement, qui connaît une langue, est homme ou femme à juger toutes les *sortes* de phrases, locutions, tournures, expressions, etc. (je ne dis pas toutes les phrases, on ne sait jamais) qui existent dans cette langue. Elle est en état de prédire des textes qui, du point de vue du grammairien, sont *corrects*.

C'est comme si les connaissances d'une langue c'était d'avoir vu, d'avance, tout ce qui se dit. Dans cette vue d'ensemble, dans ce déjà-vu, il n'y a pas d'irrégularités. Tout est comme il faut et tout est comme dit l'autre. C'est cet ensemble qui constitue la langue.

Dans un ensemble sans irrégularités, il n'y a pas non plus de régularités, parce que l'un des deux principes n'existe pas sans l'autre. Aussi, les notions de régularité et d'irrégularité proviennent-elles de la grammaire, langage des grammairiens, qui comporte toujours un point de vue, une manière de voir une langue. La grammaire, même dans le sens le plus large du terme, ce n'est jamais qu'un auxiliaire, accompagnant les recherches; elle est elle-même née des recherches. Le grammairien n'est pas maître de la langue, mais il est le porteur d'un héritage, porte-parole des grammairiens qui ont produit les notions de régularité et d'irrégularité, en développant les méthodes.

La grammaire grecque (c'est-à-dire, la méthode de grammairiens) a une histoire elle-même. De toute antiquité, les scientifiques et grammairiens, semble-t-il, se servaient d'une méthode selon laquelle les mots d'une langue sont divisés en classes. D'abord par genre: des listes d'ustensiles divers, d'articles de marchandise, etc. etc. La toute première division *linguistique*, par contre, doit avoir été une division en classes syntaxiques. Vraisemblablement, ce n'est pas comme tout s'est passé en réalité, mais c'est comme la théorie de l'histoire de l'invention du feu[2] ou de la roue: entre la période où l'humanité avait ni feu ni lieu, ou ne disposait pas de moyens de transport convenables, et la période d'aujourd'hui, il a fallu quelqu'un qui les ait inventés. Il doit avoir été quelqu'un, mais c'est difficile à se figurer que ce n'était pas du jour au lendemain.

Imaginons-nous le gros oeuvre du bâtiment grammatical des grammairiens avant la lettre: au début préhistorique de la linguistique il ne disposait que de textes, car la linguistique n'aurait jamais pu commencer sans la constatation que les gens se font entendre et sans la prise de conscience de ce qu'ils comprennent. Comment aurait-on analysé les paroles de soi-même ou du voisin? Aurait-on analysé un texte en mots ou en phrases?

Les textes sont discours et les discours se composent d'autres discours, comme les chants consistent en couplets, les romans en volumes et ceux-ci en chapitres. Si un texte a du sens, le sens consiste en plusieurs sens et les plus petites unités de sens sont les phrases. Une analyse ultérieure va au-delà du sens et il n'en reste que les parties, les parties d'un discours.

C'est ainsi qu'on peut imaginer la naissance de la doctrine des huit parties du *sens*, les huit μέρη τοῦ λόγου des grammairiens grecs qu'on trouve canonisés enfin chez Denys de Thrace. Les parties du discours sont catégories syntaxiques; c'est leur fonction syntaxique qui les fait rentrer dans une catégorie. Elles ne sont que des parties du sens, c'est-à-dire, pièces détachées, et dépourvues de sens. Elles sont particules qui n'ont pas de sens, parce qu'elles sont prises à part. Elles sont les λέξεις, "des choses qu'on dit" ou "qu'on peut dire", donc "mots décousus", "bruits de parlotte"; λέξις, c'est un mot terminant en -*sis* et dérivé de λέγειν, "parler", comme πρᾶξις, "action de faire", "l'acte d'un acte", est dérivé de πράσσειν, "faire" (en tout cas formé avec la racine πραγ-).

La signification, c'est tout ce qu'on veut dire ou ce qu'on pourrait comprendre. Elle se trouve dans la différence entre les phrases, pour ainsi dire, dans l'espace entre deux phrases. Les processus inconscients qui précéderaient ou accompagneraient l'acte de la parole, à ce que croient les linguistes depuis Hermann Paul (par. 12; et Wilhelm Wundt y a mis du sien), ne sont pas tellement intéressants que le contenu, souvent inconscient, du moins partiellement, de la différences entre les signes linguistiques distincts.

Raconter ou réécrire tout ce que signifie un texte, ce n'est pas le réciter ou transcrire, c'est rapporter son contenu. C'est expliquer tout ce qui est impliqué entre les phrases. A l'opposé de cela, la grammaire se préoccupe de ce que les phrases ont en commun. Le début de la linguistique était donc l'abandon du sens, puisqu'en divisant le discours en morceaux, c'est-à-dire, en morcelant le discours, objet concret et tangible de l'investigation qui sert à mieux comprendre le langage, on perd le sens.

Il n'en reste pas moins vrai que les parties du discours restent reconnaissables. Ainsi, on peut identifier un mot dans des phrases différentes. Toutes les phrases possibles, quoique toutes différentes les unes des autres, peuvent bien avoir quelque chose en commun, comme par exemple un ou plusieurs mots. Toutes ces significations ont des points communs qui aident à identifier un mot et parmi ces points-là on reconnaît ce que les phrases ont en commun: on reconnaît la phrase en phrase.

Ce que les phrases ont en commun, c'est, tout au moins, le sens de phrase, c'est-à-dire, tout ce qui fait reconnaître la phrase comme phrase. Elles sont plus qu'une séquence, elles ne sont pas une simple succession de mots. La signification d'un mot peut changer d'une phrase à l'autre (à condition, bien entendu, que l'on reconnaisse ce mot comme le même mot dans tous les cas où il est employé), mais c'est son identité qui revient toujours dans des phrases qui sont, pour le reste, différentes. Dans toutes ces significations, le mot est identique à soi-même; tous ces emplois peuvent révéler l'essence du mot. Les emplois peuvent avoir en commun une sorte d'emploi: c'est la fonction syntaxique primaire du mot. La fonction syntaxique d'un mot c'est la particule de sens qu'on retrouve dans tous les mots de la même catégorie syntaxique.

Il s'ensuit de là que la première particule sémantique qu'on a déterminée dans un mot, après l'avoir reconnu et identifié, c'est la fonction syntaxique, élément de la valeur d'un mot. C'est cela qui décide du sort des méthodes linguistiques, mais c'est une idée qui est loin d'être révolutionnaire. Seulement, comme il paraît, il n'y a pas eu de linguistes qui en ont tiré les conséquences.

Les huit parties du sens de la grammaire antique grecque (alexandrine) peuvent bien être les catégories syntaxiques de la langue grecque, bien que Denys de Thrace lui-même, peut-être, dans le temps, n'y ait pas pensé. En tout cas, elles ont dû être syntaxiques jadis, à l'époque où les grammairiens, de *cujus successione agitur*, se rendaient compte de ce qu'ils enseignaient.

Denys de Thrace a repris à son précepteur, Aristarque de Samothrace, la dernière mesure pour distinguer exclusivement des classes syntaxiques, en joignant deux sortes de mots (différents, selon les Stoïciens), dans une seule véritable catégorie syntaxique: ὄνομα et προσηγορία, le nom propre et l'appellatif, unis ainsi sous le nom de *nom*.

D'où viendrait, par contre, l'argument pour faire figurer le participe parmi les parties du sens? Contrairement à l'infinitif, qui n'est, selon Denys de Thrace, qu'un mode de la catégorie du verbe, le participe (μετοχή) est une catégorie parmi les autres catégories. Selon Denys, il doit son nom au fait qu'il participe à la catégorie du verbe aussi bien à celle du nom (la catégorie qui comprend les noms appelés plus tard noms substantifs et noms adjectifs). Ainsi, chez Denys, le participe en grec est une classe morphologique. En grec, sa participation à deux autres classes morphologiques consiste dans l'emploi d'un suffixe déverbal qui rend le verbe participant au nom et dans l'emploi simultané d'un suffixe nominal qui suit le suffixe de participe (l'ancien grec n'avait pas de vrai participe verbal indéclinable, comme dans d'autres langues, par exemple le дее-причастие en russe).

L'infinitif, par contre, n'a que les suffixes qu'il faut qualifier de verbaux ou de déverbaux, et qui permettent à l'infinitif d'être reconnaissable en tant que tel. L'infinitif est en état de porter un *temps* (le temps, en vérité, porte le mode, puisque les temps différents portent leurs propres modes et aussi leurs infinitifs) et cela, apparemment, a suffi pour le qualifier de forme modale d'un verbe et, par conséquent, il est, chez Denys, l'une des manifestations de la catégorie du verbe.

L'infinitif grec n'a pas de désinences personnelles, mais il a, s'il est accompagné d'un article, la capacité d'assurer la fonction de nom, quoique sa forme, en soi, soit indéclinable. Autrement que l'infinitif français, l'infinitif en grec, tout ainsi qu'un nom, que ce soit un substantif ou un adjectif, peut être déterminé par un article. Cette qualité, une qualité syntaxique, au fond, n'a pas été prise en ligne de compte. Ce n'étaient que les formes, les *morphes*, apparemment, qui comptaient pour Denys, quoique bien d'autres en aient une autre opinion, par exemple, les grammairiens phéniciens (Solá-Solé 1957).

Dans une langue, une catégorie grammaticale particulière caractérisée par la fonction syntaxique primaire de participe, pourrait néanmoins bien être possible, comme nous espérons avoir démontré ailleurs (Breunis 1986). Dans la phrase, le participe détermine en même temps le nom et le verbe. Par conséquent, l'argument en faveur de la thèse que le participe appartient à une catégorie syntaxique séparée, peut avoir été, du moins primitivement, apporté par des considérations d'un ordre syntaxique. C'est voilà la raison pour laquelle toutes les huit parties du sens grecques peuvent être considérées comme catégories syntaxiques.

Sauf le verbe, le nom, le participe, l'article, parties déjà mentionnées, il y a le pronom, l'adverbe, la préposition et la conjonction. Il y a de bonnes raisons pour assumer que le pronom se comporte dans la phrase d'une autre façon que le nom. L'article, qui a un emploi spécial en grec, peut lui aussi être conçu comme catégorie syntaxique. Non pas pour sa fonction de rendre substantif un nom adjectif (épithète, c'est la construction du type *le sourd*), parce que l'un et l'autre, le substantif et l'adjectif, rentrent dans une seule catégorie, celle du nom. Mais il est bien capable de changer l'infinitif, mode verbal, en une forme nominale. Ce qui peut-être est plus important pour démontrer que c'est la fonction de l'article et non spécialement celle de l'infinitif, c'est qu'il peut lier un nom fléchi à un autre nom (la construction du type *l'homme dans la rue* est exprimée en grec par *l'homme le dans la rue*, pour ainsi dire, sans virgule, *l'homme celui dans la rue*).

S'il est difficile, pour autant, de démontrer l'origine purement syntaxique des catégories dionysiennes, les grammairiens romains, en reprenant aux Grecs l'analyse en catégories grammaticales, ont encore plus brouillé la piste. En latin, comme on le sait, il n'y a pas d'article, l'une des huit sortes de λέξεις en grec. Pour conserver le nombre intégral des parties du discours, les Romains n'ont pas tout simplement supprimé la catégorie de l'article, mais ils l'ont remplacée par une autre, celle de l'interjection ou celle de la particule. Le grec ancien possède une profusion de particules et d'interjections, mais il n'y a pas de catégorie sous tel nom chez Denys. On pourrait expliquer cette lacune apparente par l'origine syntaxique des classes grammaticales, puisque les interjections et les particules (même celles qui occupent la deuxième place dans la phrase) admettent d'être conçues comme employées en dehors de la construction de la phrase. *Oratio*, traduction latine du terme grec λόγος, nous laisse la possibilité d'assumer une historique syntaxique (surtout si l'on accepte une interprétation pseudo-étymologique: *oratio* vient de *orare*, "raisonner", "plaidoyer" et contient, comme si ce serait une sorte de calembour, *ratio*, "la raison"; mais le sens de *oratio* suffit). Divisible en deux, parce qu'il y a deux groupes, à quatre parties du discours chacun, déclinables et indéclinables respectivement, le nombre de huit parties du discours est resté sacré au fait de grammaire (il n'y a donc pas le même nombre de caté gories grammaticales que de merveilles du monde ou de péchés capitaux).[3]

L'introduction des particules dans les *partes orationis* a rompu les liens qui peuvent avoir existé entre l'analyse de la phrase et la syntaxe. Enfin, préparée par la syntaxe d'Apollonius le Difficile, traduite (c'est, à peu près, ainsi) par Priscane, l'analyse logique du moyen-âge a achevé la séparation de la syntaxe et le sens des mots. Depuis Apollonius (Alexandrie, 2ème siècle), les grammairiens avaient déjà l'habitude de considérer le nom et le verbe comme les parties principales de la phrase. Depuis le moyen-âge on n'admet qu'une coupure dans la phrase, à savoir la coupure entre le sujet et le prédicat. D'une façon définitive, comme il semble, les parties des unités significatives les plus petites, les mots de la phrase, sont devenues *parties du discours* dans l'acception actuelle du terme. Cela signifie, qu'elles sont maintenant classes grammaticales qui supposent une différence entre les parties du discours et les parties de la phrase (comme par exemple la différence entre verbe et prédicat). La détermination des classes grammaticales d'une langue ne peut s'opérer que selon le critère de la traduction: quelque soit la langue analysée, quelque soient les fonctions syntaxiques dans la totalité de son emploi, un mot est un verbe s'il peut être traduit par un verbe latin. Il en va de même des autres mots.

Déjà au moyen-âge, la *construction*, traduction en latin du terme grec σύνταξις, commence à être conçue, au lieu de l'ensemble des rapports entre les parties de la phrase, comme un assemblage de parties de discours, la phrase elle-même. Elle est devenue égale à la phrase qui est prise pour le résultat de l'action de construire, ensuite pour l'action de construire elle-même. Autrement dit, la construction de la phrase (que d'autre pourrait-elle signifier?) est devenue l'action de parler.

Smotryćkyj

C'est sous cette forme que l'analyse grammaticale a apparu en Russie. La version slave de la terminologie latine est employée jusqu'aujourd'hui, y compris des noms de notions nées au moyen-âge, comme ceux du sujet et du prédicat (подлежащее et сказуемое). Comme les grammaires des langues occidentales, comme la grammaire latine elle-même qui, plus ou moins, a été calquée sur la grammaire grecque, la terminologie grammaticale russe a été calquée sur le latin. Y compris le nom terrible de l'accusatif (*casus accusativus*, ou même *casus accusandi*, (Varron, VIII, 66), en russe винительный падеж), le cas de l'accusation, de l'accusé ou de l'accuseur, peu importe. Le nom grec est le cas (πτῶσις, fém. en grec: αἴτια). L'adjectif αἴτιος, il est vrai, c'est "coupable", mais il désigne aussi le rapport avec quelque chose: "relatif à quelque chose". C'est exactement le nom de la circonstance, parce que l'accusatif est le cas des relations les moins spécifiques. Par exemple, l'accusatif de temps, etc., non seulement en sanskrit, mais aussi en grec et en latin. (Voir Gonda 1957). L'objet direct a été inventé au moyen-âge, mais le nom de l'accusatif était tout prêt. Autrement dit, le nom du cas a été traduit, jadis, sans que le traducteur romain n'ait jamais su ce qu'il signifie.

Le linguiste qui connaît en gros l'histoire de la grammaire d'une langue d'Europe occidentale (au sens de M.H. Jellinek, à savoir, l'histoire de la littérature des manuels grammaticaux), verra tout de suite, à la terminologie grammaticale même, que la grammaire russe est d'origine occidentale et latiniste. On verra que la notion, en soi, de l'aspect verbale, a elle aussi été prise à la grammaire antique et est restée dans la grammaire russe, jusqu'à ce que les linguistes s'en sont occupés et qu'ils en ont oublié l'origine.

Tout cela grâce à la grammaire du vieux slave (1619) du Meletij Smotryćkyj (1578-1633, né à Smotrič, à cent kilomètres de distance de la frontière nord de la Moldavie), qui, après avoir séjourné quelques années en Allemagne, à plusieurs universités, travaillait à Vilna, à l'époque, en Pologne (Horbatsch 1974). Pour autant que le latin était connu aux russes, c'était par l'Ukraine. C'est donc lui, Smotryćkyj, qui a introduit le système et la terminologie grammaticale antique en Russie, parce que sa grammaire était la première grammaire slave, non seulement assez étendue (surtout à cause des tableaux des déclinaisons et des conjugaisons), mais aussi systématique. Incompréhensible, en fait, que Smotryćkyj n'est mentionnée qu'une fois dans l'histoire de la langue russe de Vinogradov.

Les grammairiens qui ont succédé à Smotryćkyj, ont poursuivi la tradition. Avant, il y a eu, en Russie, quelques abécédaires, et, très tôt, une grammaire purement grecque, d'origine serbe, intitulée "Les huit parties du discours", qui incluait même l'article sous le nom de различие; plus tard, Dmitrij l'Interprète faisait usage du terme различие pour désigner l'interjection, mais chez les grammairiens après Smotryćkyj on n'en retrouve rien. L'influence de la traduction de l'Ars Mineur de Donat par le moine Dmitrij dit Tolmač (l'Interprète) n'est pas claire, sa terminologie (c'est-à-dire, ses traductions), comme il paraît, n'a pas été reprise par la grammaire russe postérieure à celle de Smotryćkyj.

La grammaire du vieux-slave qu'a publié Smotryćkyj est en fait la grammaire antique, mais pas entièrement à la grecque. Smotryćkyj a connu Denys de Thrace, Diomède et Donat (2ème moitié du 3ème siècle) et aussi Priscien, grammairien (du latin) byzantin du 6ème siècle, sans doute du moins d'une façon indirecte. La grammaire médiévale l'a aussi influencé, parce qu'il emploie le terme "adjectif" et le "nom substantif". Le nom est par contre toujours une seule partie du discours, bien que les notions de "nom propre" et "nom appellatif" figurent chez lui, comme chez Donat. Les huit parties du discours, parmi lesquelles l'interjection et la division en quatre déclinables et quatre indéclinables, ont subsisté intégralement. Smotryćkyj emploie des notions traditionnelles qu'on rencontre aussi dans l'art majeur de Donat, mais sa grammaire a la simplicité pratique de celle de Denys de Thrace.

Donat, commentateur et biographe de Virgile, quoiqu'il connaisse les classiques, n'a pas, semble-t-il, connu Varron, ou bien, ce qui est plus vraisemblable, il a cru que réfléchir sur la grammaire, ce n'est pas la changer, moins encore l'élaborer. Le système des temps de Denys de Thrace se retrouve dans la grammaire slave ukrainienne, un peu mieux ordonné que dans la grammaire de Donat, et est ainsi devenu la base de l'étude des verbes russes.

Ce que les verbes et les noms ont en commun, c'est ce que les grammairiens leur ont accordé, mais dès l'antiquité le système grammatical n'a pas changé essentiellement. Le verbe et le nom connaissent, selon les grammairiens, les formations dites εἶδος et σχῆμα, ou alors, en latin, *forma* et *figura*. Le dernier terme est le même chez Prisciane, mais pour εἶδος il a *species*, qui correspond mieux au terme grec, parce que l'étymologie du terme de Prisciane et de celui de εἶδος est en rapport avec "voir", "regarder" (cf. *con-spicio, con-speci, con-spec-tum*). Les verbes à *figura* "forme", "figure", et aussi "esquisse", "ébauche", d'où: начертание chez Smotryćkyj) sont créées par la composition (les verbes pourvus de préfixes, comme *indicere, praedicere, prodicere*, etc.), les autres (*forma, species*, вид chez Smotryćkyj, образ chez Dmitrij Tolmač) par la dérivation (les formations du type *dictare*, dérivé de *dictum*, en tout cas d'un participe du verbe nommé d'après son infinitif *dicere*. Une *forma* peut être *primitiva* ou *perfecta* et le dernier terme ne se retrouve pas chez Denys de Thrace, mais est emprunté à Donat ou à quelque source commune. Smotryćkyj les appelle вид первообразный ou совершенный. En grec, c'est le *prototype* (πρωτότυπον) qu'on appelle aujourd'hui forme *primaire* ou *immotivée*. Une dérivation (παράγωγον, forme secondaire ou motivée) s'appelle chez Prisciane *derivatum* (производное). La *figura* est soit *simplex* (простой), soit *compositum* (сложный) ou même *decompositum* (terme de Prisciane: пресложный, par ex. en russe: происходить). On voit bien, pour la catégorie de *forma* (donc dérivé ou non-dérivé), que le terme "parfait" est appliqué ici non à un temps verbal, mais à la forme immotivée ou primaire qui est la fondation des formes dérivées. On voit aussi que производный signifie, en linguistique aussi bien qu'en mathématique: "dérivé".

Entre les *qualités* des noms, chez Donat, il n'y a pas de terme désignant le mot dérivé ou immotivé et *figura* est l'une des six caractéristiques du nom (la "qualité", la comparaison, le nombre, le genre, *figura*, et cas). Si Smotryćkyj ne se serve pas du terme *qualité*, la comparaison (les degrés de comparaison) est bien l'une des caractéristiques du nom dans sa grammaire slave, comme chez Donat, alors qu'elle est un εἶδος, une *forma*, chez Denys de Thrace.

Il y a six cas selon la grammaire de Donat, ou, comme il le nomme, six *formae* casuelles. Au premier abord, la caractéristique de *qualitas* nominale de Donat n'est pas comparable à celle du verbe, parce que les deux qualités nominales sont le nom propre et le nom appellatif ou générique (*appellativa*). Mais entre les noms appellatifs, il y a beaucoup de *species*, parmi lesquelles les mots *derivata*, dérivés des mots *prima positione*, des mots à position primaire, c'est-à-dire, immotivés. Donat parle aussi de *positio* pour désigner le singulier et le pluriel séparément.

Pour les verbes, Smotryćkyj n'a pas pu reprendre le terme de Donat qui signifie "dérivé", parce que Donat n'emploie que les noms des dérivés eux-mêmes: *meditativus*, de *meditari*, "méditer", qui est le désidératif (*lecturio* "je veux lire"), le *fréquentatif* (*lectito* "je lis souvent") et l'*inchoatif* (*calesco* "je deviens chaud", de *caleo*, "je suis chaud"), donc trois *formae*. La forme non-dérivée, celle de la "position primaire", s'appelle *perfecta* (*lego*, "je lis"). Donat ne reconnaît pas les compositions verbales à plus d'un préfixe. Pour une raison ou une autre, il emploie le terme *qualitas*, une des sept caractéristiques du verbe, innovation et complication qui ne vient pas de Denys de Thrace. Chez Donat, *figura* est une caractéristique verbale à part et *forma* est l'une des deux *qualités* dont le mode du verbe en est l'autre. Cela peut causer la confusion de dérivation et de flexion, mais Smotryćkyj ne l'a pas repris.

Pour les caractéristiques du verbe, Donat en distingue sept: deux *qualitates* (*modus* et *forma*), ensuite *conjugatio*, *genus*, *numerus*, *figura*, *tempus*, *persona*. Denys et Smotryćkyj (nommés d'un trait ici, malgré la disparité d'âge d'environ mille sept cents ans) mettent la notion de *conjugatio* en bas de la liste, fait auquel les historiens de la grammaire attachent beaucoup d'importance. Plus important est que Smotryćkyj distingue les *formae* (виды) et les *figurae* (начертания) plus nettement que Donat. Le grammairien de l'Ukraine accorde les deux à tous les mots déclinables (le nom, y compris à l'adjectif, le pronom, le verbe, l'adverbe et le participe), donc, en fait, à cinq classes de mots, et aussi à l'adverbe. Seulement le participe n'a pas de вид, et s'il est composé, il l'est grâce au verbe dont il est, comme on dirait aujourd'hui, dérivé. Chez Donat, l'adverbe, le participe et le pronom n'ont pas de *forma*, ils n'ont que la *figura*: le *simplex* du pronom, soit dit en passant, est par exemple *quis*, "qui", composé: *quisquis*, "qui que ce soit". Smotryćkyj appelle simple: *азъ* "je"; *сам азъ* "moi-même" est composé. Trouvaille personnelle, dirait-on, mais c'est en réalité puisé aux sources: Denys de Thrace, après avoir donné des exemples de "pronoms dérivés" (des adjectifs possessifs qui sont dérivés des pronoms), il cite des pronoms composés: "moi-même", "toi-même", qui ne sont pas vraiment composés, mais plutôt contractés p.ex. σεαυτὸν (cf. γνῶθι σεαυτὸν, "connais-toi toi-même").

Quant au système verbal, pas de trace des proportions de Varron, ni chez Donat, ni chez Prisciane, ni dans la grammaire de Smotryćkyj. Pour Denys de Thrace, comme indiqué ci-dessus, il y a les trois *temps* de l'espace euclidien (avant, derrière et l'endroit où l'on est, tout à fait compréhensible pour un Alexandrin); le prétérit a quatre possibilités; de même pour Donat et Prisciane: il y a, comme si le latin a les mêmes temps qu'en grec, à côté du temps indéfini (aoriste), les temps παρατατικόν, provenu de παρατείνειν, "continuer", ce qui est traduit en latin par *imperfectum*, puis παρακείμενον, "présent", mais désignant en latin ce que les grammairiens appelaient *perfectum*, le même *temps*, en forme verbale, que "il s'est assis", mais désignant un état présent en grec, donc "il est assis". Le mot "parfait", dans la terminologie grecque, se trouve dans ὑπερσυντέλιχον, formé de "hyper" et "tout-à-fait-terminé", le *plus-quam-perfectum*. Smotryćkyj n'emploie le terme "parfait" (совершенный) que pour les verbes non-dérivés qui sont les seuls verbes, avec les verbes fréquentatifs (учащательные, qui sont dérivés), à exprimer un temps présent (настоящее). Seulement, le temps parfait (прешедшее) est *entièrement* (совершенно) fini, comme l'aoriste (непредельное). L'imparfait (преходящее) de Smotryćkyj est: *pas entièrement* (несовершенно) fini, ce qui s'appelle ici прошлое, mais le temps du parfait et de l'aoriste "fini" s'appelle прешлое. Digne d'être remarqué, à condition qu'il ne s'agisse que d'une coquille dans le texte réédité par Horbatsch.

Il ne reste maintenant que le plus-que-parfait (мимошедшее) qui est une action déjà longtemps finie: древле совершенно прешедшее et le futur simple (будущее). Pour conserver la tradition séculaire de trois temps, parmi lesquels les quatre prétérits, Smotryćkyj a classé des temps composés (passifs) parmi des autres temps. Puis, s'il a nettement fait une distinction entre *forma* et *figura* et montré dans le tableau de conjugaisons que les temps aoriste et futur sont verbes préfixés, il ne le porte pas spécialement à l'attention du lecteur.

La notion de conjugaison (συζυγία), chez Denys, remplace pour les verbes la notion de *cas* pour les noms. La notion de flexion (κλίσις), désigne le fait que l'attachement des suffixes différents, aux noms ou aux verbes, se réalise de façons différentes. Ce qui pourrait s'appeler système flexionnel, ce serait donc l'ensemble des règles pour décrire les changements phoniques qui se produisent entre la racine (ou le thème) et un suffixe. Au fond, le terme antique de flexion n'a rien à voir avec la distinction moderne (bien qu'impliquée dans la terminologie grecque), entre système flexionnel et système dérivatif. Un verbe, par exemple, peut avoir des désinences de temps, de mode, de personne, de nombre (singulier, duel ou pluriel), de voix active, moyenne ou passive (залог) et de *forma* et de *figura*.

Déjà dans les textes anciens, *forma* et *figura* d'un nom ou d'un verbe pourraient être considérés comme noms ou verbes autonomes, qui eux-mêmes peuvent avoir toutes sortes de désinences de temps, de mode, de personne, etc., comme les autres noms ou verbes. Pourtant, on ne le dit pas. Ce qui est certain, quand même, c'est que les temps, y compris l'aoriste, n'appartiennent pas à de verbes différents. Tous les grammairiens considéraient l'aoriste du verbe grec comme un *temps*. Que d'autre auraient-ils dû faire? Il n'y pouvaient rien, parce que l'aoriste, en tant que temps, quoiqu'il ait bien des modes (conjonctif, optatif, et l'infinitif, si l'on veut), il n'a pas de temps lui-même. Il est par conséquent, ce que nous appelerions aujourd'hui une forme flexionnelle d'un verbe, non pas une forme dérivée, en tout cas.

Suivant l'exemple de la grammaire classique, Smotryćkyj avait maintenu le classement de huit parties du discours et le participe était toujours rangé à leur nombre. En pratique, cependant, les participes du présent passif et du passé passif étaient censés être les représentants de la voix passive. En tant que tels, ils étaient accueillis dans le système des temps, de la sorte, que nous pouvons supposer que Smotryćkyj les regarderait comme formations flexionnelles, s'il avait été contraint à se prononcer pour ou contre. Nous ne pouvons rien conclure, à cet égard, de la circonstance que le залог, de toutes les caractéristiques du verbe, trône chez lui en haut de liste. Denys de Thrace commence par les flexions qui sont suivie par les *genera verborum*. Je n'y vois aucune hiérarchie. Chez Denys comme chez Smotryćkyj, ce sont les temps qui portent les modes et les voix (ou les genres) du verbe, non inversement.

L'ère des temps.

La première grammaire de la langue russe plus ou moins complète est celle de Lomonosov (1755). Si la grammaire de Smotryćkyj est la grammaire antique qui a passé par le moyen-âge, la grammaire de Lomonosov est la grammaire raisonnée (bien qu'elle ne porte pas ce nom). Celui-ci entendait créer une langue acceptable et utilisable, pourqu'on puisse énoncer ses pensées correctement, et à propos de choses temporelles et séculières. C'est donc une langue entre ciel et terre, une langue nationale et érudite entre la langue liturgique et la langue du peuple. En pratique, le moyen de parler divinement de la barbe.

L'air ne fait pas la chanson, mais on juge néanmoins de nos pensées, sur les apparences grammaticales. D'où une grammaire russe pour faire respecter les convenances. Une grammaire d'une langue qui en même temps doit être adaptée à la vie moderne, c'est-à-dire, une langue qui diffère par essence de la vieille langue liturgique. Pierre le Grand avait ordonné de faire imprimer, encore en 1721, une nouvelle édition de la grammaire de Smotryćkyj et de nombreux abécédaires et de livres de lecture. La nouvelle grammaire de Lomonosov devait en tout cas différer de l'ancienne qui était généralement connue. C'est certainement la raison pour laquelle Lomonosov a conçu un système qui, par rapport à la tradition, ne manque pas d'originalité.

Ce ne sont pas, certes, les faiseurs de vers et les cuistres que nous sommes, avouons-le, nous les autres grammairiens et linguistes, qui auraient pu créer une langue littéraire. Il est plutôt ainsi, que les méthodes primitives des grammairiens n'ont pas empêché la langue russe de se déployer et de prendre son élan comme porteuse d'une littérature des plus belles du monde. Pourtant, la grammaire de Lomonosov contient les phénomènes les plus importants pour faire une nette distinction entre le russe et le vieux slave d'église. Qui mieux est, par son système de temps qu'il a développé dans sa grammaire, Lomonosov a dépassé le niveau de l'épigone qu'il était.

Ce n'est pas seulemenent pour aider le commun des mortels à s'exprimer d'une façon correcte, mais aussi pour démontrer la richesse de la langue des russes, que Lomonosov, tout en répondant aux exigences d'une grammaire comme il faut (elle aussi doit être correcte à son tour), a inventé une manoeuvre toute simple. Que les linguistes, deux cents ans plus tard, devaient se précipiter sur les formes dérivatives et composées du verbe russe, il ne pouvait que l'ignorer. Aussi a-t-il supprimé la notion de dérivation et donné le droit de préférence aux *temps* qu'il a choisi pour forme de fondation dans la grammaire russe. Dix temps verbaux (deux fois plus qu'en français) et, par conséquant, encore plus de modes (l'infinitif, par tradition, puis l'impératif et le conditionnel).

Ce qui serait vraiment original, ce serait classer холодно parmi les verbes ou entrevoir dans есть что делать une construction de participe, ou, pour le moins, prendre l'infinitif pour la forme de fondation du verbe conjugué, si ce n'était pas faux. Lomonosov n'a fait rien de ce genre, mais d'un point de vue de grammairien, le système verbal de Smotryćkyj (ce qui revient à dire: le système dionysien-donatien-, etc.) se retrouve chez Lomonosov dans un état qui est entièrement modifié.

Lomonosov n'est pas vraiment sorti des catégories de la pensée des grammairiens antiques, mais il ne s'en est pas moins permis de s'en dégager un peu. Sur la conjugaison, il ne dit pas un mot de trop. Il en distingue deux, l'une à -ет, l'autre à -ит (3ème pers.; par. 285), l'infinitif étant un mode (par. 267) dont la flexion peut être différente selon le verbe. La différence entre dérivation et composition verbales est impliquée dans son système, par la façon dont il a divisé les *temps* du verbe. Il n'y a pas de division en trois temps et une subdivision des temps prétérits, mais tout simplement dix temps, parmi lesquels six prétérits, nombre assez élevé en conséquence de l'introduction de trois temps du plus-que-parfait. Il y a aussi une division en temps simples: huit sans préfixe, et deux temps verbaux à forme préfixée (par. 268).

La distinction de flexion, dérivation et composition, n'est pas très nette chez les grammairiens alexandrins (les notions, chez eux, en revanche, n'étaient pas confondues), elle l'est encore moins chez Lomonosov. Son schéma de temps verbaux rend flexionnels des formes verbales qui auraient pu aussi bien être considérées comme dérivées. Mêmes les deux formes composées (préfixées) semblent se trouver sur le plan d'une forme flexionnelle: написал est le prétérit parfait (praeteritum perfectum) d'un · verbe dont le présent est пишу. L'un des deux futurs (futurum indefinitum) de ce verbe est буду писать, l'autre (futurum perfectum) напишу. Lomonosov parle explicitement (par. 312) de verbes qui, au temps prétérit parfait *(написал)*, consistent (состоят) du prétérit indéfini et d'un préfixe, c'est-à-dire, de la forme du prétérit indéfini composée d'un préfixe.

Les temps verbaux chez Lomonosov sont d'ailleurs les temps antiques, augmentés de temps typiquement russes. Leurs noms sont classiques. Les temps existent, par conséquent, indépendamment des formes verbales dans le schéma des temps. Apparemment, quand le locuteur en a besoin, il les exprime en russe par des verbes simples (motivés ou non-motivés, comme on dirait aujourd'hui, donc les types говаривать et говорить respectivement), par des verbes préfixés (composés) ou des verbes pourvus d'un auxiliaire. Cette indépendance du fond et de la forme, Lomonosov ne s'en confesse pas ouvertement dans sa grammaire, mais c'est bien cela qui est la conséquence de l'imposition de temps grecs (quelque soit le nombre de plus-que-parfaits) à une autre langue. C'est qui découle de la grammaire logique qui sépare la pensée de son expression.

Ce système aurait pu offrir des avantages. Tout compte fait, c'est ce qui a permis à Lomonosov de distinguer un temps prétérit однократное et un futur однократное, le temps "sémelfactif", donc le temps de ce qui se passe une fois (par. 268), dans les verbes non-préfixés au suffixe -ну- et aussi dans бросить, "jeter". Le sémelfactif n'est donc pas égal au prétérit parfait (совершенное: notre passé d'un verbe qu'on appelle maintenant aspect perfectif), mais il affirme en même temps (au même chapitre, par. 313) qu'il y a des verbes (entre autres дать, простить, пустить, et... encore бросить), qui forment leur prétérit parfait sans préfixe.

D'autre part, s'il est vrai, selon l'opinion de son temps, que l'emploi de la langue ne fait qu'exprimer, c'est-à-dire, faire sortir des idées, pré-établies à l'intérieur, celles-ci, dans cette même opinion-là, sont universelles et inaltérables et se manifestent, apparemment, dans la grammaire et non pas dans la parole, selon le contexte. Mais l'idée que la significa-tion ne se manifeste que dans l'emploi de la langue, c'est-à-dire, dans le contexte, est trop moderne. Lomonosov n'a pas pu profiter de la grammaire logique pour faire plus que d'adapter la grammaire classique au nombre des formes verbales en russe. Il n'a pas vu la possibilité d'un futur antérieur (il aura écrit), qui peut se manifester dans les futurs sémelfactif et indéfini, ni un véritable plus-que-parfait dans les prétérits (voir Hamburger 1988: 243). Au lieu de cela, il a accordé le sens d'un давнопрошедшее время aux verbes fréquentatifs-itératifs.

Lomonosov a ménagé la chèvre et le chou: de l'un côté, conformément aux exigences de la grammaire antique, il a séparé les verbes simples et composés, de la sorte que, à l'en croire, il n'y aurait pas de verbes com-posés au temps présent. Il n'en cite pas un, même pas dans les para-graphes qui suivent le bordereau de dix temps au par. 268. S'il a distingué des temps en russe qui diffèrent des temps en grec, il l'a fait parce qu'il y était obligé. Ce qui en est la conséquence, c'est que dans le système verbal de Lomonosov, il y a autant de noms de temps qu'il y a des formes verbales différentes.

En confondant ailleurs les verbes "sémelfactifs" et "perfectifs", il avoue que le sens de l'un peut être exprimé par l'autre. Cela revient à dire què la composition n'a rien à voir avec le temps du verbe et qu'un classement verbal qui commence par les temps est inutile.

Ce n'est pas que Lomonosov ne soit au courant de la terminologie grammaticale grecque que partiellement. Il s'en sert lui-même. Il emploie les termes traditionnels первообразный et производный (primitivement pour désigner "immotivé" et "motivé") pour les noms de nombre cardinaux et ordinaux respectivement. Il ne l'a pas non plus fait oublier à ses successeurs. Il y a eu de différentes grammaires russes dans la période de 1755-1800 (voir Kul'man 1917). L'une d'elles, attribuée à Barsov (Краткие правила... 1771, voir Schütrumpf 1980), présente intégralement la terminologie grecque dans la traduction de Smotryćkyj. Seulement, le système verbal à dix temps est celui de Lomonosov.

C'est logique en tout cas de ne pas parler de la dérivation. Pourtant, les notions de *forma* (*species*) et de *figura* sont employées, de façon implicite, dans la grammaire de Lomonosov. Au début du chapitre sur le verbe il mentionne la faculté des verbes d'être composés, mais il n'appelle pas la chose par son nom, qui serait вид ou начертание. C'est ce qui lui permet, premièrement, d'omettre le nom de la notion de dérivation, deuxièmement, de ne pas du tout parler de la notion elle-même, et, troisièmement, de faire aux autres confondre ainsi les notions de dérivation et de flexion, du moins, de voiler leur différence.

S'il est vrai que les russes ont tiré vanité de la multitude de temps dans leur langue, c'est tout a fait compréhensible que le système temporel de Lomonosov a persisté longtemps. Peut-être, cela tient-il à l'ambiguïté sur le domaine de la flexion (chacun y trouve son compte), que la grammaire de Lomonosov a donné le ton pendant tout le reste du XVIIIème siècle. La toute première Grammaire Académique de l'an 1802 est, au fond, la grammaire lomonosovienne. A quelques nuances près: si l'affaire de la différence entre temps et *forma* est réglée pour la grammaire grecque, il n'en est pas de même de la grammaire russe. D'une manière ou d'une autre, la question de la différence entre flexion et dérivation, apparemment, n'a pas manqué de chiffonner les grammairiens, quoique, quant à la conception de la flexion, la première grammaire académique en soit restée au niveau "morphophonique" (nommé ainsi, parce que les noms des temps sont encore les noms de formes verbales différentes).

Contrairement à ce qu'a fait Lomonosov (qui en distingue deux), les auteurs de la première grammaire académique admettent quatre sortes de flexion verbale, donc quatre conjugaisons, en considérant que réduire tout le système de la conjugaison russe à deux voyelles -*e*- et -*и*-, c'est faire un tableau trop flatteur des difficultés de la langue russe. Ils s'expliquent largement là-dessus,[4] mais ils ne disent pas qu'ils cèdent à la mode de l'époque selon laquelle on commence à choisir l'infinitif comme le nom du verbe.

Pour l'expression des temps verbaux divers, cela ne ferait pas de différence, si ce n'était que, avec l'infinitif, l'identité d'un verbe est en cause. En choisissant l'infinitif d'un verbe comme le représentant d'un type spécifique, un type entre les autres types de flexion, on risque de le promouvoir en forme de fondation (sur laquelle les autres formes flexionnelles sont fondées) et on le prive de son état de mode verbal (alors qu'il s'appelle toujours modus infinitivus, неокончательное наклонение), mode dont la forme peut varier selon le verbe et aussi selon le temps. La première Grammaire Académique ne va pas aussi loin; la question de savoir si par exemple *писать* et *написать* sont, oui ou non, chacun un mode appartenant à deux temps différents du même verbe, question déjà laissée ouverte par Lomonosov, reste entière dans la première Grammaire Académique.

C'est Anton Alekseevič Barsov (1730-1791), professeur à Moscou, à qui revient l'honneur d'être le premier à avoir tenté de résoudre le problème de la cohérence des formations verbales qui expriment les *tempora* en russe. Fils de l'illustre hellénisant Aleksej Kirillovič, qui, au service de Pierre le Grand, avait traduit l'oeuvre attribuée à Apollodore (autre élève d'Aristarque), et était resté traducteur lorsqu'il était devenu chef de l'Imprimerie Nationale à Moscou, Barsov lui-même était de formation classique et aussi mathématicien. Il opère d'une façon exacte et, souvent, il rend compte au lecteur de son point de vue. On ignore, il est vrai, quelle a été l'influence de sa grammaire (1783-1788) sur la pensée des grammairiens russes. Son manuel de grammaire a été publié posthumement, il faut le dire, pour tenir compte des besoins de la linguistique moderne. Mais grâce à cette publication nous savons exactement ce que Barsov, dans son temps, a enseigné à ses élèves. Sa grammaire cadre excellemment avec l'évolution qui a mené jusqu'à la prétendue découverte du caractère spécial propre au verbe russe.

D'abord, Barsov a simplifié le système de Lomonosov. Celui-ci distinguait trois genres de "plus-que-parfait" (давнопрошедшее), deux entre eux formés à l'aide de l'"auxiliaire" *бывало* (1: *брасывал*; 2: *бывало бросал*; 3: *бывало брасывал*). Barsov a supprimé les deux temps à *бывало*, en tenant compte du caractère spécial de cette construction. Si l'on classe ce type d'emploi dans les catégories temporelles, dit-il, on devrait inclure dans le système le type avec *было*, qui s'appellerait несостоявшееся прошедшее (Barsov, éd. Uspenskij, p. 547), et qui n'est pas mentionné par Lomonosov. (Omission qui n'a été réparée par les slavisants, ne disposant pas de la grammaire de Barsov, que beaucoup plus tard; voir Barentsen 1986). On pourrait bien, selon Barsov, compter les temps ainsi construits. Alors, on aurait un несостоявшееся прошедшее et deux genres de plus-que-parfait, le давнопрошедшее первое et le давнопрошедшее второе, et ce dernier comprendrait les deux constructions, celle du type *бывало бросал* et celle du type *бывало брасывал*, réunies dans une seule catégorie, comme il ne s'agit que d'un seul type de construction. Une construction en effet qui est réalisée à l'aide d'un "auxiliaire impersonnel" (c'est ainsi qu'il l'appelle) et employée avec des formes verbales déjà traitée auparavant.

Le seul plus-que-parfait qui en reste est en réalité un fréquentatif, ou plutôt fréquentatif-habituel, lorsque le vrai plus-que-parfait en russe se cache dans le sens indifférencié du temps passé, perfectif ou non. Chez Barsov, en tout cas, le давнопрошедшее время est l'un des trois temps prétérits qui figurent entre les six temps du verbe russe qu'il a distingués. L'un des deux autres temps prétérits est le прошедшее совершенное ou прошедшее tout court, appellation qui suffit, parce que l'autre, le прошедшее неопределённое de Lomonosov s'appelle chez Barsov преходящее неопределённое, pour souligner le caractère d'une action inachevée. D'où, le temps *passant* indéfini (ou преходящее tout court), l'idée verbale que Bogorodickij devait appeler (ou aurait voulu appeler) plus tard вид совершающий.

Restent encore les autres temps de Barsov, le présent (настоящее), le futur "simple" et le futur "composé" ou indéfini (будущее неопределённое).

En réduisant les dix temps verbaux de Lomonosov à six, Barsov en finit avec l'ambiguïté du système lomonosovien (p. 543). Il distingue entre вид (*forma, species*) et начертание (*figura*), à l'endroit dans son livre où il commence à traiter le verbe, mais indépendamment de l'exposé du système verbal. Pourtant, nous pouvons admettre qu'il a cherché à expliquer ce que cela signifie pour le système verbal en tant que *système flexionnel*. Il ne le nomme pas ainsi, mais c'est ici que la notion, au moins, de flexion est étendue, de façon explicite, d'une notion purement "morphophonique" à une notion qui concerne l'identité d'un nom ou d'un verbe.

Pour Barsov, le point de départ est la forme de la première personne au temps présent, le *commencement* (начало) de tous les autres temps et les autres changements (изменения) du verbe (p. 544). Quant aux changements, il ne les appelle pas flexion et dérivation, car le nom de changement comprend l'une et l'autre.

C'est tout comme on apprend à l'école le latin et le grec, la première personne étant le nom du verbe, choisie pour *conventional citation form*, remplacée en tant que telle par l'infinitif pour les autres langues. C'est le nom à décliner. Cela ne veut pas dire que le système tel que Barsov se représente pour le russe, est exact. Le nom du verbe n'est pas nécessairement la forme de fondation des autres formes. C'est un problème qui jusqu'aujourd'hui n'est pas encore résolu. Ce qui est toujours autant de gagné, c'est que nous savons ce qu'il en pensait. Avant Barsov, le problème ne s'était pas du tout posé.

Les formes composées du verbe, chez Barsov, sont accueillies dans la catégorie du présent aussi bien que dans celle du passé dit perfectif. Il s'agit du présent et du passé de tous les verbes composés dit aujourd'hui imperfectifs, comme par exemple выбрасывать ou спрашивать. Ils se trouvent fraternellement ensemble avec des verbes non-composés, comme бросаю, dans la même catégorie du présent. Il est, cependant, allé un peu trop loin.

La séparation des verbes non-préfixés et des verbes préfixés, c'est ce qui était restée du système antique dans le système de Lomonosov. Celui-ci l'a appliquée à son système, d'une telle rigueur, qu'il n'a osé, semble-t-il, citer des verbes préfixés, en exemple d'un temps présent ou d'un temps imparfait. Quoiqu'il mentionne, à un autre endroit, des verbes non-préfixés en fonction de verbes préfixés qui expriment le passé parfait, le verbe au passé perfectif ne semble possible que s'il est préfixé. Cela a conservé l'idée que le sens, qui est propre au passé perfectif russe et au futur simple, dépendrait de la préfixation verbale (futur simple ici opposé au futur antérieur, donc le futur qui est exprimé par les mêmes verbes avec leur forme du présent).

C'est ainsi que Lomonosov a créé la condition *sine qua non* de la confusion de ce que l'on appelle aujourd'hui *aspect* et *Aktionsart* (l'un et l'autre employés ici au sens auquel, par exemple, Barentsen les emploie, en les séparant strictement).

Il y a eu et il y a toujours des linguistes qui ne font pas de distinction entre *aspect* et *Aktionsart*, confusion, dont même le grand Wackernagel s'est rendu coupable. (Décidément, Lomonosov avait le bras long). Le terme de *Aktionsart* a bien des inconvénients, mais la confusion avec ce qu'on appelle aujourd'hui *aspect* est d'autant plus regrettable, que le terme de *Aktionsart* est entièrement vide de sens, justement dans le cas où il est effectivement synonyme au aspect dit aujourd'hui perfectif.

Je garderai le mot de cet énigme pour un article qui est à suivre. Ce qui importe ici, c'est que Lomonosov a bien distingué un temps

"sémelfactif" (однократный) pour l'opposer à un temps itératif (многократный), mais il a relégué celui-ci à la catégorie du plus-que-parfait
multiple. C'était peut-être par nonchalance que le grand philosophe-
matérialiste et père de la poésie russe a ajouté *бросить* à la catégorie
des sémelfactifs. On pourrait pourtant se demander s'il y a vraiment une
différence entre le passé parfait et le passé sémelfactif. Il est de fait que
Lomonosov, l'un des derniers grands esprits universels de la civilisation
occidentale, par l'ambiguïté de son exposition du système verbal russe,
a laissée la voie libre à d'autres pour découvrir la différence entre *aspect*
et *Aktionsart*, quoique ces mots n'existent pas encore dans son temps.
Barsov, avec toute son ardeur à être exact, a claqué la porte à ceux qui
auraient voulu les séparer. On le verra:

Ayant groupé les verbes simples et les verbes composés dans la même
catégorie, Barsov a uni ainsi les temps passés однократные et parfaits
(les types *крикнул* et *написал*) et le temps futur des mêmes types. Il les
mentionne séparément, à l'intérieur de la même catégorie de temps verbal,
mais la position de verbes comme *бросить* ou *купить* a cessé d'être
ambiguë, parce que le partage, dans le passé parfait ou perfectif, entre
des temps passés "sémelfactifs" et "perfectifs" est devenu secondaire.

Les verbes simples qui n'ont pas de temps perfectif, pensait-il, em-
pruntent la forme du verbe composé, qui exprime ce temps-là, au temps
présent, donc *вяжу* tire *связал* de *связываю*. En cas de besoin, le passé
perfectif est dérivé d'une forme verbale inusitée, comme *написал* est
fondée sur *написываю*, qu'on cherchera en vain dans les dictionnaires.
Et c'est normal, parce que, dit Barsov, les verbes comme *написал* sont
défectifs (недостаточествующие), autre notion de la grammaire antique,
bien applicable au russe, comme il paraît, pour expliquer des choses qui
ne tournent pas rond.

Les verbes simples de la catégorie du futur, selon Barsov, sont verbes
appartenant à trois types: les verbes simples du type au suffixe *-ну-* ou
du type *бросить*; puis, les verbes composés de cette catégorie (les mêmes
verbes que les premiers, donc simples d'origine, mais, cette fois, pourvus
d'un préfixe, comme *с-бросить*) et, ensuite, les verbes également d'origine
simple, mais composés pour obtenir le sens du futur (p. 546). Barsov
mentionne, pour tout exemple, *сбросать*; sans doute est-il permis de
mentionner le type *напишу* composé de *на-* et *пишу*. Autrement dit,
les formes préfixées du futur (будущее совершенное) consistent (состоят)
soit de la forme simple du même futur (*брошу*) à laquelle un préfixe
a été ajouté, soit de la forme simple du présent (disons: *пишу*), également

fournie d'un préfixe (*напишу*). Ce sont les mots de Lomonosov (chez celui-ci, le par. 312, voir ci-dessus), mais dans un tout autre contexte.

Cela nous permet de dire que le "futurum perfectum" est formé, dans le cas de *напишу*, de *пишу*, et dans le cas de *сброшу*, de *брошу*. Il en va de même des verbes au passé dit perfectif: les formes composées sont dérivées soit du temps passé perfectif d'une forme simple (comme *сбросил* qui proviendrait de *бросил*), soit du praeteritum indefinitum (преходящее неопределённое, le temps *passant* indéfini) d'une forme non-composée, comme *написал* a été formé de *писал* pour obtenir un passé perfectif.

C'est ici que Barsov a commis une erreur. Si *сбросил* était fondée sur *бросил*, la différence de sens qui accompagne ce changement est une autre que celle entre *написал* et *писал*. Barsov l'a bien remarqué (p. 544), mais selon lui, l'action du verbe *сбросил* serait *plus parfaite* que celle du verbe *бросил* et il n'y aurait, donc, pas de différence entre les deux genres de changement, des changemens en soi, parce que le préfixe ne fait que rendre l'action parfaite, et si l'action l'est déjà, la préfixation le fait plus que cela, pour ainsi dire, elle fait les finitions. C'est que c'était Lomonosov lui-même qui l'avait déjà remarqué: "Par de compositions diverses de préfixes, les temps obtiennent souvent des nouveaux moyens de désignation et une plus grande force." (R. Gr. IV, I, par. 265). C'est à un endroit où Lomonosov vient de dire que le parfait exprime une action complètement achevée (полное совершенное действие), par "une plus grande force" il entendait donc autre chose que "parfait". Certes, *сбросить* peut être employé, dans un certain contexte, comme renforcement de *бросить*. Mais un tel raisonnement ne peut pas dissimuler que la méthode suivie jusqu'ici pour la description, qui a bien servi depuis Denys de Thrace jusqu'à Smotryćkyj, s'est altérée sans aucune justification. Le système traditionnel permet qu'un mot soit пресложное, non pas qu'il soit plus parfait que parfait.

Tout cela à cause de la réduction du système verbal en russe, d'abord, par Lomonosov, à une gamme de temps verbaux qui, tous séparément, correspondraient aux noms de formations verbales, ensuite par la réduction, par Barsov, à un système flexionnel qui commence par un prototype qui *génère* des temps.

Heureusement, Barsov a parti, comme Varron, de formes entières. Il n'aimait pas représenter son système flexionnel comme une machine à coller des préfixes aux verbes simples. Bien évidemment, a-t-il ajouté à son exposé, si l'on n'accepte pas qu'il y ait des verbes qui serait dérivés d'un prototype qui n'a jamais existé, on peut supposer que le passé perfectif est formé directement par la composition du temps "passant" simple avec une préposition. Le lien supposé entre *написал* et *написываю*, qui n'existe pas, n'est qu'une représentation plus précise, qui se base sur l'emploi qui montre quelle est la préposition appropriée à former le temps passé perfectif d'un verbe particulier (p. 545). Sans quoi, qui saurait dire que *писал* se compose avec *на* et *сделал* avec *с*?

C'est quand même un faut débat. Les gens disposent des formes correctes à condition qu'ils connaissent la langue. La question de Barsov est issue du système, qui présuppose que les dérivations et les compositions ne puissent exister sans mot de fondation. Pourtant, le problème une fois posé, il faut le résoudre, mais cela n'est possible que d'un point de vue historique.

Le verbe sous tous ses aspects.

Johann Severin Vater (1771-1826), polonisant et slavisant, successeur autorisé de J.Ch. Adelung, paraît avoir été le premier à se rendre compte que les formes verbales comme *писать* et *написать*, *вязать* et *связать* sont en effet des formes qui proviennent de verbes différents.[5]

Ce n'est pas tout à fait vrai, comme le dit Newman (1976), que c'est Vater, (parce que c'est ce qui en serait la conséquence), qui a été le premier à faire une distinction entre formes de flexion et formes de dérivation. La distinction en soi a existé de tout temps, car elle est impliquée dans la différence entre, de l'une part, la dérivation et la composition et, de l'autre part, quant aux verbes, les conjugaisons, les personnes, les modes et les temps. Mais, quand même, entre toutes les manifestations du thème ou de la racine d'un nom ou d'un verbe, quelles formations représentent le même nom ou le même verbe? Question qui n'est pas inutile, mais qui peut rester sans réponse tant que la distinction entre *forma* et *figura*, entre celles-ci et les conjugaisons, les personnes, les modes et les temps, et aussi la différence de ceux-ci entre l'un et l'autre sera maintenue. Barsov n'a pas pu concevoir un système flexionnel logique du verbe russe, parce que les formations temporelles russes ne constituent pas un seul système. Mais c'est Vater qui a dit le fin mot pour résoudre le problème de la *méthode* d'un inventoriage logique des verbes russes, selon les principes traditionnels.

L'honneur lui revient, à lui, de l'avoir trouvé lui-même. Les grammaires polonaises qu'il a citées dans sa contribution au Mithridates (vol. II, 1809) de J.C. Adelung, ne lui en ont pas pu inspirer. Il en a mentionné seize, en commençant par Jer. Roter, Breslau 1616, jusqu'à Kopczyński, Varsovie 1807. Un autre grammairien polonais, Jakubowicz (1825), a dit que, avant Kopczyński, il n'y avait pas, pour ainsi dire, de grammaire polonaise. C'est, effectivement, la grammaire d'Onufry Kopczyński (1807) qui est la plus récente que Vater a connu dans le temps. J'ai vu l'édition de 1817: les formes verbales différentes sont mis dans le même tableau, comme les temps verbaux chez Lomonosov. Il aurait été intéressant, soit dit en passant, si nous avions eu l'opinion de Vater sur Jakubowicz, mais il ne l'a vraisemblablement jamais connu.

Par hasard ou non, Vater s'est inspiré d'une fausse question comme celle de Barsov. Pour en terminer avec l'opinion que движуть est dérivé de двигать ou que le premier était une forme flexionnelle de l'autre (conséquence du système lomonosovien), Vater a recouru à des verbes qui n'existent pas, mais qui doivent avoir existé. En partant du participe passif du présent движемый (ce que nous pourrions faire en prenant l'ancien participe actif du présent движущий), il a désigné двину comme l'origine de двинул, et двигу comme l'origine de двигаю. Les deux formes (en -ну et en -аю) exprimaient un temps présent, двигаю l'exprime toujours, двину, étant en tant que tel, apparemment, superflu, est devenu un futur et двигу a disparu. Une explication étymologique, donc historique, de la présence dans la langue de deux verbes différents, auxquels l'état actuel de la langue où il y a deux types de futur et deux types de passé, est imputable. Vater n'a pas établi un rapport quel que ce soit entre le passé perfectif et le futur exprimé par le même verbe. Il s'était parfaitement rendu compte du sens perfectif du passé du verbe perfectif, mais il n'a pas pu comprendre le futur perfectif. Problème qui n'existait pas pour Lomonosov, encore moins pour Barsov. Mais cent ans plus tard, les savants n'avaient pas encore cessé de chercher la genèse du sens typiquement russe de perfectivité, dans le déplacement du sens de la forme du présent (comme Musić 1902: 479 sqq.).

En considérant les verbes comme autonomes, dérivés de verbes qui n'existent plus, donc dérivé de thèmes *abstraits*, Vater a aboli toute hiérarchie entre les formes verbales qui existent encore dans la langue. Il n'en a pas tiré de conséquence lui-même. Dans son manuel de grammaire russe, il a présenté les verbes en types de conjugaisons, suivant la méthode de Lomonosov. Tout à fait compréhensible, quand même, puisqu'il s'agit d'un cours pour apprendre la langue russe, non d'un ouvrage linguistique.

Vater correspondait de temps en temps avec Nikolaj Ivanovič Greč, critique et censeur littéraire à Saint-Pétersbourg (1787-1867). Quoiqu'il se plaigne souvent, auprès de Friedrich Adelung (son autre correspondant à Saint-Pétersbourg, neveu de Joh. Chr. Adelung), de ce qu'il ne reçoit pas de réponse de la part de Greč, celui-ci a dû être parfaitement au courant des idées de Vater concernant le verbe russe, mais, vraisemblablement, il n'en a pas perdu le sommeil. Pour Greč, à en juger par sa grammaire, la tradition de la grammaire russe n'était pas une obsession. En tout cas, la tradition n'a pas fait obstacle à ses propres idées. Dans son autobiographie, Greč maintient qu'il n'avait jamais lu la grammaire de Lomonosov. S'il l'a feuilletée une fois, c'était pour constater que tout celà lui était déjà parfaitement connu. Très peu probable, en plus, qu'il a suivi (à Moscou!) les cours de grammaire de Barsov qui était mort sexagénaire en 1791, mais on ne peut pas exclure que Greč a étudié la grammaire de Barsov. Quelques similitudes peuvent être des indications de ce qu'il la connaissait, comme le verbe *бросить*, qui rentre dans la catégorie des verbes однократные.

Greč a publié un manuel de grammaire russe et ce manuel a été traduit en français par Reiff. La grammaire de Greč a eu une deuxième édition en 1827, cette fois traduite en allemand par A. Oldekop (St.-Pétersbourg, 1828). C'est cette traduction allemande que j'ai étudiée. Elle contient une terminologie bilingue et a conservé les termes grammaticaux russes.

On aurait dit que Greč a seulement corrigé le système de Barsov par sa division des verbes russes en виды, en allemand *Formen* (quatrième Hauptstück, par. 63 sqq.), en français, dans la traduction de Reiff, ils sont nommés *aspects*. C'est en effet exactement ce qui manque chez Barsov pour distinguer nettement les formes flexionnelles et dérivatives, mais par suite de cette correction, tout le système change. Les temps verbaux que ces виды peuvent exprimer, sont ainsi devenus subordonnés au sens qui appartient spécifiquement à chaque type de dérivation. Certains temps sont limités à certains types de dérivation.

D'autre part, Greč semble faire marche arrière. Pour son classement des verbes, il ne distingue que виды, quatre formes simples et deux composées. La désignation explicite de начертание (σχῆμα, *figura*) manque, son classement des types de verbes est, par conséquent, ambigu et il est obligé de séparer encore les verbes du type *тронул* (parmi lesquels il compte *бросил*) et les verbes du type *написал*. Ce serait, par conséquent, seulement par rapport aux verbes composés, que les formes simples sont vraiment des verbes non-composés et c'est seulement par rapport aux verbes immotivés que les autres verbes sont motivés.

En revanche, c'est exactement cela qui lui laisse une certaine liberté. Aussi, cela signifie-t-il qu'un verbe composé peut être en même temps un verbe dérivé. C'est que, à cause de la confusion, qui est d'ailleurs apparente, de la notion de dérivation et de celle de composition, on peut dire qu'un verbe peut être dérivé d'un autre verbe non seulement par l'emploi de suffixes, mais aussi par préfixation.

Cela signifie aussi que la désignation de вид совершенный peut être ambiguë, si les verbes de la forme *perfective* (*perfectum* à l'opposé de *imperfectum*) sont en même temps *parfaite* (non-motivé, non-dérivé), donc forme de fondation d'une forme imperfective ou même, éventuellement, d'une forme simple, créée par l'enlèvement du préfixe.

Les aspects (виды) verbaux selon Greč sont:

verbes simples:

1. вид неопределённый: par exemple *пишу* qui exprime une action qualifiée d'indéfinie (indéterminée), parce que le verbe ne dit pas que l'action se produit fréquemment, ni qu'elle se passe effectivement au temps qu'on parle. Tout cela dépend du contexte.

2. вид определённый (défini, déterminé): en particulier les verbes de locomotion "concrets";

3. вид многократный: *езжать, хаживать* "l'aspect fréquentatif-habituel" ("multiple" chez Reiff);

4. вид однократный: *тронуть, шагнуть, бросить* "l'aspect sémelfactif" ("uniple", chez Reiff);

verbes composés (préfixés):

5. вид несовершенный: *рассматривать* (l'aspect qui exprime que l'action se passe ou s'est passé une fois, sans indiquer qu'elle est, ou sera, accomplie).

6. вид совершенный: *рассмотрю* (l'aspect qui exprime que l'action est, ou sera, accomplie).

Le вид неопределённый, вид определённый et le вид несовершенный (1, 2 et 5) ont trois *tempora* classiques, qui expriment le présent, le prétérit et le futur; le вид однократный et le вид совершенный (4 et 6) ont deux temps: le prétérit et le futur, le вид многократный n'a qu'un temps: le prétérit. Tout cela veut dire que selon Greč les temps s'adaptent aux виды, appelés *aspects* dans la traduction française de Reiff. Quand le вид неопределённый, le вид определённый ou le вид несовершенный expriment le passé, c'est premièrement le prétérit du temps "passant" (преходящее время). Par contre, quand le вид однократный ou le вид совершенный expriment le passé, c'est en raison de leur nature qu'ils expriment le passé perfectif, le совершенное время, le parfait. Le seul вид verbal qui n'a qu'un seul temps exprime une certaine habitude dans le passé (cf. en anglais: *he used* [ju:st] *to* ...).

La tradition de la grammaire antique présuppose toutes sortes de verbes complets, incomplets, et défectifs, etc. Les grammairiens russes le croyaient convenable de les distinguer aussi. Chez Lomonosov c'était un peu tiré par les cheveux, Barsov distinguait полные (verbes complets), puis, les verbes недостаточные (défectifs) et ce qui en est le contraire: избыточные. Greč ne l'a pas simplement reprise à Smotryćkyj (qui n'admet qu'une catégorie de verbes défectifs (лишаемые). En tout cas, il en a fait tout un système et considère les *aspects* comme dérivations d'un seul verbe, tout en laissant au lecteur la liberté de les considérer comme verbes différents.

Après l'exposition des aspects et des temps Greč procède à la discussion des groupes verbaux différents, envisageant le verbe sous tous ses aspects. Parmi les verbes simples il y a:

1. Les verbes недостаточные (défectifs), nommés ainsi, parce qu'ils ont un aspect seulement, l'aspect indéfini (неопределённый: *алеть, блистать*).

2. Les verbes qui peuvent avoir l'aspect неопределённый aussi bien que многократный sont les verbes неполные (incomplets: *гадать - гадывать; печь - пекать*).

3. Les verbes полные (complets) peuvent avoir trois aspects: однократный, неопределённый et aussi многократный, c'est le type *болтнуть - болтать* dont la forme en *-ать* a été dérivée par analogie avec les verbes défectifs (недостаточные) comme *желать*; en tout cas, s'ils n'ont que deux aspects, c'est toujours l'aspect однократный (sémelfactif) et неопределённый (indéfini), c'est ce qui les distingue des verbes incomplets, qui n'ont que les aspects неопределённый et многократный.

4. Les verbes сугубые (doubles, terme emprunté à Smotryćkyj qui en faisait usage pour désigner les compositions à deux préverbes) sont toujours des verbes désignant la locomotion et aussi *быть - бывать* et *видеть - видать - видывать*. Ils peuvent être à l'aspect неопределённый ou определённый et parfois многократный (en exemple, Greč cite *брести - бродить - браживать*).

Les verbes composés d'un préfixe, catégorie à part, sont soit de l'aspect imperfectif (несовершенный) soit de l'aspect perfectif (совершенный).

1. Les verbes formés de недостаточные (*иметь, владеть, алеть,* "dérivation" du type préfixe + verbe simple, ont seulement l'aspect perfectif (вид совершенный: *воз-иметь, за-владеть, по-алеть*).

2. D'autres verbes ont deux aspects préfixés. Ils sont "dérivés" des неполные (le type *гадать - гадывать; печь - пекать*).

a. Ainsi préfixés ils obtiennent deux formes, l'aspect perfectif et l'aspect imperfectif (*угадать - угадывать*).

b. Il y en a des verbes qui dérivent l'aspect imperfectif par la préfixation d'un verbe многократный peu usité (ainsi on obtient les deux aspects *наблюсти - наблюдать, по-спешить - по-спешать*).

c. D'autres verbes encore ont l'aspect perfectif à l'infinitif en -ить) et l'aspect imperfectif a été raccourci (comme l'exprime Greč), ou non: *умолить - умолять, прекратить - прекращать;* parmi ces verbes-ci, les verbes tels que *приварить - приваривать* ("souder", et "augmenter un repas") et *предварить - предварять* ("prévenir", "anticiper").

d. Il y a aussi les verbes dérivés de verbes en -*нуть: замерзнуть,* avec l'aspect imperfectif en -*ать: замерзать.*

e. Les verbes dérivés d'un verbe simple qui n'existe plus: *обижать - обидеть.*

f. Les verbes dont l'aspect perfectif manque (par ex. *помнить*).

3. Un nombre de verbes simples ont les propriétés des verbes composés, comme *дать - давать, пустить - пускать,* mais le type *бросить - бросать* est cité parmi les verbes complets comme *болтать-болтнуть.*

4. Les verbes préfixés, qui sont formés à l'aide d'un préfixe et un verbe simple *complet* (полный, le type *ботать - ботнуть* ou *бросать - бросить*) ont souvent, pour l'aspect perfectif, selon Greč, la forme composé des deux parties (en -*ать* et en -*нуть*): *выбалтывать - выболтать/выболтнуть.*

5. Les formations du type *выбродить* (ipf.) - *выбрести* (pf.) face à *выбраживать* (ipf.) - *выбродить* (pf.) et *проводить* (ipf.) - *провести* (pf.), "mener", face à *проваживать - проводить,* "accompagner" sont des exemples de ce qu'on peut former des verbes dits, chez Greč, doubles (сугубые).

Quant à la dernière catégorie, Greč ne dit pas ce qu'ils signifient exactement, mais ce qui est certain, c'est que les types многократные, en tant que tels, ne sont pas préfixés, et que la qualité de многократность "disparaît" quand on y "ajoute" un préfixe. Ils "deviennent" un aspect imperfectif (вид несовершенный) quand ils sont préfixés. Pour le reste, leur valeur reste pareil.

En somme, des verbes qui n'ont que l'aspect indéfini se tire un seul autre aspect, l'aspect perfectif (ou parfait), des verbes à deux aspects non-préfixés (incomplets) se tirent l'aspect perfectif et imperfectif. Les verbes simples complets et les verbes simples doubles (сугубые), sont les verbes qui ont trois aspects, trois types de dérivation non préfixés. Ils produisent par conséquent trois formes préfixées. En plus, il y a les paires verbales simples qui ne sont pas incomplètes, ni complètes, ni doubles, verbes qui se comportent comme verbes préfixés.

L'aspect fréquentatif-habituel, la catégorie des dérivations verbales qui ne sont employés qu'au temps passé, ont un sens spécifique. C'est un sens qui est propre à cette catégorie, donc propre à cet *aspect*, mais les verbes préfixés de l'aspect imperfectif peuvent également exprimer une nuance fréquentatif-habituel, mais seulement si le contexte le permet ou l'impose. Cela signifie que la distinction que Greč a faite, entre, d'une part, les formes verbales (motivées et immotivées, mais sans préfixe), et, d'autre part, les formes verbales préfixées, n'est pas, semble-t-il, sans justification. Il y a, au moins, une forme de dérivation (un aspect, chez Greč), qui ne peut être que non-composée. Par contre, la citation des verbes simples qui se comportent comme verbes préfixés (дать - давать, кончить - кончать, et aussi, dirait-on, бросить - бросать), a l'air d'une manoeuvre qui sert à tenir compte de la tradition, peut-être, pour ne pas les faire confondre avec les verbes sémelfactifs en -нуть, ou pour distinguer ces verbes-là des verbes préfixés de l'aspect perfectif qui proviennent des verbes sémelfactifs sans préfixe.

Pourtant, on aurait pu en rester là pour déterminer le caractère spécial qui est propre aux aspects différents. Conclusion étonnante, sans doute. D'autant plus qu'elle découle de ce qui a succédé à l'oeuvre grammaticale de Greč et de Reiff. J'ai failli dire logiquement. En tout cas, sans les études savantes au sujet de l'aspect verbal en russe et en d'autres langues slaves, depuis Agrell jusqu'à Barentsen et nos collègues,[6] je ne serais jamais arrivé à la conception que je vais présenter ci-dessous.

La division de Greč n'a pas l'apparence très élégante, mais elle n'a pas été faite sans intention. Pourtant, plus tard, d'autres auteurs ont réduit les six aspects de Greč à trois et, encore plus tard, Bogorodickij en a fait deux: *l'aspect perfectif* (совершенный) et *l'aspect imperfectif* (несовершенный), ce qui est devenu la pratique non seulement de l'enseignement du russe, mais aussi des recherches linguistiques. Puis, on a détaché inutilement le sens primitif de l'aspect (traduction française, répétons-le, de вид, traduction ukrainien et russe de *forma* aussi bien que de *figura*, traduction latine de εἶδος et σχῆμα, ou bien les noms respectivement des formes verbales immotivées ou dérivées et des formes simples ou composées) du sens de la grammaire grecque. Aussi, employons-nous, au moins ici, le sens originel.

Les linguistes ont opposé les notions de *l'aspect perfectif* et de *l'aspect imperfectif*, et, en beaucoup de cas, ils en on fait une qualité verbale, qu'ils ont mise sur le même pied que les autres qualités verbales comme le temps et le mode. Ces qualités ont cependant une certaine hiérarchie. Tous les verbes conjugués ont des désinences personnelles (c'est la raison pour laquelle ils s'appellent conjugués), mais les désinences personnelles ne sont pas nécessaires. Il y a des langues qui n'en disposent pas. Les temps peuvent avoir des modes, mais les modes ne peuvent pas avoir de temps. On pourrait donc rencontrer un "mode" sans temps grammatical, mais, dans ce cas, du point de vue de la description, le "mode" appartient au sens intrinsèque du verbe. Dans un système verbal binaire, où il n'y a, pour exprimer le temps, que des formes verbales qui représentent la *simultanéité* avec le moment de parler et *l'antériorité* au moment de parler (Kuryłowicz 1977: 53 sqq.), il n'y a pas de temps grammaticaux. Tout ce qu'on veut prendre pour mode, est par conséquence une dérivation verbale qu'on ne peut pas appeler mode.

Les quatre aspects simples de Greč, détournés par les linguistes qui sont venus après lui, ont été relégués à des classes de sortes d'action (*Aktionsarten*, способы действия) ou se sont égarés dans l'aspect imperfectif, sauf l'aspect sémelfactif qui s'est noyé dans l'aspect perfectif. Procédure non seulement inutile, mais inacceptable, en plus, du point de vue de méthodologie: la comparaison de langues c'est la mesure du linguiste. Les phénomènes linguistiques sont les différences entre des langues comparées. S'il n'y avait pas de langues à comparer entre eux, il n'y avait aucune langue. Seulement langage: le fait que les gens parlent et qu'ils s'entendent.

Si l'on change de point de vue, de méthode, sans en rendre compte de façon scientifique, on a deux poids et deux mesures. Aussi, d'autres scientifiques sont-ils allés chercher le phénomène linguistique de l'aspect russe dans d'autres langues. Ils l'ont trouvé un peu partout, ce qui est loin d'être étonnant: selon le contexte, on traduit un temps passé en français par le temps passé d'un verbe de l'aspect perfectif ou imperfectif en russe. Même chose pour le futur. C'est seulement dans les cas où un infinitif ou un impératif est employé qu'on a deux alternatives en russe, ce qui peut donner, pour ainsi dire, un vrai embarras de choix. Un temps verbal (imperfectif, simple ou composé) du verbe conjugué français ne peut avoir la signification d'un verbe à l'aspect perfectif russe, que si le contexte

le permet. Quand on compare le russe avec des langues slaves, donc
avec des langues affines, des petites différences intéressantes apparaîtront,
mais les comparaisons avec d'autres langues que langues slaves demandent
une mesure plus exacte. La langue russe est trop différente. Comment
veut-on découvrir cette différence, si l'on ne la mesure qu'à sa toise?

L'étude des relations dérivatives constitue une erreur méthodologique
vieille comme la linguistique elle-même. La méthode que j'estime pas
encore vieillie, regarde les dérivations et les compositions comme des mots
autonomes. C'est l'arbitraire *relatif*, il est vrai, mais on n'a pas le droit
d'assumer que les dérivations se formeraient en parlant, à l'opposition
des mots immotivés qui serait déjà, que m'on passe l'expression, prêts à
parler. Ce serait confondre la dérivation et la parole, ou la linguistique
diachronique et la linguistique synchronique. Les formes dérivées se
trouvent comme des mots parmi les autres mots, dans la langue. D'où
elles proviennent et comment elles se sont retrouvées dans la langue,
c'est une question qui ressort à la linguistique historique, quelque lien
que ce soit entre le mot de fondation et le mot fondé, et quelque
transparent et évident que ce lien puisse paraître.

Les néologismes sont formés par analogie avec un exemple qu'on a
à l'esprit, procédure qui est, techniquement, pareille au calembour. Avant
que le néologisme se soit intégré à la langue, si jamais il y sera intégré,
le nouveau mot, qu'il soit dérivé, composé, déverbal ou dénominatif,
ou même "dé-motivé", "dé-composé" ou "dé-dérivé", est une forme
occasionnelle, qui survient de temps en temps dans la parole.

La notion de thème (θέμα) ne se trouve pas chez Denys de Thrace
et n'apparaît que deux siècles plus tard, chez Apollonios le Difficile.
En fait, ce n'est pas une amélioration, parce que la grammaire classique
n'en avait pas besoin. Se servant des notions de *forma* et *figura* elle
considère les formes immotivées et motivées, apparemment, comme
formées d'une abstraction dite "le verbe".

Cela suffit pour garder de la réserve sur la question de savoir quelle
est la forme fondée et quelle la forme de fondation. Il peut y avoir,
également ici, une certaine transparence, mais le lien dérivatif n'est pas
toujours clair. Si quelqu'un réfléchit sur sa langue, il verra plus de
cohérence et découvrira qu'il y a plus de liens entre des mots qu'il n'avait
cru auparavant. L'histoire de la dérivation reste quand même inconnue,
s'il ne connaît pas l'histoire de sa langue.

Souvenons-nous en tout cas que l'emploi des notions de flexion et
de dérivation n'est qu'une méthode, le sens des flexions (invariable) et
dérivations (variable, pas prévisible) n'en est pas la norme. Ce qui compte

c'est l'application systématique de la méthode. Une fois engagée, il faut que le chercheur scientifique s'y tienne et il ne peut s'en écarter sauf si les résultats des recherches y donnent lieu. Les auteurs de la grammaire russe, avant Greč, étaient loin de là et les recherches scientifiques ultérieures de la langue russe n'y donnent lieu non plus.

Finalement, on verra qu'il n'y a pas de quoi de changer le sens de la traduction russe de *forma* et de *figura*, ni de la traduction française (quelque soit le sens que les linguistes y attachent aujourd'hui), des termes russes de la grammaire de Greč. A une condition de près: il n'était pas la peine d'étudier les aspects (formes dérivatives) des verbes russes s'il s'agissait de rien que des classes morphologiques.

Greč lui même a provoqué un petit problème. Son classement en виды, donc en formes verbales motivées et immotivées, néglige les distinctions morphologiques telles que dans *хаживать*, *езжать* (verbes cités par Greč) ou *возить*, *бегать* qui appartiennent à des conjugaisons différentes (Greč en distingue trois), mais qui, du point de vue du вид (*forma*), sont aussi des aspects (dérivations) différents, en raison de leurs suffixes de dérivation. En plus, il faut tenir compte de ce qu'il y a, parmi les dérivations déverbales, des dérivations dénominatives (comme, peut-être, *возить* et *бегать*). Cela signifie que Greč a dépassé le sens strict du mot *forma*. L'inconvénient de toutes ces extensions pourront être écarté si l'on met le terme de вид au pluriel (donc, par exemple, troisième groupe d'aspects (de dérivations): les aspects fréquentatifs-habituels, виды многократные). Reste à savoir, alors, si le rassemblement de l'aspects qui sont formellement différents (rassemblement de classes dérivatives différentes, appliqué en vertu de leur valeur sémantique) est justifié.

Revenons à Barsov. Dans toutes ses catégories temporelles, le verbe (ou le verbe principal dans la construction à auxiliaire) peut être composé... à l'exception de la catégorie du plus-que-parfait. Inconsciemment, sans doute, ce fait est caché et Barsov procède ici comme Lomonosov. Il cite quelques exemples du давнопрошедшее время, temps qu'on n'aura pas de mal à reconnaître comme fréquentatif-habituel: *двигивал*, *тряхивал*, *глатывал*, *брасывал*, *плескивал*, *ганивал*, tout comme si la liste pourrait être enrichie de beaucoup d'autres exemplaires du plus-que-parfait, mêmes préfixés. Mais il n'en est rien. On pourrait, selon Tichonov, ajouter *говаривал*, *писывал*, *сиживал*, *рабатывал*, *вязывал* et d'autres, mais selon le même Tichonov il faut supprimer tous les exemples cités par Barsov. Il est clair en tout cas que la catégorie en question est limitée et il n'y a pas, en russe, de formes fréquentativeshabituelles préfixées. Les verbes comme *покрикивать*, par conséquent, n'y rentrent pas. La composition d'un verbe de ce type avec un préfixe peut toujours être employée comme les verbes qui expriment le temps преходящее неопределенное (par ex. *связывал*) et il peut arriver que ces verbes-ci ont un sens fréquentatif-habituel. Cela ne dépend que du contexte.

En russe, l'emploi des verbes fréquentatifs-habituel que Greč appelle многократные est limité au passé (Miklosich 1926: 803). C'est vraisemblablement la raison pour laquelle Barsov y a attribué la valeur du "plus-que-parfait", au lieu de les qualifier de fréquentatifs. Pas sans raison. Au fond, les verbes fréquentatifs ne sont pas si fréquentatifs comme cela. Selon la traduction allemande, многократный signifie que l'action s'est passée quelques fois (*einige Male*, "c'est arrivé parfois").[7] A juste titre, parce qu'il s'agit ici de l'emploi spécial des verbes non-préfixés, comme en Polonais *wieczorami czytywał książkę*, "le soir il avait l'habitude de lire un livre", ce qui ne doit pas forcément être jugé comme "fréquemment", mais plutôt selon le principe: une fois n'est pas coutume.

En polonais, l'emploi de ces verbes-là, dits ailleurs itératifs, est plus répandu qu'en russe et ne se limite pas au passé: *każdy dzień jadamy o szóstej*, "chaque jour nous dînons habituellement à six heures". Mais quelque limités, ou non, en nombre et en emploi qu'ils soient, en russe (comme en polonais) les verbes en question ont leur sens indépendamment du contexte, ce qui les distingue des autres verbes, même de ceux qui sont, le cas échéant, fréquentatifs selon le contexte. Il faut en conclure que l'aspect многократный, surtout en polonais, mais aussi en russe, l'aspect "itératif" (terme à ne pas prendre à la lettre, comme l'a remarqué Van Wijk 1927) est un aspect à part, qu'on ne peut pas supprimer, à ne pas parler de le reléguer à la catégorie de l'aspect imperfectif.

L'extension au présent de l'aspect "itératif" comme en polonais, ne rendrait pas superflu un aspect défini (определенный) dans la grammaire, puisque c'est l'aspect des verbes de locomotion *concrets* (глаголы одно-направленного движения). Les pendants *abstraits* (глаголы неоднона-правленного движения) changeraient facilement de catégorie et sortiraient de la catégorie de l'aspect неопределенный, dont les verbes expriment, comme par exemple *писать*, une action qui ne se déroule pas nécessairement au moment que le verbe est employé. Ils rentreraient, comme en polonais les verbes comme *chodzić, wozić, łazić*, etc. dans la catégorie des "fréquentatifs-habituels" et ne seraient pas étonnés de se trouver ensemble, dans cette catégorie-là, avec les verbes tels que *jadać* ou *czytywać*, qui expriment une habitude durant laquelle on reste, habituellement, à sa place et qui expriment le présent aussi bien que le passé. Apparemment, tout cela s'est passé aux frais des vieux verbes fréquentatifs non-préfixés en polonais, parce que les verbes *chadzać* ou *jeżżać* non-composés n'existent plus.

Mais en russe, au moins selon Greč, il y a bien deux catégories distinctes de verbes de locomotion. Préfixés, ils sont verbes à l'aspect perfectif ou imperfectif comme les autres, mais sans préfixe, ils obligent le grammairien à maintenir trois aspects, indéfini, défini et fréquentatif.

Il s'ensuit de là que la première division que Greč a faite des verbes russes, celle en verbes préfixés et non-préfixés, n'est pas tout à fait inutile. Il ne reste que la question de savoir la raison pour laquelle il y a, dans la catégorie des verbes préfixés, des verbes simples (non-composés, sans préfixe), à une valeur quand même dite perfective.

Quant au sens, il n'y a pas, pour autant que je sache, de différence claire entre l'aspect sémelfactif et l'aspect dit perfectif. Pour le traducteur, il est intéressant d'avoir la possiblité de traduire *крикнуть*, *ахнуть* comme "pousser un cri, un soupir" et *бросить* comme "lancer d'un seul jet", traduction qui, semble-t-il, n'est pas permise dans le cas de *решить*, "prendre une 'seule' résolution". Mais la traduction, bien évidemment, ne touche pas au sens du verbe russe nommé aujourd'hui perfectif.

Et puis, les "imperfectifs" comme *решать*, *давать*, *кончать* auraient bien pu, dirait-on, être rangés parmi les verbes de l'aspect indéfini. C'est là, au bout du compte, que se trouvent les pendants non-sémelfactifs en -*ать* des verbes comme *ахнуть*, *икнуть* et aussi de *бросить*. En outre, il y a aussi les verbes en -*нуть* de l'aspect indéfini (*сохнуть*, *вянуть*). Aurait-on ajouté aux verbes sémelfactifs le verbe *бросить* pour la seule et simple raison qu'il a fallu démontrer que ce n'est pas le suffixe -*ну*- qui était le critère de mettre à part les verbes sémelfactifs?

Ni Lomonosov, ni Barsov, ni Greč, c'est à quoi on peut se fier, n'ignoraient le sens spécifique propre aux verbes однократные et aux verbes que Greč appelait les aspects perfectifs. Greč semble avoir voulu maintenir, par tradition, un aspect однократный face à l'aspect многократый. Le sens dit perfectif, propre à des verbes russes, qui, plus tard, a tant frappé l'imagination des linguistes, ne l'intéressait pas spécialement. Ce n'était pas, pourtant, seulement pour l'amour de la tradition que Greč a maintenu un aspect однократный. Cela est lié à la distinction (implicite, parce qu'il se sert d'une seule traduction de *forma* et de *figura*) entre les verbes simples et composés.

En fait, chaque verbe de l'aspect (dérivation) imperfectif a le sens spécifique qui est aussi propre à l'aspect indéfini, mais les verbes de l'aspect fréquentatif et ceux de l'aspect défini, quand ils seraient préfixés, seraient aussi des types séparés parmi les verbes de l'aspect imperfectif. Chaque verbe préfixé conserve un peu la valeur de l'aspect dont il a été tiré. Ce n'est pas tout simplement et uniquement la préfixation, quand *на-* rend *писал* perfectif ou *с* le fait de *делал*, c'est la valeur du préfixe et celle du verbe ensemble qui y contribuent. Les verbes défectifs (de l'aspect indéfini seulement), les verbes incomplets (donc les verbes qui ont l'aspect fréquentatif et l'aspect indéfini), les verbes complets (qui ont l'aspect sémelfactifs et les autres aspects) et les verbes doubles (qui peuvent avoir, eux aussi, trois aspects) sont tous différents les uns des autres. Ils diffèrent également, même spécialement, en ce qui leur arrive quand ils sont préfixés.

Les aspects, rappelons-le, sont, chez Greč, dérivations d'une abstraction verbale. Un verbe, dans l'acception que Greč y accorde, qui n'a que l'aspect indéfini, reste tout seul quand il est préfixé. Ce qui compte pour la théorie de la distinction des aspects différents, c'est que les verbes неполные ont un vrai aspect многократный. Quand ils sont préfixés, ils sont couplés deux à deux, liaison qui leur est imposée par l'ensemble des aspects dont ils sont dérivés. C'est que les verbes préfixés n'ont que l'aspect perfectif et imperfectif, puisque le dernier ne peut avoir le sens de l'aspect многократный, que si le contexte le permet ou l'impose. L'aspect многократный lui-même est non-préfixé par essence.

Les verbes non-préfixés qui auraient seulement l'aspect *indéfini* et однократный, se comportent donc comme verbes préfixés, parce qu'ensemble, ils ne sont que deux aspects. La moitié imperfective ne peut pas être многократный sans que le sens dépende du contexte.

Les verbes de l'aspect однократный n'ont pas d'autre sens typique, indépendant du contexte, que le sens spécifique des verbes préfixés de l'aspect совершенный. Le suffixe *-ну-* ne les rend pas nécessairement sémelfactifs et le sens однократный, selon les grammairiens eux-mêmes qui classent *бросить* dans cette catégorie, peut même s'en passer. Pourtant, en aspect, il n'aurait pas pu être supprimé. Le verbe auquel l'aspect sémelfactif est censé appartenir est un verbe полный et peut avoir l'aspect однократный, неопределенный et многократный qu'il forme par analogie avec la forme des многократные verbes неполные: *гадать : гадывать = бросать : брасывать*, forme inconnue de Tichonov, mais au temps de Greč, la langue russe semble avoir eu d'autres dictionnaires qu'il y en a aujourd'hui. Ce qui ne signifie pas forcément que le *système* qu'on cherche et qui se manifeste dans la langue quand on étudie son histoire, était essentiellement différent.

La dernière catégorie de verbes non-préfixés, les verbes doubles (verbes de locomotion), ont également trois possibilités d'être préfixés, parce qu'ils peuvent avoir trois aspects. Ils diffèrent du type précédent, parce que au lieu de l'aspect sémelfactif ils ont l'aspect défini. Cette différence entre les verbes complets et les verbes doubles se répercute sur la façon dont ils sont préfixés. On a vu que c'est cela qui décide de la différence entre les verbes complets (qui ont, entre autres, l'aspect sémelfactif) et les couples de verbes qui se comportent comme s'ils sont préfixés.

Il s'ensuit de ce qui précède que les deux catégories de verbes non-préfixés, celle des verbes complets (полные) qui possèdent donc trois aspects — fréquentatif-habituel, indéfini et sémelfactif — et celle des verbes "qui se comportent comme verbes préfixés" contiennent deux types sémantiques (concernant le sens spécial à l'aspect perfectif). Ces deux types-là peuvent être observés du point de vue de l'une et l'autre catégorie: l'aspect sémelfactif peut avoir la signification de l'aspect perfectif, ou inversement.

Etant donné que le type verbal complet et le type *double* ont trois aspects, du moins en beaucoup de cas, trois formes pourraient en être dérivées en théorie. Comme il y a, cependant, seulement deux aspects préfixés, il y a par conséquent deux notions opposées. Il vaut mieux, s'il y a trois verbes préfixés, formés des verbes simples à trois aspects, les qualifier de "paires" qui ont un aspect en commun, soit l'aspect imperfectif soit l'aspect perfectif. S'il y a une différence de sens dans l'aspect (forme de dérivation) qu'ils ont en commun, par exemple dans le cas du type *выбалтывать - выболтать/выболтнуть*, ce sera dû au suffixe *-ну-* qui, vraisemblablement, sert à renforcer la nuance de однократность.

De l'aspect fréquentatif-habituel ne se tire qu'une forme, qui est en tout cas imperfectif; les deux autres deviennent perfectifs: avec une différentiation de sens, en russe moderne *забрасывать - забросать - забросить*. Si l'on les considère comme verbes couplés (car il n'y en a que deux aspects préfixés), on obtient les deux paires *забрасывать - забросать*, "combler", "encombrer" et *забрасывать - забросить*, "lancer", "jeter loin" ou "abandonner", "négliger".

Les deux aspects *кончить - кончать* (ce dernier cité par Greč et aussi par Tichonov) constituent une paire qui est un exemple d'un verbe qui, comme on dirait, pourrait bien rentrer dans la catégorie du verbe qui a l'aspect sémelfactif et les deux autres. Mais ce n'est pas là que la paire en question est à sa place, parce qu'il n'y a pas de forme en -*кончать* qui est le pendant perfectif d'un autre perfectif en -*ить*.

Pourtant, il y a *скончаться* "décéder", "trépasser" qui est perfectif. Pour expliquer cela, il ne faut pas expliquer les phénomènes de la langue. Ceux-ci n'existent, si je l'ose dire, que par la grâce des grammairiens et linguistes. Il faut donc expliquer la théorie de Greč.

Le système de Greč, quelque inélégant qu'il puisse paraître, est fondé sur une théorie et, décidément, la grammaire de Greč est le résultat d'une réflexion nourrie. La pratique du russe peut être un peu changée aujourd'hui, la théorie peut être maintenue.

C'est cette théorie qui aurait dû rendre superflue la notion de "imperfectivation secondaire", notion qui repose sur un raisonnement qui est en porte-à-faux: si jamais il y aurait un lien dérivatif de *готовить* à *подготовить* et de là à *подготовлять* ou *подготавливать*, ce serait un lien historique, le terme même de "imperfectivation secondaire" étant inacceptable du point de vue de la linguistique synchronique. La théorie de Greč, par contre, admet des groupes de verbes (aspects) comme groupes fondamentaux sur lesquelles d'autres groupes, des paires de verbes préfixés, sont fondés. En même temps, la théorie est subordonnée à la pratique et le système, par conséquent, tient compte de verbes non-préfixés qui ne se laissent pas mettre sur le même plan que les verbes dits complets. C'est que, les verbes complets supposent des préfixations, sauf de verbes fréquentatifs, de verbes indéfinis et de verbes sémelfactifs. En règle générale, l'un et l'autre, quand ils sont préfixés, ont l'aspect perfectif. Il en reste pourtant une différence de forme que les verbes simples au sens de verbes préfixés, en règle général, ne possèdent pas (en règle générale, puisqu'on les trouve quand même, mais les mots comme *скончаться* ne sont pas seulement des exceptions, ce sont, en plus, des mots exceptionnels).

Dans la parole, la *concurrence* (au sens étymologique plutôt qu'au sens propre) des deux formes différentes offre la possibilité de faire des nuances subtiles. D'une façon ou d'une autre, on devra pouvoir trouver, pour l'emploi de l'un des deux, un contexte pour faire sortir la différence entre les deux formes préfixées. Jusqu'au point où je devrai avouer que Barsov avait grandement raison d'accorder la dernière perfection à la forme perfective de l'aspect sémelfactif (*сбросить*). Mais dans la majorité des cas, même des formes à l'aspect sémelfactif, la forme "la plus perfective" a évincé l'autre.

Pour expliquer la différence entre d'autres verbes, étroitement liés les uns aux autres par dérivation ou préfixation, on pourrait même étendre la théorie de Greč. On ne va pas trop loin en affirmant que le sens du terme de вид совершенный, chez Greč, est tout à fait primitif. La notion latine, qui avait remplacé le grec πρωτότυπον, de *primitivus* ou *perfectus*, qui en est le synonyme, désignant le mot immotivé et introduites par Smotryćkyj en Russe sous la forme ukrainienne de первообразный ou совершенный, peuvent bien avoir été les désignations des formes verbales immotivées comme *решить, дать, кончить*, etc. Le вид производный (*forma derivata*) serait donc *решать, давать, кончать*. Les verbes ainsi dérivés du вид совершенный, c'est-à-dire, les verbes de l'aspect *dérivé* face à l'aspect parfait ou primitif, sont différents des verbes comme *писать*, parce que ceux-ci ne sont pas dérivés, mais *primitifs*. Les verbes du type *решать* ne le sont plus, ils appartiennent donc à d'autres aspects. La création (dérivation), ainsi conçue, des formes *préfixées* correspond à la création des verbes du type *решать*, selon le fond aussi bien que selon leurs formes respectives, à partir des verbes primitifs du type *решить*.

Sous la structure des deux aspects imperfectif et perfectif de Greč (peut-être, en avait-il le brouillon), il y aurait eu, donc, quatre aspects, préfixés et non-préfixés. Et il faudrait, par conséquent, dire que les verbes préfixés se comportent comme les verbes simples du type qui serait celui des verbes полные si la langue leur aurait permis de former l'aspect многократный (on connaît leur histoire et on sait pourquoi). Le critère de sens qui a permis de rassembler des aspects différents sous un seul nom (voir ci-haut) a apparemment provoqué un fusionnement des quatre *aspects*, dont deux, l'un simple et l'autre préfixé, sont les formes dérivées, pendants dérivés d'autres verbes qui sont совершенный. On peut facilement deviner ce que signifie maintenant le contraire de несовершенный.

Retour aux six aspects de Greč. Le verbe non-préfixé a une sphère d'action plus grande que celle du verbe préfixé, puisque le verbe sans préfixe peut avoir trois aspects, les autres n'en ont que deux: perfectifs et imperfectifs. Les verbes préfixés ne sont pareils qu'*en théorie*, ils diffèrent entre eux par leur origine dérivative. Effectivement, les verbes préfixés qui sont formés à partir des verbes de locomotion se distinguent nettement des autres verbes préfixés, par leur origine.

La position du verbe de l'aspect indéfini est ambiguë. Il arrive que la forme composée d'un préfixe et de l'aspect indéfini du verbe simple, est elle aussi "indéfinie" d'une manière dont un verbe préfixé peut l'être: il se scinde en deux. C'est normal chez les verbes de locomotion, où une forme préfixée peut être dérivée de l'une des trois formes verbales (aspects, chez Greč). Les verbes doubles peuvent donc se dédoubler.

D'où les paires *проводить* (ipf.) - *провести* (pf.), "mener", face à *про-*
important (ipf.) - *проводить* (pf.!), "accompagner".

C'est normal avec les verbes de locomotion, ce n'est pas normal avec
les autres verbes, mais on en rencontre quand même. Des dérivations des
trois aspects simples de *читать* en constituent un exemple, avec une
différentiation accentuelle, dans le cas du préfixe *вы-*, qui accompagne
une différentiation de valeur: *вычита́ть* (ipf) - *вы́честь* (pf), "décompter",
"soustraire", "prélever", face à *вычитывать* (ipf.) - *вы́читать* (pf),
"collationner", ou (familier), "apprendre en lisant". D'autres dérivations
de *читывать* (Tichonov) - *читать* - *честь* ont le schéma des verbes
complets, donc deux aspects perfectifs: *зачитывать* (ipf) - *зачитать* (pf),
"donner lecture de..." face à *зачитывать* (ipf) - *зачесть* (pf), "compter",
"mettre en compte"; "certifier une épreuve subie". (Adriana Pols, à propos
de: André Mazon, *Morphologie des aspects du verbe russe*, 1908).

Il y a, par contre, beaucoup d'autres verbes, à deux aspects imperfectifs,
le type *подготовлять/подготавливать*, imperfectifs alternatifs "accouplés",
avec le perfectif *подготовить*. C'est le pendant des verbes du groupe
avec l'aspect sémelfactif en -*нуть* qui, s'ils sont préfixés, ont deux formes
de l'aspect perfectifs. La question, posée par Adriana Pols, de savoir
s'il existe, dans ce type-là (dans celui des deux formes imperfectives),
une différence de sens entre les deux manifestations de l'aspect imperfectif, est tout à fait justifiée. Ici, on peut y ajouter la question: pourrait-on
y répondre à l'aide de la théorie étendue de Greč?

Les verbes sans préfixe qui s'appellent défectifs, le sont parce que,
en pratique, ils ont un seul aspect, l'aspect indéfini. A cause de cela,
la forme préfixée de l'aspect perfectif ne peut pas être liée à un verbe
de l'aspect imperfectif. Pourtant, en théorie, tous les verbes simples en
russe ont la forme en -*ывал* ou en -*ял* de l'aspect fréquentatif-habituel.
Si la forme imperfective qui correspondrait à la forme perfective *написать*
manque, il existe bien une forme *писывал* à côté de *писал*.

L'aspect indéfini, c'est déjà beaucoup: Les formes de l'aspect многократный ne sont que peu usitées, en fait, parce qu'on n'en a pas besoin.
L'aspect indéfini implique le sens itératif ou fréquentatif, qui serait trop
explicite dans l'aspect многократный. En plus, l'aspect indéfini comprend
"l'aspect défini" des verbes autres que ceux de locomotion ("il écrit",
face à "il est maintenant en train d'écrire", et "il a l'habitude d'écrire").
Il n'est pas sûr que les verbes de locomotion "abstraits" (*ходить, возить*)
y appartiennent; Greč ne s'est pas prononcé là-dessus. Si besoin en est,
le système pourrait être enrichi d'un aspect des verbes de locomotion

abstraits, entre "indéfini" et "fréquentatif", Ils sont en tout cas encore moins défini que les verbes de l'aspect indéfini, parce que les derniers peuvent être nettement "concret" ou "défini". Il en résulteraient des verbes non-préfixés à quatre degrés de détermination: fréquentatif, "encore moins défini qu'indéfini", indéfini, défini et sémelfactif.

En fait, on peut se figurer toute une gamme de genres d'action. Les verbes préfixés n'ont que deux aspects et les aspects perfectifs sont "sémelfactifs" ou "perfectifs". Les aspects imperfectifs peuvent donc prendre en charge tous les autres "Aktionsarten", depuis sémelfactif, ou un peu après, jusqu'au degré le plus haut de fréquentatif-habituel, que permet le contexte.

La pratique d'un système verbale se laisse expliquer, grâce à l'invention de Johann Severin Vater, par la théorie qui part de verbes qui n'existent plus. En théorie, pour élever l'étude du système verbal au niveau de la linguistique synchronique, on peut élargir l'application de cette invention-là à des verbes qui n'ont jamais existé, à condition qu'ils aient pu exister, c'est-à-dire, si leurs formes sont impliquées, d'une façon ou d'une autre, dans les formes qui sont réellement employées.

Il n'y a pas, pour autant que je sache, de différence fixée entre les suffixes de dérivation -ыва-(-ива-) et -а-(-я-): *хаживать* aurait pu être "*хаждать*": cf. le polonais (*przechadzać* [*się*]) et, *езжать*, semble-t-il, aurait pu être quelque forme en -ыва-(-ива-) (cf. *выезживать*, qui contient l'un et l'autre suffixe). Aussi, *en théorie*, les deux formes dérivatives existent-elles dans la langue, et, en effet, elles y *concourent*. Sinon, d'où viendrait les deux formes de l'aspect imperfectif *подготовлять/подготавливать* auxquelles Mme Pols a dédié sa thèse? A ne pas oublier les paires verbales comme *выходи́ть* (ipf) - *вы́йти* (pf), "sortir", face à *выха́живать* (ipf) - *вы́ходить* (pf), "sauver", "élever".

Les deux formes ont la même valeur, l'une des deux, dirait-on, est donc superflue et l'existence, en russe, de *хаживать* au lieu de "*хаждать*" n'est imputable qu'au hasard. Pourtant, Greč ressentait les dérivations imperfectives en -а-(-я-) (*научать*) comme *raccourcies* par rapport aux formes en -ыва- (*выучивать*). Il y a donc un peu plus de différence, ou de nuance, entre les deux formes qu'on pourrait évoquer, en s'aidant de leur différence formelle, quand on pèse ses paroles et les oppose par l'emploi dans un texte. Comme les verbes en -ать (-ять) sont "raccourcis" par rapport aux verbes à l'autre suffixe "itératif", qui en est, prétendument, le synonyme (s'ils sont les aspects imperfectifs alternatifs), on pourrait s'imaginer que ce sont eux qui ont un peu plus de "détermination", qui

86

sont donc un peu plus spécifique que les autres, les verbes en -ывать (-ивать). C'est Greč lui-même qui le dit de sa propre façon (Pols 1993: 20), et tout porte à croire qu'il a raison. On peut en tout cas découvrir dans le système de la grammaire de Greč les liens de dérivation entre les trois aspects virtuels du verbe simple et les deux aspects préfixés, qui confirment son opinion. Mais le linguiste peut amasser trop de formes verbales (très beaucoup, en tout cas, par rapport au nombre que le simple lecteur de journaux et de livres rencontre), pour le prouver. Les recherches de Mme Pols ne le démentent pas: la forme "courte" de l'imperfectif alternatif est, en effet, un peu plus "perfectif" (1993: 107), que j'appellerais un peu plus spécifique.

En général, pour les synonymes, on en a le choix pour de diverses raisons, mais, à mon goût, l'emploi de la langue qui tient compte du sens étymologique des synonymes n'appartient qu'au style d'un bon écrivain. Greč lui-même, à ce propos, n'avait pas l'étoffe d'un bon écrivain, mais il avait l'art et la manière de raconter savoureusement de sa vie et de ses ancêtres.

Pour finir, il faut remarquer que dans la gamme des degrés différents de détermination, les limites sont floues. On ne peut pas, cependant, dire qu'elles n'existent pas, puisque les verbes, en russe et dans les autres langues slaves, ont les formes dérivatives des aspects différents, et ils entrent inévitablement dans des catégories de détermination différentes.

Université de Leyde

NOTES

[1] Du moins pour des formes occasionnelles, comme, par exemple, *obaczyć*, "regarder", en polonais factitif ou itératif (sinon, on ne pourrait pas expliquer le *-a-* de la racine) qui vient de *oko*, "oeil", d'où: *ob-aczyć*, mais "dépréverbé" peut-être par analogie avec *patrzyć - opatrzyć* (donc, *opatrzyć* > *patrzyć* = *obaczyć* > *baczyć*) (Vaillant 1946).

[2] Des moyens, bien évidemment, de le dominer et de le posséder. Voir: Goudsblom 1992.

[3] Pour illustrer comme les romains, ou du moins les grammairiens-analogistes, attachaient de l'importance aux proportions harmonieuses, je cite l'exemple que donne Varron (X, 46) de la *cithara* à sept cordes. Sept n'est pas divisible par deux, mais on regarde la *cithara* quand même comme pourvue de deux paires de quatre cordes. La proportion d'accord de la première corde et la quatrième, la corde du milieu, est égale à celle de la quatrième et la septième. C'est ce qui peut importer pour la théorie des proportions linguistiques.

[4] Ch. VIII, par. 222, remarque pp. 159-160. C'était un événement! Vater raconte: "Man darf nur die Menge der, durch eine ganz abweichende Bildung ihrer Tempora unterschieden, Arten der Verba auf den angeführten Tafeln [dans le livre de Vater] anblicken, um einzusehen, daß es unmöglich war, aus blos zwei Paradigmen alle diese Formen zu übersehen, welche Formen dann in eine Menge einzelner Regeln zerteilt, und zum Teil aus dem Auge verloren werden mußten. Deswegen ist neuerdings von der Kaiserlichen Russischen Akademie zu St. Petersburg eine Einteilung der verba auf Ю in *vier* Conjugationen eingeführt worden." (1814, 85-86)

[5] Je cite de la seconde édition (Vater 1814: 116): "Eine beträchtliche Anzahl von Verbis auf АЮ oder ЯЮ und auch einige auf Ю mit vorhergehendem Consonant oder auf У haben auch noch ein anderes Verbum desselben Stamms bei sich, bei welchem statt jener Endung НУ zu dem Endstammconsonanten tritt; und welches die Bedeutung einer einmaligen, aber auch völlig zu Ende gebrachten Handlung oder Begebenheit, und in jener Präsensartigen Form auf НУ auch die Bedeutung eines Futuri (exacti) hat, z.B.; ..."

[6] C'est le moment, bien qu'il n'en soit pas l'endroit indiqué, d'exprimer ma gratitude à Mme Ania 't Hart-Waślicka, assistente, à l'époque, à l'institut de langues orientales et de linguistique indo-européenne (depuis longtemps fermé) de l'université d'Utrecht. Elle m'a beaucoup aidé à étudier à fond le livre d'Agrell et d'autres ouvrages, de mes collègues.

[7] Ce n'est pas une chose trop bizarre que de qualifier la forme en question de plus-que-parfait, comme l'a fait Lomonosov. Il aurait été un drôle de grammairien s'il n'aurait pas su ce qu'elle signifie, lui, qui disait que dans sa propre langue russe, on trouve la magnificence de la langue espagnole, la vivacité de la langue française, la puissance de la langue allemande, la tendresse de la langue italienne, et, en plus, la richesse et la force de l'imagination des expressions lapidaires des langues grecque et latine. Ce fameux dicton, paraît-il, comme Lomonosov a dit dans la préface à sa grammaire, est inspiré d'un mot célèbre de l'empereur Charles Quint qui y connaissait, parce que dans son empire, où le soleil ne se couchait pas, il y avait plus de langues que dans celui de Mithridate. Enfin, Lomonosov raconte que Charles avait l'habitude de dire (говаривал, p. 6), qu'il convient de parler avec Dieu en espagnol, avec les amis en français, avec les ennemies en allemand, avec les femmes en italien. Bien évidemment, Charles n'en avait pas l'habitude. Il ne parlait que le français et, semble-t-il, un peu le néerlandais. Il était bègue. Bref, il ne l'a pas dit trop souvent, si tant est qu'il l'ai dit jamais. Mais ce qui est sûr, c'est que la translation de говаривал est correcte, si l'on dit qu'il l'avait dit *jadis*, autrement dit, *une fois*.

Il est évident que notre représentation du système verbal russe est en fonction de la présence, dans la langue, de la forme fréquentative, forme courante à l'époque de Puškin et Greč. La langue littéraire russe d'aujourd'hui est différente, mais on ne peut pas maintenir que cette forme-là n'y existe plus. Elle a joué un rôle fondamental dans l'histoire de la langue moderne et il n'est pas sûr que son rôle soit terminé, si la situation qu'elle a aidé à créer, existe encore. Le traitement de ce problème a été retenu pour un article qui est à suivre: *A propos de la genèse du sens caractéristique des verbes perfectifs en russe.*

88

BIBLIOGRAPHIE

Adelung, J.C.
1807   *Mithridates oder allgemeine Sprachenkunde* mit dem Vater Unser
            als Sprachprobe in beynahe fünf hundert Sprachen und Mundarten.
            I. Berlin.
1809   *Mithridates* II. Großenteils aus dessen Papieren fortgesetzt und
            bearbeitet von Dr. Johann Severin Vater. Berlin.
1812-17   *Mithridates* III et IV, fortgesetz von ... Dr. Johann Severin Vater...
            Berlin.
AG 1802
1802   *Rossijskaja grammatika* sočinennaja Imperatorskoju Rossijskoju
            Akademieju vъ Sanktpeterburgu ... Nachdruck besorgt von Michael
            Schütrumpf, München 1983.
AG 1980
1980   *Russkaja Grammatika*. Ak. Nauk SSSR. Institut Russkogo Jazyka.
            Moskva.
Agrell, S.
1908   *Aspektänderung und Aktionsartbildung beim Polnischen Zeitworte.*
            Ein Beitrag zum Studium der idg. Präverbia und ihre. Bedeutungs-
            funktionen. Diss. Lund, 1908. Lund.
Barentsen, A.A.
1973   "'Vid' i 'vremja' v predloženijax, soderžaščix slovo *poka*", *Dutch
            Contributions to the Seventh International Congress of Slavists,*
            (ed.: A. van Holk), 33-94. La Haye.
1986   "The use of the particle BYLO in modern Russian", *Dutch Studies
            in Russian Linguistics* (= *Studies in Slavic and General Linguistics,*
            Vol. 8), 1-68. Amsterdam: Rodopi.
Barsov, A.A.
1981(1773) *Rossijskaja Grammatika*, podgotovka teksta i tekstologičeskij kom-
            mentarij pod red. i s predislovijem B.A. Uspenskogo. Moskva.
Benfey, Th.
1869   *Geschichte der Sprachwissenschaft und Orientalischen Philologie in
            Deutschland seit dem Anfange des 19. Jahrhunderts, mit einem
            Rückblick auf die früheren Zeiten.* München.
Berezin, F.M.
1979   *Istorija russkogo jazykoznanija.* Moskva.
Boissier, G.
1861   *Etude sur la vie et les ouvrages de Marcus Terentius Varron.* Paris.
Bogorodickij, V.A.
1907   *Obščij kurs russkoj grammatiki* (iz universitetskich čtenij), Izd.
            vtoroe. Kazan'.
Breunis, A.
1983   "Sur la phrase nominale en russe", *Dutch Contributions to the Ninth
            International Congress of Slavists. Linguistics* (= *Studies in Slavic and
            General Linguistics,* Vol. 3), 37-51. Amsterdam: Rodopi.

1986   "L'analyse logique de la phrase du type *možno kurit'* ", *Dutch Studies in Russian Linguistics* (= *Studies in Slavic and General Linguistics*, Vol. 8), 69-85. Amsterdam: Rodopi. (Erratum: p.74, ligne 2 d'en bas, lire: *le passé* non *le présent*).

1994   "L'analyse de la phrase du type *nečego delat'/ est' čto delat'* ", *Dutch Contributions to the Eleventh international Congress of Slavists, Bratislava. Linguistics* (= *Studies in Slavic and General Linguistics*, Vol. 22), 51-60. Amsterdam: Rodopi.

Chase, W.J.
1926   *The Ars Minor of Donatus*, for one thousand years the leading textbook of grammar translated from the latin, with introductory sketch. Madison.

Colson, F.H.
1919   "The analogist and anomalist controversy", *Classical Quarterly* 13, 24-36.

Dahlmann, H.
1932   *Varro und die Hellenistische Sprachtheorie.* Berlin.

Delbrück, B.
1893   *Vergleichende Syntax der Indogermanischen Sprachen.* Strasbourg.
1919   *Einleitung in das Studium der Indogermanischen Sprachen,* ein Beitrag zur Geschichte und Methodik der vergleichenden Sprachforschung, sechste, durchgesehene Auflage. Leipzig.

Desnickaja A.W. & Kacnel'son, S.D. (éds.)
1980   *Istorija lingvističeskix učenij.* Leningrad.

Gonda, J.
1940   "Taalbeschouwing en Taalbeoefening I", *Bijdr. tot de Taal-, Land-en Volkenkunde van Ned.-Indië*, 99, 35 sqq.

1957   "The Character of the Sanskrit Accusative", *Miscelanea Homenaje à André Martinet "Estructuralismo e Historia"*, T. I. (éd. Diego Catalan), 47-65.

1962   *The aspectual function of the Rigvedic present and aorist.* La Haye.

Goudsblom, J.
1992   *Vuur en Beschaving.* Amsterdam.

Greč, N.
1930   *Zapiski o mojej žizni.* Moskva-Leningrad. (première éd. complète: 1886).

Gretsch, N. (= Greč, N.)
1828   *Grundregeln der Russischen Grammatik,* Aus dem Russischen übersetzt von August Oldekop. St-Peterburg.

Hamburger, H.
1988   "The nature of the perfect and the aorist in Russian", *Dutch Contributions to the Tenth International Congress of Slavists, Sofia. Linguistics* (= *Studies in Slavic and General Linguistics*, Vol. 11), 235-252. Amsterdam: Rodopi.

Holtz, L.
1981   *Donat et la tradition de l'enseignement grammatical*; étude sur l'*Ars Donati* et sa diffusion (IVe-IXe siècle) et éd. critique. C.N.R.S. Paris.

Horbatsch, O.
1974   *Meletij Smotryćkyj, Hrammatiki Slavenskija pravilnoe syntagma*, 1619;
            Kirchenslavische Grammatik (Erstausgabe), Herausgegeben und
            eingeleitet von Olexa Horbatsch. Frankfurt a/M.
Issatschenko, A.
1974   "Vorgeschichte und Entstehung der modernen russischen Literatur-
            sprache," *Zeitschr. f. Slav. Phil.* XXX vii, heft 2, 235-273.
Jakubowicz, M.
1825   *Grammatyka Języka Polskiego*. 2 Vol. Wilna
Jagić, V.
1896   *Codex Slovenicus Rerum Grammaticarum*. Berlin-St-Peterburg.
            Ré-éd. München 1968.
Jellinek, M.H.
1913   *Geschichte der Neuhochdeutschen Grammatik von den Anfängen bis
            auf Adelung*, I, 1. Heidelberg.
Keil, H.
1961   *Prisciani institutionum grammmaticarum libri XVIII.* Grammatici
            Latini ex recensione Henrici Keilii Vol. I, II, III. Hildesheim.
            (Leipzig, 1895).
Kent, R.G.
1977   *Varro on the Latin Language*, with an English translation by R. G.
            Kent; in two volumes, I.
1979   *idem*, II; Loeb Classical Library. Cambridge (Massachusetts)-London.
Kopczyński, O.
1817   *Grammatyka Języka Polskiego*. Varsovie. 4e éd.
Kožin, A.N.
1989   *Literaturnyj jazyk dopuškinskoj Rossii.* Moskva.
Kul'man, N.
1917   *Iz istorii russkoj grammatiki.* Nachdruck besorgt von Peter Kosta,
            München 1982.
Kuryłowicz, J.
1973a   "Szerzenie się nowotworów językowych; na przykładzie pewnych
            końcówek koniugacyjnych germańskich", *Esquisses Linguistiques* I,
            109-118. München. (*Sprawozdania Polskiej Akademii Umiejętności.*
            1946.)
1973b   "La nature des procès dits 'analogiques'", *Esquisses Linguistiques* I,
            66-86. München. (*Acta Linguistica.* 1949.)
1977   *Problèmes de Linguistique Indo-Européenne.* Wrocław - Warszawa
            etc.
Lomonosov, M.
1755   *Rossijskaja Grammatika*. St-Peterburg. Ré-éd. Photom. Leizig 1972.
Miklosich, F.
1926   *Vergleichende Grammatik der Slavischen Sprachen; IV. Band:
            Syntax.* Manulneudruck der Erstausgabe van 1866-1874. Heidelberg.
Musić, A.
1902   "Zum Gebrauch des Praesens verbi perf. im Slavischen", *Archiv f.
            Slav. Philologie*, 24.

Newman, L.W.
1975   "The unpublished Grammar (1783-88) of A.A. Barsov", *Russian Linguistics* 2, 283-301.
1976   "The notion of verbal aspect in eighteenth century Russia", *Russian Linguistics* 3, 35-53.
Okenfuss, Max J.
1995   *The Rise and the Fall of Latin Humanism in Early-Modern Russia*; Pagan authors, Ukrainians, and the Resiliency of Muscovy (Brill's Studies in Intellectual History) Leiden-New York-Köln.
Paul, Hermann
1975   *Prinzipien der Sprachgeschichte.* 9. Auflage. Tübingen.
Pols, Adriana
1993   *Varianty pristavočnyx glagolov nesoveršennogo vida v russkom jazyke.* (= *Studies in Slavic and General Linguistics* 19). Amsterdam: Rodopi.
Rieger, Janus
1989   *Z dziejów języka rosyjskiego.* Varsovie.
Robins, R.H.
1951   *Ancient and Mediaeval Grammatical Theory in Europe.* Londres.
1957   "Dionysius Thrax and the western grammatical tradition, *Transactions of the Philological Society*, 67-106.
Schütrumpf, M
1980   *Kratkije pravila rossijskoj grammatiki, 1773*; Nachdr. besorgt von Michael Schütrumpf. Munich.
Solá-Solé, J.M.
1957   "Sur les parties du discours en phénicien", *Bibliotheca Orientalis*, 14, 2.
Stender-Petersen, Ad.
1970   *Den russiske litteraturs historie II.* 2. oplag. København.
Tichonov, A.N.
1985   *Slovoobrazovatel'nyj slovar' russkogo jazyka.* 2 Vol. Moscou.
Uhlig, G.
1883   *Dionysii Thracis Ars Grammatica qualem exemplaria vetustissima exhibent...* edidit Gustavus Uhlig. Leipzig.
Vaillant, J.
1946   "La dépréverbation", *Revue des Etudes Slaves*, 22.
Vater, J.
1814   *Praktische Grammatik der Russischen Sprache* in bequemen und vollständigen Tabellen und Regeln. 2. Auflage. Leipzig.
1984   *Johann Severin Vater - Ein Wegbereiter der Deutsch-Slawischen Wechselseitigkeit.* (Zu Vaters slawistischen Studien im Lichte seiner Briefe an Friedrich Adelung in Petersburg, herausgegeben und eingeleitet von E.Winter und E. Eichler). Berlin: Akademie-Verlag.
Vinogradov, V.V.
1978   *Istorija russkogo literaturnogo jazyka.* (Izbr. trudy, IV). Moscou.
Vostokov, A.X.
1863   *Grammatika cerkovno-slovenskago jazyka.* St-Peterburg. Photom. Nachdr. Leipzig 1980.

Wackernagel, J.
1920   *Vorlesungen über Syntax* I, mit bes. Berücksichtigung von Griechisch, Lateinisch und Deutsch. Basel.
1924   *Vorlesungen über Syntax* II, etc. Basel.
Wijk, N. van
1927   "Die sogenannten Verba iterativa und die Bezeichnung der wiederholten Handlung im Altkirchenslavischen", *Indogermanische Forschungen* 45, 93-104.
Worth, Dean S.
1984   *The origins of Russian Grammar*; Notes on the state of Russian Philology before the advent of printed grammars; *UCLA Slavic studies* 5. Ohio.

Dutch Contributions to the Twelfth International Congress of Slavists,
Cracow, Linguistics (= Studies in Slavic and General Linguistics Vol 24),
93-123. RODOPI, Amsterdam - Atlanta, GA 1998.

DIE PHONOLOGISCHE ENTWICKLUNG DES SCHLEIFER DIALEKTS IM 19. UND 20. JAHRHUNDERT

HÉLÈNE BRIJNEN

0. Vorwort

Der sorbische Dialekt von Schleife wird heute in sieben Dörfern der gleichnamigen evangelischen Parochie und zwar in *Slěpe* (Schleife), *Rowne* (Rohne), *Trjebin* (Trebendorf), *Mulkecy* (Mulkwitz), *Miłoraz* (Mühlrose), *Brězowka* (Halbendorf) und *Dźěwin* (Groß-Düben) gesprochen. Die Dörfer liegen im nordosten des Freistaates Sachsen auf der Muskauer Heide, im heutigen Landkreis Weißwasser. Ehemals gehörten sie zu der Oberlausitzer Standesherrschaft Muskau.

Bis zum Ende des 19. Jahrhunderts waren fast alle Einwohner dieser Dörfer einsprachig Sorbisch. Sie lebten traditionell von der Land- und Waldwirtschaft. Im Laufe des 20. Jahrhunderts wurde das Sorbische durch die erzwungene Germanisierung in der Zeit des Nationalsozialismus, den Zuzug von Heimatvertriebenen aus Schlesien und die Entwicklung des Braunkohlenbergbaus stark zurückgedrängt.

Heutzutage (1998) ist der größte Teil der sorbisch sprechenden Bevölkerung über 60 Jahre alt, die jungen Leute sprechen den Dialekt nicht mehr. In *Dźěwin* wird nur noch vereinzelt Sorbisch gesprochen. Der Kern des Dialektgebiets wird von den südlichen Dörfern *Rowne*, *Trjebin*, *Mulkecy* und *Miłoraz* gebildet. Die Zukunft dieser Dörfer ist unsicher; ihre Abbagerung ist bis zum Jahre 2020 vorgesehen.

1. Die Position des Schleifer Dialekts innerhalb des sorbischen Sprachkomplexes

Der Schleifer Dialekt ist ein Übergangsdialekt zwischen dem Obersorbischen und dem Niedersorbischen, mit Kennzeichen beider Sprachen. Bei seiner Entstehung im späten Mittelalter hat möglicherweise auch der Einfluß der östlich der Neisse, zum Polnischen übergehenden Dialekte eine Rolle gespielt (Schuster-Šewc 1995a: 70). In der Literatur wird der

94

Dialekt nach Muka (1891) im Hinblick auf seine geografische Lage öfters der "östliche Grenzdialekt" genannt.

Der Schleifer Dialekt unterscheidet sich vom Dialekt von *Mužakow* (Muskau), der östlich von ihm gesprochen wurde und in den fünfziger Jahren dieses Jahrhunderts ausgestorben ist. Der Muskauer Dialekt wurde von Wjelan (1869) und später in der Monographie von Ščerba (1915) beschrieben. In beiden Beschreibungen wird auf die Unterschiede mit dem Schleifer Dialekt hingewiesen. Stieber klassifizierte beide Dialekte als niedersorbisch; dem Schleifer Dialekt schrieb er aber mehr niedersorbische Kennzeichen als dem Muskauer Dialekt zu (Stieber 1934: 77).

Nur einige Kilometer südlich von Slěpe liegt *Nowe Město* (Neustadt), das von 1744 bis 1918 zur Schleifer Parochie gehörte. Nowe Město liegt an der nordöstlichen Grenze des obersorbischen Sprachgebiets. In diesem Dorf wird obersorbischer Dialekt gesprochen, der sich ebenfalls von dem Schleifer Dialekt unterscheidet. Der Dialekt von Neustadt wurde von S. Michalk in einer Monographie beschrieben (Michalk 1962). Diese Monographie enthält zahlreiche interessante Bemerkungen über den Schleifer Dialekt. Eine Monographie des Schleifer Dialekts ist nicht vorhanden.

2.   Rukopisy Hansa Nepile-Rowniskeho

Die älteste und vollständigste Wiedergabe des Schleifer Dialekts sind die Handschriften des Hanso Nepila (1761-1856), einem Bauern aus dem Dorf Rowne. Die Handschriften sind größtenteils autobiografisch und stammen aus der ersten Hälfte des 19. Jahrhunderts. Kulturhistorisch sind sie besonders wertvoll; ein schriftkundiger Bauer war in dieser Zeit eine Ausnahme. Für die Sprachwissenschaft stellen sie ein einzigartiges Dokument dar, das unter anderen zahlreiche lexikale Elemente enthält, die heute verloren gegangen sind.

Ein Teil dieser Handschriften wurde vom Pfarrer und Slawist Matej Handrik (1864-1946) in den Jahren 1896 bis 1900 in der Zeitschrift *Časopis Maćicy Serbskeje* unter den Namen *Rukopisy Hansa Nepile-Rowniskeho* veröffentlicht. Durch diese Herausgabe wurde Nepila einem breiten Leserkreis bekannt. Mit der Beschreibung seiner Jugend auf dem Lande, des Hungerjahres 1770 und des Wiederaufbaus der Wirtschaft in dem *prěni pisany rukopis* erwirbt er sich den Ehrennamen 'serbski Turgenjew'.

Nepilas Sprache wurde bisher jedoch wenig untersucht. Handrik selbst hat eine kleine grammatische Analyse an seine Publikation hinzugefügt

(Handrik 1900c) und separat ein Lexikon des Schleifer Dialekts veröffentlicht (Handrik 1905-1906). Muka, der Handriks Lehrer auf dem Bautzener Gymnasium war, hatte ebenfalls sprachwissenschaftliches Interesse für den Dialekt und seine Laute (s. Muka 1891, 1898, 1911-28). Einige seltene Lexeme aus Nepilas Wortschatz wurden von Schuster-Šewc etymologisch analysiert (Schuster-Šewc 1978-1989 und 1997).

In der zur Verfügung stehenden Literatur beruht das Kennen von Nepilas Handschriften meist auf Handriks Ausgabe; an die Originale wird kaum direkt referiert. Das gilt für sprachwissenschaftliche Arbeiten wie den *Sorbischen Sprachatlas* (s. z.B. Faßke 1988: 10), sowie für literarische wie *serbska čitanka* (Lorenc 1981) oder *Slěpjańska cytanka* (Richter 1995).

Auch meine phonologische Analyse der Sprache Nepilas (Brijnen 1994) stützt sich auf Handrik. Originalhandschriften standen mir damals nicht zur Verfügung. Eine solche Analyse erwies sich aber als unbefriedigend. Nepila schrieb in Schwabacher Schrift; Handrik hat diese Schrift in lateinische Buchstaben übertragen und nach eigenem Ermessen diakritische Zeichen hinzugefügt. Zwischen der Zeit, in der Nepilas Sprache sich gebildet hat, und Handriks Veröffentlichung liegt ein Jahrhundert.

3. Die unveröffentlichte Originalhandschrift Nepilas

Über das Vorhandensein von Originalhandschriften Nepilas bestand lange Zeit Unklarheit. Aus meiner Nachforschung 1994 im Bautzener Kulturarchiv hat sich ergeben, daß die mit Handrik übereinstimmenden autobiografischen Schriften größtenteils nicht mehr aufzufinden sind. Vom Original des *prěni pisany rukopis* fehlt heute jede Spur. Das Manuskript ist im Zweiten Weltkrieg verloren gegangen oder befindet sich vielleicht noch in Privatbesitz.

Dahingegen befindet sich im Restarchiv der Maćica Serbska eine unveröffentlichte Originalhandschrift Nepilas. Diese Handschrift wurde mir mit der Hilfe des Bibliothekars Franz Schön vom sorbischen Kulturarchiv zur Verfügung gestellt; ich habe sie transliteriert. Die Transliteration wurde in den Computer eingeführt, so daß Lexeme und Sequenzen leicht aufzufinden sind. Das Manuskript wurde in Schwabacher Minuskel-Schrift geschrieben und umfaßt 186 Seiten. Die ersten sieben Seiten stimmen mit Handriks: *Z druheju dweju pisaneju rukopisow* (Handrik 1900b) überein; der Rest bildet die Fortsetzung. Die Handschrift ist unvollständig, sie hat keinen Anfang und kein Ende; sie ist jedoch gut erhalten und gut lesbar geblieben. Die Buchstaben sind sehr klein (die Vokale sind ± 1 mm hoch), aber regelmäßig geschrieben. Das Format der Seiten ist 10 x 17 cm; auf jeder Seite befinden sich 34 Zeilen. Sie sind verschiedene Male numeriert worden, eine fortlaufende Numerierung befindet sich unten an der Seite. Die Blätter sind zusammengebunden; möglich haben wir mit einem der beiden Bündel zu tun, auf dessen Veröffentlichung Handrik damals verzichtet hat (s. Handrik 1900b: 30).

Die Handschrift beinhaltet den letzten Lebensabschnitt Nepilas, in der Periode zwischen 1826 und 1841; Nepila hat sie vermutlich mit 80 Jahren geschrieben. Das Manuskript erzählt von dem alten Vater, der als Kostgänger bei seinen Kindern wohnen muß. Hauptthema sind Nepilas Konflikte mit seiner Schwiegertochter, die hauptsächlich zurückzuführen sind auf den *wumionk* oder das Ausgedinge (das Altenteil). Der *wumionk* war die Leibrente, die ein Bauer von seinen Erben ausbedungen hatte: ein Lebensunterhalt in Natura. Die Handschrift enthält zahlreiche Details aus dem täglichen Leben; anders als bei Handrik findet man hier viel Dialog und viele familiäre Ausdrücke.

4. Inhalt und Ziel dieser Arbeit. Die benutzten Quellen

Es ist Nepila und Handrik zu verdanken, daß der Schleifer Dialekt über eine längere Periode dokumentiert worden ist; verschiedene Zeitabschnitte seiner Geschichte sind schriftlich belegt. Wie erwähnt, datiert Nepilas Originalhandschrift (ab jetzt: Nepila) aus den ersten Jahrzehnten des 19. Jahrhunderts; Handriks Arbeit ist am Ende des 19. Jahrhunderts erschienen. Aus dieser Zeit datiert auch der *Deutsche Sprachatlas* von Georg Wenker (1926-1956). Für diesen Atlas wurden 1879/1880 in Trjebin, Miłoraz, Mulkecy und Dźěwin Fragebogen in Schleifer Dialekt ausgefüllt (s. Stone 1994). Der Umfang dieses Materials ist jedoch bescheiden.

In den dreißiger Jahren des 20. Jahrhunderts wurde erneut Dialektmaterial gesammelt. Stieber (1934) hat in seiner historisch-vergleichenden Untersuchung der sorbischen Dialekte den Schleifer Dialekt mit einbezogen. Wirth und Schroeder, zwei Schüler von Vasmer, verrichteten ebenfalls Feldarbeit in Slěpe. Wirth, der Gründer des *Sorbischen Sprachatlasses* (SSA), publizierte eine Übersicht der Charakteristika des Schleifer Dialekts mit Bemerkungen über das Lautsystem und Dialekttexte; eine Schallplatte mit Dialektaufnahmen, Nr. LA 1324 der Staatsbibliothek Preußischer Kulturbesitz zu Berlin, ist verloren gegangen (cf. Wirth 1936b: S. 34). Schroeder (1958) liefert in seiner Dissertation die erste vollständige Beschreibung der Laute des Schleifer Dialekts. Schroeders Interesse galt der Phonetik, nicht der Phonologie; seine Arbeit ist besonders wichtig, da sie in phonetischer Transkription aufgeschrieben wurde. Wirth und Schroeder sind beide im Zweiten Weltkrieg umgekom-

men; Schroeders Arbeit wurde postum herausgegeben und 1959 von

men; Schroeders Arbeit wurde postum herausgegeben und 1959 von Schuster-Šewc rezensiert. Neuere Lautaufnahmen datieren aus den sechziger Jahren; sie wurden von dem 1992 gestorbenen sorbischen Dialektologen S. Michalk registriert. Die Tonbänder befinden sich im Bautzener Lautarchiv und wurden mir von dem sorbischen Institut zur Verfügung gestellt. Die wichtigste Aufnahme ist ein 45minutiges Interview mit einer Frau aus Trjebin, Marja Kudźelina. Marja Kudźelina wurde 1902 geboren; ihre Mutter kam aus Rowne, der Vater aus Trjebin; sie hat ihr ganzes Leben in Trjebin gewohnt. Sie war eine markante Figur, die gern erzählte und auch gut singen konnte; auf dem Tonband erzählt sie über Legenden und Traditionen aus dem Dorfsleben. Mit der Hilfe von Dorothea Šołćina wurden ihre Erzählungen niedergeschrieben. Später wurden die teilweise sehr schnell gesprochenen Aufnahmen mit dem Lautanalyseprogramm Gipos (einem Computerprogramm, das vom niederländischen Institut für Perzeptionsforschung IPO in Zusammenarbeit mit der Technischen Universität Eindhoven entwickelt wurde) von mir weiter analysiert. Feldarbeitaufnahmen, die ich 1991 in Rowne gesammelt habe, wurden an das Material hinzugefügt. Anschließend habe ich das damals für den SSA zusammengebrachte gesammte Material des Informationspunkts Trjebin (56) analysiert. Ein Teil dieses Materials wurde in dem SSA 13 (*Synchronische Phonologie*, Faßke 1990) und SSA 14 (*Historische Phonologie*, Faßke 1993) verarbeitet.

Im Vergleich zu meiner früheren phonologischen Beschreibung (Brijnen 1994) ist das verwendete Material somit stark ausgebreitet und ergänzt worden; eine Revision erwies sich als notwendig. Einige damals offen gebliebene Fragen können jetzt beantwortet, andere Ergebnisse bestätigt oder korrigiert werden.

Mit dieser Arbeit stelle ich mir die Aufgabe das phonologische System des Schleifer Dialekts, wie es in Rowne und Trjebin gesprochen wird, zu rekonstruieren und seine Entwicklung bis in die Gegenwart zu verfolgen. Dabei werde ich mich auf die drei Zeitabschnitten: Nepila (1826-1841), Handrik (1896-1900), und dem 20. Jahrhundert (1930 - heute) beziehen. Die Verwendung von Quellen aus verschiedenen Perioden der Geschichte bringt mit sich, daß diese Arbeit sowohl einen synchronen als auch einen diachronen Charakter hat.

5. Probleme bei der phonologischen Analyse sorbischer Dialekte

Die bisherigen phonologischen Analysen sorbischer Dialekte sind nach dem Zweiten Weltkrieg erschienen. Monografisch orientierte phonologische Beschreibungen haben wir von dem Dialekt von *Nowe Město* /Neustadt (Michalk 1962), *Wětošow*/Vetschau (Faßke 1964), *Rozdece* /Rodewitz-Spree (Jentsch 1980) und neulich auch von *Dešno*/Dissen (Steenwijk 1996). Die Phoneme des heutigen Schleifer Dialekts wurden von Schuster-Šewc (1959) und von Faßke (1990) besprochen. Brijnen (1994) stützt sich, wie erwähnt, auf Handrik. Alle Analysen wurden auf strukturalistischer Grundlage erstellt.

Die oben erwähnten phonologischen Beschreibungen stimmen nicht in jeder Hinsicht miteinander überein. In den phonologischen Beschreibungen von Faßke, Michalk, Schuster-Šewc und Steenwijk werden die Vokale *i* und *y* wie Varianten eines Phonems /*i*/ dargestellt, obwohl Michalk (1962: 35) und auch Steenwijk (1996: 88) Argumente für eine biphonematische Interpretation anführen. Dagegen betrachten Jentsch (1980) und Brijnen (1994) *i* und *y* als separate Phoneme. Die meisten Autoren, wie auch Jentsch, halten zugleich an einem phonematischen Unterschied zwischen palatalen und nicht-palatalen Konsonanten fest.

Die Interpretationsunterschiede beziehen sich somit auf:
- den Status der Vokale *i* und *y*;
- den Status des Unterschieds zwischen palatalen und nicht-palatalen Konsonanten.

Beide Problemfragen stehen in engem Zusammenhang zueinander; nachfolgend werde ich sie getrennt betrachten.

Der Vokal *i* ist ein hoher Vokal der vorderen Reihe; *y* ist (nach Schroeder 1958: 20) ein 'ungespannter Vokal der mittleren Reihe mittlerer bis erhöht mittlerer Hebung'. Im Folgenden werde ich zuerst eine Zusammenfassung der Distribution von *i* und *y* in Handrik mit einer Darstellung der Umgebungen, in denen *i* und *y* kontrastieren, geben. Da die Vokale *i* und *y* auf Grund dieses Materials von mir als zwei selbständige Phoneme analysiert wurden, ist jetzt die Frage, ob man die Annahme von zwei separaten Phonemen *i* und *y* bei Nepila ebenfalls aufrecht halten kann, und, falls dies so ist, ob die Argumente dafür dann dieselben sind. Die Antwort auf diese Fragen wird es ermöglichen, auch über den Status der Konsonanten in Beziehung zur Palatalität Aussagen zu machen. Anschließend werde ich die Ergebnisse mit denen der heutigen Situation vergleichen. Auch andere problematische Laute, wie z.B. die Vokale *ó* und *ě* werden dabei betrachtet.

6. Die Distribution der Grapheme *i* und *y* in Handrik

In seiner Transliteration verwendet Handrik die Vokalgrapheme: *a, i, y, e, ě, o, ó, u*. Die Distribution der Vokale *i* und *y* ist die folgende:

- *i* und *y* stehen entweder zwischen zwei Konsonanten oder nach einem Konsonanten im Wortauslaut; im Wortanlaut kommt weder *i* noch *y* vor.
- Weder *i* noch *y* findet man nach den folgenden, häufig auftretenden Graphemen:

  ṕ, b', ḿ und *ẃ*;
  ' *ń* und *ŕ*;

  und nach den seltenen Graphemen:

  č (beschränkt auf den Diminutivsuffix -*učki*);
  ś (nicht in *'tś*; nur in *wóść* 'Vater');
  v (nur in den Lehnwörtern *revěr* 'Revier', *verš* 'Vers' und *vort* 'fort').

6.1 Kontrastive Umgebungen

Wie sich aus meiner Analyse von Handriks *Rukopisy Hansa Nepile-Rowniskeho* ergeben hat, kommt der Kontrast zwischen *i* und *y* nur in bestimmten Umgebungen hervor. Diese Umgebungen sind jedoch für die Feststellung einer phonologischen Distinktion wichtig. Ausgedrückt in den von Handrik verwendeten Graphemen, sind die kontrastiven Umgebungen in Handrik die folgenden:

- nach *ch, k* und *h*,
- nach *š*,
- nach *d*.

Nach *ch, h, š* und *d* tritt in der Regel *y*, in bestimmten Fällen jedoch auch *i*, in derselben Umgebung auf; nach *k* kommt in der Regel *i*, in einem Fall jedoch *y* vor.

Einen Sonderfall bilden die Grapheme *p, b, m, w, n* und *r*, nach denen sowohl *i* als *y* auftreten können; diese Konsonanten können palatal bzw. nicht-palatal interpretiert werden. Der Vokal *i* gibt hier die Palatalität des vorhergehenden Konsonanten wieder und *y* die Abwesenheit dieser Palatalität. Demzufolge sind Beispiele, in denen diese Sequenzen auftreten, zum Beweis der Opposition zwischen *i* und *y* nicht geeignet, solange wir keine Entscheidung hinsichtlich des phonematischen oder nicht-phonematischen Status der Palatalitätsopposition in diesen Konsonanten getroffen haben; sonst wäre die Beweisführung zirkulär.

6.2 Nicht-kontrastive Umgebungen

Die Umgebungen, in denen der Kontrast zwischen *i* und *y* nicht hervortritt, sind geteilt in Umgebungen, in denen nur *i* vorkommt, und diejenigen, in denen nur *y* auftritt.

- nur *y* findet man nach den Graphemen *t*, *s*, *z*, *c*, *ž* und *ł*;
- nur *i* findet man nach *ć*, *'tś*, *dź*, *l*, *j*, *g* und *f*.

Nach den seltenen Graphemen *ř* und *ź*, die beide nur in einer orthographischen Variante eines einzigen Wortes vorkommen, bzw. *tři* 'drei' und *łóchźi* 'Ellen', folgt ebenfalls nur *i*.

7. Einige Bemerkungen zu Nepilas Schrift

Wie erwähnt, schrieb Nepila in Schwabacher Schrift; Diakritika verwendete er nur selten. In manchen Wörtern findet man die Grapheme *ä* und *ö* zur Wiedergabe von *e*; diese Schreibweise erinnert an die Krakauer-Berliner Handschrift, in der mit *ä* möglicherweise ein breites *e* und mit *ö* ein verengtes *e* gemeint ist (s. Schuster-Šewc 1996: 24). Das Graphem *y* wird stets mit einem Umlaut und *u* mit einem Bogen versehen. Die halbhohen Vokale *ě* und *ó* werden von Nepila nicht extra bezeichnet; wo man sie erwarten würde, findet man in der Handschrift bzw. *ie* oder *e*, und *o*.

Die Konsonanten werden alle ohne Diakritika geschrieben; es gibt z.B. nur ein Graphem *l*. Die Rechtschreibung der Handschrift ist nicht immer konsequent; manche Konsonanten werden doppelt oder sogar dreifach geschrieben. Die Palatalität wird oft gar nicht wiedergegeben, oder der Konsonant wird von *i* gefolgt. Ansonsten ist die Schreibweise ziemlich einheitlich: für den Laut [š] z.B. findet man konsequent *sch*; [s] und [z] und [ž] werden grafisch nicht voneinander unterschieden; sie werden durch *s*, durch *ss* oder am Wortende durch *ß* wiedergegeben. Nach *s* steht nur *y*; die Sequenz **si* kommt nicht vor. Die Grapheme *cz* und *z* werden abwechselnd für sowohl [c] als [ć] verwendet; je nachdem wird nach ihnen *y* oder *i* geschrieben. Die von Nepila verwendeten Grapheme sind in meiner Transliteration wiedergegeben.

8. Die Distribution von *i* und *y* nach *ch*, *k* und *h*

8.1 *chi* und *chy*

Die Sequenzen *chi* und *chy* kommen im Schleifer Dialekt nur in wenigen Lexemen vor. Es handelt sich um einige Verben, z.B.: *třechić/ trjechić* 'treffen', *chytać* 'werfen', *chylić* 'neigen' und nur wenige Substantiva, z.B.: *sochi* 'Pfähle', *grěchi* 'Sünden', *měchi* 'Säcke', *chyla* 'Weile', *pchy* 'Flöhe' und Adjektiva, z.B.: *suchi* 'trocken', *chytry* 'beträchtlich'. Der geringe Korpus bringt mit sich, daß eine eventuelle Opposition zwischen *i* und *y* nach *ch* sich nur auf einige seltene Fälle beschränkt.

8.1.1 *chi* und *chy* in Handrik

In Handrik gibt es die folgende Distribution der Sequenzen *chi* und *chy*: im Auslaut findet man *chi* in der Endsilbe mehrsilbiger Nomina, z.B.: *sochi* 'Pfähle', *grĕchi* 'Sünden' und in der Stammesendsilbe des Verbs *třechić* 'treffen', ein Lehnwort aus dem Deutschen, wo *ch* < **f*; z.B.: *třechi* 'traf'. Im Nominativ masculinum singularis des Adjektivs *suchi*/*suchy* 'trocken' findet man entweder *chi* oder *chy*; an allen anderen Stellen findet man nur *chy*.

Die Tatsache, daß sich in der Verbform *třechi chi* niemals mit *chy* abwechselt, während man bei den Nomina im Auslaut eine Abänderung *chi/chy* antrifft, ohne daß dies vorhersehbar wäre, ist der Grund, in Handrik eine marginale Opposition zwischen *i* und *y* nach dem Velar *ch* anzunehmen.

8.1.2 *chi* und *chy* in Nepila

In Nepilas Handschrift findet man einen anderen Sachverhalt. Im Wortauslaut tritt nur *chi* auf, z.B.: *miechi* 'Säcke', *suchi*, *trechi*. Im Inlaut steht *chi* nur in der Endsilbe des Verbs: *trechicz* 'treffen', *trechich* 'ich traf', *pschetrechil* 'traf', oder des Adjektivs, z.B.: *gluchich* 'tauben'. Die Sequenz *chy* findet man nur im Anfang eines Wortstammes, z.B.: *chyttry* 'beträchtlich', *chyttaiu* 'sie werfen', *wuchyttuio* 'wirft heraus', *pochyli* 'neigte'. Das von Handrik (1906) in seinem Lexikon belegte Wort *pcha*, gen. sg. *pchy* 'Floh' kommt in Nepila nicht vor.

8.1.3 *chi* und *chy* in der heutigen Mundart

In Schroeder (1958) findet man *trjechili su* 'sie trafen' und *njetrjechi* 'wird nicht treffen' nur mit *chi* und *pchy* 'Flöhe'. Bei Kudźelina findet man dieselbe Situation wie in Nepila.

Die Distribution von *i* und *y* nach *ch* ist laut Faßke (1990: 167) in Slĕpe komplementär und positionsabhängig: nicht im Morfemanlaut *chi*, im Morphemanlaut *chy*; *pchy* wird dabei als Morfemanlaut betrachtet. Diese Erklärung ist meines Erachtens jedoch wenig befriedigend. Erstens sind Morfemanlaut und Morfemauslaut oft nicht eindeutig von einander zu trennen, wie z.B. der Fall *pchy* zeigt. Auch ist es die Frage, ob eine solche positionsabhängige Erklärung den fonetischen Fakten recht tut; eher ist *chi* in *trjechić* lexikal gebunden.

102

8.2 *ki* und *ky*

Anders als nach *ch* das öfters sowohl von *i* als von *y* gefolgt wird, tritt nach *k* nur *i* auf. In einem einzigen Lexem: *kyrk* 'Gurgel', findet man jedoch die Sequenz *ky*.

8.2.1 *ki* und *ky* in Handrik

Nach *k* tritt in Handrik immer *i* auf, mit der Ausnahme von *kyrk* 'Gurgel', das einmal in einem religiösen Abschnitt vorkommt (Handrik 1898: 68). Auch in anderen Dialekten findet man Lexeme, in denen der Velar *k* von *y* gefolgt wird (s. Muka 1891: 122). Das Vorkommen von *kyrk* begründet, in Handrik nach *k* eine Opposition zwischen *i* und *y* anzunehmen.

8.2.2 *ki* und *ky* in Nepila

Der *Druhi čiščany rukopis* (Handrik 1898), in dem das Wort *kyrk* auftritt, wurde von Nepila ursprunglich in Majuskel geschrieben; Nepila verwendete die Majuskelschrift für Dokumente religiösen Inhalts. Die Originalhandschrift befindet sich in der Form einer Fotokopie im Restarchiv der Maćica Serbska in Bautzen. In dieser Handschrift findet man ebenfalls *kyrk*; es handelt sich also nicht um eine Verschreibung Handriks.

8.2.3 *ki* und *ky* in der heutigen Mundart

Die Tatsache, daß *kyrk* auch in Schroeder (1958) belegt ist, zeigt, daß dieses Wort keinesfalls auf einem religiösen Kontext beschränkt ist. Außerdem wird deutlich, daß es über eine lange Periode zu dem Schleifer Wortschatz gehört. Im Material des SSA tritt ebenfalls *kyrk* auf.

Das Wort *kyrk* (oder *gyrk*) ist in mehreren sorbischen Dialekten belegt worden. Das Vorkommen des Wortes *gyrk* in Neustadt spricht nach Michalk (1962: 35) für eine Wertung von *i* und *y* als zwei selbständige Phoneme. Auch in Slĕpe ist dies der Fall.

8.3 *hi* und *hy*

Der Laryngal *h* tritt nur im Wortanlaut vor Vokalen auf. In dieser Position kontrastiert er mit anderen Konsonanten und vor *a* auch mit Null; demzufolge ist *h* als selbständiges Phonem /h/ zu werten. Das Vorkommem der Sequenzen *hi* und *hy* ist nur auf einige Lexeme beschränkt: *hišći/hyšći* 'noch', *hižo(n)* 'schon', *hyć* 'gehen', *hynak* 'anders' und Ableitungen.

8.3.1 *hi* und *hy* in Handrik

Der Laryngal *h* steht bei Handrik stets im Anlaut, vor allen Vokalen außer *ě*. Betrachten wir die Distribution von *i* und *y* nach *h*, dann ist *hy* die übliche Sequenz, z.B.: *hyć* 'gehen', *hyšći* 'noch'. Die Sequenz *hi* findet man nur in einem einzigen Lexem *hižo* 'schon'. *Hižo* alterniert in Handrik mit *južon* oder *jižo(n)* (mit Verengung *ju* > *ji*), und *hyšći* mit *jěšći*. Die Tatsache, daß *ji* in *jižon* nur mit *hi* alterniert (und nicht mit *hy*, also nicht *hyžo*), und *jě* nur mit *hy*, begründet, in Handrik eine marginale Opposition zwischen *i* und *y* nach *h* anzunehmen.

In Georg Wenkers Fragebogen treten, neben Formen mit *hy*, die Formen mit der Sequenz *hi* häufiger auf; für 'schon' findet man jedoch nur *hižom* (neben *hužom*). Leider ist über die Personalia der Befragten wenig bekannt; das Material ist deswegen nicht vollkommen zuverlässig.

8.3.2 *hi* und *hy* in Nepila

In den Lexemen *hycz* 'gehen', *hynak* 'anders' und Ableitungen steht in der Regel die Sequenz *hy*; daneben tritt in diesen Lexemen mehrmals die freie Variation von *i* und *y* auf, z.B.: *hycz/hicz* 'gehen', *hyndzion/ hindzio* 'woanders'. Für 'noch' findet man *jeschzi, jeschzien, hieschczi, hieschzien*; *hy* kommt in diesem Lexem nicht vor. Nepilas Handschrift gibt somit eine ältere Stufe in der Lautentwicklung wieder, in welcher der Dissimilationsprozeß *j* > *h* noch im Gange war; die Änderung *hie* > *hy* hat bei ihm noch nicht stattgefunden.

Für 'schon' verwendet Nepila sowohl *jusson* als *hisson*. In *hisson* alterniert *hi* niemals mit *hy*; *hysson* kommt nicht vor. Die Tatsache, daß man in *hisson* die freie Alternanz von *i* und *y* nicht findet, ohne daß dies vorhersehbar wäre, weist auf eine marginale Opposition von *i* und *y* nach *h* hin.

8.3.3 *hi* und *hy* in der heutigen Mundart

Im neueren Dialektmaterial des 20. Jahrhunderts ist die Distribution von *hi* und *hy* nicht sehr eindeutig. Schroeder (1958) stellte die Sequenz *hi* nur in dem Verb *hijać* 'hü-rufen' fest, in allen übrigen Lexemen findet man *hy*; z.B.: *hyć* 'gehen'; *hyši* 'noch'. Kudźelina verwendet für 'gehen' stets *hyć* und für 'noch' überwiegend *hišći*, manchmal auch *hyšći*. Es gibt jedoch keine freie Variation von *i* mit *y* in *hižon*; auch im Lehnwort *hica* 'Hitze' tritt nur ein sehr hohes *i* auf. Obwohl das Material beschränkt ist, bestätigt es eine Opposition zwischen den Vokalen *i* und *y* nach *h*.

9. Die Distribution von *i* und *y* nach *š*

Im Schleifer Dialekt, so wie im Niedersorbischen, ist der Alveolar *š* < **š* ein harter Laut. Allgemein wird angenommen, daß die Depalatalisierung **ši* > *šy* im frühen Mittelalter stattfand; laut Stieber (1934: 64) verläuft dieser Prozeß bis ins 16. Jahrhundert. Im Obersorbischen ist dieser Laut weich geblieben und tritt nur *ši* auf.

9.1 *ši* und *šy* in Handrik

In Handrik kommt in der Regel *šy* vor; die einzige Ausnahme ist *nejwušši* 'höchster'. *Nejwušši* tritt nur einmal und zwar in einem religiösen Abschnitt auf und kann deswegen als Obersorbismus erklärt werden.

9.2 *schi* und *schy* in Nepila

In Nepila findet man viele Doubletten *schi/schy*; es dominiert jedoch die Sequenz *schy*, z.B.: *schiczko/schyczko* 'alles'; *naschiiu* 'auf den Hals', *zasschyiu* 'an den Hals'; *mudreischi* 'vernünftiger', *sslabpschy* 'schwächer'.

In bestimmten Fällen kommt jedoch nur *schi* vor. Es handelt sich 1) um Lehnwörter aus dem Deutschen und 2) um den Kontinuanten der urslavischen Lautverbindungen **pri* und **kri* (der Reflex von **tri* ist *tczi/czi*).

9.2.1 *schi* in deutschen Lehnwörtern

Das aus dem Deutschen entnommene Lehnwort *schindowacz* (deutsch: *schinden*) und dessen Ableitungen (z.B.: *wotschindowany* 'abgearbeitet', *schindowanie* 'Schinderei', *schintliuder* 'Schindluder') sind in Nepilas Sprache völlig integriert, wie z.B. das palatale *l* in *schintliuder* zeigt; sie werden deswegen in die phonologische Analyse miteinbezogen. In diesen Lehnwörtern alterniert *i* niemals mit *y*: man kann deswegen feststellen, daß *i* und *y* nach *sch* opponiert sind.

9.2.2 *pschi* und *kschi* < **pri*, **kri*

Man findet in Nepila die Sequenz *schi* nach dem Labial *p*: es handelt sich dabei um den Reflex von **pri*, z.B.: *pschi* 'bei' oder das Verbalpräfix *pschi*- in *pschigottowane* 'vorbereitet'. In dieser Sequenz tritt nie *y* auf. Auch in *kschisch* 'Kreuz', mit *kschi* < **kri*, kommt niemals *y* vor.

Einen von *schy* gefolgten Labial findet man in *sslabpschy* und in *pomschy* 'nach dem Gottesdienst'. In *sslabpschy* hat man mit einer Morphemgrenze zu tun; in *pomschy* jedoch nicht. *Pomschy* und *namschy* 'in der Kirche' treten mehrmals in der Handschrift auf; *y* alterniert hier niemals mit *i*. Man könnte zwar eine Regel benennen, daß innerhalb eines Morphems nach dem plosiven Labial *p* nur *schi* und nach dem nasalen Labial *m* nur *schy* folgt; eine solche Regel würde den fonetischen Fakten aber nicht entsprechen, da sich diese Labiale im Lautsystem sonst ähnlich verhalten. Demzufolge könnte man sagen, daß die Sequenzen *schi* und *schy* nach diesen Labialen in einer ähnlichen Umgebung auftreten; *i* und *y* sind hier opponiert.

9.3 *ši* und *šy* in der heutigen Mundart

In Schroeder wie in Wirth findet man einen neuen Kontrast zwischen *ši* und *šy*, wobei *ši* aus der Vereinfachung von *šć* in *hyšći* > *hyši* hervorgeht. Demzufolge kommt nach *š* nicht nur *y*, sondern auch *i* vor (s. Schroeder 1958: 47; Wirth 1936b: 34-35).

In Kudźelinas Sprache alterniert *hišći/hyšći* ebenfalls mit *hiši/hyši*. Es ist jedoch die Frage, ob man hier mit einer Oppositionsumgebung zu tun hat. Das klusile Element in den Affrikaten *ć* und *dź* ist manchmal sehr schwach, wie auch die Alternanz *chójdźiła/chójźiła* zeigt.

Der Verlust des klusilen Elements *šći* > *ši* in *hiši* ist hier fakultativ, und *ši* ist als eine freie Variante von *šći* aufzufassen.

In manchen anderen Lexemen tritt bei Kudźelina eine Variation von *ši* und *šy* auf, z.B.: *wususyć* 'austrocknen', *wususił* 'trocknete aus'. Dagegen findet man nur *ši* in *šindować* 'schinden', *našindowane* 'abgearbeitet' und auch in *starejši* 'Eltern'. In diesen Lexemen alterniert *i* niemals mit *y*; sonst kommt im Auslaut nur *šy* vor; *i* und *y* sind hier opponiert.

9.4 Die Entwicklung von *pŕ, *kŕ, *tŕ

Die Assibilierung des Vibranten *ŕ* nach *p*, *k*, *t* hat vor *i* und in einigen Lexemen auch vor *e* stattgefunden (s. SSA 14, S. 133). Wie erwähnt, sind die Reflexe in Nepila bzw. *psch*, *ksch* und *tcz/cz*; in seltenen Fällen tritt *pcz* statt *psch* auf, z.B.: *wobpcziiecz* 'erfassen', *pczimam* 'ich werde anfassen', *pschecze/pczecze* 'immer'; einmal findet man *kŕ > schcz* in *schcziwei* 'schief'.

In Handrik ist der Kontinuant von *pŕ* eine Affrikate; das *p* ist verschwunden. Handrik transkribiert Nepilas *psch* < *pŕ* wie *'tś*, mit einem Komma zur Wiedergabe des weggefallenen *p*. Die übriggebliebene Affrikate ist mit *ć* zusammengefallen; die Wörter *'tśi* < *pri* 'bei', *ći* 'dir' und *tśi* < *tri* 'drei' sind in Handriks Zeit wohl Homonyme. Nur in einigen Fällen, wie z.B.: *zaptśěg* 'Vorspann', ist das *p* erhalten geblieben. Die Wiedergabe von Nepilas Sequenz *ksch* < **kŕ* ist in Handrik stets *šć*, z.B: *šćiž* 'Kreuz'. Die heutige Lage ist dieselbe wie in Handrik.

Die Entwicklung des Vibranten **ŕ* nach *p*, *k*, *t* wird von manchen Sprachwissenschaftlern (s. z.B. Michalk 1962: 126; Schaarschmidt 1988) auf der folgenden Weise erklärt:

- Die Assibilierung von **ŕ* nach *p*, *k*, *t* hat nach der Depalatalisierung *ši* > *šy* möglicherweise zwischen dem 13. und dem 16. Jahrhundert stattgefunden;

- Der neu entstandene palatale Sibilant ist im Obersorbischen mit dem weich gebliebenen Sibilant *š(i)* zusammengefallen, z.B.: *pŕi* [pši]; im Niedersorbischen und in den Grenzdialekten konnte er sich nicht bei dem harten Sibilant *š* anschließen und identifizierte er sich angeblich mit dem nächstverwanten palatalen Laut *ć*;

- Später, als im Niedersorbischen die Abänderung *ć* > *ś* stattfand, änderte sich dort laut dieser Theorie auch *pć* > *pś*; im Schleifer Dialekt, in dem die Änderung *ć* > *ś* nicht durchgeführt wurde, blieb *pć* jedoch erhalten (Schaarschmidt 1988: 91);

Zusammenfassend wäre die Entwicklung im Niedersorbischen **pŕ* > *pć* > *pś* und in Schleife **pŕ* > *pć* > *ć* gewesen. Der Vibrant **ŕ* nach *p*, *k*, *t* wurde laut dieser Chronologie zum Sibilant nach der Depalatalisierung *ši* > *šy* und vor der Lautänderung *ć* > *ś*, welche bis in das 15. Jahrhundert datiert wird (s. SSA 14, S. 138). Zur Unterstützung dieser Chronologie wird außerdem argumentiert, daß die Affrikate im Kluster *pć* artikulatorisch nur über den Konsonanten *ŕ* entstanden sein könne (s. Schaarschmidt 1988: 88); und auch, daß ein neu entstandener Laut sich sofort bei einem im Lautsystem vorkommenden Laut anschließen würde (s. SSA 14, S. 138).

Die in Nepila vorkommenden Formen mit *pschi* sind mit diesem Vorgang jedoch in Widerspruch. Man müßte sie entweder als Niedersorbismen (obwohl die Affrikate *ć* in Schleife erhalten ist) oder als Obersorbismen (obwohl in Schleife die Depalatalisierung *ši* > *šy* stattgefunden hat) erklären; die seltenen Formen mit *pczi* wären laut dieser Theorie als Archaismen zu betrachten. Ob mit *schi* nach *p* oder *k* in Nepila nun der palatale Sibilant *ś(i)* oder der präpalatale Sibilant *š(i)* gemeint ist, ist jedoch nicht festzustellen, so daß sich die Frage Nieder- oder Obersorbismus nicht beantworten läßt. Es bleibt dann noch die Frage, ob die Formen mit *pcz* älter oder neuer sind als die Formen mit *psch*.

Handrik (1898: 74) hat auf Grund von Nepila eine andere Chronologie angenommen: *pŕ > pš > pć > ć. Für eine solche Chronologie sprechen die folgenden Argumente:

- Die Schreibweise prczi < *pri in Jakubica 1548 deutet möglich darauf hin, daß das vibrantische Element des ŕ in diesem ostniedersorbischen Dialekt erst später im 16. Jahrhundert aufgegeben wurde. Da der Schleifer Dialekt in mancher Hinsicht sprachlich mit diesem Dialekt verbunden ist, wäre es durchaus möglich, daß der Vibrant auch in Schleife länger bewahrt geblieben ist (s. SSA 14: S. 138; Schuster-Šewc 1995a: 70).

- Die häufigen Doubletten schi/schy in Nepila weisen darauf hin, daß eine palatale Realisierung des Sibilanten [ši] dem Lautsystem nicht fremd war, worauf auch die Schreibweise kschiesszianstwie 'Christentum' möglicherweise hinweist (s. Michalk 1962: 125). Der neue, aus *pŕ entstandene Sibilant könnte sich deswegen zum palatalen š(i) entwickelt haben.

- Obwohl die Entstehung der Affrikate ć über ŕ (*pŕ > pć) vor der Hand liegt, ist die Entwicklung pš > (p)ć artikulatorisch keinesfalls unmöglich; sie wird heute (1998) auch in der Umgebung von Bautzen wahrgenommen, z.B.: ćećelka < pŕećelka 'Freundin'.

Es kann mehrere Jahrzehnte dauern, bis sich eine neu entstandene Lautverbindung dem System angleicht. Es ist bemerkenswert, daß in Nepila in Ableitungen von dem deutschen Lehnwort butra 'Butter', z.B.: butrianku 'Buttermilch' und butrianniczu 'Butterfaß', die Sequenz tri erhalten ist. In Handrik findet man butśanki; bei Kudźelina bućanku und butranicu. Diese Lexeme weisen möglich darauf hin, daß der Assibilierungsprozeß noch nicht abgeschlossen war.

Auch Schuster-Šewc (1997: 35) geht davon aus, daß Formen mit pś oder kś älter sind als jene mit der Affrikate ć. Seine Erklärung, daß pś > pć in den Grenzdialekten nach Analogie des Obersorbischen entstanden sei, scheint aber nicht zuzutreffen, da sich gerade die relevanten Sequenzen im Ober- und Niedersorbischen, bzw. [pš] und [pś], akustisch ähnlich sind.

Über die Chronologie der Entwicklung von *ŕ nach p, k, t ist auf Grund des Materials keine entgültige Aussage möglich. Es ist jedoch nicht anzunehmen, daß es sich bei den regelmäßigen Formen mit pschi und kschi in Nepila um eine Innovation oder eine Entlehnung handelt. Es ist durchaus möglich, daß wir hier mit zwei parallelen Entwicklungen, die vorübergehend koexistierten, zu tun haben: *pŕ (> prš) > pš und *pŕ > pć. Die Chronologie *pŕ > pš > pć (> ć) würde vielleicht auch die seltenen Formen mit psć, z.B. Nepila: pscecze 'immer', besser erklären.

10. Die Distribution von *i* und *y* nach den Dentalen *t* und *d*

Die Dentale *t* und *d* sind hart; nach ihnen folgt in der Regel der
Vokal *y*. Diese Regel wird jedoch durch die Aufnahme von Lehnwörtern
aus dem Deutschen durchbrochen.

10.1 *i* und *y* nach *d* in Handrik

In Handrik werden die Dentale *t* und *d* nur von *y* gefolgt; das Lehnwort *paradizu* 'Paradies' bildet die einzige Ausnahme. Bezieht man dieses
Lehnwort in die Analyse ein, dann kommen nach dem Dental *d* in Handrik
i und *y* in derselben Umgebung vor (s. *'dyž* 'wenn') und bilden deswegen
eine Opposition. Nach *t* findet man nur *y*.

10.2 *i* und *y* nach *d* und *t* in Nepila

Bei Nepila ist die Lage nach dem Dental *d* dieselbe wie bei Handrik.
Die Sequenz *di* tritt, außer in *parradissu*, auch noch in *parradissagrotcze*
'Paradiesgarten', *diabel* 'Teufel', *diablowala* 'behandelte teuflisch', *dichtigk*
und *dicht* 'tüchtig' auf.

Nach *t* sind *i* und *y* bei Nepila ebenfalls opponiert. Obwohl in der
Regel *ty* vorkommt, z.B.: *tykach* 'ich steckte', *tykaince* 'Kuchen', *tyran*
'Tyrann', findet man in den aus dem Deutschen entlehnten Formen
tichtuiosch 'denkst dich aus' (deutsch: *dichten*), *nietichtuio* 'denkt sich
nicht aus', *wutichtowala* 'sie hat sich ausgedacht' und *tintu* 'Farbe' nur *ti*.
Im Pronomen *ty* 'du' alterniert *y* mit *i*, z.B.: *ti tyran niemudry* 'du dummer
Tyrann', *ti gnillei, ty ty gnileiaty* 'du Faulenzer, du du Faulenzender'.

10.3 *i* und *y* nach *d* und *t* in der heutigen Mundart

Schroeder (1958) erwähnt für 'Teufel' *djas* und für 'tüchtig' *dichtich*;
die Verbform *tychtował* neben *tichtował* zeigt eine weitere Integration
des deutschen Lehnworts; in *tinta* 'Farbe' (Material des SSA) ist dies
nicht der Fall. Michalk (1962: 35) zeichnete in *Židźino* ebenfalls *t'i* für *ty*
im emotionellen Sprachgebrauch auf.

11. *i* und *y* nach *p, b, m, w, n, r* im Vergleich zwischen Handrik, Nepila und heute

Wie erwähnt (s. 6.1), können in Handrik die Konsonantengrapheme
p, b, m, w, n, r sowohl von *i* als auch von *y* gefolgt werden und, abhängig
von den folgenden Vokalen *i* oder *y*, palatal bzw. nicht-palatal interpretiert werden. Im Unterschied zu Handrik kommt bei Nepila noch der

Konsonant *l* dazu, den man in der Sequenz *li* palatal und in der Sequenz *ly* nicht-palatal interpretieren kann (für Nepilas Grapheme *cz* und *z* siehe 7.). Die heutige Lage ist in dieser Hinsicht wie in Handrik.

12. Die nicht-kontrastiven Umgebungen in Handrik, Nepila und heute

In den übrigen Umgebungen, in denen *i* oder *y* vorkommen können, tritt keine kontrastive Opposition auf. Vergleichen wir die Umgebungen, in denen *i* und *y* in Handrik nicht kontrastiv sind (s. 6.2) mit den äquivalenten Umgebungen in Nepila oder mit der heutigen Lage, kommen wir zu den gleichen Ergebnissen, mit Ausnahme der oben erwähnten Opposition nach *t*.

Die Äquivalente von Handriks Konsonanten *s*, *z*, *c* und *ž* werden bei Nepila nur gefolgt von *y* und nicht von *i*, z.B.: *sy* 'du bist', *symie* 'im Winter', *zynila* 'sie tat', *ssyweniu* 'Leben' (in Handrik bzw. *sy*, *zymje*, *cyniła*, *žyẃenju*); auch heute sind diese Konsonanten stets hart.

Die Äquivalente von Handriks Konsonanten *ć*, *'tś*, *dź*, *j*, *g* und *f* werden bei Nepila gefolgt von *i* und nicht von *y*, z.B.: *dzieczi* 'Kinder', *pschi* 'bei', *jesdzicz* 'fahren', *praiil* 'sagte', *drugi* 'ein anderer', *fillku* 'Weilchen' (in Handrik bzw. *dźěći*, *'tśi*, *jězdźić*, *prajił*, *drugi*, *filku*). Die bei Handrik erwähnten Ausnahmen *tři* und *łóchźi* werden bei Nepila *czi* und *lochzi* geschrieben (s. 6.2).

12.1 Progressive Assimilation in der Lautgruppe *chw* vor *i*; Erhöhung des Vokals *ě*

In dem bei Handrik auftretenden Lexem *filu*, *filku* ist *f* die Folge progressiver Assimilation in der Lautgruppe **chw* vor *i*. Bei Handrik kommt **chw* nicht vor; *filu* wird dagegen mit *chylu* abgewechselt.

Bei Nepila findet man für 'Weile', 'Weilchen' die folgenden Ausdrücke: *chwilliu*, *chwielliu*, *filliu*, *fieliu*, *fillku*. Die Formen mit *chw* sind sehr häufig, der Veränderungsprozeß *chw* > *f* ist noch nicht abgeschlossen; das Lexem *chylu* findet man in Nepila nicht.

In Schroeder, Wirth oder bei Kudźelina kommt die Sequenz *fi* nur noch in deutschen Lehnwörtern vor. Für 'Weile' findet man, wie im Niedersorbischen, *chylu*; von zwei möglichen parallelen Entwicklungen *chwilliu* [chwilu] > *filu*, und *chwilliu* [chwilu] > *chylu* (vielleicht über *chwielliu*), dominiert jetzt die letzte.

Handriks Grapheme *ć* und *'tś* werden heute beide mit dem Symbol *ć* wiedergegeben. Bei Kudźelina tritt nach dieser Affrikate mehrmals *y* statt *ě* in freier Variation auf, z.B.: *cył* statt *ćěł* 'wollte'. In Handrik

110

findet man für 'wollte' *'ćeł* oder *'cył*; bei Schroeder *ćěł*; die Erhöhung
des Vokals *ě* vor einem harten Konsonanten wurde durch ihn bemerkt
(Schroeder 1958: 17).

13. Die Opposition *i* - *y* in Handrik, Nepila und in der heutigen Mundart

In Handrik haben wir eine marginale Opposition zwischen *i* und *y*
nach den Velaren *ch*, *k*, *h* und nach dem Dental *d* festgestellt.

In den originalen Handschriften Nepilas finden wir ebenfalls eine
Opposition zwischen *i* und *y*, und zwar nach *ch*, *k* und *h*, nach *š* (*sch*),
nach *d* und nach *t*.

In der heutigen Lage sind die Oppositionsumgebungen dieselbe wie bei
Nepila. Auch hier kann man *i* und *y* als zwei separate Phoneme betrachten.
Nach den Dentalen *d* und *t* wird die Opposition ausschließlich durch
Lehnwörter aus dem Deutschen verursacht.

Auffallend ist die häufig auftretende freie Variation von *ši* und *šy*,
sowohl in Nepila als auch in der Gegenwart bei Kudźelina; nach *ž* tritt
dagegen nur *y* auf; die beiden Sibilanten *š* und *ž* verhalten sich nicht auf
derselben Weise. Auch nach *h* tritt die freie Alternanz zwischen *i* und *y*
häufiger auf als nach den Velaren *ch* und *k*.

14. Der Palatalitätsunterschied bei den Konsonanten

Die Analyse der palatalen Konsonanten als selbständige Phoneme neben
nicht-palatalen steht in direktem Zusammenhang mit der Frage, ob man
die Vokale *i* und *y* entweder als Allophone eines einzigen Phonems /i/
oder als zwei verschiedene Phoneme betrachtet. Dieser Zusammenhang
trifft sowohl im Schleifer Dialekt als auch in den übrigen sorbischen
Dialekten und in anderen slawischen Sprachen, z.B. dem Polnischen, zu.

Den labialen Konsonanten wird, wenn sie palatal sind, in phonologischen Beschreibungen sorbischer Dialekte durchaus den Phonemstatus
anerkannt. Die Lautbeschreibungen von Ščerba (1915) und Schroeder
(1958) unterscheiden sich von den übrigen Analysen dadurch, daß die
Frage nach dem Phonemstatus keine wichtige Rolle spielt. Schuster-Šewc
(1959) analysiert die palatalen Labiale wie selbständige Phoneme. Faßke
(1990) betrachtet den Unterschied zwischen palatalen und nicht-palatalen
Labialen in Slěpe ebenfalls als phonematisch.

In der folgenden Abhandlung über den möglichen Palatalitätsunterschied der Konsonanten in Handrik, Nepila und in der heutigen Lage,
werde ich der Deutlichkeit halber mit den Konsonanten der labialen Reihe
beginnen. Danach betrachte ich die Situation bei den Velaren, bei den

Resonanten *n*, *ń*, *r*, *ŕ* und bei den Lateralen *ł* und *l*. Konsonanten, die nicht mit einem palatalen oder nicht-palatalen Pendant in Korrelation stehen, werden außer Betracht gelassen; sie sind phonetisch zu sehr voneinander entfernt, um komplementäre Paare bilden zu können. Bei diesen Konsonanten spielt die distinktive Palatalität keine Rolle.

14.1 Der Palatalitätsunterschied der labialen Konsonanten: phonematisch oder nicht?

Sowohl bei Handrik wie bei Nepila als auch heute sind die labialen Konsonanten *p*, *b*, *m*, *w* in bestimmten Stellungen zweifellos phonetisch palatal. Handrik gibt die Palatalität entweder mittels diakritischer Zeichen oder mittels des Graphems *j* nach dem Konsonanten wieder; Nepila schreibt *i* nach dem Labial. Die Graphik in Schroeder und Wirth weicht nur sehr wenig von Handriks Schreibweise ab; in der folgenden Diskussion ist die Lage in Handrik auch eine Wiedergabe der heutigen Situation.

Palatale Labiale kommen bei Handrik vor allen Vokalen außer *y* und *ó* vor. Vor den Vokalen *i* und *ě* wird die Palatalität des Labials nicht explizit angegeben, weil der Labial in dieser Position automatisch palatal ausgesprochen wird. Vor anderen Vokalen ist die Palatalität des Labials nicht automatisch und muß deshalb angegeben werden. Handrik versieht einen palatalen Labial vor *e* mit einem diakritischen Zeichen, wenn nach *e* wieder ein palataler Konsonant folgt, z.B.: *wob'edźe* 'Mittagessen'; folgt ein nicht-palataler Konsonant, dann findet man Labial plus *j*, z.B.: *wobjedował* 'er aß'; vor *u*, *o*, und *a* wird der Konsonant von *j* gefolgt, z.B. *żywju se* 'ich nähre mich', *mjo* 'mich', *drobjaty* 'brockig'. Im Inlaut vor einem Konsonanten oder im Auslaut trifft man keine palatalen Labiale an.

Auch bei Nepila kommen palatale Labiale nur im Inlaut vor einem Vokal vor. Vor dem Vokal *i* findet man dieselbe Lage wie bei Handrik; vor den Vokalen *a*, *u*, *o* und *e* schreibt Nepila Labial plus *i*, z.B.: *ssemia*, *ssemiu* 'Erde', *mio* 'mich', *wiesolly* 'froh'. Die Sequenz *ee* weist möglicherweise ebenfalls auf einen vorhergehenden palatalen Konsonanten hin; so findet man neben *wiesolly* auch *weesolly*.

Die phonetische Palatalität bei den labialen Konsonanten ist jedoch kein genügender Grund um anzunehmen, daß der Unterschied zwischen einem palatalen und einem nicht-palatalen Labialen auch phonematisch ist; man kann den palatalen Labial auch wie /*pj*/, /*bj*/ u.s.w. analysieren.

Vor *i* und *y* wird noch bei Handrik noch bei Nepila zwischen palatalen und nicht-palatalen Labialen ein Unterschied gemacht. Man kann eventuell annehmen, daß der Unterschied zwischen *i* und *y* die Palatalität des vorhergehenden Konsonanten reflektiert, aber das ist hier irrelevant, denn wir haben eine marginale Opposition zwischen *i* und *y* festgestellt; wenn einer von beiden, nämlich *i*, Palatalität des hervorgehenden Konsonanten mit sich bringen würde, ist dies noch kein Grund anzunehmen, daß diese Palatalität bei den Konsonanten distinktiv wäre; eher geht es um eine Allophonie von [p'] vor *i* und von [p] vor *y*.

Der einzige Grund, wodurch man annehmen könnte, daß die Palatalität bei den Konsonanten distinktiv ist, wäre, wenn die palatalen Labiale auch in anderen Positionen als vor einem Vokal, wo sie nicht von einem folgenden Vokal beeinflußt werden, stehen könnten. Dies ist aber weder bei Handrik noch bei Nepila noch in der heutigen Mundart der Fall.

Zusammenfassend können wir feststellen, daß phonetisch palatale labiale Konsonanten sowohl bei Handrik als bei Nepila wie auch heute vor den Vokalen *i*, *e*, *a*, *o* und *u* vorkommen können; bei Handrik und in der heutigen Mundart auch vor *ě*. Phonologisch kann man sie wie /Labial/ vor /i/ und /ě/ (mit einem automatisch palatalen Allophon) und /Labial/ + /j/ vor /e/, /a/, /o/ und /u/ beschreiben.

14.1.1 Die Depalatalisierung der palatalen Labialen

Einen interessanten Fall bilden in Nepila die Labialen vor dem Vokal *e*. Bei manchen Wörtern schreibt Nepila stets Labial (*L*) plus *e*, z.B.: *nowe* 'neu' (Adjectiv); bei anderen wieder Labial plus *ie*, z.B.: *prawie* 'richtig' (Adverb); dieser Unterschied wird von Handrik genau so wiedergegeben. Es gibt jedoch auch Wörter, die bei Nepila *Le*, hingegen bei Handrik *L'e* geschrieben werden, z.B. Nepila *penieß* 'Geld', *perrei* 'vor', *weczerrial* 'aß Abendessen', *wönebessach* 'in den Himmeln'; Handrik *ṕenjez*, *ṕeŕej*, *wecerjał*, *we ńebjesach*. Auf Grund dieser Formen könnte man annehmen, daß bei Nepila ein Depalatalisierungsprozeß bei den palatalen Labialen vor *e* angefangen hat, der von Handrik korrigiert wurde.

Die heutige Situation zeigt aber, daß die Depalatalisierung der Labialen vor *e* einen fakultativen Charakter hat. In Schroeder findet man *pjenjez/penjez*; *pjerei/perej*; im Material des SSA: *njebjo*, *wecor*; bei Kudźelina *wjecora*.

Die Lage in Nepila und in Handrik war in dieser Hinsicht möglicherweise dieselbe wie heute.

14.2 Der Palatalitätsunterschied bei den velaren Konsonanten

14.2.1 Der Palatalitätsunterschied bei den Velaren vor *e*

In Handriks Ausgabe findet man vor dem Vokal *e* keine als palatal markierte Velare. Zwei Ausnahmen weisen auf eine mögliche Palatalität vor *e* oder auch vor *ě* hin: *kěrliše* 'Kirchenlieder' und *cygjel* 'Ziegel' kommen jeweils einmal in freier Variation neben *kerlišami* und *cygel* vor. Bei Nepila alternieren die Sequenzen *ke* und *kie* in freier Variation, z.B.: *pschesskerrssycz/pschesskierrssycz* 'anklagen'; *sekerru* 'Axt', *sessekierru* 'mit der Axt'; *taike/taikie* 'solche'.

Die Sequenz *ge* findet man, mit Ausnahme des Verbs *sgiesz* 'essen', wo man mit einer Morfemgrenze zu tun hat, konsistent im Anlaut und im Inlaut; z.B.: *gernyschk* 'Töpfchen', *dogersszi* 'gegen die Hand', *wogen* 'Feuer', *cygellia* 'Ziegel'. Im Auslaut alterniert *ge* mit *gie*, z.B.: *nage/nagie* 'nackt'; *druge* 'andere', *poldrugie* 'anderthalb'.

Nach dem velaren Frikativ *ch* folgt in Nepila konsequent *e*. Die einzige Ausnahme ist die einmalig vorkommende Variation im Lehnwort *zycher/zychier* 'sicher'. Die Tatsache, daß im Schleifer Dialekt *ch* vor *e* stets erweicht wäre (s. Faßke 1990: 167), wird in Nepila nicht bestätigt. Die Sequenz *che* kommt jedoch nur in wenigen Lexemen vor.

In der heutigen Lage findet man die freie Variation von palatalen und nicht-palatalen Velaren vor *e* in allen Positionen. Es ist durchaus möglich, daß die Lage in Nepila und Handrik dieselbe war wie heute; im Inlaut erscheint die Sequenz *ge* öfters nicht erweicht.

14.2.2 Der Palatalitätsunterschied bei den Velaren vor Vokalen der hinteren Reihe

Sowohl in Handrik wie auch in Nepila kommt in den Lexemen *kjarla* bzw. *kiarrlia* 'Kerl' und *třechjony* bzw. *trechiona* 'getroffen' ein palataler Velar vor einem Vokal der hinteren Reihe vor; bei Nepila erscheint außerdem die Verbalform *kiakoczo* 'gackert'.

Das Auftreten von einem palatalen Velar vor einem Vokal der hinteren Reihe in *kjarla* war für Schuster-Šewc (1959: 777) ein Grund, ihn als ein selbständiges Phonem zu betrachten. Wie sich schon in meiner Analyse der palatalen Labiale herausgestellt hat, ist die Anfangssequenz in *kjarla* wohl biphonematisch /*kj*/ zu interpretieren.

14.3 Der Palatalitätsunterschied bei den Resonanten _n_, _ń_, _r_, _ŕ_

In Handrik kommen die palatalen Resonanten _ń_ und _ŕ_ nicht nur vor
Vokalen, sondern auch im Inlaut vor einem Konsonanten und im Auslaut
vor, z.B.: _góspodaŕ/góspodajŕ_ 'Wirt'; _twajŕ_ 'Gebäude', _twajrc_ 'Zimmermann'; _kóń_ 'Pferd', _kójncarje_ 'Pferdehändler'; _swaŕbje_, _swaribu_ 'Hoch-
zeit'; _tykajnce_, _tykanicy_, _tykańcaj_ 'Kuchen'. Die Schreibweise vor Konsonanten und im Auslaut entspricht der Aussprache, wie sie von Schroeder
(1958: 37) beschrieben wurde.

In Nepila finden wir dieselbe Situation wie bei Handrik. Sowohl im
Inlaut vor einem Konsonanten wie im Auslaut wird die Palatalität der
Resonanten deutlich mittels _i_ angezeigt, z.B.: _hainibu_, _haniby_ 'Schande';
konicz 'Ende', _tykaincze_ 'Kuchen'; _schraibari_ 'Schreiber'; _gospodarrisstwo/
gosspodairsstwo_ 'Wirtschaft'; _twarricz_ 'Zimmermann'.

Vor dem Vokal _e_ wird die Palatalität nicht immer angegeben, z.B.:
wönebessach 'in den Himmeln'; die Lage ist vergleichbar mit der der
palatalen Labialen (s. oben 14.1.1).

Die palatalen Resonanten _ń_ und _ŕ_ kontrastieren mit ihren nicht-palatalen
Pendants in mehr Umgebungen als die palatalen Velare und Labiale:
vor den Vokalen _a_, _e_, _o_, _u_, im Inlaut vor Konsonanten und im Auslaut;
auch in der heutigen Mundart ist dies der Fall. Schroeder (1958: 39)
ordnete sie wohl aus diesem Grund bei den 'normalen Konsonanten' ein,
während er die palatalen Labiale und Velare als kombinatorische
Varianten betrachtete.

Es wäre durchaus möglich _ń_ und _ŕ_, analog zu den palatalen Labialen
und Velaren, phonologisch wie /n/ + /j/ und /r/ + /j/ zu analysieren;
eine solche Analyse ist jedoch aus distributionellem Grund nicht er-
wünscht. Eine phonologische Beschreibung, in der der Halbvokal _j_
zwischen zwei Konsonanten oder im Auslaut stehen würde, bzw. /CjC/
oder /Cj/, würde den fonetischen Fakten und der Wortstruktur in Slěpe
nicht entsprechen; _ń_ und _ŕ_ sind deswegen als selbständige Phoneme /ń/
und /ŕ/ zu betrachten (s. Brijnen 1994: 79). Die Opposition /n/ - /ń/ und
/r/ - /ŕ/ ist vor den Vokalen _i_ und _ě_, wo nur palatale Konsonanten, und
vor _y_, wo nur nicht-Palatale zutreffen, aufgehoben. In Handriks Schrift
wird in diesen Fällen _n_ bzw. _r_ geschrieben.

14.4 Der Palatalitätsunterschied bei den Lateralen

Im Schleifer Dialekt ist der harte Lateral ein velarisierter Laut _ł_, der
nicht wie in den meisten anderen sorbischen Dialekten mit _w_ zusammen-

gefallen ist (s. Wirth 1933, Karte 7); *l* ist ein nicht=velarisierter palataler Lateral.

In Handrik wie auch heute werden für die Laterale zwei Grapheme: *ł* und *l* verwendet; in Handrik findet man das Graphem *ł* vor allen Vokalen außer *i* und *ě*; und *l* vor allen Vokalen außer *y*. Beide Laterale kommen im Anlaut, im Inlaut vor einem Konsonanten, z.B.: *wełmy* 'Wolle', *kulki* 'Kartoffel', und im Auslaut vor; da *ł* und *l* in derselben Umgebung vorkommen, sind sie als zwei selbständige Phoneme zu betrachten. Die Lage ist hier dieselbe wie bei den Resonanten.

Wie erwähnt, verwendet Nepila nur ein einziges Graphem *l*, das sowohl von *i* wie von *y* gefolgt wird, z.B.: *dali* 'sie gaben', *zely* 'ganz'. Die Doppelschreibung *ll* ist unsystematisch und hat nichts mit dem Unterschied palatal/nicht-palatal zu tun; z.B.: *kullkach* 'Kartoffeln' (palatal), *sniedall* 'frühstückte' (nicht-palatal). Vor Vokalen der hinteren Reihe wird die Palatalität des *l* stets mittels eines *i* bezeichnet, z.B.: *liubo* 'lieb', *rosstyllia* 'auseinander'; bzw. *valliowal* 'fehlte', *liassowanie* 'das Lesen'. Auch im Inlaut vor einem Konsonanten wird die Palatalität eines *l* ab und zu mit einem hinzugefügten Graphem *i* wiedergegeben, z.B.: *potkoillniu* 'unter den Schuppen'; die Lage war wohl dieselbe wie in Handrik oder heute.

Die in Handrik in seltenen Fällen auftretende Schreibweise *jl* oder *lj* statt *l*, z.B.: *kujlkate* 'kuglig'; *roztylja* 'auseinander' wurde wohl aus Versehen von Nepila übernommen.

15. Übersicht der Konsonantenphoneme

In der nachfolgenden Übersicht (1) findet man die Konsonanten-phoneme, wie man sie aus der Originalhandschrift Nepilas ableiten kann; die Wiedergabe entspricht der heutigen Schreibweise. Es fällt auf, daß der Inventar der Konsonanten in Nepila mit dem Inventar der Konsonanten-phoneme, den ich vorher basierend auf Handrik festgestellt hatte, oder mit der heutigen Lage identisch ist. Es ist aber nicht immer so, daß ein Konsonant aus einer bestimmten Phase in einer anderen Phase mit demselben Konsonant übereinstimmt, z.B.: Nepila: *pschi*, heute: *ći*. Der Konsonant /v/ wird als selbständiges Phonem bei den Lehnwörtern gewertet; einen dritten Lateral, der entweder palatal oder velarisiert wäre, gibt es nicht (s. Brijnen 1994: 81, 83).

		Velare	Palatale (hart)	Palatale (weich)	Alveolare (velarisiert)	Alveolare (einfach)	Labiale
Explosive	Stimmlos	*k*				*t*	*p*
	Stimmhaft	*g*				*d*	*b*
Affrikaten	Stimmlos			*ć*		*c*	
	Stimmhaft			*dź*			
Frikative	Stimmlos	*ch*	*š*			*s*	*f*
	Stimmhaft		*ž*			*z*	*v*
Nasale				*ń*		*n*	*m*
Vibranten				*ŕ*		*r*	
Laterale				*l*	*ł*		
Halbvokale		*h*		*j*			*w*

Übersicht 1

16. Übersicht der Vokalphoneme ·

16.1 Die Vokalphoneme in Handrik

Basierend auf Handrik habe ich die folgenden Vokalphoneme festgestellt:

	vor	zentral	hinter
hoch	*i*		*u*
mittel, erhöht	*ě*	*y*	*ó*
mittel		*e* *o*	
niedrig		*a*	

Übersicht 2

16.2 Die Vokalphoneme in Nepila

In Nepila gibt es ebenfalls zwei Vokalphoneme /i/ und /y/; außerdem kann man die Vokalphoneme /u/, /e/, /o/ und /a/ unterscheiden. Da Nepila keine Diakritika verwendete, ist es jedoch schwer, Aussagen über die Vokale *ě* und *ó* zu machen.

16.2.1 Der Vokal *ě* in Nepila

Bei Handrik haben wir zwei Phoneme /e/ und /ě/ auf Grund von minimalen Paaren wie *ćěło* 'Körper' - *ćeło* 'es wollte'; *njebě* 'war nicht' - *ńebje* 'Himmel' festgestellt. Bei Nepila finden wir diese Lexeme in bzw. *cziello* 'Körper' - *ziell* 'er wollte'; *nebiescho* 'war nicht' - *nebieskiego/niebieski* 'des Himmels'. Auf Grund dieser Beispiele ist es nicht möglich, zwei unterschiedliche Vokale festzustellen.

Man kann jedoch konstatieren, daß Nepila dort, wo man *ě* erwartet, ständig *ie* schreibt, z.B.: *miechi* 'Säcke', *griecha* 'Sünde', *piecz* 'fünf'; Ausnahmen gibt es nur wenige, z.B.: *melli* 'hatten'. In einem Lexem alterniert *ie* mit *i* : *dzierrow/dzirrow* 'Löcher'. Obwohl dieses Lexem nur manchmal auftritt, wäre es ein Hinweis dafür, bei Nepila ein Phonem /ě/ anzunehmen.

16.2.2 Der Vokal ó in Nepila

Man findet in Nepila keinen einzigen Hinweis für die Existenz eines Vokals ó. Nach Labialen und Velaren alterniert o niemals mit u wie in der Krakauer-Berliner Handschrift (s. Schuster-Šewc 1996: 25). Nepila schreibt nur o; die einmalig auftretende Form *schtu* 'wer' steht in einem religiösen Abschnitt und ist wohl Obersorbisch (*štó*); in Nepilas Sprache ist 'wer' *chta*.

Bei Handrik steht ó in der Regel in der ersten Silbe eines Wortes, nach einem labialen oder velaren Konsonanten, wenn kein Labial oder Velar folgt. Ein Grund dafür, bei Handrik ein Phonem /ó/ anzunehmen, ist das Vorkommen von o nach einem Labial vor *j*, wenn *j* < *wj*, in z.B.: *pojedać* 'erzählen' < *powjedać*, *spojedźi* 'Beichte' < *spowjedźi*. In dieser Umgebung tritt normalerweise ó auf, z.B.: *wójo* 'Deichsel'.

Bei Nepila findet man hauptsächlich Formen mit *w*, neben Formen mit *i*, z.B.: *powedacz/poiedaz* 'erzählen', *spowedzi* 'Beichte'; der Änderungsprozeß *wj* > *j* ist noch nicht abgeschlossen. Diese Tatsache, und daß Nepila immer o schreibt, wo man bei Handrik ó findet, liefern kaum Argumente dafür, um bei Nepila ein Phonem /ó/ anzunehmen.

16.2.3 Die Vokalphoneme in Nepila

In der folgenden Übersicht (3) findet man die Vokalphoneme, die man bei Nepila feststellen kann. Für den Phonemstatus eines möglichen Vokals ó findet man in Nepilas Handschriften keinen Hinweis; der Phonemstatus eines Vokalphonems ě ist unsicher.

	vor		zentral		hinter
hoch	i				u
mittel, erhöht	(ě)		y		
mittel			e		o
niedrig			a		

Übersicht 3

16.3 Die Vokalphoneme in der heutigen Mundart

Der Inventar der Vokalphoneme ist in der heutigen Mundart derselbe wie bei Handrik. Der Vokal ě steht in der ersten Silbe eines Wortes in Opposition zu *i* und zu *e*, z.B. Kudźelina: *lězć* 'kriechen' - *ležej* 'leichter'; *wěc* 'Ding' - *pjec* 'backen' - *bic* 'Dreschflegelklöppel. Die Vokale *o* und *ó* sind als zwei unterschiedliche Phoneme zu betrachten. In der Regel tritt *ó* nach Labialen und Velaren, falls kein Labial oder Velar folgt, in der ersten Silbe eines Wortes auf. Diese Regel wird jedoch durchbrochen in z.B.: *porjom* 'ich trenne auf', und in deutschen Lehnwörtern wie z.B.: Kudźelina: *gor* 'gar, ganz', *porty* 'Parte', *poru* 'paar' und *korwejdu* 'Kümmel'.

17. Schlußfolgerungen

17.1 Das Phonemsystem

Das Phonemsystem des Schleifer Dialekts hat sich im Laufe des 19. und 20. Jahrhunderts nur wenig geändert. Im Gegensatz zu den bisherigen Phonemanalysen werden von mir zwei unterschiedliche Phoneme /i/ und /y/ angenommen. Manche Oppositionsumgebungen wurden auch von anderen Sprachwissenschaftlern festgestellt, aber bei der Analyse außer Betracht gelassen, weil es Einzelfälle (*kyrk*) oder Lehnwörter aus dem Deutschen betrifft. Lexeme wie *trjechić, tichtować, šindować* oder *dichtich* werden jedoch zu Unrecht unbeachtet gelassen, da es um für den Schleifer Dialekt sehr charakteristische Lexeme geht, die schon zwei Jahrhunderte zum Wortschatz gehören.

In Handrik habe ich, im Gegensatz zu der Lage in Nepila oder in der heutigen Mundart, keine Opposition *i* - *y* nach *š* und nach *t* festgestellt; ein Grund für diese Annahme ist, daß die Verben *tichtować* und *šindować* in Handrik nicht vorkommen. Nepilas Germanismen wurden von Handrik öfters korrigiert und durch slawische Ausdrücke ersetzt; Handrik änderte z.B. *wotschindowane* 'abgearbeitet' in *wótdźěłany*. Auch manche familiäre Ausdrücke wurden von ihm verbessert; seine Herausgabe ist deswegen für die phonologische Analyse weniger zuverlässig. Es ist anzunehmen, daß der Kontrast zwischen *i* und *y* in den verschiedenen Entwicklungsphasen des Dialekts stets nach denselben Konsonanten, und zwar nach den Velaren *ch, k, h,* nach *š* und nach den Dentalen *t* und *d*, zum Ausdrück kommt.

Der Vokal *ó* wird heutzutage von mir als selbständiges Phonem, und nicht als Allophon von *o* gewertet. Auch hier spielen deutsche Lehnwörter wie *gor* oder *poru* eine wichtige Rolle. In Nepilas Handschrift habe ich keinen Hinweis für die Existenz eines Vokals *ó* angetroffen. Für das Vorhandensein eines Vokals *ě* in Nepila spricht nur ein Lexem; es ist deswegen schwer, hierüber entgültige Aussagen zu machen.

Die palatalen Konsonanten *ń*, *ŕ*, und *l* werden von mir aus phonetischen und aus distributiven und nicht aus ökonomischen Gründen, als selbständige Phoneme neben ihren nicht-palatalen Pendanten *n*, *r*, *ł* analysiert.

17.2 Phonologische Entwicklung

Im Vergleich zu Handrik und zu der heutigen Mundart stellt die Originalhandschrift Nepilas eine ältere Entwicklungsstufe des Dialekts dar. Handriks Transkription war nicht nur eine Transliteration, sondern auch eine Anpassung der Sprache Nepilas an der Sprachsituation am Ende des 19. Jahrhunderts. Am Anfang des 19. Jahrhunderts waren die folgenden Lautentwicklungsprozesse in Nepila noch nicht abgeschlossen:

1) Die Dissimilation *j* > *h* vor Vordervokalen: Nepila: *jeschzi/hieschczi*; Handrik: *hyšći*, heute: *hyśći/hyši/hišći/hiši*; bei Nepila hatte in diesem Lexem die Abänderung *hie* > *hy* noch nicht stattgefunden.

2) Die Abänderung *chw* > *f* vor *i*. Die Form *chwilliu* in Nepila läßt zwei parallele Entwicklungen sehen: *chwilliu* [chwilu] > *filu* (Nepila und Handrik); und *chwilliu* [chwilu] > *chylu* (Handrik und Gegenwart).

3) Die Abänderung *owje* > *oje*: Nepila *powedacz/poiedaz*, *spowedzi*; Handrik *pojedać*, *spojedźi*.

4) Im Reflex der Lautgruppe **pri* war bei Nepila das *p* noch erhalten, z.B.: *pschi*; in Handriks Zeit war das *p* abgefallen. Möglicherweise fand im Laufe des 19. Jahrhunderts auch die Abänderung *pš* > *pć* (> *ć*) statt.

5) Das Auftreten eines *k* im Reflex der Lautgruppe **kri* in Nepila scheint darauf hinzudeuten, daß auch die Abänderung *kš* > *šć* in z.B: *kschisch* [kšiš] > *šćiž* im 19. Jahrhundert stattfand.

6) Der Erhalt in Nepila der Sequenz *tri* im deutschen Lehnwort *butrianka* und das Vorkommen einer Affrikate in Handrik und in der heutigen Mundart *bućanka* zeigen, daß der Prozeß *tri* > *ći* im 19. Jahrhundert noch nicht abgeschlossen war.

7) Da in Nepila kein Hinweis für einen Vokal *ó* angetroffen wurde, könnte man annehmen, daß die Entwicklung *o* > *ó* im 19. Jahrhundert stattgefunden hat.

8) Da in Nepila nur in einem Lexem *dzierrow/dzirrow* durch die Alternanz *ie/i* ein Hinweis für einen Vokal *ě* angetroffen wurde, hat sich möglicherweise auch dieser Vokal erst im 19. Jahrhundert weiterentwickelt.

17.3   Der Schleifer Dialekt heute

Der Schleifer Dialekt ist ein konservativer Dialekt; das Lautsystem hat sich im Laufe des 19. und 20. Jahrhunderts gut erhalten. Auch heute is das harte *l* velarisiert und wird *r* apikal und nicht uvulär ausgesprochen. Sehr auffallend ist die Satzmelodie und die Betonung der vorletzten oder auch der ersten Silbe des Wortes; manchmal tritt eine sehr starke Nebenbetonung der vorletzten Silbe auf. Die Prosodie in Schleife wurde leider noch nicht untersucht oder beschrieben; eine Analyse wäre eine zukünftige Aufgabe.

Universität Groningen

LITERATURVERZEICHNIS

Arnim-Muskau, H. Graf von, & Boelcke, W.A.
1979   *Muskau, Standesherrschaft zwischen Spree und Neiße.* Berlin/Frankfurt/Wien: Ullstein.
Autorenkollektiv
1990   *Die Folklore der Schleifer Region*, Heft 1-4. Bautzen: Haus für sorbische Volkskultur.
Autorenkollektiv
1993   *"..da sah ich sie liegen schön, unsere Dörfer". Sorben im Landkreis Weißwasser/Oberlausitz.* Heimatkundliche Beiträge für den Landkreis Weisswasser/Oberlausitz, Heft 9. Landratsamt: Weißwasser/Oberlausitz.
Brijnen, H.B.
1994   "On the phonology of the Sorbian dialect of Slĕpe", in: Barentsen, A.A., Groen, B.M., & Sprenger, R. (Hrsg.) *Dutch Contributions to the Eleventh International Congress of Slavists, Bratislava. Linguistics.* (= Studies in Slavic and General Linguistics, Vol. 22), 61-91. Amsterdam: Rodopi.
1997   "An incipient literary tradition in Slĕpe Sorbian: Nepila's manuscripts and their transcription by Handrik", in: Synak B. & Wicherkiewicz T. (Hrsg.) *Language Minorities and Minority Languages in the changing Europe*, 305-309. Gdańsk: Wydawnictwo Uniwersytetu Gdańskiego.
Faßke, H.
1964   *Die Vetschauer Mundart.* Bautzen: Domowina.
Faßke, H. (Hrsg.)
1988   *Sorbischer Sprachatlas, 12: Morphologie.* Bautzen: Domowina.
1990   *Sorbischer Sprachatlas, 13: Synchronische Phonologie.* Bautzen: Domowina.
1993   *Sorbischer Sprachatlas, 14: Historische Phonologie.* Bautzen: Domowina

122

Handrik, M.
                "Rukopisy Hansa Nepile-Rowniskeho", *Časopis Maćicy Serbskeje*
                (*ČMS*):
1896   "Ćišćany rukopis", *ČMS* XLIX, 73-89.
1898   "Druhi ćišćany rukopis", *ČMS* LI, 65-74.
1899   "Prěni pisany rukopis", *ČMS* LII, 42-55 und 88-115.
1900a   "Prěni pisany rukopis", *ČMS* LIII, 14-30.
1900b   "Z druheju dweju pisaneju rukopisow", *ČMS* LIII, 30-38.
1900c   "Wo rěči Nepilowych pisanych rukopisow", *ČMS* LIII, 38-41.
1901   "Slěpjanska swaŕba", *ČMS* LIV, 18-37.
1902a   "Zběrka mjenow ze Slepjanskeje narěče", *ČMS* LV, 46-50.
1902b   "Zběrka přisłowow ze Slepjanskeje narěče", *ČMS* LV, 50-52.
1904   "Druha zběrka (101) přisłowow ze Slepjanskeje narěče", *ČMS* LVII,
                145-147.
1905   "Słownik Slepjanskeje narěče", *ČMS* LVIII, 81-100.
1906   "Słownik Slepjanskeje narěče", *ČMS* LIX, 41-58.
Jentsch, H.
1980   *Die sorbische Mundart von Rodewitz/Spree*. Bautzen: Domowina.
Jentsch, R.
1954-60   *Stawizny serbskeho pismowstwa, I, II*. Bautzen. [1870-1918]
Lorenc, K. (Hrsg.)
1981   *Serbska čitanka*. Leipzig: Reclam.
Michalk, S.
1962   *Der obersorbische Dialekt von Neustadt*. Bautzen: Domowina.
Muka, A.
1898   "Samozynk ó w Slepjanskej narěči", *ČMS* LI, 86-88.
1965 [1891]   *Historische und vergleichende Laut- und Formenlehre der nieder-
                sorbischen (niederlausitzisch-wendischen) Sprache*. Bautzen: Domo-
                wina.
1966-80   *Wörterbuch der niedersorbischen Sprache und ihrer Dialekte*.
                Bautzen: Domowina. [1911-1915, 1928]
Richter, H.
1995   *Slěpjańska cytanka (Schleifer Lesebuch)*. Bautzen: Domowina.
Schaarschmidt, G.
1988   "Phonological Space and System Simplification: Coronal Spirants and
                Affricates in Sorbian and Other West Slavic Languages", *Canadian
                Contributions to the X International Congress of Slavists. Sofia 1988.
                Canadian Slavonic Papers*, Vol. XXX, No. 1, 81-95.
Schroeder, A.
1958   *Die Laute des wendischen (sorbischen) Dialekts von Schleife in der
                Oberlausitz (Lautbeschreibung)*. Tübingen: Max Niemeyer Verlag.
Schulenburg, W. von
1985 [1882]   *Wendisches Volkstum in Sage, Brauch und Sitte*. Bautzen: Domo-
                wina.
Schuster-Šewc, H.
1959   Rezension: "A. Schroeder. Die Laute des wendischen (sorbischen)
                Dialekts von Schleife in der Oberlausitz (Lautbeschreibung)", *Zeit-
                schrift für Slawistik*, Bd. IV, 5, 771-780.

1978-89   *Historisch-etymologisches Wörterbuch der ober- und niedersorbischen Sprache.* Bautzen: Domowina.

1995a   Rezension: "Synchronische und diachronische Phonologie des Sorbischen (Sorbischer Sprachatlas - Serbski rěčny atlas, Bd. 13. und 14.)", *Zeitschrift für Slawistik* 40, 1, 68-91.

1995b   "Michała Frenclowy rowjenk Jan Cichorius a jeho rukopis z lěta 1663", *Lětopis* 42, 2, 3-29. Bautzen: Domowina.

1996   *Das Neue Testament der niedersorbischen Krakauer (Berliner) Handschrift. Ein Sprachdenkmal des 17. Jahrhunderts.* Bautzen: Domowina.

1997   Mikławša Jakubicowy přełožk Noweho zakonja do serbšćiny z lěta 1548. Pospyt noweho hladanja na wosobinu přełožowarja a jeho rěč", *Lětopis* 44, 2, 31-52. Bautzen: Domowina.

Sorbischer Sprachatlas (SSA): s. Faßke, H. (Hrsg.)

Steenwijk, H.

1996   "Phonologie des niedersorbischen Dialekts von Dissen/Dešno", *Lětopis* 43, 1, 75-96. Bautzen: Domowina

Stieber, Z.

1934   *Stosunki pokrewieństwa języków łużyckich.* Kraków.

Stone, G.

1994   "Material k serbskej historiskej dialektologiji z archiwa Němskeho rěčneho atlasa", *Lětopis* 41, 2, 52-66. Bautzen: Domowina.

Ščerba, L.V.

1973 [1915]   *Vostočnolužickoe narečie (Der ostniedersorbische Dialekt).* Bautzen: Domowina.

Wenker, G.

1926-1956   *Deutscher Sprachatlas.* Marburg.

Wirth, P.

1931   "Studien zur sorbischen Sprachgeographie, 1: Zur 'ostsorbischen' Mundart", *Zeitschrift für slavische Philologie.* Bd. VIII.

1975   Beiträge zum sorbischen (wendischen) Sprachatlas. Bautzen: Domowina. [1933, 1936a]

1936b   "Ze Slepjanskeje narěče", *ČMS* XVIII, 31-39.

Wićaz, P.

1949   "Zakitowar Serbstwa w Mužakowskej holi. K 85. narodninam Mateja Handrika", *Nowa Doba*, č. 41.

Wjelan, J.E.

1869   Namjezno-Mužakowska wotnožka serbšćiny", *ČMS* XXII, 57-93.

Dutch Contributions to the Twelfth International Congress of Slavists, Cracow, Linguistics (= *Studies in Slavic and General Linguistics* Vol 24), 125-150. RODOPI, Amsterdam - Atlanta, GA 1998.

THE LANGUAGE OF THE RUSSKAJA PRAVDA IN THE NOVGOROD KORMČAJA OF 1282

CLAIRE GELDERMANS

1. Introduction[1]

This article is devoted to the language of the oldest extant copy of Russian medieval law, the Russkaja Pravda in the Novgorod Kormčaja of 1282 (henceforth: RPK). Despite the reputation of this manuscript and the large amount of research into its historical and legal features that has been carried out in the course of time, the language of the RPK has never been described in detail. Available studies are few and not up to date.[2] In particular the discovery of the Novgorod birchbark letters and, as a result, the new insights in Old Russian and its dialects, make some features of the RPK more understandable than they were formerly.

This article has the intention of making a start with a description of the phonology and morphology of the RPK (section 4 and 5). In addition, some attention will be drawn to the orthography of the manuscript (section 3).

2. Russkaja Pravda (1282)

Reading the RPK, one is struck by the purity of its Old Russian. Indeed, the RPK is one of the very few early Old Russian manuscripts that reflect a very pure Old Russian instead of the mix of Old Russian and Church Slavonic found in most 13th-century documents. Church Slavonic elements are rare and seem to have sneaked in during the copying process of the original manuscript. Taking into account that the copyists must have spent most of their time copying religious texts in Church Slavonic, the presence of a few slips of the pen of this type cannot come as a surprise.

The RPK is included in the Novgorod Kormčaja of 1282. Its Novgorod origin has left traces in the language. The most obvious example of dialectal influence is the absence of difference between the graphemes ц and ч. Other dialectal features (both phonological and morphological) are dealt with in the following sections.

The recording of Russian oral law in the Russkaja Pravda dates back to the 11th and 12th century, the age of Jaroslav the Wise and his descendants. The history of oral and written versions of the Russkaja Pravda that preceded the copy of 1282 is practically unknown. This adds a significant element of uncertainty to the analysis of the language of the RPK.

3. Orthography

As far as the orthography is concerned, this article will pay attention to a feature of the RPK that has not yet been described: the presence in it of *bytovoj* elements in the sense established by Zaliznjak.[3] This is one of those characteristics that have become understandable as a result of the research of the birchbark corpus. Due to lack of space, other characteristics are not discussed.

The presence of *bytovoj* elements is the result of the *bytovoj* orthographic practices, in accordance with which о, є and ѣ can render jers and *vice versa*. In the period the RPK was copied, *bytovoj* practices were very common in texts of a non-religious nature (see further NGB 8: 100-109).

While reading the RPK, one does not have the feeling of reading a *bytovoj* text: generally, jers are written etymologically correctly (ъ, ь), are vocalized (о, є) or are not written in weak position (see section 4.11). After detailed examination of the manuscript, however, the number of words with interchange of the letters ь – є – ѣ and ъ – о turns out to be far from negligible. The question arises whether these words reflect the application of *bytovoj* spelling rules or point to other phenomena.

In order to evaluate this question, it is necessary to examine all examples of interchange of the types ь/є/ѣ and ъ/о and to distinguish between (1) those cases that obviously are instances of *bytovoj* spelling or at best mistakes, and (2) those that can plausibly be attributed to other factors as well, e.g. analogy or phonetic/morphological causes.

(1) The RPK contains the following examples of interchange of ь/є/ѣ and ъ/о that can hardly be intepreted as anything else than instances

of *bytovoj* spelling or downright mistakes: а|жь 615ob., клъпалъ 617, помоченаго| 617, тъгда| 618, нь|тоуть 619 (later, with other ink, the ь was changed to ѣ, Grekov 1947: 126), клъпати| 620, пьрегаславьскаго 620ob., трьтьіаго 620ob., плъдъ 626.

In addition, it should be noted that the final ъ in ютрокъ 627 and торгъ 627 is the outcome of a correction of о. The photographs in Karskij (1930) do not enable one to tell whether these corrections were made by the copyist or arose at a later stage, as is the case in нь|тоуть. Grekov (1947) does not mention the words; Karskij (1930: 61) does mention торгъ, but does not give his opinion about the stage at which the correction took place.

(2) The text contains the following examples of interchange of ь/є/ѣ and ъ/о that can be regarded as instances of *bytovoj* spelling, but could plausibly be attributed to other factors as well:

– во юди|номь городѣ 618. It is conceivable that the spelling *vo-* really renders /vo/ (see NGB 9: 259).

– ютови|ютьса 624ob. Karskij suggests that *o* is the outcome of analogical vocalization of a weak jer (Karskij 1930: 14). It is to be noted, though, that the position of the vocalized jer is ambiguous. As a matter of fact, the *i* that is regarded as causing the jer to be weak, probably reflects a Proto-Slavic *ь (Leskien 1990[10]: 44-45), which, hence, introduces the possibility of a strong position. Finally, it should be mentioned that the grapheme *o* looks like the outcome of a correction of ъ and that ютови|ютьса is the only case of the verbal prefix *ot-* not being written with the ligature $\widetilde{w}$- but as ют-.

– въ чеіен перевесє 625. The form is inappropriate because перевесъ is masculine. All other copies of the Russkaja Pravda show a Lsg masc (чьіємь). Since the copyist obviously made a mistake, this word loses reliability.

– моуже 617ob. Krys'ko (1993: 138-139) considers this word evidence of the existence for the ending *-e* in the masc *jo*-stems (see further section 5.1(a)).

– и ієметє| и 625ob. Possible vocalization of a jer which, due to its position preceding Proto-Slavic *jь, could be regarded as a strong jer. Obnorskij (1960: 133) argues that the form has its origin in a southern (Ukrainian) *Vorlage*: "Как известно, подобные формы [i.e. ієметє и and познаієти и, C.G.], возникшие ассимиляционным процессом, характерны для южнорусских памятников старшего периода; ..." (cf. познаієти и| in section 4.11(g)).

– тъ (used as conjunction) 14x тъ vs. 155x то. Possible analogy with нъ (*nъ). The pronoun to is always spelled etymologically as то (15x).

– 18x *e → ѣ (vs. 698x *e → є: 3% – 97%), e.g. нѣ|волѣ 617, въ|з-мѣтъ 620. The rendering of e with ѣ could be the result of a possible phonetic merger of /e/ with /ě/ (cf. section 4.10). In addition, in the case of a Ukrainian Vorlage some of the forms could reflect what is known as a "secondary jat'", i.e. a ě reflecting Proto-Slavic *e before a syllable containing a weak jer.

– 73x *ě → є (vs. 269x *ě → ѣ: 21% – 79%), e.g. слове|нинъ 615ob., всєхъ| 623ob. The rendering of ě with є could be the result of a merger of /e/ with /ě/ as well.

– 6x *ь → ѣ: челѧдѣхъ| 617ob., wвѣль| 620ob., воіарѣхъ 621ob., wвѣль|нъıн 624, смѣрдѣ| заглавие статьи 624ob., дѣтѣмъ 626. These words are ambiguous, because it is impossible to tell whether ѣ still renders /ь/ or already /e/ (*ь (vocalization) > e → ѣ). In the latter case, ѣ could reflect a merger of /e/ with /ě/.

In view of the fact that, generally speaking, spelling errors involving a single letter are very rare in the RPK, the examples of category 1 force one to assume that the copyist was familiar with bytovoj spelling systems.[4] It follows that in all likelihood not only all of the examples of category 1, but also some of those of category 2 are to be regarded as bytovoj elements in a knižnyj text. This pattern of a knižnyj text with sporadic bytovoj elements is not unusual in Old Russian (NGB 8: 105).

Now that we are aware of the bytovoj influence on the RPK, we can say with confidence that many of the words with є rendering *ě and ѣ rendering *e reflect bytovoj spelling. In this context, the following facts are important: (1) most birchbark letters that contain examples of o and є rendering jers and vice versa, contain forms with є and ѣ rendering ě and e respectively as well; (2) in northern manuscripts the orthographic practice that permitted the use of є and ѣ to render ě and e is far more common than the practice of using o and є to render jers and vice versa. However, this conclusion by no means rules out the possibility of a merger of /e/ – /ě/ or the possibility of a Ukrainian Vorlage (cf. section 4.10).

4. Phonology

This section describes the phonology reflected in the RPK. The relevant positions will be dealt with one by one. For positions not mentioned, the RPK does not deviate from Old Russian 13th-century standards.

4.1 Second Palatalization of velars

The Second Palatalization of velars displays its usual reflexes c (= $č$, see 4.8), z and s, with the single exception of the Isg of $kъto$, attested twice in the RPK: передъ къ|мьже 619, съ| къıмъ 627ob. Since $kutь$ is a rare exception among an overwhelming majority of palatalized forms, the k must be due to analogical restoration of the velar and, consequently, not to the Novgorod absence of the Second Palatalization (NGB 8: 117-118; NGB 9: 195-197; Zaliznjak 1995: 37-38). Undoubtedly, the fact that all other forms of $kъto$ and, in addition, the pronoun kyj, have inherited k-, has stimulated to the analogy. Kyj is attested twice: аже пьрьстъ оутьнеть| къıи любо 617 and къıмь| любо wбразомь 625ob. The use of -y- instead of *-$ě$- may also point to influence of *kyj on *$kъto$ (see section 5.3 (a)).

4.2 Progressive (or Third) Palatalization of velars

In case of *k and *x, the Progressive Palatalization consistently displays its regular Old Russian reflexes c (= $č$) and s, e.g. лице 618, все 615ob. The reflex of *g, to the limited extent that it is attested, does not deviate from the Old Russian norm: кънѧзь (12 times, always with -z-: кнѧзю (9x) e.g. 618, кнѧзь 619ob., кнѧзѧ 621ob., кнѧ|земъ 622ob.), варѧгъ 617ob., колбѧгъ 617ob.

4.3 Proto-Slavic *tl/dl

Examples of *tl are absent. The four attestations of *dl display the regular reflex: крало 619, кра|лъ, крали (2x) 627ob.

4.4 Proto-Slavic *tj, *kt/gt + front vowel, *dj, *sj and *zj

With the single exception of аще 617, the RPK shows the normal Old Russian reflexes $č$ (= c), $ž$, $š$ and $ž$, e.g. аче 615ob., помоченаго| 617, поклажаи| 620, прашавъ 617ob., порежеть 625. The reflex in аще appears to be an intrusion from Church Slavonic.

130

4.5 Proto-Slavic *stj/skj and *zdj/zgj

All forms with *stj/skj display the regular Old Russian reflex šč, e.g. ицютъ| 615ob., възицетъ| 619ob. Examples of *zdj and *zgj are absent.

4.6 Sequences of the type *TьrT

In general, sequences of the type *TьrT display their normal Old Russian reflex TьrT, e.g. вьрви 615ob., сме|рдии 616ob., кормилца 616ob., полнага 617ob. Five exceptions have however jers, in some cases vocalized, on both sides of the *r and *l: полотъ 616ob., пьрьстъ 617, ворътьноую 621, полъ|тъ 621ob., испоръ|титъ 623. This feature, traditionally known as *второе полногласие*, is widespread in northern dialect areas (NGB 9: 265-266).

Since the frequent loss of weak jers in the RPK (see 4.11(a)) may have caused coalescence of the possible reflexes TьrT and TьrъT, it is necessary to distinguish between *TьrT sequences in strong and weak positions in order to get a clear insight into the ratio Old Russian reflex – Novgorod *второе полногласие*. Strong positions give a reliable indication: 17% of the attestations have *второе полногласие* (4 of 19). In weak positions the outcome of *второе полногласие* has in most cases been masked by the loss of the weak jer: only a single example (out of 37) shows a second jer: испоръ|титъ.

The attested form вирьвноую 'общинный' 615ob. has not been taken into account in the numbers above. In all likelihood вирьвноую displays *второе полногласие* as well; the i instead of ь must be a spelling error: вирьвноую instead of вьрьвноую. The chances are that the copyist confused the word with вира 'денежная пѣня, замѣняющая смертную казнь' and its derivations, which happen to be frequent in the same part of the manuscript. Compare: вира/-ы/-оу/-ою/-ахъ 616, 616ob., 617, вирьникоу 616, вирникоу 616ob., вирьнии, вирнии 616 – вьрвь/-и 615ob., 616, вьрвинънѣ| 616, вирьвноую 615ob.

Finally, it is to be noted that of the five examples with *второе полногласие*, the TьrъT sequence is put in line-final position twice. It is possible that there is a connection between these reflexes and the convention in the RPK of writing a vowel or jer at the end of each line. With a single exception, all lines end on (1) a vowel (including *ъ (ъ), *ь (ь) and *jь (и)), (2) ѿ, (3) a numeral notated with letters, preceded by a vowel or ѿ, or (4) an abbreviation (e.g. гн 617ob.). The single exception is the *заглавие статьи* а се оу|стави володимир·:·| 620ob.

The fact that *второе полногласие* is common in Novgorod Church Slavonic manuscripts as well (cf. for example the Minea of 1095, Sobolevskij 1907: 26), in combination with the striking frequency of the use of *ТългъТ* in manuscripts that display *второе полногласие*, suggests that the threshold to use the Novgorod reflex was quite low. Apparently, words with *второе полногласие* were not strongly perceived as dialectal, and, therefore, their use was acceptable even in non-private texts like the RPK.

4.7 Sequences of the type *TorT

In general, Proto-Slavic *TorT, *TolT, *TerT is reflected with *полногласие* (respectively 35, 57 and 31 times), e.g. гороχογ 616ob., головог 615ob., переди 616ob. In addition, пьрегаславьскаго 620ob. appears to display the normal Old Russian reflex as well, however, spelled with the *bytovoj* effect є = ь (cf. section 3).

Three exceptions have metathesis with lengthening of the vowel, thus being among the sporadic Church Slavonicisms in the RPK: въ среᴰ 'on Wednesday' 616ob. (to be read as *vъ srědu*, hence with the effect ѣ → є, see section 3), чрєво 621ob. (with ѣ → є as well) and враждогь 623ob. Note that modern Russian has the Church Slavonic reflex in these words as well: *чрево, среда, вражда*.

4.8 Цоканье

Although Proto-Slavic *č and *c are written etymologically correctly most of the time (187 of 209: 89%), there are some examples of *цоканье*, i.e. loss of the distinction /c/ – /č/ (22 of 209: 11%), for example: пл|тничю 616ob., личє 619, задница 622, володи|мирица *заглавие статьи* 615ob., ѡтьцимъ 626. It is a familiar fact that *цоканье* is characteristic of the Old Novgorod dialect: similar use of ч and ц is common in Novgorod birchbark letters and manuscripts from an early date (NGB 8: 109; NGB 9: 200; Zaliznjak 1995: 34).

It is to be noted that the percentage of *цоканье* fluctuates according to the etymological position of *č and *c. For example, the percentage of similar use of ч and ц in position of the First Palatalization is 3%, while the percentage in the position of the Second Palatalization is as high as 39%. According to Živov (1984, 1986), this pattern implies the use of orthographic rules: the Novgorod absence of a phonological distinction between /c/ – /č/ forced copyists to apply "искусственные орфографические правила". The number of mistakes copyists made

132

while applying these rules was related to the complexity of a particular orthographic rule, and, therefore, fluctuated according to the position involved (Živov 1984: 271).[5]

4.9 Шоканье

Examples of шоканье, i.e. loss of the distinction /s', z'/ – /š', ž'/ (NGB 9: 200; Zaliznjak 1995: 43), are absent.

4.10 Proto-Slavic *ě and *e

The RPK contains many forms with ѣ rendering *e and є rendering *ě. In section 3 it was argued that interchange of the letters ѣ and є is purely graphic in at least some of the forms. It is hard to say whether other phenomena, like a possible merger of /e/ with /ě/, have stimulated the interchange of ѣ and є as well. It is to be noted though, that:

– interchange of ѣ and є in the RPK is not restricted to particular phonetic positions and is distributed proportionally over hard, soft (i.e. in front of a hard/soft consonant) and final positions;
– the effect *ě → є (21%) is far more frequent than the effect *e → ѣ (3%).

Both patterns can be considered evidence against a phonetic merger (cf. NGB 8: 108). On the other hand, the fact that the interchange ѣ – є is not equally distributed among various etymological categories could be considered an argument for a possible phonetic explanation. The effect *ě → є, for example, is concentrated in the endings of nouns: 37% of all endings containing *ě are spelled with є (51 of 137). In other positions the effect *ě → є is consistently less frequent, e.g.: *ě as a stem vowel in verbs 4% (2 of 51); *ě as a stem vowel in adjectives or pronouns 15% (13 of 89); *ě in adjectival endings (compound form) 20% (1 of 5); *ě in pronominal endings 14% (5 of 35); *ě in nětutь 14% (1 of 7). Such a distribution suggests the presence of orthographic rules which, in turn, could imply merger of /ě/ with /e/.

Evidence for the northern merger of Proto-Slavic *ě with *i, such as attested in 13th-century birchbark letters, is virtually absent. There is only a single example: наимѥтоу 623ob. (*i = ě → є). Most of the copies of the Russkaja Pravda have наимиту. One copy has наимѣтоу. It is very interesting though, that some of the few words that have been written in the margin (cf. Karskij 1930: 45: "выноска более поздняя, написанная киноварью полууставным почерком"), do contain an example of merger of *ě and *ī: а се ѡ за|дн҃кцѣ 621ob. These words must have been written down in the period of Novgorod merger of *ě with *i (NGB 8: 108; Zaliznjak 1995: 57).

4.11 Proto-Slavic *ъ and *ь

(a) Weak jers in non-final position

If one compares the spelling of jers in the RPK with Zaliznjak's analysis of the reflex of jers on birchbark (NGB 9: 243-255), it turns out that the RPK is conservative compared with contemporary birchbark letters. In the RPK, 22% of weak jers in non-final position are spelled etymologically correctly, while 78% are not written.

The exact distribution is shown in Table 1[6] (I: medial, i.e. non-initial, non-final, position; II: initial position; I*/II*: special positions that impede or prevent elimination of the jer, e.g. complex consonant clusters; see further NGB 9: 243-244):

Table 1: presence or absence of weak *jers*						
	I	II		I*	II*	
ъ present	6	12	74 (22%)	6	18	58 (47%)
ь present	49	7		32	2	
ъ absent	·7	102	267 (78%)	5	34	66 (53%)
ь absent	120	38		4	23	

Novgorod birchbark letters of the second half of the 13th century show nearly complete absence of non-final weak jers (NGB 9: 269-270).

Obviously, the difference is caused by use of orthographic rules. The RPK dates from a phase between two opposed spelling norms: consistent spelling of jers in conformity with their etymology versus loss/vocalization of weak/strong jers (cf. Živov 1984: 262). The assumption of a copyist steering a middle course (with some jers being retained, other being eliminated), seems reasonable. The influence of a *Vorlage* that reflected a more archaic phase of language, may have been a contributing factor.

(b) Comparing non-final weak *ъ with non-final weak *ь

Just as is the case on birchbark (NGB 9: 255), the RPK displays different percentages of eliminated *ъ and *ь: loss of *ъ is more frequent (109 of 127 = 86%) than loss of *ь (158 of 214 = 74%) (see

134

Table 1, positions I and II). The difference is due to the new function that *ь developed, namely the rendering of palatality of consonants (NGB 9: 255-256).

(c) Initial weak *ъ- and *ь-
The loss of weak jers in initial position is significantly more frequent than in medial position: 88% (140 of 159) versus 70% (127 of 182) (see Table 1, positions II and I).

(d) Final *-ъ in prepositions
Just as in other Old Russian manuscripts, the spelling of final *-ъ in prepositions varies depending on the consonant or vowel that follows. The RPK displays the following distribution: 30% loss of *ъ preceding a voiceless consonant (20 out of 66), 0% loss preceding a voiced consonant (0 out of 18) and preceding a vowel (0 out of 5; always in front of o-). Examples of prepositions on *-ъ preceding /j/ are absent.[7]

The fact that the *ъ is written most of the time implies that prepositions were treated as separate words, independent of subsequent words (cf. NGB 9: 257). The spelling of въ о̲вчі| 616, съ ш̲|трокомъ 616ob., во ѡди|номь 618 (see section 3 for во), съ| ѡтрокомъ 621ob. and съ ѡтрокомь 626 with o and ѡ, graphemes only used in initial position in the RPK, confirms this implication.

(e) Final *-ъ and *-ь
As is well-known, loss of final weak jers can only be determined by means of indirect evidence, of which the writing of -мъ for Proto-Slavic *-mь is the most important (see NGB 9: 263). The RPK contains 67 relevant forms; 54 are reflected as -mь and 13 (19%) as -mъ. These examples belong to various grammatical categories: nominal and pronominal Isg masc/neuter 11x (vs. 33x -mь), e.g. ѡ|трокомъ 616ob., т︮ѣ︯мъ 624, кымъ 627ob., во|лшимъ 620; pronominal Lsg masc/neuter 2x (vs. 18x -mь): сельско|мъ 616ob., верестовомъ| 620ob. It is only in jestmь (admittedly attested only three times: 618ob., 627 (2x)) that Proto-Slavic *-mь is consistently spelled as -мь. If these examples are representative, the picture concurs with that in the birchbark corpus, where attestations of ксмъ (or -мо) are very sporadic (Zaliznjak 1995: 63).

It is to be noted that the RPK also contains two forms with -мь instead of -мъ. Both examples involved are pronominal masculine plural datives:

– то ити по| немь т҄ѣмь видоко|мъ на търгоу 618ob. Here the copyist used a Dpl instead of an expected dual.

– аже воудоу|ть двою моужю д҄ѣ|ти а ѡдинои мт҇ри|, а ѡнемь свонго 622ob. Compared with other copies of the Russkaja Pravda, the RPK lacks a few words (here underlined): ... ѡдинои мт҇ри <u>то он҄ѣмъ свонгѡ ѡц҇а задница</u>. а он҄ѣмъ свонго (cf. Obnorskij 1960: 127). It is obvious that the copyist made a mistake.

(f) Vocalization of strong jers and jers in * *ТъrТ* position

As usual, loss of weak jers is coupled with vocalization of strong jers and jers in * *ТъrТ*-position: 55% of the relevant jers have been vocalized, while a sizeable minority of 45% are rendered as ъ and ь. The distribution is as follows:[8]

Table 2: vocalization of *jers*			
position	*vocalized*	*retained*	*percentage vocalized*
strong ъ	22	18	55
strong ь	31	17	65
* *ТъrТ* – strong ъ	11	5	69
* *ТъrТ* – weak ъ	13	9	59
* *ТъrТ* – strong ь	4	5	44
* *ТъrТ* – weak ь	4	15	21

(g) Other irregularities involving jers

In items (a) through (f) the reflexes of Proto-Slavic jers in the RPK were evaluated. In order to complete the picture, this final item will survey all other irregularities involving jers (the *bytovoj* forms mentioned in section 3 are not considered here):

– вирьвноую 615ob. instead of вьрьвноую: see 4.6;

– ·з҃·| в҄ѣдеръ 616-616ob. (Gpl в҄ѣдро): a non-etymological vocalized ь;

– а познакти и| 617ob.: Karskij (1930: 16) gives a phonological explanation: "... конечный ь изменился в и перед следующим *j*: и вин. п. = *jь*". Obnorskij (1960: 133) argues that the form has its origin in an Ukrainian *Vorlage* (see section 3). In addition, it should be kept in mind that и may have arisen as a spelling error under influence of the following и;

– въ ... клѣтъ 619 instead of клѣти (Lsg): probably a spelling error;

– володимир·:–| 620ob.: the final *-ъ is not written. This is the only line in the RPK that does not end in a vowel or jer (cf. section 4.6).

4.12 Proto-Slavic *ъjь and *ьjь

Proto-Slavic *ъjь is in nearly all cases reflected as yj (19x), for example: съкрꙑ|іетьсѧ 617ob., клѣ|тьнꙑи 618, знамеіннꙑи 621. The contracted variant -y- is attested once: мц̃кнꙑ 620. It is noteworthy that the RPK does not contain a single example of the reflex oj; oj has been regarded as the reflex of northern dialects spoken to the east of Novgorod (cf. NGB 9: 205-206) and is widely attested in Novgorod manuscripts and birchbark texts. Since the RPK more than once shows (east) Novgorod influences, one would expect examples of *ъjь > oj in the RPK as well.

In soft position, the RPK does show both possible reflexes: ij and ej; ij is attested eight times: конюшии 616ob., сме|рдии 616ob., третии 617ob., конечнии 618ob., чии 624, людии 621, 624ob., лю|дии 625ob.; ej is attested three times: дѣтеї 622, треиі (Gpl) 622ob., влижеи (comp. Nsg masc) 626.[9]

4.13 Proto-Slavic *vl' and *ml'

The RPK displays the regular Old Russian reflexes vl' and ml' (4 and 14 times respectively), for example гавлено| 616, ловле|но 621, землѧмъ| 618, ино|чимлѧ 622ob., ѥмь|леть 625ob. (with softening of the m indicated by means of ь, cf. 4.16). Attestations of the northern developments *vl' > l' and *ml' > n' (for which see NGB 9: 202-204) are absent.

4.14 Proto-Slavic *y after velars

With the single exception of паки 616 (vs. 10x пакꙑ), the RPK displays y: *ky > ky 17x, e.g. пакꙑ 618, къ|мь 619, кꙑневьского| 620ob., воискꙑ|и 623ob.; *gy > gy 8x, e.g. погꙑвло 618, многꙑмъ| 623, погꙑнеть 623ob.; *xy > xy 5x: послоухꙑ 619, 620, 625, 626ob., послоухꙑ| 620. The consistent spelling of y after velars suggests a Novgorod phonological background, because in the south the change *y > i after velars had already taken place. The earliest examples in northern texts date from the second half of the 13th century (Sobolevskij 1907: 130-131; NGB 8: 119; Zaliznjak 1995: 74).

Superficially, паки 616 reminds one of another early Novgorod attestation, namely паки in birchbark letter 421 (mid 12th century) (Zaliznjak 1995: 259-260). However, there is an important difference: whereas the birchbark example can be interpreted as a mistake (паки ли: -i instead of -y under the influence of the following i, cf. Zaliznjak 1995: 74), the RPK's example cannot be so explained and may therefore actually constitute early evidence of the change *-y > -i after velars (паки людинъ то|).

4.15 Proto-Slavic *-i in infinitive, 2sg present/imperative and particle ti

Word-final *-i has been retained in the three verbal positions (e.g. платити| 616, юси 618, воуди 616ob.), with the exception of the following infinitives: воро|тить 618ob., дьржа|ть 622ob. and possibly also пла|тить 623 (the context is ambiguous: this verb could be a 3sg present as well).

As for the particle ti, it is necessary to distinguish between a "свободное (т. е. не связанное с соседством тех или иных конкретных словоформ) употребление" and a "несвободное употребление" (see NGB 9: 299-308):

– ti in free position is attested once and has -i: на послоушьство холо|па не ск[л]адають: но| оже не воудеть свобо|дьнааго, то по ноу|жи ти сложити на| вогарьскаго тиоуна| 621 (cf. NGB 9: 303).

– ti in несвободное употребление is attested more frequently and testifies to reduction in some cases. In NGB 9: 305, Zaliznjak quotes the following examples from the RPK: а и своюго города въ чю|жю землю свода нѣ|тоуть 619; искавше| ли послоухъа и не налѣ|зоуть а истьца начь|неть головою клепа|ти, то ти имъ правь|доу желѣзо 617;[10] а желѣзнаго| платити ·м̃· коу|нъ, а мечникоу ·е̃·| коунъ а полъ грвне| дѣтьчьскомоу, то| ти желѣзнъи оу|рокъ 625ob.; оже за ковълоу ·а̃· коунъ а за волъ гри|вноу ....., то ти оуроци смьрдо|мъ 619ob. In order to complete the picture, the following instances can be added: нѣтоуть (617, 621ob., 627 (3x)), нетоуть| 620 and оть 618ob. (оть идеть до конечь|наго свода). It turns out that the -i of -ti is reduced in all seven instances of nětuti and the single example of oti, whereas no reduction is found in the three (or perhaps two) attestations of toti.

138

4.16 Consonant clusters

Consonant clusters of the type "consonant + ь + hard consonant" are written sometimes with ь (30 times, e.g. татѣ|ва 618, свободьна 618оb., кл‘ѣ|тьнꙑи 618, wльгова 619оb., wвьльнꙑи| 624) and sometimes without (30 times, e.g. татвоу| 624оb., свободна 624, съме|тнаіа 617, толко 620, wвьлноіе| 626оb.) It cannot be determined whether the latter spelling indicates that the first consonant is hard; it is possible that the copyist pronounced the consonant palatal without expressing its palatality in writing.

The RPK contains two examples of a hard consonant that has become soft under influence of a following soft consonant: въ коупь|лю (Nsg коуплаа) 620, іемь|леть 625оb. It is possible that the position of these words at the end of the line (where the RPK displays a vowel or jer, see section 4.6), stimulated the use of ь.

Consonant clusters of the type "voiced consonant + ъ/ь + voiceless consonant" or "voiceless consonant + ъ/ь + voiced consonant" retain their voiced – voiceless opposition, whether the jer is written or not.[11] For example: вчелꙑ| 624оb., оукрадъше 619, кдѣ 618, татвѣ 617, татьвꙑ 619.

In five cases a consonant in a consonant cluster has been dropped: исвоіего города 619, росѣчена 621, разнаменаіеть| 621, wвинить 625оb. (2x). Note also the contraction in придеть 617оb. (3x) (cf. принметь| 623оb.) and мцѣнꙑ 620 (у < уj (*ъjь), see section 4.12).

In the case of three forms an additional consonant has been inserted: тиву°|на/ъ 615оb. (versus 4x тиоунъ) and вездрадоу 626оb. (versus 3x везрадоу).

Finally, the peculiar spelling of the words тꙑсачьскꙑи and дѣтьскꙑи should be mentioned: тꙑсачького 620оb. (3x), дѣчькꙑ|и 622оb., дѣтьчьскомоу 625оb.

4.17 Variation of *ь and *i in position for */j/

The RPK contains numerous forms with interchange of i and ь in position before /j/, e.g. оувьіеть 615оb., оувиіеть| 615оb., людьіе 616, лю|діе 619, знаменьіе| 621, знаме|ниіе 621. As is well-known, this is a common feature of many Old Russian and Church Slavonic texts.

4.18 Proto-Slavic *jь

Depending on position, Proto-Slavic *jь is reflected as je (strong position) or i (weak position), for example: переıемъ, пе|реıемъ 626ob., поиметь 618ob., имати| 620, переıима 626ob.

Two forms are irregular: ıемати| 620 instead of imati (this form is attested in other Old Russian manuscripts as well, cf. Sreznevskij 1893-1903) and и ıемете| и на желѣзо 625ob., which must be a mistake instead of ıемлеть (imperfective aspect) or иметь (perfective aspect). The context is inconclusive and other copies of the Russkaja Pravda show both imperfective and perfective forms. Note that this form is unusual because of its final -e as well (cf. section 3 and 5.5).

4.19 Proto-Slavic *orT- and *olT- in initial position

Most relevant forms display the East Slavic reflex: Proto-Slavic *orT- > roT- (21x), e.g. рова| 616ob., росѣчена 621; Proto-Slavic *olT- > loT- (5x): лоньцµиноу 619ob., лодью 624ob. (2x), лодию 624ob., локотъ 625ob. Six examples have the Church Slavonic reflex: развои 615ob., 616 (2x), разво|иника 616, разграблени|ıе 616, разнаменаıеть| 621.

4.20 Proto-Slavic *e- in initial position

Initial *e- has its regular Old Russian reflex in во wди|номь 618, wдинъ| 619 and other attestations of the same word. The Church Slavonic reflex je- is found twice in ıеже 'if' 622, 623ob. (opposed to 58x ože 'if'). Obnorskij (1960: 139) argues that both examples are part of an "испорченное место". However, this point is not explained and remains unclear.

4.21 Merger of early Russian *a with *e between soft consonants in /e/

The word metelьnikъ, which is attested three times, is spelled as ме|телникоу 616ob., 622ob. and мѧтелникоу 622ob. The latter case is the outcome of a correction; cf. Karskij (1930, 47): "В мѧтелникоу ѧ исправлен из другой буквы, вероятно ıе". Sobolevskij (1886: 377) connects metelьnikъ with the word *metlь, 'coat' (a borrowing from Latin or a Germanic language): originally, metelьnikъ denotes the person who administers the metli of the prince. In later days, metelьnikъ denoted a particular legal function. It is obvious that copyists soon did

140

not understand the word; many copies of the RPK have *metalьnikъ* instead of *mętelьnikъ*.

The fact that *ę is twice reflected as *e* might be due to the northern merger of *a* (< *a/*ę) with *e* between soft consonants in /e/. The correction of є into ѧ implies that, according to the orthographic rules, *a and *ę had to be spelled in conformity with their etymology.

4.22 An interesting detail

Finally, the secondary imperfective помогати 616 should be noted. This type of imperfective, which was derived from its perfective counterpart with the help of the suffix -(j)a-, originally had -a- alternating with -o- in the stem in such examples as *pomagati* (perf *pomoči*), *prašati* (perf *prositi*). At a later stage the difference between imperfective -a- and perfective -o- was obliterated by analogical replacement of -a- with -o- (cf. Kiparskij 1967: 215-216).

In the case of помогати the analogy has taken place. The imperfectives помаѓгають 616 and праѓшавъ 617ob.-618, on the other hand, still display the original form with -a-.

5. Inflexion

Section 5 is devoted to the inflectional morphology of the RPK. It is beyond the scope of this article to give a complete survey of all (pro)nominal, adjectival and verbal forms and a complete summary of the declension and conjugation of these forms. Therefore, the discussion will be focused on those positions that are interesting, e.g. because the RPK either shows or, on the contrary, does not show dialectal influence. These special features of the manuscript are described against the background of the Old Russian standards, usually followed by the RPK. If a position has not been mentioned, the RPK does not show deviations from the Old Russian 13th-century standards.

5.1 Nominal inflexion

(a) *o-, jo-* and *u-*stems

With the single exception of Nsg моужє 617ob., the *o-, jo-* and *u-*stems consistently display their regular Old Russian endings. Novgorod dialectal characteristics are absent.

Krys'ko has argued that моужє should be considered an example of the Novgorod Nsg on *-e* (1993: 138-139). If right, this would be remarkable, because the northern Nsg in -*e*, which is frequent in *o*-stems, is rarely if ever attested in *jo*-stems. In view of section 3, however, моуже can be considered a *bytovoj* element as well.

Besides, this form is not reliable because of the peculiar position of its first letters (моу) in the margin. Gippius (1996: 53) convincingly argues that this peculiarity points to a graphic (instead of a morphological) cause for the ending -є: the copyist involuntary copied the first two graphemes of the preceding line (consisting of an initial ◊ followed by жепридетькроъвавъ), then realized that he had omitted the initial syllable of the word, and therefore added the graphemes моу to the margin, right under the initial ◊ of the previous line.[12]

Like other 13th-century Old Russian manuscripts, the RPK contains examples of analogical carry-over of endings from *o*- to *u*-stems and vice versa. The examples are the following: Gsg *o*-stem горохоу 616ob., сводоу 618 (vs. 5x свода), Dsg *u*-stem снѹ| 615ob. (vs. 2x снви|), по полоугрвнѣ 619ob., Npl *u*-stem снви 622ob. (*-*ove* has been changed into -*ovi* under the influence of the *o*-stem ending *-*i*; снве is attested three times). In the Gpl of the masc *o*-stems the original *u*-stem ending has already become standard (7x, e.g. оуворوковъ| 616ob.); only a single exception shows *-ъ: колико воу|детъ возъ оукраде|но 625.

(b) *ā*- and *jā*-stems

In an overwhelming majority the *ā*- and *jā*-stems display their regular Old Russian endings; however, there are some interesting exceptions. All but one are concentrated in the Gsg, DLsg and NApl:

– *ā*-stem Gsg -*ě* (3x): полоугрвнѣ 619ob., полъ грвне| 624ob. (ѣ → є), полъ грвнѣ| 625ob., opposed to 22x -*y*;
– *jā*-stem Gsg -*i* (3x): земли 622ob., opposed to 29x -*ě*;
– *jā*-stem DLsg -*ě* (3/4x): ноуже 621, даче 626ob., прода|же 627ob. (ѣ → є) and probably also тяжие 621; opposed to 8x -*i*;
– *ā*-stem NApl (preceded by the numerals 3 or 4) -*ě* (3x): ·г· грвнѣ 623ob., ·г· грвне 624ob., 625 (ѣ → є), opposed to 18x -*y*. If not preceded by a numeral the ending is always -*y* (23x).[13]

The Gsg and NApl *grivně* unambiguously point to influence from the Novgorod dialect, which had generalization of -*ě* in the GDLsg and NApl (NGB 9: 212-217). In the case of the Gsg -*i* and DLsg -*ě* in *jā*-stems, it is impossible to tell whether they reflect some Novgorod dialectal form as well, or are due to the rise of the *литературная система* (cf. Zaliznjak 1988: 72).

The example DLsg тѧжк 621 needs some additional discussion. It is the only word in the RPK that has к (instead of є) in postconsonantal position. Karskij (1930: 43) assumes that "к исправлено из н", which implies that the normal Old Russian ending -*i* was replaced with the Novgorod ending -*ě* (with the graphical effect ѣ → є/к). This does not seem reasonable, but the alternative, a possible correction of є into н does not seem plausible either in the light of the photographic reproduction. If the copyist would first have written є, what would have caused him to leave more space between this grapheme є and its preceding ж than usual?

Finally, the NAdu of the *jā*-stems must be mentioned. This position is attested twice, once with the regular Old Russian ending -*i* and once with -*ě*: ·ві· в’ккшє| 616ob. (ѣ → є). Obviously, the -*ě* may reflect two different developments; both connect the RPK to the northern dialects:

– The tendency to eliminate the distinction between NApl, NAdu and Gsg resulted in an analogical replacement of the NAdu ending *-*i* with the NApl/Gsg ending *-*ě*. The loss of distinction between NApl, NAdu and Gsg is characteristic for the northern dialects; in the southwest of the East Slavic area this innovation did not take place or only at a later stage (cf. NGB 9: 219-220 and Sobolevskij 1907: 207-208).

– The soft NAdu ending *-*i* has been replaced with the hard NAdu ending *-*ě*: *věkši* → *věkšě*. According to Zaliznjak, obliteration of the difference between hard and soft endings is characteristic for what he calls Ilmen Slovene. With the exception of the area near Lake Seliger, the Ilmen Slovene dialects generalized hard endings (NGB 9: 215-216). Another example of generalization of the hard ending might be the Apl овци 619: -*i* instead of inherited *-*ě* in analogy with the ending -*y* of the *ā*-stems; *-*ě* is attested five times (3x Apl and 2x Npl).

(c) Loss of distinction between nominative and accusative plural

Although the Npl and Apl in general show their inherited endings, a few forms anticipate the future loss of the distinction Npl – Apl: по| слоуси Apl 619ob.-620 (the fact that the Npl *-*i* has been used, while eventually the Apl *-*y* will be generalized, stresses that the elimination of the difference between Npl and Apl is still in its initial stage), кони Apl 625ob. (-*i* instead of *-*ě*), людї| Npl 621 (it is possible that lack of space at the end of the line stimulated the use of -*i* instead of *-*ьje*; -*ьк/ик* is attested 7x).

(d) Interesting details

Finally, against the Old Russian background, the following details deserve attention:

– в͠раи 622ob. (воу|детъ ли потер͠ъ сво|юго иночима что|, а wнѣхъ w͠ца а оумре|ть, то възворота|ть в͠раи, на нь же| и людые въıлѣзу|ть, что воудеть оц͠ь| юго истералъ ино|чимла): the -i instead of -ьja is unusual. The form reminds of the соудии, кн͠агъıни and вог͠ъıни-type, where -i is the inherited ending. Besides в͠раи the regular form is used as well: в͠рага 622 and вратьıа 622ob.

– погоувивъши 623ob. (нъ юже да|лъ юмоу г͠нъ плоугъ| и вороноу, w него же| ковоу юмлеть, тъ| то погоувивъши ю|моу платити): Sobolevskij (1907: 225) correctly interprets the form as an early example of the loss of the congruence between participles and nouns: "Причастія стали употребляться неправильно, не согласуясь съ именами в родѣ, числѣ, и падежѣ, довольно рано" (cf. also Zaliznjak 1995: 166).

– шедъши 627 (а|же кто своюго холопа| самъ досочитьс͠а| въ чи|юмь любо [го]родѣ|, а воудеть посадникъ| не вѣдалъ юго, то, по|вѣ-давше юмоу, пога|ти оу него wтрокъ, и| шедъши оувазати| и, и дати юмоу вла|зевною ·і· коунъ|, а переима нѣтоуть|): this form can be regarded as an instance of the loss of congruence between participles and nouns as well.

5.2 Adjectival inflexion (the compound form)

The nominative and accusative consistently display their regular Old Russian endings. In oblique forms however, several deviations from the Old Russian standard occur (non-standard endings have been underlined): Gsg masc (including Asg = Gsg) -ого/юго (6x), -аго/ыаго/гаго (11x), -ааго (1x); Dsg masc -омоу/юмоу (4x); Lsg masc -омь (2x), -ѣмь (3x); Gsg fem -ои (4x), -ога (1x); Lsg fem -ои (1x), -ѣи (2x). Examples: тъıсачь|кого къıювьского| 620ob., чюжего 624, помоченаго| 617, пьрегаславьскаго| 620ob., вогарьскаго 621, конечнаго 618, свово|дьнааго 621; дѣтьчьскомоу 625ob., мьншемоу 626; сельско|мъ 616ob., верестовомъ| 620ob., ратаинѣ|мь 616ob., мцьнѣмь заглавие статьи 620, своводнемь (ѣ → е) 624; пьрвои 622, вортьнои| 622ob., всако|га 616; кото|рои 619, во|гарьстѣи, дроужинн| заглавие статьи 621ob.

If one wants to account for the relative large number of non-standard endings, once again one realizes the importance of the birchbark letters for our understanding of medieval Russian: the birchbark letters make clear that adjectives ending in -(*j*) *ago*, -*ětь* and -*ěi* not only may prove of Church Slavonic influence, but of Novgorod dialect influence as well (NGB 8: 141-142; NGB 9: 220-224; Zaliznjak 1995: 100-108).

Thus, while in former days we would have struggled with a mysterious frequency of Church Slavonic forms in a manuscript that otherwise contains sporadic Church Slavonic elements, today we can attribute this frequency to Novgorod influence. It must be considered that, in the RPK, endings of the nominal ending + **jь* type are attested only in cases that have identical endings in Novgorod and Church Slavonic (Gsg masc, Lsg masc, Lsg fem), while in case of a difference between the Novgorod and the Church Slavonic ending (Gsg fem), the pronominal ending is used (see below for the Novgorod dialectal form -*oi*). Apparently, due to the difference between the Novgorod dialect and Church Slavonic, the Novgorod Gsg on -*ěě* was strongly perceived as locally restricted; as a consequence, copyists preferred the regular Old Russian ending -*oě* or the Novgorod variant -*oi*. On the other hand, Novgorod forms in -(*j*) *ago*, -*ětь* and -*ěi* continued to be used in Novgorod manuscripts for quite a long time, thanks to the parallel forms in Church Slavonic.

The Gsg feminine ending -*oi* (4x of 5x) testifies to Novgorod influence as well: the distinction between Gsg (**-oě*) and DLsg (**-oi*) is lost, the DLsg-ending has been generalized. The inherited Gsg-ending has been preserved only in one case, though in Church Slavonic form: вс҄ако|ꙗ 616. According to Gippius, this use of Church Slavonic -*oja* instead of -*oi* is due to graphical reasons: "Во всех остальных случаях [...] односложную флексию -ои находим в середине строки. Употребив ее и в данном случае, писец вынужден был бы перенести на новую строку одиночное и, не обозначающее слога. Между тем, использовав двусложную цсл. флексию, он получил возможность перенести слово по всем правилам" (Gippius 1996: 51).

In addition to -*oꙗ*, the RPK contains another Church Slavonic adjectival ending, namely -ааго: свобо|дьнааго 621. The word appears to be an intrusion from Church Slavonic (cf. Gippius 1996: 50-51: "[...] нестяженное окончание -ааго, которое можно рассматривать как случайно сорвавшееся с пера писца, набившего руку в переписке церковной книжности").

5.3 Pronominal inflexion

(a) Other than personal pronouns

Regular Old Russian forms predominate. Sporadic exceptions can be divided into two types: (1) exceptions that are attested consistently, and (2) sporadic exceptions that may have sneaked in by accident.

To the first type the Gsg of the (j) a-stems belongs, which always ends in -oi/ei instead of *-oě/eě: мтри своієн (2x) 622, ієн 622, ѡдиноιн мтри| 622ob. With this the RPK, again, testifies to the loss of the distinction Gsg – DLsg, and, hence, again betrays influence from the Novgorod dialect.

The second type is more varied and contains the following pronouns:

(1) къимь 619 and къимъ 627ob. (нъ тако же| въивести іємоу по| слоухъи любо мъи|тникa, передъ къ|имь же коупивъше| and любо въидати и съ| къимъ боудеть кра|лъ). Both the absence of the Second Palatalization (see section 4.1) and the ending are unusual: **kymь instead of inherited *cětь/*kětь. In theory, two explanations might account for this: (1) the use of -y- instead of *-ě- is due to influence of the pronoun къин, in which -y- is inherited (Isg къимь/къимь), on forms of къто, (2) the use of -y- is connected with the Novgorod substitution of -ě- with -i- in pronominal o-stems (see NGB 9: 225-226); the development would have been *kětь > kitь > (generalization hard endings) > kytь.

The fact that къимь also has been attested in the Житие Нифонта (1219), a manuscript from Rostov that does not contain any dialectal features (Sobolevskij 1907: 187), in combination with the complete absence of the Novgorod substitution of -ě- with -i- elsewhere in the pronominal system of the RPK, render the former explanation the most plausible. In addition, this explanation concurs with the picture of the outcome of the Second Palatalization being cancelled under the influence of къto.

(2) двоу| 621ob. and 626 (а самомоу ієхати съ| ѡтрокомъ на двоу| коню and а мость|никоу ієхати само|моу съ ѡтрокомъ на| двоу коню). These two attestations are the earliest examples of GLdu dvu in Old Russian manuscripts (Kiparskij 1967: 174). Two other attestations of the GLdu still show the old form *dvoju: ѡли до двоію гривноу 617 and аже боудоу|ть двою моужю дѣ|ти 622ob.

In the Novgorod birchbark corpus, the original ending -*oju* is completely absent. As a matter of fact, even one of the earliest texts contains a Gdu on -*u*: кєз дъкоѵ (birchbark letter 526, mid 11th century, see further Zaliznjak 1995: 112).

(3) всє 622 (нъ| комоѵ мѓти дастъ|, томоѵ жє взѧти. да|стъ ли всѣмъ, то всє| роздѣлѧтъ). In all probability, всє is the result of coalescence of Npl (-*i̯) and Apl (*-ě) in the Apl, with the effect ѣ → є. Theoretically, the form could be an Asg neuter as well.

(4) чєѥи 625 (въ чєѥи пєрєвєсє). See Karskij (1930: 54): "Повидому, чєѥи описка вм. чьѥмь" (cf. also section 3).

(5) а 627ob. (а ѡ|жє воѵдоѵтъ с̃ нимь| крали и хоро̂ни̃ли, то| всєхъ въıдати, па|къı ли а̲ въıкоѵпаѥ|тъ гн̃ъ). See Karskij (1930: 61): "пакъı ли а – здесь *a* вм. га = ѥ̈ их". Thus, instead of the Old Russian Apl ѣ, the Church Slavonic form has been used. The use of the grapheme а for *ja* in postvocalic position is remarkable. In other cases, postvocalic *ja* is spelled as га.

(b) Personal pronouns

Since the RPK contains only few personal pronouns, it is possible to give a complete survey of all occurrences (with the exclusion of сѧ and the clitic Dsg си and ти). Forms that need some explanation, have been underlined: Nsg азъ (1x), Gsg мєнє (1x), Asg тѧ (2x), Gsg сєбє (3x), DLsg собѣ (7x), Isg собою (1x).

The use of the Church Slavonic азъ instead of the Old Russian газъ in нъ азъ ѥмлю тѧ, а| нє холопъ 625ob. has been convincingly dealt with by Gippius, who states that "вся фраза представляет собой перформативный речевой акт, и в этом отношении употребление азъ перекликается с его использованием в формуле сє азъ... древнерусских грамот (ср. «это я...» в переводе)" (Gippius 1996: 51).

The distribution Gsg сєбє – DLsg собѣ is a common feature of most early manuscripts (Kiparskij 1967: 133). Hence there is no reason to suppose that the distinction *seb*- versus *sob*- suggests any dialectal influence of, for example, Old Novgorod, that had Gsg *seb*- and DLsg *sob*- as well (NGB 9: 228).

5.4 Numerals

Due to the large number of punitive measures, there is hardly any page in the RPK that does not contain a numeral. Nevertheless, due to the notation of numerals with letters, information about their morphological form is limited. Alongside pronominal *odinъ* (always spelled with *-i-*), the manuscript contains only fourteen forms.

Thirteen of them involve the numerals *dъva* and *tri*, which have a regular declension (pronominal and substantival respectively). The fourteenth form is сорокъ 616 (паки людинъ, то| сорокъ гривенъ·:·|). With this sentence, the RPK shows the earliest attestation of the use of сорокъ ("ursprünglich *Hülle, Sack für Pelzwerk*", Kiparskij 1967: 179) as a numeral.

With respect to ordinals and collective numerals there are no irregularities.

5.5 Conjugation

Three verbal forms deviate from the Old Russian norm:

(1) съвѣдитеса| 618 (съвѣдитеса| кто боудеть вино|ватъ, на того татьба снидеть): in all probability, what is meant is the imperative of съвѣстиса 'сойтись на очную ставку для выясненія виновности' (Sreznevskij 1893-1903), in which case the ending *-ite* is due to analogical replacement of the inherited hard ending **-ěte* with the corresponding soft ending *-ite*. Since analogical replacement of hard endings with the corresponding soft ones in the plural and dual of the imperative of thematic verbs is a characteristic of the Novgorod dialect (NGB 8: 145; NGB 9: 229), the RPK, again, seems to betray its Novgorod origin. However, it cannot be ruled out that съвѣдитеса| is the imperative of съвѣдѣтиса 'знать о себе самом' (cf. Karskij 1930: 112). In this case the ending *-ite* would be the inherited ending (Leskien's class V, cf. Leskien 1990: 167).

(2) познаютⷮи и| 617ob. and имете| и 625ob.: the origin of these forms is uncertain. They have been attributed to a southern (Ukrainian) *Vorlage* (cf. Obnorskij 1960: 133), but this is not strictly necessary. Present verbs in *-ti* are attested in some other Novgorod manuscripts as well (Sobolevskij 1907: 38). The ending might be due to phonological reasons or an ordinary spelling error, see section 4.11(g). In case of *-te* one could assume vocalization of the jer or *bytovoj* spelling (see section 3).

6. Summary

This article has made a beginning with a description of the language of the Russkaja Pravda in the Novgorod Kormčaja of 1282. On the basis of the orthography, it has been argued that the copyist of the manuscript must have been familiar with *bytovoj* spelling practices, which are known to have been very popular in the 13th century. The phonological characteristics have been described in detail. It turns out that the RPK in almost every respect displays regular Old Russian reflexes. Exceptions are sporadic and usually point to northern dialectal influence or Church Slavonic. Finally, the article gives an overview of the inflexion of the RPK, with special attention for positions in which the RPK deviates from the Old Russian norm. In most of these positions the RPK shows a northern dialectal form.

NOTES

[1]   I am indebted to Willem Vermeer for his comments on early versions of this article.

[2]   Most important are Karskij's book *Русская Правда по древнейшему списку* (1930), which contains an edition of the text and photographs of the manuscript, and the following articles: Obnorskij (1934/1960), Seliščev (1957) and Gippius (1996).

[3]   In the absence of suitable English terms the Russian words *bytovoj* and *knižnyj* are used here throughout in the sense in which they are used by Zaliznjak (1995: 19).

[4]   Such spelling errors are attested four times: въвкоупати| 615ob. (instead of въккоупати), начтеть 620 (instead of начнеть), скадають 621 (instead of складають), пюсчю 621ob. (instead of писчю).

[5]   The distribution of *цоканье* in the RPK differs from the distribution attested in the manuscripts examined by Živov. Živov's manuscripts show comparatively many examples of *цокание* in the position of the Progressive (Third) Palatalization (i.e. *c/č* preceded by *i/ь*), but comparatively few examples in the position of the First and Second Palatalization (Živov 1984: 266-272). The RPK, by contrast, contains more instances of *цокание* in the position of the Second Palatalization (7 of 18 (39%)) than in other positions (First Palatalization: 3 of 95 (3%); First Palatalization in position of the Progressive Palatalization: 3 of 16 (19%); Progressive Palatalization: 9 of 58 (16%)).

The difference could reflect a difference between the spoken language of the copyists of Živov's manuscripts and that of the copyist of the RPK, namely absence (Živov 1984: 267; 1986: 291-294) vs. presence (cf. section 4.1) of the Second Palatalization of velars. Since the spelling rules formulated by Živov presuppose absence of the Second Palatalization, the copyist of the RPK must have used different rules, resulting in a different pattern of mistakes.

[6]   The ten forms with *ь* preceding *sja* have not been taken into account. Since reflexive *sja* was still treated as a separate word (cf. its free pre- and postposition, e.g. wже см почнеть за|пирати·:· 620, заидоуть ли см коунъ до| того же года 620), these jers were final jers. In all likelihood, prepositions were treated as

separate words in the RPK (see section 4.11(d)). Therefore, jers in initial position that are preceded by a proclitic, are counted as initial jers. Example: въ свадѣ 616.

[7] The jers in въ чени 625 and въ чинемь 627 have not been taken into consideration. As a result of the variation of respectively *ь – e* and *ь – i*, it is impossible to tell whether these jers are strong or weak. The preposition *отъ* is always spelled with the ligature ѿ, and, therefore is not counted. The prepositions *bezъ* and *izъ* have been left out of consideration as well. Their original forms are **bez* and **iz*; the jor has been introduced in analogy with other prepositions.

[8] The six forms with **ь* rendered as ѣ have not been taken into account, because it is impossible to determine whether the ѣ renders a vocalized jer (**ь > e → ѣ*) or is an instance of a *bytovoj* effect (**ь → ѣ*).

[9] The examples дѣтunderстии 622ob. and переднии 624 have not been taken into account, because they are not reliable. On the basis of other copies of the Russkaja Pravda, it is probable that которꙑи дѣчькꙑи дѣтии ихъ дѣлиⷮтъ has been written instead of originally дѣчькꙑи идѣть ихъ дѣлиⷮтъ (Karskij 1930: 48), and переднии instead of переди (Karskij 1930: 52).

Among the words written in the margin of page 626 ("выноска более поздним почерком – полууставом", Karskij 1930: 58) there is another example: дѣтен.

[10] This example is ambiguous. Judging by the context on the one hand and by other copies of the Russkaja Pravda on the other, ти may have to be read as [да]ти.

[11] The voice assimilation of the final consonant of *bez(-)*, *raz(-)* and *iz(-)* (e.g. ростераютъ 622, бес трен коунъ 622ob., исплатить 625) is not to be considered an exception, because the Proto-Slavic forms of **bez*, **raz* and **iz* lack a final -ъ, hence loss of the opposition voiced – voiceless is not due to elimination of a weak jer.

[12] Gippius (1996: 53) observes that the RPK also contains an example of Asg моуже: "оже кто оубнетъ женоу то тѣмь же соудомь соудити гакоже и моуже. оже боудеть виноватъ... 621ob.". As far as I can judge, the photograph in Karskij (1930) shows моужа.

[13] Gippius (1996: 53) gives different figures.

REFERENCES

Gippius, A.A.
1996   "'Russkaja pravda' i 'Voprošanie Kirika' v Novgorodskoj Kormčej 1282 g. (k xarakteristike jazykovoj situacii drevnego Novgoroda)", *Slavjanovedenie* 1996/1, 48-62.
Grekov, B.D. (ed.)
1947   *Pravda russkaja* II. *Kommentarij.* Moskva-Leningrad.
Janin, V.L. and Zaliznjak, A.A.
1986   *Novgorodskie gramoty na bereste (iz raskopok 1977-1983 gg.).* Moskva.
1993   *Novgorodskie gramoty na bereste (iz raskopok 1984-1989 gg.).* Moskva.

150

Karskij, E.F.
1930   *Russkaja pravda po drevnejšemu spisku*. Leningrad.
Kiparskij, V.
1967   *Russische historische Grammatik* II. Heidelberg.
Krys'ko, V.B.
1993   "Obščeslavjanskie i drevnenovgorodskie formy Nom. sg. masc. *o-sklo-
            nenija", *Russian Linguistics* 17, 119-156.
Leskien, A.
1990[10]   *Handbuch der altbulgarischen (altkirchenslavischen) Sprache*. Heidel-
            berg.
NGB 8   See Janin and Zaliznjak (1986).
NGB 9   See Janin and Zaliznjak (1993).
Obnorskij, S.P.
1960   "'Russkaja pravda', kak pamjatnik russkogo literaturnogo jazyka",
            Izbrannye raboty po russkomu jazyku. Moskva. (First edition 1934.)
Seliščev, A.M.
1957   "O jazyke 'Russkoj Pravdy' v svjazi s voprosom o drevnejšem tipe rus-
            skogo literaturnogo jazyka", *Voprosy jazykoznanija* 4, 57-63.
Sobolevskij, A.I.
1886   "Jazyk Russkoj Pravdy", *Žurnal Ministerstva Narodnago Prosvěščenija*
            52, 374-382.
1907[3]   *Lekcii po istorii russkago jazyka*. Moskva.
Sreznevskij, I.I.
1893-1903   *Materialy dlja slovarja drevne-russkago jazyka po pis'mennym pamjat-
            nikam*. Sankt Peterburg.
Zaliznjak, A.A.
1988   "Drevnenovgorodskoe kojne", *Balto-slavjanskie issledovanija 1986*,
            60-78.
1995   *Drevnenovgorodskij dialekt*. Moskva.
Živov, V.
1984   "Pravila i proiznošenie v russkom cerkovnoslavjanskom pravopisanii
            XI-XIII veka", *Russian Linguistics* 8, 251-293.
1986   "Ešče raz o pravopisanii *c* i *č* v drevnix novgorodskix rukopisjax",
            Russian Linguistics 10, 291-306.

Dutch Contributions to the Twelfth International Congress of Slavists, Cracow, Linguistics (= Studies in Slavic and General Linguistics Vol 24), 151-173. RODOPI, Amsterdam - Atlanta, GA 1998.

THE USE OF THE LONG AND SHORT ADJECTIVAL FORMS
IN
CONTEMPORARY STANDARD RUSSIAN*

B.M. GROEN

0. Introduction

0.1   There is a rich literature on the subject of the long and the short adjectival forms in contemporary standard Russian (henceforward CSR). But in spite of this wealth, a recent survey describing into some detail the basic semantics of the short and long adjectival forms opposed to each other in the same context, and the syntactical and stylistical phenomena involved, hardly exists. In most grammars, including the more recent ones, the treatment of the long and short forms is inadequate, incomplete and not seldom incorrect. This concerns grammars of CSR written by native speakers as well as those by foreigners.

The aim of this paper is, therefore, to present an overview which will take into account the principal factors determining or influencing the choice which a speaker of CSR has between a long form and a short form of the adjective in given contexts and situations. While it is not so much my goal to start a polemic on this subject, however useful this may appear to be, I will mainly try to summarize the state of affairs on the subject of the long and short forms.

I shall limit myself to a treatment of predicates with a zero verbal form, where the adjective as the nominal part of the predicate can have either the long form in the nominative case or the short form. I will not describe into any detail predicates containing other than a zero form. As the reader may know, if the predicate contains a copula other than a zero form, a speaker of Russian has in principle three, instead of two, forms available for the adjective: a short form, a long form in the nominative and a long form in the instrumental case. This aspect of the problem about the choice of the form of the adjective as the nominal part of the predicate goes beyond the aim of this paper, although examples of short form usage in utterances with

152

a non-zero copula will be used to illustrate the fact that short forms can be used with non-zero copulas as well, a fact which is not always recognized in the literature, especially grammars of CSR.[1]

0.2   As we know, most of the so-called qualitative adjectives, adjectives like *новый*, *синий*, *молодой*, have long and short forms. Relational adjectives, like *золотой*, do not normally have short forms. However, in artistic language usage, e.g. poetry, short forms of the relational adjectives do occur. But such forms take a special place, because, strictly spoken, they lie beyond the boundaries of current CSR and carry a specific stylistic load. The possessive adjectives, like *рыбий*, *отцов* and *сестрин*, do not have the formal possibilities to express the semantic difference between long and short forms.

In attributive usage the short forms are only found as relics of older times. In fairy tales, folk songs, epics (*былины*), one can find examples of short adjectival forms used attributively, illustrating their different functions in older stages of Russian. In CSR we only find short forms in attributive function as traces of older forms of Russian, in a number of idiomatic expressions, with archaic oblique cases, like *средь бела дня* 'in broad daylight', *на босу ногу* 'barefoot', *по белу свету* 'in the whole wide world', *от мала до велика* 'young and old'. In poetry again, with its large autonomous position as a literary *genre* towards the rules of the standard language, short forms can also be encountered attributively.

In standard usage, however, the choice between the long and short forms only exists predicatively.

In the following *exposé* I will first try to summarize the semantics of the opposition of long and short forms. Then I will describe into some detail the syntactics and stylistics implied in the use of the short form.

1.   Semantic difference between the long and short forms

1.1   A description of the semantic difference between the long and short forms should start from the supposition that the lexical meaning of the adjective remains the same in both long and short forms.

The short form presents the lexical meaning of a qualitative adjective in a given situation. The quality mentioned is not attributed to the subject as such, but it is part of the situation. The quality is actualised in this situation and the subject manifests itself with this quality in the given situation.

The long form, on the other hand, categorizes, classifies the subject into a class of subjects which possess the same quality. It attributes the quality referred to by the long form as an inherent quality to the subject.

A few examples should illustrate this semantic opposition.

The short form in *Эта книга интересна* 'this book is interesting' should be interpreted as 'the book makes an interesting impression in the given situation', 'it looks interesting to me', etc., while *Эта книга интересная* means 'this book belongs to the class of interesting books'.

Костюм готов 'the suit is ready'; this is not presented as a 'class of ready suits', it just means that 'the suit is ready to wear', 'one can pick it up at the tailor's', it is a feature that appears in the given situation, whereas *костюм готовый* 'the suit is ready-made', means indeed that the quality of the suit is such that it belongs to a 'class of suits made in a clothing-factory', this quality is an inherent quality.

У него пятница как раз свободна 'he is free right on (this) Friday', the unique reference to one Friday does not exclude that 'he is free every Friday', but this is not the message, this message only says that 'he is free in the given situation on this Friday, while *у него пятница свободная* 'he is free on Friday's', indeed implies that 'his Fridays can be categorized as his days off'.

1.2 A characteristic of the general meaning of the short form is that the given situation in which the meaning of the adjective is actualised, very often entails one or other **restriction**. This restriction can be different in nature: it can be temporal, spatial, conditional, or other, including subjective judgments of a situation. However, a restriction is not a necessary prerequisite of the short form. At the most, it is a very frequent phenomenon as a consequence of the fact that the quality of the short form adjective is only manifest in the given situation in a certain way.

Examples for this are:

Мать сегодня больна 'mother is ill to-day', i.e. mother's illness is presented as being part of a situation we are confronted with; the short form is fully responsible for this, but the adverb *сегодня* makes explicit that the restriction of mother's illness lies in its temporary nature; on the other hand *мать больная* must be interpreted as something like 'mother belongs to the category of ill people/of people with a bad health';

Он здоров 'he is healthy, not ill at the moment', but *он здоровый*

154

'he has a strong constitution';

Врачи совершенно беспомощны перед этим 'the doctors are completely helpless in this case', in which the quality of 'helplessness' is evidently related to a certain case in a certain situation; the restriction lies here in the words *перед этим*, while *она стала совершенно беспомощная* 'she became completely helpless' where the quality of 'helplessness' is presented as an inherent quality, which classifies the subject into a 'class of helpless people' (examples from RRR 1973: 202).

1.3 A few more examples, some of them taken from the press or contemporary literature, may illustrate the use of the short form with non-zero copulas:

"Особенно дороги мне были стихи Пастернака о музыке" 'Pasternak's poems on music were especially dear to me' (Независимая газета, 26.VI.1993), in which case the restriction lies in the person, who wrote these words, the quality *дороги* 'dear' must be applied to the poems with respect to the writer and it is not given as an inherent quality of the poems as such;

"[...] контакт с народом в тот день был невозможен по причине алкогольного опьянения всех манифестантов" '[...] contact with the people was impossible on that day because of alcoholic intoxication of all demonstrators' (Независимая газета, 2.VI.1993). Here there is a combination of a temporal *в тот день* and a causal restriction *по причине ...*, which limits the scope of the quality and explains the use of the short form;

"Генка, ты мне друг, – я всегда был хорош для тебя?" 'Genka, you are a friend to me, I have always been good to you, haven't I ?' (В. Тендряков, Ночь после выпуска);

Они были с ним очень дружны 'They were like friends to him', and *Да-а, вообще люди были дружные* 'Yes, these people were friendly anyway' (RRR 1973: 202). In the first sentence 'they' are not classified as friendly people, but their behaviour was considered friendly towards 'him', they made an impression of being friendly with him, while in the second sentence 'these people' are indeed classified as 'friendly people';

Это в тридцатых годах были модны новые имена 'New names were in vogue in the thirties', where the quality again manifests itself only in the given situation, but *Платье модное, а туфли никуда* 'The dress is stylish, but the shoes are poor' (RRR 1973: 203), where the quality mentioned by *модное* is presented as inherent to the subject, the dress is classified as 'a stylish dress'.

As said before, the short form actualises a given quality in a given situation. The difference between short and long form is nicely illustrated in the following literary example:

"«*В молодости была красива*», – *думает Мария Николаевна, глядя на соседку. Аксинья Кузьминична улыбается и говорит: – Смолоду я была кра-а-сивая, ой какая.*" (Н Баранская, День поминовения, p. 9). The short form *красива* stresses the subjective vision of the person thinking the words: 'her neighbour makes the impression that she was beautiful in her youth', the given quality is attributed to the given situation and is given as a subjective judgment, while the second person speaks about herself 'as having belonged to the category of beautiful persons'.

More examples of short forms with a zero verbal form taken from literature and the press are:

"*Такие майки с портретом Андреотти в виде спрута сейчас в Италии очень актуальны*" 'These T-shirts with Andreotti's portrait in the form of an octopus are very popular in Italy at the moment' (Литературная газета, 19.V.1993);

Насколько велики его шансы? 'What are his chances?' (RRR 1973: 205), where the 'chances' are related to the person referred to by *его* and something present in the given situation, but not mentioned in this sentence;

"*Ротшильдам не безразличны беды других людей*" 'The Rothschilds are not indifferent towards other people's misfortune' (Известия, 22.V.1993), i.e. the way the misfortunes of other people are described here is within a context in which the Rothschilds care about other's misfortune; these misfortunes cannot be classified in one or other way;

"*Выход этой книги сейчас, видимо, не случаен?* " 'The appearance of the book now, evidently, is not accidental?' (Московские новости 13, 19-26.II.1995);

"*В Боснии зачехляют орудия, однако перспективы мира все еще не ясны*" 'In Bosnia they have put away their guns, but the prospects for peace are still unclear' (Известия, 22.V.1993).

2. Situations which require the use of a short form

For certain semantic relationships which are present in the context and/or the situation, the meaning of the short form fits better than that of the long form. It concerns the relationship of reciprocity of the subject, the idea of 'oversize', apodictic statements and definitions, and the expression of a degree or intensity of the quality mentioned. In the latter case, however, the use of the short form is not obligatory.

2.1 To express **reciprocity** the short form must be used. This is a consequence of the above described meaning of the short form which implies the actualisation of the quality mentioned in a certain situation. In the case of reciprocity the quality specified by the short form functions only in relation to the subjects mutually. The subject is always plural.

Examples:

Эти улицы параллельны 'These streets run parallel';

Петя и Саша неразлучны 'Petja and Sasha are inseperable';

Приведенные случаи аналогичны 'The quoted examples are analogous';

Наши силы равны 'Our forces are equal';

"Партия и народ едины!" 'The Party and the people are one!' (Э. Тополь, Завтра в России, p. 63);

"Они не были близки, хотя и жили вместе" 'They were not close, although they lived together'. (Н. Баранская, День поминовения, p. 40).

The following examples (taken from RRR 1973: 201) give a good illustration of the short form expressing reciprocity, while the long form does not and cannot express this:

Они семнадцать лет уже женаты 'they have already been married for 17 years' and *они все женатые* 'they are all married'. In the first sentence the short form indicates that 'they' are married to each other, while the second sentence only means that 'they all' possess the wedded state, but we do not know, without any more context, to how many people this applies, nor do we know anything about their sex; this could be said about a group of men, all married.

2.2 The short form is also used to express **'oversize'**. This is because the idea of 'oversize' presupposes a relationship between the quality mentioned and somebody or something in a certain situation: 'something is too big for me, for the room, in the given circumstances', etc. It is the opposite of categorization.

Compare:

Чемодан ему тяжел 'The suitcase is too heavy for him', the quality mentioned is related only to a certain person, while in:

Чемодан тяжелый, the quality of 'heaviness' is given as an inherent characteristic of the suitcase, the suitcase is classified as 'a heavy suitcase'.

More examples of 'oversize' are:

Эти ботинки мне узки 'These shoes are too tight for me'
Он уже стар для этого 'he is already too old for that'
Я еще молод 'I am too young [for that]'
Этот стол высок для меня 'This table is too high for me'
Наш дом велик для нашей семьи 'Our house is too big for our family'
Вода холодна для купания 'The water is too cold for bathing'
Платье ей немножко свободно 'The dress is a bit too loose for her'.

In a sentence like " *Территория слишком велика*" 'The territory is too large' (Литературная газета, 19.V.1993), the 'oversize' is also expressed by the adverb *слишком*.

2.3 In **apodictic statements** and **definitions** the short form is used. The basic idea here is that in an utterance like 'Life is difficult' the word 'life' is used as a unique entity in a generic sense, in which case it cannot be categorized. The impossibility of categorizing 'life' in the generic sense into a "class of difficult lives" accounts for the fact that the long form cannot be used in an utterance like the above. The Russian formula can only be *Жизнь трудна*. On the other hand a sentence like 'Life there is very hard' in which the word 'life' is used in the sense of living conditions, it can be categorized; it can be understood as 'The way of life there can be classified as difficult': *Жизнь там очень трудная.*

Other examples are: *Пчелы трудолюбивы* 'Bees are industrious' versus *Ребята у нас трудолюбивые* 'The children with us are hard-working'. In the first sentence the bees are not being categorized as 'industrious creatures', but 'bees as a species manifest themselves as being industrious'. But 'these children of ours' in the second sentence are categorized as 'hard-working children', they may be compared to other children who would not be so diligent.

Other examples of the short form in statements and definitions where the noun-subject is used as a unique entity in its generic sense are:

Курение вредно 'Smoking is harmful'
Корь заразна 'Measles is contagious'
Любовь слепа 'Love is blind'
Охота на хищников опасна 'Predator hunting is dangerous'
Мир тесен 'It's a small world'
"*Жизнь коротка, коррупция вечна*" 'Life is short, corruption is everlasting' (Литературная газета, 16.IV.1997).

158

2.4   The short form is especially suitable when the speaker wants to emphasize the **degree** or **intensity**, whether high or low, of a given quality. The short form is very frequently used, especially colloquially, when an adverb expressing degree or intensity, like *слишком, (не) очень, настолько, довольно, немножко*, etc., or a comparison accompanies the adjective (RRR 1973: 205f.). The presence of such an element stresses the fact that the given quality is being actualised in the situation and should not be understood as a categorization:

Она необыкновенно красива 'She is exceptionally beautiful'
Ты очень строга к себе 'You are very strict on yourself'
Он далеко не глуп 'He is far from stupid'
Он не больно умён 'He is not very bright'
Он бесстыден до невозможности 'He is shameless to the last degree'
Он глуп как пробка 'He is as stupid as a donkey'
"Совокупный риск крайне велик и для этой огромной территории, и для соседних стран, [...]" 'The combined risks are extremely great for this enormous territory as well as for the neighbouring countries [...]' (Независимая газета, 22.XI.1994).

We are not maintaining that a long form would not be possible when adverbs of degree or intensity are being used, but it seems that expressing 'quantification' or 'intensification' far more frequently evokes a short form of the adjective.

The competing semantics of the long and the short forms may become clear in the following example, (again taken from RRR 1973: 205-206):

Очень он самоуверенный, безумно самоуверен 'He is a very self-assured person, he is [acts, manifests himself] terribly self-assured'.

It is for the same reason (of degree or intensity) that adjectives provided with the attenuative suffix -*оват*- are very frequently used in their short form (RRR 1973: 207):

Этот сыр суховат 'This cheese is a bit dry'
Он немножко странноват вообще 'He is somewhat strange'
Я на это дело туповат 'I'm rather stupid in that matter'.

3.   The role of the lexical meaning of an adjective

The lexical semantics of an adjective may imply that a long form can hardly be used predicatively, because the grammatical meaning of the long form in predicative function does not match very well the lexical meaning of the adjective.

It is, e.g., less obvious to use a long form like *склонный к* 'inclined to' predicatively, because the lexical meaning does not 'easily' fit the idea of categorization or classification, like 'somebody belongs to a class of people who are inclined to (do something)'. It seems that the earlier mentioned restriction forms an inherent part of the lexical meaning of this adjective. One is 'inclined to do something' or 'inclined *to* somebody or something', while just 'being inclined' without any further complement simply does not make sense. In other words, the lexical meaning entails a restriction, which requires the use of the short form, which makes the quality mentioned manifest in a certain situation.

Another example is the adjective *благодарный* 'grateful'. It is a very common thing to say *Я очень ей благодарен* 'I am very grateful to her'. Indeed, 'one is grateful *in a certain situation, to somebody, for something*', while it is less common, though not impossible, to say *Я благодарный* 'I am grateful' in the sense 'I belong to the category of grateful people'. But a long form is acceptable in a sentence like: *Обидно когда [родители] вкладывают всю жизнь, и дети неблаго-дарные* 'It's a shame when [the parents] invest their whole life, and the children are ungrateful' (RRR 1973: 201). The feature of 'ungratefulness' is indeed projected as a more permanent, inherent one, the children are classified as 'ungrateful children'.

The choice between a long and a short form in the predicate is maintained, but the lexical semantics of these adjectives makes categorization of the subject into a 'class of subjects which share the same quality' less probable. And especially when a restriction is not only explicitly mentioned, but the lexical meaning of the adjective requires a complement as such, the choice between long and short form is almost non-existent, the short form is then the only one suitable to be used as part of the predicate: *Он мне должен 1000 рублей* 'He owes me a thousand roubles'. The long form *должный* hardly ever occurs in the predicate, because this adjective needs a complement, which then functions as a restriction in the above mentioned sense.

Compare:
Пётр способен на всё 'Peter is capable of everything', *Анна способна к математике* 'Anna is good at mathematics' where only short forms are possible, but in *Пётр способный* 'Peter is (a) capable (person)' the long form categorizes 'Peter' into 'the class of capable people' in a sentence which does not contain any kind of restriction of the quality mentioned.

160

One more comparison:
Ты мне нужна, не уходи! I need you, don't go away!'; *"Нужны ли России советы Европы?"* 'Does Russia need Europe's advice?' (Московские новости 13, 19-26.II.1995), versus *Эта книга очень нужная* 'This book is very necessary'. In the first two examples the relevance of the utterance is related to a given situation, while the last example is a more general statement, in which the quality mentioned is presented as an inherent quality of the book.

4. Difference in lexical meaning between the long and the short form

Related to the problem pointed out above is that of the lexical meaning of the long and short forms compared with each other. As a starting point for our analysis we took for granted that the lexical meaning of long and short forms is always the same. This, however, is not the case. We may have to do with a complex of different semantic relationships between the long and the short forms. The lexical meaning(s) as such may be different, but more often we will have to handle different kinds of polysemy.[2] Apart from that, metaphorical or metonymical usage may influence the choice between the long and the short forms.

As lexicographers know, there is no sharp boundary between different lexical meanings of a form and polysemy. As a most evident case of different meanings are often considered the long form *видный* 'distinguished, prominent' and the short form with the same root *виден* 'visible, conspicuous'. It is not too difficult, however, to consider this case too as one of polysemy, if one is prepared to relate the 'concrete meaning' of 'visibility' to the more 'abstract meaning' of 'prominency'. For our treatment of the grammatical meaning and the use of the long and short forms this seems, however, not very important. I will therefore not try to draw a line between a 'difference in meaning' and 'polysemy', but I will use the term 'meaning' covering both meaning and polysemy in the following discussion (see 4.1). I will, however, try to discriminate between meaning and polysemy on one side and metaphorical or metonymical usage on the other (4.2).

4.1 (Partly) different meanings

As is already said before, the semantic relationship between the long and the short forms may be different. The case is rare, if at all existent, that long and shorts forms have completely different meanings, which are not shared by the opposite member. But there are quite a few cases in which the lexical meaning(s) of the short form cover(s) only part of the lexical meaning(s) of the long form, or the other way round: the short form has meanings, only part of which is shared by the long form.

The following lists a number of adjectives which show (partly) different meaning(s) for the long and the short forms:

виден 'visible, conspicuous'   видный 'distinghuished, prominent; (rare) visible'
волен 'free, at liberty'   вольный 'free, unrestricted'
грешен 'guilty'   грешный 'sinful, culpable'
должен 'owing; must'   должный 'due; fitting, proper'
дурён 'ugly'   дурной 'bad (of character/habits)'
жив 'alive'   живой 'lively; keen; animated'
зол 'angry'   злой 'evil; bad; wicked'
намерен 'intend'   намеренный 'intentional, deliberate'
одинок 'lonely'   одинокий 'alone; solitary'
плох 'poorly, indisposed'   плохой 'bad (of character, etc.)'
прав 'right, correct'   правый 'right-hand; right-handed; just, righteous'
свободен 'free, unhampered'   свободный 'free, for nothing'
симпатичен 'be liked'   симпатичный 'nice; attractive'
согласен 'agree'   согласный 'concordant, harmonious'
счастлив 'happy'   счастливый 'happy; lucky; successful'
хорош 'pretty, good-looking; good'   хороший 'good; nice'.
цел 'whole, intact, safe'   целый 'whole, entire'.

The forms хороший/хорош are examples of an adjective, where only part of the meaning is shared by both long and short forms: this is the meaning 'good', but the meaning 'pretty, good-looking' is only present in the short form.

Examples are:

Она хороша (собой)   Она очень хорошая
'She is pretty'   'She is good'
Весна в этом году особенно хороша   Сегодня погода хорошая
'Spring is this year exceptionally fine'   'The weather is fine to-day'
Хорош все-таки мороз, да?
'Quite a sharp frost, isn't it?'
"Даже лучший автомобиль хорош

162

лишь настолько, наколько хорош
водитель." (Приложение к «Московские новости», август 1995).
Even the best car is good only in
so far as the driver is good.'

Examples of some of the other adjectives are:

Она дурна собой
'She is ugly'

Она дурная
'She is nasty'

Ребенок еще жив
'The child is still alive'

Ребенок очень живой
'The child is lively'

Она одинока
'She is alone/lonely'

Она одинокая
'She is alone/has no relatives'

Больная очень плоха
'The patient is in a critical condition'

Она очень плохая
'She is very bad/nasty'

Он прав
'He is right'

Он правый
'He is righthanded'

Наше дело правое
'Our cause is just'

Путь свободен
'The road is clear'

Путь свободный
'The road is free/no toll bar'

После обеда я буду свободен
'After dinner I am off'

Вход свободный
'Free entrance'

Он ей симпатичен
'She likes him'

Он симпатичный
'He is nice; good-looking'.

Она была очень счастлива
'She was very happy'

Она была очень счастливая
'She was (a) very happy (woman)'

"Ну, какой же он счастливый,
что вы ему такое имя дали"
'Well, how lucky he is that you
gave him such a name' (RRR
1973: 202)

Все ваши вещи целы
'All your things are safe/intact'

Яблоко целое
'The apple is whole/entire'

"Я знаю у вас одну книжку, она
у вас еще цела?"
'I know you've got a book, do you
still have it?' (RRR 1973: 201).

There are a few adjecives of which the meaning of the short form
differs colloquially considerably of that of the long form:

здоров [+inf.] 'strong, good at'   *здоровый* 'healthy'

прост 'silly, foolish'	простой 'simple'
силён в [+L] 'good at'	сильный 'strong'
смешон 'ridiculous'	смешной 'funny'.
не далёк 'not clever/bright'	(не) далёкий '(not) far/remote'
неравнодушен к 'in love with'	(не)равнодушный '(not) indifferent'

The short form in the latter two meanings is always negated.

Examples:

она не очень далека 'she is not very bright'
он здоров врать 'he is a good liar'
он к ней неравнодушен 'he is in love with her'.

4.2 Metaphorical or metonymical usage

When the meaning of an adjective is used metaphorically or metonymically, it is predominantly the long form which can be used in these cases. It is seldom the short form, but it seems they cannot be used both. In other words, the speaker has no longer a choice between the long and short forms.

Examples:

беден 'poor'	бедный 'poor; miserable'
В это время она была очень бедна	*Она была очень бедная*
'She was very poor in those days'	'She was very poor'

but only the long form is possible in the metaphorical meaning:

Какая она бедная!
'What a poor thing she is!'

благодарен 'grateful'	благодарный 'grateful'
Люди очень неблагодарны	*Люди очень неблагодарные*
'People are very ungrateful'	'People are very ungrateful'

but only the long form in the metonymical meaning:

Работа в опере [...] гораздо трудней [...] и менее благодарная
'The job in the opera [...] is harder [...] and less rewarding' (RRR 1973: 201)

болен	больной
Ты у меня больна	*Она больная*
'You are ill'	'She is a sick woman'

but only the long form in the metaphor:

Он больной
'He is a bit soft in the head'

верен	верный
Она осталась верна себе	*Он такой верный*
'She remained true to herself'	'He is such a loyal person'

but only the long form in the metonymical usage:

Мои часы верные

'My watch is right'

весел	*веселый*
Девушка весела	*Девушка веселая*
'The girl is cheerful'	'The girl is (a) cheerful (girl)'

but only a long form in the metonymy:

Песня веселая

'The song is cheerful'

гениален	*гениальный*
Этот артист гениален!	*Этот артист гениальный*
'This artist is great!'	'This artist is a genius'

but only a long form in the metonymy:

пьеса гениальная

'the play is brilliant'

глух 'deaf'	*глухой* 'deaf; voiceless; remote'
Он глух на оба уха	*Он глухой*
'He is deaf in both ears'	'He is (a) deaf (man)'

but only the long form in the metaphorically derived meanings:

Стена глухая

'This is a blind wall'

Эти согласные глухие

'These consonants are voiceless'

умён	*умный*
Человек очень умён!	*Человек очень умный*
'How clever the man is!'	'The man is very intelligent'

but only the long form in the metonymy:

Голова у него очень умная

'He is very clear-headed'

фальшив	*фальшивый*
Он был фальшив	*Он был фальшивый*
'He was false'	'He was (a) false (person)'

but only a long form in the metaphorical meanings:

деньги фальшивые; музыка фальшивая

'the money is forged; the music is false'.

5. No long forms available

It is a well-known fact that a few adjectives do not have long forms. The most notable case is here *рад* 'glad', but there are a few more: the colloquial form *квит* 'quits', mostly used in its plural form *квиты*, the obsolete and folkloristic *люб* 'dear' and the slang (*просторечное*) form *горазд* 'good (at), clever (at)'. One may wonder why these forms do not possess a long form. The most obvious explanation for *квит(ы)* will be because its meaning will always be used in a reciprocal situation (cf. 2.1). Forms like *люб* and *горазд* will, due to their meaning, always be accompanied by a complement, which functions as a restriction to the quality in question. The meanings of these adjectives are only actualised in a certain situation which entails a restriction.

For the adjective *рад* one could argue that 'being glad' is a state of mind which is necessarily related to a situation and cannot be seen as an inherent property on the basis of which one can categorize the subject.

6.   Fixed expressions

Short forms can form a permanent part of fixed expressions. We will not go into any detail of discussing the use of short forms in such expressions. For the sake of illustration I list a few examples:

С него взятки гладки 'You'll get nothing out of him'
Он жив и здоров 'He is safe and sound'
Мал золотник, да дорог 'Little bodies may have great souls'
Забот полон рот 'To be up to one's neck in worry'.

7.   Syntactic means for the expression of a restriction

As already stated, the short form is very often, but not necessarily, restricted in one way or other. This restriction is syntactically most frequently expressed by an adjunct which in a given situation determines the scope of the effect of the quality. It is not said that every adjunct functions as such. The following may make that clear:

Он глухой от рождения 'He is deaf since his birth'
Он глух к моим просьбам 'He is deaf to my requests'.

The person in the first sentence is classified as a 'deaf person', the quality of deafness is an inherent one; the adjunct does not function as a restriction of the quality mentioned, but it supplies complementary information about the person's deafness. But the subject in the second sentence is only 'deaf' in the given situation, only to my requests, this on top of the fact that 'deaf' in this sentence is used metaphorically.

Summarizing: an adjunct is neither a necessary element for the use of a short form, nor does it necessarily imply the use of a short form.

But the adjunct I have in mind here, which functions as the expression of a restriction to the scope of the quality, decidedly entails the use of a short form.

An adjunct in this sense can be formed by a noun or pronoun, a prepositional phrase, an infinitive or a subordinate clause, or it can have the form of a comparison introduced by *как*. A brief survey of these syntactic means to overtly express the potential restriction follows here.

7.1 A noun or a pronoun in an oblique case:

пустыня бедна водой 'the desert is poor of water'
очень вам благодарен 'I'm very grateful to you'
он мне дорог 'he is very dear to me'
чем она жива? 'what makes her tick?'.

Also in complex sentences:
Рассказ увлекателен тем, что в нём захватывающий сюжет 'the story is appealing because it has a gripping subject'.

7.2 A prepositional phrase

The short form is here followed by a preposition which in its turn demands a certain case, e.g.:

[+G] *характерен для* 'characteristic of'
[+D] *близок к* 'close to', *готов к* 'prepared for'
[+A] *благодарен за* 'grateful for', *глух на* 'deaf in'
[+I] *бессилен перед* 'powerless towards', *близок с* 'intimate with'
[+L] *виноват в* 'guilty of', *наслышан о* 'familiar with', *силён в* 'good at'.

Examples:
Я далёк от того, чтобы желать 'I am far from wishing'
Она равнодушна к сладостям 'She is indifferent to sweets'
Он похож на мать 'He takes after his mother'
Я не виноват перед вами 'I feel no guilt towards you'
Я в этом не властен 'I have no competence in that matter'.

7.3 An infinitive or a subordinate clause

Examples:
Он молод занимать этот пост 'He is too young for that post'
Ты молод, чтобы меня учить and the more colloquial version:
Молод ты меня учить 'You are too young to teach me'
Он слишком слаб, чтобы работать 'He is too weak to work'

Я вынужден / готов / намерен / способен / согласен / склонен это сделать
'I am forced / am prepared / intend / am capable / agree / am inclined to do that'.

7.4 The conjunction *как* introducing a comparison

Этот район известен, как родина Чехова 'This region is famous as Chekhov's birthplace'
Шулейкин пунцов, как пересевший помидор 'Šulejkin is as crimson as an overripened tomato' (Булат Окуджава, Повести и рассказы, p. 224).

8. Syntactic factors which require the use of the short form

In contrast with the adjunct described above, there are syntactic elements and constructions which force the use of the short form. This can be explained by scrutinizing once again the meaning of the short form. This form means basically that the subject manifests itself as 'such and such' in a certain situation, where 'such and such' is the lexical content of the adjective in its short form. In a sentence like *Это интересно* the subject *это* displays itself to the person saying or writing these words as *интересно*, and not as something which can be classified as such. In *Завидовать не умно* it is the act of 'being jealous' which is considered by the speaker or writer as 'not wise', but it is not categorized as such.

The following sections give a brief survey of the syntactic elements forcing a short form.

8.1 Impersonal sentences

When the adjective[3] forms the predicate of an impersonal sentence the short form must be used:
Здесь очень холодно 'It's very cold here'
Зимой жарко, а летом знойно 'In winter it is hot, but in summer it is burning'.
The short form is also used in exclamations with *как*:
Как хорошо! 'How good!'.

8.2 Pronominal or numerical subject

The short form must be used when the subject is expressed by *это*, *то, что, всё, всё что, (всё) остальное, одно, другое, первое,* and *кто* and *что* in relative clauses:

Это очень интересно 'That is very interesting'
Одно хорошо, что ... 'One thing is good, and that is that ...'
Всё ясно 'Everything is clear'
Всё хорошо, что хорошо кончается 'All's well that ends well'
(Всё) остальное ясно '(All) the rest is clear'
Прав тот, кто искренен 'He is right, who is sincere'.

8.3 Infinitive or subordinate clause

The short form must be used when the subject is formed by an infinitive or a subordinate clause:

Мне больно это слышать 'It hurts me to hear that'
На него было больно смотреть 'It was painful to look at him'
Как хорошо быть здесь! 'How good to be here!'
Как хорошо, что ты здесь! 'How good that you are here!'
"Хотя понимаю, что завидовать не умно." 'Though I know it is not wise to envy' (Московские Новости 49, 16-23.VII.1995).

9. The construction *у* [+G]

It is often remarked that a short form cannot occur in sentences which are constructed with the preposition *у* followed by the genitive case. From several examples presented above (see 1.1 *свободна* and 4.2 *болен*) it becomes clear that this standpoint cannot be held. However, it is true that it is not always possible to determine whether the adjective, which stands in a postpositive position in a sentence with the construction *у* [+G], is used attributively or predicatively. This syntactic ambiguity may be a reason why the long form seems to be typical for this construction.

A sentence like

Конечно у нас церкви красивые в Москве

can be interpreted as either:

'Of course, we have beautiful churches in Moscow', or
'Of course, the churches we have in Moscow are beautiful.'

Another (colloquial) example (taken from RRR 1973: 210) is

Говорят у верблюдов очень глаза какие-то умные и добрые.

This sentence may mean:

'They say, camels have in a way very wise and kind eyes' or
'They say, that the eyes of camels are in a way very wise and kind.'

10. Syntactic agreement

When the pronouns *как/какой* and *так/такой* accompany an adjective, they must agree in long or short form with the form of the adjective:

Как она хороша! — *Какой он хороший!*
'How beautiful she is!' — 'How good is he!'
Она так счастлива! — *Она такая счастливая!*
'She feels so happy!' — 'She is so happy/lucky!'.

The form *самый*, used with an adjective to express the superlative, does not possess a short form in this function. This means that a short form of this superlative formation does not exist, e.g.:

Эта книга самая интересная 'This book is the most interesting'
Это самое интересное 'This is most interesting'.

A superlative short form does occur, however, with *наиболее*:
Наиболее важен вопрос снабжения 'Most important is the question of supplies' (cf. 11.2).

11. Stylistic considerations concerning the use of the short form

11.1 Whenever a speaker has a real choice between the long and the short form, the short form is considered the more expressive and/or emotional one.

An utterance like *Ты глупая* 'You are stupid' is of a much more 'neutral' kind than *Ты глупа* 'How stupid you are!'. Apparently, the meaning of the short form as the 'evocation of the quality mentioned with reference to a situation' makes this form very suitable for emotional and expressive usage.

11.2 The use of the short form seems almost obligatory in sentences where inversion is being used for reasons of expressiveness. Utterances of this type very often have the character of an exclamation. This inversion is especially characteristic for literature, prose and poetry, but one can also encounter this device in journalistic prose.

Examples are:

Широка страна моя родная! 'How big my native country is!';
"Поразительна судьба этой книги: [...]" 'Amazing is the destiny of this book: [...]' (Независимая газета, 12.III.1998, in an article about Анна Ахматова's «Вечер»);
"Загадочны и потому прекрасны темные чащи лесов" 'Mysterious and beautiful are the dark thickets of the woods (К.Г. Паустовский);
"О, милая бабушка! Как ласкова и прекрасна ты была [...]" 'O, dear

170

grandmother! How gentle and beautiful you were [...]' (Московские новости 15, 11.IV.1993);
"Очень важен вопрос снабжения" 'Very important is the problem of supplies' (cf. Isačenko 1968: 149).

11.3   The intensity of the quality attributed to a person or an object in a given situation can be reinforced with a particle or an interjection. This is particularly a device in the spoken language (and in literature which imitates spoken language). Irony may be the result.
Ну, умён! 'How clever!'
Ты тоже хорош! 'You are a nice one!'

11.4   Of a stylistic nature is also the difference between constructions like *весёлость его неприятна* 'his cheerfulness is unpleasant' and *неприятно, что он такой весёлый* 'it's unpleasant that he is so cheerful'. In the first construction there is a noun which is modified by (the genitive form of) another noun or pronoun; this type of construction is typical for the written language, or for the spoken language under less spontaneous conditions. The second utterance belongs more to the spoken language in unconstrained and spontaneous circumstances. In this case different constructions are available, such as the construction *у* [+G] or an infinitive as subject of the sentence.
   More examples (taken from RRR 1973: 210f.) are:

работа Иванова интересна	*у Иванова работа интересная/*
'Ivanov's work is interesting'	*у Иванова интересная работа*
	'Ivanov has interesting work'
лицо её бледно	*лицо у неё бледное*
'her face is pale'	'she has a pale face'.
проверка этого трудна	*проверить это трудно*
'verification of this is difficult'	'to verify this is difficult'.

   In the latter example a short form is also used in the 'colloquial' version, which is motivated by the infinitive as subject of the sentence (cf. 8.3).

12.   Weather descriptions

   Finally, I would like to make a remark on the fact that in utterances describing weather conditions the nominative case of the long form seems to be by far the predominant choice. This is irrespective of the form of the verbal predicate, whether zero or non-zero. In the latter case the long form instrumental, of course, also occurs.

Examples:

Погода хорошая 'The weather is fine'
Погода была/стояла хорошая 'The weather was fine'
Зима в этом году на редкость тёплая и мягкая 'The winter this year is unusually warm and soft'
Август выдался сухой и тёплый 'August happened to be dry and warm'
Ветер стал сильный 'The wind became strong'
"Весна наступила в этом году ранняя и дружная" 'Spring was very early this year, and steady' (А.И. Куприн, see Xrekova 1981: 46).
Вечер был морозный/морозным 'It was a frosty evening'
Зима в Приморье бывает суровой 'Winter in Primor'je happens to be severe'.

Apparently, in describing the weather a speaker of Russian is more inclined to classify the weather and compare it, as it were, with other weather conditions, more than just describing a certain type of weather on a given moment in a certain situation.

Leiden University

NOTES

* I am very grateful to dr A.A. Barentsen of the University of Amsterdam for his very useful commentary on an earlier version of this article. This has led to a considerable improvement in the consistency of this paper.

[1] The reader is kindly referred to Johanna Nichols for a detailed analysis of nominal predicates in a non-zero copula context (1985: 342-387).

[2] This is dangerous ground. We start here from the supposition that different meanings between the long and the short forms can really be established. This seems the more so by using English translations. But this, of course, is misleading. One should wonder whether it concerns different meanings without respect to the language used. A watertight proof of different semantics would be provided by minimal pairs of the type *Путь свободен* 'The road is free, accessible' versus *Путь свободный* 'The road is free (of charge)', in which the short and the long form alone account for the difference in meaning. But minimal pairs like this are rarely available.

[3] What is called here an adjective functioning as the predicate of an impersonal sentence is also called 'predicative', 'adverb' or 'категория состояния' by other researchers. There is enough ground for the supposition that the opposition between the syntactic categories of adjective and adverb is neutralised in sentences of this structure.

172

AkGr
1970   *Grammatika sovremennogo russkogo literaturnogo jazyka.* Otvetst-
            vennyj redaktor N.Ju. Švedova. AN SSSR. M.
1980   *Russkaja Grammatika.* Tom I. Fonetika. Fonologija. Udarenie.
            Intonacija. Slovoobrazovanie. Morfologija. Tom II. Sintaksis.
            AN SSSR. M.
Barnetová, V. et al. (eds.)
1979   *Russkaja Grammatika.* 1. 2. Praha: Academia.
Comrie, B., G. Stone & M. Polinsky
1996   *The Russian Language in the 20th century.* Second edition, revised
            and expanded, of *The Russian Language since the Revolution.*
            Oxford.
Gabka, K. (ed.)
1975   *Die russische Sprache der Gegenwart.* Band 2. Morphologie. Band 3.
            Syntax. Düsseldorf.
Garde, Paul
1980   *Grammaire russe.* Tôme 1. Phonologie. Morphologie. Paris.
Graudina, L.K.
1977   "Razgovornye i prostorečnye formy v grammatike", *Literaturnaja
            norma i prostorečie,* M.
Isačenko, A.V.
1968   *Die russische Sprache der Gegenwart.* Teil 1. Formenlehre. Halle
            (Saale).
Juxas, J.
1957   "Atributivnye konstrukcii s prostoj formoj sravnitel'noj stepeni
            prilagatel'nyx v roli opredelenija v sovremennom russkom literatur-
            nom jazyke", *Studia Slavica Academiae Scientiarum Hungaricae,*
            299-326.
Leitfaden
1975[10]   *Leitfaden der russischen Grammatik.* Leipzig.
Mulisch, Herbert
1966   *Einführung in die Morphologie der russischen Gegenwartssprache.*
            Berlin.
1993   *Handbuch der russischen Gegenwartssprache.* Leipzig.
Nichols, Johanna
1985   "Padežnye varianty predikativnyx imen i ix otraženie v russkoj
            grammatike", *Novoe v zarubežnoj lingvistike,* vypusk XV, 342-387.
Offord, D.
1993   *Modern Russian. An andvanced grammar course.*
1996   *Using Russian. A Guide to Contemporary Usage.* CUP.
R R R
1973   *Russkaja razgovornaja reč'.* Otv. red.: E.A. Zemskaja. M.
1981   *Russkaja razgovornaja reč': Obščie voprosy. Slovoobrazovanie.
            Sintaksis.* Pod red. E.A. Zemskoj, M.V. Kitajgorodskoj &
            E.N. Širjaeva. M.

Rozental', D.È. & M.A. Telenkova
n.d.(1974³) *Praktičeskaja stilistika russkogo jazyka.*
Tauscher, E. & E.-G. Kirschbaum
1968⁷ *Grammatik der russischen Sprache.* Berlin.
Timofeev, V.I.
1958 "O perexode nekotoryx kratkix prilagatel'nyx v kategoriju sostojanija", *Voprosy jazykoznanija* 5, 93-98.
Vinogradov, V.V.
1972² *Russkij jazyk (grammatičeskoe učenie o slove).* M.
Vsevolodova, M.V.
1971 "Upotreblenie kratkix i polnyx prilagatel'nyx. Stat'ja pervaja", *Russkij jazyk za rubežom* 3, 65-68
1972 "Upotreblenie kratkix i polnyx prilagatel'nyx. Stat'ja vtoraja", *Russkij jazyk za rubežom* 1, 59-64.
Wade, Terence
1992 *A Comprehensive Russian Grammar.*
Xrekova, L.F.
1981 "Imenitel'nyj i tvoritel'nyj padež prilagatel'nyx v imennoj časti skazuemogo", *Russkij jazyk za rubežom* 6, 44-49.

Dutch Contributions to the Twelfth International Congress of Slavists, Cracow, Linguistics (= *Studies in Slavic and General Linguistics* Vol 24), 175-262. RODOPI, Amsterdam - Atlanta, GA 1998.

SOME METHODOLOGICAL NOTES ON MEL'ČUK'S
COURS DE MORPHOLOGIE GÉNÉRALE

W. ANDRIES VAN HELDEN

Mel'čuk, Igor: 1993, *Cours de morphologie générale (théorique et descriptive). Volume 1: Introduction et première partie: le mot*, Les Presses de l'Université de Montréal / CNRS Éditions, 412 pp.

Introduction

Igor Mel'čuk was one of the leading Russian theorists during the Golden Age of Central and East European formal linguistics, which lasted from the late 1950s to the early 1970s. He also became one of the most prominent victims of the shift in Soviet science policy of the early 1970s, when Soviet humanities and social sciences were no longer allowed to accommodate mathematical linguistics, structuralism and other disciplines which were censured for their cynical and amoral approach to mankind. The new tack forced Mel'čuk to leave the Soviet Union. But his vicissitudes did not prevent him from continuing to build up his impressive *oeuvre*, comprising hundreds of papers and numerous books. After his migration he enriched western linguistic theory not only with his own original ideas, but also with the legacy of the Golden Age, as well as with elements from the Russian and Soviet traditions that had nurtured it.

Mel'čuk's feats in linguistics include not only robust theoretical constructs, such as his major contributions to the development of the *Meaning ⇔ Text Model* (e.g. Mel'čuk 1974c), but also subtle empirical observations, such as his 500-page study on the syntax of Russian numeral expressions (Mel'čuk 1985a). Mel'čuk excels in linking up theory and empirical observation in a variety of subdisciplines of the science, such as semantics, syntax and lexicology. His achievements also cover a field which might be called *metalinguistics* and which deals with the terms and concepts that are used in making statements about linguistic phenomena.

176

0.1 The *Cours de morphologie générale*

In his ongoing work on the metalanguage of morphology, Mel'čuk presents and discusses a large quantity of linguistic material from a wide variety of languages, as in most of his research. This time, the material is assembled and arranged not only for its own interest, and not just in order to prove or reject a theory, but also with the aim of explaining and underpinning proposals for the coinage of terms and for the calibration of the concepts that we must have if we are to discuss morphological phenomena.

In his *Cours de morphologie générale* (henceforth *CMG*), the first volume of which appeared in 1993, Mel'čuk has condensed the results of thirty years of research in this field. Many ideas found here will look familiar to those who are acquainted with Mel'čuk 1975 (45 pages) and Mel'čuk 1982 (160 pages), which treated the same subject matter. But the *CMG* is much more ambitious than Mel'čuk's older work.

The *CMG* promises to be a monument. It consists of seven parts, to be published in five volumes, all devoted to morphology in its narrow sense, i.e. excluding diachronic morphology, morphological typology, etc. Each volume comprises at least 300 pages. Mel'čuk's ideas have now been synthesized into a self-contained, well-structured whole. The monograph is intended not so much for the morphologists among Mel'čuk's traditional audience as for those who have thus far been unacquainted with the subject or Mel'čuk's ideas on it: linguists with a different paradigmatic background and (advanced) students of linguistics. The *CMG* is meant to be a textbook as well as a reference book and a research monograph: the text is sprinkled with simple and complex exercises, the solutions of which are given in the back of each volume.

The publisher's notes make a bid for the status of a classic: the book is destined to play the same *rôle unificateur* in the science that was once played by the works of Meillet, Bloomfield, Sapir and Nida. The publisher does not mention Saussure but the title of Mel'čuk's monograph speaks for itself.

It is true that efforts to develop a broadly accepted "unified metalanguage" of linguistics are rarely undertaken. Mel'čuk himself refers to Bloomfield 1933 and Hjelmslev 1953 as predecessors of the *CMG*. It seems to be an almost impossible task to simultaneously meet the relevant requirements: rigour, readability, avoidance of a simplistic view of language, and exhaustiveness for at least one coherent subdiscipline of linguistics. And even if such requirements are met, the prospects of such proposals gaining broad acceptance can only be speculated on. Too often, the fate of a major contribution to a science depends on factors that have little to do with its contents.[1]

At the time of writing the present paper, most volumes of the *CMG* are still to appear. As a result, its prospects of becoming a classic are particularly hard to assess. The detailed forward references, suggesting that the manuscripts of the forthcoming volumes are all but completed, give some idea of things to come. Nevertheless a conclusive appraisal can only be given when the complete book is available.

Rather than being an appraisal of the *CMG*, therefore, the present discussion is an effort to inform potential readers about its author's underlying frame of reference, to discuss some of his major methodological choices and fundamental concepts, and indicate where, how and why the latter converge with or diverge from existing or possible alternatives.

This implies that certain important aspects of the *CMG* will be neglected here. One aspect which will be painfully ignored below is the quality and diversity of the adduced material, which includes spectacular examples from a broad variety of languages. The examples enrich the collection of classic touchstones for the testing of theories considerably. Their study is a must for any theoretical linguist who takes the universality of his statements seriously. In the present paper, however, more familiar examples will be used wherever possible, as they take less space to explain and less time to understand.

0.2 Volume I

The present paper, which purports to discuss the methodological aspects of the *CMG,* deals almost exclusively with *Volume I.*[2] This volume contains, besides "Part 1", the 100-page "Introduction". It describes the general conceptual framework on which the other volumes are based. Being the ground-breaking volume, *Volume I* has two special functions.

0.3 Didactic function

The first function is of a didactic nature: *Volume I* must initiate the reader into the goals and methods of the book.

The didactic function barely needs any comment, as it speaks for itself. In *Volume I,* the *CMG's* function as a textbook is taken so seriously that almost everything is immediately clear. Mel'čuk takes his time, explicitly announces almost every step he takes, and illustrates every proposal with numerous well-chosen, well-glossed and well-explained examples.

178

0.4   Methodological function

The present discussion will concentrate on the second function of *Volume I*, the presentation of the methodological foundations for the author's proposals and the fundamental concepts on which his system is based. Most of his fundamental choices are made transparent in this volume. The other volumes deal with the proposed rules of the morphology talking game, but the very terrain on which the game is to be played is smoothed out in *Volume I*.

What follows below is an attempt to identify and explain its author's most essential implicit and explicit paradigmatic choices, while suggesting a few technical improvements here and there. The discussion consists of four sections.

- § 1 deals with Mel'čuk's metalinguistic choices: what does it mean to define a concept?
- § 2 presents his linguistic choices: what is the object to which his definitions are applied?
- § 3 discusses Mel'čuk's conception of what he considers the core unit by which the domain of morphology is distinguished from that of syntax: 'word'.
- § 4 discusses the way in which the author identifies the domain of morphology as distinct from that of lexicology.

1.   Mel'čuk's metalinguistics: morphology as a system of concepts and terms

The author starts with explaining the *raison d'être* of the *CMG*, viz. the crucial importance to a serious science of having a rigorous system of terms and concepts. He demonstrates this in his first deed, on p. 10 (unless indicated otherwise, page numbers refer to the French version of *Volume I*): the disambiguation of the term *linguistic*. His *linguistic₁* henceforth means 'pertaining to language'; his *linguistic₂* means 'pertaining to linguistics'.

A concern for terminological clarity is not always evident in linguistics. Exponents of the generative tradition, for example, tended to regard linguistic terminology as an issue of minor importance. Chomsky observed in 1964 that linguistic concepts are eventually to be defined in terms of formal properties of grammars. He proposed to regard linguistic labels for the time being as purely conventional (Chomsky 1964: 60). For a long time since, the distribution of labels seemed a relatively trivial business of little theoretical interest. According to Brandt Corstius (1974:

42), for example, "transformational linguistics answers the ancient question *what is a verb?* in a silly, but explicit and adequate way: the words which are located in the right-hand strings of the rewrite rules that have *verb* in the left-hand strings".

But in Russia, in the same period, linguists took the terminology issue seriously and developed an interesting linguistic tradition around it, in which the author of the *CMG* played an active role. As early as 1957, Mel'čuk took part in a seminar of linguists and mathematicians on such questions as: "what exactly do we mean when we say that two nouns are in the same case?" (Uspenskij 1957/93: 1202). He came up with answers to this particular question at regular intervals afterward (e.g. in Mel'čuk 1977 and Mel'čuk 1986) and will return to the issue in *Volume II* of the *CMG* (Mel'čuk 1994: 271-293).[3]

1.1 Metalinguistic intuition

At first sight, the Soviet way of dealing with terms is not so distinct from the one adopted by Chomsky in the 1960s. Mel'čuk himself, for example, states that a conceptual system for a domain is equivalent to a theory of that domain (pp. 9-10), meaning that the concepts to be defined should reflect formal properties of whatever we identify as the object of linguistics. Many exponents of the Soviet tradition, however, considered that the choice of concepts and labels should not be <u>arbitrary</u>. They attributed an independent existence to their linguistic$_1$ concepts. Instead of just representing slots in a specific theory, concepts were supposed to correspond to deeply rooted intuitions among speakers concerning the properties of language. According to these linguists, a full-fledged theory of language should account for such intuitions.

An example of this approach is Mel'čuk's defense of the necessity of providing a morphemic analysis for the Russian diminutive *lámpočka* (p. 307). Its meaning ⸢light-bulb⸣ cannot be reduced to the meanings of its etymological sources, i.e. of its stem *lamp-* ⸢lamp⸣ and *-očk-* ⸢diminutive⸣: a light-bulb is not the same as a little lamp. It may therefore be argued that a morphological analysis of /lámpočk/ into the morphs /lámp/ and /očk/ is not to the point, since the combination must be accounted for in the dictionary anyway. Mel'čuk does not think so. He points out that speakers are perfectly aware of the morphemic structure of *lámpočka*. The internal structure of such words is available and used for puns and metaphors, explains slips of the tongue and deviations in aphasic speech, and serves as a model for artistic occasionalisms and neologisms. Thus, a metalanguage which fails to furnish concepts identifying the components of *lámpočka* is an incomplete tool for talking about morphology.

Speakers' attitudes toward linguistic$_1$ analysis make up what Revzin (1978: 15), another theorist belonging to this tradition, called *metalinguistic intuition*. Metalinguistic intuition tends to precipitate in observations about language. It is not unlikely, therefore, that existing linguistic$_1$ concepts of many linguistic$_2$ traditions to a certain extent reflect naïve speakers' awareness of the structure of language. Many Soviet theoretical linguists took traditional grammar seriously. As the mathematician Gladkij (1983: 188), co-author of some of Mel'čuk's work, put it, "there can be no question of ignoring traditional language science and rejecting the concepts which it has developed and which have been used successfully for a very long time. The problem consists in giving just these notions a basis which could satisfy today's requirements on the logical structure of scientific concepts." This is what Mel'čuk is after in the *CMG*. His goal is to construct a consistent and explicit system of concepts covering existing implicit notions (p. 28) while retaining the traditional terms wherever he can. In this respect, his enterprise is opposed to Hjelmslev's: the latter insisted on shaking off the burden of tradition and inventing an entirely novel terminological system (p. 26).

This does not imply that traditional terminology provides absolute guidance for the choices made in the *CMG*. At several junctures, considerations of consistency or mnemonic elegance induce its author to invent new terms and concepts or to propose deviations from traditional usage of existing terms.

1.2 Terminology as a deductive system of definitions

About 250 definitions of morphological concepts make up the backbone of the *CMG*. They constitute a network, in the sense that concepts which are defined in one definition may be used to define new concepts in another definition. *Volume I* contains 47 definitions. The author specifies the logical and practical conditions which his system of definitions must satisfy. These include:

- absence of ambiguity, as in the usage of the term *linguistic* mentioned above;
- absence of logical contradictions (p. 13) and circularity (p. 19), meaning, for example, that two concepts may not be used to define each other;
- *naturalness*, meaning that the concepts as defined do not contradict intuitions on what belongs together and what is different (p. 14).

Mel'čuk's network of definitions is a *deductive system.* In this respect, his enterprise resembles Hjelmslev's (1953) glossematics, and is opposed to Nida's (1949[2]) inductive approach (p. 16). Nida's system is presented as a procedure. It practices a gradual ascent from the particular to the general. Nida's linguist starts out from a body of linguistic[1] observations, classifying them according to the properties which he identifies in his observations, and distributing labels to the identified classes. Mel'čuk's (meta-)linguist starts out, at least in the presentation of his system, from a given (i.e. conventional, agreed) set of properties of language, which are not necessarily observed or even observable. He then proceeds to define, at least in principle, the categories that can be derived from this set. His system of definitions is a *calculus,* a conceptual grid which accommodates any objects which possess the specified properties, irrespective of whether their existence in the actual world has been established. Mel'čuk's deductive calculus is in a sense the metalinguistic analogue of a generative grammar. A generative grammar generates and characterizes the possible (grammatical) sentences of a language, no matter whether they have ever been produced in the real world. Mel'čuk's calculus generates and characterizes the linguistic[1] concepts that are possible once a certain conception of language is agreed upon. As he puts it, "if we say that natural languages possess four types of affixes, it is exactly four, and as long as we remain within the framework of the adopted criteria, a fifth type will never be found: each affix, however eccentric, will always end up in one of our prefabricated cells" (p. 17).

The cells that are generated by a given conception of language may turn out to be empty: the system may produce concepts which do not materialize in any attested languages. This situation is not unusual in other disciplines. Mel'čuk refers to Mendeleev's periodic table of chemical elements (p. 17). This system not only characterizes existing elements but also generates combinations of mutually compatible properties characterizing elements which have not, or not yet, been discovered or synthesized. Within linguistics, a similar practice is found in phonetics. We can draw up, for example, a table of properties of possible clicks (e.g. 'central' vs. 'bilateral' vs. 'unilateral'; 'bilabial' vs. 'alveolar' vs. 'retroflex' vs. 'velar') without having to provide evidence that each combination of (physically compatible) properties generated by the table has actually materialized in some natural language. As early as 1964, Mel'čuk himself used a simple Mendeleevan calculus to generate and characterize possible combinations of semantic, syntactic, morphosyntactic and linear order relationships between elements, and adduced examples from various languages to fill up each cell (Mel'čuk 1964).

The system of definitions which is presented in the *CMG* is not, however, intended to guide us in finding instances of the defined concepts. Although description is part of the subtitle of the monograph, and although Mel'čuk's deductive system will not fail to inspire us in our ways of dealing with particular languages, it is not a discovery procedure (p. 29). It pinpoints relationships between properties that may characterize objects, but, being a calculus, it is not an *algorithm* that tells us <u>how</u> to pinpoint the objects carrying these properties.[4]

Methodologically speaking, therefore, the author considers the linguistic₁ material adduced in the *CMG* to be of minor importance (p. 11), in spite of its abundance. The examples in the book serve for illustration, not falsification. They do not prove or disprove the truth of anything stated in the definitions. Mel'čuk points out that the linguistic₁ material presented may be incomplete and even incorrect without affecting his definitions in any way (p. 30).

In the Soviet Union of the 1970s, such statements, reminiscent of Hjelmslev's "decadent idealist structuralism" (Degtereva 1964: 77-86, in what was perhaps the earliest attack on Mel'čuk and his colleagues), were used to denounce theoreticians. Opponents qualified them as "language-less linguists", "who consciously neglect the study of living human languages and their genuine regularities, and overtly replace the science of the true object of linguistics by nebulous and opinionated linguo-philosophical arguments" (Axmanova & Dolgova 1979: 37). It goes without saying that Mel'čuk's deductive method is perfectly legitimate. He points out that his linguistic₁ examples must not be read as absolute but as conditional truths: if the facts are such and such, then the consequences are so and so. In the type of effort presented in the *CMG*, the truth of a fact is less important than the validity of its implications (p. 30). The only thing required of the linguistic material is that it fit a set of specified properties of language. At some places in the *CMG*, non-existing languages (e.g. on p. 141) or adapted versions of existing ones (e.g. on p. 197) are used to illustrate a point.

Yet the importance of the hundreds of examples from 67 different languages (among which French and Russian are particularly well represented) which are adduced in *Volume I* should not be underestimated. Besides successfully guiding the reader through the complex network of definitions, the examples fulfil another crucial function. They are implicitly used in lines of reasoning of the following type. "If we operate

183

definition ξ of concept 'x', then phenomenon *w* in a given language *L* will be treated as an instance of 'x'. Do we consider this consequence acceptable? (I.e. does *w* intuitively look like an x?) If not, we must reject definition ξ and devise a new definition ξ' of 'x'." Here the examples serve as a falsification tool after all: they can be used to assess the naturalness of the definitions and the necessity to deviate from linguistic₂ tradition.

This imposes another condition on the examples to be chosen. They need not necessarily represent adequate descriptions of genuine languages but, if they are to be used as a tool for measuring naturalness, they must to a certain extent be plausible specimens of such descriptions. The plausibility of the linguistic material determines the range within which the naturalness of the definitions can be verified. One cannot require the results of definition ξ for a given language *L* to be more natural than language *L* itself: if the linguistic material of *L* has zero plausibility, a resulting zero naturalness for application of definition ξ to *L* cannot be a reason for rejecting ξ. So what we may require from a system of definitions is that there be no loss of naturalness.[5] Of course, all this does not take away the legitimacy of using entirely fictitious and implausible languages as a means of checking the logical consistency of a system of definitions.[6]

Thus, Mel'čuk's deductive system meets an important requirement for a meaningful formalism. There is, at least in principle, an external criterion which we can use to evaluate the system, by giving us reasons for preferring one definition to another. In this respect, Mel'čuk's naturalness can be regarded as a metalinguistic analogue of grammaticality: in a way, his terminological system is a falsifiable theory of naturalness. It may be objected that naturalness is a fuzzy phenomenon, whose contours cannot be sharply defined. But the same applies to grammaticality if one is prepared to have a close look at it.[7]

1.3 The technical metalanguage

In his "Introduction" to the *CMG*, Mel'čuk expounds the properties and structure of the definitions which are used in the monograph.

In order to provide definitions of a metalanguage for talking about language, another, auxiliary, metalanguage is needed in which we can denote the definitions themselves. So as to avoid circularity, this technical metalanguage must not include any linguistic₁ concepts. Its terms and symbols can be left undefined within the framework of the *CMG*: other disciplines can take care of them.

The auxiliary metalanguage introduced in the *CMG* contains general scientific concepts, mainly originating from mathematics, set theory and symbolic logic (pp. 81-85). It is implied that these concepts can be combined according to the rules of their respective disciplines so as to make up meaningful statements. Some symbols are used in a rather loose or shorthand fashion in order to simplify presentation. Such deviations from mathematical rigour are mostly specifically indicated, as in the case of Mel'čuk's use of the equation symbol = (p. 91).

In the body of the book, Mel'čuk's definitions are not normally expressed in formulas but in a restricted form of French that unambiguously evokes the underlying canonical concepts, i.e. which does not present an obstacle to readers who are not versed in the formal disciplines.

1.4 Mathematical and logical concepts

Most enumerated concepts in the auxiliary metalanguage speak for themselves, although the list (pp. 81-82) contains a few "difficult" concepts, such as:
- 'part': a concept which is hard to define; it is certainly not a synonym of the concept 'subset', although Mel'čuk's typography suggests that this may be the case;
- 'much' (or 'many'): this concept usually entails implicit reference to a standard of "muchness"; its use as a mathematical or logical concept would seem to require that such a standard be made explicit;
- 'nearly' (or 'almost' or 'all but'): besides entailing implicit reference to a standard of "nearness", it may refer to notions which are referentially quite distinct: compare *nearly 100%*; *nearly twelve o'clock*; *nearly pregnant*.

The list of logical concepts also contains a few expressions which probably involve a conception of time, such as 'simultaneously', 'change', 'never' ($\neq$ 'not'?).

1.5 Quasi-logical concepts

Mel'čuk adds some concepts which he calls *quasi-logical* because they are insufficiently rigorous to be qualified as logical. These include such concepts as 'sufficiently' and 'similar' (p. 83). The difference between this group and the other auxiliary concepts is not always clear. 'Type', for example, is considered a mathematical concept and 'identical' is classified as a logical concept, but the concept 'of the same type', which would seem to be made up of these two concepts, is only assigned quasi-logical status.

Due to the use of certain quasi-logical concepts, such as 'sufficiently', the linguistic$_2$ definitions in the *CMG* are not as rigorous as mathematical or logical definitions. Mel'čuk wants them to be just <u>sufficiently</u> rigorous, introducing what he calls a *vague voulu* (pp. 90-91). He considers this necessary to cope with the fuzzy nature of language, which does not always allow for clear-cut distinctions. This being granted, the term *sufficiently* may be somewhat infelicitous. We shall return to it in § 3.2 and § 3.24 ff.

1.6 Undefined linguistic concepts

Besides the "technical" auxiliary concepts as described above, the *CMG* makes use of undefined concepts of an entirely different nature. As was pointed out in § 1.2, deductive systems deal with conditional truths. A formal system presupposes certain primitive concepts and unproven axioms expressing their mutual relationships, which specify the conditions under which the definitions are held to be true. Linguistic$_1$ concepts are defined on the basis of such *assumptions* or *conventions* concerning the object of linguistics. The question whether the assumptions are true in an absolute sense is not in order here. Within the deductive system, the assumptions are simply regarded as given. But they must be made explicit.

The expression of such assumptions on the object of linguistics involves the use of a set of <u>given</u> linguistic concepts. The "Introduction" to the *CMG* contains a non-exhaustive but substantial list of such undefined items. Here Mel'čuk seems to show less methodological purism than Hjelmslev, who wished to avoid the use of linguistic concepts in defining the object of linguistics altogether (cf. Vogt 1944: 97). Unlike Hjelmslev's deductive system, however, the *CMG* only covers morphology. The undefined items on Mel'čuk's list are not necessarily indefinable in an absolute sense. Their definition may simply be entrusted to other subdisciplines of linguistics and assumed to be ultimately expressible in terms of non-linguistic concepts.

More specifically, phonemes and phonological representations are considered given in the *CMG*, as are syntactic structures and syntactic roles, such as 'subject', 'direct object', 'indirect object' and 'modifier' (pp. 86-88). Given semantic concepts include the semantic counterparts of syntactic relations and roles, such as ʿlogical subjectʾ, etc.

1.7 The universal semantic core

In addition, Mel'čuk introduces a set of given semantic units which belong to what he calls the *universal core* of the set of meanings in natural language (pp. 89-90). This list includes such concepts as 'event', 'time', 'space', 'instrument', 'sex', 'ownership', 'respect', 'intimacy', 'disapprove', 'want/wish'. The universal core meaning 'part' is not to be confused with the homonymous mathematical concept 'part', which is employed in the technical metalanguage of the definitions.

It is not quite clear here what universal core status implies and why some meanings deserve it while others do not. Their use in the definition of morphological concepts (p. 89) alone cannot justify singling out a set of specific universal core units within the total set of meanings. This would introduce circularity in the system of definitions. One cannot simultaneously refer to a specific semantic unit 'X' from the universal core in the definition of a morphological concept 'x' and use the same concept 'x' as a justification for identifying the very unit 'X'. One cannot use, for example, the concept of 'gender' as a criterion for singling out 'sex' from the set of meanings and assigning it universal core status, and simultaneously use 'sex' as a criterion in the definition of 'gender'. It will be interesting to see how the author will handle his universal core in the forthcoming volumes of the *CMG*.

For the time being, we must assume that the specific units in the universal core are somehow special in representing defining properties of a natural language (implying that languages without 'sex', 'respect', and 'intimacy' are not natural).

2. Mel'čuk's language: the Meaning ⟺ Text Model (MTM)

Mel'čuk's assumptions regarding the object of linguistics are not restricted to a simple set of given concepts. In order to develop a consistent deductive system, the relevant relationships between the given concepts must also be indicated. This presents a problem for anyone who pursues a unifying role in a paradigmatically divided discipline. Mel'čuk's intention is to give linguists a formal metalanguage that is maximally independent of the particularities of any specific theory, a tool that can be used by linguists of any theoretical persuasion (p. 31). But a specific set of assumptions about the object of linguistics is nothing less than a theory of language. A theory implies choices. And choices imply that you cannot please everyone.

In trying to mitigate the conflict between the necessity of a theoretical framework and the wish to be as independent as possible of any particular one, the author adopts the *Meaning ⇔ Text Model* (henceforth *MTM*) as the theoretical setting for the *CMG*. It seems to him the most neutral theory, especially as far as morphology is concerned (p. 31). The "Introduction" contains a 40-page presentation of the model.

Mel'čuk and other Soviet linguists developed the MTM in the late 1960s. It is in several respects typical of the period. The prospects of mechanical translation and automatic analysis of texts had induced science policy makers of the 1950s to raise a new generation of researchers, trained in both linguistics and formal methods, who were to conduct the corresponding research. As these researchers became aware of the complexity of language and of the impossibility of developing straightforward surface-to-surface algorithms, they emancipated themselves from their applied research tasks, and adopted a more fundamental approach to language. They started developing broad theoretical frameworks, which no longer immediately supported the original practical goals. Generative grammar was among the first of such frameworks.

As usually happens with innovations, the new conceptions were moulded into models that had been developed to serve the original needs. The first cars looked a lot like carriages. Generative grammar, which regarded syntax as the most urgent problem on the linguistic$_2$ agenda, started out as a calculus that generates text, i.e. strings of symbols, quite like the format that makes up the interface of a 1950s computer. This does not imply that linguists worked with actual computers. Both in the east and in the west, swimming was mostly practised on land (cf. Brandt Corstius 1978: 20-24). But the capacities of existing or imagined computers determined the frame of reference of a great deal of 1950s theoretical thought (cf. Bar-Hillel 1968/70: 293 ff.).

The MTM originated somewhat later, when the idea of developing text-to-text machine translation had been largely given up and the idea of artificial intelligence had grown more prominent. Priorities had shifted to the study of meaning. The MTM, which was developed more or less simultaneously with Schank's models of semantic analysis in the United States,[8] is not a calculus and does not, therefore, generate sentences. It is an *equative* or *transductive* system (p. 44): a complex function, which matches the texts of a language with its meanings and *vice versa*.

2.1 The MTM as a system of representations

The MTM reflects a stratificational approach to language, representing it as a set of objects each consisting of seven correlated representations of an utterance. The semantic representation is the *deepest* level and coincides with the *meaning* of the utterance. The phonetic representation is the shallowest or *surface* level and coincides with its *text*.

deep

semantic level (= meaning)
deep syntactic
surface syntactic
deep morphological
surface morphological
(deep) phonological
phonetic (= surface phonological) (= text)

surface

The correspondences between meanings and texts are ensured by context-sensitive rules which relate units from adjacent levels to each other. As indicated by the two-headed double arrow in the name of the MTM, the rules are bidirectional. But, arguing the priority of linguistic$_1$ synthesis over analysis (pp. 46-47), the author presents and denotes his rules as textward transformations, i.e. they transform units of a given non-surface representation into units of a shallower representation.[9]

2.2 Canonical representations

Within a single level, different representations of the same utterance or fragments thereof coexist (p. 148). The most analytical representation of a fragment within a level is called its *canonical representation*. Consider, as an example, the morphological representation **borral** of Hungarian *borral* 'wine, instrumental'. (Following the author's convention, signs are denoted in bold type.) It can be substituted by **bor** ⊕ **ral**, splitting up the word into the morphs of which it consists. Its canonical representation is **bor** ⊕ **vel**: here the morphs are denoted without taking account of the assimilation and vowel harmony rules (p. 149) which apply when the morph **vel** is combined with **bor**. Mel'čuk's symbol ⊕ indicates *linguistic$_1$ union*, a "meta-operation" by which fragments of a representation are combined, according to the combination rules of the language, into larger fragments, and ultimately into utterances (p. 138).

2.3 The reality status of the MTM

As in western linguistic theories originating in the same period, the MTM's roots in automatic text processing are apparent. The MTM is described as a *functional* or *cybernetic model* (pp. 42-43). The meanings and texts of a language are regarded as directly observable by its speakers, unlike the rules and intermediate representations which express the correspondences between meanings and texts. The real process of cor- relating texts and meanings takes place in a *black box*: it is not available for inspection. The investigator can only simulate the process by a system of formal rules in the best possible way, and this is what a cybernetic model purports to do. A cybernetic model is an agnostic investigator's theory. We do not have to <u>believe</u> that language really works like the model: the only thing which counts is the *functional equivalence* of the rules of the model to the unobservable "real" rules in establishing the correspondences between meanings and texts.

Although the rules connecting the meaning and text representations of the MTM only emulate those of natural language, the author refers, throughout *Volume I*, to the elements of the MTM as if they were genuine properties of real language. This is perfectly in line with the accorded status of the MTM as the conventional object on which the deductive system in the *CMG* is <u>assumed</u> to be based. It implies that, when the author states that certain $linguistic_1$ elements do not exist (e.g. on p. 111), he may, depending on the type of unit, mean either that they do not exist in the MTM or that they do not exist in natural language. It is perhaps a useful additional exercise for the reader to disambiguate Mel'čuk's use of $linguistic_1$ 'pertaining to language', by determining for each occurrence whether he means:
- $linguistic_{1a}$ 'pertaining to language as an observable or postulated phenomenon in reality', or:
- $linguistic_{1b}$ 'pertaining to language as modelled in the MTM'.

2.4 The semiotics of the MTM

The computer-oriented origins of the MTM also betray themselves in the way in which the observable levels of representation are handled. Consider the word *text* in the title of the model. It goes without saying that it no longer refers to strings of characters from an alphabet, as it did in the early days, when theoretical linguistics was immediately asso- ciated with computers. Nowadays *text* implies a phonic representation of an utterance, including prosodic features. But in some respects, MTM texts are still treated as if they were real texts. Text-oriented linguistic$_2$ practice has left its traces in the way in which such semiotic key terms as *utterance, langue, parole* and *sign* are used. In the text-oriented varieties of linguistics which were developed in the 1950s and 1960s, these terms underwent a shift of meaning, which must be recognized in order to gain a proper understanding of the MTM. They will be dwelt upon presently.

2.5 Speech-oriented vs. text-oriented linguistics

Consider an essential difference between speech in classic, pre-information-age conditions on the one hand, and written utterances on the other.[10] In classic speech conditions, the situation in which an utterance is encoded and decoded is unique. An utterance is produced for single usage only. The situation of encoding and the situation of decoding are closely intertwined: the main difference between them is the relative position of the speaker and the hearer with regard to the utterance. Text, on the other hand, acquires, after its unique encoding, an independent existence, which allows for multiple decoding events. The situation of encoding text and the situations of decoding it do not usually coincide. As Ehlich (1982: 318) puts it, "a text is an undertaking of a kind such that a transfer between situations is made possible".

These differences have produced two distinct schools of linguistic$_2$ conceptualization, which often employ the same terms but mean different things by them without making the distinction explicit. The schools can be labelled *speech-oriented* and *text-oriented*.

2.6 Utterance

In both orientations, the term *utterance* usually refers to the rawest material of analysis. To speech-oriented linguists, this implies that an utterance is a concrete linguistic$_1$ event in a concrete setting. When I say *come here* to my gorilla one day, and my wife says *come here* to me the next, speech-oriented linguists are likely to agree that we are dealing here with two different utterances. Analysis of the invariant features shared by the two speech events may eventually produce identical representations, implying that the two events of *come here* are instances of the same sign.

Text-oriented linguists, on the other hand, tend to take the process leading to the first representation of utterances, their denotation, for granted. Their rawest unit of analysis, a text, is already a representation, produced by a writing language user. The text-oriented linguist's raw material is a dilettante version of the speech-oriented linguist's first abstraction.

Now consider the way in which the term *utterance* is used in the *CMG*. The author characterizes a (*complete*) *utterance* as a "linguistic$_1$ manifestation" which is "capable of appearing between two major or absolute pauses" (p. 84). This is a typical text-oriented linguist's definition: it implies that the existence of utterances is independent of specific situations. The use of the word *capable* indicates that, unlike a speech-oriented linguists' utterance, Mel'čuk's utterance is not a unique event: a single utterance may occur in different circumstances, between pauses or elsewhere, without becoming a different utterance. In terms of the MTM, the events of *come here* described above are two instances of the same *manifestation*. Mel'čuk's utterance is a special case of a manifestation, not an instance of it. So, like a text, an MTM utterance is a first abstraction, registering properties which different speech events may have in common.

2.7 *Langue* and *parole*

This terminological choice has implications for Mel'čuk's use of the concepts *langue* and *parole*. In a speech-oriented approach, it is not uncommon to reserve *parole* for the set of utterances of a language, and *langue* for the set of signs which underlie (potential) utterances. Text-oriented linguists of the 1950s and 1960s, on the other hand, may use *parole* to refer to their set of utterances, i.e. units of text, usually sentences. Thus, *qua* level of abstraction, the text-oriented linguist's *parole* corresponds to the speech-oriented linguist's *langue*.

If, in turn, text-oriented linguists employ the term *langue*, they tend to refer to units which are abstractions from their own *parole*, viz. to the complex of building bricks and combination rules which are used to compose the sentences, say a lexicon and a grammar. In text-oriented linguistics, utterances (i.e. observable phenomena) and sentences (i.e. their first-level abstractions) tend to conflate. Bar-Hillel (1967/70: 167) signalled this for 1960s generative grammar.

In the *CMG,* the distinction between *langue* and *parole* is not explicitly introduced. It is used, however, in the definitions of *word form* (pp. 187-188, 247; we shall return to this term in § 3: for the time being, a word form is the same as a word). Here the author introduces a distinction between two concepts: *word form of the langue* and *word form of the parole*. The former covers "autonomous" word forms, which can be related to dictionary entries without the help of other word forms (p. 247). A word form of the *parole*, on the other hand, is regarded as a separate word form in certain contexts only, and must be related to a dictionary entry by means of another word form. The element *an* in the German sentence *ich rufe ihn an* 'I call him up' is a word form of the *parole* (p. 201). In other contexts, such as *daß ich ihn anrufe* 'that I call him up', *an-* is a part of *anrufe*, a word form of the *langue* which provides the key to the relevant dictionary entry. All this reflects the text-oriented linguist's conception of *langue* and *parole*: the *langue* consists of building bricks; the *parole* consists of sentences and fragments thereof.

Utterances and sentences are units belonging to the same level of abstraction in the MTM. An utterance may coincide with a sentence, consist of several sentences, or be a non-sentence like *Merci!* 'thanks' (p. 85). All this shows that the MTM adheres to the text-oriented linguist's conception of the *langue-parole* distinction.[11]

2.8 Sign

The shift of usage has also affected Mel'čuk's use of the term *sign*, which is a key concept in his deductive system. The author regards 'sign' as a rather concrete and transparent notion: "a linguist who has not yet been poisoned by philosophical germs will not find any subject matter in it for a long discussion" (p. 125). One can readily agree with this. Nevertheless, for a proper understanding of the MTM, it must be pointed out that Mel'čuk's 'sign' deviates considerably from the classic sign concept as ascribed to Saussure. The latter's 'sign' is a two-sided entity, a correlation of an acoustic image, called its *signifiant*, and a mental image, called its *signifié*. Mel'čuk's 'sign', on the other hand, is a three-sided entity. Its components are referred to as its *signifiant*, its *signifié* and its *syntactique* (*syntactics*).

2.9 *Signifiant* and *signifié*

The *signifiant* and *signifié* of a sign in Mel'čuk's sense are hardly related to Saussure's. Any pair of units of two different representations that are correlated by the rules in the MTM represent the *signifiant* and *signifié* of a sign. Consequently, the precise nature of a sign in Mel'čuk's sense varies considerably depending on the position of the *signifiant* and *signifié* in the network of representations representing the correspondence between a meaning and a text. Here are some examples.

- In French, the deep syntactic relation 'modifying' is a *signifié* when correlated with a surface syntactic construction N$_{(gender)}$ number $\oplus$ Adj$_{gender, number}$ (i.e. a specified combination of word classes, word order and concordance features) as its *signifiant* (p. 114).
- The English deep morphological unit 'plural' correlates as a *signifié* in a sign with a surface morphological entity /s/ as its *signifiant*.
- The *signifiant* of 'plural' may also be a rule, for example the *Ablaut* (*apophonie*) rule /al/ $\Rightarrow$ /o/ in French *chevaux* 'horses' /ʃəvo/, the plural of *cheval* /ʃəval/ (p. 124).

In fact, any linguistic$_{1b}$ element which correlates with another linguistic$_{1b}$ element which is closer to the phonetic surface is its *signifié*. Conversely, any linguistic$_{1b}$ element which correlates with another linguistic$_{1b}$ element which is more remote from the phonetic surface is its *signifiant*. Consequently, a unit of level n may be simultaneously the *signifié* of a unit of level $n + 1$ and the *signifiant* of a unit of level $n - 1$ (p. 115).

2.10 *Syntactique*

The *syntactique* of a sign X contains the information that is necessary to combine X with other signs and make up signs of a higher order, at least as far as this information cannot be deduced from the properties of *signifiant* and *signifié* (p. 117). It specifies the signs with which X can be combined, and indicates the behaviour of the *signifiant* of the unit resulting from the combination.

Thus, the *syntactique* Σ of the Russian sign **gorod** = ‹'gorod'; /górat/; Σ› 'town' may contain information on:
- the part of speech of **gorod** (i.e. noun, implying that it can occur in the noun slot in syntactic constructions);
- its gender (i.e. masculine, implying that it selects specific options among the possible *signifiants* of modifiers and verbs);
- its government properties (none, it seems, in the present example);
- the alternations in its *signifiant* in combination with other signs (e.g. ... $\Rightarrow$ /górad/ with **genitive singular**);
- the alternations which it triggers in the *signifiants* of other signs (e.g. ... $\Rightarrow$ /á/ in **nominative plural**);
etc. (pp. 117-118).

It is not immediately clear how the *syntactique* is computed when two signs are united into signs of a higher order. When introducing the meta-operation $\oplus$ of linguistic$_1$ union, the author states that the *syntactique* of the new sign simply consists of the set-theoretical union of the *syntactiques* of the composing signs (p. 141). But this hardly ever happens in the examples. In the German example **wälder** = **wald** ⊕ **er** 'forest, plural' it seems logical, when denoting the combination, to delete the instruction /a/ ⇒ /ɛ/, which is contained in the *syntactique* of **er** (p. 141), since the result of the instruction materializes in the resulting *signifiant* /vɛldər/. On the other hand, the author states that **er** adds nothing to the *syntactique* of the root **wald** (p. 142), although it would seem to be responsible for plural agreement of articles and adjectives with **wälder**. Elsewhere we see *signifiés* of composing signs being transformed into elements of the *syntactique* of a resulting sign. Thus, the element 'infinitive' in the *syntactique* of French **marcher**, 'walk', is the *signifié* of the composing sign **er**, 'infinitive' (p. 121).

This shows, incidentally, that a morph like **er** as in *marcher* is a sign (p. 126), since it contains a *signifiant* and a *signifié*, as well as a *syntactique* which governs its compatibility with verb stems. Morphemes and lexemes, on the other hand, are not signs but sets of signs (p. 128).

In the case of gender endings of articles or adjectives as well, the *signifié* of a morph may contain no more than the *syntactique* of another sign. Thus, in French *la montagne*, 'the mountain', /a/ in *la* is not regarded as a part of a potentially discontinuous morph -*a* ... *montagne*, an allomorph of the morpheme **montagne**, which is the type of morphological analysis Martinet (e.g. 1962: 16) would provide. In the approach adopted in the *CMG*, it seems, /a/ is rather the *signifiant* of a morph whose *signifié* is the element 'feminine' as occurring in the *syntactique* of **montagne**.[12]

2.11 Sentences

Thus, a sign in the *CMG* is a building brick. It is used to construct (text-oriented linguists') utterances but is not an utterance itself. An utterance is qualified as a complex of signs (p. 132). Sentences are not signs in *CMG*, for they are two-sided entities which lack a *syntactique* (p. 128). Their combinability with other signs is possibly controlled by pronominal reference and semantics, which the author does not regard as syntactic phenomena.[13] This shows that, in contrast to the given general rule that the *syntactique* of a sign is the set-theoretical union of the *syntactiques* of its composing signs, the ultimate result of all the operations of linguistic$_1$ union, i.e. the sentence, must be a construct with an empty *syntactique*, instead of containing the set-theoretical union of all the *syntactiques* of its composing signs.

2.12 Conclusion on Mel'čuk's sign concept

Once the use of the term *sign* is understood, the framework of the MTM turns out to be consistent. The author of the *CMG* does not feel that he deviates from tradition by adopting his usage. He refers (p. 102) to Meillet (1921: 30), who defines a word as resulting from the association of a given meaning to a given group of sounds which is liable to a given grammatical use. Nonetheless, Mel'čuk's use of *sign* for pairs of matching units of any two levels of representation finds less justification in linguistic tradition.

2.13 Morphology and phonology

The shallowest representation which Mel'čuk uses in his deductive system for morphology is the phonological level. The ultimate *surface phonetic* representation of the MTM is not regarded as relevant to morphology.

The phonological representation employed in the *CMG* consists exclusively of strings of phonemes. Phonemes are treated as inaccessable entities: no reference is made to the distinctive features that compose them. For all practical purposes, the "text" level of the author's morphology is a set of strings of symbols. This again recalls the computer science origin of the MTM.

The use of morphological considerations in defining the phonemic representation is banned, as is that of subphonemic considerations in defining the morphological representation. This has the advantage of reducing the risk of circularity in the deductive system: the adoption of a single interface between the phonological and the morphological compartments prevents a situation in which phonologists depend on morphological concept 'x' in defining phonological concept 'y', while morphologists simultaneously depend on 'y' to define 'x'. On the other hand, as will be shown presently, the modular structure of the MTM seems to jeopardize the naturalness of certain of Mel'čuk's choices.

2.14 Banning morphology from phonology

The ban on the use of morphological considerations in defining the phonemic representation results in certain deviations from traditional linguistic₁ analysis. Mel'čuk is prepared to accept these, as in the classic case of German *ch* juncture (p. 87). The traditional allophones [x] and [ç] corresponding to graphemic *ch* are generally considered to belong to the same phoneme /x/ on account of their complementary distribution:

the choice between [x] and [ç] is conditioned by the environment. This complementarity is partly governed by morpheme boundaries: in *tauchen* **tauch** ⊕ **en** 'dive' we find ['tauxən]; in *Tauchen* **tau** ⊕ **chen** 'small rope' we find ['tauçən] (example from Leopold 1948/66[4]: 215). Eager to avoid circularity, Mel'čuk does not involve morphological considerations in his phonological representation and is therefore forced to split up traditional /x/ into /x/ and /ç/.

We can apply the naturalness test here and ask ourselves whether we are prepared to accept all the consequences. Consider some implications for Dutch.

In the traditional analysis, the vowel phonemes /e/ and /o/ have allophones which are used only before final /r/ of a morph but not before /r/ belonging to the next morph. So there is an audible distinction between:

- *(dat hij) meer eist* **meer** ⊕ **eis** ⊕ **t** '(that he) demands more' ['me̦əʀɛjst],

and:

- *(dat hij) meereist* **mee** ⊕ **reiz** ⊕ **t** '(that he) travels together' ['muiʀɛjst].

This distinction is not denoted in the traditional phonological representation because it is conditioned by morph boundaries (cf. Cohen & al. 1972[2]: 14). Ignoring morph boundaries here, as Mel'čuk proposes, results in the addition of two vowels to the traditional Dutch system.

Such distinctions are not necessarily located on boundaries. Some Dutch speakers operate a length distinction in /ɛ/, /ɑ/ and /ɔ/ before /r/ indicating whether there is a morpheme boundary between /r/ and /s/ following it. These speakers have the following oppositions.

[vɛːʀst] *verst₁* **ver** ⊕ **st** 'farthest' vs. [vɛʀst] *verst₂* **vers** ⊕ **st** 'freshest';
[bɑːʀst] *barst₁* **bar** ⊕ **st** 'most barren' vs. [bɑʀst] *barst₂* **bars** ⊕ **st** 'sternest',
  barst₃ **barst** ⊕ **t** 'bursts',
  barst₄ **barst** 'burst';
[dɔːʀst] *dorst₁* **dor** ⊕ **st** 'most withered' vs. [dɔʀst] *dorst₂* **dors** ⊕ **t** 'threshes',
  dorst₃ **dorst** ⊕ **t** 'thirsts',
  dorst₄ **dorst** 'thirst'.

Such distinctions force us to add three more vowels to the traditional system for these speakers, each with a restricted distribution. These are not the only cases of juncture in Dutch, nor is Dutch a special language in possessing these phenomena.[14] So consistent banning of morphological criteria in phonological representations may result in a proliferation of phonemes. The limits of naturalness may come into sight here.

There may be reasons for examining alternatives for a strict compartmentalization of phonology and morphology. It is interesting to confront Mel'čuk's policy with the non-modular design presented in Ebeling 1978. Ebeling's deductive system, whose methodological objectives resemble those of the *CMG*, is intended to deal with syntax and semantics but, due to numerous feedback loops between linguistic₁ levels, it also covers a great deal of the area treated in the *CMG*. Ebeling defines morphological concepts on the basis of provisional phonological units, which themselves do not involve morphological concepts. His provisional phonemes, which include German */x/ and */ç/, are used in his morphological definitions. But later on in his deductive system, Ebeling revisits phonology: his definitive phonological definitions do involve morphological concepts and produce a merger of */x/ and */ç/. "Since no description can dispense with morph boundaries, the notation of a phonemic opposition between /x/ and /ç/ would indeed furnish superfluous information." Ebeling's definitions uniting morphologically conditioned allophones (Ebeling 1978: 495-499) even take account of the difference between lexical and grammatical morphs, whose boundaries sometimes condition phonemic distribution in different ways. It may be suggested that Mel'čuk's phonemes, too, be qualified not as definitive phonemes but only as operational units used for morphological analysis.

2.15 Banning phonology from morphology

We have seen that morphological concepts are banned in defining phonological representations in the *CMG*. Conversely, subphonemic concepts are banned in morphological definitions. From a morphological viewpoint, Mel'čuk's phonemes are black boxes.

Here, too, the naturalness test may be applied. Can we dispense with subphonemic concepts in our efforts to separate things that are felt to be different and to bring together things that we feel are the same? Consider the possibilities which manipulation of strings of complete phonemes leaves us for combining signs. Combining the *signifié* of a string x of phonemic material with another *signifié* may result in the addition of another string to x; or to the insertion of one or more strings in x; or to repetition of (a part of) x; or to the substitution of another string for (part of) x.[15] Here are some examples.

- The plural form *trees* is analysed as **tree** ⊕ **s**.
- The Arab plural form *rusūm* 'drawings' is analysed as **r-s-m** 'drawing' ⊕ **-u-ū-** 'plural') (p. 159).

- The Indonesian "plural" form *anak-anak* 'children' must be analysed as **anak** 'child' plus a repetition operation.
- The plural form *men* is analysed as **man** plus an operation which substitutes /ɛ/ for /æ/.[16]

The question is what happens when meanings correspond wholly or partly to a subset of the distinctive features constituting a phoneme, either partially or completely.

2.16 Overlapping morphemes

For the partial case, consider *wolves*, where the addition of the plural suffix entails voicing of the stem-final consonant /f/ of *wolf*. Mel'čuk's Russian example is *nesët* **neset** = **nes** ⊕ **et** 'carries', where the third person singular ending /ót/ entails palatalization of the preceding verb stem final /s/ (p. 118). Here the feature 'palatal' is not part of the *signifiant* /ót/ of **et**: it is accounted for in the *syntactique* of **et**, which contains an alternation instruction that takes care of the substitution of soft consonants for the corresponding hard consonants.

Such instances of alternation are likely to be quite frequent, since they cover not only changes of distinctive features which are conditioned by the morphological environment, as in *wolves* or *nesët*, but also those motivated by the phonological context. The phonological representation does not handle neutralization, which would involve morphological criteria. It does not, therefore, accept archiphonemes.[17] Thus, the stems of Russian singular *naród* **narod** 'people' and plural *naródy* **narody** must be denoted as /narót/ and /naród/ in the phonological representation used in the *CMG*. Whereas traditional structuralists would account for their correspondence in terms of the phonological ban on word-final voiced consonants in Russian, the *CMG* accounts for it in terms of morphological rules. (The rule which accounts for this particular alternation must probably be found in the *syntactique* of the stem morpheme, not that of the ending.)

A morphological *signifié* may even correspond exclusively to one or more phonemic features within a phoneme. The plural of Romanian masculine nouns may be a case in point. Let us assume, as Mel'čuk does, that it is derived from the singular by palatalization of the final consonant of the singular form. This implies that, say, /pom'/ is considered a plausible phonological representation of the plural form *pomi* corresponding to singular *pom* /pom/ 'tree'.[18] Here Mel'čuk assumes, as the *signifiant* of 'plural', a substitution rule in which the stem-final consonant is replaced by its palatalized counterpart. Although he employs the term *palatalization* (p. 159), suggesting reference to phonological alternation, the rule is purely morphological. *Pomi* is characterized as a *megamorph*, produced by an *Ablaut* operation on *pom*. The same type of rule is employed to express the *signifiant* of the preterite in German *las* 'read, preterite', as derived from the present tense stem *les* 'read, present tense' (p. 165).[19]

The naturalness test may fail to fully corroborate this practice, as some linguists may feel that there is a difference between these cases. The relationship between German *les* and *las* can only be expressed in a rule which lists the pairs of phonemes involved in *Ablaut* correspondences, as well as, for each pair, the lexical items to which they apply. Romanian plural palatalization, on the other hand, involves phonological features and enables a broader generalization. Due to the ban on dissecting phonemes into distinctive features, the *CMG* seems to assign to the morphology the work that the phonology may handle more elegantly.

In the above examples, the ban on dissecting phonemes seems to bring about a situation in which things which some linguists may feel are different are subsumed under a single heading. In other instances, it may lead to the splitting up of phenomena which tend to be regarded as belonging together. Mel'čuk adduces the Russian adjective *flótskij* **flot** $\oplus$ **sk** $\oplus$ **ij** 'of the navy' /flóck'ij/. One would like to see *flótskij* be treated on a par with, say, *kapitánskij* **kapitan** $\oplus$ **sk** $\oplus$ **ij** 'of the captain' /kapitánsk'ij/. This is prevented by the merger of stem-final /t/ of **flot** and initial /s/ of the suffix **sk** into the single phoneme /c/. This makes /flóck/ an indivisible megamorph (p. 159), while /kapitánsk/ is segmented into distinct strings /kapitán/ and /sk/. Of course it may be expected that Mel'čuk's further analysis will bring the two words together, but the problem will not arise in the first place if /c/ can be dissected into distinctive features, such that 'fricative' can be assigned to the ending and 'occlusive' to the stem.[20]

It may be concluded that, by adopting a linear phonological representation without feedback loops between phonology and morphology as the basis for his system of definitions, the author of the *CMG* stretches the limits of naturalness here and there, and deviates more from the the average linguistic$_2$ theory than his ambition to present a "neutral" theory suggests. In return, his choice for a tight compartmentalization of phonology and morphology yields the advantage of operating on a relatively simple and straightforward surface structure. It may be argued that the "intuitive" fit of his phonological representation may be enhanced at a later stage, after the establishment of the morphological definitions.

2.17   Morphology and semantics

If, on the surface side, the linear phonological representation is relatively simple to handle, the operational deep representation on which the definitions of the *CMG* are based is more complex. Technically, the surface syntactic representation of the MTM represents the upper bound for definitions of morphological units; but this level contains units that have passed unmodified from deeper representations.

Consider the *signifié* of the morphological unit **diamonds**. It contains the semantic units 'diamond' and 'plural', as expected. But the element 'diamond' can be dissected, within the same level, into a network consisting of more basic elements. Its canonical representation may contain such elements as 'precious' and 'stone'. Both representations can be a *signifié* of a morph **diamond**. This implies that users of Mel'čuk's deductive system must have an inkling of the devices used in the semantic representation level of the MTM. Here also, the computer-oriented origins of the MTM are transparent, as will be shown presently.

Speech-oriented linguists studying utterances in their search for invariant properties are confronted with speech as an interactive instrument, involving a particular typical division of labour between the encoder and the decoder(s). The frames of reference of speakers and hearers overlap to a considerable degree. Speakers are usually aware of the state of hearer's frames of reference, or think they are. A speaker's main goal will be to induce the hearer to apply changes to his frame of reference. In their interaction, speaker and hearer constantly adjust for changing circumstances. For speech-oriented linguists, a representation of invariants of meaning in utterances will in the first place reflect the means which a speaker uses in efforts to effectuate a change in the hearer's frame of reference. To them, the meaning of *Elvis is not dead* is not so much the fact that Elvis is alive but rather the appeal to the hearer to change the state of his frame of reference which contains (or rather: which the speaker assumes to contain; or even: which the speaker pretends to assume to contain) the *datum* that Elvis is reportedly dead.

Text involves a different division of labour between the encoder and the decoder. The encoder is rarely present in situations in which the text is decoded, and depends on the willingness and ability of the decoders to change their own frame of reference by means of the text. It is up to the decoder to secure the circumstances in which such changes are possible. The encoder cannot make a direct appeal to the decoder: he can only facilitate decoding by excluding reference to situational factors that are not guaranteed to be present in the situation of decoding.

This applies *a fortiori* to the type of text that interested the people who commissioned automatic semantic analysis and mechanical translation. They were not interested in a representation of the means and strategies that a speaker uses to convey a message. What they wished to see represented is information, i.e. the result of the change in the frame of reference that can be brought about by decoding the text. Text-oriented theoretical linguists were, consequently, set to develop a representation device that serves these goals: a representation model that registers the inferences that can be made from text in technical and newspaper articles. To them, the meaning of *Elvis is not dead* is the registered belief that Elvis is alive.

The resulting differences between the approaches adopted by speech- and text-oriented linguists can be illustrated by their treatments of two phenomena: pronominals and synonymy. They are dealt with below, followed by Mel'čuk's way of handling them.

2.18 Pronominals in the MTM

Speech-oriented linguists study the meaning of a pronoun by analysis of situations and potential situations in which it is used. Consider, as an example, a speech event featuring an occurrence of the pronoun *it*. When determining his communicative strategy, a speaker operates a set of assumptions regarding the state of the frame of reference of the hearer at the moment of the speech event. One of the assumptions is that the hearer will be able to identify an appropriate referent for *it*. Where do the appropriate referents in the situation come from? How do they enter the situation? In concrete speech situations, recent linguistic$_1$ utterances are one of the possible sources prompting appropriate referents for *it*. But they are not the only source of appropriate referents. In living speech, textual sources of pronominal reference compete with other elements in the spatial, temporal and communicative environment of an utterance: as often as not, pronominals refer directly to non-linguistic$_1$ elements in the concrete speech situation. *It* may point to something just mentioned, but just as well to any other item that is assumed to be relatively prominent in the hearer's frame of reference and may have been brought in there by being physically present in the situation or otherwise.[21] Speech-oriented linguists have to take account of all possibilities.

For text-oriented linguists, the relevant situational factors of an utterance are <u>only</u> its contiguous utterances, i.e. sentences preceding and following it. Reference to other situational factors is ruled out in a well-formed text inasmuch as their presence cannot be guaranteed in the situation of reading. Thus, text-oriented linguists are mainly interested in the use of pronominals insofar as they are instances of anaphora and (rarely) cataphora, i.e. insofar as 'they refer to preceding and following bits of text.[22] To them, pronominals organize the meaning of a text.

This is also Mel'čuk's conception of pronominals. In the *CMG*, pronominals are characterized as units which refer to other linguistic[1] units (p. 86). This definition is characteristic of the type of linguistics that is geared to written text.

2.19 Synonymy in the MTM

Now consider synonymy. Speech-oriented linguists hesitate to acknowledge its existence: even the minutest difference between words or utterances may reflect a difference in the communicative strategy of the speaker. *Elvis is alive* and *Elvis is not dead*, or an active and a passive construction, or even *oculist* and *eye-doctor*, to mention two classic examples (cf. Chomsky 1955 for references), are not synonymous to them. Bolinger 1977 provides an enlightening exposition of the minimal synonymy viewpoint.

Text-oriented linguists, on the other hand, are fond of synonymy. To them, semantic representations should only differ if they correspond to differences between communicated states of affairs. It was Schank's (1972: 105) goal to "represent the content of an utterance in such a way that the representation that we use is the same for paraphrases and translations of that utterance as for the utterance itself".

The *CMG*, too, seems to adhere to the text-oriented linguists' maximal synomymy viewpoint. Typically, the *signifié* of a passive suffix is a change in the *syntactique* of the verb, i.e. the distribution of the formal properties of the actants (pp. 147-148).[23] A meaning is the invariant shared by utterances that are paraphrases of each other (p. 42). A single not-too-complex meaning may correspond to numerous *signifiants*. Mel'čuk demonstrates how a French newspaper sentence consisting of 36 words can have over 50 million paraphrases, implying that a single meaning corresponds to that many different texts (pp. 44, 76-77). This approach to synonymy follows from the conception of meaning that is operated in the MTM.

2.20 Semes, meanings and *signifiés*

The semantic representation or meaning of an utterance consists of a complex network of primitive semantic elements called *semes* (p. 52). The semes in a representation are sometimes tagged, and are connected by tagged arrows indicating a predicative relationship between the connected elements. Elsewhere the term *meaning* (*sens*) is also used to refer to fragments of meanings (pp. 112-113).[24]

A meaning is not necessarily a *signifié*. The meaning 'first person' in French, for example, is not a *signifié* because it does not correspond to any *signifiant*: person is only expressed in the verb endings e and ons in, e.g., *je joue* 'I play' and *nous jouons* 'we play', which simultaneously express the meanings 'person' and 'number' (pp. 112-113). Conversely, a *signifié* is not necessarily a meaning, as it does not necessarily comprise units of the deepest, semantic, level of representation.

A semantic representation is not necessarily unique. The primitive status of semes may be only relative: a single node in a network of semes may, on closer inspection, stand for another network of semes. Thus, a three-node network that is read as α *is before* (*avant*) β may be replaced by an equivalent seven-node network in which the element 'before' is dissected into more primitive semes, and which is read as "t_1, which is the time of α, is larger than t_2, which is the time of β" (p. 51). In this analysis of *avant*, the author has apparently preferred an *AD* conception of time measurement to a *BC* one: time is viewed as something which inherently increases, not decreases. But Mel'čuk does not insist on this particular treatment, adducing it just for the sake of an example. Further semantic research may ultimately yield the most viable elementary representation.

The semantic network provides in the first place a formal representation of the part of the real world which a sentence allows the hearer to infer. As a result, in a combination of two signs, the meaning of one sign may *subtract*, i.e. cancel, meanings carried by the other sign in the *signifié* of the combination. "By adding the meaning (*sens*) of *false* to that of *diamond*, we modify the meaning of the latter lexeme by removing from it elements like 'precious', etc." (p. 143). So the semantic representation adopted in the *CMG* reflects the final result of the process of decoding the utterance in the hearer's frame of reference, viz. the absence of the element 'precious'. It does not represent the speaker's strategy for arriving at this result, since this representation should be expected to include the speaker's consideration that something which is presented as being as precious as a diamond, is not so after all. The MTM allows for the expression of speaker's intention by splitting up the semantic representation into a (*semantic-*)*communicative structure* and a *rhetoric structure* besides the *semantic structure* in its proper sense (p. 50), but the semantic representation as used in the *CMG* is restricted to the latter. The type of semantics practised in the *CMG* is *referential* or *real world* semantics, in which the meaning of *7 + 1* coincides with that of *2³* (cf. Ebeling 1978: 507).[25]

The question which arises here is whether the use of this type of semantics in the *CMG* excludes linguists who practise divergent approaches as potential users of Mel'čuk's morphological nomenclature. As pointed out above, Mel'čuk himself suggests that the MTM's treatment of morphology is even more neutral than that of the other components of language (p. 31). In other words, even if linguists may have different opinions on the exact semantic representation of *false diamond*, their differences do not affect its morphological treatment. This is the case if any discrepancies between the treatments of false and genuine diamonds are removed long before the morphological representation is reached. Whether all morphological choices in the *CMG* are independent of the adopted type of semantics remains to be seen. As far as the present writer is aware, *Volume I* contains only one instance of reference to real world semantics where a different type of semantics would yield different results. This instance, which illustrates the German *coordinative tmesis* problem, will be discussed in § 3.23.

3.   Mel'čuk's word: delimitating morphology from syntax

No treatment of the basic concepts of morphology can afford to ignore the word problem. Generally speaking, we face a choice between two conceptions of the discipline.

On the one hand, there is the classic conception, in which morphology is identified with the study of the changes of words. In this conception, the goal of morphology consists in pinpointing and organizing the differences and shared properties of words.

On the other hand, there is a more recent conception, in which morphology deals with morphemes, the conditions under which they change, and the conditions in which the variants of a morpheme occur. Linguists of the latter persuasion adopt an "agnostic" stance with respect to words.

The concept may play an auxiliary role, often depending on the language, but is not the central unit from which the discipline derives its *raison d'être*.

The choice between the conceptions is related to one's belief in the separability of morphology and syntax. To those who believe in a clear-cut distinction between these disciplines, 'word' is a pivotal concept, representing the lower bound of syntax: morphology begins where the linear arrangement of signs in a sentence is no longer free, i.e. is no longer capable of carrying independent meaning. Here linear arrangement must be described in terms of properties of the composing signs themselves. The agnostics point to numerous borderline cases, such as French clitics or Turkish suffixes, point to the arbitrary decisions which underly word division even in a language like English, and do not wish to be forced to mould their data of exotic languages into unsuitable or uninteresting models. Some of them end up with dividing up morphology between syntax and phonology.

As a result, the discussion on 'word' has been both popular and unpopular. The older literature is enormous. In the early twenties, Noreen provided and classified over twenty available definitions of the concept (Noreen 1923: 433-447). A great deal of the 1949 VIth International Congress of Linguists was devoted to the existence of a universal distinction between syntax and morphology. The stream of contributions to the discussion abated in the 1960s,[26] when the subject went out of fashion in the west.

In the Soviet tradition, on the other hand, 'word' always was a cornerstone of linguistic theory, not only in traditional grammar but also in theoretical linguistics, and especially after the "linguistic$_2$" wars of the late 1940s, in which Vinogradov 1972[2], whose first edition appeared in 1947 and which carries the programmatic subtitle *učenie o slove* 'teaching of the word', was targeted by the faction which was eventually defeated (cf. L'Hermitte 1987: 54).[27] In line with this tradition, and with the title of "Part I", Mel'čuk makes a clear choice in favour of the classic conception of morphology. To the author of the *CMG*, morphology is identical to the study of the word (p. 25). Most concepts in the *CMG* are defined with respect to their position in, or relation to, 'word'.

3.1 Universal vs. language-specific words

The problem of the universality of words imposes itself. The option to decide that 'word' is an undefined universal primitive concept, or that the definition of 'word' does not belong to the domain of morphology, lacks plausibility. But when it comes down to defining 'word', many linguists believe that, even though 'word' is both a universal and a definable concept, a universal definition is not attainable. It is not unusual for linguists who believe in words to provide language-specific definitions of 'word'.

Smirnickij once questioned this approach in a footnote. "If we do not operate with a general word concept, i.e. do not generalize from facts from different languages, we would not even be entitled to speak of a *Russian word*, or of a *French* or an *English word*. These very expressions already presuppose that we refer to certain common properties, besides properties which may vary between languages. We would have to speak about the Russian *slovo*, the French *mot* and the English *word*, analogously to the way in which we speak about the Russian *ruble*, the French *franc*, and the English *shilling*" (Smirnickij 1952: 184).

Nevertheless, after all these years, no universal definition of the concept has become commonplace. This has forced the author of the *CMG* to go to considerable lengths in order to identify the common properties of words in all languages, to discuss numerous problems and *nuances*, and to define a number of subtypes. The roughly 150 pages which are devoted to the concept could well be a self-sufficient monograph on the subject.

In his word definition, Mel'čuk makes an effort to reconcile the universal and the language- specific viewpoints. Before details will be dealt with, a general characterization of the definition is provided here.

3.2 Gradual properties and threshold levels

The definition of 'word' consists of a series of partial definitions identifying the properties which words of all languages have in common. The identified properties themselves are of a gradual nature: signs may posses them in different degrees. The properties are also to a certain extent interchangeable: in some cases, a sign is required to possess only a certain number (e.g. two out of three) of the identified properties in order to qualify as words. This means that the definitions as such cannot be applied unequivocally.

At several places, the author therefore introduces the term *sufficiently* (*suffisamment*) to indicate the degree in which a given defining property must be present. Thus, after defining a concept called autonomy, he indicates that a sign must be <u>sufficiently</u> autonomous to be a word (p. 187). He assumes what will be called here a *threshold level* for a property, which a sign must reach in order to qualify for the defined status.

To some readers, the use of the term *sufficiently* in definitions may arouse the suspicion of implicit circularity. Compare definitions of the type: *adults are people who are old enough.* But there are other ways of looking at the threshold level problem. We may assume, for example, that *sufficiently* implies that the required level of autonomy is left unspecified. Then, the results of the application of the definitions in the *CMG* to the languages of the world may vary according to the adopted threshold level. We may decide that fixing the threshold level itself is not a conceptual problem, and as such is not necessarily part of a deductive system of linguistic concepts. (Besides, in actual practice the relevant quantitative choices in linguistic analysis tend to be of a qualitative nature: they oppose 'zero' to 'something', or 'one' to 'more than one', or 'few' to 'many'.)

3.3 Language-specific criteria

In fact, Mel'čuk provides criteria which are used to determine threshold levels. The levels are fixed accordingly so as to make the outcome of the definition for a given language more regular from a morphological, phonological or syntactic viewpoint. Application of these criteria is, therefore, based on language-specific properties, and consequently provides language-specific threshold levels (e.g. on p. 187).

Operating language-specific considerations is risky in a deductive system. There is nothing wrong with a universal criterion whose application to specific languages produces trivial results in some languages. A definition which produces words which coincide with morphemes in one language (it is sometimes said that Chinese approaches this situation) and with sentences in another (Yukaghir is sometimes thought to approach this situation) is, methodologically speaking, perfectly acceptable. But if we are told to adapt our criteria when applying them to specific languages in order to produce the desired results, we are far from developing a universal system of concepts. If the properties needed to define words vary from one language to another, 'word' ceases to be a single concept.

Picking up Smirnickij's analogy, as we speak of a *French franc*, a *Belgian franc* and a *Swiss franc*, we could also speak of a *French word*, a *Russian word* and a *Turkish word*, each with a different definition. But, as we can spend French francs in Belgium and Belgian francs in France, we can define French words in Russian and Russian words in French. Every definition based in turn on the concept of word should therefore, technically speaking, be marked for the type of word used, as we would like to know whether we are dealing with French or Belgian

208

centimes, or with French franc or Belgian franc millionaires: we must account for the absence of a common francness. Failing to do so would turn all typological comparison of languages into sand castles: the parallels and differences between languages would be by-products of the parallels and differences of the definitions which we impose on them, not of the languages themselves.

Nevertheless, as we shall see below, a case can be made for the practice adopted in the *CMG*. In principle, the language-specific properties on the basis of which a threshold level is determined for a language are based on properties which can be expressed without mentioning specific languages. The language-specific criterion can be formulated as a universal condition: "if the phonology, morphology or syntax of a language has properties X and Y, then the following threshold level for the word definition results for that language". In Smirnickij's terms, Mel'čuk provides us with exchange rates.

The remaining question is, then, whether properties X and Y can be established without using the word definition for which X and Y are needed; in other words, whether we can avoid circularity. This question can be dealt with when the complete *CMG* is available.

3.4 Defining words

In what follows, three aspects of Mel'čuk's word definition will be treated. We shall start by discussing the status of the units to be defined in the MTM (§ 3.5). Then we shall discuss the definition itself (§ 3.6 to § 3.23). Finally we shall deal with the threshold conditions which are imposed in order to fine-tune the definition for specific languages (§ 3.24 ff.)

3.5 Word forms vs. lexemes

Before tackling the actual definition of 'word', Mel'čuk starts with some seemingly trivial but actually extremely useful preliminary distinctions that are not specific to 'word' but facilitate talking about sign systems in general. The necessity of the distinctions to be introduced becomes obvious when we try to count the words in a sentence containing homonyms, different forms of the same word, several occurrences of the same word, etc., as in the author's phrase (p. 98):

Quand je me suis levé, les deux hommes se   sont aussi levé
When I me am lifted the two men   themselves are also lifted

du   siège et   se   sont approchés de moi.
from the seat   and themselves are approaced of me
'When I rose, the two men also rose from the seat and approached me'

Are the two occurrences of *se* 'oneself' one or two words? Are *levé* 'lifted, singular' and *levés* 'lifted, plural' one or two words? Are *suis* 'am' and *sont* 'are' the same word? And *les* 'the' and *du* 'from the'? Etc. The result of the count varies according to whether we count:

- *signifiants*, *signifiés* or signs;
- items of the *langue* (in the text-oriented linguists' conception, i.e. dictionary entries) or items of the *parole* (i.e. occurrences).

Applying these distinctions, we can set up a grid containing six possible ways of singling out and identifying manifestations of 'word' (the numbers which identify the resulting conceptions of 'word' are in accordance with the list in Zaliznjak 1969: 43-52).

- by their *signifiants* in the dictionary (the text-oriented linguists' *langue*):   'word$_2$';
- by their *signifiants* in running text (the text-oriented linguists' *parole*):   'word$_1$';
- by their *signifiés* in the dictionary: 'word$_5$';
- by their *signifiés* in running text: 'word$_6$';
- by their signs in the dictionary: 'word$_4$';
- by their signs in running text: 'word$_3$'.

The grid can be visualized as follows.

	dictionary item	items in running text
signifié	word$_5$	word$_6$ word$_6$ word$_6$
sign	word$_4$	word$_3$ word$_3$ word$_3$
signifiant	word$_2$	word$_1$ word$_1$ word$_1$

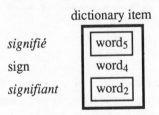
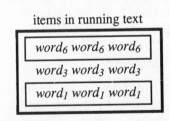

All six word concepts have been used in Soviet linguistics. Zaliznjak identified most cells of the grid. 'Word$_3$' in its purest form is found in Gladkij 1983: 193-194 (as *lexically meaningful segment*). 'Word$_6$' was implicitly used in Uspenskij's (1957) definition of 'part of speech'.

Mel'čuk focuses on two word concepts, which he considers to be the really pertinent ones (p. 99).

His first 'word' is a sign in the sense of the MTM, i.e. a building brick in the *langue* made up of a *signifiant* and a *signifié*. In order to avoid confusion with the other conceivable word concepts, he refers to it as *word form* (*mot-forme*), a term whose Russian original *slovoforma* was introduced in Smirnickij 1954: 18. Mel'čuk distinguishes two types of word forms:

- *word forms of the parole*, i.e. Zaliznjak's *concrete* word forms and more or less correspond with words$_3$, and:
- *word forms of the langue*, i.e. Zaliznjak's *abstract* word forms and more or less correspond with 'word$_4$'.

(Cf. Zaliznjak 1969: 44, where *forme lexicale* is used instead of *mot-forme*.)

Mel'čuk's distinction between word forms of the *parole* and word forms of the *langue* will be dealt with in § 3.19.

The author's second word concept unites word forms which have identical lexical *signifiés*. It is referred to as *lexeme*, which corresponds to 'word$_5$' of the grid which was presented above (or 'word$_6$' when occurring in running text) and whose precise definition will be discussed in § 4. The word *word* (*tout court*) is banned altogether in technical discourse in the *CMG*.[28]

In Mel'čuk's French example given above, the two occurrences of *se* are instances of the same word form se, since they have the same *signifiant* and the same *signifié*. Since me has the same *signifié* (at least in the author's analysis) as se, the two word forms belong to the same lexeme SE.

Since lexemes are sets of word forms, 'word form' is the key concept to be defined first. Before doing so, Mel'čuk defines a number of auxiliary concepts.

3.6 Autonomy

Most word definitions are based on some conception of autonomy, i.e. a constellation of properties which characterize words as such and cannot be attributed to parts of them. Generally, three types of autonomy are used, which will be discussed below:
- phonological autonomy (§ 3.7);
- prosodic autonomy (§ 3.8 to § 3.11);
- syntactic autonomy (§ 3.12 ff.).

3.7 Phonological autonomy

The complications of basing word definitions on phonological properties have by now become well known. In some languages, words are not marked by phonological properties. Trubeckoj compared phonological properties indicating word boundaries with traffic signs marking road crossings and the like: they are present at some crossings in some towns but most crossings are not marked and there are towns which lack them altogether (Trubetzkoy 1939: 242). In languages where phonological properties characterize words, such as Russian, they do not fully coincide with the other characteristics of words: many prepositions make up a single "phonological word" with the word which follows it: the group *v górode* 'in a town', possesses all phonological properties which characterize independent words.

In linguistic practice, the discrepancies between the results of phonological definitions of 'word' and definitions which employ alternative criteria are nearly always resolved in favour of the latter. Thus, the observation that the Russian preposition *v* 'in' behaves phonologically as if it were a part of a contiguous word is no reason for linguists to deny it its autonomous word status.

What is more important, no phonological criteria seem to be universally applicable: they must be specified for each language, which contradicts the principle of a universal system of definitions.

Unlike earlier word definitions in the Russian tradition, which strongly involve phonological criteria,[29] the definition of 'word form' in the *CMG* makes only limited use of them. As we shall see in § 3.27, Mel'čuk assigns a certain role to phonological properties when determining his threshold levels.

3.8 Prosodic or strong autonomy

Mel'čuk's central word form definition rests on two types of autonomy, called *strong* and *weak*. They can be regarded as manifestations of prosodic and syntactic autonomy, respectively.

Strong autonomy is based on the principle of the *free form*, as proposed in Bloomfield 1926/66[4]: 27. A sign X is said to be strongly autonomous if there is a complete utterance (p. 84; cf. § 2.6 above) which contains just X, i.e. if it can be bounded by pauses (p. 170). Thus, *professeur* 'teacher' represents a strongly autonomous sign since it can be used as an answer to the question *quel est le métier de ton père?* 'what is your father's occupation?'.

3.9 Minimum free forms

Bloomfield goes on to define words as strongly autonomous signs which cannot contain other such signs: his *minimum free forms*. But, as he

212

acknowledges, strong autonomy does not include all words (Bloomfield 1933: 179). Some items which we would like to treat as words (*the*, *a*) do not occur independently between pauses.[30] French finite verb forms, for example, require a subject and are not, therefore, strongly autonomous. But at least it may be assumed that strongly autonomous signs do not include signs that are smaller than words. The *CMG* contains refinements of Bloomfield's definition.

3.10 Metalinguistic statements

Mel'čuk mentions the usual *caveat* (cf. Nida 1949[2]: 81; Lyons 1971: 201) that metalinguistic statements must be excluded (p. 170), since they may include utterances in which signs smaller than words occur referring to themselves, Thus, a possible utterance *ez*, in which the suffix of the French second person plural verb ending is used as an answer to the question *quel est le suffixe de cette forme?* 'what is the suffix of this form?', must be prevented from turning the sign **ez** into a strongly autonomous sign. This should not be a problem, since in metalinguistic statements the *signifié* 'ez' (or even 'ez') of -**ez** is distinct from its usual *signifié* 'second person plural'. In other words, we are dealing with two different signs.

3.11 Intonation features

Mel'čuk does not treat the problem of separating miscarriages from full-term utterances. The former often occur in ordinary speech, e.g. as a result of interruptions or because the speaker changes his mind. They regularly contain fragments of words, which must be set aside when applying the definition. Nida (1949[2]: 81) points out that the type of free forms that is intended by the definition is characterized by special intonation features. It is not so much the pauses that make a sign strongly autonomous but its potential to sustain a complete intonation contour. It seems attractive, therefore, to define a complete utterance in terms of intonation patterns instead of pauses. This entails the assumption that every language possesses a category of signs whose *signifiants* are intonation patterns and whose *signifiés* contain a 'complete message' seme. A strongly autonomous sign can then be defined as a sign whose *syntactique* allows it to be combined with the category of signs containing the 'complete message' seme.

In the approach adopted in the *CMG*, assuming a 'complete message' seme should not be a problem: such *signifiés* are more likely to belong to the universal semantic core than some of the meanings which the author mentions as belonging there. Being a communication device, a language is bound to possess means to mark the organization of a message. A language in which 'sex' or 'ownership' cannot be expressed is implausible in the biological or sociological frameworks which are part of the foundations of Mel'čuk's referential semantics, but is anthropologically conceivable. Nevertheless, as pointed out in § 1.7, the assumption of the very universal core may arouse the suspicion of circularity.

3.12 Syntactic or weak autonomy

The cases that strong autonomy cannot solve, i.e. signs which are part of strongly autonomous signs but are not strongly autonomous signs themselves (p. 171), include v 'in' in v górode 'in a town', a in a diamond, fume 'smokes' in papa fume une pipe 'father smokes a pipe', and -ish in boyish. The author introduces three syntactic criteria, "at least some" of which must be satisfied to qualify for weak autonomy (p. 171). The criteria are separability, distributional variability and permutability. They are discussed below.

3.13 Separability

A non-strongly autonomous sign X which is part of an autonomous sign Y is separable if another autonomous sign Z can be inserted between it and the remaining part of Y without affecting the semantic relationships and semantic contents of Y (p. 173).

Thus, the article a, whose signifié occurs in 'a' ⊕ 'diamond' in the autonomous sign a diamond, is separable if we assume that there is a strongly autonomous sign genuine whose signifié 'genuine' occurs along with 'a' ⊕ 'diamond' in the autonomous sign a genuine diamond. The circumstance that this does not work if false would be inserted, false changing the meaning of a diamond in Mel'čuk's semantic conception, does not affect the definition.

Similarly, the sign v, whose signifié occurs in 'in' ⊕ 'town' in the autonomous sign v gorode, is separable if we assume that there is a weakly autonomous sign bol'šom whose signifié 'large, locative' occurs along with 'in' ⊕ 'town' in the autonomous sign v bol'šom gorode 'in the large town'.

214

3.14 Recursive definitions

The sign Z to be inserted may be either strongly or weakly autonomous (p. 173). This makes the definition look circular: weak autonomy is apparently used as a criterion in the definition of weak autonomy. In fact it is not. We are dealing with a *recursive definition*, in which a concept is defined in an incremental manner. Definitions of this type were introduced into linguistics by Bar-Hillel (1953/70: 304 ff.) and were popular in Soviet mathematical linguistics since their introduction in Revzin 1961. Their structure is as follows.

1. First, a *catalyst* concept X^s (say, strong autonomy) is defined or assigned. Concept X^s is employed in a definition of X^w (weak autonomy).
2. Subsequently, X^s and X^w are collapsed into a concept X (autonomy *tout court*).
3. Concept X is substituted for X^s in the definition which was used to define X^w, in order to define a new concept which is also labelled X^w. So after step 3, the contents of X^w as defined in step 1 have changed.
4. Step 2 is repeated with the new X^w.
5. Etc. This goes on until the domain of the definition is exhausted, i.e. until the results of the nth application of the definition coincide with those of the n-1th.

So the semblance of circularity is due to the practice of shifting the label (X^w) to the outcomes of subsequent definitions.[31]

Thus, the sign **bol'šom**, being a locative form, which does not occur without a preposition, does not necessarily have to be strongly autonomous itself. It may have been isolated as a weakly autonomous sign from the strongly autonomous sign **v bol'šom** 'in the big one' by means of the insertion of the strongly autonomous sign **očen'** 'very'.

3.15 Distributional variability

A non-strongly autonomous sign X is *distributionally variable* if it makes up autonomous signs in combination with signs Y^1, ..., Y^n belonging to different distribution classes without changing its semantic contents or its relationship with Y^1, ..., Y^n (p. 176).

The *distribution class* of a sign Y is the set of signs which occurs in the same (linear and semantic) contexts as Y (p. 85). In his exemplification, Mel'čuk indicates that he conceives of parts of speech as making up distribution classes.

The Russian question particle *li* seems to provide a likely example of distributional variability. (The author himself adduces an example from

Quechua on pp. 176-177.) The sign li marks the focus of the question, which can be expressed by a noun, an adjective, an adverb or a verb. At the same time, li cannot be separated from the focused item.

Distributional variability looks like an easy criterion to fulfil. Consider English ish, which occurs with both nouns and adjectives (boyish, greenish) without changing its *signifié*, as a result of which it qualifies as distributionally variable. On the other hand, ish, like in fact most suffixes, is not compatible with all items within a part of speech (?familyish, ?ferociousish). So nouns and adjectives each are split up into several distribution classes. As a consequence, even the plural suffix s may qualify for distributional variability: it combines with most distribution classes that arise as a result of the irregular behaviour of suffixes like ish (boys, families). The author makes clear, however, that distributional variability is a matter of degree. It is obvious that Russian li is much more distributionally variable than is English plural s. It is plausible, therefore, that a threshold level can be fixed for this criterion which can be reached by li while being out of reach for s.

3.16 Permutability

Finally, a non-strongly autonomous sign is *permutable* if its position in the linear order with respect to the sign(s) with which it makes up an autonomous sign may change without prompting a change of semantic contents (p. 177).

Mel'čuk uses this criterion to handle movable clitics, such as Spanish le 'him' in *le encontré en Granada* and *encontrele en Granada*, both meaning 'I met him in Granada' (p. 179).[32]

So far, it has been assumed that the units on which autonomy is defined are complete signs. But some uncertainty arises when studying the author's treatment of French clitic pronouns. These represent a classic touchstone for word definitions. They are hardly separable. They occur only with verbs and are not distributionally variable. They must gain their autonomy on account of their permutability. But permutation of French clitics entails a change in the *signifiants* of such words. Compare *ne me quitte pas* 'don't leave me' and *quitte-moi* 'leave me', where me and moi must be regarded as the same sign if we want permutability to yield autonomous signs. The author accepts this practice, not only for clitic and full forms of pronouns but also for finite forms and the infinitive of verbs. He generalizes it to all autonomy definitions (p. 178).

As far as the present writer is aware, this new interpretation of autonomy implies that neither the *syntactiques* nor the *signifiants* of signs

216

216

are in fact involved in its definitions.[33] The identity of the operated sign unit is determined by the *signifiés* and the <u>positions</u> of the corresponding *signifiants* in the linear strings. We are not dealing here with word forms but with Uspenskij's mysterious words$_6$ referred to in § 3.5: *signifiés* in running text.

If this conclusion is correct, French clitics can be handled in a simpler way. If **me** and **moi** are treated as interchangeable, then, since **moi** is strongly autonomous, **me** automatically has the same status. This renders the permutability criterion redundant.

Even if we split up clitic **moi**$_1$ and independent **moi**$_2$, considering them to have different *signifiés*, collapsing of verb forms will take care of separability, as in the author's example (p. 179): cf. *il le raconte* 'he tells it' vs. *il l'entend raconter* 'he hears it told', in which **le/l'** 'it' is separated from **raconte/raconter** 'tell' by a strongly autonomous sign **entend/entendre/entends** 'hear'.

We may conclude here that permutability fails to assign autonomy status to French clitics when applying the original complete-sign interpretation, in which **me** and **moi** are regarded as different signs, whereas it is superfluous when applying the new interpretation, in which **me** and **moi** are regarded as the same sign.

The joint application of separability, distributional variability and permutability determines weak autonomy. A sign X is weakly autonomous if there exists a sign Y of which X is a part and in which X is separable, variable or permutable (p. 171). As pointed out above, a sign does not have to satisfy all criteria to qualify as a word. Moreover, the <u>degree</u> in which a sign satisfies the criteria plays an important role in determining autonomy.

The definition of autonomy involves thresholds on various parameters: many or few contexts involved; many or few distribution classes, etc. (cf. pp. 181-182). The threshold must be high in the case of distributional variability, in order to keep derivative suffixes such as **ish** out. It must be low in the case of permutability, in order to keep the French clitics in. The thresholds for weak autonomy are language-specific (p. 171). The criteria for establishing the thresholds will be dealt with in § 3.24 ff.

3.17· Word forms of the *langue*

After defining strong and weak autonomy, Mel'čuk merges them into a single concept (p. 187), to be used in his definition of 'word form'. The concept to be defined is that of *word form of the langue*, which is an <u>autonomous sign which cannot be broken up into autonomous signs</u> (p. 188).[34]

Thus, the autonomous sign **papa fume une pipe** is not a word form, because it can be represented as a series of autonomous signs: **papa** ⊕ **fume** ⊕ **une** ⊕ **pipe**. These individual signs, on the other hand, are words, since they cannot be represented in smaller autonomous signs. The autonomous sign **boyish** is a word form. It can be represented as **boy** ⊕ **ish** but **ish** is not autonomous.

3.18 The non-uniqueness of word forms

Note that, technically speaking, the definition does not guarantee unique word segmentations. Consider, for example, a language containing the following signs.

A; A ⊕ B; A ⊕ B ⊕ C; B ⊕ C; C;

as well as many other signs composed of signs **D**, ..., **Z**.

Since A and C are strongly autonomous, A ⊕ B ⊕ C must be split up into words. Now what to do with sign B? It cannot be a word, since it is not even weakly autonomous, so it must be joined to A or C. The two remaining options are:

- A ⊕ B and C;
- A and B ⊕ C.

In this symmetric situation, the word definition does not indicate a preference.

An approximative instance of **B** is the French sign **ès**, which is normally used to indicate fields of arts and science in which degrees can be obtained: cf. *bachelier ès sciences* 'bachelor of science', *diplomé ès lettres* 'arts graduate', *spécialiste ès otages* '(ironically) hostage specialist'. **Ès** is not strongly autonomous, hardly separable and hardly distributionally variable, and not permutable. We have to settle for a non-unique solution here.

The description of Mel'čuk's word definition given above is a simplification. The definition includes some additional conditions and variants in order to provide for special cases. Two of them are discussed below.

3.19 Word forms of the *parole* vs. word forms of the *langue*

In some languages, fragments of what many of us would like to regard as word forms are permutable or separable. Consider German prefix **an** in the word form **anrufe** 'call up (on the telephone)', which alternates in certain syntactic circumstances with **rufe ... an** (cf. § 2.7 above for details). According to the definition of word forms of the *langue* as described above, this makes **an** weakly autonomous, and turns it into a separate word form.

Mel'čuk adduces Hungarian examples in which such prefixes can even make up independent utterances and be strongly autonomous. The question *megkapta a levelemet?* 'did you receive my letter?' can be answered with *meg* 'yes', which literally means 're-' (p. 202). According to the definition of word forms of the *langue* as described above, this makes **meg** strongly autonomous, and turns it into a separate word form.

We might call **an** and **meg** *floating prefixes*. They raise two questions. How do we wish the definition to treat them, and how does the definition treat them?

As to the first question, Mel'čuk prefers to regard a floating prefix as a part of the word form to which it belongs. His main argument is that prefixed verbs such as **an** ⊕ **rufen** are lexemes, whose behaviour coincides with that of other prefixed verbs in German or Hungarian, (e.g. German **unter** ⊕ **liegen**, 'be susceptible to'), except, of course, for their separability (p. 203). A word definition which produces separate treatments for the two groups should be avoided. (The language-specific criterion which is invoked here is language-specific *paradigmatic attraction*, and will be discussed in § 3.26.) Mel'čuk's bottom line is that here, as in numerous other cases, the traditional description of German or Hungarian has been adopted as the norm to be emulated by the system of definitions, even if our knowledge does not permit us to be certain whether it has been sufficiently well-founded (p. 203).

If we treat **an** and **rufen** as parts of the same lexeme, how should we handle specific occurrences of **an**, as in *ich rufe ihn an* 'I call him up'? Mel'čuk accepts discontinuous word forms in certain circumstances (viz. when a clitic is inserted in a word form; see the Portuguese example in § 3.28 and § 3.29) but not in this case.

Here, the author introduces this distinction between *word forms of the langue* and *word forms of the parole*: the former are signs which are always autonomous, the latter only in a particular context (p. 200). The sign **an** is a word form of the *parole* because it is autonomous in *ich rufe ihn an* but not in *daß ich ihn anrufe* 'that I call him up'. The sign **anrufe** is a word form of the *langue* because it is autonomous in all contexts.

The idea is clear and attractive but the corresponding formal definitions are less so, at least as far as the present writer can see. The

219

definition of word forms of the *parole* requires that there is a context
in which they are sufficiently autonomous (p. 187). (Also, they may not
be split up and must resemble other word forms of the language in
accordance with language-specific criteria.) It would seem that just about
every word form will pass this simple test, so the definition does not
single out a special group of floating prefixes.

We may suspect that the underlying intention is to single out word
forms which fulfil this weak criterion but fail to satisfy stricter conditions
which apply to full-fledged word forms of the *langue* as described earlier.
In other words: word forms of the *langue* are intended to be a subset
of the word forms of the *parole*. Both **an** and **anrufen** should be word
forms of the *parole* but only **anrufen** should have the chance to attain
the status of word form of the *langue*.

But then it is not clear why floating prefixes would fail to meet the
requirements for word forms of the *langue* as formulated in the *CMG*.
Consider the definition of strong autonomy as given on p. 170. It says
that a sign **X** is strongly autonomous if there <u>exists</u> an utterance in
which **X** occurs in zero context. The *parole* sign **papa** 'father' in *papa
fume une pipe* 'father smokes a pipe' is autonomous because there is also
a *parole* sentence consisting of the same *langue* sign in zero context:
papa! 'father!'

This fully applies to our Hungarian example **meg**. Since it cannot be
split up, there is, formally speaking, no way of preventing it from ob-
taining the status of word form of the *langue*.

The same goes for weak autonomy. According to its definition on
p. 171, a sign **X** is weakly autonomous if there <u>exists</u> an utterance in
which **X** occurs in a context Ψ in which it is separable or permutable,
i.e. there exists another context Ψ' in which **X** is separated from its
immediate environment in **Y** without affecting its semantic and syntactic
relationships. The *parole* sign **une** 'a' is autonomous because there exist
a *parole* context (*une*) *pipe* '(a) pipe', and a *parole* context (*une*) *grande
pipe* '(a) big pipe'.

All this applies to our German floating prefix **an**. In view of existence
of the utterance *ich rufe an* 'I call up', in which **an** can be separated from
anything in front of it almost endlessly (*rufe ihn an* 'call him up', *rufe
ihn morgen an* 'call him up tomorrow'), **an** can only be qualified as a
word form of the *langue*.

Thus, one instance of autonomy of a sign is enough to grant autonomy
to all its occurrences, at least according to the definition as described
above. After establishing the autonomy of **an** or **meg** on the basis of

220

comparison of two occurrences, all of their occurrences must be considered word forms. As a result, *anrufe* and *megkapta* are split up into *an rufe* and *meg kapta*. Once a floating prefix, always a separate word form.

This calls for a revision of the pertinent definitions. What seems to be needed is a consistent and explicit distinction between *langue* and *parole* (in the text-oriented linguists' sense), not just in the definition of 'word form', but all the way, starting with the signs themselves, and applied in all autonomy definitions.

Let X indicate a sign of the *langue* and X', X'', ... occurrences of X in the *parole*. (It must be borne in mind that occurrences exist only in specific contexts.) Then autonomy could be defined first for occurrences in the *parole*. We shall start with weak autonomy.

Basically, a definition of weak autonomy of the *parole* might run as follows. An occurrence X' of X, in context Ψ' in which semantic and syntactic relationships ρ_1, ... ρ_m hold between X' and occurrences A', ..., N' of signs A, ..., N, is strongly autonomous if there exists an occurrence X'' of X in a context Ψ'' such that semantic and syntactic relationships ρ_1, ... ρ_m hold between X'' and occurrences A'', ..., N'' of signs A, ..., N, in which the position of the *signifiant* of X' with respect to the adjacent *signifiants* of A', ..., N' in the linear order is not fully identical to that of the *signifiant* of X'' with respect to the adjacent *signifiants* of A'', ..., N''. (This definition is not complete. Conditions on ρ_1, ... ρ_m must be added.)

Strong autonomy for the *parole* could be defined as follows. An occurrence X' of X in context Ψ', is strongly autonomous if there exists an occurrence X'' of X in context Ψ'' such that Ψ'' is zero.

A word form of the *parole* could, then, be defined as an undivisible *parole* sign which is either weakly or strongly autonomous. This provides us with a segmentation of *parole* signs into word forms of the *parole*, which can serve as a basis for the definition of word forms of the *langue*. A word form of the *langue* could perhaps be defined as a *langue* sign such that all of its occurrences are word forms of the *parole* (or whatever modifications are deemed necessary in order to keep the clitics on board).

This approach seems to take care of the German floating prefixes. The occurrence of **an** in rufe $\oplus$ **an** qualifies as a word form of the *parole* but, since **an** in **an** $\oplus$ rufe does not qualify as such, the *langue* sign **an** cannot gain word form status.

The **meg** problem, however, has not been solved. It holds for every occurrence of **meg** that there is another occurrence in zero context.

Consequently, all occurrences of **meg** qualify as strongly autonomous, which makes **meg** a word form of the *langue*. Maybe strong autonomy is not such a strong idea after all. We shall return to it in § 3.22.[35]

It is interesting to compare Ebeling's way of handling floating prefixes with Mel'čuk's approach. In his deductive system, the need for a homogeneous treatment of *rufe ... an* and *anrufe* is acknowledged, but its author adopts a solution which is precisely the opposite of Mel'čuk's. He introduces a rule which splits up *anrufe*. The existence of such phrases as *rufe ihn an* 'call him up' is for him an argument to split, in spite of the non-separability of the constituents of *anrufe* (Ebeling 1978: 433-434): once a word boundary, always a word boundary.

So we see that, whereas Mel'čuk, unlike Ebeling, makes no bones about deviating from the results of structuralist tradition in phonological matters (as in the classic case of German *ch* juncture discussed in § 2.14), the latter is, more than Mel'čuk, prepared to ignore certain achievements of traditional grammar in morphology.

For Mel'čuk's system, it might be suggested to accept floating suffixes for the time being as full-fledged word forms, and to remove them at a later stage by means of a revised definition of the concept. After the definition of 'lexeme', for example, the unitary semantic structure of **anrufen** may provide useful new criteria for revising or refining the present definition of 'word form'. After all, the reason for wishing to assign a special status to **an** is that we want to treat it as part of **anrufen** in the lexicon (p. 201), where facilities for assigning a morphological structure to phraseologisms are needed anyway.

3.20 Truncation

Mel'čuk makes another special provision in order to include cliticized words, such as **'ve** in English *could've*, in the set of word forms of the *langue*. Although **'ve** is neither strongly nor weakly autonomous, it should be a word form. Therefore the definition of 'word form of the *langue*' includes the rule that, if there is exactly one word form which can replace a non-autonomous sign in all contexts, that sign is regarded as a word form itself.

Thus, since there is a sign **have**, which can always replace **'ve** without affecting the grammaticality or meaning of the sentence, **'ve** counts as a word (p. 188). The sign **spec** in Russian *speckomíssija* **spec** ⊕ **komissija** 'special committee', however, is not a word form, there being no word form which can <u>always</u> replace it. Depending on the case, gender and number of the noun to which it is attached, **spec** must be replaced by different flexional forms of the adjective *speciál'nyj* 'special': *speciál'naja* 'special (feminine)', *speciál'noe* 'special (neuter)', etc. (p. 189).[36]

This does not prevent the author from assigning word form status to 'd, which may stand for *had*, *should* or *would*, or to 's$_1$ although it may stand for either *has* or *is* (p. 191; 's$_2$ is the possessive and will be dealt with in § 3.27). A possible argument in favour of distinguishing the relationship between *had* and *should* from that between, say, *speciál'nyj* 'special, masculine' and *speciál'naja* 'special, feminine' is the lexical nature of the first distinction as opposed to the flexional nature of the second. Anticipating the author's definitions of lexemes and flexion, which will be dealt with in § 4, we can observe that circularity in the system of definitions can probably be avoided for these instances, but may turn up in such cases as 'll, which may stand for **shall** or **will** in *I'll* but only for **will** in *you'll*. But we'll have to see the forthcoming volumes of the *CMG* to find out.

3.21 Conflict between strong and weak autonomy

In his word form definitions, Mel'čuk no longer distinguishes between strong and weak autonomy: the two types are considered equivalent (p. 187). But what happens if the two criteria contradict each other?

Consider English or German compound nouns, such as **horse** ⊕ **race**, **fremd** ⊕ **sprache** 'foreign language'. The composing signs are strongly autonomous, so since the definitions of weak autonomy apply only to signs that are not strongly autonomous, one would expect the combinations to split up. But the author applies the separability criterion: *Fremd* and *sprache* cannot be separated or interchanged without affecting the semantic relationships between them.

He therefore decides that such combinations are single word forms, without indicating how it can be prevented that **fremd** and **sprache** carry over to all contexts the strong autonomy status which they acquire in zero context. The only possible consideration which the present writer can imagine, is that **fremd**$_1$ occurring as a free form is not the same sign as **fremd**$_2$ in **fremdsprache**.

It is quite plausible that there is a semantic difference between *Fremdsprache* and *fremde Sprache*, which may be assumed to contain **fremd**$_1$.[37] But the question is whether the difference can be ascribed to the presence of two homonymous signs **fremd**$_1$ and **fremd**$_2$ in the language. Compound nouns are an open class in German, involving not only adjectives but also verb stems and other nouns. Splitting up **fremd** would entail splitting up innumerable morphs into homonymous pairs expressing a <u>systematic</u>

semantic difference. It seems more plausible that the compound as a whole carries the specific meaning shared by all compounds. But this type of meaning does not differ essentially from the meanings carried by syntactic constructions: we cannot use it to prevent strong autonomy from splitting up *Fremdsprache* into two word forms.

3.22 Exit strong autonomy?

Now if strong autonomy is too strong to produce the desired results, it might be proposed to do without it altogether. The concept has shown to be quite dubious: the problems in applying the minimum free form criterion were pointed out in § 3.9 ff.

More important, strong autonomy may well turn out to be a superfluous criterion. Minimum free forms are undoubtedly an important tool in a discovery procedure, and they will serve well to identify a large majority of word forms by means of a simple procedure. But since our deductive system is not a discovery procedure but a calculus, and since a sophisticated system of definitions must be developed anyway in order to cover the last 10%, it may be worth examining whether weak autonomy can do the job of strong autonomy as well. The present writer is not aware of strongly autonomous signs which are not at the same time weakly autonomous (usually separable), with the exception of instances like Hungarian **meg**, which, as discussed in § 3.19, represents the very instances of strong autonomy which we would like to dispense with.

A likely objection to this proposal is the function of strong autonomy as a catalyst in the recursive definition of separability. The signs to be inserted when applying the separability "test" should be autonomous themselves: without strongly autonomous signs, there would be no reliable signs to start with. Consider the Russian sign *karadašóm* **karandaš** ⊕ **om**, 'pencil' 'instrumental singular', discussed in the *CMG* (pp. 173-174). If just any sign may be inserted to yield separability, we allow the diminutive suffix **ik** in *karandášikom* **karandaš** ⊕ **ik** ⊕ **om** 'pencil' 'little' 'instrumental' to endow **om** with word form status (assuming that **ik** does not affect the semantic relationships between the noun stem **karandaš** and the instrumental ending **om**).

But additional syntactic criteria might be explored in order to prevent this unintended result. Ebeling (1978: 428), for example, proposes to reinforce the separability criterion by requiring that the class of signs that can be inserted should be open, and that it should be possible to insert another sign on either side of the inserted sign. Thus, in order to isolate *une* 'a' in *une pipe* 'a pipe', it is not enough, according to

224

Ebeling, that a phrase like *une grande pipe* 'a big pipe' may exist. We must also be convinced that, whatever number of signs we find to replace **grande**, another one will always be found. Moreover, we must also find phrases like *une très grande pipe* 'a very big pipe' and *une grande belle pipe* 'a big beautiful pipe'. This criterion is likely to solve the **karandašom** problem: the number of signs that can fulfil the same function as **ik** is limited, and no additional signs can be inserted around it in **karandašikom**. But the new criterion may sacrifice word form status for the French clitic pronouns in the process.

3.23 Coordinative tmesis and referential semantics

Mel'čuk points out that even the syntactic approach does not immediately produce obvious results for noun compounds. He adduces instances of *coordinative tmesis*. Although tradition and intuition treat a German noun like *Fremdsprachen* **fremd** ⊕ **sprache** ⊕ **n** 'foreign languages' as a single word form, it is possible to separate **fremd** and **sprachen** in expressions such as *Fremd- und Muttersprachen* 'foreign and native languages', apparently without affecting the semantic relation between **fremd** and **sprachen**. Consequently, the criterion of preservation of semantic contents dictates that *Fremd-* and *-sprachen* should be treated as separate word forms.

Mel'čuk rejects this counter-example. He argues that the semantic contents of *Fremdsprachen* do change as a result of the split since we are dealing with different sets of languages. The languages covered by *sprachen* in *Fremd- und Muttersprachen* do not coincide with the languages covered by *Muttersprachen* (p. 204).

This example can be used to illustrate the risks of dealing with semantics in terms of referents. The author's treatment is likely to prompt a diverging treatment for the parallel constructions involving a single object. Consider the parallel Dutch example *boekhandel* 'bookshop' and *boek- en tijdschriftenhandel* 'book and magazine shop'. As most bookshops sell magazines nowadays, I can use the two terms to refer to the same shop, thus causing the referents of the two expressions to coincide.

It may be argued that one should not compare particular referents of specific utterances, but rather the <u>potential</u> referents of the signs: as long as there is one bookshop left which does not sell periodicals, the sets of potential referents of *boekhandel* and *boek- en tijdschriftenhandel* do not coincide. But this line of reasoning would jeopardize the Mel'čuk's own example. One person's *Muttersprache* is always someone else's *Fremd-*

sprache. Since all pidgins have turned into creoles and a few children were raised in Esperanto-speaking families (Lins 1988: 69), the sets of foreign and native languages coincide. Consequently, the sets of potential referents of *Fremdsprachen* and *Fremd- und Muttersprachen* coincide, which is contrary to the author's intention.

This is not to say that *Fremdsprachen* should be split into two words, or that the author's criterion of preservation of semantic contents should be rejected. But the referential semantics of the MTM does not thus far seem to provide a semantic basis to apply it.

An approach in which the coordinating **und** interferes with the semantic relationship between **fremd** and **sprachen** is conceivable. This analysis is produced by Ebeling's semantics, in which there is a direct relationship between **sprachen** and **und**, while **und** in turn dominates **fremd** and **mutter**, thus affecting the original relationship between **fremd** and **sprachen** (Ebeling 1978: 425). This would take care of splitting up **fremd** and **sprachen**.

A possible drawback of Ebeling's semantic representation is that, in factoring **fremd** and **mutter**, the insertion of **und** affects not only the relationship between **fremd** and **sprachen** in *Fremd- und Muttersprachen*, but also that between **mutter** and **sprachen**. This produces two signs **muttersprachen₁** and **muttersprachen₂**, the latter occurring in expressions involving factorization through **und** or similar conjunctions and the former elsewhere. If **muttersprachen₂** occurs only after such conjunctions, it is not separable, as a result of which **und** ⊕ **muttersprachen₂** must be regarded as one word.

Elsewhere, however, Mel'čuk treats coordination in a way which possibly offers a solution for this unintended side-effect. He points out that conjunctions do not necessarily represent conjoined items as being in a symmetrical relation. Although he views the items in *John and Mary* as interchangeable, he points to the semantic difference between *he stood up and gave me the letter* and *he gave me the letter and stood up* (Mel'čuk 1988: 26). In this example, the difference is registered in Mel'čuk's type of referential semantics because of the obvious temporal interpretation of *and.*

But in a type of semantics which is based on the speaker's communicative strategy, any instance of conjunction is asymmetric, if only because a·speaker always chooses the order in which the conjoined items are presented, thus manipulating the hearer's decoding process. Consider, for example, the sentence *for thirty years I made coffee for three: for myself, for my wife and for the kitchen sink.* It is obvious that changing the order of the items, while keeping the intonation pattern constant, results in a different message. In this approach, the concept of coordination ceases to be a linguistic concept, at least as far as coordination implies even-handed treatment of conjoined linguistic items.

Consequently, even if Mel'čuk's semantics of *Fremd- und Mutter-sprachen* is rejected, it is not excluded that a semantic analysis can be found in which the insertion of **und ⊕ mutter** between **fremd** and **sprachen** affects the semantic relationship between **fremd** and **sprachen** while leaving the semantic structure of **muttersprachen** intact.

3.24   Criteria for sufficiency

As pointed out in § 3.3, the criteria in Mel'čuk's autonomy definitions are of a gradual nature and allow for language-specific application. In order to avert the risk of arbitrariness in assessing whether a sign fulfils the criteria to a sufficient extent, Mel'čuk introduces a few language-independent criteria which guide such language-specific application. Four such criteria are mentioned: *morphological coherence* (p. 192), *paradigmatic attraction* (p. 181), *phonological coherence* (p. 190) and *syntactic coherence* (p. 196). They will be discussed below.

3.25   Morphological coherence

As Mel'čuk puts it, a candidate for word-form status must fit naturally in an overall system of morphological description which is considered reasonable for the language (p. 192).

The French clitic pronouns are, again, the ideal example. We have seen that their performance on the autonomy scales is poor. But the author argues, in a long discussion, that giving up the autonomy of French clitic pronouns and regarding them as a part of the corresponding verb forms would upset French morphology. It would complicate the structure of the French verb considerably. Among other things, no fewer than 14 flexional categories would be added to the traditional description (pp. 192-195; the definition of the term flexional category will be dealt with in § 4). Therefore, the criterion of morphological coherence allows us to lower the threshold levels for autonomy in French so as to allow just a little bit of permutability to be sufficient to accept clitic pronouns as autonomous (but see the discussion on permutability in § 3.16 for complications in the methods applied to obtain even this little bit of permutability).

3.26 Paradigmatic attraction

The way in which a language treats most signs of a given paradigm determines the level that is required for assigning autonomy to all signs of the paradigm. This principle is called *paradigmatic attraction*.

Paradigm, the concept used to formulate the principle, has not yet been defined. It is defined provisionally as a set of signs which are semantically, syntactically and morphologically akin and oppose and exclude each other in a given position (p. 182). Note that the definition given here is not equivalent to the official definition of the concept, which is given much later (p. 356). The latter definition is useless at this stage, since it is based on concepts that are yet to be defined on the basis of concepts being defined here.[38]

An example of the language-specific application of paradigmatic attraction is Mel'čuk's way of dealing with the Polish preterite. Here the indicators of the first and second person do not necessarily follow the verb. Compare *pisałem* 'I wrote', where the first person ending **m/em** follows the preterite suffix **ał**, and *kiedym pisał* 'when I wrote', where it is attached to the conjunction **kiedy** 'when'. This instance of permutability is at least as evident as that of the French clitics, and would therefore seem to prompt autonomy status. But it is limited to the preterite. The suffixes of the first and second person of the present tense forms of Polish verbs, which belong to the same paradigm, are not permutable. Mel'čuk prefers to treat **em/m**, which he refers to as a *migrant suffix*, as a non-autonomous sign (p. 182).

Thus, we see that the high score of Polish **em/m** on the permutability scale does not result in autonomy status, because it would upset the morphological description of the Polish verb.

The effects of paradigmatic attraction are inverse to those of morphological coherence. The results of the application of these principles are best illustrated in the author's example in which the Hungarian and Arabic possessive suffixes are compared (pp. 237-239). Consider the Hungarian sign **könyv** ⊕ **em** and its Arabic counterpart **kitāb** ⊕ **ī**, both meaning 'my book'. Mel'čuk shows how none of the autonomy criteria yields a decisive difference between the two signs. But the Hungarian sign **em** 'my' fits in all respects in the morphological system: it is followed by case endings and its expression is in many contexts obligatory. Treating it as a separate word form would wreak havoc in Hungarian morphology. The Arabic sign **ī** 'my', on the other hand, stands alone and is not necessarily expressed. Considering it as part of the word which precedes it would complicate the morphological description of Arabic. Thus, the principles of morphological coherence and paradigmatic attraction differentiate the threshold levels for autonomy between the two languages.

3.27 Phonological coherence

The phonological coherence criterion implies that the *signifiant* of a sign which is a candidate for word-form status must resemble the *signifiants* of evident word forms in the same language (p. 190).

Thus, Russian prepositions such as *v* 'in' and *na* 'on' do not carry independent stress and in this fail to resemble the overwhelming majority of Russian word forms. This deviating phonological characteristic gives them a low score on the phonological coherence criterion. This should discourage us in regarding them as word forms. Their score is not low enough, however, to prevent their convincingly high score on the separability autonomy criterion from establishing their word-form status.

Things are different in the case of the English possessive 's₂ in the hackneyed example **the king's hat**. This sign is separable, as illustrated by *the king of England's hat*. Mel'čuk rejects treating 's₂ as having word-form status. His main argument is that there are no word forms in English which consist of one phoneme (p. 191): accepting 's₂ as a word form would upset the phonological description of the language.

This argument strikes us as somewhat artificial. The *signifiant* of the article **a** also consists of one phoneme. As we saw in § 3.20, the author goes to considerable lengths to obtain word-form status for English auxiliaries with truncated *signifiants* consisting of one phoneme, such as 've, 'd and 's₁. If we have introduced a back door rule in order to include these signs in the set of word forms, why should we make an effort to exclude such word forms if they acquire such status through the front door of separability? The author's back door argument is that the possessive 's₂ does not correspond to a full form, unlike the truncated auxiliary forms (p. 191). This point needs further examination. In colloquial Dutch, the cliticized form *z'n* of the possessive pronoun *zijn* 'his' is used in the same way as English possessive 's₂. Cf. *mijn broer z'n vrouw* 'my brother's wife'; *de buurman van boven z'n fiets*, lit. 'the neighbour of upstairs's bicycle'. Although it is about as troublesome to replace *z'n* by *zijn* here as it is to replace *'s* by *his* in ?*the king of England his hat* in English, *z'n* is generally considered a separate word form. Thus, the present writer has not seen any cogent examples which justify the use of the phonological coherence criterion.[39]

3.28 Syntactic coherence

The syntactic coherence criterion implies that the *signifiant* of a sign which is a candidate for word-form status must fit naturally in an overall system of morphological description which is considered reasonable for the language (p. 196).

Mel'čuk's most familiar example is the famous case of the Portuguese future ending, which, at least in the formal style of a now obsolescent variety of written European Portuguese, allows itself to be separated from the rest of the verb by clitic forms of personal pronouns. Thus, the first person plural ending **emos** in *mostraremos* 'we shall show' can be separated from the infinitive of the verb **mostrar** 'show', which is used as the future stem, by the third person indirect object clitic **lhe** to obtain *mostrar-lhe-emos* 'we shall show him'. Since **lhe** is, in other circumstances, a word form, **emos** makes a positive score on the separability criterion, albeit a very low one. But treating it as a separate auxiliary would upset the syntactic description of Portuguese, in which auxiliaries normally precede the verb, and therefore word-form status is rejected for it. Mel'čuk indicates that he would be ready to pay the price of a more complex syntactic description if *mostraremos* could be split up by a larger variety of items than just the clitic pronouns (p. 197). So he more or less applies Ebeling's reinforced version of separability which was discussed in § 3.22.

3.29 Intraclitics and discontinuous word forms

This brings us to the question of what happens with *mostrar-lhe-emos*. This instance is now comparable to that of the infinitive markers **zu** in German and **te** in Dutch. These are normally treated as separate word forms, as in German *zu suchen* and Dutch *te zoeken* 'to look for', but are inserted between the prefix and the stem of compounds such as *aufsuchen* and *opzoeken* 'look up, visit' (**auf** and **op** 'up' are floating prefixes of the type discussed earlier, cf. § 3.19). Does the *CMG* prefer the one-word solution reflected in German orthography, which has *aufzusuchen*, or the three-word practice of Dutch spelling, which has *op te zoeken*?

Mel'čuk chooses neither. He continues to regard **lhe** as a word form, calling it an *intraclitic*, which is inserted in *mostraremos* (p. 198). The separated signs **mostrar** and **emos** continue to make up one word form, in spite of their separation.

If there is one instance supporting the author's case for discontinuous word forms, it is Tegey's Pashto example, which is adduced on p. 228. A series of intraclitics may be inserted after the stressed syllable of a verb form, right in the middle of the verb. Thus, the future tense clitic **ba** and the third person object clitic **ye** are inserted after the accentuated syllable of the verb if no other accentuated word precedes it (cf. Tegey 1975: 578).[40]

tór	ta	<u>ba</u> <u>ye</u>	ráwri
Tor	to	fut 3rd sing/plur. obj.	bring - 3rd sing. subj

'he will bring it to Tor'

wər	ta	rá<u>bayew</u>ri

'he will bring it to him'

The chapters on word definition conclude with a taxonomy of word forms, in which *perfect primary* word forms are distinguished from *defective primary* word forms, such as clitics, and from *secondary* word forms which result from syntactic and morphonological maneuvers, such as German *Fremd-* resulting from coordinative tmesis, and the French megamorph *au* resulting from à $\oplus$ le 'to the', respectively.

The numerous examples represent a most important aspect of these chapters. Mel'čuk treats the implications of his definitions for a large number of interesting problem cases in a broad variety of languages, ranging from Quechua to Tocharian to Breton. This makes *Volume I* of the *CMG* a gold mine of touchstones for word definitions, which no future work on the subject can afford to ignore.

4. Mel'čuk's domain of morphology

After the definition of 'word form', Mel'čuk proceeds to define a series of concepts which enable him to identify the domain of morphology as distinct from that of lexicology, and to introduce a number of subdomains. As pointed out above, morphology in Mel'čuk's view deals with changes in word forms, i.e. with paradigmatic relationships between words. This requires a distinction between the parts and aspects of words which change on the one hand, and the parts and aspects which remain the same on the other. This distinction involves such concepts as 'category', flexion, derivation, 'lexeme' and 'paradigm'.

4.1 Significations

Most concepts defined in the last part of *Volume I* are based on what Mel'čuk calls *significations*. Due to what looks like a text management flaw, an official definition of this concept is lacking. In one place, significations are provisionally identified with *signifiés* (p. 154). In another, *signifiés* are said to contain significations (p. 345). Significations cannot be identified with meanings (*sens*), as the latter occur only in the semantic representation, while some significations are featured in the syntactic representation (p. 325). The present writer conjectures that significations are the smallest identifiable elements in a *signifié*, whether semantic or syntactic.

If this is true, Mel'čuk's example, quoted in § 2.20, which illustrates that meanings are not necessarily *signifiés*, should be replaced. It was stated there that the <u>meaning</u> (*sens*) 'first person' is not a *signifié* in French, because it cannot be expressed separately. Later in the *CMG*, however, French 'number' and 'person' are adduced as examples of *syntactic significations*, which do not occur in the semantic representation (p. 332). It seems, therefore, that the French verb number example illustrates the relationship between significations and *signifiés*, rather than that between meanings and *signifiés*.

Throughout § 4, the term *signification* will be used to render Mel'čuk's *signification* wherever it is used in the *CMG*.

4.2 Categories

The definition of flexion involves that of 'category'. A category is a maximal set of significations that exclude each other in the same semantic of logical position (p. 261). Mel'čuk's examples include colour terms ('red', 'blue'), vehicle terms ('car', 'lorry', 'bus') and grammatical categories, such as gender ('neuter', 'feminine') and number ('singular', 'plural').

The presentation of such logical and (referential) semantic examples of categories may confuse the reader who expects linguistic ones. The examples illustrate mutual exclusion as enforced by logic or reality, not that enforced by the language itself. The author argues, for example, that no 'X' can be red and blue simultaneously (p. 262). This may be correct from a referential viewpoint but most of us have been taught that, linguistically speaking, an 'X' may be simultaneously green and colourless.

Conversely, if, as the author states, the plural of a noun in French or English may express several distinct significations, such as 'more than one X' and 'different sorts of X' (p. 269), it is logically and referentially speaking possible to pluralize 'X' for one signification without doing so for the other. It is, for example, logically and referentially possible to identify a group of two or more 'X's belonging to only one sort. But the expression of such combinations by means of the category of number is blocked in certain languages by the way in which they organize their categories: when I talk about cheeses in French of English, the plural cannot assist me in making clear whether I am referring to more than one cheese or to different sorts of cheese.

4.3 Flexional categories and grammemes

The *flexional category*, which is a special type of category, is the central concept of the last part of *Volume I*. A flexional category 'F' of a class K of signs is defined as a category which consists of significations for which the following conditions hold (p. 263).

1. Each occurrence of K requires the occurrence of exactly one element of 'F'.
2. The elements of 'F' must be expressed in a regular way.

The elements of a flexional category are called *flexional significations* or *grammemes* (p. 264).

Four aspects of the definition of flexional categories are commented on below: the nature of class K (§ 4.4); the two criteria of the definition, viz. regularity (§ 4.5 to § 4.7) and obligatory expression (§ 4.8); and the adopted terminology (§ 4.9).

4.4 Distribution classes

The properties of class K are not specified in the definition, but Mel'čuk makes clear elsewhere that he intends K to refer to a distribution class (p. 264), i.e. a set of signs which occur in the same context (p. 85), i.e. which exclude each other in the same position. We see that the definitions of categories and distribution classes are very much alike, the difference consisting in the domain of the definition: categories, including flexional categories, contain significations, while the distribution classes to which K is intended to refer contain complete signs.

In practice, K is intended to refer to large classes (p. 263), such as the parts of speech of a language. Nevertheless, small Ks are not excluded. The small class of French personal pronouns, for example, is the only one in its language to be inflected for 'case' (p. 264).

The two main criteria for flexional categories are regular expression (criterion 2 of the definition on p. 263) and obligatory expression (criterion 1). The regularity criterion consists of three subcriteria, which are, again, of a gradual nature.

4.5 Productivity

Each grammeme should be expressible with most elements of K (criterion 2c): defective paradigms, such as that of *mečtá* 'daydream', which lacks a genitive plural, should be rare. A complication is that, if K is a distribution class, the impossibility of combining the sign of the stem **mečt** with a genitive plural puts it in a different K, since its distribution differs *ipso facto* from that of other nouns.[41]

4.6 Regular expression

As a second subcriterion of regularity, it is required that the number of ways in which a grammeme is expressed be limited (criterion 2b). Mel'čuk points out the relative value of this criterion. He provides spectacular examples of diversity of expression of grammemes, such as the 70 plural suffixes in Burushaski (p. 284). Only the unitary zero expression of the singular ensures for number the status of a flexional category in this language (p. 282). For languages in which an intended grammatical category may be expressed by a large variety of *Ablauts*, as with number in Hausa, the author speaks of zero *Ablaut* (p. 282).

The zero argument is vulnerable as long as we have no criteria for the direction of *Ablaut* rules. Consider a hypothetical language which contains only strong verbs with a large variety of *Ablaut* rules. Correspondences between the present tense and preterite are of the following type.

schrijf 'write'	:	*schreef* 'wrote';
lees 'read (present)'	:	*las* 'read (preterite)'.

Here zero *Ablaut* is warranted if we assume, as *Ablaut* rules, either *ij* ⇒ *ee* and *ee* ⇒ *a*, or *ee* ⇒ *ij* and *a* ⇒ *ee*. We then find consistent zero treatment in either present or preterite. But if we have *ee* ⇒ *ij* and *ee* ⇒ *a*, we lose regularity on both sides. It will be interesting to see in one of the forthcoming volumes of the *CMG* which criteria will be used for assigning the direction of *Ablaut* arrows.

As to the necessity of including the criterion of regular expression in the definition of 'flexional category', Mel'čuk is prepared to give it up if

234

there is a natural language in which an indisputable flexional category is found of which no grammeme has a standard marker. "Until such a language is found, it is more prudent to retain criterion 2b in the definition" (p. 270). Intuitively, the present writer finds it hard to disagree with this practice. But it entails a logical problem. Technically speaking, as long as regular expression is part of the definition of a flexional category, categories without it cannot be indisputable. The author's practice is tantamount to defining quadrupeds as having four feet and a tail, while adding that we can drop the tail from the definition if we find a quadruped without it. In that case, there is no reason to include the tail in the first place. Here definition and observation, which the author strives to separate, seem to conflate. A definition of quadrupeds which does not include the tail enables us to observe that quadrupeds have tails. This, in turn, may be a starting point for empirical research: some of us will start looking for quadrupeds without tails, others for explanations why quadrupeds have tails. But the observation that quadrupeds have tails should be no reason for including the tails in the definition. (The matter becomes more complex if the tail is needed in order to exclude listing unwanted objects as quadrupeds, e.g. tables and chairs. But Mel'čuk does not indicate that the regular expression criterion was introduced with problems of this type in mind.)

4.7 Transparency

As a third subcriterion of regularity, the signification of a sign consisting of an element of K and a grammeme should be computable from its composing elements (criterion 2a). The signification of **apples** should be predictable on the basis of that of **apple** and that of **s**. This applies to most combinations of signs and is hardly distinctive for grammemes.

4.8 Obligatory expression

The basic distinctive criterion on which the definition of flexion is based, is the classic property of obligatory expression.[42] Mel'čuk adduces numerous examples which show how a language forces its speakers to express certain significations while leaving the expression of other significations up to the individual speaker (e.g. pp. 258-259). In English, expression of definiteness and number is obligatory, in Russian that of aspect and number.

As the author points out, even this criterion fails to be absolute. The obligatory expression of number with French nouns, which forces us to choose between *Marie a un enfant* 'Mary has a child' and *Marie a des enfants* 'Mary has children', can be avoided by saying *Marie est mère* 'Mary is a mother' (p. 279). This does not seem to be a grave matter, since it may be argued that the meaning of the latter phrase is not simply that of *Marie a des enfants* minus 'plural', or that of *Marie a un enfant* minus 'singular'. The verb *avoir* 'have' does not necessarily imply mother-hood, even if this relationship may be inferred in many situations in which *avoir* indicates a relationship between female persons and children.

The author points out that obligatory expression occurs also in non-grammatical categories. For example, when translating Russian *stól* 'table' into French, we must choose between *table* 'table' and *bureau* 'desk'. We are forced to specify the type of *stól*. Such instances are ruled out on account of their being non-systematic and non-regular (p. 280). Yet there is room for intermediate instances here, as in the case of the Russian verbs of motion, where a systematic distinction, viz. 'determined' vs. 'non-determined', is applied to a closed set of verbs and expressed in a semi-regular morphological pattern.

The obligatory expression criterion also entails a technical problem. It appears to be insufficiently distinctive. Let us assume that K is the set of nouns. It is true that the use of a noun in a language like French forces us to express either definiteness or indefiniteness. But the converse also holds: the use of a definite or indefinite article implies the obligatory expression of the signification of a noun. Nouns fulfil the author's regularity requirements even better than suffixes. This implies that his definition, as it is, qualifies nouns as flexional categories and, consequently, fails to distinguish lexical significations and grammemes.

It seems expedient, therefore, to introduce another criterion for the definition of flexional significations, which is based on the most prominent characteristic of flexional categories as compared with other categories: their size. It might be proposed to define a flexional category as a category containing a small, closed set of significations. Non-flexional categories, such as nouns, contain many significations. A possible consequence is that, in the case of the French personal pronouns mentioned above, we are dealing with two flexional categories: 'personal pronoun' and 'number'.

4.9 Terminology

Although many linguists take the term *flexion* to refer to changes within words, and although all given examples of flexional categories illustrate word-internal flexion, the definition of flexional categories on

p. 263 does not involve word forms. Articles and auxiliaries, i.e. grammemes which are expressed outside the words expressing the significations of the signs in **K**, are not excluded from flexional categories. As Mel'čuk points out on p. 330, this is intentional. The author labels *flexional categories* what some linguists would have preferred to call *grammatical categories*; such linguists would reserve the former term for the subsets of their grammatical categories which operate within word forms.

Adoption of the term *grammatical category* instead of *flexional category* would solve the terminological problem which the author faces with his term *grammeme*. As far as the present writer is aware, the latter term was coined by Pike in 1957 as *grameme*, changed into *grammeme* after a few months, and subsisted for another few months before being supplanted by *tagmeme* (cf. Pike 1957a, 1957b, 1958). The short life of the grammeme in tagmemics was nevertheless long enough to secure it a solid position in the Soviet tradition. The term returned into North American linguistics when Mel'čuk moved to Canada in the 1970s. In the *CMG*, Mel'čuk admits that he would like to abandon *grammeme* in favour of something like *flexioneme* in view of the discrepancy between his *grammeme* and his usage of the term *grammatical*, but does not wish to dissociate himself from the well-established tradition of which *grammemes* are a part. He therefore tolerates this terminological anomaly in his system (p. 265). Abandoning the use of terms containing *-flex-* for phenomena crossing the word boundary and reserving the term *grammatical* for the broader concept would restore consistency in a different way.

This is not so simple as it looks, however, as it entails terminological shifts elsewhere in Mel'čuk's system: as we shall see in § 4.11, the author uses *grammatical* for an even broader concept.

4.10 Derivatemes and quasi-grammemes

As illustrated by the *lámpočka* 'light-bulb' argument in § 1.1, Mel'čuk regards word formation as an integral part of morphology. After defining flexional categories, he introduces a concept called *derivational signification* or *derivateme*, which is to cover all non-flexional morphological changes in a word. Derivatemes are defined as significations which, without being grammemes, are expressed by *signifiants* which resemble *signifiants* which express grammemes (p. 288). The French diminutive signs, such as *ette* in *maisonnette* 'little house', are less regular than grammemes: most nouns do not admit them. Moreover, they are not an element of a category: when using the word *maison* 'house', we do not

237

have to choose between a big and a little house. Since such signs resemble grammemes in their being expressed by endings, they are classified as derivatemes (p. 288).

For signs which resemble grammemes and also fulfil the regularity criteria set for grammemes (but are not obligatorily expressed), the author coins the term *quasi-grammeme* (p. 303). Some further definitions introduce various types of derivation (pp. 311, 312).

The basis for formal resemblance of *signifiants* is not specified. Which properties determine whether two *signifiants* are alike and which are to be ignored? Here, as in other instances, the author resorts to a *vague voulu*, allowing for discretionary decisions on the part of the individual linguist (p. 289). The resemblance criterion is not without problems. We shall return to it in § 4.22.

4.11 Grammatical vs. lexical significations

The term *grammatical signification* is used to include grammemes as well as quasi-grammemes and derivatemes. This explains Mel'čuk's reluctance to use the term *grammatical* to qualify the concepts for which he uses *flexional*: his *grammatical* includes derivation.

Significations which are not grammatical are *lexical significations* (p. 323).

At several places, the *caveat* is made that the borderline between grammatical and lexical significations is vague. Sometimes the same signification can be expressed both by lexical and grammatical means. Thus, the signification of the Spanish sign **golpe** 'blow' is expressed by the suffix **azo** in the word form *garrotazo* 'blow with a stick' (p. 255). The signification 'inhabitant of Paris' can be expressed by lexical means in French, as in *habitant de Paris* 'inhabitant of Paris', as well as by the suffix **ien** in *Parisien* 'Parisian' (p. 324). It would seem that this problem can be largely solved in a more precise approach to semantics. The present writer, for example, is an inhabitant of Paris but has given up hope of ever becoming a *Parisien*.

4.12 Semantic vs. syntactic significations

Mel'čuk furthermore distinguishes *semantic significations* (*semantemes*) and *syntactic significations* (*syntaxemes*) (pp. 324-325). Semantic significations consist of fragments of the semantic representation, i.e. semes or networks of semes. The apparent tautology in the term is due to the author's idiosyncratic sign concept. The significations in the *signifié* of a sign may be units of any level of representation which is deeper than the phonological one. This includes syntactic units.[43] Syntactic significations consist of syntactic relations only. They affect the semantic representation only indirectly (p. 325). Examples of syntactic significations are prepositions governed by verbs and gender endings, such as the feminine ending -e of *importante* in *catégorie importante* 'important category' (p. 326).

The author points out that the same preposition may have a semantic signification in one context and a syntactic one in another: cf. *Jean insiste sur cette table* 'Jean insists on that table', where *sur* 'on' indicates the syntactic relation between *insiste* and *table*, and *le magazine se trouve sur cette table* 'the magazine is on that table', where *sur* indicates a spatial relationship (p. 335).

Gender endings would seem to show the same behaviour. Compare, for example, the apparently syntactic signification of the feminine ending **aja** in, say, *nóvaja* 'new' in *nóvaja kníga* 'a new book' and its apparently semantic signification in the utterance *Nóvaja!* 'a new female person'. But the author adduces gender significations as purely syntactic (p. 332).[44] The person and number endings of French verbs are treated in the same way (p. 332), the apparent reason being that these meanings are already expressed in the non-omissible subject. Compare *vous mangez* 'you eat, plural' vs. **mangez*. It may nevertheless be suggested that these endings obtain semantic significations in the imperative: cf. *mangez!* 'eat, plural'.

4.13 Morphological significations, reference significations

Mel'čuk's final distinction being used to determine the domain of morphology is that between *morphological* and *non-morphological significations*. As he points out, morphology in principle deals with linguistic₁ significations which are expressed within word forms in combination with other significations (p. 327). But, as he continues, this criterion is too broad by itself. In some languages, almost every signification is expressed within a word form in combination with other significations. In Russian, only a few adverbs, such as *óčen'* 'very', would be excluded. Therefore, an auxiliary concept called *reference signification* (*signification repère*) is introduced.

The definition of 'reference signification' varies depending on whether ‹X› is a grammatical or a lexical signification (p. 327).
- The reference signification of a grammatical signification is "its corresponding lexical signification".

- The reference signification of a lexical signification ⟨X⟩ is another lexical signification ⟨Y⟩ such that ⟨X⟩ either modifies ⟨Y⟩ or is a complement of ⟨Y⟩.

A signification ⟨X⟩ is morphological if its reference signification is expressed in the same word form as ⟨X⟩ (p. 327-328).

Thus, the signification of **ette** 'little' in *maisonnette* 'little house' is morphological because its corresponding lexical signification **maison** 'house' is expressed in the same word form.

We must assume that the word *corresponding* in the first definition refers to some type of syntactic relationship. Syntactic relations are considered given in the MTM. The root of a verb is regarded as the reference signification of the first person suffix of Polish *pisałem* 'I wrote'. The definition does not cover instances of migrant suffixes, as in the case of Polish *kiedym pisał* 'when I wrote', discussed in § 3.26. The latter require a separate solution, which will be presented in future volumes of the *CMG* (p. 328).[45]

The second type of reference signification must apparently cater for compounds, making clear that in *Fremdsprache* 'foreign language', discussed in § 3.21 and § 3.23, the signification ⟨fremd⟩ is morphological to the signification ⟨sprache⟩ and not the other way round.

4.14 The domain of morphology

Mel'čuk presents a grid in which the twelve possible combinations of the introduced distinctions (i.e. morphological vs. non-morphological; semantic vs. syntactic; flexional vs. derivational vs. lexical) are checked (pp. 331-334). Only one type (morphological lexical syntactic significations) appears to remain empty. The three types of lexical signification are referred to the domain of lexicology. The remaining eight combinations, viz. all those with flexional and derivational significations, whether morphological or non-morphological and whether semantic or syntactic, are covered by the author's conception of morphology. The following matrix shows the structure of the domain of Mel'čuk's morphology. Each cell contains a putative example.

240

	flexional significations (grammemes)	derivational significations (derivatemes)
morphological significations	semantic: noun number: table ⊕ s	semantic: diminutives: maison ⊕ ette
	syntactic: adjective gender: nov ⊕ aja	syntactic: nominalization: déplace ⊕ ment
non-morphological significations	semantic: articles: the ⊕ table	semantic: analytical derivation: bale ⊕ bet
	syntactic: infinitive marker: to ⊕ walk	syntactic: syntactic nominalization: to, čto

The various subdivisions of morphology are discussed below.

4.15 Semantic flexional morphological significations

All morphological conceptualization commences in the top left corner of the matrix. Linguists regard semantic flexional morphological significations as manifestations of morphology *par excellence*. The question is how far the domain of morphology extends around this archetype.

4.16 Syntactic flexional significations

Most linguists also tend to include syntactic flexional morphological significations in the domain of morphology. It is hard to conceive of a better place to deal with **aja** in *nóvaja* 'new' (cg. § 4.12). As shown in the matrix, the author of the *CMG*, too, includes this type in the domain of morphology.

His definitions, however, do not seem to justify this choice. We saw in § 4.3 that flexional significations are elements of categories. We saw in § 4.2 that categories are sets of significations which exclude each other in the same semantic position. But syntactic significations have been defined (in § 4.12) as consisting of syntactic relations only. They do not figure in the semantic representation. This implies that syntactic significations do not make up categories and cannot, therefore, be flexional. Here are some examples.

We can say that the preposition **sur** in *Jean insiste sur cette table* 'Jean insists on that table' contains a syntactic signification by virtue of the fact that we do not implicitly oppose it to other signs, e.g. to **sous** 'under' in *Jean insiste sous cette table* 'Jean insists under that table'. If we do oppose **sur** to **sous**, **sur** obtains a different signification. Both

sous and **sur** then indicate spatial relationships and their significations are semantic. Syntactic significations are syntactic by virtue of the fact that they are not opposed to other signs *in absentia*. This also applies to gender. In contexts where the feminine signification of **aja** in *nóvaja* can be replaced by the masculine signification **oj** to yield the masculine form *nóvyj*, as in *nóvaja sirotá* 'new female orphan' vs. *nóvyj sirotá* 'new male orphan', **aja** is no longer syntactic but semantic, its signification being 'female' instead of 'feminine'.[46]

We have a problem here. Our definition of morphology is obviously incomplete if it does not cover syntactic flexional significations. As far as the present writer is concerned, finding a foolproof solution would require a separate study. But the following three options for developing the relevant criterion may be suggested for further consideration.

4.17 The syntactic role criterion

We may propose to introduce a special criterion on the basis of which syntactic significations could be assigned flexional status.

It is not Mel'čuk's intention to regard all syntactic significations as flexional. Nominalization, for example, is seen as a syntactic derivateme: the French suffix **ment** in *déplacement* endows a (potential) event described by the verb *déplacer* 'shift, move' with the syntactic properties of a noun (cf. p. 332). But certain types of syntactic relations, such as predication, valency marking and modification, may perhaps be identified as special relations, which generate flexional syntactic significations. As we saw, flexional status is assigned to semantic significations on account of their being elements of categories, i.e. on acount of their mutual exclusion in the same position. Syntactic significations do not exclude each other in the same position, but they may serve to distinguish co-occurring positions with respect to each other. In *otéc ljúbit sýna* 'the father loves the son', the nominative of *otéc* 'father' and the accusative of *sýna* 'son' mark the different roles fulfilled by these actors with respect to the verb *ljúbit* 'loves'. This circumstance, i.e. the potential to mark contrasting roles, may perhaps provide a criterion in a definition of syntactic flexional significations.[47]

A possible disadvantage of this solution is that prepositions may fulfil the same role as case endings. Compare, again, *Jean insiste sur la table*. Here *sur* marks what is insisted on. This implies that a definition which employs this property as a criterion will treat governed prepositions, which Mel'čuk regards as syntactic lexical significations (p. 332), as (non-morphological) syntactic flexional significations. So the present option blurs his distinction between lexical and flexional significations and therewith affects his intended domain of morphology.

4.18 The formal resemblance criterion

As a second option, we may regard syntactic significations as flexional if their formal expression resembles that of flexional morphology. This would imply that syntactic gender of adjectives, as in aja, must be included because it is expressed by endings with, say, phonological properties resembling those of semantic flexional significations.

A disadvantage of this solution is that the resemblance criterion is already used for derivational significations, such as that of ment in déplacement. The criterion would, consequently, blur the distinction between syntactic derivational significations and syntactic flexional significations and, moreover, share with derivational significations the problems connected with the resemblance criterion, which will be discussed in § 4.22.

4.19 The desemantization criterion

Finally, we may decide to regard syntactic significations as flexional if their corresponding signifiés coincide with those of semantic flexional meanings. This would imply that syntactic gender of adjectives should be included in morphology because its formal expression coincides with that of semantic gender.

A possible disadvantage of this solution is that signifiés which are never used to express semantic significations would be excluded from the domain of morphology. The present writer is not aware of an example of a syntactic signification which should intuitively be included in this domain but fails to correspond to a semantic signification. But research should be undertaken in order to verify this observation. If no signifiés can be found which serve exclusively to express syntactic significations, we should also look for an explanation: is their absence accidental, or a by-product of the definitions used?

The above does not exhaust the list of possible solutions. But none is fully satisfactory. Further efforts to solve this urgent problem are needed.

4.20 Morphological derivational significations

If linguists generally agree on including the top left cells of the matrix in the domain of morphology, some may hesitate on the top right cells.

They will be inclined to assign what the author calls *derivational morphology* to a special division of *word formation*, jointly with compounds of the *Fremdsprache* type. There is not, however, a fundamental barrier to a joint treatment of flexional and derivational morphology, which facilitates dealing with such intermediate cases as the Russian participles. Also the convenience of jointly treating, e.g., the many morphonological properties which are common to flexional and derivational *signifiés* is attractive.

4.21 Non-morphological flexional significations

The case for including the bottom left cells in the domain of morphology is somewhat more unusual. To many linguists, morphology stops at the border of word forms. According to them, significations which are carried by separate words should be dealt with in the grammar of a language, but not in its subdivision called morphology. There is not, however, a fundamental barrier to a joint treatment of all significations which belong to small categories. Moreover, the convenience of a joint treatment of categories whose *signifiants* are expressed partly within and partly outside a word form, as in the author's example of the Danish articles, is undeniable. Cf. *en bog* 'a book' vs. *bogen* 'the book' (pp. 344).[48]

4.22 Non-morphological derivational significations

The bottom right cells cover the most disputable areas of Mel'čuk's domain of morphology. To end up in one of the bottom right cells, a signification must resemble non-morphological flexional significations, such as those of composite verb forms or case markers which make up separate word forms.

This seems to be the case in the author's Amharic example of a semantic non-morphological derivational signification. Here the word form *balɛ*, literally meaning 'master, boss', is used for functions that are expressed by suffixes like *-er* or *-ist* in English: cf. *mɛkina* 'car', *balɛ mɛkina* 'driver'; *bet* 'house', *balɛ bet* 'house owner'; etc. (p. 333).

For its syntactic counterpart, the author adduces syntactic nominalization in Russian. Here (potential) events described in sentences can be endowed with the syntactic properties of a noun by means of the inflecting neuter demonstrative pronoun *tó* 'that' followed by the conjunction *čto* 'that' introducing the sentence describing the event (p. 333). Cf. *já govorjú o tóm, čto ón otsútstvoval* 'I am talking about that, that he was absent', where *tóm* is the locative case of *tó*, motivated by the

244

preposition *o* 'about'. As shown by the *déplacement* example, such nominalization is also often expressed by morphological derivation.

The problem with non-morphological derivational significations is that the resemblance criterion may allow us to stretch up the domain of morphology indefinitely. Consider the future of the Russian imperfective as formed with the auxiliary verb *búdu* 'will', which Mel'čuk regards as a flexional signification (p. 355). If there is one verb which closely resembles *búdu*, it is *stánu*, which, when used with imperfective verb infinitives, means almost the same thing. Cf. *já búdu pisát'* 'I shall write' and *já stánu pisát'* 'I am going to write'. It is not clear how we can prevent the latter expression from being qualified as derivational and, consequently, from being assigned to morphology. Nor is there an obvious reason why *já načináju pisát'* 'I am beginning to write' and *já končáju pisát'* 'I finish writing' should not share the same treatment. In fact, since we are dealing with formal resemblance, there is no clear reason why we should exclude any verb at all from carrying a non-morphological derivational signification.

Of course, we may eliminate this example by rejecting Mel'čuk's reasons for assigning a flexional signification to *búdu*.[49] But it seems easy to find other examples of unintended proliferation of non-morphological derivation. We can think, for example, of the English demonstrative pronouns *this* and *that*. Bloomfield already noted their formal resemblance with articles (both types of significations contain the rare phoneme /ð/: cf. Bloomfield 1933: 147) and used the distributional resemblance of articles and demonstrative pronouns as a criterion for classing articles as separate words (Bloomfield 1933: 179). In fact, if derivatemes are defined as significations whose formal expression resembles that of grammemes, and if grammemes can be expressed by separate word forms, then any separate word form can express a derivateme.

The present writer is not aware of any means to prevent unintended proliferation of non-morphological derivation as a result of the application of the resemblance criterion. It would perhaps be better to simply keep the bottom right cells out of morphology. Arguments in support of such a decision are available. We have seen that the prototypical morphological significations in the top left cells qualify as morphological on account of positive scores on two criteria. The signs containing them have:

1. morphological *signifiants*, and
2. flexional *signifiés*.

The significations in the top right cells are assimilated with the proto-types on account of their positive scores on just criterion 1: they have morphological *signifiés*.

The significations in the bottom left cells, on the other hand, are assimilated with the prototypes on account of their positive scores on criterion 2: they have flexional *signifiants*.

The significations in the bottom right cells have neither the morpho-logical *signifiants* nor the flexional *signifiés* of the prototypes: they fail to score on criterion 1 and they fail to score on criterion 2. So at first sight, there are no cogent reasons to assimilate them to the prototype significations and include them in the domain of morphology.

4.23 Lexes and syntagms

The definition of 'lexeme' requires a preliminary identification of the units which can be part of lexemes. These units, called *lexes*, comprise all word forms, as well as *syntagms* containing no more than one non-flexional signification,[50] which is expressed in a single word form (p. 342). Syntagms are linear strings of two or more word forms in a text which are connected in the syntactic representation (p. 128).

As a corollary, lexes may overlap. In *nous avons été vus* 'we have been seen', all separate word forms represent lexes, but **avons été vus** 'have been seen' is also a lex. The sign **avons été** 'have been' is apparently excluded, since, in this context, it is neither a word form nor a syntagm containing a non-flexional meaning. Presumably, the given definition of 'syntagm', which requires that its components may not be separated in the linear string, must be adjusted, as we may expect that **avons été vus** should also be treated as a syntagm in *nous n'avons pas été vus* 'we have not been seen'.[51]

4.24 Lexeme

Lexemes are defined as maximal sets of lexes which differ only in their flexional significations (p. 346). For some reason, *flexional* must include here quasi-grammemes as well as grammemes. The author adds a complex second condition, which takes care of splitting up synonyms, such as Russian *smotrét'* and *gljadét'* 'watch' or *dogmatičeskij* and *dogmatičnyj* 'dogmatic' (p. 349). This condition employs concepts which will be defined in the forthcoming volumes of the *CMG* and is given in *Volume I* for the sake of completeness. It is left out of consideration here.

The definition does not imply that all lexemes have lexical significations. Articles or auxiliary verbs make up lexemes which consist exclusively of flexional significations (p. 348). There is an unintended side-effect here. Since all lexes which contain only flexional significations differ from each other in their flexional significations only, they will all end up in the same lexeme. The definition, as it is, unites articles, auxiliary verbs, etc. into one great lexeme.

If one wishes to avoid this unintended result, one might add a condition which stipulates that, in order to belong to the same lexeme, word forms in a lexeme be characterized by the same flexional categories. This separates articles and auxiliary verbs, whose flexional categories diverge. But the precise formulation of such a condition is not as simple as it looks. The German article, for example, is characterized for 'gender' in the singular but not in the plural, and would therefore be split up under the present wording. Defective paradigms may also cause complications here. Nevertheless, its seems likely that a satisfactory formulation can be found.

4.25 Paradigms

After discussing a few interesting problem cases, such as the negative forms of Finnish verbs (p. 353-354), the author defines the concept of *paradigm₁* more or less along the lines of Zaliznjak's (1967: 30) classic definition. A paradigm₁ is a matrix containing cells for all possible combinations of grammemes which may characterize a lexeme or class of lexemes, filled with the lexes which express these combinations (p. 356). A further definition takes care of defective paradigms₁, such as that of *mečtá* discussed in § 4.5.

It is one thing to be characterized by the same grammemes, but another to express these grammemes by the same *signifiants*. Therefore, the author defines *paradigm₂* as the type of a paradigm₁ (p. 361). The term *type* used here does not refer to the homonymous undefined mathematical concept (p. 81), but to the specification of the flexional affixes contained in the *syntactique* of a stem (p. 118). Thus, Russian *učitel'* 'teacher' and *čitátel'* 'reader' belong to the same paradigm₁: they can be combined with the same grammemes. They do not share their paradigm₂, since the nominative plural ending of *učitel'* is á, while that of *čitátel'* is i (cf. p. 362).

247

5. Conclusion

At the end of *Volume I,* the *CMG* is ready to really take off. The author provides a three-page survey of the forthcoming parts of the book (pp. 367-369), which will be devoted to concepts and distinctions touching the heart of the matter:

- *signifiés,* or morphological significations;
- *signifiants,* or morphological means;
- morphological *syntactiques*;
- morphological signs, i.e. signs with morphological significations;
- morphological models, i.e. correspondence rules between representations (cf. p. 42);
- the principles of morphological description.

Volume II of the *CMG,* which has since become available (Mel'čuk 1994), shows the direction in which the work will further develop. It is even richer in empirical material.

In the meantime, *Volume I* leaves us little to be desired. If anything, the present writer would have liked to see a transparent road map or system of sign posts for the logical relationships among the definitions in the network, which would indicate which concepts are used in a definition, whether they are primitive of defined, where their own definitions can be found, and where apparent circularity is accounted for.[52]

A most important virtue of the volume is its agenda-setting function. The subject of linguistic terminology has been marginalized by mainstream linguistics for too long. In several areas, such as case theory (cf. Wierzbicka's comment in 1980: xi), the usurpation of existing labels for new functions has given rise to confusion in linguistic communication without really giving an increase in rigour in return. Now here is a book which takes the terminology problem seriously and inspires both young and experienced investigators to search for solutions for the numerous and complex problems existing in this area. If the forthcoming volumes will continue to fulfil this function, the impact of the *CMG* on linguistic thought should be greater than if it were a hermetic construction, aspiring to bring the final word on all aspects of the subject matter. Viewed in this light, the prospects of Mel'čuk's book playing the intended *rôle unificateur* in the science may be brighter than those of Hjelmslev 1953.

Dutch UNESCO Delegation, Paris, June 1996

NOTES

[1] E.g. on mere chance, on fashions or on personal relationships within a scientific community, and on a phenomenon to which certain Soviet linguists (e.g. Gladkij 1966: 58) used to refer as the "cyclical" (kon"junkturnyj) conditions in linguistics, i.e. conditions imposed by funding agencies and their structures, by science administrators and politicians. The important role played by cyclical factors is by no means restricted to the Soviet context.

[2] In the meantime, Volume II (Mel'čuk 1994) and Volume III (Mel'čuk 1996) have seen the light, as well as the Russian version of Volume I (Mel'čuk 1997).

[3] In Mel'čuk 1994: 272, the author of the CMG refers to Mel'čuk 1986 for his most complete definition of 'case'. This definition was briefly discussed in Van Helden 1993b: 1146-1154.

[4] Kolmogorov & Uspenskij (1958: 3) define an algorithm as "a system of computations which, for a class of mathematical problems, enables us to arrive, with the aid of a uniquely determined sequence of operations which can be executed "mechanically", i.e. unaided by human creative capacities, from a representation A of "conditions" for a problem, at a representation B of solutions to the problem". In Gladkij & Mel'čuk 1983: 120, the term constructive is used to refer to linguistic definitions in Nida's sense, i.e. models of procedures of linguistic research.

The explicit distinction between 'algorithm' and 'calculus' in Soviet theoretical linguistics is probably due to Apresjan (1973: 118). The essential property of an algorithm is that it consists of instructions, which fix a process. A calculus, on the other hand, consists of permissions, which fix possibilities.

[5] As the mathematician Dobrušin (1973: 439) put it in one of the many apologetics of Soviet theoretical linguistics which appeared in the 1970s, "mathematical theory makes it possible to establish the ultimate consequences of precisely formulated postulates, the plausibility of the consequences being no less than the plausibility of the ·postulates".

[6] Interestingly, the first, 1946, edition of Nida 1949[2] contained a great deal of hypothetical data, which were subsequently replaced whenever possible by data from real languages in the second edition (Nida 1949[2]: v). So the difference between Mel'čuk's "deductive" and Nida's "inductive" approaches may be smaller than advertised.

Mel'čuk's own hypothetical examples are plausible and his examples from actual languages are, of course, correct or at least carefully documented with the most authoritative sources.

[7] The fuzziness of grammaticality is dealt with in, for example, Al 1975. Mel'čuk himself employs the concept of grammaticality (in the sense of grammatical correctness) only once: as a criterion in Definition I.23 (p. 188).

[8] The thorough analysis of Schank's model in Mel'čuk 1974a and Mel'čuk 1974b brings to light the analogies and differences between the two approaches.

[9] As one of his arguments in favour of the primacy of linguistic encoding over decoding, Mel'čuk points out that languages usually have special words for producing

speech as opposed to other sounds (cf. English *speak*) but lack, to his knowledge, words for mentally processing perceived speech: *hear*, *listen* and *understand* are not restricted to speech processing (pp. 46-47).

Standard Dutch is a counter-example. It has the verb *verstaan* to express precisely this action, i.e. it exists alongside *horen* 'hear', *luisteren* 'listen' en *begrijpen* 'understand'. People distinguish between *Ik hoor hem wel maar ik versta hem niet* 'I can hear him all right but I cannot decode him', and *Ik versta hem wel maar ik begrijp hem niet* 'I can decode him all right but I do not understand what he means'.

[10] Intermediate varieties, such as recorded utterances, broadcast utterances and telephone utterances, as well as formalized works of oral art, are left out of consideration.

[11] Mel'čuk does not employ the terms *type* and *token*, which are subject to the same kind of confusion among theoretical linguists of the same period. Herdan (e.g. 1960) adopts the text-oriented viewpoint in his type-token mathematics, which deals with counting tokens (e.g. occurrences of a word) of types (e.g. dictionary entries) in texts. Bar-Hillel, although initially adopting a text-oriented interpretation of the type-token distinction, (Bar-Hillel 1964: 3) develops toward a speech-oriented interpretation (Bar-Hillel 1954/64: 41).

[12] Mel'čuk acknowledges instances of discontinuous morphs elsewhere, e.g. in the Semitic languages, where grammatical and derivational meanings are expressed by vowels between consonants carrying lexical meanings (p. 159). See also note 40.

[13] The author does acknowledge a *deep syntactic anaphoric structure*, where anaphoric relations within sentences are registered (p. 54).

[14] Note that these Dutch examples are more complex than the classic instances of juncture, such as *nitrate* vs. *night rate* in certain varieties of English. In the classic cases, the juncture features can perhaps be treated as constituting an isolated phoneme: either assigned to both contiguous morphs, as proposed in Nida 1949[2]: 86, or positioned between them, as proposed in Hockett 1958: 54-55. But this is hardly feasible in the above example [vɛɪʁst] vs. [vɛʁst], since the distinctive phonetic feature, vowel length, is separated from the relevant morpheme boundaries by a consonant, viz. [ʁ]. This feature can plausibly be assigned to the phoneme /r/, but it is improbable that it could be assigned to anything following /r/. Accounting for juncture as a suprasegmental feature, as proposed in Joos 1966[4]: 216, seems to be the only solution.

[15] Inversion and truncation are left out of consideration here. This list of possibilities is not exhaustive. The forthcoming volumes of the *CMG* will undoubtedly provide us with a calculus.

[16] Mel'čuk uses unidirectional arrows ($\Rightarrow$) in these substitution rules. His criteria for determining their direction, i.e. which indicate that the plural is made up by processing the singular instead of the other way round, are dealt with in later volumes of the *CMG* and fall outside the scope of the present discussion.

[17] This is confirmed in some Russian examples containing reduced unstressed vowels. In their phonological representation, the first vowels of *nesút* **nesut** 'carry,

third person plural' (p. 118) and *nosý* **nosy** 'noses' (p. 140), are identical to /i/ and /a/, respectively.

[18] In the *CMG* (p. 159), the author uses the more complicated example *creang* 'branch' but elsewhere (e.g. Mel'čuk 1985b: 190) he uses examples which are fully comparable with *pom*.

[19] Compartmentalizing morphology and phonology also enforces complex morphological descriptions for instances of what the author calls *external sandhi*, where the occurrence of a morpheme belonging to another word is accompanied by phonological mutations in the adjacent phonemes of a given morpheme, as in Tuscan dialect, where the initial [k] of *casa* 'house' is pronounced [χ] in *due case* 'two houses' but [kː] in *tre case* 'three houses' (cf. Grassi 1967: 86), or possibly in Mel'čuk's Breton example *ho penn* 'your (plural) head' vs. *e benn* 'his head' vs. *ma fenn* 'my head' (p. 227). Such instances are perhaps described more naturally in terms of overlapping phonological features on word boundaries than in terms of consonant *Ablaut*. The feature 'length' in *tre case* can then be accounted for as a part of the *signifiant* of the sign **tre** 'three' instead of a morphological alternation in **casa** 'house'.

This does not rule out, of course, the possibility that alternations exist which cannot be accounted for in phonological terms and where complex morphological statements are inevitable.

[20] Nor does the problem occur if one adopts a phonological analysis in which /c/ is split up in /ts/, as many phonologists do. In traditional phonology, since /t/ + /s/ in *flótskij* **flot** ⊕ **skij** (as well as /t/ + /s'/ in *kážetsja* **kažet** ⊕ **sja** 'seems', and /t'/ + /s'/ in *kazát'sja* **kazat'** ⊕ **sja** 'seem') coincides with morph-internal [ts], spelt *c* as in *úmnica* 'clever one', there is no reason to introduce a special phoneme /c/ for the phonetic sequence [ts]. The author's reason for introducing the phoneme /c/ is perhaps his observation that /t'/ + /s'/ does not always coincide with [ts]: after verb stems, i.e. in the imperative, as in *trát'sja* **trat'** ⊕ **sja** 'spend your own money', we find [ʦ] (p. 144). This argument may not be conclusive, as imperatives, along with vocatives and interjections, often have a phonology of their own. In common descriptions of French, for example, (such as Léon & Léon 1976: 44), the distribution of stressed [ə] is almost exclusively restricted to the imperative: *prenez-le!* 'take it', where *le* 'it' is stressed. (But speakers consulted by the present writer pronounce [œ] here.)

[21] Expanding on proposals made in Ehlich 1982, it may be suggested that English *it* (but not necessarily its French and Russian counterparts) implies an instruction of the speaker to the hearer to refrain from refocusing on an appropriate non-personal actant in his frame of reference in the ongoing process of communication. This in contrast to deictic *this* and *that*, which are appeals to refocus. Hearing *it*, the hearer has various inferences to choose from. The following list of options is not exhaustive.
- In his preceding utterances (or earlier in the same utterance), the speaker has ensured that he may reasonably assume that the hearer is already focusing on the intended referent: *This is my new painting. What do you think of it?*
- Recent utterances on the part of the hearer leave little doubt to the speaker as to what referent the hearer is focusing on: – *I am trying to get a taxi. – You won't find it easy.*

- Pragmatic clues give the speaker reason to believe that the hearer's frame of reference is already focused on the intended referent. *It is drowning*, when both interlocutors are looking at a wasp in a glass of lemonade.
- The speaker intends to provide the necessary information shortly, e.g. when *it* is a provisional subject: *It was hard to get a taxi*; or in the case of cataphora: *Once its terminology is understood, the book turns out to be interesting.*
- No specific actant should be focused on. This is the impersonal use of *it*, as in *it is raining*: for default of a specific appropriate rainer, the use of *it* assures the envisaged "empty" interpretation.

22 An interesting exception is reference to the text itself, or to its carrier, which may be assumed to be present in every decoding situation. In order to avoid confusion between this type of reference and intratextual reference, some writers in some languages have adopted special formulas: *the present paper*, or Russian *nastojáščaja stat'já* 'the present paper'.

23 The voices of the verb are dealt with extensively in Volume II of the *CMG*, where it is made clear that replacing active sentences by passive ones affects the communicative structure of a sentence but does not change its semantic structure (Mel'čuk 1994: 145). It would be interesting to learn Mel'čuk's comment on Chomsky's sentences *everyone in the room knows at least two languages* vs. *at least two languages are known by everyone in the room*, which text-oriented linguists used time and again in the 1960s and 1970s when discussing the putative semantic equivalence of active and passive sentences: under the normal interpretation of these sentences, the languages referred to in the passive sentence should be identical for all persons in the room, whereas they may vary between persons for the active sentence (Chomsky 1957: 100-101).

24 The *CMG* contains more terms which refer to semantic units. *Semanteme* is introduced as referring (*"grosso modo"*) to a lexical unit, i.e. a network of semes kept together by a distinct label in the dictionary (p. 50). Later on, a definition of *semanteme* is provided which includes non-lexical meanings as well (p. 324). The term *signification* will be discussed in § 4.1.

25 Interestingly, Mel'čuk's real world *signifiés* are not mirrored by real world *signifiants*. While endorsing subtraction on the semantic side, he points out that subtraction of *signifiants* does not exist. Even truncation (i.e. the removal of a part of a morph expressing the addition of a meaning) is additive, since it is the result of the addition of an operation (p. 143).

26 Classic contributions include Jespersen 1924: 92-95, Togeby 1949, Rosetti 1947²/1965, Reichling 1967², Krámský 1969.

27 The wars were decided in 1950, in Stalin's *Pravda* articles on Marxism and linguistics. Key Soviet contributions on word theory include Smirnickij's work of the early fifties (1952, 1954, 1955, 1956) and Kuznecov 1968, as well as the relevant parts of Zaliznjak 1967.

The origins of the divergence between American and Soviet theoretical linguistics on the importance of 'word' can be speculated on. It is sometimes ascribed to the relative abundance of morphological categories operating within the word in Russian as compared with languages like English. In mechanical language processing, storing all forms of a Russian word separately would burden the memory of a 1950s

252

computer much more than a word in a non-inflected language. Morphological analysis
of words became, then, much more of a research priority in the USSR than in the
west. It may not be a coincidence that the earliest work of the author of the *CMG*
(e.g. Mel'čuk 1958) includes algorithms for automatic translation from Hungarian,
a language with an elaborate but regular morphology, enabling relatively simple
rules to yield considerable efficiency gains.

On the other hand, to text-oriented linguists the availability of words in written
text may have been a factor in selecting them as convenient units of syntactic analysis.
(In Mel'čuk 1961: 207, for example, a word form is defined as a string of characters
between spaces, an act for which he was to be branded a criminal during the attacks
on modern linguistics in the 1970s: cf. Budagov 1972: 407.) But then the question
why the convenience of identifying words in text was ignored in the west remains
unanswered. A possible reason is the circumstance that the interests of several
theoretical linguists populating the American East Coast in the early 1950s included
communication theory as well as computer linguistics: word boundaries are not
available when one studies sound waves. As Bar-Hillel suggests, the work of Cherry,
Halle and Jakobson has been particularly influential here (cf. Cherry & al. 1953).

28 The distinction between word forms and lexemes is a recurrent theme in Soviet
linguistic discussion. Vinogradov, who in 1944 illustrates the distinction on Puškin's
sentence *gluxój gluxógo zvál na súd sud'í gluxógo* 'the deaf man called the deaf man
to the court of the deaf judge', refers to Peškovskij's 1925a proposal to distinguish
the corresponding concepts by the labels *slovo-člen* and *slovo-tip* (Vinogradov
1944/75: 36).

29 The most sophisticated definitions of this type are probably found in Kuznecov
1968 and Revzin 1978: 44-46. Cf. Van Helden 1993a: 276-306 for a full discussion.

30 Bloomfield therefore intends to increase the power of strong autonomy by adding
the criterion of *parallelism* (Bloomfield 1933: 179). In the *CMG*, this criterion appears
as *generalized strong autonomy*. Its definition extends strong autonomy to all signs
belonging the same distribution class as a strongly autonomous sign (p. 170). It
enables us to treat all nouns like **professeur**, without having to find situations for each
of them separately in which they can occur as minimum free forms (p. 171).

The gains made by introducing generalized strong autonomy are not immediately
clear to the present writer. The distribution class of x is the set of objects with the
same distribution as x (p. 85). The criterion 'same' necessarily produces a *partition*
of the total set of objects involved, the distinctive power of which cannot be further
extended (as proved in Kulagina 1958: 206). In other words, since **professeur** can
occur between pauses, any sign which cannot occur between pauses does not belong
to the distribution class of **professeur**, whereas any sign in its distribution class can
occur between pauses and is therefore strongly autonomous in its own right. Moreover,
if the system of definitions is not intended to be a discovery procedure (p. 29), there
seems to be little point in introducing practical shortcuts for them.

· The same applies to the author's subsequent definition of generalized weak
autonomy (p. 172).

31 Mel'čuk's present autonomy definition is in fact more complex because concept
X is also "fed" by the outcome of the other criteria for weak autonomy, to be discussed in § 3.15 ff.

32   Mel'čuk uses the term *transmutability*, which covers two criteria: *permutability* as discussed here, and *transferability*, which implies the possibility of moving a non-strongly autonomous sign from one strongly autonomous sign to another without affecting the original semantic relationships, as in Spanish clitic raising: cf. *quiero poder hacerlo* 'I want to can do-it' vs. *quiero poderlo hacer* 'I want to can-it do' vs. *lo quiero poder hacer* 'it I want to can do' i.e. 'I want to be able to do it' (p. 179). Since transferability implies separability or permutability, it is left out of consideration here.

33   We assume that the author allocates to the *syntactique* properties which distinguish clitic forms from non-clitic forms, or finite forms of a verb from its infinitive form. If, on the other hand, they are supposed to affect the *signifié* of a sign, we have a problem, since we then must distinguish between semes which should be ignored when collapsing two forms of a verb on the one hand, and semes which should be taken into account on the other. Of course there is such a distinction, viz. that between lexical meanings and grammatical meanings, but these have not yet been defined. Although the author uses the term *lexeme* to explain why **m'** and **moi** must be identified with each other (p. 178), he cannot <u>formally</u> base their merger on this concept, since the definition of 'lexeme', i.e. a set of word forms with the same lexical meaning, presupposes a definition of 'word form', which in turn presupposes a definition of autonomy. The use of lexemes to define autonomy would therefore produce circularity.

34   In fact, the author states that an autonomous sign which cannot be broken up into word forms is a word form itself (p. 190). This is presented as another recursive definition, in which the defined word forms and the word forms which are used in the definition are not identical. Unlike the definition of separability, however, the given definition does not contain a catalyzing concept: we do not have a prototype word form to start with and use in the subsequent applications of the definition. The interpretation given above seems to cover Mel'čuk's intention.

35   Perhaps it is also possible to get rid of floating **meg** by denoting the meaning 'yes' for it instead of 're', as a result of which we would be dealing with different signs. Not being an expert on the MTM, the present writer hesitates to propose it. Moreover, even if we could dispose of **meg** in this fashion, there may be other instances of strongly autonomous prefixes to replace it.

36   Mel'čuk's gives a second reason, viz. that the syntactic behaviour of **spec** is not altogether like that of its sources: cf. *óčen' speciál'naja komíssija* 'very special commission' vs. **óčen' speckomíssija*. This argument is less useful because, as Mel'čuk points out elsewhere, the same applies to '**ve**: cf. Mel'čuk's examples *have you been there?* vs. **'ve you been there?* (p. 217). (But an American informant of the present writer considered the last sentence perfectly acceptable.)

37   The difference can perhaps be expressed in terms of speakers' strategies. *Fremde Sprache* might be said to contain an appeal to the hearer to carry out separate operations: search and find the set of features constituting the notion 'language', as well as those constituting the notion 'foreign, strange', and apply the latter set to the first. *Fremdsprache*, on the other hand, is rather an appeal to the hearer to search and present a ready-made parcel of semantic features constituting the notion 'foreign language' as assumed to be present in the hearer's frame of reference.

254

38 In both definitions, the author's *paradigm₁*, is the defined concept. His *paradigm₂*, which is defined on p. 361, is not pertinent here.

39 One objection could be that 's₂ may stand for **his** and **her**, whereas there are different clitics for male and female possessors in Dutch. But this argument does not apply to several southern dialects of Dutch. Here z'n is used for male and female possessors indifferently, while the distinction exists in stressed forms of the possessive pronoun **zijn** 'his' and **haar** 'her'.

40 In the example given by Mel'čuk, the clitics separate the verb from a prefix (cf. Tegey 1978: 107). Elsewhere, Tegey (1978: 88-90) provides examples in which clitics actually split up morphemes: cf. *axistálə me* and *ámexistálə*, both meaning 'I was buying them'. Tegey insists that the verb stem *axist-* 'buy' is unanalysable in the modern language.

41 When making up paradigms, this can be corrected with additional definitions, by which Ks with flexional categories which are a subset of those of another K are merged with the latter. A technical problem nevertheless remains if no noun exists which can be combined with all grammemes of a flexional category. The complete case paradigm of Russian nouns, for example, hinges on a few words such as *snég* 'snow', which possess both a partitive and a locative. Even then, we have to assume, unlike Jakobson, that the nominative and accusative of *snég* are separate cases, which are not syncretized but whose expression happens to coincide (cf. Jakobson 1936/71: 67).

42 For the classic status of this criterion, cf. Jakobson 1959/71: 492.

43 *Signification* renders Russian *značénie*, the meaning of which is broader than that of *meaning* (*sens*) or French and English *signification*. In scientific texts, for example, *značénie* is used to refer to, e.g., a value on a variable. It is perhaps this circumstance that induced or allowed Mel'čuk to stretch up the Saussurean sign concept. Perhaps the French term *valeur* would have rendered *značénie* more transparently.

44 The treatment of gender is a rather thorny problem in view of the question of the status of the utterance *nóvaja!* when used to refer to a book (i.e. an object which can be referred to by a feminine noun) present in the speech situation. The present writer is looking forward to Mel'čuk's way of dealing with it.

45 The problem is not in fact restricted to migrant suffixes. We also find non-migrant suffixes without immediate syntactic relationships within the word form of which they are considered to be a part. It will be interesting to learn how the author will treat such complex cases as the West Flemish subordinate conjunction *da* 'that' adduced in Mel'čuk 1988: 121-122, which is reputed to inflect according to the number of the subject of the subordinate clause, with which it does not have a direct syntactic relation. Compare *k weten da Jan goat weggoan* 'I know that (singular) Jan is going to leave' vs. *k weten dan Jan en Marie goan weggoan* 'I know that (plural) Jan and Marie are going to leave' in the dialect of the area between Bruges and the coast (examples from Haegeman 1983: 87).

46 We could save the syntactic status of gender endings in this case by assuming the existence of two homonymous signs **sirota₁** 'male orphan' and **sirota₂** 'female

orphan', requiring masculine and feminine agreement respectively, an option proposed in Zaliznjak 1967: 67-68. It may be surmised that Mel'čuk does not favour this option, in view of his *principle of maximal localization*, expounded elsewhere in his work (e.g. Mel'čuk 1988: 397). The principle necessitates localizing all difficulties and peculiarities observed when describing a linguistic₁ phenomenon within its narrowest "neighbourhood". In the case of *nóvaja sirotá*, we face the choice between two explanations for the choice of *nóvaja* instead of *nóvyj*:

- We correlate to /aja/ the syntactic relation 'modifier' as conditioned by the element feminine in the *syntactique* of the noun *sirotá₂* which means 'female orphan' and is homonymous with the noun *sirotá₁* , meaning 'male orphan'.
- We correlate the meaning ⁽female⁾ directly to /aja/.

It would seem that the principle of maximal localization favours the latter explanation: here the semantic difference is localized on the spot where the corresponding formal difference occurs.

⁴⁷ The treatment of word stress in phonology represents a remote analogue for this treatment of syntactic significations. It is not meaningful to describe stress in terms of categories: a stressed vowel does not make up a category with unstressed vowels. But stress must nevertheless be dealt with in the phonology of a language. A stressed vowel is described in terms of its contrasts with other vowels in the same utterance.

⁴⁸ It would be interesting, however, to present a foolproof instance of a category which mixes morphological and non-morphological significations. It may be argued that the Danish article is always non-morphological, the definite article sign **en** in *bogen* being not a suffix but a separate word form: **en** is separated from *bog* 'book' when this noun is modified: cf. *den nye bog* 'the new book'. The same seems to apply to Mel'čuk's Romanian example (p. 344). Several other instances of mixed expression of categories and significations in the literature are also doubtful. The English dative, which is said to be expressed either by morphological means or by the separate word *to*, can, on closer inspection, be split up into different meanings. Consider *Jack lost me a lot of money* vs. *Jack lost a lot of money to me*: the person affected by the loss in the dative does not necessarily coincide with the goal of the movement evoked by *lose* expressed by *to* (examples from Oehrle 1978: 215).

⁴⁹ The treatment of expressions with *búdu* as flexional follows from the application of Smirnickij's heuristic (or discovery) criterion: if a signification is expressed morphologically somewhere in the language, or at least if other significations in its category are expressed morphologically, its non-morphological expression should be treated as flexional (pp. 354-355, cf. Smirnickij 1956: 45, where especially the second condition is worked out). According to Mel'čuk, perfective verbs express the future morphologically, viz. by means of the present tense forms: cf. *já napišú* 'I shall write, perfective'. Its imperfective expression by means of *búdu* should therefore be treated as flexional.

This treatment is, again, based on referential semantics: both actions of writing are projected in the future. But it may be argued that we are dealing with different types of future. Some linguists (e.g. Ferrell 1953: 368) prefer a description in which the present tense forms of both perfective and imperfective verbs express the same meaning, say ⁽non-past⁾. In this view, the association of reference to the future with present tense perfective forms is not due to meaning but to <u>inference</u>, drawn from the combination of ⁽non-past⁾ and ⁽perfective⁾. Assuming that the perfective expresses an action as a total event, then if such an event has not taken place before the moment of speech, in which case it must be expressed by means of the preterite, its completion can only take place in the future (cf. Vinogradov 1972[2]: 451-452), at least in a straightforward communication on events. But this does not mean that the present tense expresses the meaning of the future.

If the present tense of perfective verbs does not mean the future, Smirnickij's criterion would no longer invite us to regard expressions with *búdu* as flexional, and Mel'čuk's example would no longer be valid. The perfective forms *búdu* and *stánu* could then be regarded as lexical means to project the completion of the beginning of an action expressed by the infinitive in the future.

Of course there are counter-arguments to this analysis, such as the impossibility to put *búdu* in the preterite: cf. **ón býl rabótat'*. This objection may not be conclusive, as modal-like verbs are often defective. Think of Russian **já xočú móč' sdélat' èto* or its English translation **I want to can do it*. Nevertheless, the syntactic freedom of *búdu* seems to be more limited than that of "normal" modal verbs. Cf. Grenoble's examples *já ne mogú ne kurít'* 'I cannot not smoke' vs. **já ne búdu ne kurít'* 'I shall not not smoke' (Grenoble 1995: 188, 191).

[50] The definition as printed speaks of "no more than one lexical signification", the other significations being flexional. This would fail to accommodate derivational significations.

[51] The author's distinction between *syntagm₁* and *syntagm₂* (p. 128) is not pertinent here. Note that syntagms could not be used in the definition of 'reference signification' (§ 4.13), as the latter involves syntactic relationships between parts of words. Perhaps syntagms are defined on surface syntactic relationships, while reference significations involve deep syntactic relationships.

[52] The book supplies an index of numbered definitions but their mutual relationships are not indicated. Also, not all definitions have made it to the official list (e.g. that of 'reference signification' on p. 327 is not included) and not all official definitions are definitions in the author's sense (e.g. Definition I.1 of the linguistic sign on p. 123 looks more like an axiomatic statement on the relationships holding among the initial objects).

REFERENCES

(Page references are to the most recent editions mentioned. Titles which the present writer has not seen are marked with an asterisk.)

Al, B.P.F.
1975   *La notion de grammaticalité en grammaire générative-transforma-tionelle: Étude générale et application à la syntaxe de l'interrogation directe en français parlé* (= *Publications romanes de l'Université de Leyde* 22). Leyde.
Apresjan, Ju.D.
1973   *Principles and Methods of Contemporary Structural Linguistics* (= *Janua linguarum, series minor* 144). The Hague - Paris.

Axmanova, O.S., O.V. Dolgova
1979   "Sintaksičeskaja teorija i znanie jazyka", *Voprosy jazykoznanija 28*,
            1, 33-39.
Bar-Hillel, Y.
1953/70   "On Recursive Definitions in Empirical Sciences", *Proceedings of the
            Eleventh International Congress of Philosophy 5*, 160-165. Brussels.
            Reprint: Bar-Hillel 1970, 302-307.
1954/64   "Logical Syntax and Semantics", *Language 30*, 2, 230-237. Reprint:
            Bar-Hillel 1964, 38-46.
1964   *Language and Information: Selected Essays on their Theory and
            Application*. Reading, Mass. - Palo Alto - London - Jerusalem.
1967/70   Review of Fodor & Katz 1964, *Language 43*, 2-1, 526-550. Reprint:
            Bar-Hillel 1970, 150-181.
1968/70   "Cybernetics and Linguistics", *Information und Kommunikation*
            (S. Moser, ed.), 29-38. München - Wien. Revised reprint: Bar-Hillel
            1970, 289-301.
1970   *Aspects of Language: Essays and Lectures on Philosophy of Language,
            Linguistic Philosophy and Methodology of Linguistics*. Jerusalem -
            Amsterdam.
Bloomfield, L.
1926/66[4] "A Set of Postulates for the Science of Language", *Language 2*, 3,
            153-164. Reprint: Joos 1966[4], 26-31.
1933   *Language*. New York.
Bolinger, D.L.
1977   *Meaning and Form*. London.
Brandt Corstius, H.
1974   *Algebraïsche taalkunde*. Utrecht.
1978   *Computer-taalkunde* (= *Randgebieden* 3). Muiderberg.
Budagov, R.A.
1972   "O predmete jazykoznanija", *Izvestija Akademii nauk SSSR, Serija
            literatury i jazyka 31*, 5, 401-412.
Cherry, E.C., M. Halle, R. Jakobson
1953   "Toward the Logical Description of Languages in their Phonemic
            Aspect", *Language 29*, 1, 34-46.
Chomsky, N.
1955   "Logical Syntax and Semantics: Their Linguistic Relevance", *Lan-
            guage 31*, 1-2, 36-45.
1957   *Syntactic Structures* (= *Janua linguarum, series minor* 4). London -
            The Hague - Paris.
1964   *Current Issues in Linguistic Theory* (= *Janua linguarum, series
            minor* 38). London - The Hague - Paris.
Cohen, A., C.L. Ebeling, K. Fokkema, A.G.F. van Holk
1972[2]   *Fonologie van het Nederlands en het Fries*. 's-Gravenhage.
Degtereva, T.A.
1964   *Puti razvitija sovremennoj lingvistiki 3: strukturalizm i principy
            marksistskogo jazykoznanija*. Moskva.
Dobrušin, R.L.
1973   "Matematizacija lingvistiki", *Izvestija Akademii nauk SSSR, Serija
            literatury i jazyka 32*, 5, 438-441.

258

Ebeling, C.L.
1978   Syntax and Semantics: A Taxonomic Approach. Leiden.
Ehlich, K.
1982   "Anaphora and Deixis: Same, Similar or different?", Speech, Place
            and Action (R.J. Jarvella, W. Klein, eds.), 315-338. Chichester -
            New York.
Ferrell, J.
1953   "On the Aspects of byt' and on the Position of the Periphrastic
            Future", Word 9, 4 (= Slavic Word 2), 362-376.
Fodor, J.A., J.J. Katz (eds.)
1964   The Structure of Language: Readings in the Philosophy of Language.
            Englewood Cliffs, N.J.
Gladkij, A.V.
1966   "O formal'nyx metodax v lingvistike", Voprosy jazykoznanija 15, 3,
            52-59.
1983   "Toward a Formal Definition of Grammatical Case and Gender of
            Nouns" (= "Supplement II"), Gladkij & Mel'čuk 1983, 188-218.
Gladkij, A.V., I.A. Mel'čuk
1983   Elements of Mathematical Linguistics. Berlin - New York - Amster-
            dam.
Grassi, C.
1967   Elementi di dialettologia italiana. Torino.
Grenoble, L.
1995   "The Imperfective Future Tense in Russian", Word 46, 2, 183-205.
Haegeman, L.
1983   "Die and dat in West-Flemish Relative Clauses", Linguistics in the
            Netherlands 1983 (= Publications in the Language Sciences 12)
            (Bennis, H., Van Lessen Kloeke, W.U.S., eds.), 83-91. Dordrecht -
            Cinnaminson, N.J.
Herdan, G.
1960   Type-token mathematics. The Hague.
Hjelmslev, L.
1943   Omkring sprogteoriens grundlæggelse. København.
1953   Prolegomena to a Theory of Language (= International Journal of
            American Linguistics, Memoir 7). Baltimore.
Hockett, C.F.
1958   A Course in Modern Linguistics. New York.
Jakobson, R.
1936/71   "Beitrag zur allgemeinen Kasuslehre", Travaux du Cercle Linguisti-
            que de Prague 6, 240-288. Prague. Reprint: Jakobson 1971, 23-71.
1959/71   "Boas' View of Grammatical Meaning", The Anthropology of Franz
            Boas: Essays on the Centennial of his Birth (= Memoir 89 of the
            American Anthropological Association) (= the American Anthropolo-
            gist, 61, 5, Part 2) (W. Goldschmidt ed.), 139-145. Reprint: Jakobson
            1971, 489-496.
1971   Selected Writings II: Word and Language. The Hague - Paris.
Jespersen, O.
1924   The Philosophy of Grammar. London.

Joos, M. (ed.)
1966⁴   *Readings in Linguistics I: The Development of Descriptive Linguistics in America 1925-1956.* Chicago.

Kolmogorov, A.N., V.A. Uspenskij
1958   "K opredeleniju algoritma", *Uspexi matematičeskix nauk* 13, 4 (82), 3-28.

Krámský, J.
1969   *The Word as a Linguistic Unit* (= *Janua linguarum, series minor* 75). The Hague - Paris.

Kulagina, O.S.
1958   "Ob odnom sposobe opredelenija grammatičeskix ponjatij na baze teorii množestv", *Problemy kibernetiki* 1 (A.A. Ljapunov, ed.), 203-214. Moskva.

Kuznecov, P.S.
1968   "Vvedenie k ob"ektivnomu opredeleniju granic slova v potoke reči", *Semantičeskie i fonologičeskie problemy prikladnoj lingvistiki* 3, 191-222. Moskva.

Léon, P., M. Léon
1976   *Introduction à la phonétique corrective.* (Paris.)

Leopold, W.F.
1948/66⁴   "German *ch*", *Language* 24, 2, 179-180. Reprint: Joos 1966⁴, 216-217.

L'Hermitte, R.
1987   *Marr, marrisme, marristes.* Paris.

Lins, U.
1988   *Die gefährliche Sprache: Die Verfolgung der Esperantisten unter Hitler und Stalin.* Gerlingen.

Lyons, J.
1968   *Introduction to Theoretical Linguistics.* Cambridge.

Martinet, A.
1962   *A Functional View of Language.* Oxford.

Meillet, A.
1921   *Linguistique historique et linguistique générale.* Genève - Paris.

Mel'čuk, I.A.
1958   "O mašinnom perevode s vengerskogo jazyka na russkij", *Problemy kibernetiki* 1 (A.A. Ljapunov, ed.), 222-264. Moskva.
1961   "Morfologičeskij analiz pri mašinnom perevode", *Problemy kibernetiki* 6 (A.A. Ljapunov, ed.), 207-276. Moskva.
1964   "Tipy svjazej meždu èlementami teksta i tipologija jazykov", *Aktual'nye voprosy jazykoznanija i lingvističeskoe nasledie E.D. Polivanova* 1, 57-59. Samarkand.
1974a   "Ob odnoj modeli ponimanija reči (semantičeskaja teorija R. Šenka I): Zadači lingvističeskoj teorii i semantičeskoe predstavlenie vyskazyvanij", *Naučno-texničeskaja informacija, Serija* 2, 6, 35-46.
1974b   "Ob odnoj modeli ponimanija tekstov (semantičeskaja teorija R. Šenka II): Obščee stroenie modeli "Tekst ⇔ Smysl" i ispol'zuemye v nej semantičeskie sredstva: sistemy SPINOZA i MARGIE", *Naučno-texničeskaja informacija, Serija* 2, 8, 33-44.
1974c   *Opyt teorii lingvističeskix modelej "Smysl ⇔ Tekst".* Moskva.

260

1975   "Opyt razrabotki fragmenta sistemy ponjatij i terminov dlja morfologii
            (k formalizacii jazyka lingvistiki)", *Semiotika i informatika* 6, 5-50.
            Moskva.
1977   "Le cas", *Revue des études slaves* 50, 1, 5-36.
1982   *Toward a Language of Linguistics.* München.
1985a   *Poverxnostnyj sintaksis russkix čislovyx vyraženij* (= *Wiener sla-
            wistischer Almanach, Sonderband* 16). Wien.
1985b   "Three Main Features, Seven Basic Principles, and Eleven Most
            Important Results of Roman Jakobson's Morphological Research",
            Roman Jakobson, Verbal Art, Verbal Sign, Verbal Time (K. Pomor-
            ska, S. Rudy, eds.), 178-200. Minneapolis.
1986   "Toward a Definition of Case", *Case in Slavic* (R.D. Brecht, J.S.
            Levine, eds.), 35-85. Columbus, Ohio.
1988   *Dependency Syntax: Theory and Practice.* Albany, N.Y.
1993   *Cours de morphologie générale (théorique et descriptive), volume I:
            Introduction et première partie: le mot.* Montreal.
1994   *Cours de morphologie générale (théorique et descriptive), volume II:
            deuxième partie: significations morphologiques.* Montreal.
1996   *Cours de morphologie générale (théorique et descriptive), volume III:
            troisième partie: moyens morphologiques et quatrième partie: syn-
            tactiques morphologiques.* Montreal.
1997   *Kurs obščej morfologii, tom I: Vvedenie, Čast' pervaja: Slovo* (=
            Wiener slawistischer Almanach, Sonderband 38, 1). Moskva - Vena.

Nida, E.A.
1949[2]   *Morphology: The Descriptive Analysis of Words* (= *University of
            Michigan Publications; Linguistics* 2). Ann Arbor.

Noreen, A.
1923   *Einführung in die wissenschaftliche Betrachtung der Sprache.* Halle
            (Saale).

Oehrle, R.D.
1978   "Semantic Import of an Investigation of the English Double Object
            Construction", *Proceedings of the Twelfth International Congress of
            Linguists (Vienna 1977).* (W.U. Dressler, W. Meid, eds.), 214-217.
            Innsbruck.

Peškovskij, A.M.
*1925a   "Ponjatie otdel'nogo slova", Peškovskij 1925b, 122-140.
*1925b   *Sbornik statej.* Leningrad.

Pike, K.L.
1957a   "A Note on the Term "Grammeme" ", *General Linguistics* 3, 1,
            29-29.
1957b   "Grammemic Theory", *General Linguistics* 2, 2, 35-41.
1958   "On Tagmemes, née Gramemes", *International Journal of American
            Linguistics* 24, 4, 273-278.

Reichling, A.
1967[2]   *Het woord.* Zwolle.

Revzin, I.I.
1961   "O logičeskoj forme lingvističeskix opredelenij", *Primenenie logiki
            v nauke i texnike,* 140-148. Moskva.
1978   *Struktura jazyka kak modelirujuščej sistemy.* Moskva.

Rosetti, A.
1947²/65   *Le mot.* Copenhague - Bucureşti. Reprint: Rosetti 1965, 11-46.
1965   *Linguistica* (= *Janua linguarum, series maior* 16). London - The
           Hague - Paris.
Schank, R.C.
1972   "Semantics in Conceptual Analysis", *Lingua* 30, 101-140.
Smirnickij, A.I.
1952   "K voprosu o slove (problema "otdel'nosti slova")", *Voprosy teorii i
           istorii jazyka v svete trudov I.V. Stalina po jazykoznaniju* (G.F.
           Aleksandrov, V.V. Vinogradov, G.D. Sanžeev, B.A. Serebrennikov,
           D.I. Česnokov, eds.), 182-203. Moskva.
1954   "K voprosu o slove (problema "toždestva slova")", *Trudy Instituta
           jazykoznanija AN SSSR* 4, 3-49. Moskva.
1955   "Leksičeskoe i grammatičeskoe v slove", *Voprosy grammatičeskogo
           stroja* (V.V. Vinogradov, N.A. Baskakov, I.S. Pospelov, eds.), 11-53.
           Moskva.
1956   "Analitičeskie formy", *Voprosy jazykoznanija* 5, 2, 41-52.
Tegey, H.
*1975   "The Interaction of Phonological and Syntactical Processes: Examples
           from Pashto", *Chicago Linguistic Society, Papers from the Eleventh
           Annual Regional Meeting*, 571-582. Chicago.
1978   *The Grammar of Clitics: Evidence from Pashto (Afghani) and Other
           Languages* (Thesis University of Illinois at Urbana-Champaign, 1977).
           Kabul.
Togeby, K.
1949   "Qu'est-ce qu'un mot?", *Recherches structurales 1949* (= *Travaux
           du Cercle linguistique de Copenhague* 5) (C.A. Bodelsen, P. Dide-
           richsen, E. Fischer-Jørgensen, J. Holt, eds.), 97-111. Copenhague.
Trubetzkoy, N.S.
1939   *Grundzüge der Phonologie* (= *Travaux du Cercle Linguistique de
           Prague* 7). Prague.
Uspenskij, V.A.
1957   "K opredeleniju časti reči v teoretiko-množestvennoj sisteme jazyka",
           Bjulleten' ob"edinenija po problemam mašinnogo perevoda 5 (V.Ju.
           Rozencvejg, ed.), 22-26. Moskva.
1957/93   "K opredeleniju padeža po A.N. Kolmogorovu",: *Bjulleten' ob"edine-
           nija po problemam mašinnogo perevoda* 5 (V.Ju. Rozencvejg, red.),
           11-18, corrigenda 83. Moskva. Reprint: = "Appendix A", Van Helden
           1993b, 1201-1206.
Van Helden, W.A.
1993a   *Case and Gender: Concept Formation between Morphology and
           Syntax, Volume I* (= *Studies in Slavic and General Linguistics* 20).
           Amsterdam - Atlanta, GA.
1993b   *Case and Gender: Concept Formation between Morphology and
           Syntax, Volume II* (= *Studies in Slavic and General Linguistics* 21).
           Amsterdam - Atlanta, GA.
Vinogradov, V.V.
1944/75   "O formax slova", *Izvestija AN SSSR, Otdelenie literatury i jazyka* 3,
           1, 31-44. Reprint: Vinogradov 1975, 33-50.

262

1972[2]   *Russkij jazyk: grammatičeskoe učenie o slove.* Moskva.
1975   *Izbrannye trudy: issledovanija po russkoj grammatike.* Moskva.
Vogt, H.
1944   Review of Hjelmslev 1943, *Acta linguistica* 4, 94-98.
Wierzbicka, A.
1980   *The Case for Surface Case* (= *Linguistica extranea, studia* 9). Ann
            Arbor.
Zaliznjak, A.A.
1967   *Russkoe imennoe slovoizmenenie.* Moskva.
1969   "La morphologie nominale en Russe", *La linguistique en U.R.S.S.*
            (= *Langages* 15) (R. L'Hermitte, ed.), 43-56. Paris.

Dutch Contributions to the Twelfth International Congress of Slavists, Cracow, Linguistics (= *Studies in Slavic and General Linguistics* Vol 24), 263-281. RODOPI, Amsterdam - Atlanta, GA 1998.

CAUSATIVE MEANING IN RUSSIAN: STOPPING A PROCESS

WIM HONSELAAR

0. Introduction

The Dutch causative/permissive verb *laten* has a great many translations into Russian. This comes out clearly in the extensive entry *laten* in Van den Baar's Dutch-Russian dictionary (Van den Baar 1989: 557-58) where we find seven general translations (namely: бросить, отказаться от, заставить + inf., приказать, велеть, поручить, оставить, допустить, позволить and разрешить) and many contextual and collocational translational variants. The German equivalent of *laten*, *lassen*, shows a similar "richness" of translations (Götz 1988); Götz has pointed out that this enormous "fanning out" has to do with the multiple and complex polysemy of *lassen*. Given the great variety of meanings and sub-meanings of the Dutch verb *laten* in the standard Dutch monolingual Van Dale dictionary (Van Dale 1992: 1630-31), we can conclude that Götz's statement holds for Dutch *laten* as well.

The polysemous character of *laten* does not, however, explain the fact that *laten* in one of its specific meanings can have a number of different translations, viz. the translation of the imperative phrase *Laat dat!* 'Hold it/stop it/don't do that'. The preferred Russian translations are the following perfective imperative forms: Брось(те), Перестань(те) and Оставь(те). Although these three Russian forms reflect one Dutch form, they are not mutually substitutable in all contexts, at least not without effecting various pragmatic changes. In order to be able to examine the pragmatic characteristics of брось(те), перестань(те) and оставь(те), I have collected all occurrences of these forms from the texts in the Amsterdam Russian Corpus and in the Uppsala Corpus; all these texts are original Russian texts, not translations.

In the following section I will sketch a "frame" (in the sense of Fillmore (1976), Werth (1995) and Van Brederode (1995)) for *Laat dat!*; subsequently I will discuss the way in which the forms брось(те), перестань(те) and оставь(те) fit into this frame.

1. The frame of the Russian correspondences of *Laat dat!*

The expressions брось(те), перестань(те) and оставь(те) are imperative forms. The situations associated with these imperatives, can be characterized by a "frame" specified by four categories:

1. the *moment of speaking*;
2. the *speaker* who gives an order at the moment of speaking;
3. the *addressee* who is urged to stop a certain activity in which he is the agent;
4. the *activity* that has to be stopped.

Basically, this frame looks very simple but this simplicity is only superficial, for the frame only specifies the categories and not their relevant values, nor the interrelations of these values.

Within the frame we can expect at least the following potential relations between the categories of *activity* and *moment of speaking*:

-   the activity is actually going on at the moment of speaking;
-   the activity is a habitual activity which is not necessarily in progress at the moment of speaking;
-   the activity was planned before the moment of speaking, and not yet in progress at the moment of speaking.

Correspondingly, the order to stop the activity is an order:

-   to cease the activity immediately or in the near future;
-   to give up the habitual activity;
-   to refrain from the planned activity in the future.

The activity may be stopped permanently or temporarily; in the first case the activity will not (or never) take place, in the latter case the activity is merely interrupted or postponed until later.

The activities involved must necessarily be controlled somehow; otherwise it would be pragmatically inappropriate to give an order to stop them. All the same, the degree of control may vary from case to case: from absolute control in *stop smoking!*, where the addressee is urged to do his best to give up a bad habit, to indirect control in *stop sleeping so long!*

A relevant factor seems to be the amount of energy which the addressee must spend to stop the activity: from experience we know that to stop smoking requires considerably more will power from a chain smoker than from somebody who smokes only occasionally.

The motives for the speaker to give his order may range from relatively subjective and personal (such as "I don't like your activity") to relatively objective (such as "your behaviour is not appropriate in the given circumstances").

In the following sections we will see how these categories, their values and relations, combine in the case of брось(те), перестань(те) and оставь(те), and in what respect these forms differ.

2. *Брось(те)*

In its literal sense the verb бросить means 'throw (away)' and it is associated with an accusative or instrumental object, referring to concrete objects, such as stones:

(1)   бросить камень$_4$ в [4]
(2)   бросить камнями$_5$ в [4]

In certain contexts the meaning of 'throwing away' is associated with the idea of stopping the activity in which the object would have played an important role. In the following example Гущин is urged to throw away his knife; by implication he is asked not to use it:

(3)   Он заметил, что его напарника, дежурившего в этот день без оружия, гущинские дружки оттеснили. **Брось** нож, – тихо сказал он Гущину. – Не дури... (Uppsala Corpus)

In other contexts, this implication is softened by the suggestion to use another object instead:

(4)   – Тогда что ж ты возишься с кисточками, Кай Юлий Цезарь? **Брось** их, вооружись чем потяжелее. Чтоб видели и боялись – можешь проломить голову. (Uppsala Corpus)

Although it cannot be excluded that, in (4), Кай Юлий Цезарь is asked to throw away his brushes, the general message is that he should replace the brushes by more powerful weapons.

The bigger, or the less concrete, this object is – the less "throwable" in other words –, the more the idea of physical movement of an object is backgrounded:

(5)   – Я украл эту машину, – сказал я.
– **Брось** ее здесь и пойдем, – сказал он. Пойдем в село.
(Аксенов: *Ожог*)
(6)   И он помахал в темноте ярко тлевшим шнуром. – **Брось** огонь! Разведчик в ватнике, с автоматом на шее, неслышно появив-

шийся перед ними, ударил его по руке, сапогом втоптал огонь в снег. (Uppsala Corpus)

(7) — Ладно, — сообщил Остап, прощаясь, — сейте разумное, доброе, вечное, а там посмотрим! Прощайте и вы, служивые. **Бросьте** свои масляные краски. Переходите на мозаику из гаек, костылей и винтиков. Портрет из гаек! Замечательная идея. (Ильф и Петров: *Золотой теленок*)

(8) — Ну, я тебя надолго не задержу, — сказал Дик и посмотрел на часы. — Слушай, Рэд, **брось** ты свои мелочи, возвращайся в институт. (Стругацкие: *Пикник* ...)

(9) — Я тебя по старой дружбе предупреждаю: **брось** это дело, **брось** навсегда. Ведь во второй раз сцапают — шестью месяцами не отделаешься. А из института тебя вышибут немедленно и навсегда, понимаешь? (Стругацкие: *Пикник* ...)

(10) На крыльце с клюкой или ухватом в руках появлялась Хавронья, бойкая крупная баба. Федя не шутя предупреждал ее: — Ты **брось** эту моду — сразу за клюку хвататься. А то я когда-нибудь отобью руки-то. (Шукшин: *Любавины*)

In (8), (9) and (10) the "concrete" objects do not refer to objects that are thrown from one place to another. Instead they refer to activities: мелочи means 'insignificant activities', дело means 'the things your are occupied with', and эту моду is paraphrased as the habit 'сразу за клюку хвататься'.

A more explicit way to refer to activities is to use verbs rather than nouns. And indeed, I have found numerous examples with an infinitive as the object of брось(те):

(11) Но тут владычица буфета, вся белая, как белый свет, воскликнула: — Да что же это! Уйдёшь ты всё же или нет? Ах, деточка, мой месяц ясный, пойдём со мною, **брось** тужить! Мы в роще Марьиной прекрасной с тобой, две Марьи, будем жить. (Ахмадулина: *Стихи*)

(12) — **Брось** считать, что ты выше других... что мы мелкая сошка, а ты Каин и Манфред... (Ерофеев: *Москва-Петушки*)

(13) Он подошел к зеркалу, прихорошился, подмигнул самому себе и, обернувшись, пропел: — **Брось** сердиться, Саша, ласково взгляни! (Незнанский: *Фауст*)

(14) Из коридора со скрежетом выехала скамеечка и на ней вытянулся, балансируя, Филипп Филиппович в синих с полосками носках.

– Иван Арнольдович, **бросьте** вы отвечать. Идите в спальню, я вам туфли дам. (Булгаков: *Собачье сердце*)

(15)   Вам нравится такой способ дележки?
– Нет, не нравится, – вырвалось у Паниковского.
– **Бросьте** шутить, Бендер, – недовольно сказал Балаганов. – Надо разделить по справедливости.
– Этого не будет, – холодно сказал Остап. (Ильф и Петров: *Золотой теленок*)

In a considerable number of cases the infinitive objects as well as the noun objects suggest that the activity in question has a negative connotation: свои мелочи in (8), эту моду – сразу за клюку хвататься in (10), тужить in (11), считать, что ты выше других in (12), сердиться in (13), and шутить in (15). In one way or another, the speaker evaluates the activity as 'negative', 'not appropriate', in short, 'unsuited to the occasion', and therefore urges the addressee to stop this activity.

The link between the literal and the metaphorical senses of бросить is quite transparant (cf. Lakoff and Johnson: 1980):
- lit.: if X throws Y, then, X uses some power to move Y, X throws Y in order to get Y at another place, X's activity has a rather abrupt character, X gets rid of Y, and therefore loses his direct contact with Y and can no longer manipulate Y.
- metaph.: if X "throws" Y, then, X uses some power with respect to Y, X "throws" Y in order to stop Y, X's activity has a rather abrupt character, X loses his direct contact with Y and can no longer perform Y.

In many cases the activity is not explicitly mentioned, but what it is, is implicitly clear from the context:

(16)   «Ну, что тебе приснилось? Говори.»
«Да я ж тебе сказал о разговоре с комиссией.»
«Да **брось** ты, не хитри. Я сам его подслушал в коридоре.»
(Бродский: *Из старых стихов*)

(17)   – Управлюсь, – недовольно отвечал отец, – материал есть, и председатель обещал еще подкинуть. Вот только вернулся из правления с Иваном. Теперь мне сам бог не брат и черт не кум!
– **Брось**, Степан, рано еще песни-то играть.
(Солоухин: *Не жди ...*)

(18)   – По признаку незаметности, – ответил Павор. – Если человек сер, незаметен, значит, его надо уничтожить.

268

- А кто будет определять, заметный это человек или нет?
- **Бросьте**, это детали. Я Вам излагаю принцип, а кто, что и как это детали. (Стругацкие: *Гадкие лебеди*)

(19) – А почему так официально? Садитесь, Лева...
- Я буду говорить стоя, – сказал Лев Абалкин.
- **Бросьте**, Лева, что за церемонии? Садитесь, прошу вас. Нам предстоит долгий разговор, не правда ли? (Стругацкие: *Жук ...*)

In the metaphorical sense the idea of power is associated with manifest decisiveness on the part of the speaker (and reluctance on the part of the subject):

(20) – Почему же не объясняет? – возразил Валентин.
- Могла ведь какая-нибудь девчушка забыть на лужайке любимого заводного медвежонка...
- Ну, это Вы **бросьте**, – <u>решительно</u> сказал Нунан.
- Ничего себе медвежонок – земля трясется... Впрочем, конечно, может быть и медвежонок. (Стругацкие: *Пикник ...*)

(21) – Пистолет, – буркнул Артур и закусил губу.
- Зачем он тебе?
- Стрелять! – сказал Артур с вызовом.
- **Брось, брось**, – <u>строго</u> проговорил Рэдрик и сел прямо. – Давай его сюда. В зоне стрелять не в кого. Давай.
(Стругацкие: *Пикник ...*)

(22) – <u>Сию же минуту</u> **брось** накладывать!
Серый побледнел.
- Нет, дела я не брошу. Дела мне нельзя бросать.
(Бунин: *Деревня*)

With respect to the speaker's perspective – cf. Zaitseva (1995) – it is important to notice that the speaker often has a strongly negative attitude towards the (continuation of the) activity and/or towards the addressee. This claim is supported by the fact that in the immediate context of брось(те) we often find explicit signals reflecting the deprecatory attitude of the speaker, such as:

- a negative evaluation of the addressee's behaviour or state of mind:

(23) – Эх, здорово я их усек, сейчас бы сшиб подряд, не успели бы пикнуть, – сдерживая дыхание, проговорил тот, что целился.
- **Брось**, <u>дурило</u>! С пулей не шутят, не целься зря, – ответил ему другой, ... (Айтматов: *Ранние журавли*)

– a deprecatory expression for the activity, such as тужить in (11), and:

(24) – Кирюшка! **Бросьте** <u>трепаться</u>! Что вы, с ума сошли?..
      (Булгаков: *Мастер и Маргарита*)
(25) – Вы, – кричал гражданин, сопровождаемый свистящими
      мальчишками, – **бросьте, бросьте** <u>дурака валять</u>! Не выйдет это!
      (Булгаков: *Мастер и Маргарита*)

– a deprecatory expression for the object:

(26) А ты, мой скучный проповедник, Умерь ученый вкуса гнев!
      Поди, кричи, брани другого И **брось** <u>ленивца</u> молодого, Об нем
      тихонько пожалев (Пушкин in: Смирнов: *Кастрационный* ...)
(27) А ты что, жаловаться побежишь, что я тебя опозорил? А?
      Что ты все строчишь? **Брось** свои <u>писульки</u>.
      (Петрушевская: *Три девушки* ...)

– an indication of the uselessness of the activity:

(28) – Хоть халат-то запахни ему. Ведь неудобно, я тут. Проклятые
      черти. Пить не умеете. Витька! Витька! Что с тобой? Вить...
      – **Брось**. <u>Не поможет</u>. Николушка, слушай.
      (Булгаков: *Белая гвардия*)

With брось(те) the activity may or may not actually be in progress at the moment of speaking: in (28) брось obviously refers to the arguments the first speaker is producing at the moment of speaking, in (10) it refers to the habit of grasping at a stick, a habit which is, by the way, shown at the moment of speaking, and in (7) брось refers to a habit which is not manifest at the moment of speaking, but which is relevant to the present situation.

It may be concluded that брось(те) is an appropriate choice when a personal, subjective position of the speaker with respect to the addressee and his activity is at issue, and when the speaker is, or feels himself, in a position where he has the authority to disqualify the activity of the addressee.

3. *Перестань(те)*

Syntactically, перестань(те) differs from брось(те). Whereas брось(те) may (occasionally) take a noun as an object, перестань(те) never does. Перестань(те) only accepts infinitive objects (29) or ∅-objects (30):

(29) — Любимой игрушкой, — улыбнулась Зиночка. — Просто игрушкой я быть не согласна.

— **Перестань** болтать глупости! — прикрикнула Искра. — Мне противно слушать, потому что все это отвратительно. Это буржуазные пошлости, если хочешь знать. (Uppsala Corpus)

(30) Старик Базаров глубоко дышал и щурился пуще прежнего.

— Ну, полно, полно, Ариша! **Перестань,** — заговорил он, поменявшись взглядом с Аркадием, который стоял неподвижно у тарантаса, между тем как мужик на козлах даже отвернулся. (Тургенев: *Отцы и дети*)

Semantically, перестань(те) differs from брось(те) in that it carries the meaning of 'stopping' directly, not metaphorically. The idea of 'power', which is so characteristic of брось(те), is not explicitly present in перестань(те). Therefore, we may find all kinds of "softeners" in the immediate context of перестань(те). These softeners are realised as:

— specific verbs of speaking:

(31) Ну... **перестаньте,** — она <u>бормотала,</u> дергая за локоть Димыча и одновременно ногой под столом Санечку пихая. (Uppsala Corpus)

— adverbials with the verb of speaking:

(32) — **Перестань,** — <u>тихо</u> сказал дедушка, хотя он ничего не делал. (Uppsala Corpus)

(33) — Повторяю тебе, но в последний раз: **перестань** притворяться сумасшедшим, разбойник, — произнес Пилат <u>мягко и монотонно,</u> — за тобою записано немного, но записанного достаточно, чтобы тебя повесить. (Булгаков: *Мастер и Маргарита*)

(34) Маргарита заговорила, криво и <u>жалко улыбаясь:</u>

— **Перестаньте** вы меня мистифицировать и мучить вашими загадками... (Булгаков: *Мастер и Маргарита*)

— sympathetic forms of address:

(35) — **Перестань,** <u>моя хорошая,</u> — говорил он, — поплакала — и будет... (Чехов: *Дама с собачкой*)

The most frequent interpretation of перестань(те) is: stop your actual activity for it is not appropriate. The non-appropriateness of the activity comes out clearly in the paraphrase не надо плакать in (36) and не надо in (37) (for the meaning of надо, see Honselaar 1992), or in the fact that it prevents the speaker from speaking in (38).

(36)   — Не плачь... **Перестань**. <u>Не надо</u> плакать.
       (Шукшин: *Любавины*)

(37)   — Какое роковое заблуждение! **Перестаньте**, Юрий Андреевич, <u>не надо</u>. (Пастернак: *Доктор Живаго*)

(38)   И она заплакала, опустив голову на руки.
       — **Перестань**, мне <u>надо</u> тебе что-то сказать.
       (Рыбаков: *Дети Арбата*)

Other examples of inappropriate activities are:

(39)   — Но вы же... «Галина Па-а-а-авловна»... «царица вы наша»... Примадонна... Так и выходите...
       — **Перестаньте** ехидничать, Борис Александрович, я в самом деле не знаю. Всю роль отчетливо представляю, но не выход.
       (Вишневская: *ГАЛИНА*)

(40)   — Петя, сынок, что же сделаешь?.. Что же теперь сделаешь? **Перестань**, сынок, люди услышат, **перестань**. Их теперь не вернешь... (Шукшин: *Любавины*)

(41)   — Я вас предупредил, любезный мой посетитель, — начал Василий Иванович, — что мы живем здесь, так сказать, на бивуаках...
       — Да **перестань**, что ты извиняешься? — перебил Базаров. — Кирсанов очень хорошо знает, что мы с тобой не Крезы и что у тебя не дворец. Куда мы его поместим, вот вопрос.
       (Тургенев: *Отцы и дети*)

(42)   И неизвестно было по-прежнему, что их ждало впереди, когда вдруг лодка сильно вздрогнула и он услышал испуганный возглас отца:
       — Мылгун! Мылгун! Что ты делаешь? **Перестань**!
       (Айтматов: *Пегий пес*)

A personal evaluation by the speaker stands out in:

(43)   — Слушайте, — перебил я его, — да **перестаньте** же вы называть меня этим идиотским именем. Если уж вы вообще не можете обойтись без подобных кличек, называйте меня просто Классик, но без всяких Никитичей. (Войнович: *МОСКВА 2042*)

(44)   ... Семенова, из скольких томов состоит собрание сочинений Гениалиссимуса?
       — Из шестисот шестнадцати, — охотно отвечала Семенова.
       — Неправильно. Вчера вышли еще два новых тома. Комков,

перестань вертеться. Так вот, дети, этот памятник представляет собой скульптурную группу, центральной фигурой которой является сам Гениалиссимус. (Войнович: *МОСКВА 2042*)

The personal evaluation may result in something like a reproach: "you are exaggerating" in (45) and (46), and "your statement does not hold" in (47):

(45) И поклонницы мои плакали. А я смотрел на них и думал: Боже мой, как летит время! Вот эту я знаю уже 30 лет, а эту – 20, и какие они уже все старые, и какой же я-то старый...
 – Да **перестаньте**, Сергей Яковлевич. Вы выглядите моложе любого нашего молодого тенора. Посмотрите на их сутулые спины и унылые физиономии – и ходят-то, как старики, ноги волочат. (Вишневская: *ГАЛИНА*)

(46) – Господи, Слава, что это – война, что ли?
 – Да **перестань** – маневры. (Вишневская: *ГАЛИНА*)

(47) – Так кто ж тебя отсюда гонит? Почему ты как сумасшедший работаешь и носишься по всему миру?
 – Я работаю для семьи.
 – **Перестань**, нам уже ничего не нужно. Ты купил третью машину, а нам хватило бы и одной. Остановись, посиди дома, с детьми позанимайся, кто им может помочь в музыке так, как ты... (Вишневская: *ГАЛИНА*)

The speaker's discontent is made explicit in "Надоело наконец!" (48) and in "противно/отвратительно" (49):

(48) – Ай-яй-яй... – начала она прежним тоном, но мать Навы нервно сказала:
 – **Перестаньте!** Надоело наконец! Уходи отсюда, – сказала она Кандиду. (Стругацкие: *Улитка* ...)

(49) – **Перестань** болтать глупости! – прикрикнула Искра. – Мне противно слушать, потому что все это отвратительно.
 (Uppsala Corpus)

In addition to saying that the addressee should stop his activity, the speaker may also suggest a more desirable alternative: "drink" instead of "become angry" in (50), "improve things" instead of "go out boozing" in (51), and "drink tea" instead of "be upset" in (52):

(50) — Йося, да **перестань** ты сердиться! Ишь, какой обидчивый! Давай лучше выпьем и – кто старое помянет, тому глаз вон!.. (Вишневская: *ГАЛИНА*)

(51) — Ну, Кузьма, **перестань** гулять – надо дело исправлять. (*Русские волшебные сказки*)

(52) И все, и **перестаньте** переживать, давайте лучше чай пить. Отнесите соседям эту присоску. (Незнанский и Тополь: *Журналист для Брежнева*)

In this context it is significant that the activity itself is often expressed by words having an deprecative meaning, such as болтать in (53), врать in (54), ныть in (55), бренчать in (56), ваньку валять in (57), молоть чушь in (58), and наивничать in (59):

(53) — **Перестаньте** болтать, Размыткин. Отвечайте на вопросы. (Ардов: *Двое в ...*)

(54) — Знаю, – сказал Голем. – Догадываюсь, потому что мне так хочется... И **перестаньте** врать, Вы же торговали у Тэдди Погодник и прекрасно знаете, что это такое. (Стругацкие: *Гадкие лебеди*)

(55) — Вот балда! Я же тебе сказал: никого не убивал! И **перестань** ныть, а то вышвырну к едреной матери из квартиры! (Незнанский и Тополь: *Журналист для Брежнева*)

(56) — Виктуар, **перестаньте** бренчать, – сказал Голем. (Стругацкие: *Гадкие лебеди*)

(57) — Господин Сумман, – сказал Виктор. – **Перестаньте** ваньку валять. (Стругацкие: *Гадкие лебеди*)

(58) Чебриков побагровел: — **Перестаньте** молоть чушь! Учились вместе – хорошо. А теперь нечего об этом болтать! (Незнанский: *Фауст*)

(59) — **Перестань** наивничать, – резко сказал Родионов: шрам его потемнел. (Шукшин: *Любавины*)

In order to enforce his order, the speaker may add a threat (*а то*) to "punish" the addressee if he shows any reluctance to obey the order:

(60) — **Перестань** брать слово, когда мне спится, а то на тебя заявление подам! (Платонов: *Котлован*)

(61) — **Перестань**, а то в зубы заеду! (Шукшин: *Любавины*)

The speaker may also point out other negative consequences of the activity if it is not stopped:

274

(62)   – **Перестань**, дурак, с огнём баловать! – крикнули на него
        братья. – Ещё избу сожжёшь. (*Русские волшебные сказки*)
(63)   Когда он говорил ему, царь отвечал: разве советником царским
        поставили тебя? **перестань**, чтобы не убили тебя.
        (Библия: *Ветхий завет*)
(64)   – **Перестань**, мама, тебе вредно так, – предостерегла Тоня.
        (Пастернак: *Доктор Живаго*)

In conclusion we can say that перестань(те) is an order or request
to the addressee to stop his actual activity, which without the addressee
obeying the order would continue. The motives for the speaker to give
his order are <u>evaluative</u> (<u>personal</u> and <u>situational</u>), rather than <u>objective</u>:
the speaker finds the activity inappropriate.

4.   *Оставь(те)*

Whereas перестань(те) accepts infinitive objects (or Ø-objects), оставь-
(те) accepts only (pro)nouns) (or Ø-objects).

Just like перестань(те), оставь(те) conveys a relatively mild order
to stop an activity. It is an order to spend no more energy to continue
an activity:

(65)   **Оставьте** ваши занятия. Остановитесь вместе со мной, и почтим
        минутой молчания то, что невыразимо.
        (Ерофеев: *Москва-Петушки*)
(66)   Говорил он, естественно, о ребенке, о том, что мальчик
        нуждается в отце, но Вероника его оборвала:
        – **Оставь**, пожалуйста, стыдно слушать, умный человек, а туда
        же ... зачем ему нужен отец-дурак? (Uppsala Corpus) [= (77)]

This meaning is also clear in other cases where the verb оставить is
used, such as in the very frequent collocation оставить кого-л. в покое:

(67)   – Ну, чего еще делать?
        – **Оставь** меня в покое и сама присядь наконец, не мелькай
        у меня перед глазами! (Вишневская: *ГАЛИНА*)

and in many other syntactic environments, such as:

– with a nominal direct object:

(68)   — Слушай, тетенька, — сказал я, к ней повернувшись, — **оставь меня**, ради Бога, и без тебя тошно. (Войнович: *МОСКВА 2042*)

— with a nominal direct object followed by a predicative modifier:

(69)   — Только не изменяйте ничего. **Оставьте** все как есть, — сказал он дрожащим голосом. (Толстой: *Анна Каренина*)

(70)   Тут Пилат вскричал: — Вывести конвой с балкона! — и, повернувшись к секретарю, добавил: — **Оставьте** меня с преступником наедине, здесь государственное дело.
(Булгаков: *Мастер и Маргарита*)

— with an object with infinitive construction:

(71)   Список же с этого указа выставив на всяком месте открыто, **оставьте** Иудеев пользоваться своими законами и содействуйте им, чтобы ... (Библия: *Ветхий завет*)

— with a nominal direct and indirect object:

(72)   Насчет золота: мама все боится войны, говорит, в случае чего живи как Нора: ничего не продавай, все **оставь** детям.
(Петрушевская: *Три девушки*)

Usually, оставь(те) does not have an explicit direct object. If the object is expressed, it is a noun, not an infinitive. The noun refers to an action, for example, ваши занятия in (65). Occasionally the object does not directly refer to an activity, as, for example, принципы in (73):

(73)   — Но это против моих принципов.
       — **Оставьте** свои принципы для другого места и не доказывайте здесь никому ничего. (Вишневская: *ГАЛИНА*)

The implicit activity in (73) is "talking about, referring to". Other cases are:

(74)   — Мы все сами купим, — возразил племянник.
       — Представляю! — Варвара Тихоновна всплеснула руками. — Нет уж, **оставь** свое «сами» на другой раз. Лучшие костюмы в городе — мои. (Солоухин: *Не жди ...*)

(75)   — Кушай, чего это ты?
       — Наелась.
       — Ну-ка **оставь** свое «наелась». Тебе надо, нечего экономить, все равно мука кончается. (Солоухин: *Не жди ...*)

The phrase эти мрачные мысли in (76) refers to something intermediate between an activity and an actant in an activity:

(76)　— Не кажется ли вам, – сказал Генрих своему новому другу Бомзе, – что мне заплатили деньги зря? Я не выполняю никакой работы.
　　　— **Оставьте**, коллега, эти мрачные мысли! – вскричал Адольф Николаевич. (Ильф и Петров: *Золотой теленок*)

If оставь(те) is used without an overt object, the form generally refers to the speech process of the addressee: he is requested to keep his mouth shut because the speaker has negative feelings about what the addressee has just said:

— the speaker may be embarrassed:

(77)　Говорил он, естественно, о ребенке, о том, что мальчик нуждается в отце, но Вероника его оборвала:
　　　— **Оставь**, пожалуйста, стыдно слушать, умный человек, а туда же ... зачем ему нужен отец-дурак? Да еще к тому же пошлый дурак, убежденный в своей незаурядности? (Uppsala Corpus) [= (66)]

— the speaker finds it inappropriate that somebody (in (78)) or something (in (79)) is brought up in the discourse:

(78)　— Этот Долго-Сабуров покончил жизнь самоубийством, у меня есть магнитофонная запись с его словами...
　　　— **Оставь!** – лениво прервал он мягким жестом руки. – Дело не в нем. (Незнанский и Тополь: *Журналист для Брежнева*)
(79)　Сергей Иванович еще раз улыбнулся. «И у него там тоже какая-то своя философия есть на службу своих наклонностей», – подумал он.
　　　— Ну уж об философии ты **оставь**, – сказал он. – Главная задача философии всех веков состоит именно в том, чтобы найти ... (Толстой: *Анна Каренина*)

- the speaker does not agree with the words of the addressee:

(80)　Жареный заяц – вещь великолепная. Но выводить отсюда, что деревня благоденствует, это, простите, по меньшей мере смело, это скачок весьма рискованный.
　　　— Ах, **оставьте**, – возражал Юрий Андреевич. – Посмотрите

на эти станции. Деревья не спилены. Заборы целы. А эти рынки! Эти бабы! Подумайте, какое удовлетворение! (Пастернак: *Доктор Живаго*)

– the speaker does not find the words of the addressee realistic:

(81)   – Ты абсолютно прав. И если мне скажут, что твое письмо появится в советской печати, я первая подпишусь под ним, и пусть тогда меня хоть и растерзают на глазах у всех. Но глупо отдавать жизнь на подлое и тайное ее удушение.
– **Оставь**, не те теперь времена. Я знаю, что письмо не напечатают, и все же какой-то круг людей узнает о нем от сотрудников редакций газет. (Вишневская: *ГАЛИНА*)

– the speaker is bored by the words of the addressee:

(82)   «Забилась в угол, глядишь упрямо... Скажи, согласна? Мы ждем давно». – «Ах, я не знаю. **Оставьте**, мама! **Оставьте**, мама. Мне все равно!» (Цветаева: *Стихотворения*) [= (93)]

– the speaker disagrees with the addressee's reasoning in (83) and with the addressee's statement about the value of the paintings in the museum in (84):

(83)   – Черт знает что... Сколько же ты думаешь так скитаться, прятаться? А вышибут немца, тогда как?
– Я веру принял, клятву дал не брать в руки оружия.
– **Оставь**, Лазарь, этим не прикроешься. Ты боец Красной Армии, первая клятва давалась Родине, что ж так легко клятвы меняешь? Ты – дезертир, и власть с тебя спросит!
(Солоухин: *Не жди ...*)

(84)   – Я вовсе не против театров и музеев. Но ассигнования на городской театр в прошлом году недоиспользованы, а в музеи ходят одни туристы...
– Похитители картин, – вставил человек с пластырем.
– **Оставьте**, пожалуйста. У нас нет картин, которые стоило бы похищать. (Стругацкие: *Хищные ...*) [= (88)]

– the speaker thinks that the addressee is not talking seriously:

(85)   – Нашей публике нужна хорошая оккупационная армия, сказал человек с пластырем.
– Ах, **оставьте**, пожалуйста, вы ведь так не думаете... Охват кружками у нас на безобразном уровне. Боэла мне жаловалась

вчера, что на ее чтения ходит только один человек, ...
(Стругацкие, *Хищные* ...)

Even if there is an overt object, this usually refers to the addressee's
words, for example, the object все это in (86):

(86) Ты щадишь его, дитя мое, я угадала тебя, и, бог видит, какими
горькими слезами обливала я подушку мою!..
– Да **оставьте** все это, маменька! – прерывает Зина в невыра-
зимой тоске. (Достоевский: *Дядюшкин сон*)

Other activities are less frequently referred to; an example is "shooting"
in (87):

(87) Мылгун опустил вскинутый винчестер – добивать нерпу теперь
не было смысла.
– **Оставь**, все равно утонет, – проговорил Эмрайин.
(Айтматов: *Пегий пес*)

The appeal to inactivity makes the order оставь(те) relatively mild.
Elements in the context, such as particles and phrases, confirm this:

(88) – Похитители картин, – вставил человек с пластырем.
– **Оставьте**, пожалуйста. У нас нет картин, которые стоило бы
похищать. (Стругацкие: *Хищные* ...) [= (84)]
(89) – Ах, **оставьте**, пожалуйста, вы ведь так не думаете...
(Стругацкие: *Хищные* ...)
(90) Её губы слегка побледнели...
– **Оставьте** меня, – сказала она едва внятно.
(Лермонтов: *Герой нашего времени*)
(91) – **Оставьте**, Галя, прошу вас, не надо, – сказала Софья Алексан-
дровна, – ведь вы хорошая, добрая женщина, зачем вам это?
(Рыбаков: *Дети Арбата*)
(92) – Маменька, **оставьте** это, я сейчас пойду. Я не для того при-
шёл. Пожалуйста, выслушайте меня.
(Достоевский: *Преступление и наказание*)

The mild character of the order is sometimes related to lack of interest
of the speaker in what will happen:

(93) «Забилась в угол, глядишь упрямо... Скажи, согласна? Мы ждем
давно». «Ах, я не знаю. **Оставьте**, мама! **Оставьте**, мама. Мне
все равно!» (Цветаева: *Стихотворения*) [= (82)]

In three examples the meaning of оставь(те) is made clear by the parallel phrase забудь(те) 'do not pay attention to ... any more':

(94)   – Забудь все это! – кроткого привета раздался всплеск, и образ просиял. Отбор довел до совершенства лица: лишь рознь пороков оживляет их.
       – Забудь! Оставь! – упрашивал и длился печальный звук, но изнемог и стих. (Ахмадулина: *Стихи*)

(95)   Что же скажу тебе, кроме: – Ты это забудь и оставь! Ведь не растревожишь же! (Цветаева: *Стихотворения*)

(96)   Оставьте меня! Оставьте меня одного! Я так решил, еще прежде... Я это наверно решил... Что бы со мною ни было, погибну я или нет, я хочу быть один. Забудьте меня совсем. Это лучше... (Достоевский: *Преступление и наказание*)

In conclusion, оставь(те) is an order or request to spend no more energy on something, generally by no longer talking about it or no longer paying attention to it. The main motive for this order is that the speaker has negative feelings about the addressee's words.

5. Conclusion

Syntactically, брось(те) is more flexible than перестань(те) and оставь (те): although all three can be used absolutely (i.e. with a Ø-object), only брось(те) combines with both infinitives and noun objects; перестань(те) takes only infinitives and оставь(те) only noun objects.

Semantically, брось(те) conveys greater emotional involvement than перестань(те) and оставь(те): it is the most emotional, personal and powerful expression of the three forms. It is especially used in cases where it is difficult for the addressee to stop his activity, where the speaker has an aversion to this activity, or where the speaker has or feels authority over the addressee. Перестань(те) and оставь(те) are less explicit in this respect. Перестань(те) is an order or request to stop an ongoing activity because the speaker finds it inappropriate in the given situation. It is associated with the expectation that the addressee would continue the activity otherwise. Оставь(те) says that the addressee is ordered or requested to spend no more energy on some ongoing activity because the speaker has negative feelings about this activity; the default activity is 'talking/speaking'.

University of Amsterdam

REFERENCES

Baar, A.H. van den
 1989   *Nederlands-Russisch Woordenboek*. Deventer-Antwerpen.
Brederode, T. van
 1995   *Collocation Restrictions, Frames and Metaphor*. Amsterdam.
Dale, van
 1992   *Groot Woordenboek der Nederlandse Taal*. Utrecht, Antwerpen.
Fillmore, Ch.
 1976   "Topics in Lexical Semantics". In: Roger W. Cole (ed.), *Current Issues in Linguistic Theory*. Bloomington
Götz, D.
 1988   "Zur Wiedergabe von "lassen" im Russischen", *Praktika* 1, 3-6.
Honselaar, W.
 1992   "The Russian modals ПРИХОДИТЬСЯ/ПРИЙТИСЬ, НУЖНО and НАДО: semantics and pragmatics", *Studies in Russian Linguistics* (= *Studies in Slavic and General Linguistics* Vol. 17), 125-149. Amsterdam: Rodopi.
Lakoff, G., and M. Johnson
 1980   *Metaphors We Live By*. Chicago and London.
Werth, P.N.
 1995   *Text Worlds*. London.
Zaitseva, V.
 1995   *The Speaker's Perspective in Grammar and Lexicon. The Case of Russian*. New York.

SOURCES

Uppsala Corpus

Amsterdam Russian Corpus:
 Чингиз Айтматов: *Ранние журавли*
 Василий Аксенов: *Ожог*
 Виктор Ардов: *Двое в одной проруби*
 Белла Ахмадулина: *Избранное. Стихи*
 Библия (Ветхий завет)
 Иосиф Бродский: *Из старых стихов*
 М.А. Булгаков: *Белая гвардия*
 М.А. Булгаков: *Мастер и Маргарита*
 М.А. Булгаков: *Собачье сердце*
 И.А. Бунин: *Деревня*
 Владимир Войнович: *МОСКВА 2042*
 Г. Вишневская: *ГАЛИНА. История жизни*
 Ф.М. Достоевский: *Дядюшкин сон*
 Ф.М. Достоевский: *Преступление и наказание*
 Венедикт Ерофеев: *Москва - Петушки*

Илья Ильф и
Евгений Петров: *Золотой теленок*
М.Ю. Лермонтов: *Герой нашего времени*
Фридрих Незнанский: *Операция «Фауст»*
Фридрих Незнанский и
Эдуард Тополь: *Журналист для Брежнева или смертельные игры.*
                       (Детектив)
Б. Пастернак: *Доктор Живаго*
Людмила Петрушевская: *Три девушки в голубом*
А. Платонов: *Котлован. Повесть*
Анатолий Рыбаков: *Дети Арбата. Роман*
Русские волшебные сказки. Изд. «Детская литература». Москва 1970
Игорь П. Смирнов: "Кастрационный комплекс в лирике Пушкина
                       (методологические заметки)" In: *Russian Literature*
                       XXIX-II, 1991: 205-228.
Валентин Солоухин: *Не жди у моря погоды. Роман*
А. и Б. Стругацкие: *Гадкие лебеди. Повесть*
А. и Б. Стругацкие: *Жук в муравейнике*
А. и Б. Стругацкие: *Пикник на обочине*
А. и Б. Стругацкие: *Улитка на склоне. Фантастическая повесть*
А. и Б. Стругацкие: *Хищные вещи века*
Л.Н. Толстой: *Анна Каренина*
И.С. Тургенев: *Отцы и дети*
Марина Цветаева: *Стихотворения*. In: *Стихотворения и поэмы в пяти*
                       томах: Том первый. New York: 1980.
А.П. Чехов: *Дама с собачкой*
В. Шукшин: *Любавины. Роман*

Dutch Contributions to the Twelfth International Congress of Slavists,
Cracow, Linguistics (= Studies in Slavic and General Linguistics Vol 24),
283-307. RODOPI, Amsterdam - Atlanta, GA 1998.

THE DIALECT OF OSTROVCY IN THE PSKOV OBLAST

ZEP HONSELAAR

1. Introduction

1.1 The aim of this article

The aim of this article is to give a short impression of the most interesting features of the Russian dialect spoken in the village of Ostrovcy in Northwestern Russia. The data in this article are based on tape-recordings I made during four periods of field-work between 1995 and 1997. I taped 56 hours during sessions with informants in Ostrovcy and about 20 hours in the neighbouring villages. My three main informants are Ekaterina Filippova (born in 1908), Marija Usova (born in 1911) and Marija Ekimova (born in 1918). Other informants were taped a little less frequently: Vera Žandarova (born in 1918) and Tatjana Žandarova (born in 1912). All informants were born in Ostrovcy and did not live anywhere else for a long period of time. All of them have spent a half year in another village in the Pskov region when having been evacuated after the war. One informant, Vera Žandarova, spent the whole war in the Kalinin oblast (nowadays Тверская область). All informants went to school and have elementary reading and writing skills.

In the present article only the most striking characteristics of the dialect are discussed. A complete description of the dialect is planned to appear in the course of 1998. When giving examples of the dialect I shall use a notation (in italics) which is in principle phonemic, but with some modifications:
- [i] and [ɨ], both allophones of the phoneme /i/ are written as i and y;
- in unstressed syllables the oppositions between /o/, /a/ and sometimes /e/ are often neutralised. The resulting archiphoneme is written as ə or α according to its (approximate) phonetic realisation.

1.2   Ostrovcy

Ostrovcy is a village on the shore of Lake Peipus in the Gdov district of the Pskov oblast. The village has about 200 permanent inhabitants, most of whom were born there. Fishing was – and still is – the inhabitants' main occupation. The village is situated on a kind of peninsula, surrounded by marshes, woods and Lake Peipus. Until quite recently most of the villagers' external contacts were with the inhabitants of neighbouring fishing villages. Nowadays a paved road connects Ostrovcy with the Gdov-Pskov highway.

Ostrovcy was founded in the last quarter of the sixteenth century. The whole village, except for two stone storehouses, was burned to the ground on 7 January 1941, when the Germans retreated. All inhabitants could escape, but were forced to live in a village in the inland until Estonia on the opposite side of Lake Peipus had been reconquered by the Red Army.

2.   Phonology

2.1   Phoneme inventory

The inventory of phonemes in maximally distinctive positions is given in the table below.

Vowels   Consonants

i	u		p	p'	t	t'		k	k'
e	o		b	b'	d	d'		g	g'
a					c	č			
			f	f'	s	s'	š	x	
			v	v'	z	z'	ž	γ	
			m	m'	n	n'			
					l	l'			
					r	r'			
						j			

2.2   Vowel system in the first pretonic syllable

2.2.1   Preliminary remarks

One of the most salient features of the Ostrovcy phonological system is the vowel system in the first syllable before the stress. The presence

or absence of oppositions between /a/, /o/ and /e/ in the first pretonic syllable depends on three factors:
— whether the consonant immediately preceding is palatalised (which includes /c/ and the historically palatalised /č/, /š/, /ž/ as well) or not;
— the stressed vowel;
— whether the consonant immediately following is palatalised (which includes /c/ and the historically palatalised /č/, /š/, /ž/ as well) or not.

In 2.2.2 and 2.2.3 the term 'palatalised consonants' will include /č/, /š/, /ž/ and /c/.

2.2.2 Vowel system in the first pretonic syllable after a non-palatalised consonant

The opposition between /a/ and /o/[1] is maintained before stressed /a/, /o/ or /e/. Before stressed /i/ or /u/ the opposition is neutralised. The resulting archiphoneme is realised as [a].

taká - vojná	Nsg f 'such' - Nsg 'war'
art'él' - ob'ét	Nsg 'team' - Nsg 'lunch'
takój - vojnój	Nsg m 'such' - Isg 'war'
tak'íx - vajný	Gpl 'such' - Gsg 'war'
takúju - vajnú	Asg f 'such' - Asg 'war'

2.2.3 Vowel system in the first pretonic syllable after a palatalised consonant

The phonemes /a/, /o/ and /e/ are distinguished before a stressed /o/ and a non-palatalised consonant.

časóf - s'ostrój - r'ekój   Gpl 'hour' - Isg 'sister' - Isg 'river'

Before a stressed /a/, the opposition between /a/ and /e/ is neutralised. The resulting archiphoneme is realised as [ɛ, æ, ʌ]. The phoneme /o/ remains distinct in this position: its phonetic realisation ranges from [o] to [ə].

p'atnácət' - r'aká - s'ostrá 'fifteen' - Nsg 'river' - Nsg 'sister'

The opposition between /e/ and /o/ is neutralised before a stressed /e/. The resulting archiphoneme is realised as [e]. The same neutralisation takes place before a stressed /o/ when the consonant immediately after the vowel in question is palatalised. The phoneme /a/ remains distinct in the above-mentioned positions.

gl'ad'ét' - n'ed'él'u - pr'iv'ed'é   Inf 'look' - Asg 'week' -
                                       PR3sg 'bring'
v'az'ó - m'ešók - pr'iv'ed'ó   PR3sg 'knit' - Nsg 'bag' -
                                       PR3sg 'bring'

Before a stressed /i/ or /u/, the oppositions between /a/, /o/ and /e/ are neutralised. The resulting archiphoneme is realised as [a].

gl'ad'ít' - s'astrý - r'ak'í   Inf 'look' - GDLsg 'sister' - GDLsg 'river'
v'ažú - s'astrú - r'akú   PR1sg 'knit' - Asg 'sister' - Asg 'river'

2.3 Cokan'je

One of the best known features of the Pskov dialects is 'cokan'je', i.e. a consonant system where one phoneme, /c/, corresponds to two phonemes, /c/ and /č/, in most other Russian dialects.[2] In recordings made for the Диалектологический Атлас Русского Языка (ДАРЯ) in the second half of the 1940's, cokan'je was found in the western part of the Pskov oblast including Ostrovcy. However, in the taped interviews I made in Ostrovcy I found very few traces of cokan'je except for some lexicalised forms such as *coló* 'stoking hole'. It seemed that cokan'je had died out in the dialect of Ostrovcy. But in the winter of 1997 I taped Marija Usova and Tatyana Žandarova, who thought they were conversing in the absence of strangers. They were not aware they were being taped and, surprisingly, the speech of one of them, T.Ž., differs substantially from that on previous recordings. On this recording, which lasts for about 24 minutes, she consistently does not distinguish /č/ and /c/, pronouncing both of them as [c]:

zəmacýt'   Inf 'moisten'
fcarás'   'yesterday'
nəcynájə   PR3sg 'begin'

Cokan'je might be hidden from strangers because dialect speakers consider it to be one of the most striking features of the dialect.[3]

3. Noun

3.1 Inventory of desinences

The substantival endings are shown in the table below. The apostrophe before the ending /i/ indicates that the preceding consonant is always palatalised.

	sg				pl			
	I		II	III	I		II	III
	m	n			m	n		
N	-∅	-o	-a	-∅	-i, -a	-a, -i	-i	-i
G	-a		-i	-i	-of, -ej, -∅		-∅	-ej
D	-u		-i	-i	-am			
A	A=N/G	A=N	-u	A=N	A=N/G			
I	-om		-oj	-ju	-am			
L	-'i, -u	-'i	-i	-i	-ax			

As can be seen in the table above there are six primary cases (nominative, genitive, dative, accusative, instrumental and locative) and one secondary case (second locative). A second genitive in ⟨-u⟩, as in Standard Russian, has not been attested. Nouns can be assigned to one of three genders: masculine, feminine and neuter. Their distribution does not show significant differences from Standard Russian, except for *myš* 'mouse' m., *ikró* 'spawn' n., *pom'ál* 'mop' m. and *stúlə* 'chair' n. All nouns can be grouped into three declension classes according to their declensional patterns.

3.2 Npl neuter ⟨-a⟩ - ⟨-i⟩

Two nominative plural endings have been attested for neuters: ⟨-a⟩ and ⟨-i⟩. There are some rules regarding the distribution of both endings:

1) If the substantive belongs to accentuation type c (see 3.3), only ⟨-a⟩ occurs:

d'alá	Npl 'thing, case'
oz'orá	Npl 'lake'
pol'á	Npl 'field'

2) If the stem ends in /j/ in plural forms, Npl takes ⟨-a⟩. This /j/ can be a part of the stem both in singular and in plural, but it can also be the result of a morphological alternation such as extension. Several neuters form their plurals by extension of the stem with -j- or -əvj-. The neuters extending their stem with -j- are the same as in Standard Russian, whereas those with the extension -əvj- in plural forms have no equivalents in Standard Russian. All six attested neuters with the extension -əvj- in plural will be given below together with some examples of neuters with the extension -j-.

dónəvjə	Npl 'bottom'
górləvjə	Npl 'net opening'
gúmnəvjə	Npl 'threshing-floor'
karýtəvjə	Npl 'trough'
odánəvjə	Npl 'haystack'
ud'ajáləvjə	Npl 'blanket'
d'er'évjə	Npl 'tree'
stúljə	Npl 'chair'

3) If the stem of a neuter not belonging to accentuation type c ends in /k/, Npl takes ⟨-i⟩ only:

ack'í	Npl 'glasses'
jáblək'i	Npl 'apple'
okóšk'i	Npl 'window'

4) úxə 'ear' always takes ⟨-i⟩ in Npl: úšy Npl 'ear'.

There are, of course, many neuters which do not fit into one of the above-mentioned groups. Of the remaining 17 attested neuters in Npl five have been attested with a Npl ending in ⟨-a⟩, seven with a Npl in ⟨-i⟩ and five taking both ⟨-a⟩ and ⟨-i⟩ in the nominative plural.

⟨-a⟩	gl'an'íššə	Npl 'top of a boot'
	p'ís'mə	Npl 'letter'
⟨-i⟩	ókny	Npl 'window'
	voróty	Npl 'gate'
	v'ódry	Npl 'bucket'
⟨-a⟩/⟨-i⟩	drová/dróvy	Npl 'firewood'
	jájcə/jájcy	Npl 'egg'
	st'óklə/st'ókly	Npl 'glass'

3.3 Some remarks on accentual patterns of nouns

As in Standard Russian, the stress in the dialect of Ostrovcy is free, i.e. it can fall on any syllable of a word. The stress can fall on a syllable of the stem or it can fall on a syllable (mostly the first one) of the desinence. The majority of nouns has fixed stress, i.e. the stress remains on the same syllable throughout the whole paradigm, but there is a small group of frequent nouns with mobile stress. In this case the stress falls on the stem in one part of the paradigm and on the desinence in another part. Following Zaliznjak (1987: 31-32) every noun can be assigned to one of the six accentuation types and one accentuation sub-type according to: 1) the stress paradigm in the singular, except Asg, 2) the place of the stress in the Asg form, 3) the place of the stress in the Npl form and 4) the stress paradigm in the other plural forms.

accentuation type	sg forms (not Asg)	Asg	Npl	other pl forms
a	+	+	+	+
b	-	-	-	-
c	+	+	-	-
d	-	-	+	+
e	+	+	+	-
f	-	-	+	-
f'	-	+	+	-

In the table above '+' means stem stress, '-' means ending stress.

Accentuation type a: fixed stem-stress throughout the paradigm.

xl'ep Nsg, *xl'ébu* Dsg, *xl'éby* Npl, *xl'ebəf* Gpl 'bread'
bolótə Nsg, *bolótəm* Isg, *bolótə* Npl, *bolótəx* Lpl 'marsh'
z'aml'ánk'i Gsg, *z'aml'ánk'i* Npl, *z'aml'ánkəx* Lpl 'dug-out'
krovát' Nsg, *krovátju* Isg, *krovát'əj* Gpl 'bed'

Accentuation type b: fixed stress on the desinence throughout the para-digm, unless the desinence is zero. In that case the stress falls on the final stem-syllable.[4]

mužýk Nsg, *mužyká* Gsg, *mužyk'í* Npl, *mužykám* Dpl 'man'
šyluxá Nsg, *šylux'í* Gsg, *šylux'í* Npl 'skin (vegetable)'
put'í Lsg, *put'ám* Dpl 'road'

290

Accentuation type c: stem-stress in singular and stress on the desinence in plural.

bókəm Isg, *boká* Npl, *bokám* Dpl 'side'
d'élu Dsg, *d'éləm* Isg, *d'alá* Npl, *d'elóf* Gpl 'matter'

Accentuation type d: stress on the desinence in singular and stem-stress in plural.

l'ist Nsg, *l'istóm* Isg, *l'ístjə* Npl, *l'ístjəf* Gpl 'leaf'
v'odró Nsg, *v'adrú* Dsg, *v'ódry* Npl, *v'ódrəx* Lpl 'bucket'
travá Nsg, *travú* Asg, *travój* Isg, *trávy* Npl, *trávəm* Ipl 'grass, herbs'

Accentuation type e: stem-stress in singular and Npl; stress on the desinence in the other plural forms.

v'ek Nsg, *v'ék'* Gsg, *v'ék'i* Npl, *v'ekóf* Gpl 'age'
d'er'évn'i Gsg, *d'er'évn'u* Asg, *d'er'évn'i* Npl, *d'ir'avn'ám* Dpl 'village'
lóšəd'i Gsg, *lóšəd'i* Npl, *lošad'ám* Dpl 'horse'

Accentuation type f: stem-stress in Npl only, stress on the desinence in all other forms.

boraný Gsg, *boranú* Asg, *bórəny* Npl, *boronám* Ipl 'harrow'

Accentuation sub-type f': stem-stress in Asg and Npl, stress on the desinence in other forms.

golavý Gsg, *góləvu/golavú* Asg, *góləvy* Npl, *golovám* Ipl 'head'

All of the above-mentioned accentuation types exist in Standard Russian as well. There is, however, a sub-type d' in Standard Russian which includes nouns with stress on the desinence in the singular, except for Asg, and stem stress in the plural forms and Asg (Zaliznjak 1987: 31-32). This accentuation type has not been attested in the dialect of Ostrovcy.

Accentuation sub-type f' in the Ostrovcy dialect consists of two groups: the first group are nouns with Asg-forms which are always stem-stressed:

góru Asg   'hill'
sr'édu Asg   'Wednesday'

stórənu   Asg 'side'

Nouns belonging to the second group admit both stem-stressed and ending-stressed Asg-forms:

dósku/daskú	Asg 'blackboard'
góləvu/golavú	Asg 'head'
íz'bu/iz'bú	Asg 'house'
lódju/ladjú	Asg 'boat'
nógu/nagú	Asg 'leg, foot'
rúku/rukú	Asg 'arm, hand'
tón'u/tan'ú	Asg 'fishing-ground'
z'éml'u/z'aml'ú	Asg 'ground'
vódu/vadú	Asg 'water'

The ending-stressed forms are more frequent than the stem stressed ones, except for *rúku/rukú*.

The main difference in accentuation between Standard Russian and the dialect of Ostrovcy is the distribution of the nouns assigned to a particular accentuation type: several frequent nouns in the Ostrovcy dialect belong to a different accentuation type or admit two stress variations in certain parts of their declination.

Accentuation type d is confined mainly to neuters and to feminine nouns in -a. But I have attested two fairly frequent masculine nouns of the first declension which also belong to type d:

kon' Nsg, *kon'á* Gsg, *kan'ú* Dsg, *kan'í* Lsg,
kón'i Npl, *kón'əm* Dpl, *kón'əx* Lpl 'horse'

The following nouns which belong to type f in the dialect of Ostrovcy belong to a different accentuation type in Standard Russian:

boradú	Asg 'beard' (Standard Russian: f')
boranú	Asg 'harrow' (Standard Russian: f'/f)
polasú	Asg 'slot, plot' (Standard Russian: f/f')
r'akú	Asg 'river' (Standard Russian: d'/d/f')
skovoradú	Asg 'frying pan' (Standard Russian: f/f')

Needless to say that we can assign nouns to a certain accentuation type only when all the necessary forms have been attested.

4. Adjective

4.1 Preliminary remarks

Short form adjectives have been attested a lot less frequently than in Standard Russian. The only short form I am certain of is the neuter singular which can function as an adverb. It is often impossible to determine whether a given form is short or long since contracted long forms occur in the predicate as well. Even when a given form is attested with a short ending only, it still might be a contracted long form. Therefore, I only recognise short forms as such 1) if they take an exclusive short form ending or 2) if they have a different stress.

1) Adjectives ending in ⟨-∅⟩ are always masculine singular short forms because the sg m long form ends in ⟨-oj⟩:

fs'ak	sg m 'each'
gotóf	sg m 'ready'
núžən	sg m 'necessary'
róv'ən	sg m 'flat'
žyf	sg m 'living'

Adjectives in the dative which take ⟨-u⟩ and are preceded by a preposition are always neuter short forms, because the Dsg n long form ends in ⟨-om⟩:

po-mnógu	Adv 'much'
po-mal'énku	Adv 'a bit'
pó-rəvnu	Adv 'equally'

2) Since the stress of long form adjectives remains on the same syllable throughout the paradigm, forms with a different stress and a short ending must be short forms:

pravá	sg f 'right' (comp. *právəj* Nsg m, *právəj* Isg f)

The following forms are probably short, because they have been attested only in the predicate and with short endings. But again: we cannot prove that they are short forms and not contracted long forms.

doložná sg f, *doložnó* sg n, *dolažný* pl 'obliged'

293

4.2 Accentuation types

Following Zaliznjak (1987: 32-33) adjectives are assigned to an accentuation type according to: 1) the place of the stress in the long forms and 2) the stress paradigm in the short forms.

Accentuation type a/a:	the stress falls on the stem in both the long and the short form(s).
Accentuation type a/b:	the stem is stressed in the long forms, the ending is stressed in the short form(s).
Accentuation type b/a:	the ending is stressed in the long forms, the stem is stressed in the short form(s).
Accentuation type a/c':	the stem is always stressed in the long forms. In the short forms of prefixed adjectives, however, the prefix is stressed.
Accentuation type b/c:	the ending is stressed in the long forms and in the sg f of the short forms, the stem is stressed in the sg m and pl of the short forms (sg n has not been attested).

Examples:

a/a:	*vysókəj* Nsg m - *vysókə* Adv 'high'
a/b:	*xoróšəj* Nsg m - *xorošó* Adv 'good'
b/a:	*r'etkóvə* Gsg m - *r'étkə* Adv 'rare'
a/c':	*kr'épkəjə* Nsg n - *kr'épkə* Adv, *ná-kr'əpkə* 'strong'
b/c:	*žyvójə* Nsg n - *žyf* masc, *žyvá* fem, *žývy* pl 'living'

Accentuation type b/c is rare since few short forms other than the adverb have been attested.

Several adjectives with a place of stress different from Standard Russian have been attested. Long forms with:

1) stem stress instead of ending stress:

molódəj Nsg m 'young'
pr'áməjə Nsg n 'straight'
rónnəjə Nsg f 'relative, native'

2) ending stress instead of stem stress:

blagój	Nsg m	'bad'
r'etkóvə	Gsg n	'rare'
t'ixój	Nsg m	'quiet'
žarkójə	Nsg n	'hot'

Some neuter singular short forms have been attested with stem stress opposed to the Standard Russian forms with ending stress:

dal'ókə	Adv	'far'
glybókə	Adv	'deep'
l'ókkə	Adv	'light'
šyrókə	Adv	'wide'
t'ómnə	Adv	'dark'
vysókə	Adv	'high'

4.3 Inventory of adjectival desinences

case	masc	neut	fem	plur
N	-oj	-oa	-aa	-ia
		-o	-a	-i
G	-ova		-oj	-ix
D	-om		-oj	-im
A	A=N/G	A=N	-uju	A=N/G
			-aju	
			-u	
I	-im		-oj	-im
L	-om		-oj	-ix

The endings Nsg n ⟨-oa⟩, Nsg f ⟨-aa⟩, Npl ⟨-ia⟩ and Asg f ⟨-uju⟩ have contracted doublet forms: ⟨-o⟩, ⟨-a⟩, ⟨-i⟩ and ⟨-u⟩ respectively. The doublet forms occur independently of the place of stress or the syntactical position of the adjective.

Examples of doublet forms:

bol'šój/bol'šó	Nsg n	'big'
molódəjə/molódə	Nsg f	'young'
bal'šýjə/bal'šý	Npl	'big'
xoróšəju/xoróšu	Asg f	'good'

5. Verb

5.1 Preliminary remarks

In this section on the verb I will concentrate on the endings and the stress patterns of the present tense, the endings of the simple past tense and the secondary imperfectives. The dialect of Ostrovcy distinguishes between three past tenses: simple past tense, perfect and pluperfect. Section 6 deals with the construction and use of the perfect and pluperfect.

5.2 Inventory of desinences of the present

The verbs can be divided into two conjugations depending on the thematic vowel in the second and third persons singular and the first and second persons plural forms of the present. The first conjugation is characterised by the thematic vowel <-o-> or <-e> in the 2sg and 3sg. The second conjugation contains the thematic vowel <-i-> in the above mentioned forms.

	1st conj.	žyt' 'live'	2nd conj.	stoját' 'stand'
1sg	-u	žyvú	-u	stajú
2sg	-oš/-eš	žyv'óš/ dožyv'éš 'live till'	-iš	stajíš
3sg	-o/-e	žyv'ó/žyv'é	-i	stají
1pl	-om	žyv'óm	-im	stajím
2pl	-ot'a	žyv'ót'ə	-it'a	stajít'ə
3pl	-u	žyvú	-a	stojá

Since the opposition between /o/ and /e/ is neutralised in posttonic syllables, we can distinguish <-o-> and <-e> only when the ending is stressed. The thematic vowel <-e> occurs in all verbs with end stress in the relevant forms. It is present in the speech of all informants, but those with more archaic dialect features (T.Ž., M.U.) tend to use it more often. Some doublet forms are given below:

b'er'óš/b'er'éš	PR2sg 'take'
pr'in'es'óš/pr'in'és'eš	PR2sg 'bring'
žyv'ó/žyv'é	PR3sg 'live'
pjo/pje	PR3sg 'drink'

5.3 Third sg and pl forms of the present

The table shows that the 3rd person singular and plural forms of the present tense do not end in a ⟨-t⟩ as in Standard Russian. In fact, the northern part of the Pskov region is about the only East Slavonic dialect area which does not have the 3rd person endings ⟨-t⟩/⟨-t'⟩ in both singular and plural, in stressed and unstressed endings and in both conjugations (ДАРЯ, том II Морфология, карта 80, 81). Only in some scattered areas south of Lake Ladoga and around Porkhov (central Pskov region) ⟨-t⟩/⟨-t'⟩ is also lacking. The examples taken from the dialect of Ostrovcy show that ⟨-t⟩ does not occur at all irrespective of the conjugation, number or place of stress.

1st conjugation	*p'ek'ó* PR3sg, *p'akú* PR3pl 'bake'
	d'éləjə PR3sg, *d'élƏju* PR3pl 'do'
2nd conjugation	*govar'í* PR3sg, *govor'á* PR3pl 'speak'
	xód'i PR3sg, *xód'ə* PR3pl 'go'

The 3rd person form of reflexive verbs, however, shows a different picture. Whereas all other reflexive verbs are formed by adding the reflexive suffix *-s'ə/-sə*[5] to the verb form, reflexive 3rd person forms end in *-cə*. This suffix must have originated from a former 3rd pers. ending ⟨-t⟩/⟨- t'⟩ in combination with the reflexive suffix *-sə*.[6]

– *b'arúcə*	PR3pl 'take'
gul'ájucə	PR3pl 'walk'
d'élƏjcə	PR3sg 'do'
žyv'ócə	PR3sg 'live'
– *bajícə*	PR3sg 'be afraid'
bojácə	PR3pl 'be afraid'
pondráv'icə	PR3sg 'please'
účƏcə	PR3pl 'study'

5.4 Some remarks on accentual patterns in the present tense

Stress plays an important role in the verbal morphology of the Ostrovcy dialect. Its role is even more important than in Standard Russian, because the place of stress is sometimes the only way to distinguish a 1st person singular form from a 3rd person plural:

| *pr'idú* | PR1sg | - | *pr'ídu* | PR3pl 'come' |

In the present tense the stress can fall on the stem, on the first syllable of the ending or on the prefix. According to the stress paradigm in the present tense we can assign each verb to one of the four stress-patterns.[7]

stress pattern	PR 1sg	PR 2sg - 3pl
a	+	+
b	-	-
c	-	+
c'	-	# /-

In the table above '+' means stem stress, '-' means ending stress, '#' means stressed prefix.

Stress pattern a: fixed stem-stress throughout the paradigm.

Stress pattern b: fixed stress on the desinence throughout the paradigm.

Stress pattern c: stress on the ending in the 1st person singular, stem stress in the other forms.

Stress pattern c':   stress on the ending in the 1st person singular and permitting stress both on the prefix and on the ending in the other present tense forms.

Examples:

a   *robótəju* PR1sg, *robótəjəš* PR2sg, *robótəjə* PR3sg, *robótəju* PR3pl 'work'

b   *govar'ú* PR1sg, *govar'í* PR3sg, *govar'ím* PR1pl, *govor'á* PR3pl 'speak'

c   *magú* PR1sg, *móg'əš* PR2sg, *móg'ət'ə* PR2pl 'be able'

c'   *vaz'mú* PR1sg, *vóz'm'əš/voz'm'óš* PR2sg, *vóz'm'ə/voz'm'ó* PR3sg, *vóz'm'əm/voz'm'óm* PR1pl, *vóz'm'ət'ə/voz'm'ót'ə* PR2pl, *vóz'mu* PR3pl 'take'

Some more examples of stress-pattern c' are given below:

valjú PR1sg, *vóljəš/voljóš* PR2sg, *vólju* PR3pl 'pour in'
pajdú PR1sg, *pójd'əš/pojd'óš* PR2sg, *pójd'ə/pojd'ó* PR3sg, *pojd'óm* PR1pl, *pojd'ót'ə* PR2pl, *pójdu* PR3pl 'go'

As can be seen in the examples not all forms have attested doublet forms. Most probably these missing doublet forms would have been attested, if more recordings could have been made.

It is obvious that stress pattern c' can occur with prefixed verbs only. Their non-prefixed counterparts can be divided into two groups. The first group includes verbs without any vowel in the present tense who have automatically pattern b.

/b'i/ ~ /Bj/   b'it' Inf, bju PR1sg, bjoš PR2sg 'beat'
          ub'íl'i LPpl, ubjú PR1sg, úbjəš PR2sg 'kill'

The second group consists of only one verb, it'í 'go', which can have both patterns b and c. However, it must be noted that only the 2nd and 3rd person singular and the 3rd person plural admit stress both on the ending and the stem. These doublet accentuation forms have been attested in the speech of all informants. No stem stressed 1st and 2nd person plural forms have been attested. Forms of it'í with stress on the ending are more frequent than those with stem. All attested present tense forms of it'í are listed below:

idú PR1sg, id'óš/id'éš/íd'əš PR2sg, id'ó/íd'ə PR3sg,
id'óm PR1pl, id'ót'ə PR2pl, idú/ídu PR3pl

5.5   Simple past tense masc sg in -e[8]

The table below shows the simple past tense forms.[9]

	masc	fem	neut
sg	-l-Ø	-l-a	l-o
	-l'-e		
pl	-l'-i		

The table shows that the masc sg is expressed by two endings: ⟨-Ø⟩ and ⟨-e⟩ (with palatalisation of the preceding affix -l). When stressed, ⟨-e⟩ is realised as [-ɛ], when unstressed as [-ə].

pov'el'é   LPsg m 'bring'
pr'išl'é   LPsg m 'come'
brál'ə   LPsg m 'take'
dál'ə   LPsg m 'give'
l'ub'íl'ə   LPsg m 'love'
uv'íd'əl'ə   LPsg m 'see'

The zero desinence is the most frequently attested one, whereas ⟨-e⟩ has been attested in the speech of one informant (T.Ž.) only. Moreover, she avoids forms in ⟨-e⟩ in the presence of strangers. Only on one recording, made when T.Ž. thought no strangers could hear her (see 2.3 as well), I have attested masc sg simple past tense forms in ⟨-e⟩. I counted 78 examples of the masc sg simple past tense: 32 of them end in ⟨-e⟩, 36 in ⟨-∅⟩. Below some examples of masc sg forms taking both ⟨-e⟩ and ⟨-∅⟩.

atkrýl/atkrýl'ə   LPsg m 'open'
pr'ijéxəl/pr'ijéxəl'ə LPsg m 'arrive'
zasnúl/zasnúl'ə   LPsg m 'fall asleep'

5.6 Secondary imperfectives containing a velar

Dialects spoken in the western part of the Pskov region are characterised by a series of verbs with root final /k/, /x/ and /g/ instead of the /č/, /š/ and /ž/ found in every other Slavonic dialect.[10] These verbs are all secondary imperfectives formed from perfective verbs in *-it'* by means of the suffixes ⟨-ova⟩ or ⟨-a⟩. In the Ostrovcy dialect /s'/, /t'/ and /č/ immediately before the final stem vowel *-i* alternate with /x/, /k/ and /k/ respectively. In the neighbouring village of Dragotina I have attested the alternation /d'/ ∼ /g/ as well. All attested verbs showing these alternations are listed below:

⟨-s'-i-⟩ ∼ ⟨-x-ova-⟩	*spras'ít'* Inf 'ask' - *spráxəvəjəš* PR2sg 'ask'
	snas'ílə LPsg f 'wear out' - *snáxəvəcə* Inf 'wear out'
⟨-č-i-⟩ ∼ ⟨k-ova-⟩	*zəmačíl'i* LPpl 'moisten' - *zamákəvəl'i* LPpl 'moisten'
⟨-s'-i-⟩ ∼ ⟨-x-a-⟩	*v'és'it'* Inf 'hang' - *'éxət'* Inf 'hang'
	m'és'iš PR2sg 'mix' - *m'axáj* PR3sg 'mix'
⟨-t'-i-⟩ ∼ ⟨-k-a⟩	*zam'ét'it'* Inf 'notice' - *zəm'akát'* Inf 'notice'
	pust'ít' Inf 'let' - *puskát'* Inf 'let'
⟨- -i-⟩ ∼ ⟨-k-a-⟩	*nəučíl'i* LPpl 'teach' - *nəukál'i* LPpl 'teach'
	polučít' Inf 'get' - *polukáju* PR3pl 'get'
⟨-d'-i-⟩ ∼ ⟨-g-a-⟩	*rad'íləs'ə* LPsg f 'be born' - *ragájəš* PR2sg 'give birth' (Dragotina)

6. Syntax

6.1 Preliminaries

6.1.1 Simple past

The Ostrovcy dialect distinguishes three past tenses: the simple past, perfect and pluperfect. The simple past is a simple form made up of the *l* -participle (see 5.5). It expresses an action which has no relation to the present or to another past action.

(1) *p'ésn'i garás xoróšy p'éjəl'i*
songs very good-pl sing-LPpl (*l*-participle)
'they were singing very good songs'
(2) *vot ny k istóncəm pašl'í xl'ébə pras'ít'*
so we to Estonians-Dpl go-LPpl bread-Gsg demand-inf
'so we went to the Estonians, in order to ask for bread'

6.1.2 Perfect[11]

The perfect expresses an action completed in the past but still relevant for the present or related to it. It exhibits a split: most intransitive verbs use the past active participle in order to form the perfect tense. Most transitive verbs use the past passive participle for the perfect tense. This two-fold way of forming the perfect tense has been attested in all north-western Russian dialects (its isoglosses are given in Kuz'mina 1993: 136). There are, however, some transitive verbs using the past active participle to form the perfect and pluperfect tense and some intransitive verbs using the past passive participle to do so (see 6.4):

(3) *ot jovó n'étu i ot sos'éd'əj zd'es' n'étu p'ís'əm*
from him-G Neg and from neighbours-Gpl here Neg letters-Gpl
oj tóčənkə - dúməju kudá jon d'éfšy
oh right (I) think where-to he-N get-to-ActPart
'there aren't any letters from him and neither from the neighbours here. Oh right, I think: where has he gone?'
(4) *my žýl'i vot tám gd'e Makáryč žyv'ó prót'i məgaz'ínə*
we-N live-LPpl well there where M.-N lives across shop-Gsg
iz'bá étə v m'a pródənə jamú
cottage-Nsg that-Nsg at me-G sell-passpart him-D
'we used to live there; where Makáry lives. The cottage opposite the shop. I sold it to him'

6.1.3 Pluperfect

The pluperfect denotes an action completed in the past and relevant for a subsequent action in the past. The pluperfect exhibits a similar split as the perfect tense: intransitive verbs form the pluperfect by means of the simple past of the verb *byt'* 'be' and the past active participle. Transitive verbs form the pluperfect from the simple past tense of *byt'* and the past passive participle. The agent is expressed in the same way as in the perfect tense.

(5) *i žaná býlə pr'ijéxəfšy s'udá tóžə tr'i m'és'əcə*
and wife-Nsg was arrive-ActPart here also three months
s jim adžýl'i zd'és'ə
with him live-LPpl here
'and his wife had arrived and they spent three months here together'

(6) *v'odró býlə v jej pr'in'es'ónə tóžə atúdə s*
bucket was at her-G fetch-PassPart also from-there out-of
podválə
cellar-Gsg
'she had fetched the bucket out of the cellar, too'

6.2 (Plu)perfect tense formed with the past active participle

6.2.1 Preliminary remarks

The perfect of intransitive verbs is expressed by the past active participle in *-fšy*. The agent stands in the nominative. The pluperfect is formed by adding a past tense form of the verb *byt'* to the perfect tense form. The distinction between reflexive and non-reflexive verbs is neutralised: the reflexive suffix *-s'ə* cannot follow the past active participle.

(7) *top'ér' Natáxə ross'ard'ífšy*
now Natasha get-angry-ActPart
'now Natasha is angry'

(8) *ny býl'i pr'iznakóm'ifšy*
we were get-acquainted-ActPart
'we got acquainted'

6.2.2 Subjective resultative

Trubinskij (1962, 1984) distinguishes three types of the (plu)perfect tense expressed by the past active participle: subjective, possessive and objective resultatives. The subjective resultative expresses an action completed by the subject which resulted in the present state of the subject or its state on the moment of speech (pluperfect). This includes changes in space (*pr'ijéxət*'arrive'), changes in the physical state (*pom'er'ét*'die'), changes in the 'readiness' (*pr'ivýknut*'get used') of the subject.

(9) *nəpugál'i   l'ud'éj   štə   xtó   tam   v   takój*
     frighten-LPpl people-Gpl that   who-N there in   such-Lsg f
     pogódy   výjəxəfšy?
     weather-Lsg go-out-ActPart
     '(we) frightened people (and they were wondering:) "who has gone out in such a weather"?'

(10) *v m'an'á i sup jes' rýbnəj da nav'érnə výstyfšy*
     at me   also soup is   fish   but probably become-cold-ActPart
     'I also have fish soup but it has probably become cold'

(11) *v jix   býl'i dvójə glúxə-n'amýx a   joná govar'íĺə no*
     at them   were two   deaf-mutes   and   she   spoke   but
     on'átnə   pojm'óš   ny býl'i pr'ivýkšy ·
     understandably understand-PR2sg   we were use-to-ActPart
     'they had two deaf-mute ones (children), and she (one of them) could talk, but understandably − you would understand it − we were used to it'

6.2.3 Possessive resultative

The possessive resultative is used in combination with a subject and an object. This type is very rare in the dialect of Ostrovcy. In fact, it has been attested twice with one verb only: *adžýt'* 'live'. The object belonging to this verb always denotes a period of time.

(12) *Nu, zabl'úd'iššə   da i   srázə   i   výjd'əš.*
     Well, get-lost-PR2sg but then immediately also get-out-PR2sg
     Fs'ó-tək'i   fs'u   žýz'in' adžýfšy   zd'és'ə
     After all   whole-Asg f life-Asg live-ActPart here
     'Well, you may get lost (in the woods) but then you will find the way out immediately. After all, you've spent your whole life here'

6.2.4 Objective resultative

The objective resultative expresses an action which is related to the present state of the subject or its state at the moment of speech but

303

which the subject itself did not complete. Actually, the objective resultative is a form of the passive voice.

(13) a   ný   býl'i   s   d'er'év'ní   výs'əl'ifšy
      and we   were   from village   evacuate-ActPart
      'and we had been evacuated from the village'

6.3 (Plu)perfect tense formed with the past passive participle of transitive verbs

Transitive verbs usually form the perfect and pluperfect tense with the past passive participle. The past passive participle usually ends in an unstressed -ə. Since the phonological opposition between /a/ (feminine singular ending) and /o/ (neuter singular ending) is neutralised when unstressed it is impossible to determine whether the past passive participle agrees with its grammatical subject. In case of a masculine singular or a plural grammatical subject and a past participle ending in -ə, it is clear that there is no agreement. The following example shows that the adjective and the simple past form agree with the grammatical subject košal'í which is plural, whereas the past passive participle does not do so.

(14) v   jix   košal'í   bal'šýjə nab'ítə   býl'i   s'énəm
      at them-Lpl bag-Npl big-Npl filled-PastPart were-pl hay-Isg
      'they had filled the bags with hay'

The agent is expressed by a combination of the preposition v 'at' and the agent in the genitive (singular) or locative (plural).[12] The patient stands in the nominative, as is shown by šúpkə 'fur coat' in the following example.

(15) v   káždəvə   i   šúpkə   kúpl'ənə   dl'a óz'ərə
      at each-Gsg m also fur-coat-Nsg bought-PassPart for lake-Gsg
      'each one has bought a fur coat for the lake, too'

The preposition v is also used to express possession. This can cause ambiguity: a sentence can sometimes be interpreted both as a perfect tense and as a possessive construction. For example the following sentence:

(16) z'en' v   m'an'á   n'a   páxənə
      floor at me   not   swept-PassPart
      a) 'I have not swept the floor'
      b) 'I have the floor in an unswept state'

304

There are, however, a lot of sentences containing the construction
described above which are clearly not possessive constructions. For
instance: on one recording the informant (E.F.) explains how she got the
fruit tree standing in her garden:

(17) *jáblən'ə (...)*, *étə*   *s*   *l'in'ingrádə va vnúkə*
apple-tree-Nsg that-Nsg f from Leningrad   at grandson-Gsg
mojóvə   pr'iv'ed'ónə
my-Gsg m brought-PassPart
'the apple tree, my grandson brought that one from Leningrad'

(18) *a t'ep'ér' snóvə p'ir'ižyvájəm   v nas étə p'ir'ažýtə*
and now   again go-through-PR1pl at us   that go-through-
       fs'o
PassPart all
'and now we are going through it again – we have been through
it all'

**6.4   (Plu)perfect tense formed with the past passive participle of
intransitive verbs**

There is a small number of intransitive verbs which can form the perfect tense with the past passive participle. All of these verbs are imperfective and most of them are verbs of motion ('go', 'drive', 'run'). This
construction describes a habitual, repeated action in the past which is
related to the present moment. It is usually accompanied by a perfective
formed with a transitive verb. The first example given below is from
Ostrovcy, the second one is taken from recordings made in the neighbouring village of Dragotina.

(19) *v nas p'ir'ažýtə   fs'o   ·i   v lapt'áx*
at us   went through-PretPass everything and in bast shoes
xóžənə
walked-PassPart
'we have been through it all. We have walked in bast shoes'

(20) *byválə   skól'kə   d'et'éj róššənə   nocám n'a*
used-to-be how many children raised-PassPart nights not
spánə
slept-PassPart
'(I) used to raise so many children, I did not sleep at night'

NOTES

*   The work reported here was supported by the Foundation for Language, Speech and Logic Research which is part of the Netherlands Organisation for Scientific Research, grant 300-72-022.

1   The phoneme /e/ is not mentioned here because it does not occur after non-palatalised consonants or − in other words − the phonological opposition between palatalised and non-palatalised consonants is neutralised before /e/ in a palatalised archiphoneme.

2   This phenomenon has been amply attested in the Novgorod birchbark documents, for example Gram. 752 *cъtъ* 'what', *ocъju* 'eye' Gdual (Zaliznjak 1995: 229).

3   Cf. Čekmonas (1997: 183-184): "цоканье как неразличение исторических *ц и *ч, и их реализация как /ц/ в настоящее время является не столько территориальной, сколько социолингвистической характеристикой носителей псковских говоров (...) некоторые информаторы могут сознательно избегать цоканья в беседе с посторонними; (...)", and (idem: 184-185): "Информаторы, отошедшие от цоканья либо освоившие его от старших, объясняют это влиянием школы и речи образованных людей. Они подчеркивают, что цокали именно неграмотные люди, что цоканье - черта "серой" деревенской речи."

4   The only exception to this rule is *úgəl* 'corner' which has stress on the first stem syllable when the desinence is zero.

5   The reflexive suffix has three allomorphs: *-s'ə*, *-sə* and *-s'*:
− *-sə* occurs after consonants such as /t/, /t'/ and /š/;
− both *-s'ə* and *-sə* occur after /l/ and /m/;
− after vowels usually *-s'ə* occurs, but sometimes *-s'* as well.

6   The Old Novgorod dialect shows a similar picture. Its 3rd person forms of the present tense end in a vowel when not followed by enclitics:
   bude PR3sg 'be', *boudou* PR3pl 'be', *žive* PR3sg 'live', *ide* PR3sg 'go', *xoce* PR3sg 'want', *xъtę* PR3pl 'want' (Zaliznjak 1995: 119).
   When followed by pronominal enclitics, however, the 3rd person present forms end in ⟨-t'⟩:
   zapirajutьs(ę) PR3pl 'will be closed', *kupętь ti* PR3pl 'buy for you', *n[e o]stanetь ti sę* PR3sg 'will not be left for you', *xoсьtь ti* PR3sg 'wants for you' (Zaliznjak 1995: 120).

7   Verbs can also be divided into accentuation types according to the stress patterns of the present and the simple past tense.

8   The ending ⟨-e⟩ has been amply attested in the Novgorod birchbark documents. It is the normal nominative singular ending for masculine *o*-stem nouns, whereas *-ъ* is used to mark the accusative singular. The (nominative) masculine singular forms of adjectives, *l*-participles, passive participles and some pronouns also take *-e*. The birchbark documents show a gradual decline in the use of *-e*: from 80% between the 11th and 13th centuries to 58% in the 15th century (Zaliznjak 1995: 83). In this period *-e* is replaced by *-ъ*. Tönnies Fenne's Gesprächsbuch, a Russian-Low German phrase

306

book written in Pskov and published in 1607, shows us that -e is still used, but mainly as a masculine singular marker for the past tense (Schaeken 1992: 286-288). The data indicate that -e has been retained when the verbal stem ends in a consonant or when the form is followed by the reflexive suffix (idem: 287). In the modern Ostrovcy dialect the use of -e is not restricted in the above mentioned way.

9 Verbs with a stem in a consonant in the past tense forms do not take the suffix ⟨-l-⟩ in the masculine singular form:
pag'íblə - pag'íp LPsg f - LPsg m 'die'
pr'in'oslá - pr'in'ós LPsg f - LPsg m 'bring'

10 Various hypotheses have been proposed in order to explain this alternation: Gluskina (1979), Nikolaev (1988: 128-137 and 1990: 57-59), Krys'ko (1994: 32-42) and Bjørnflaten (1997).

11 The formation and use of the perfect and pluperfect in Russian dialects have been extensively discussed by Kuz'mina & Nemčenko (1971) and Trubinskij (1984).

12 The preposition v has several meanings: 'in, into, to, at'. When meaning 'in' it governs the locative; when meaning 'into' or 'to' it governs the accusative. But when v means 'at' it governs the genitive in singular and the locative in plural forms:
fs'ó   zd'élənə   v sámyx v rybakáx
everything done-PassPart at self-Lpl at fisherman-Lpl
'The fishermen did everything by themselves'

REFERENCES

Bjørnflaten, J.I.
1997   "Opyt lingvogeografii pskovskoj oblasti", Pskovskie govory. Istorija i dialektologija russkogo jazyka, 8-30. Oslo.
Čekmonas, V.N.
1997   "Osobennosti realizacii soglasnyx /c/ i /č/ v govorax pskovskoj oblasti", Pskovskie govory. Istorija i dialektologija russkogo jazyka, 182-208. Oslo.
ДАРЯ
1986   Dialektologičeskij Atlas Russkogo Jazyka. Vypusk I. Fonetika. Moskva.
1989   Dialektologičeskij Atlas Russkogo Jazyka. Vypusk II. Morfologija. Moskva.
Gluskina, S.M.
1979   "Morfologičeskie nabljudenija nad pskovskimi govorami", Pskovskie govory, 113-125. Pskov.
Honselaar, Z.
1997   "Sledy okončanija -E m. ed. muž. o-sklonenija", Russian Linguistics 21, 271-274.
Kasatkin, L.L.
1989   Russkaja dialektologija. Moskva.

307

Krys'ko, V.B.
1994   "Zametki o drevnenovgorodskom dialekte (I. palatalizacija)", *Voprosy jazykoznanija* 5, 28-45.

Kuz'mina, I.B.
1993   *Sintaksis russkix govorov v lingvogeografičeskom aspekte.* Moskva.

Kuz'mina, I.B., Nemčenko, E.V.
1971   *Sintaksis pričastnyx form v russkix govorax.* Moskva.

Nikolaev, S.L.
1988   "Sledy osobennostej vostočnoslavjanskix plemennyx dialektov v sovremennyx velikorusskix govorax. I. Kriviči", *Balto-slavjanskie issledovanija 1986*, 115-154. Moskva.

Schaeken, J.
1992   "Zum nordrussischen Nominativ Singular auf -e im Gespächsbuch des Tönnies Fenne (Pskov 1607)", *Studies in Slavic and General Linguistics* 17, 285-293.

Trubinskij, V.I.
1962   "O leksičeskoj baze predikativnogo deepričastija v pskovskix govorax", *Pskovskie govory* I, 162-178. Pskov.

1984   *Očerki russkogo dialektnogo sintaksisa.* Leningrad.

Zaliznjak, A.A.
1987   *Grammatičeskij slovar' russkogo jazyka.* Moskva.

1995   *Drevnenovgorodskij dialekt.* Moskva.

Dutch Contributions to the Twelfth International Congress of Slavists,
Cracow, Linguistics (= Studies in Slavic and General Linguistics Vol 24),
309-315. RODOPI, Amsterdam - Atlanta, GA 1998.

ROUNDED NASAL VOWELS IN THE FREISING FRAGMENTS*

FREDERIK KORTLANDT

Twenty years ago I argued that the reflexes of jers and nasal vowels
in the Freising Fragments reflect the Proto-Slavic accentual system existing before the operation of the progressive accent shift which is
characteristic of all Slovenian dialects (1975, cf. also 1996). This view
was opposed by Holzer, who argues that in I and II (but not in III) the
rounded nasal vowel yielded u(n) in final syllables of polysyllabic words
(unless the following word began with a nasal consonant) and o(n)
elsewhere (1986). The latter view is now endorsed by Woodhouse, who
claims that in III the rounded nasal vowel is reflected as o after hard
and u after soft consonants (1996). As I have not been convinced by
these proposals, there may be reason to clarify my position here.

The hypothesis that the Proto-Slavic accentual system is reflected
in the Freising Fragments is based primarily on the preservation of
weak jers under the stress. Thus, we find initial stress in III 21 **Ki-
bogu**, I 27 **zenebeʒe**, II 22 **pulti**, II 26 **mirze**, as opposed to II 83
ctomu, I 32 **ztemi**, II 5 **flzna**, III 58 **mrtuim**. Similarly, the rounded
nasal vowel is stressed o in II 13 **(boi)do**, 25 **(pre)ſtopam**, 81 **boði**,
112 **bo(dete)**, and posttonic u in II 8 **zavuiztiu**, 9 **(ne)priiazninu**, 20
trebu, 104 **naſu praudnu vuerun iprauðnv izbovuediu**. A crucial point
in the argumentation is that the choice between the inflectional endings -o and -u is lexically conditioned. Thus, we find 1st sg. -u nine
times with five verbs and -o four times with three other verbs, but
never both -u and -o with the same verb. Similarly, in the a-stems
we find -u nine times with five nouns and -o twice with two other
nouns. Even the exceptions to the accent rule show a regularity
which requires an explanation: the contracted nasal vowel is written
-o in mo (3x), **tuo, to,** whereas the uncontracted ending of the possessive pronoun is written -u in I 11 **moiv izpovued,** III 66 **moiu
dufu,** III 51 **tuuoiu milozt,** never -o, which suggests that the ending

of the pronoun was unstressed before the initial stress of the following noun.

According to Holzer (1986: 32), my theory predicts 52 reflexes of the rounded nasal vowel correctly, yields 10 contrary examples, and allows no conclusion for 21 instances. The latter are largely the result of his disregard of the accentological evidence. In the following I shall first discuss the allegedly contrary instances and then proceed to a discussion of the allegedly inconclusive cases.

(1) II 49 bòzzekacho, II 98 ſtradacho, III 42 boðo. The word-final -o in these forms is indeed unexpected in my theory and can be compared with the occurrence of -o for -u in II 60 vuirch|nemo, as I pointed out already (1975: 410).

(2) I 11 moiv (izpovued), III 51 tuuoiu (milozt), III 66 moiu (duſu). In these instances I assume that the stress of the possessive pronoun was lost before the initial accent of the following noun (see above).

(3) II 88 iuſe. Here I also assumed weak stress (1975: 411). I now think that the nasal vowel was pretonic in this word (1996: 143, 149).

(4) II 104 naſu. Here I assume a short nasal vowel. Note that after the loss of intervocalic *j vowels in posttonic syllables were contracted before the operation of Dybo's law, which can be dated at least 200 years before the Freising Fragments (cf. Kortlandt 1975a: 39). Later uncontracted forms are partly the result of back-formations which took place when the conditioning factor was lost as a result of the retraction of the stress from final jers, Dybo's accent shift, and the loss of the acute tone.

(5) III 38 ptiuuo | bogu beside I 19 protiubogu iprotiu me|mu creʒtu. Here I assume retraction of the stress of bogu to the preceding nasal vowel in the first instance (1996: 142, 151).

(6) II 19 ſunt. This is clearly Latin orthography (cf. already Kolarič 1968: 54).

(7) I 29 poronſo, III 61 poruſo, III 54 (na)ʒudinem, III 57 ʒodit, and II 88 iuſe have a nasal vowel in pretonic position. Holzer does not explain why different reflexes in the same root are only found in pretonic syllables.

(8) I 7 choku, III 48 chocu, I 13 pomngu (2x), I 22 and 24 tuoriv have initial stress because they belong to the mobile accent paradigm (c), as is clear from modern Slovene 3rd pl. hotę́ and from the comparative Slavic evidence (cf. Kortlandt 1975: 409, with refer-

ences).[1] Holzer ignores the comparative evidence and pretends that the choice is arbitrary in these instances. One can only wonder how much longer some colleagues will go on disregarding the work done by Stang, Dybo, Illič-Svityč, Ebeling, Garde and the present author and ignoring what has been achieved in the field of Slavic accentology in the last forty years (cf. Kortlandt 1978 for an introduction).

(9) I 29 poronſo, III 61 poruſo, III 11 izco, III 1 ӡaglagolo have final stress because they belong to accent paradigm (b) according to the comparative evidence.

(10) I 14 vuolu (2x), I 32 vueliu, II 8 ne|priiazninu, II 34 boſiu, II 104 naſu prau|ðnu vuerun ipraudnv | izbovuediu all have the short case ending, which is hardly remarkable in such an old text. Here again, Holzer maintains his agnostic view.

(11) III 22 (Dabim) ciſto (iz|pouued ztuoril) "that I may make a clean confession". Here I admit that one should rather expect an uncontracted ending, yielding -u after the stress.

(12) II 87 izio prio, III 10 Iӡ|emlo have final stress as a result of Dybo's law. The final accentuation in the latter example is very archaic and attested in Kajkavian and Old Russian (cf. Kortlandt 1975: 410, with references). In view of the comparative evidence I now think that zio was disyllabic (1996: 149, against Kolarič 1968: 213, Kortlandt 1975: 409, Logar 1993: 76).

Thus, I conclude that my theory predicts 73 out of Holzer's 83 instances correctly and allows for the doublets in the 5 pretonic reflexes (which Holzer does not explain). There is an unexpected lowering of final -u to -o in 4 instances, as there is in II 60 vuirch|nemo (which Holzer does not discuss). The form ſunt is Latin orthography. Holzer does not count I 5 muſenicom, which is a counter-example to his theory and which may be a loanword.

In order to compare Holzer's theory with mine, it seems useful to list those instances where the rounded nasal vowel is reflected as o(n) in final syllables of polysyllabic words and u(n) elsewhere because these constitute counter-evidence to his principal rule:[2]

I 29	poronſo	I 5	muſenicom
II 12	boi|do	II 19	ſunt
II 49	bozzekacho	II 88	iuſe
II 87	zio	III 54	ӡudinem
II 87	prio	III 61	poruſo
II 98	ſtradacho		

II 107   vue|lico
III 1   ӡaglagolo
III 10   ӡ|emlo
III 11   izco
III 22   cifto
III 38   ,ptiuuo
III 42   boðo
III 61   porufo

It turns out that unexpected -o for -u is Holzer's major problem. Note that I 5 mufenicom, III 54 ӡudinem, III 61 porufo are matched by III 16 mofe|nic, III 57 ӡodit, I 29 poronfo (see above).

In order to accommodate the counter-evidence, Holzer modifies his rule in two respects. Firstly, he assumes that the word-final reflex of the rounded nasal vowel -u was lowered to -o before an initial nasal consonant of the following word. This is an unnatural condition because one would rather expect raising before a nasal consonant. Moreover, the additional rule only applies to 4 out of the 14 contrary examples, and all of them have a syntactic boundary after the nasal vowel: I 29 (Miloztivui bofe) tebe poronfo me telo "(Merciful God,) I commend to thee my body", II 12 ftrazti Ipetzali boi|do neimoki "came pain and sorrow, sickness", II 48 malo mogoncka | uime bofie bozzekacho | mrzna zigreahu "visited the infirm in the name of God, warmed the cold", II 97 preife naffi zefztoco | ftradacho nebo ie te|pechu "our predecessors suffered cruelly, for they beat them" (Stone's translations, 1993). There is neither lowering in II 46 bozza | obuiachu naga ode|achu malo mogoncka "shod the barefooted, clothed the naked, [...] the infirm", nor in II 98 nebo ie te|pechu metlami "for they beat them with birches", III 50 (Daimi | bofe goӡpodi) tuuoiu | milozt "(Give me, Lord God,) thy grace", in spite of the close syntactic connection in the last two examples. It follows that we can safely discard the alleged influence of the following word-initial nasal consonant.

Secondly, Holzer happily removes FF III from his corpus, in spite of the fact that II and III are written in the same hand, as opposed to FF I. This eliminates 7 of the 14 counter-examples of -o for -u and 2 of the 5 instances of -u- for -o-. He is left with 6 counter-examples against 23 correct predictions of -u and with 2 contrary instances against 9 correct predictions of -o- for FF II. Though this is better than his score of 9 counter-examples against 11 correct predictions for FF III, it is not impressive. The main objection to Holzer's methodology, however, is that there is no reason to suppose that it should lead to a meaningful result in the first place.

In a recent article, Woodhouse has proposed to modify Holzer's rule by means of an additional series of ad hoc assumptions (1996):

(1) Far from rejecting the lowering of final -u to -o before an initial nasal consonant, he observes that the reflex of the rounded nasal vowel is -u if the vowel of the preceding syllable is the same as the vowel which follows the initial nasal consonant of the following word, while the reflex is -o if the vowel of the preceding syllable is different from the vowel which follows the initial nasal consonant of the following word: II 46 **bozza | obuiachu naga ode|achu malo mogoncka** and II 98 **te|pechu metlami** versus I 29 **poronſo me telo**, II 12 **boi|do neimoki**, II 49 **bozzekacho | mrzna zigreahu**, II 98 **ſtradacho nebo ie te|pechu**. On the basis of this bizarre rule Woodhouse rejects the usual emendation of II 13 **neimoki** to **inemoki** because this eliminates his explanation of the final -o in **boido**. He evidently does not feel the need to discuss III 51 **tuuoiu | milozt**, which would constitute another counter-example.

(2) Woodhouse attributes the -u- in II 19 **ſunt** to the fact that it is the only closed monosyllable with a rounded nasal vowel in the corpus.

(3) He adduces the -o of II 107 **vue|lico** as "precious evidence that the assimilation of adjectival to pronominal desinences, which was to become such a prominent feature of South (and East) Slavonic, though not necessarily of Slovenian, began, as is to be expected, with adjacent items in concord in the same noun phrase" (1996: 53f) and maintains that this "precious harbinger of a future important morphological change appears to have been sadly overlooked" and that it is one of the two "hitherto unsuspected Serbo-Croatisms" which he has detected in the FF (1996: 57).

(4) Woodhouse interprets -i- before -o in II 87 **prio** as a sign of palatalization so that the -r- is nonsyllabic, in spite of the comparative evidence.

(5) He suggests that the -u- of II 88 **iuſe** is "due to the paradoxical fact of a morphologically final nasal being located nevertheless medially within a phonetic disyllable" (1996: 54).

It seems to me that all of these considerations are quite useless. For FF III Woodhouse submits another series of additional hypotheses. According to his main rule, the rounded nasal vowel is reflected as o after hard and u after soft consonants. This rule accounts for 14 out of 20 instances and yields 5 contrary examples: III 1 ʒaglagolo, 10 Iʒ|emlo, 54 (na)ʒudinem, 61 poruſo (root vowel), and either 61 poruſo (desinence) or 66 duſu. In order to eliminate the counterevidence, Woodhouse assumes that *l* in ʒaglagolo and ʒemlo and *č* in poruſo are hard while *š* in duſu is soft, adducing the alleged depalatalization of *č* as the second of his "hitherto unsuspected Serbo-Croatisms" in the FF. He attributes the -u- in poruſo to the preceding -r- and the -u- in ʒudinem to the jer in the following syllable. It remains unclear how his article has been accepted for publication in a scholarly journal.

The two articles under review have not given me reason to change my opinion that the reflexes of the jers and nasal vowels in the Freising Fragments reflect a very archaic system of accentuation. The archaic character of this accentual system is no surprise because we are dealing with a very old text. The remarkable fact is that the attested forms fit our expectations so nicely and thereby confirm our reconstructions.[3] It turns out that the Freising Fragments provide the oldest documentary evidence for the Proto-Slavic accentual system.

University of Leiden

NOTES

* A Slovene translation of this article has appeared in *Slavistična revija* 44/4 (1996), 393-398.

[1] The accent marks in line 2 of Kortlandt 1975: 409 are clearly the result of a printer's error.

[2] The unfortunate interchange of III 1 ʒaglagolo with 5 uze molgoki, 10 Iʒ| emlo, 11 izco in Kortlandt 1975: 409 (which Holzer mistakenly interprets as my attribution of the latter forms to FF II) is clearly the result of a printer's error.

[3] The full preservation of the nasal vowels in the FF can be inferred from the accent marks on I 7 chokú, 8 vueruiú, 17 ʒpé (2x), 22 tuoriv́, 23 ze´, 24 tuoriv́,

315

28 otél, 30 mó (2x), 30 dufú, 32 tuó, which originally marked tautosyllabic nasality (cf. Kortlandt 1994 = 1996a).

REFERENCES

Holzer, Georg
1986   "Die Reflexe des hinteren Nasalvokals *ǫ in den Freisinger Denkmälern", *Wiener slavistisches Jahrbuch* 32, 29-35.
Kolarič, Rudolf
1968   "Sprachliche Analyse", *Freisinger Denkmäler: Brižinski spomeniki* (ed. J. Pogačnik), 18-120. München: Rudolf Trofenik.
Kortlandt, Frederik
1975   "Jers and nasal vowels in the Freising Fragments", *Slavistična revija* 23, 405-412.
1975a   *Slavic accentuation: A study in relative chronology*. Lisse: Peter de Ridder.
1978   "On the history of Slavic accentuation", *Zeitschrift für vergleichende Sprachforschung* 92, 269-281.
1994   "O naglasnih znamenjih v Brižinskem spomeniku I", *Slavistična revija* 42, 579-581.
1996   "The accentual system of the Freising Manuscripts", *Zbornik: Brižinski spomeniki*, 141-151. Ljubljana: SAZU.
1996a   "On the accent marks in the First Freising Fragment", *Studies in Slavic and General Linguistics* 23, 167-171.
Logar, Tine
1993   "Fonetični prepis", *Brižinski spomeniki: Znanstvenokritična izdaja*, 65-81. Ljubljana: SAZU.
Stone, Gerald
1993   "Angleški prevod", *Brižinski spomeniki: Znanstvenokritična izdaja*, 120-129. Ljubljana: SAZU.
Woodhouse, Robert
1996   "Notes on the reflexes of the Proto-Slavonic back nasal vowel in the Freising Fragments", *Australian Slavonic and East European studies* 10, 51-58.

Dutch Contributions to the Twelfth International Congress of Slavists, Cracow, Linguistics (= *Studies in Slavic and General Linguistics* Vol 24), 317–327. RODOPI, Amsterdam – Atlanta, GA 1998.

KAZANIA ŚWIĘTOKRZYSKIE: A TEXT EDITION*

FREDERIK KORTLANDT AND JOS SCHAEKEN

1. Introduction

The following edition is based on Diels (1921) and Łoś and Semkowicz (1934). Where these editions differ, both readings are adduced, separated by a slash / for single letters and a double slash // for sequences of letters. Original superscript is rendered as superscript. New readings in the later edition and resolutions of abbreviated forms are presented in subscript. Textual emendations of lacunae are enclosed in square brackets [ ]. Superfluous elements are enclosed in braces { }. Latin text is italicized. For a bibliography we refer to Wydra and Rzepka (1995: 89, 436).

2. Text edition

Text lines
– first digit: page number (ar, av, br, bv, cr, cv, dr, dv)
– last two digits: line number

Special characters
– φ stands for a nasal vowel
– 7 stands for *et*

100 [... zi]
101 douskego [uiego] mesce use slaua c_r^ola use$_{mog\varphi ce}$^{go} · y[moui crol pogan]
102 sky doc$_r^o$la ezehiasa . c_r^ola zidouske^{go} v/ydol$_{ud[a\ iego\ ...]}$
103 aue^m p$_r^a$u$_i$ puace . vmoch boga uasego . n/uadφcy/i [sφ smocφ crola moc]
104 neysego . vslisew to c_r^ol eze$_{hias}$. yusic$_{ek}$ lud i/jego . secl/s$_{[i\ odene}$ y]

318

105   kaiφch ydehφ pospesihφ sφ docos$_{co}$la namodlituφ p$_{re}$d bog^{a}
use$_{mogφce}^{go}$ y

106   pocφhφ sφ modlich izbi $_{ie}$ bog zbauil . o$_{tmo}$cy c$_{r}^{o}$la poganske^{go} .

107   Tegdis nagle bog uslusal . modlituφ luda sm$_{e}^{r}$[nego yposlal ...]

108   gim napomoch . angela suego s$_{uφte}^{go}$. je^{n}ze ang$_{el}$ c$_{s}$[ni sneba slecew y]

109   $_{s}$stφpiu p$_{r}^{a}$ui . ang$_{el}$ bozy . vzastφpy poganske$_{go}$ [crola pobil ...]

110   vel/sbore asirske^{m} toie poganske^{m} sto tysφccy . [osmdesft ti]

111   sφcy ypφc tysφcy . luda poganskego taco lud bozy [prez bozego an]

112   g$_{e}$la uicφzstuo odirzely/i . apogany sm$_{i}^{r}$c podiφly bo [angeli suφci da]

113   ny sφ na^{m}. na$_{otu}$adene nasego ust$_{r}^{a}$sena . ¶ apφte [dani sφ nam]

114   ang$_{e}$li suφcy . nanaucene nasego neumena . [praui taiem]

115   nichah . *Quod* ang$_{e}$l$_{u}$s h$_{ab}$ebat ap$_{er}$t$_{u}^{m}$ lib$_{r}^{v}$m . p$_{r}^{u/a}$ui tage$_{[m]}$

116   nychah . videh p$_{r}^{c/a}$ui ang$_{e}$la bo$_{ze}^{go}$ mochne^{go} sneb$_{[a sle]}$

117   cew p$_{r}^{a}$ui postaui p$_{r}^{a}$uφ nogφ namory ale$_{[uφ nazemi]}$

200   [...]

201   *[fili recordare] quia rece$_{pisti}$. bon^{a} i^{n} uita tua 7 la$_{zarus}$. si$_{militer}$. ma$_{la}$.* ¶ aosme [angeli]

202   [suφci dani nam] sφ . naosuecene nasego sφmnena . *j/Iudic$_{u}^{m}$. Cu^{m}*

203   *[que loqueretur angelus] do$_{min}^{i}$ om^{n}ia u$_{e}^{r}$ba hec ad filios isr$_{ae}$l eleua$_{ue}^{r}$unt*

204   *[ipsi vocem suam et] fle$_{ue}$runt .* Cce sφ taco . uekxφgah sφdskih . ang$_{el}$

205   praui suφti . $_{s}$stφpi do galaa cusino^{m} isl$_{a}$reskim . Galaa $_{u}$ip$_{r}^{a}$ua

206   sφ masto pluφcih . toie neustauichstuo ludy g$_{r}^{e}$snih yzmo

207   [uil to] . sl$_{ouo}$. sam p$_{r}^{a}$ui . p$_{re}$smφ p$_{r}^{i}$sφgl iesm . iz ua^{m} hochal

208   [iesm podac z]emφ urogow uasih . izbisce cugih bogom

209   [nehodili to]go iesce neucinily . ale potφpiusy bog^{a} uasego

210   [usemogφcego poganskim] bogo^{m} modlφ iesce vzdaualy p$_{re}$toz p$_{r}^{a}$ui da^{m}uas

211   [urogom uasim] yugih ulodane . agdas p$_{r}^{a}$ui . ang$_{el}$ zmo^{uil} ta . usic/t

212   [ca sloua z]aplacahφ p$_{r}^{a}$ui . use^{m} sirce^{m} . yobetnicφ bogu vzdahφ

213   [izbi ... bog] sφ nadnímy smiloual . Toc y . i$_{esc}$. to yze ang$_{e}$li

214   [suφci dani sφ n]a^{m} naosuecene nasego sφ^{m}ne^{na} . ¶ ad^{e}uφte dany

215   [sφ suφci angeli utoua]ristuo uecnego c$_{r}^{o}$leuana . gdes . i$_{esc}$. bog vt$_{r}^{o}$y

216   [ci iedini ssui]my su$_\varphi$ti^{my} izbiho^m gih touaristua . yneb^{e}s$_{ke}^{go}$ c$_r^o$leu stua

217   [dost$_\varphi$pili ceg]o^z nas douedy bog usemog$_\varphi$cy *am$_e{}^n$* .

301   *surge* p$_{ro}$p$_{er}$a *amica m$_e$a* 7 *ue^{n}i* Ta sloua pise m$_\varphi$d$_r^i$ salo$_{mon}$. as$_\varphi$

302   slo$_{ua}$ si$_{na}$ bo$_{ze}^{go}$ t$_\varphi$to su$_\varphi$t$_\varphi$ d^{e}uic$_\varphi$ kat$_e^r$in$_\varphi$ vslau$_\varphi$ c$_r^o$la . neb^{e}ske^{go} vab$_\varphi$

303   cego . vstan p$_r^a$ui . pospeys$_\varphi$ milut/cka m$_{oia}$ ypoydy . yzmouil

304   sin bo^{zi} sloua uelmy zna$_{meni}^{ta}$. gimis casd$_\varphi$ dus$_\varphi$ zbosn$_\varphi$ pobu

305   da pon$_\varphi$cha y pouaba . pobucha . reca vstan [pon$_\varphi$]cha

306   rek$_\varphi$ ta . pospeys$_\varphi$. pouaba reca . y poydy . y[moui sin bozi]

307   vstan . Otb/k$_\varphi$d p$_r^a$ui . stadla g$_r^e$snego . pospey s$_\varphi$ vl[epse zdo]

308   b$_r^e$go posydy t/camo$^{o/c}$ doc$_r^o$leustua neb^{e}ske^{go} . y$_m$[oui sin bozi]

309   vstan . ale vsu$_\varphi$te^m pis$_a^{ny}$. ctuoraki^m lude^m . pobudai$_\varphi$ ie mo$_{ui}$ [bog]

310   vse$_{mog\varphi}^{cy}$ vstan . pocazuí$_\varphi$ izs$_\varphi$ g$_r^e$sni^{cy} ctuoracy . bo mo$_{ui}$. to slou$_o$

311   albo sed$_\varphi$cim . albo sp$_\varphi$cim albo lez$_\varphi$cim albo um$_a$[rlim]

312   sed$_\varphi$cy s$_\varphi$ giz s$_\varphi$ kdobremu oblenai$_\varphi$. lez$_\varphi$cy s$_\varphi$ giz s$_\varphi$ u[ez]

313   s/le^m cohai$_\varphi$. Sp$_\varphi$cy s$_\varphi$ gis s$_\varphi$ vg$_r^e$seh zap$_e^c$clai$_\varphi$. vmarly s$_\varphi$ giz

314   vmiloscy bozey rospachai$_\varphi$. ati^m usem t$_{ec}$to bog mylosciuy

315   mo$_{ui}$. reca vstan . ¶ ymouy p^i_ruey sed$_\varphi$ci^m vstan giz s$_\varphi$ kdob$_r^e$m[u]

316   oblenai$_\varphi$. ctuorodla . jz nab$_\varphi$d$_\varphi$ce dob$_r^o$ negl$_\varphi$dai$_\varphi$. iz $_v$vre

317   m$_e^n$ne^m dobre lubui$_\varphi$. iz chego gim doych . nepam$_\varphi$tai$_\varphi$. iz

318   osobe nyiedne pece neymai$_\varphi$. atogodla i$_z$ [boga nehc$_\varphi$ uz]

319   rech kdob$_r^e$mu vstac s$_\varphi$ oblenai$_\varphi$. p$_{reto}$ p$_{re}^z$ [slepego ...]

320   dob$_r^e$ s$_\varphi$ zna$_{monu}^{i\varphi}$. Ogemze pise su$_\varphi$ti lucas . *Cecus se*[debat secus viam]

321   . slepy bo nab$_\varphi$d$_\varphi$ce dob$_r^o$ negl$_\varphi$dal . sedese . bo udob[re uremennem luboual]

322   podle d$_r^o$gy bo che/ogo iemu bilo doych nepa$_m$[$_\varphi$tal zebr$_\varphi$ci bo use]

323   be nics dob$_r^e$go neymal . ap$_{reto}$ iz su$_\varphi$ta kat$_e^r$in$_{[a}$ ... dobrego]

324   s$_\varphi$mnena . bila . cuglosu si$_{na}$ bo$_{ze}^{go}$ vstac s$_\varphi$ [...]

325   bila . *No$_t^a$ i^n uita sua i^n p$_r^i$ncip$_i^o$. Cu^m aute^m max*[encius imperator omnes]

326   *ta^m diuites qu$_u^a$m paup$_{er}$es ad alexand$_r^i$a^m co^{n}uocass$_{et}$* [ut ydolis ymmo]

327   *lare^{n}t . ka$^t_{erina}$ i^{n}quiri íuss$_i^t$ cel$_e^r$it$_e^r$ p$_{er}$nu^{n}ciu^m qu$_i^d$ h$_{ec}^{'}$*

assu^{n}t//ess$_e$nt · [Katerina]

328 *stat$_i^m$ surgens* . 7 signo c$_r^v$cis se muníe^{n}s illuc acc$_{essit}$ [et
imperatorem in]

329 *crepauit* . u^t ï^n uita $_{narracio\ patet}$ sic$_u^t$ melius scis . ¶ autore [ustan]

330 moui bog milosciuy . lezφci^m giz sφ uezlem cohaiφ . atacy

331 dob$_r^e$ sφ pre^s $_{one}$/ogo nemoch$_{ne}^{go}$ paralitica t$_r^v$dnφ nemocφ
urazone^{go}

332 znamonuíφ . Ogemze pise s$_{u\varphi}$ti lucas . *Off$_e^r$ebant ei*
mis$_{erum}$//inqu$_u^i$t paraliti

333 c$_u^m$. *iace^{n}te^m* ï^n l$_e$cto . *Cui dix$_i^t$* . *S$_u^r$ge q/7 surrexit* . cso na^m
prestogo nemoch

334 nego naloz$_{cu}$ lezφcego zna$_{mo}^{na}$. zau$_e^r$ne nics ynego . c$_r^o$me
clo$_{ue}^{ca}$ g$_r^e$s

335 nego uezlih skutceh $_{pre}$speuaiφcego . je^{n}ze nepamφtaiφ dob$_r^a$ ue

336 kuiego . Obφzal sφ tomu csoz . i$_{esc}$. urem$_e^n{}_{ne}^{go}$. leníu . i$_{esc}$.
cuvstanu . cy

337 nich casd^{e}go skutka dob$_r^e$go . *qu^i $_{propter}$ mom$_e^n$taneu^m* [questum
non ti]

338 *met . et$_e^r$nu^m suppliciu^m q$_{uod}$ c$_r^v$ciat* . suφta kat$_e^r$ina [kdobremu]

339 nemeskacy . i$_{esc}$. stala . uezle^m nelezala . asy yty [... iez sφ]

340 vblφdne^m stadle lez$_{aly}$. ty . i$_{esc}$. suoiφ naukφ o$_t$uodila . jac/kos

341 sφ cce vie suφte^m ziuoce . *No$_t^a$ d^e qu$_u^i$nqu$_u^a$g$_i^n$ta sapie^{n}tib$_{us}$* . *qu$_u^o$s*
a

342 *remotis* re$_{nunci}$andos ab ï^{m}p$_e$ratore . q/$_{conu}e^r$tit ad x$_{pistu}^m$ us$_{que}$
ad illu^m

343 loc$_u^m$. qu$_u^o$m$_{od}^o$ ign$_i^b$us s$_{unt}$ c$_r^e$mati . ï^n qu$_u^i$b$_{us}$ illu$_u^d$ mirab$_i$le
accid$_i^t$ q$_{uod}$ eo$_{rum}$ capilli

401 7 uestim$_e^n$ta abigni/e illesa p$_{er}$ma^{n}s$_e^r$unt s$_{ed}$ uelud u$_e^r$na$_{li}$s $_{ro}$

402 *sa facies* eo$_{rum}$ p$_{ost}$ ign$_i^s$ ï^{n}cendiu^m app$_{aruer}$unt ¶ . at$_r^e$ce toto/a
slo

403 vo vstan moui bog . spφci^m gizsφ ug$_r^e$seh zap$_e^c$claiφ . bo g$_r^e$snik

404 ugreseh zap$_e^c$clony . jesc j/iaco klodnik uce^{m}nicy scouany . Oge^m

405 [ze praui suφti luka]^s . *in ip$_s$a nocte* . *erat petr$_{us}$ dor$_{miens}$* . *Requ$_u^i$re*
super$_{ius}$ ï^n s$_e^r$mo^{n}e

406 [de transfiguracione Domini ...] foli^o . *No$_t^a$ qu$_u^o$m$_{od}^o$ surrexit b$_{ea}$ta* .
$_k$aterina · *que non* solu^m ï^n p$_e^c$

407 [cato sed eciam in inqu]in$^{aci}o_{ne}$ dormire noluit veru^m 7$_{iam}$//eciam
dormie^{n}tes

408 $_a$d p$_{\{ma\}}$//p$_{eni}$tenci$_a^m$ ï^{n}citau$_i^t$. ut pat$_{et}$ ï^n regina 7 porphirio

321

$p_r{}^i ncipe$

409   *[m]ili$c$/t$_u{}^m$. q$_u{}^i$ audie^{n}tes . d^e ip$_s$a q$_u{}^a$lit$_e{}^r$ fuit ex$_s$poliata . 7 scorpionib$_{us}$*

410   *mac$_e{}^r$ata . 7 xij dieb$_{us}$ i^n c$^a{}_r$c$_e{}^r$e fame 7 siti mac$_e{}^r$ata . 7 q$_u{}^o$m$_{od}{}^o$ p$_{ost}$ xij*

411   *$_d$ies . p$_{er}$ ang$_e$los 7 do$_{minu}{}^m$ uisitata . 7 consolata . ad ea^m i^n c$^a{}_r$c$_e{}^r$em i^n*

412   *t$_r{}^a$ntes . 7 q$_{ue}$ d^e ip$_s$a audiera^{n}t uid$_e$ntes . 7 consiliu^m b$_{ea}$te kat$_e{}^r{}_i{}^n$e*

413   *seq$_{ue}$ntes . $_{con}$u$_e{}^r$si s$_{unt}$ ad x$_{pistu}{}^m$. 7 p$_{er}$palma^m martirii ad x$_{pistu}$m migr^a*

414   *u$_e{}^r$unt . h$_{ic}$ no$_t{}^a$ d^{e}martirio regíne . 7 rotis . q$_{ue}$ m$_u$lta miliu^m occid$_e{}^r$unt*

415   *[agmina et alii sunt]* conu$_e{}^r$sy 7 martirio ad x$_{pistu}{}^m$ migr^{a}u$_e{}^r$unt ¶ ac

416   *[tuarte toto slo]*ne//uo mo$_{ui}$. bog vstan . vmarlim giz vmy

417   *[losci bozey]* rospachaiφ . 7 c$_e{}^r$te taliu^m i^nfinit$_{us}$ e$_{st}$ n$_{ume}{}^r$us .

418   *[et non est dom]*us i^n qua no^n iac$_e{}^r$et mortuus . 7 c$_e{}^r$te v

419   *[erba Domini]* . surge . jsta . $_e$n$_{im}$//n$_{obis}$. sign^{i}fica^{n}t$_u{}^r$ p$_{er}$ filiu^m ui

420   *[due unicum vide]*lic$_{et}$ m$_{at}$ris eccl$_{esi}$e . Tum . q$_{ue}$ erat m$_u$l

421   *[titudo affectus carit]*atis . $_v$idelicet . m$_u$ltitudo i^nt$_e{}^r$ced$_e$nciu^m ex

422   *[animi affectu]* karitatis . ad cui$_{us}$ ub$_e{}^r$es lac$_r{}^i$mas . 7 ad

423   *[multas preces]* deuotas . dicit ih$_{esu}$s/c . adolesc$_e$ns t$_{ib}{}^i$ dico . sur

424   *[ge et resedit et]* surrex$_i{}^t$ et reddid$_i{}^t$ illu^m m$_{at}$ri sue . $_v$idelicet . eccl$_{esi}$e . Tu

425   *[in desper]*ac$_i$one mortuus no^n iaceas s$_{ed}$ ad uoce^m ih$_{esu}$ xp$_{isti}$

426   pie excitantis . surge . Cauens . ne modo maxencij i^m

427   p$_{er}$atoris . c$_u{}^m$ i/jp$_s$o desp$_{er}$ando ad inf$_e{}^r$nu^m d^{e}sc$_e$ndas . No$_t{}^a$ erg^o q$_u{}^o$m$_{od}{}^o$

428   i^mp$_{er}$ator maxencius . c$_u{}^m$ b$_{ea}$tam . ka$_{terinam}$. d^{e}collari iussiss$_{et}$. 7 cu^m

429   ad morte^m duc$_e{}^r$et$_u{}^r$ 7 orass$_{et}$ 7 i^n om^{n}ib$_{us}$ exaudita fuiss$_{et}$. 7 p$_{ost}$

430   d^{e}collac$_i$on$_e$m . d^e cor$_{por}{}^e$ eius lac p$_{ro}$ sangui^{n}e fluxiss$_{et}$ 7 corp$_{us}$

431   eius p$_{er}$ ang$_e$los i^n mo^{n}te^m synay . sep$_u$lt$_u{}^m$ fuiss$_{et}$. *[et]* p$_{ost}$ morte^m e$_{ius}$

432   i^mp$_{er}$ator no^n potuit diu uiu$_e{}^r$e . q$_u{}^i$ p$_{er}$desp$_{er}$ac$_i$on$_e$m mortu$_{us}$ fu$_e{}^r$at

433   *[nam in domes]*ti$_{co}$ bello c$_u{}^m$ i^mp$_{er}$atore $_{con}$stantino d^{e}uict$_{us}$ ab ip$_s$o uo

434   *[catus repent]*e p$_{er}$ponte^m i^n equo c$_u{}^r$rens . d^{e}ponte oc//cecidit 7

435
$c_u{}^m$

[in fluvio periisset] ad $i^n f_e{}^r nu^m$ $d^e sc_e ndit$. 7 quia i^n hiis uiciis no^n sed$_i{}^t$ n$_e{}^c$

436 iacuit $b_{ea}ta$ $k_{aterina}$ · sed e_{ius} $ex_{emp}l^o$ te do_{minus} . ad idem excitat orta$_{tu}{}^r$

437 7 uocat . dic$_e$ns . surge $_s$stadla $gr^e s_{ne}{}^{go}$. $pro_p er$a ulepse . sdob$_r{}^e$go . ve

438b ni do $c_r{}^o{}_{leu}{}^{stua}$ neb$_e s_{ke}{}^{go}$ a/Am$_e{}^n$

438a $Di^{le} c_t us$ $d^e o$ 7 $hom_{in}ib_{us}$. cui_{us} memoria

439 $i^n b_e n_e d_{icci}{}^o ne$ e_{st} . Timy sloui . mϕdre/osc faly . suϕtego Nicolaia

440 [ssk]utka duoiakego $b^a{}_{rzo}$ zna$_{menite}{}^{go}$. yfaly gy $p^i{}_r$uey ziego

[...]

501 yde tobe $c_r{}^o$l . zbauicel . izbi nas otuecne $sm_i{}^r$cy zbauil *[Salvum rex]*

502 faciet $po_p ulu^m$ suu^m $ap_e{}^c catis$ eo_{rum} . Tet/cto . $p_r{}^a{}_{ui}$. gdaz $p_r{}^i$yde sbaui l[ud suoy ot ...]

503 uelikih $g_r{}^e$how . $za u_e{}^r ne$ nícsby $_{nam}$ nemescach . aleb$_y$ [nasego ...]

504 zbauícela . y iego $p_r{}^i$sca pozϕdach . by on racil . tog[o dna una]

505 sa sircha zauitach . ynas uro^{gow} . nasih uidomih yneuidomih uhouach .

506 Onihze . mo$_{ui}$. $J_e{}^r$emias jn desc$_e$nsu corrozaím ululat$_u{}^m$ $con_t r^i c_i onís$ host$_{es}$

507 audiera/u^{n}t . fugite 7 saluate $a^n i^m as$ $u_{est}ras$. vistϕpaiϕch zm$_a$

508 sta corrozaím nep$_r{}^i$iacele to sϕ dyably urocy cloueca $g_r{}^e sne^{go}$

509 gloz sϕ $p_r{}^a{}_{ui}$ s$c_r{}^v$sena vslisely . pospecsicesϕ . acamo^c na$_{s[usi}$ bϕdece se]

510 dech . izbisce duse uase zdrϕky urogow uasih d[iablow zuol]

511 níly . vidce . $b_r{}^a{}_{ca}$. mila zba$_{ue}{}^{ne}$. y/vidce uelike si_{na} bo$_{ze}{}^{go}$ $p_r{}^i$iazny [To slouo]

512 Corrozay^m uíp$_r{}^a$uasϕ taynícha moia mne . azna$_{monu}{}^{ie}$. sϕ $s_{i[rce}$ ...]

513 taynímy $g_r{}^e$hy scalano . yothtogo zba$_{uice}{}^{la}$. zlymy vcína$_{n[mi}$ ottargnone]

514 yute^{m}to mesce corrozaím . vp$_e{}^c{}_{kle}$ uekuiem . $sm_i{}^r$tn$_{y[mi}$ grehi zano]

515 rone . yutonϕlo . knem$_{uz}$ gdaz clouek $g_r{}^e$sny . rospam$\phi_{[tai\phi s\phi}$ ...]

516 $_s$stϕpy . tochu sam sebe vspomene . staynego sircha [strumene gor]

517 skih slez zag$_r{}^e$hi uilige yto uzna^{ie} . kegdy sg$_r{}^e$sil . vkake uremϕ

sg$_r^e$sil . kilko

518 croch sg$_r^e$sil . ktorimy g$_r^e$hi t$_{uor}$cha sue^{go} nagnew pouabil . aiaco

519 coly to g$_r^e$sny clouek . uciny taco nagle sirce iego iemu doracy

520 yzbi g$_r^e$ha ostal . suogih g$_r^e$how sirdec^{ne} zalo^{ual} . y$_s$su$\varphi^{t\varphi}$ cyrek$^{u\varphi}$. dínsa za

521 uolal . *veni do$_{min}^e$ 7 noli tardare relaxa fasci^{nora} . plebi tue isr$_{ael}$. Tochto*

522 y . iesch p$_r^a$uda ize yde tob^e c$_r^o$l zbauicel . izbi nas $_{otu}$echne sm$_i^r$cy zba^{uil}

523 ¶ at$_r^e$ce yde tobe vboky izbi ty wbostue nestiscoual . jacoz p$_{ro}$

524 rok d$_{aui}$d uznamonaw ogego silne^m ^{vbostue} . i$_{esc}$. suadec^{stuo} dal . reca . *Exiuit*

525 *h$_o^m$o ad op$_{us}$ suu^m* . Naktore nato iez sam ziaua reca . *Paup$_{er}$*

526 *su^m ego 7 ín laborib$_{us}$ aíuue^n$_{tu}^{te}$. m$_e$a* . Toch ubo$_k$y c$_r^o$leuich bil . ize

527 neymal gdeby suoiφ glouφ podklonil . *wlpes fo$_{ueas}$. h$_{abe}$nt 7 uo$_l$ucres*

528 *celi . ny$_{dos}$. fi$_l$ius . a$_{utem}$ ho$_{minis}$. no^n h$_{abet}$ ubi cap$_u^d$ suu^m recli$_{[net]}$* ap$_{re}$to ize

529 neymal wsue^m narodeny gdebi suφ g$_{[lou\varphi}$ podklonil]

530 togodla p$_{re}$duole^m . a p$_{re}$doslem vyaslkah s$_{[\varphi}$ polozic ...]

531 bil . bo deuicha maria az pelusek dob$_{ri}$h [uiego narodeni]

532 neymala . a togodla gy uezle hustky ogar$_{[n\varphi la]}$ *[Invenerunt]*

533 *eu^m pannis i^{n}uolu$_{tum}$. 7 po$_{situm}$. i^n p$_{re}$se$_{pio}$* . Nalezly gy p$_r^a$ui p[eluskami ...]

534 ogarno/e^{nego} . auiaslkah polozone^{go} . toc ue^m uelike u[bostuo crola]

535 taco csnego . iz . i$_{esc}$. taco sm$_e^r$ne p$_r^i$sce ytaco sm$_e^r$ne narodene · sina bozego

536 ienze p$_{re}$zpocφthka . sboge^m occe^m . j$_{esc}$. c$_r^o$leual . Toch y . i$_{esc}$. ize yde tobe

537 c$_r^o$l . vbogy nato izbi ty wbostue nesticoual ¶ at$_r^e$ce yde tob$_e$

538 c$_r^o$l sm$_e^r$ny . nato izbi ty nebuíal . izbi one/ogo buynego c$_r^o$la dyabla

539 nenasladoual . *qu^i e$_{st}$ rex sup$_{er}$ om^n$_e$s filios sup$_{er}$bie . quia ut [Augustinus?]*

540 *Sup$_{er}$b$_i^a$. dici^t ip$_s$e om^n$_e$s u$_r^i$rtutes deb$_i$litat . 7 eneruat p$_r^a$[vitates vero multiplicat]*

541 *7 confor$_{lat}$. O$_{mni}$no sup$_{er}$b$_i^a$ eo$_{rum}$ qu^i te od$_e^r$unt asc$_e$n$_{dit}$. s$_{em}$p$_{er}$* . Ne na/e$_{[... touari]}$

324

542 stua luda $yc_r{}^o$la buynego . ale $b\varphi$chmy stouaristua $c_r{}^o$la $sm_{[ernego}$
$_{izbihom]}$

601 [$ust\varphi$pili na ui]sokosc $c_r{}^o leu^{stua}$. $neb^e s_{ke}{}^{go}$. $a_{ugustinus}$ *an dubitas*
$d_{ici}{}^t ip_se q_{uod} no^n dab_i{}^t$

602 *[tibi bona sua qui non] dedig_n{}^a t_{us} est mala tua* . $Aue^m p_r{}^a$ui
rospachas . clouece

603 [ize ne da tobe] $dob_r{}^a$ suego ienze $s\varphi$ nezadal $p_r{}^i i\varphi$ch lichoth clouec

604 [ih $zapraud\varphi$] vcemze ty $clo_{ue}{}^{ce}$. mozez buíach . atogo ize ide
tob^e

605 $c_r{}^o$l sm_{er}ny nehces $pam\varphi$tach . $a/Au_{gustinus} i^n l_{ibr}{}^o d^e v_e{}^r b_o$
$d_{omi}ni$. *Si ig_{itur} tanta hu^m ilitate*

606 *se $d^e p_r{}^i m_i{}^t$ {hu^mana $i^n f_i{}^r_r$mitas}* [tam potens deitas] . $supe_r$bire $inq_u{}^o$
$aud_{et} hu^m$ana $i^n f_i{}^r_r$mítas . gdas $s\varphi$

607 $p_r{}^a$ui usmerilo taco mochne bostuo . w/vcem buiach moze nase
mdle

608 clouechstuo . bo iaco mo_{ui} . G^regorius *vnígenit_{us} d^e i app_{ar}uit*
$d^e sp_e{}^c t_{us}$ contume

609 *[liarum ludi]$br^{e/i}a$. illusionu^m obbrob_r{}^{e/i}a passionu^m torme^n ta*
{$torme^n ta$} $toll_e{}^r a$

610 *[vit ut su]$per b_u{}^m$, $ho_{mi}nem doc_e{}^r et hu^m ilis d^e_u s$* . O toch iesmy
[slihali] ize yde

611 [tobe crol prau]diui bo $níkome^{mu} c_r{}^i$udy neucincal $_y$de tob^e crol .

612 [uecni i]zbi ty sním naueky $c_r{}^o$leual . yde tobe $c_r{}^o$l . vboky bi ty

613 [wbostue] nesticoual . yde tobe $c_r{}^o$l $sm_e{}^r$ny bi ty nebuíal . $ap_{re}$to

614 [moui tota slo]ua $c_r{}^o$l tuoy ide tob^e . izbi ty snim naueky $ueko^m$

615b $c_r{}^o$leual . Jegoz . $c_r{}^o leu^{stua}$. do_{mesci} .

615a *[Ubi est qui] nat_{us} e_{st} rex íud^e o_{rum}* . Su_φti

616 [euangelista] $t_r{}^o$iaky $skut_{ek}$. znameniti . $pocazu^{ie}$. vtih uethreh

617 $c_r{}^o$leh poganskih . gih $z\varphi$dne $c_r{}^o$leuicha $d^e uic\varphi$ porodo/enego

618 pitane . Gih w/$v_e{}^r$ne $kz\varphi$zicha $pocoy_{ne}{}^{go} posna^{ne}$. {Gih} *vidi*

619 $m_{us} stel_{lam}$. e_{ius} . $i^n ori_{ente}$. agih rihle [ysc]$od_r{}^e c_r{}^o$la mocnego
odarouane

620 *ubi . 7 ue^n im_{us} c_u{}^m mu_{neribus} ado_{rare} . do_{minu}{}^m* . ymoui
$ew_{angelist}{}^a Su_\varphi$ti

621 $podob_r{}^a ze^m$ trsy $c_r{}^o$lew poganskih . Gde . i_{esc} . t_{ec} . ienze

622 $s\varphi$ narodil $c_r{}^o$l zidowsky . ¶ bo pismo togo $c_r{}^o$le

623 uicha $d^e uic\varphi$ porochonego . $vt_r{}^o iake^m$ mesce $pism^a$

624 naziua $c_r{}^o$lem luda zidowskego . ¶ viego $díune^m narod^e$

625 ny . ¶ wyego $ucesne^m$ uelikih chud cyneny . ¶ . au yego $t_r{}^v dne^m$

626    $_v$mφceny . ypo$_c$azuie ew$_{angelist}^a$ ize t$_{ec}$ to c$_r^o$l yc$_r^o$leuich nebesky

627   vt$_r^o$iakey recy znamenitey ine usic/tky c$_r^o$le zmyía . ¶ ato ute^m iz

628   [iesc milosciuey]^{sy} . ¶ iz . i$_{esc}$. moch$_{ney}^{sy}$. ¶ iz . i$_{esc}$. scedressy . vzna

629   [li oni tre] c$_r^o$le poganscy c$_r^o$leuicha yc$_r^o$la $_{mi}$loscíuego

630   [u Betleem ubo]g$_φ$ deuic$_φ$ porodonego . Nics nemeskai$_φ$ch

631   [gdi guazd$_φ$] uzrely . nagle dary . zloto . cacydlo amírr$_φ$

632   [uzdac mu ...] pospesily . bo c$_r^o$l milosciueysy ¶ p$_{re}$dni^m pocl$_φ$ly

633   [bo crol mocneysi] dar^y iemu vsdaly bo crol . scedreysy . ¶

634   ypocazuie na$_m$ ew$_{angelist}^a$ s$_{uφ}$ty . iz t$_{ec}$ to c$_r^o$l . i$_{esc}$. miloscyueysy . ato urecy t$_r^o$ia^{key}

635   ¶ vmile^m uab^{e}ny izbiho^m pocut$_φ$ v$_e^r$ne cyníly . ¶ wdlugem chacany izbi

636   hom s$_φ$ knemu z$_φ$dne pospesily . ¶ wrihle^m othpusceny . izbiho^m vyego

637   miloscy nerospacily . O kaco . i$_{esc}$. tito c$_r^o$le . mile pouabil . iz gi^m nou$_φ$.

638   [guazd$_φ$ poca]zal yz$_y$auil . Taco ize nícs nemeskai$_φ$ch usrewsy kuas

639   [d$_φ$ udrog$_φ$ s$_φ$] vst$_φ$pily . d$_r^o$ky s$_φ$ neothlozily uce^m rady si$_{na}$. bo$_{zego}$ slusaly

640   *[Et tu ne tardes] conuerti · ad do$_{minu}^m$. 7 ne diff$_{er}$as d^e die in die^m* . Taco tih c$_r^o$lew

641   [sin bozi z$_φ$dne tam]o chacal . ize zat$_r^i$nadesce dny otnarodena gih

700   [... usi]

701   scy . nasladouach y$_{[tecto\ crol\ milosciueysi\ cloueca\ suoim\ zlo]}$

702   te^m . toie ^{skuthkem} milosirdi^m . cadidle^m toie . nabo$_z$ni^m modlením

703   mirr$_φ$ toie . chala udr$_φ$ceni^m . b$_φ$d^e darouach yp$_{re}$sti

704   dari . milosc sina deuicego moze ot$_r^i$mach . ¶ autore

705   ew$_{angelist}^a$ s$_{uφ}$ti . pocazuie . ize tet/cto c$_r^o$l . yc$_r^o$leuich [nebeski]

706   iesc mochneysi . ¶ bo t$_r^o$iaka rech c$_r^o$la $_{m[ocneysego\ po]}$

707   cazuíe . ¶ vstauichne uic$_φ$zstuo . ¶ moch$_{ne}$ [ulodic]

708   stuo . ¶ velike bogathstuo . ¶ vstauichne uic$_φ$stuo

709   *sic$_u^t$ d$_{icitu}^r$ ad thimotheu^m . Sol$_{us}$ pot$_{ens}$. es . rex reg$_u^m$ & do$_{minus}$ d$_o$*

710   *mina^{n}ciu^m . 7 h$_{abet}$ i^{m}mortalitate^m . alij . e$_{nim}$. reges . modica*

711   *i^{n}f$_r^i$mitate u$_{el}$ mor^{te} . u$_i^n$cu^{n}t$_u^r$. sic$_u^t$. d$_{ici}^t$ mag$_{iste}^r$. vado mo*

712   *ri rex sum q$_u^i$d honor q$_u^i$d gl$_{ori}$a regny* . ¶ vtore c$_r^o$la

713 uelikego moch pocazuie . csne ymochne ulodics$_{[tuo]}$

714 *sic$_u^t$ d$_{icitu}^r$ apocalipsis* . *ex$_e^r$cit$_{us}$ cely sequ$_e$bat$_u^r$ eu^m* . *7 h$_a$bebat i^n uesti*

715 *m$_e^n$to* . *7 i^n femore sc$_r^i$pt$_u^m$ rex reg$_u^m$ 7 do$_{minus}$ domina^{n}ciu^m*

800 [...]

801b ¶ abi na$_s$ p$_{re}$sti dary c$_r^o$la . neb$_e$skego

802b ¶ domescily

801a *vid$_e$r̲unt oc$_u$li m$_e$i saluta$_{re}$*

802a *tuu^m* . Ta slo$_{ua}$ pise s$_{uφ}$ti . lucas nacesch ynafalφ

803 godom nyneysim . asφ ta ista sloua zmo$_{uona}$ ochce^m suφti^m

804 iem$_{uz}$ bese ymφ symeon . s$_{uφ}$ti . p$_r^a$udiui bogoboyny . an/ua tih slo$_v$

805 [uiklad ziφzi]ka laci^{n}ske^{go} vpolski/y iesc taky . videle p$_r^a$ui ocy moy

806 [zbauene tuoie] t$_{ochu}$ sina tuego . Tato sloua t$_{ec}$to oc$_{ec}$ suφti . sy

807 [meon pouada na y]mφ bogu ochchu use$_{mogφce}^{mu}$. iz . i$_{esc}$. seslal sina suego . na

808 [pocesene po]colena clouecego . ypouada na^m duoie utih slo$_{ueh}$. s$_{uφ}$ti

809 symeon . Suoie p$_{re}$sm$_e^r$ne ucessene . . asina bo$_{ze}^{go}$ slaune p$_{re}$

810 iauene . Suoie p$_{re}$sm$_e^r$ne ucessene zuidena . si$_{na}$. bo$_{ze}^{go}$. moui

811 *vid$_e$r̲unt o$_{cu}$li* . *m$_e$i* . sina bo$_{zego}$ slaune p$_{re}$iauene [ilkoz] do [uide]n^a [sina boze]go . tu//*tu$_{um}$* . gdes zbauene

812 tuoie . ¶ ypouada na^m t$_{ec}$to oc$_{ec}$ s$_{uφ}$ti . sy$_{meon}$. suoie p$_{re}$sm$_e^r$ne ucese

813 ne . ilkoz douidena . bo moui . videle ocy moy zba$_{ue}^{ne}$. tuo^{ie} .

814 ¶ rosmagite uidene nalazimy vsuφtem pis^{any} . bog^a use$_{mogφce}^{go}$

815 Oua gi p^i_ruey u$_{id}$al hab$_r^a$ha^m podob$_r^a$zem t$_r^i$ mφzy pod$_r^o$ce ydφ

816 cego . ¶ au$_{to}^{re}$ gy uidal moyses uekru polaiφcego . ¶ at$_r^e$ce

817 gy uidal . {uidal} e$_z$echiel nauisokem stolcy sed$_φ$cego ¶

818 actuarte . gy uidal . s$_{uφ}$ti jan . podob$_r^a$ze^m barancha sm$_e^r$nego

819 ¶ apφte gy uidal . t$_{ec}$to oc$_{ec}$ s$_{uφ}$ti symeon . podoblcením clouech

[im ...]

University of Leiden
University of Groningen

NOTE

* An electronic version of the present edition is available on the Internet at "www.let.rug.nl/~schaeken/fk-kazsw.html".

REFERENCES

Diels, P.
1921 *Die altpolnischen Predigten aus Heiligenkreuz.* Berlin: Weidmann-
sche Buchhandlung.
Łoś, J. and W. Semkowicz
1934 *Kazania t.zw. Świętokrzyskie.* Kraków: Polska Akademja Umiejętności.
Wydra, W. and W.R. Rzepka
1995 *Chrestomatia staropolska.* Wrocław etc.: Ossolineum.

Dutch Contributions to the Twelfth International Congress of Slavists, Cracow, Linguistics (= Studies in Slavic and General Linguistics Vol 24), 329–349. RODOPI, Amsterdam – Atlanta, GA 1998.

ON ONE CASE OF ANOMALY IN CZECH PHONOTACTICS

ADELA RECHZIEGEL

> *An expressive word without*
> *an extraordinary shape*
> *has not the ghost of a chance*

1. Introduction

One of the rules in synchronic Czech phonotactics applies to specific CV combinations. According to this rule the consonants classified as palatal do not combine with the vowels /o/, /u/ and with the diphthong /ou/ and, furthermore, velar consonants do not combine with the vowel /e/. This rule was formulated for the first time in 1947 by Mathesius, who still much earlier described Czech sound combinations in general, in words consisting of four phonemes (Mathesius 1929). His examination is later on expanded by Vachek (1940) with words consisting of five phonemes. Mathesius enumerated the palatal and the velar consonants, respectively, as follows: /c č ďj ň ř š ť ž; h x k/.[1] This means that combinations like /ďo/, /ňu/, /ťou/, /he/, /xe/, /ke/ should not appear in the vocabulary of the contemporary Czech language. However, Mathesius stated that there are a few exceptions to this rule. He observed that the combinations may occur in special groups of words and, additionally, in a morphologically determined position, namely:

a. in expressive words,
b. in loanwords,
c. at a morpheme boundary.

In his article Mathesius also provides us with some examples of these exceptions, cf.:

a. *čuměti* 'gape', *kňučeti* 'whine', *křupati* 'crack', *ťukati* 'knock', *čochňati* 'cuddle', *ďobati* 'peck', *čouhati* 'stick out'; *chechtati se* 'howl with laughter', *ochechule* 'hag';

330

b. *chemie* 'chemistry', *čokoláda* 'chocolate', *žumpa* 'cesspool', *šňůra* 'line', *jód* 'iodine';

c. *bojovati* 'fight', *krajový* 'regional', *klíčů* 'key gen.pl.'; *hochem* 'boy instr.sg.'.

As may appear already from the title of his article, which is 'On the expressional validity of certain groups of speech sounds in Czech', Mathesius was primarily concerned with the words representing the exception under **a.** The unusual sound combinations in expressive words he considered justified by their function which is to create contrast to all other, non-expressive ('intellectual') words. Although Mathesius did not go into particulars about the notion of expressivity, he stressed the necessity of its further investigation.

It is surprising that Mathesius did not include the vowel /a/ into his account, nor did other authors who elaborated on his findings (e.g. Zima, Hubáček, see below). In our opinion the vowel /a/ belongs with respect to combinability to the other two non-front vowels and in expressive words it is even more prominent than /o/ and /u/. In the present paper we will deal with the question how the mentioned phonotactic constraint came into being and how it maintained itself until today. We think it useful to look at this problem on the one hand from the synchronic point of view, as Mathesius did, and on the other hand from the diachronic point of view. The former tackling will show that the combinations that in contemporary Czech occur in non-expressive words and thus follow the rule are in phonetic sense more appropriate than the exceptional combinations found in expressive words. The latter, diachronic, approach makes it possible to shed some light on the relationship between the mentioned phonotactic rule and certain sound proccesses that took place in the historical development of the Czech language. We start, however, with some notes on the study of expressivity in Czech linguistics.

2. Studies on expressivity

The phenomenon of expressivity manifests itself on each level of language analysis. As a stylistic characterization it draws an important dividing line between the two main groups of language means. On the one hand there are the stylistically neutral language means, and this is the majority, on the other hand there are the stylistically contrastive, expressive language means, representing a small minority. The expressive language means can be assumed to have a system of their own, partly overlapping with and partly differing from the system which applies to the non-expressive language means. The expressive language means always transmit a subjective, and for this reason emotional, evaluation. As regards expressive words, their phonological structure is in most cases specific: either the stem or the derivational morphemes (or both) are characterized by unusual sound combinations.

In Czech linguistics due attention has already been paid to expressivity. The first book on this theme was that of Machek (1930), an outstanding etymologist in the field of the Slavic and Baltic languages and the author of the Czech etymologic dictionary (1971). In his study on expressivity he first of all makes the distinction between 'intellectual' words and 'affective' words (i.e. words of affection, words which express an emotional attitude of the speaker). Machek's division goes hand in hand with a kind of sociolinguistic characterization of the two types. In his approach the 'intellectual language' is seen as dignified, traditional and conservative, being spoken by the nobility. On the other hand, the 'affective language' is spoken by servants and other working people, it creates countless pet-names and runs over with colourful words, distinguishing themselves by unusual sound formations (Machek 1930: 4).

Machek's results are still valuable for contemporary language analyses because of the exhaustive description of the processes in the development of a language that took place when speakers had the intention to express their emotional attitude in the circumstances of the given communicative situation. One important way for expressing affection is, according to Machek, the use of palatal consonants /č ď ň š ť ž/ and of palatalization (also secondary palatalization). He devoted a whole chapter, called 'affective palatalization' to this matter (1930: 10ff). Moreover, Machek quotes Jespersen's observation that the articulators can be moved to action not only for the purpose of communication, but also for the purpose of reaching an expressive effect, by which they take on various changes. This applies especially to the lips. These affective modifications have led in the past – according to Jespersen – even to sound changes (Machek 1930: 12).

In Machek's study we find some thoughts which are important for the theme with which we are concerned in this paper. Firstly it is the distinction Machek made between the functional varieties of language, even though we perhaps would choose other characteristics in order to describe them. Another thought which is relevant for our reasoning is Machek's conviction that affective modifications of the sound structure have a physiological aspect, namely that the speaker is aware of the specific movements of his articulators, particularly of the lips, and of the extent of the contact of the tongue with the palate.

The next monography on the expressivity in Czech comes from Zima (1961). The author examines many procedures by which the expressivity in a language can be reached and gives an extensive review of the literature on this question. He, too, quotes the well-known results of Mathesius. It is not clear, why he includes /a/ in the enumeration of vowels that cannot be combined with the palatal consonants (1961: 12). He neither gives any comment on this point, nor does he give other examples than those of Mathesius where /a/ is not included, as already said. Zima also mentions some statements of Hodura (1953), e.g. his distinction of expressivity into a 'direct' one and a 'non-direct' one with their characteristics (see Note 15).

Moreover, we find a short paragraph on the combinability of the Czech phonemes in Hubáček (1981). With respect to the groups we are concerned with, he observes that the combinations of /ď ň ť/ and sometimes also /č ř š ž/ with the back vowels /o u/ are an indication of expressive words (1981: 68).

The most recent reference to the phonotactic rule discussed is made in the academic grammar of Czech *Mluvnice češtiny* (1986). It is here, that the phenomenon is given the striking characterization of *anomalous phoneme configurations* (*anomální konfigurace fonémů*) (1986: 158). A short remark tells us that, as regards /u/, its anomalous behavior results from old sound changes.

3. The phonotactic rule from the synchronic point of view

Mathesius's observation obliges us to ask what underlies the phonotactic suitability of certain CV combinations and unsuitability of others. We think that the answer should contain two aspects: the description of the suitability of the CV combinations judged on synchronic phonetic grounds and, on the other hand, the explanation how the recent state came into being. We will start with the first aspect, i.e. with the description of the relevant features which make in the contemporary Czech language the joining of a certain consonant with a certain vowel appropriate.

The features derived from the vowel triangle, i.e. [high], [mid], [low], [front], [central], [back] apply to the Czech vowels as follows: in the horizontal direction /i/ and /u/ are assigned the feature [high], /e/ and /o/ are [mid] and /a/ is [low]; in the vertical direction /i/ and /e/ are [front], /a/ is [central] and /o/, /u/ are [back] (Kučera 1961: 25). These distinctive features cannot, in this arrangement, account for the suitability

333

of CV combinations, because they place in the same group the Czech vowels /e/ and /o/, of which we already know that they combine differently. Moreover, /a/ is isolated, although it has the same capacity for combination as /o/ and /u/, as will be shown later.

In order to indicate the joint articulatory basis, we will use distinctive features which are uniform for both vowels and consonants. This concerns the features [high], [low], and [back]. They belong to the *Cavity features* (Chomsky and Halle 1968) and are called in Sloat-Taylor-Hoard (1978: 84) *Tongue body features*, as they relate to the position of the tongue. Chomsky and Halle determined as a starting-point the tongue position at the articulation of [ɛ] which they regard as neutral. Vowels with higher position of the tongue have the feature [+high], those with lower position have [+low]. In this classification the vowels /e/ and /o/ have the features [−high,−low]. In the horizontal direction, when the tongue body is retracted from its neutral position, the vowels produced have the feature [+back]. Thus the central and back vowels /a/, /o/, /u/ are [+back]; /i/ and /e/ are [−back]. For our purposes of describing the articulatory basis of the CV combinability it is sufficient to use the features [high] and [back], the latter being the determining feature for the potential combination.

The relevant features are represented in Czech vowels as follows:

Table 1

	/i/	/e/	/a/	/o/	/u/
[high]	+	−	−	−	+
[back]	−	−	+	+	+

In Czech consonants these features apply as follows:[2]

Table 2

	[high]	[back]
labials	−	−
alveo-dentals	−	−
palatals	+	−
velars	+	+
glottals	−	+

334

3.1 The relevant combinatory features of consonants

With regard to the articulation of consonants we have to take into consideration the pair of features, by means of which we can sufficiently distinguish the groups of phonemes with equal and different combinability (hence the term *combinatory* features). These are the above specified Tongue body features [high] and [back] which are found in the consonantal repertory with either the value + or −, so that there are four combinations of features possible. We make use of these combinations to distinguish three groups of consonants. In order to refer to these groups, we shall use the terms 'soft', 'hard' and 'neutral' and we will explain what they stand for.[3]

The first group is characterized by the following combination of the Tongue body features: [+hi,−bk], producing together the feature [+pal] (Sloat-Taylor-Hoard 1978: 113). These features occur in the consonants /č ď j ň ř š ť ž/. Henceforth it is these that will be referred to as 'soft' consonants (symbolized C^s). These consonants combine regularly with the front vowels /e/ and /i/.

The second group possesses the mentioned features with the values: [−hi,−bk] and the consonants can be indicated as 'neutral'. These are the consonants /b c d f l m n p r s t v z/[4] (we shall symbolize them C^n.) There are no constraints on their combination with vowels, they join all of them (including the diphthong /ou/) (Mathesius 1947: 88, cf. also Note 1). Probably the determining factor for this maximum combinability is the place of the tongue: it is situated in the neutral position (cf. Sloat-Taylor-Hoard 1978: 84 and Jakobson-Fant-Halle 1976: 18).

The third group displays two combinations of the relevant features, i.e. [+hi,+bk] which is found with /g/, /x/, /k/ and [−hi,+bk] which is assigned to the phoneme /h/. It is these consonants which will be referred to as 'hard' (symbolized C^h). The three types of consonants and their combinability can now be summarized as follows:

Table 3

'soft'	[+hi,−bk]:		
	/č ď j ň ř š ť ž/	+	/e/, /i/
'neutral'	[−hi,+bk]:		
	/b c d f l m n p r s t v z/	+	/e/, /i/, /a/, /o/, /u/, /ou/
'hard'	[+hi,+bk]:	[−hi,+bk]:	
	/g x k/;	/h/	+ /i/, /a/, /o/, /u/, /ou/

To the mentioned phonetic features by which we can differentiate between 'soft' consonants on the one hand and 'neutral' and 'hard' consonants on the other hand, we might add others. They are found in the reference book of Hála (1923). In his comprehensive description of the articulation of consonants and vowels Hála includes the jaw angle (i.e. the angle of the jaw during the articulation of a particular sound,)[5] and, additionally the contact of the tongue on the hard palate. These data supply support to my view that the basis of the combinability on the one hand and non-combinability on the other hand has to be sought synchronically in such phonetic parameters which can be readily checked by a native speaker without mechanical assistence. Hála did not record any tongue contact during the articulation of /a/ and /o/, and only the slightest contact at the edges of the soft palate with /u/, but in the articulation of /i/ and /e/ he found clear contact with the hard palate continuing onto the soft palate (Hála 1923: 31ff). Contact with the palate means that /i/ and /e/ are the most natural partners for 'soft' consonants. Conversely, the absence of palatal contact during the articulation of /a/, /o/ and /u/ accounts for the fact why combinations of these vowels with 'soft' consonants are felt to be unusual or inappropriate.[6]

As regards the jaw angle, it is usually smaller for 'soft' consonants than for 'neutral' and 'hard' consonants. This has to do with the movement of the tongue, during the articulation of 'soft' consonants, up towards the hard palate (or to where the alveoli meet the palate), which requires the lower jaw to be withdrawn slightly backwards. The greater jaw angle with the 'neutral' and 'hard' consonants probably contributes to their easier combinability with vowels of various articulatory types.

In addition to the phonetic features and speaking in terms of markedness - non-markedness I believe the 'soft' consonants may be treated as marked, 'hard' and 'neutral' as unmarked. 'Soft' consonants have a greater signalling capacity resulting from the higher degree of tension needed in their articulation. Both these facts limit their combinability. Compared to the 'hard' and 'neutral' consonants, 'soft' consonants also reveal a lower overall incidence which again is typical of marked entities in the language, cf. Mázlová (1946), Kučera (1961) and Ludvíková and Kraus (1966).

3.2   The relevant combinatory features of vowels

As appeared from Table 1 the phonetic basis of the combinatory features in vowels is, just as in consonants, complex. The Tongue body features occur in the vowels in various combinations: with /i/ the features are [+hi,–bk], with /e/ they are [–hi,–bk], with /a/ and /o/ we have [–hi,+bk], and with /u/ we have [+hi,+bk].

Only one of the mentioned features, [back], operates in a fundamental manner, since [–back] gives a sufficient characterization of /i/ and /e/ and [+back] is adequate to the characterization of /a/, /o/ and /u/. The same feature with the mark [–], i.e. [–back] is found, as has been said, to be decisive with all 'soft' consonants without exception.

Thus in the vowel triangle we can draw the dividing line as follows:

/i/		/u/
/e/		/o/
	/a/	

Vowels having similar capacities for combination with consonants are in this way put in the same group.

The above mentioned works present also statistical data on Czech vowels. Kučera states rightly, that the relative frequency of individual groups of segmental phonemes shows a correspondence to the distributional limitations on such phonemes (1961: 40).

In Table 4 the frequency of occurence of the vowels is shown, based on data drawn from Kučera (1961: 42). (As we are primarily interested in the frequency of the place of articulation, we combined the figures of short and long vowels.)

Table 4

/i/	/e/	/a/	/o/	/u/
10,19	10,51	8,91	8,24	3,67[7]

Thus, from the viewpoint of frequency, too, there are differences which are in accordance with the other characteristics of the vowels, which together form the basis for their phonotactic behavior.

4. The phonotactic rule from the diachronic point of view

In order to obtain more clarity about the phonotactic rule mentioned and about its constraints, we looked at the old sound changes which are assumed to have caused the given situation. In considering how these changes came about, we can gain advantage from modern linguistic theory, among other things from the very extensive study of the phenomenon of coarticulation (and coarticulation resistence). It has been introduced by Öhman (1966) on the basis of the data obtained from his spectrographic measurements in VCV utterances in Swedish. Herewith Öhman achieved a breakthrough in the domain of speech production and perception. In addition to the results which his analysis has brought to light, it gave rise to many relevant questions, some of which have not yet been answered. Since the beginning of the eighties coarticulation enjoys a lot of renewed attention, to which fact testifies, among other things, the conference held in Venice in 1991 (Symposium on Coarticulation, Venice 23-25 October, 1991). The contributions presented at the conference were published in *Language and Speech* 1993, volume 36 (2, 3). The papers deal with divergent aspects of coarticulation, including those which have not been studied before, such as the parsing problem or the relationship between the segmental and prosodic structure of an utterance. In respect to the complex question of the Czech sound combinations we found helpful some of the claims in this volume as well as other studies which will be mentioned in the next sections.

4.1 Sound combinations which conform to the rule

In an early stage of Czech, between the end of the 10th and the end of the 14th century, some sounds were combined in newly developed CV (or CVC) segments. The new sequential arrangement was the result of processes which took place before this period, i.e. contraction, the decline of the 'jers' (reduced vowels) and of nasal vowels. Historians of Czech describe the situation at the beginning of the 10th century as the *new vowel system* (cf. e.g. Lamprecht, Šlosar, Bauer 1986: 50).

The newly joined combinations were found in the word stems, but also in the final position of words and word-forms. They contained consonants with the feature [+pal] and vowels with the feature [+back].[8] Such combinations are not easy to pronounce, because the articulatory movements are antagonistic. The notion of *articulatory antagonism* (Öhman 1966, Farnetani 1990) applies to those situations when one and the same articulator is instructed to perform simultaneously two (or more) conflicting tasks.[9] Because the articulatory cooperation, then, is not possible, this situation can also be identified as a case of *coarticulatory resistence*. However, as the coarticulation is an expected, predictable and, according to the principle of minimal effort, a necessary procedure, the language system can modify the obstructive segment by means of a sound change. In his analysis of the nature of sound change Boersma (1998) emphasizes that it is automatic and not a goal of anyone at any time. The result of the sound change is an improvement in the outlined piece of phoneme inventory. The reason why languages never stop changing simply is, Boersma claims, that "there will always be a better system" (Boersma 1998: 3).

A convincing formulation of such modifications is put forward by Kohler (1990). He made an important distinction between two articulatory processes, namely *coarticulation* as a temporary overlapping of partly similar articulatory gestures and *assimilation* as a permanent "reorganization of articulatory gestures" (1990: 83). In the latter process certain movements are eliminated and certain places of articulation are moved. Thus, it also means that the *energy expenditure* is minimized and that the number of moving organs involved in speech production is reduced (Kohler 1990: 88).

In order to explain the Czech sound changes concerned, the notion of articulatory antagonism causing sound change, which had resulted in permanent *assimilation* can be considered appropriate. The sound changes were:

1/ *a* > *ě* [ie], *á* > *ie* [ié] (in the 12th century)
2/ *o* > *ě* [ie], *ó* > *ie* [ié] and *u* > *i*[10] (in the 14th century).

Ad 1/ <u>Before the sound change</u> /a/ occurred after a 'soft' consonant:
  a/ in stems: $\qquad\qquad$ C^s + V^h + C^s, e.g. *čáša* 'cup';
  b/ in word-final position: $\quad$ C^s + V^h, $\qquad\qquad$ e.g. *náša* 'our f.'.

In the case under 1a/ the sound change only took place when a 'soft' consonant not only preceded, but also followed.[11] In other positions (1b/) the sound change always took place in two phonemes of the indicated type. The combinations were modified as follows:

<u>After the sound change</u> the 'soft' consonant is followed by /ě/:
a/ + b/ = C^s + V^s, e.g. *čiešě, nášě.*

Ad 2/ <u>Before the sound change</u> /o/, /u/ occurred after a 'soft' consonant:
in all positions: C^s + V^h, e.g. *našo* 'our n.', *polo* 'field'; *břuch* 'belly', *juh* 'south', *cut* 'feeling'.
<u>After the sound change</u> the 'soft' consonant is followed by /ě/, /i/:
C^s + V^s, e.g. *naše, pole; břich, jih, cit.*[12]

The new sequential arrangement which can be typified as *articulatory agreement* displays articulatory gestures which are better adjusted to each other. This would make coarticulation in the segments possible.

If we are dealing with historical sound changes, we should regard them as dynamic processes which proceed along many preliminary stages. The speech mechanisms seek the way to a better articulatory structure by modifying the unsuitable one, to begin with an intuitive free variation. Sound variation has already been recognized as an important phenomenon with respect to sound change, cf. Ohala (1989): "Sound change is drawn from a pool of synchronic variation" or according to Boersma (1998: 13) "the pool of free variation" can be considered "the breeding place for sound change". Rightly Lamprecht claims that, when examining sound changes, we must not neglect the obvious variation in vowels, as it was perceived by listeners in the given speech community and written down by scribes (Lamprecht 1986: 50-52, 63-75).

All Czech vowels had at the end of the 10th century at least two variants, distinguished by the features [front] vs [back], according to the nature of the preceding consonant being soft or hard (Lamprecht 1986: 52). In the case of /a/ there were even four variants, differentiated on the one hand by the above criterion and on the other hand by the degree of openess: symbolized as ä was the more open variant of the /a/ which originated from the nasal ę, and it has a front variant 'ä and a back variant ä. The same applies to the more close a which has a front variant symbolized as 'a and a back variant symbolized as a. These variants, attested in old writings, are exactly the preliminary stages in the process of sound change which have prepared the new situation of achieving more appropriate combinations with the 'soft' consonants. The combinations of palatal consonants with those variants gradually changed their articulatory and acoustical structure, to the effect that listeners might identify them as new phonemes in a new sequential arangement.[13]

The role of synchronic variation as the pre-condition cause of sound change, and that of misparsing of the speech signal as a potential source of sound change is illustrated by Ohala (1989, 1993: 157) with various examples. One such instance from the French language shows how a misinterpretation of a modified sound can lead to establishing a new phoneme, cf:

6a <u>speaker</u> pronounces: /e/ > [ę] / _n
 b <u>listener</u> identifies: [ę] > /e/ / _n
but after a period of modified production it can happen that:
7a <u>speaker</u> pronounces: /e/ > [ę] / _n   and
 b <u>listener</u> identifies: [ę] > /ę/

If we would apply this model of successive modifications to the case of the Czech sound changes described above, we would obtain:

1a speaker pronounces: /a/ > ['ä] / _C[+pal]
 b listener identifies: ['ä] > /a/ / _C[+pal],
but successively
2a speaker pronounces: /a/ > ['ä] / _C[+pal]
 b listener identifies: ['ä] > /ě/[14]

In this way a new phoneme is added to the users' phonemic inventory.

4.2 Sound combinations which do not conform to the rule

In this section we would like to comment on the specific phoneme combinations of $C^s + V^h$ which did not change when the majority of those combinations did as we have shown in 4.1. They represent one of the exceptions, enumerated in section 1 under a., b. and c. The exceptions under b. and c. scarcely need any explanation for not conforming to the rule: in b. the instances concern loanwords, and in c. the exception applies to combinations situated at a morpheme boundary. Here, obviously, the law of analogical forms for identical morphological functions and of the paradigmatic regularity have gained priority over the phonetic rule. These concurrent mechanisms have been described already by Jakobson (1948: 16), who also referred to the idea of Horn that phonemes with a morphological function resist sound laws (Horn 1923: 131ff). So only the exceptions in a. are left over and they confront us with the question, what is the decisive factor of their resisting the sound change in the past and therefore of their preserving the status of an anomalous sound combinations until today.

In recent literature on coarticulation and sound change there is also much attention to the factors which inhibit these procceses. The most prominent of them is word stress which goes mostly hand in hand with *hyperarticulation*. According to De Jong, Beckman, Edwards (1993) the stressed nuclear segments display time patterns which allow for less coarticulatory overlap, thus resulting in *hyperarticulation*. In these stressed segments the tongue dorsum is more retracted (and the position of the jaw is lower) which makes the articulation of back vowels more distinct (De Jong, Beckman, Edwards 1993: 197).

This resistence factor certainly played a role in the preservation of the anomalous sound combinations found in Czech expressive words. As is well known, the first syllable in Czech words always carries word stress. It is, thus, a very "obstinate" combination to be changed by assimilation. Of course, this raises a new important question: why was this resistence factor productive in a small part of the vocabulary (i.e. in the expressive words), while in the overwhelming part of the vocabulary (i.e. in all other, non-expressive words) it gave way to the sound change in spite of the presence of stress?

In our view the most important factor which determined the application of the sound change in one part of the lexicon and the preservation of the given sound combinations in the other part, is the linguistic function of the words involved. The special communicative power of expressive words, connected with their meaning, regularly manifests itself in a specific, strong stress, on top of the word accent and the sentence stress which they can carry too. If an expressive word stands for a whole sentence, as do e.g. onomatopoetic words, cries and swear-words, the three types of stress accumulate on the one unit. This kind of stress can perhaps best be referred to as *emphasis*. Long ago the phenomenon of stress accompanying a special meaning has been given due attention by Jones (1972 [1918]). He differentiated two kinds of this stress, i.e. *emphasis for contrast* and *emphasis for intensity*. Jones also observes that "a fuller or strong form (of a word) is used in emphasis" (Jones 1972: 297). Words carrying this kind of "semantic stress" can with respect to their function be compared with expressive words, as they function in the Czech language. The accumulation of stress demands an articulatory effort which presumably yields hyperarticulation as a systematic procedure, in contrast to neutral words where semantic stress is lacking. In the following discussion we look for still more specific features of expressive words which may contribute to their resistence against sound changes.

5. Discussion

It is obvious that the exceptions from the rule mentioned do not concern a handful of single words or word-forms, but, on the contrary, that they represent a *type of words* which can be clearly defined from both the functional and the formal point of view. Taking off from some assumptions as to the causes of their anomalous phonotactic behavior, made in Czech publications (Machek, Mathesius, Hodura,[15] Zima, *Mluvnice češtiny*), we would like to emphasize the connection between the semantic and phonetic structure of the expressive words under discussion.

As regards their function, expressive words are − in short − signals of the personal attitude of the speaker towards the listener as well as towards the theme of the conversation and the situation. Whereas each neutral word is an indispensable link in the chain of the ongoing message, expressive words are carriers of a specific piece of information, which is added to the transmitted communicative content. The oral or the written context plays an essential role in the understanding of a neutral word in a communication, but it is less important when expressive words are involved, because of their considerable semantic independence. If an expressive word performs the function of a whole sentence only the non-textual context is present to support the correct transmission of the message. This is one of the reasons why their communicative capacity has to be strong.

The unusual phonetic structure which in the neutral vocabulary is felt as a disadvantage (and therefore there is a continual effort to remove it by sound changes) is, on the contrary, a profitable feature of expressive words. It is in perfect agreement with their typological characterization and their function (for English cf. Bloomfield 1933). The fact that they are strongly stressed and therefore hyperarticulated make it easily imaginable that what is felt as a difficult pronunciation, e.g. the combination of $C^s + V^h$ can cause a pleasant feeling on the part of the speaker and the listener, because of its exclusiveness and, consequently, of the possibility to 'taste' the meaning involved. It is like cracking nuts. We are reffering here to the kinesthetic perception which enables the speaker to be aware of his articulatory movements (Vieregge 1985: 19). In this case this concerns the contact with the palate (Hála 1923) and the movement of the lips. It can be observed that while speaking in a neutral style it is habitual to pronounce the /o, u/ without rounding, as this feature is in Czech redundant. However, if we use these phonemes in an affective utterance, the rounding is extensive. Moreover, the more distinct pronunciation of back vowels, as reported by De Jong, Beckman and Edwards, can in these combinations also be desirable in order to bring about a contrasting effect in their production and perception.

Speaking in terms of markedness - unmarkednes, the expressive words belong no doubt to the former type. The characteristic features of marked entities apply to them nicely, as they are more complex formally as well as semantically than the neutral words. The form of most expressive words is characterized by sound combinations that otherwise do not occur. They are always typically semantically loaded, because they contain the additional information of the subjective, emotional evaluation. As is common with marked entities, they are much less numerous and occur with incomparably lower frequency.

As regards their lower frequency of occurrence there can possibly be a connection with an interesting claim made by Trudgill (1989) in his investigation into language varieties. He distinguishes between high- and low-contact language varieties with respect to their capacity to submit to changes. Trudgill concludes that the low-contact variety shows a strong inclination to preserve unchanged forms, whereas the high-contact variety continues to perform many changes due to intensive contact among the language users and, as a result of it, among the language units. Although Trudgill's observation applies to the situation among language varieties, it might perhaps be taken into consideration also when it concerns stylistically differentiated parts of the lexicon. Expressive words are not frequently used, and therefore make little contact with other words, expressive or non-expressive. This might be still another factor contributing to the fact that the combinations of C^s+V^h stayed unchanged in expressive words.

In the present discussion we would also like to make some remarks upon the position of /a/. As already said, it is lacking in the original statement of Mathesius. In the preceding sections 3 and 4, we have explained that /a/ shares with /o/ and /u/ the relevant combinatory characteristics, namely the feature [+back]. Besides, as we have shown, /a/ also has been partly modified in the historical development by sound change similar to that with /o/, /u/.

The phonotactic behavior of /a/ in contemporary Czech, resembles that of /o/ and /u/, as it does not regularly combine with C^s in preposition (except for the cases mentioned in section 1 under a., b. and c.). The occurence of /a/ in expressive words is still more prominent that that of /o/ and /u/. This results from the morphological function of /a/: it is a very important and frequent inflexional suffix of feminine substantives, in the nominative singular. The forms containing /a/ in this position thus represent dictionary entries.[16] Significantly, this /a/ is felt by the language users as a pre-eminent marker of feminine gender, probably because the most essential roles of a woman are designated by substantives ending in -a, cf. *dcera* 'daughter', *sestra* 'sister', *milenka* 'sweethart, mistress', *snoubenka* 'fiancée', *nevěsta* 'bride', *žena* 'wife', *manželka* 'wife', *matka* 'mother', *babička* 'grandmother', *vnučka* 'granddaughter'. The /a/ in this position, moreover, is used in order to generate numerous hypocoristics, also for masculine persons, e.g. *Pepča, Jarča, Vláďa, Kája, Máňa, Bóřa, Máša, Váša, Rosťa, Bóža.*[17]

The above mentioned prominent semantic feature of /a/ is, interestingly, also the basis of the use of /a/ when derivatives are formed which

344

bear a quite different, i.e. pejorative meaning assigned to masculine persons (we have found as many as 80 of them), e.g. *tlučhuba* 'windbag', *nekňuba* 'nincompoop', *mrťafa* 'numskull', *halama* 'lout', *protiva* 'nuisance', *nemrava* 'immoral fellow', *pápěra* 'threadpaper of a fellow' etc.

To conclude this paragraph we give some more examples of expressive words containing the combination C^s + /a/ in the stem or in the final position: *čahoun* 'lanky fellow', *žďabec* 'pinch', *ďas* 'deuce', *ňafat* 'yelp', *řachnout* 'bash', *šašek* 'buffoon', *ťapka* '(small) paw', *žaves (metoda -)* 'slapdash'; *káča* 'hussy', *véča* (slang) 'dinner', *méďa* 'teddy bear', *říďa* (slang) 'director', *frája* 'masher', *dvója* (slang) 'second-best mark', *huhňa* 'indistinctly speaking man', *fouňa* 'nob', *šáša* 'clown', *ťuňťa* 'dunce'.

New expressive words with "anomalous" sound combinations as described in this article come continually into existence.

6. Conclusions

In the present paper we have tried to make clear that the given phonotactic rule functioning in contemporary Czech reflects a case of articulatory antagonism which occured in the old Czech language approximately in the 10th century. This antagonism had been removed in the majority of cases by changing the articulatory parameters. In a minor part of the vocabulary, i.e. in the expressive words, it has been preserved. Here the unusual combinations of C^s + V^h are important carriers of the specific meaning of these words. It is our assumption that the fact that the stylistic feature of expressivity keeps unusual sound combinations in existence, is one of universal validity. In this sense it can be suggested that an articulatory antagonism is a potential phonetic basis of expressivity.

Whenever sound changes are performed this brings about an improvement of the organization in the given system of phonemes. The development of the part of the Czech phonemic system discussed in this article satisfies this claim, even in two ways: firstly, by eliminating the articulatory antagonism coarticulation has been made possible, and, secondly, by preserving the original sound combinations in expressive words a dividing line has been drawn through the vocabulary, separating two different subsystems of lexical units. In each subsystem a higher agreement has been reached between their respective form and function. In non-expressive words the cognitive meaning generally goes hand in hand with a neutral form following the valid phonotactic rules and therefore appropriate for a smooth, easy running production. On the other hand, the expressive words, carrying affective meaning, often possess an extraordinary form as a phonetic correllate of their signalling function.

345

As regards the vowels taking part in the discussed phonotactic pattern, there are reasons for adding the /a/ to the /o/, /u/ (and /ou/) as it behaves combinatorily in the same way. The numerous studies on reduction, coarticulation and sound change, and on speech production and perception in general report of all imaginable conditions under which speech can be performed: stress, prepared or spontaneous speech, spoken or read text, rate and loudness and others. However, the stylistic parameter also should be made use of in the examinations. With regard to the case of Czech "anomalous" sound combinations the possibility that in the hierarchy of the conditions the highest position will be taken by semantic characteristics, cannot be excluded.

Expressive words deserve in general much more attention than they have been given until now. They are very valuable for gaining insight into the structure of any language and also for being the messengers of the emotional substance of life.

University of Amsterdam

NOTES

1 The actual formulation of Mathesius's rule runs as follows: "Rozbor domácích slov povahy intelektuální ukazuje, že v češtině se v mezích tohoto materiálu nespojují volně všechny souhlásky se všemi samohláskami, nýbrž že jazyk se vyhýbá spojování některých souhlásek s některými samohláskami. Můžeme po té stránce mluviti o souhláskách palatálních, které se nespojují se samohláskami *u, o* a s dvojhláskou *ou,* o souhláskách velárních, které se nespojují se samohláskou *e,* a konečně o souhláskách neutrálních, které se volně spojují se všemi samohláskami i s dvojhláskou *ou.* K řadě palatální v tomto smyslu patří souhlásky *c, č, ď, j, ň, ř, š, ť, ž.* K řadě velární náleží souhlásky *h, ch, k.* Ostatní souhlásky jsou netrální". ["Analysis of intellectual words in native stock reveals that within the limits of this material in Czech not all consonants combine freely with all vowels, the language avoiding combinations of certain consonants with certain vowels. In this respect we may mention the palatal consonants which do not combine with the vowels *u, o* and the diphthong *ou,* the velar consonants which do not combine with the vowel *e,* and finally the neutral consonants which do combine freely with all vowels and the diphthong *ou.* In the sens meant the palatal series includes the consonants *c, č, ď, j, ň, ř, š, ť, ž,* the velar series the consonants *h, ch, k,* all other consonants being neutral"] (Mathesius 1947: 88).

2 Since Kučera does not describe the Tongue body features for consonants it is thought useful to show how they apply.

3 Mathesius used the labels: 'palatal', 'velar' and 'neutral', but this is questionable, because 'neutral' is not a phonetic term, while 'palatal' and 'velar' are.

[4] Mathesius and the general practice of Czech language handbooks include /c/ among the [+pal] consonants, but in line with the articulatory features to which I have referred, I include it among the neutral consonants.

[5] It is remarkable that in recent studies on coarticulation the factor of the position of the jaw is given renewed attention, cf. for instance De Jong, Beckman, Edwards 1993: 197 or Farnetani 1990: 100.

[6] Hála also mentions the extent to which the upper incisors project beyond the lower and concludes that in general the projection with the 'soft' consonants is bigger.

[7] Also in English the vowels /a u o/ have low frequency as compared to /e i/, which have the highest frequency of all phonemes (Hirsch Weir, R. 1962: 42).

[8] In our discussion we use the term 'palatal' only in the sense of having the feature [+pal], according to the explanation in the preceding paragraphs. Synchronic Czech phonology classifies the consonants with which we are concerned partly as alveolar (č ř š ž), partly as palatal (ď j ň ť) (Mluvnice češtiny 1986: 37, Palková 1994: 209); Kučera (1961: 30) classifies them as palatal, distinguishing the /č š ž/ as apico-alveopalatal, and the /ď j ň ť/ as lamino-palatal.

[9] On the pronunciation cf. Trávníček's claim (1935: 33): "Today we would without difficulty pronounce duša, noža 'soul', 'knife gen.sg.', but in the older period, when here the sound change a-ě (duše, nože) took place, the preceding consonants š ž etc. were not non-palatal as they are now, but palatal." ("Dnes bychom bez obtíží vyslovovali duša, noža atd., ale v starší době, kdy tu nastala přehláska a-ě (duše, nože), nebyly předcházející souhlásky nepalatální jako dnes, nýbrž palatální.") (see Note 8).

[10] The mentioned processes have been still in this period completed by the change of the phoneme ě, called loss of jotation. This means that the new ě > e in all positions, except after labial consonants. The ě which was then the only diphthong in the system, became at the same time a monophthong, e.g. cěna > cena 'price', řěka > řeka 'river', kašě > kaše 'porridge', but pěna 'foam', věří 'he believes', město 'town' (see also Note 14).

[11] In the positions in the stem where the consonant after the vowel was not 'soft', the sound change was not realized, cf. jahoda 'strawberry', jaro 'spring', žába 'frog', šat 'vesture'.

[12] We have to be aware of the very important role which in this process is played by children during the acquisition of their first language from the parents (Romaine 1989).

[13] Referring to Note 10 we would like to mention that, indeed, in the Czech phoneme inventory the /ě/ existed only during the period when the above introduced sound changes were in progress, firstly (to 1150) as an isolated diphthong and later (from 1150 to 1300 and from 1300 to 1400) as an isolated phoneme (Press 1986: 92).

[14] Hodura (1953: 22) wrote: "Slova přímo expresívní napodobují skutečnost, mají k ní přímý vztah. Nepodléhají hláskovým změnám, běžným u ostatních slov". ["Directly expressive words [Hodura's term, A.R.] imitate the reality, they have a direct relationship to it. They are not liable to sound changes, which are common with other words."].

347

[15] /a/ is used in many other inflectional positions, but there it is not relevant with respect to the lexical semantics of the word involved.

[16] In these hypocoristics we see an interesting instance of the ways a sound change sometimes can take. According to historical accounts, in the first period of the sound change of a > ě these declensions have changed as well. However, after some time, the pet-names and a few other words recovered their original phonetic shape (Trávníček 1935: 74). This is somehow in conflict with Boersma's claim, cf.: "...if a certain sound change would 'improve' the sound system and would therefore be allowed to take place, the reverse change would not be allowed to take place" (1998: 12). As the sound change did take place and did improve the sound system, the mentioned return into the original state should not have happen. But, obviously, there are hierarchically higher placed demands of improvement, which has been satisfied by the return into the state before the sound change.

REFERENCES

Bloomfield, L.
1933   Language. London: Allen & Unwin.
Boersma, P.
1998   Sound change in functional phonology. Forthcoming.
Chomsky, N. and Halle, M.
1968   The sound pattern of English. New York: Harper and Row.
Cuřín, F. and coll. of authors
1964   Vývoj českého jazyka a dialektologie. Praha: SPN.
Farnetani, E.
1990   "V-C-V lingual coarticulation and its spatiotemporal domain", Speech
            production and speech modelling (Hardcastle, W.J. & Marchal, A.,
            eds), 93-130. Dordrecht/Boston/London: Kluwer Academic Publishers.
Fowler, C.A. and Saltzman, E.
1993   "Coordination and coarticulation in speech production", Language
            and speech 36, 2, 171-195.
Hála, B.
1923   K popisu pražské výslovnosti. Praha.
Hirsch Weir, R.
1962   Language in the crib. The Hague: Mouton & Co.
Hodura, Q.
1953   O slohu. Učební texty vysokých škol. Praha.
Horn, W.
1923   Sprachkörper und Sprachfunktion. Leipzig: Mayer und Müller.
Hubáček, J.
1981   O zvukové stránce českého jazyka. Praha: SPN.
Jakobson, R.
1948   "The phonemic and grammatical aspects of language in their inter-
            relations", Actes du Sixième Congrès International des Linguistes.
            Paris: Librarie C. Klincksieck.

348

Jakobson, R., Fant, C.G.M. and Halle, M.
1976   Preliminaries to speech analysis. The distinctive features and their
            correlates. Cambridge: The MIT Press.
Jones, D.
1972   An outline of English phonetics. Cambridge: Heffer. [First published
            in 1918.]
De Jong, K., Beckman, M.E. and Edwards, J.
. 1993   "The interplay between prosodic structure and coarticulation",
            Language and speech 36, 2, 197-212.
Kohler, K.J.
1990   "Segmental reduction in connected speech in German: Phonological
            facts and phonetic explanations", Speech production and speech
            modelling (Hardcastle, W.J. & Marchal, A., eds), 69-92. Dordrecht/
            Boston/London: Kluwer Academic Publishers.
Kučera, H.
1961   The phonology of Czech. The Hague: Mouton & Co.
Lamprecht. A., Šlosar, D., Bauer, J.
1986   Historická mluvnice češtiny. Praha: SPN.
Ludvíkvá, M., J. Kraus
1966   "Kvantitativní vlastnosti soustavy českých fonémů", Slovo a slovesnost
            XXVII, 334-344.
Machek, V.
1930   Studie o tvoření výrazů expresivních. Praha: UK.
1971   Etymologický slovník jazyka českého. Praha: ČSAV.
Mathesius, V.
1929   "La structure phonologique du lexique du tchèque moderne", TCLP
            1, 67-84.
1947   Čeština a obecný jazykozpyt. Praha: Melantrich.
Mázlová, V.
1946   "Jak se projevuje zvuková stranka češtiny v hláskových statistikách",
            Naše řeč 30, 101-111, 146-151.
Mluvnice češtiny
1986   Mluvnice češtiny I. Praha: Academia.
Öhman, S.E.G.
1966   "Coarticulation in VCV utterances: Spectrographic measurements",
            JASA 39, 151-168.
Ohala, J.J.
1989   "Sound change is drawn from a pool of synchronic variation", Trends
            in Linguistics 43. Language Change. Contributions to the Study of
            its Causes (Breivik, L.E. and Jahr, E.H., eds), 173-198. Berlin/NY:
            Mouton de Gruyter.
1993   "Coarticulation and phonology", Language and speech 36, 2, 155-170.
Palková, Z.
1994   Fonetika a fonologie češtiny. Praha: UK.
Press, J.I.
1986   Aspects of the phonology of the Slavonic languages. The vowel y and
            the consonantal correlation of palatalization. (= Studies in Slavic and
            General Linguistics 7). Amsterdam: Rodopi.

349

Romaine, S.
1989   "The role of children in linguistic change", *Trends in Linguistsics 43*.
            Language Change. Contributions to the Study of its Causes (Breivik,
            L.E. and Jahr, E.H., eds), 199-225. Berlin/NY: Mouton de Gruyter.
Romportl, M.
1985   *Základy fonetiky*. Praha: SPN.
Sloat, C., Taylor, S.H. and Hoard, J.E.
1978   *Introduction to phonology*. Englewood Cliffs, N.J.: Prentice-Hall.
Trávníček, F.
1935   *Historická mluvnice československá*. Praha: Melantrich.
Trudgill, P.
1989   "Contact and isolation in linguistic change", *Trends in Linguistics 43*.
            Language Change. Contributions to the Study of its Causes (Breivik,
            L.E. & Jahr, E.H., eds), 227-237. Berlin/NY: Mouton de Gruyter.
Vachek, J.
1940   "Poznámky k fonologii českého lexika", *LF* 67, 1940, 395-401. Praha.
Vieregge, W.H.
1985   *Transcriptie van spraak*. Foris Publications, Holland - U.S.A.
Zima, J.
1961   *Expresivita slova v současné češtině*. Praha: ČSAV.

Dutch Contributions to the Twelfth International Congress of Slavists, Cracow, Linguistics (= *Studies in Slavic and General Linguistics* Vol 24), 351-376. RODOPI, Amsterdam – Atlanta, GA 1998.

PALAEOSLOVENICA.
WÜRDIGUNG NEUENTDECKTER HANDSCHRIFTEN

JOS SCHAEKEN

Meinem Sohn Teun

1. Einleitung

Der Titel des vorliegenden Beitrags greift zurück auf die wohlbekannte Studie *Glagolitica. Würdigung neuentdeckter Fragmente* von Vatroslav Jagić (1890), in der er nicht nur die 1889 entdeckten kroatisch-glagolitischen Wiener Blätter allseitig beschrieben, sondern auch die fünfzehn Jahre früher aufgefundenen Kiever Blätter musterhaft herausgegeben hat. Das Jahr 1890 markiert mehr oder weniger das Ende einer Epoche, die etwa im zweiten Viertel des 19. Jahrhunderts angefangen hat und in der fast alle heutzutage als "klassisch" bezeichneten altkirchenslavischen Handschriften entdeckt – und erstmals ediert – worden sind: 1823 der Codex Suprasliensis, 1843 der Codex Zographensis, 1843/1845 der Codex Marianus, 1850 das Psalterium Sinaiticum und der Sinaitische Služebnik, 1866 die Savvina kniga, 1874 die Kiever Blätter, und 1880 das Euchologium Sinaiticum (nur der Glagolita Clozianus und der Codex Assemanianus waren schon früher bekannt). Im selben Zeitraum wurden auch die kleineren altkirchenslavischen Sprachdenkmäler, darunter die Blätter von Ohrid, Rila und Hilandar sowie die Blätter Undol'skijs, aufgefunden.

Nach der Veröffentlichung der *Glagolitica* sind bis etwa 1960 kaum handschriftliche Funde gemacht worden: lediglich die fragmentarischen Blätter von Zographos (1906) und ein zusätzlicher Teil der Blätter von Rila (1936) kamen zu Tage. Im Hinblick auf diese Entwicklung bezüglich der Entdeckung altkirchenslavischer Handschriften ist es nicht verwunderlich, daß Lunt zu Ende der fünfziger Jahre prophezeite: "The study of Old Church Slavonic has reached a stage where sensational discoveries are unlikely, barring the now remote possibility that an extensive new text might come to light" (1959: 9). Kaum ein Jahr später wurden 39 Blätter eines aus dem Ende des 11. Jahrhunderts stammenden Aposteltextes entdeckt, drei Jahre danach kam ein Bruchstück eines Triodions zu Tage und Anfang der siebziger Jahre ein glagolitisches Fragment eines Aprakosevangeliums, einige Jahre später wurden im Katharinenkloster am Sinai geradezu sensationelle Handschriftenfunde gemacht, und letztendlich entdeckte man Anfang der achtziger Jahre in der Vatikaner Bibliothek ein fast hundert Blatt zählendes kyrillisches Aprakosevangelium des 11. Jahrhunderts.

Die ab 1960 entdeckten altkirchenslavischen − oder jedenfalls als solche bezeichneten − Handschriften sind in den neueren Grammatiken, Chrestomathien und Wörterbüchern bisher nur erst teilweise berücksichtigt worden. So ist etwa im *Slovník jazyka staroslověnského* (1958ff.) lediglich der Wortschatz des Apostolus van Enina (siehe unten, 2.1) verzeichnet (vgl. dazu Hauptová 1993), was auch für den einbändigen *Staroslavjanskij slovar'* von Cejtlin u.a. (1994; vgl. Schaeken 1996: 183-184) gilt. Die breit angelegte altbulgarische Grammatik von Duridanov u.a. aus dem Jahre 1991 bietet zwar ganz kurze Beschreibungen einiger Neufunde (1991: 55-57), hat aber das einschlägige Sprachmaterial offensichtlich nicht verarbeitet (vgl. ähnlich auch Trunte 1997[4]: 21-22). Die im vorigen Jahr von Hauptová und Večerka herausgegebene Chrestomathie altkirchenslavischer Texte gibt nur eine Textprobe des Apostolus von Enina (1997: 37-38). Dagegen finden sich in der Sammlung von Slavova und Dobrev (1996) schon Textauszüge dreier Sinai-Funde aus dem Jahre 1975.

Im Hinblick auf die Tatsache, daß die neuentdeckten Sprachdenkmäler in den jüngeren Synthesen des Altkirchenslavischen nur teilweise Eingang gefunden haben, bietet der folgende Abschnitt eine Übersicht und Würdigung der bisherigen Forschungsergebnisse, wobei besonders die Sinai-Neufunde erörtert werden sollen. Hinzugefügt werden im dritten Abschnitt Beschreibungen dreier Palimpsesttexte, die zwar bereits seit Mitte des vorigen Jahrhunderts bekannt waren, aber erst viel später − Ende der fünfziger und Anfang der siebziger Jahre − z.T. entschlüsselt worden sind und somit auch zum "neuen" Sprachmaterial des Altkirchenslavischen gerechnet werden können.

2. Die neuentdeckten Sprachdenkmäler

2.1 1960: Apostolus von Enina (ApEn.)

Aufbewahrungsort: Sofia – NBKM 1144.
Schriftart und Umfang: kyrillisch, 39 fol.
Die aus dem Ende des 11. Jahrhunderts oder kurz danach stammende Handschrift enthält Textpartien aus einem Apostolus (ein genaues Verzeichnis bieten Mirčev und Kodov 1965: 258).
ApEn. wurde 1960 während Aufräumungsarbeiten in einer Kirche im Dorf Enina (in der Nähe von Kazanlăk, Bulgarien) entdeckt. Fünf Jahre später veröffentlichten Mirčev und Kodov eine Edition, einschließlich Faksimile (übrigens auch nochmal bei Kodov 1983; vgl. dazu Smjadovski 1987) und Glossar (vgl. dazu die vielen Rezensionen, wie z. B. von Bernštejn 1966, Bláhová 1966, Dostál 1966, Kopylenko 1966, Minčeva 1966, Stanislav 1966, Večerka 1966, Nedeljković 1967 und Schütz 1967). Einzelstudien bieten Mirčev (1963), Demirčeva-Chafuzova (1964), Simonov (1967), Ugrinova-Skalovska (1970), Hauptová (1971), Moszyński (1971), Šima (1971), Aitzetmüller (1978-79), Atanasov (1980), Dogramadžieva (1985) und Koceva (1985). Sprachliche Analysen finden sich weiter noch bei Tóth (1978: 247-248), Cejtlin u.a. (1994: 34), Hauptová und Večerka (1997: 37-38, mit Textprobe) und Birnbaum und Schaeken (1997: 140-141).

2.2 1963: Triodion von Sofia (Triod.)

Aufbewahrungsort: Sofia – BAN 37.
Schriftart und Umfang: kyrillisch, 1 fol.
Triod. ist die obere Schrift eines Palimpsestblattes, dessen nicht entzifferter, ebenfalls kyrillischer Grundtext nach Kodov (1969: 61) aus der Mitte des 11. Jahrhunderts stammt. Es handelt sich um ein Fragment aus dem Offizium für den Donnerstag der fünften Fastenwoche. Auf der Rückseite des Blattes befindet sich übrigens eine Glosse in glagolitischer Schrift: ⰒⰑⰒⰅ ⰀⰁⰠⰞⰤⰘⰀⰂⰠⰡ ⰕⰀⰰⰀ ⰈⰂⰑⰟⰗⰠⰞⰠⰉ (попе ⰀⰓⰀⰃⰑⰔⰎⰀⰂⰅ ⰈⰎⰑⰕ ⰔⰕⰂⰑⰓⰊⰞⰟ).
Das Bruchstück wurde 1963 von Kodov in Gabrovo (Bulgarien) entdeckt. Derselbe besorgte drei Jahre später die Edition (1966: 128-131, samt Faksimile) und datierte Triod. zu Ende des 11. oder ("naj-kăsno") zu Beginn des 12. Jahrhunderts (1966: 121). Auch Popov (1985: 69) meint, Triod. sei ein altkirchenslavisches (altbulgarisches) Sprachdenkmal, und zwar aus dem Ende des 11. Jahrhunderts. Momina (1988), die

im Jahre 1982 in der kyrillischen Handschrift Nr. 203 der Sofioter NBKM ein zweites Palimpsestblatt mit einem Fragment eines Triodions gefunden hat (vgl. Popov 1985: 64), kommt jedoch zum Schluß, daß beide Bruchstücke erst aus dem 12. Jahrhundert herrühren, und daß sie im selben Skriptorium, aber von verschiedenen Händen, abgefaßt worden sind. Zum Inhalt von Triod. siehe weiter noch Hannick (1985: 109-110) und zum Wortschatz die Bemerkungen bei Birnbaum und Schaeken (1997: 142).

2.3   1971: Fragmentum Sinaiticum (FragSin.)

Aufbewahrungsort: Katharinenkloster, Sinai – MS 39/O.

Schriftart und Umfang: glagolitisch, 1 fol.

Über den aus der 2. Hälfte des 11. Jahrhunderts stammenden glagolitischen Grundtext auf fol. 45 der kyrillischen Handschrift MS 39/O wurde im 12. Jahrhundert eine mittelbulgarische Zugabe zum Text des Praxapostolus geschrieben. FragSin. ist ein Bruchstück eines Aprakosevangeliums und enthält zufälligerweise genau dieselben Evangelien-Perikopen (Mt 13: 28-30, 36-42 und Mk 5: 26) wie die ebenfalls fragmentarischen Blätter Undol'skijs (Mt 13: 24-30, 36-43 und Mk 5: 24-34).

Das Palimpsestblatt wurde im Jahre 1971 von Lunt und Altbauer während eines Besuches in der Bibliothek des Katharinenklosters gefunden und neun Jahre später von Altbauer und Mareš in kyrillischer Transkription (einschließlich Faksimile) herausgegeben (1980). Ergänzende Bemerkungen zu dieser Ausgabe finden sich bei Altbauer und Mareš (1981) und Koch (1983).

2.4   1975: Euchologium Sinaiticum pars nova (Euch. 1/N)

Aufbewahrungsort: Katharinenkloster, Sinai – MS 1/N.

Schriftart und Umfang: glagolitisch, 28 fol.

Die im Jahre 1975 im Katharinenkloster am Sinai während Bauarbeiten zu Tage gekommenen slavischen Handschriften des 11. bis 16. Jahrhunderts wurden 1988 von Tarnanidis in einem ausführlichen Katalog beschrieben (vgl. die Rezensionen von Alekseev 1988, Velčeva 1988, Birnbaum 1989, Bláhová 1989, Parenti 1989, Tkadlčík 1989, Dobrev 1989-90, Mareš 1989-90, Drobena 1990, Špadijer 1990, Mathiesen 1991 und Momina 1991; siehe weiter auch Mareš 1991, 1993). Unter den Neufunden befinden sich fünf glagolitische Handschriften (Sin. Slav. 1/N bis 5/N, wobei "N" die neue Sammlung – im Gegensatz zu "O" =

"old" – bezeichnet), die hier in den Abschnitten 2.4 bis 2.8 erörtert werden.[1] Euch. 1/N bietet 28 zusätzliche Blätter zum bereits seit 1880 bekannten Teil Euch. 37/O (105 fol.) und enthält weitere Gebete sowie Evangelien- und Apostolusperikopen. Eine ausführliche Beschreibung und ein vollständiges Faksimile finden sich bei Tarnanidis (1988: 65-87 bzw. 219-247; siehe auch die Abbildung unten). Eine textkritische Edition wird z.Z. von einer Forschungsgruppe (I. Dobrev, H. Miklas, S. Parenti, M. Schnitter, I. Tarnanidis und E. Velkovska) vorbereitet. Inzwischen liegt der vollständige Text in glagolitischer Schrift (mit Worttrennungen) bei Schnitter und Miklas (1993: 162-220) vor, während die ersten vier Blätter von Minčev (1993: 29-35) in kyrillischer Umschrift veröffentlicht wurden. Weiter hat Bakker den Text der neutestamentlichen Perikopen (ab fol. 13; vgl. auch Alekseev 1988: 194-195, Bláhová 1989: 66-68 und Dogramadžieva 1994) in eine "operational edition" verarbeitet (1994: 184-208; ähnlich auch 1996: 66-83, 93-107 – siehe dazu die Rezension von Fetková 1997). Die kyrillische Transkription von vier neutestamentlichen Perikopen findet sich auch in der Chrestomathie von Slavova und Dobrev (1996: 44-45); siehe auch die Umschrift von fol. 12b bei Velkovska (1996: 19). Zum Lexikon von Euch. 1/N siehe besonders Hauptová (1993) sowie Birnbaum und Schaeken (1997: 144).

Im oben bereits erwähnten Beitrag Minčevs (1993) findet sich eine auffallende Notiz über einen früheren, jetzt freilich überholten Aufsatz Ševčenkos (1982), dem damals zwei Fotos von Euch. 1/N zur Verfügung standen. Minčev schreibt: "Po-važnoto v slučaja e, če I. Ševčenko publikuva tekstove ot dve neizvestni i nepublikuvani po-kăsno v opisa na Tarnanidis molitvi za večernjata (No. II i III) (vž. Ševčenko [...], il. X + A). Te bez sămnenie sa ot Sin. Ne e jasno kakvo e stanalo s tozi list, izguben (?) meždu 1982 i 1988 g. (godinata na publikuvane na opisa na Tarnanidis). Da se nadjavame, če v bădešte listăt s fragmenti ot molitvi II i III ot večernjata šte se nameri" (1993: 23, Fn. 7). Der angebliche Verlust der von Ševčenko mit den Nummern 5 und 6 verzeichneten Gebete (1982: 136-137) wurde 1988 auch schon von Arranz erwähnt, der zu der Beschreibung von Euch. 1/N bei Tarnanidis (1988) bemerkt: "On ne trouve plus trace par contre des prières 5 et 6 signalées par Ševčenko (Nos. II et III des vêpres)" (1988: 74, Fn. 118). Wenn man jedoch das Faksimile "fol. X + A verso" der Gebete 5 und 6 bei Ševčenko (1982: 125) unter die Lupe nimmt und mit dem Faksimile bei Tarnanidis vergleicht, so stellt sich ganz eindeutig heraus (vgl. die Ab-

356

bildung unten), daß es sich hier um einen durch ein Loch auf fol. 2b sichtbaren Teil von fol. 1b handelt (Gebet 5 = fol. 1b 13-16, Gebet 6 = fol. 1b 18-20), was übrigens bereits von Ševčenko selbst im Nachtrag zu einem Neudruck seines Aufsatzes (1991: 739) angemerkt wurde. Es ist also nichts verlorengegangen.

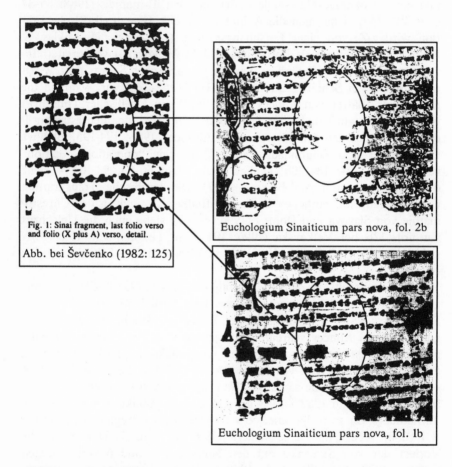

Fig. 1: Sinai fragment, last folio verso and folio (X plus A) verso, detail.

Abb. bei Ševčenko (1982: 125)

Euchologium Sinaiticum pars nova, fol. 2b

Euchologium Sinaiticum pars nova, fol. 1b

Weitere Bemerkungen zu Euch. 1/N (sowie eine zusätzliche Abbildung) finden sich unten, 2.8.

2.5   1975: Psalterium Sinaiticum pars nova (Ps. 2/N)

Aufbewahrungsort: Katharinenkloster, Sinai – MS 2/N.
Schriftart und Umfang: glagolitisch, 32 fol.

Zur Entdeckungsgeschichte siehe oben, 2.4.
Der schon seit 1850 bekannte Teil Ps. 38/O (177 fol.) wurde durch
Ps. 2/N um 32 Blätter bereichert. Das neuentdeckte Stück schließt un-
mittelbar an den altbekannten Teil an und enthält die Psalmen 138 bis
151, 14 biblische Cantica, das Vaterunser (unten abgebildet), das Mor-
gengebet Слава къ вышьннихъ боу und abschließend einen Teil des Ves-
per-Offiziums nach byzantinischem Ritus. Tarnanidis (1988: 87-91,
249-281) bietet eine kurze Beschreibung und ein vollständiges Faksimile
von Ps. 2/N. Unter der Schriftleitung von Mareš hat eine Prager Ar-
beitsgruppe 1997 den Text in kyrillischer Transkription (samt Einführung, kritischem und parakritischem Apparat sowie Wörterverzeichnis)
herausgegeben (vgl. die Rezension von Birnbaum 1998). Zwei ausge-
wählte Textproben (Ct 1 und Ct 5) bieten neuerdings auch Slavova und
Dobrev (1996: 52-53). Einzelstudien zum Text des Vaterunsers und des
Morgengebets finden sich bei Mareš (1990, 1995; vgl. auch 1991:
227-229); siehe dazu auch die Bemerkungen bei Alekseev (1988:
196-197). Der Wortschatz von Ps. 2/N wird weiter noch bei Dobrev
(1989-90: 176-177), Hauptová (1993) sowie Birnbaum und Schaeken
(1997: 144-146) besprochen.

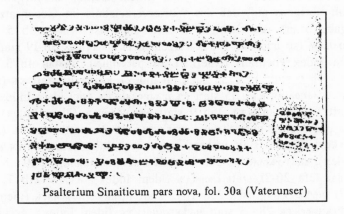

Psalterium Sinaiticum pars nova, fol. 30a (Vaterunser)

Zu der bereits genannten Edition von Ps. 2/N (Mareš u.a. 1997)
seien hier noch einige Berichtigungen und andere Bemerkungen hinzugefügt. Erstens werde ich mich punktweise mit dem Kommentar zur
Texterstellung (1997: XX) befassen:
– "Abkürzungen unter Titlos werden nicht ergänzt und fehlende Titlen
nicht restituiert". Siehe jedoch въ 21b 22, wo auf dem Faksimile ganz
deutlich бъ zu lesen ist.

358

– "Sonderligaturen [werden] aber aufgelöst (auch darauf wird im para-
kritischen Apparat verwiesen)". Nicht verzeichnet sind aber die Ligatu-
ren -жд- in хожда|ахъ 4a 17-18, -зг- in възглⷶжтъ 7b 5 (im Apparat
steht irrtümlich "litterae ligatae -гл-"), -тв- in сътво|ритъ 19a 24-25
und -ст- in der Glosse ѥст 30a 16 (siehe die Abbildung oben). Weiter
ist пⷶ̈ 27b 9 wohl viel eher als пⷶ̈, also mit -ꙇн- statt -ꙇꙁ-Ligatur,
aufzufassen: 🙰 (vgl. abgekürztes пⷩкнь 31b 2, freilich "sine compendii
ṣigno"). Schließlich handelt es sich bei мⷰци 28b 13 nicht um "litterae li-
gatae -мц-", sondern um eine komplizierte -мчц-Ligatur: 🙰.
– "Von Schreiberhand vorgenommene Korrekturen über oder unter der
Zeile sind über Kleindruck verdeutlicht". Zu beachten ist jedoch ѥмоу
11a 15 statt richtigem ѥмоу, вьсѣхъ 16a 20 statt вьсⷷхъ, намъ 32a 22
statt намъ, und опра|в(ь)д(а)нъѥмъ 32b 2-3 statt опра|в(ь)д(а)нъѥмъ.
– Leider wurde in der Ausgabe die Originalinterpunktion vereinheit-
licht (es steht überall "·") und sind die Rand- und Füllornamente sowie
die vereinzelten supralinearen Zeichen nicht wiedergegeben. Dagegen
gibt es ganz am Ende der Edition (1997: 201) eine Liste "Voces signo
formae spiritus exornatae", die jedoch nicht erschöpfend ist; es fehlen ꙇ
1a 11, ꙇхъ 16b 15 und мнⷩѣ 1a 12, 13.
Zweitens seien noch weitere Fehler in der Edition hervorgehoben.
Dabei fällt übrigens auf, daß das Wörterverzeichnis im Gegensatz zur
Textausgabe öfters die richtigen Formen aufweist: въꙇнѫ 3b 5 statt
richtigem вꙇнѫ (so auch im Index verzeichnet), расоушꙗ 3b 19 statt ра-
соусꙗ (im Index ebenfalls fehlerhaft als расоуцꙗ), земли 4b 3 statt
земли, отъ 4b 6 statt отъ (so auch im Index), кь 5a 10 statt къ (idem
Index), възглаголꙗжтъ 7a 15 statt възглаголлꙗжтъ (sic; idem Index), гⷪ̈ь
9a 13 statt гⷪ̈ъ, отьврашⷮѫ 15b 9 statt отъврашⷮѫ (idem Index), не-
їстⷷкленⷩ 16a 6 statt неїстⷷкленъ, съвⷶтъ 16a 21 statt съвⷶ̈тъ (idem
Index), нѣстъ 17a 20 statt нⷷстъ, ѥтиопьскаꙗ 18b 5 statt ѥтиопъскаꙗ
(idem Index), вьстрⷷмлениѥ 18b 10 statt въстрⷷмлениѥ, вь 19a 7 statt
въ, съни|дь 21a 20-21 statt съни|дъ (idem Index), лъжꙗ 21b 7 statt
лъжꙗ (?), прⷷвьз(но)|симъ 27b 11-12 statt прⷷвъз(но)|симъ (idem In-
dex), прⷷвьзносите 28a 5 statt прⷷвъзносите (idem Index), ѥвгнⷩлиⷷ
28b 21 statt ѥвгнⷩлиⷩⷷ (idem Index), сильнⴑꙑи 28b 27 statt сильнⴑꙑи,
гꙇлѥвъ 29a 16 statt гꙇлвъ (idem Index), вⴑсꙗ 31b 12 statt вⴑсꙗ. Frag-
würdig sind weiter die Worttrennungen съ|творит и 8a 9-10 (съ-
творити?), (зижд)ꙑꙇ̈ гꙇлⴑа 9a 3 statt (зижд)ꙑꙇ гꙇлⴑа (vgl. гꙇлⴑѥ 9b 10,
гꙇлⴑъ 25b 25) und по срⷷдⷷ 13a 2 statt посрⷷдⷷ (idem Index).
Schließlich bietet die Edition die Liste "Voces, quae in Lexico linguae palaeoslovenicae non occurrunt" (1997: 201). Hinzuzufügen sind

359

die ebenfalls nicht im *Slovník jazyka staroslověnského* verzeichneten *hapax*-Formen вешта̨дити (вешти̨дитъ 16a 10; übrigens auch im Pogodin-Psalter belegt), das possessive Adjektiv анинъ (анина 21b 14) und сѫгласъ (сѫгласъ 31b 27).

2.6 1975: Psalter Dimitrijs (PsDim.)

Aufbewahrungsort: Katharinenkloster, Sinai – MS 3/N.
Schriftart und Umfang: glagolitisch, 145 fol.
Zur Entdeckungsgeschichte siehe oben, 2.4.
Die aus dem 11.-12. Jahrhundert stammende Handschrift enthält die Psalmen 1 bis 151 sowie einige zusätzliche Notizen und zwischen fol. 141 und 142 drei eingefügte Blätter medizinischen Inhalts. Aufgrund einer Eintragung auf fol. 1a, wo es am Zeilenende азъ дъмтръ грѣшникъ ол heißt (vgl. auf fol. 141a die Notiz азъ д⟨ъ⟩мтрън писахъ се | не оумѣи̯а), schlägt Tarnanidis (1988: 92-93) für die letzten zwei Buchstaben die Lesung ольтарьникъ vor und bezeichnet die Handschrift folglich als "Psalter des Dimitrij Ol'tarnik". Da diese Konjektur jedoch gar nicht gesichert ist, wie Tkadlčík (1989: 166) mit Recht hervorhebt (vgl. auch Bláhová 1989: 65 und Mareš 1991: 229), ist es besser die Handschrift einfach "Psalter Dimitrijs" zu nennen.

Eine vollständige Edition (samt Faksimile) von PsDim. fehlt bis jetzt. Tarnanidis (1988: 91-100) gibt eine allgemeine Beschreibung der Handschrift, kyrillische Transkriptionen der zusätzlichen Notizen und eingefügten ärztlichen Vorschriften sowie leider nur eine einzige Abbildung, und zwar von fol. 126b (auf S. 192, und nicht irrtümlicherweise auf S. 193 des Katalogs), wo wir Psalm 119 und einen Teil von 120 lesen können (vgl. die kyrillische Transkription bei Velčeva 1988: 127).

Der Haupttext von PsDim. soll nach Tarnanidis (1988: 92) von zwei Schreibern stammen: "The first, scribe A, wrote folios 1v-2r, 3r, 35v-141v, 142r-145v", und "The second scribe, B, wrote folios 2v and 3v-24r". Nach den verzeichneten Textpartien von Schreiber A zu urteilen ist bei B statt "3v-24r" vielleicht "3v-34r" zu lesen; letztere Seite enthält einen Teil des Textes von Psalm 24 und fol. 34b scheint, abgesehen von einer kurzen Notiz (siehe unten), leer zu sein (1988: 94). Tarnanidis hebt einige Sprachmerkmale des Haupttextes hervor, darunter die Wiedergabe der reduzierten Vokale: "the indiscriminate use of *jer* (ь) and *jor* (ъ), though the latter is more prevalent [...]. The tendency to turn the *poluglas* (reduced vowels) into vowels" (1988: 91). Letztere Erscheinung läßt sich tatsächlich auf dem Faksimile von fol.

126b nachweisen: при|шел҃ъствова 14-15, мирен҃ъ 16, со м҃ъ|ною 17-18 und во съм҃атение 23. Dagegen ist jedenfalls auf fol. 126b (also bei Schreiber A) nicht so sehr von einem "indiscriminate use" der Jerzeichen die Rede, sondern vom exklusiven Gebrauch von ъ. Weiter weist fol. 126b zwar den etymologisch richtigen Gebrauch der Nasalvokale ѧ = є, ꙗ = ѭ und ѫ auf, dagegen fehlt ѩ völlig (vgl. д҃шѫ мою 3 und со м҃ъ|ною 17-18 sowie земꙵѫ 22), obwohl das Zeichen nach Tarnanidis (1988: 91) doch vorzukommen scheint. Die letztgenannte Form zeigt übrigens, daß das *l*-epentheticum beibehalten wird (so auch in въздрѣмлетъ 126b 24 und въздрѣꙵметъ — mit -мл-Ligatur — 126b 25). In orthographischer Hinsicht scheint Schreiber A sich durch den fast ausschließlichen Gebrauch von і (т) für *i* (auch ꙑ für *y*) von Schreiber B zu unterscheiden, welch letzterer hauptsächlich и (в) verwendet. Tarnanidis bezeichnet PsDim. als "c. 12th c." (1988: 91) und bemerkt über das Alter: "Its close resemblance to the Sinai MS 38/O [Psalterium Sinaiticum; siehe oben, 2.5 — JS] on the one hand, and its simplified language on the other, indicate to me that this Psalter belongs to the same tradition as, though it is clearly of later date than, MS 38/O" (1988: 98). Velčeva meint jedoch, daß die paläographischen und sprachlichen Merkmale von PsDim. eine frühere Datierung zulassen: "Răkopisăt e cenen za ustanovjavaneto na razvoja na bălgarskata glagolica prez XI-XII vek. Sklonna săm da go otnesa po-rano ot datata XII vek, kojato dava Tarnanidis. Interesno e, če se sreštat slučai s ю vmesto ѭ v teksta. Văzmožno e knigata da e văzniknala v manastirsko središte, v koeto sa si davali srešta različni govorni čerti. Văv vseki slučaj tazi osobenost ima značenie za rannoto razprostranenie na glagolicata sred južnite slavjani" (1988: 128).

Die Notizen von "д҃ъмтр҃ъ", die an den offengelassen Stellen eingetragen sind (wo eigentlich nachträglich Illuminationen eingefügt hätten werden sollen), umfassen:
— zwei kurze Eintragungen, in denen von "д҃ъмтр҃ъ" die Rede ist (fol. 1a und fol. 141a; siehe oben);
— eine weitere kurze Eintragung auf fol. 34b, dessen Wortlaut nicht ganz klar ist (vgl. die Mutmaßungen bei Tarnanidis 1988: 94);
— ein unvollständiges glagolitisches, griechisches und lateinisches Abecedarium (fol. 1a); letzteres auch noch einmal auf fol. 2a;
— eine Beschwörung gegen die wilden Tiere: ... азъ влжꙗ звѣръ и оуслꙑ|ишитъ мѧ с‹ва›тъи д‹ъ›митръ от|ъ солоуна ... (etwa 17 Zeilen auf fol. 1a; siehe auch den Text bei Dobrev 1990: 11-12, Dobrev und Slavova 1995: 67-68 und Slavova und Dobrev 1996: 55);

361

– ein Gebet "ο κλѣцѣ да не к|ѣлазитъ къ кошаѫ" (etwa 18 Zeilen
auf fol. 2a und weitere 8 Zeilen auf fol. 3a; siehe auch Dobrev 1990:
12-13, Dobrev und Slavova 1995: 68 und Slavova und Dobrev 1996:
55-56);
– ein Gebet des hl. Grigorij (untere Hälfte von fol. 140a sowie fol.
140b und fortgesetzt auf fol. 144b; siehe auch Dobrev 1990: 17-20).

Die verschiedenen Eintragungen stammen nach Tarnanidis (1988: 94)
alle von ein und derselben Hand (vielleicht mit Ausnahme von der Notiz auf fol. 34b), also von "дѣмтръ", den wir hier als Schreiber C an-
deuten werden. Da es keine Abbildungen der Notizen gibt, läßt sich
kaum etwas Sinnvolles über ihre Sprachgestalt sagen, nur daß Schreiber
C dem Anschein nach nur éin Jerzeichen, und zwar ъ (vgl. aber ключь
auf fol. 140b), verwendet. Ob der Haupttext und die Textpartien von
Schreiber C (ungefähr) aus derselben Zeit stammen, ist nach Tarnanidis
unklar: "It is still unknown when these notes were written" (1988: 96).
In bezug auf ihr Alter sind die Bemerkungen von R. Marti über das
glagolitische Abecedarium in PsDim. besonders aufschlußreich (siehe
weiter unten, 2.8).

Auch für die eingefügten medizinischen Rezepte (крачѣка козминаа
'Heilmittel des Kozma') gilt, daß wegen des Fehlens eines Faksimiles
noch wenig über ihre Sprache zu bemerken ist. Nach Tarnanidis handelt es sich um éinen anderen Schreiber (bei uns D), der sowohl и (в)
als ı (т) für i benutzt (bei C scheint nur и vorzukommen). Schreiber D
verwendet, ebenso wie C, fast ausschließlich das Jerzeichen ъ, obwohl
Tarnanidis (1988: 99) viermal кь кинѣ sowie einmal отрочамь transkribiert. Weiter sei die einzigartige Nominativ Singularform крьı 'Blut'
(anderswo im Altkirchenslavischen nur крькь) hervorgehoben.

Gerade wegen ihres außergewöhnlichen (da nicht religiösen) Inhalts
haben die medizinischen Blätter schon viel Aufmerksamkeit auf sich ge-
lenkt. Sie wurden bereits mehrmals aufgrund der von Tarnanidis gelie-
ferten Transkription veröffentlicht und vor allem in lexikalischer Hinsicht erörtert: Dobrev (1989-90: 168-172, mit englischer Übersetzung;
1990: 13-17, mit bulgarischer Übersetzung), Rosenschon (1991, 1993,
1994), Velčeva (1991; vgl. auch 1988: 128), Dobrev und Slavova (1995:
66-67) sowie Slavova und Dobrev (1996: 54-56). Weitere Bemerkungen
liegen noch bei Šiškova (1992), Mareš (1993, 1994: 131-133) sowie Birnbaum und Schaeken (1997: 146-148) vor.

2.7 1975: Menaeum Sinaiticum (MenSin.)

Aufbewahrungsort: Katharinenkloster, Sinai – MS 4/N.
Schriftart und Umfang: glagolitisch, 2 fol.
Zur Entdeckungsgeschichte siehe oben, 2.4.
Das in das 11. oder 12. Jahrhundert datierte Doppelblatt ist ein
Bruchstück eines Fest-Menäums und enthält einen Teil der Liturgie zur
Geburt Johannes des Täufers (fol. 1a und 1b 1-15) sowie einen der älte-
sten Kanons zu Ehren der hll. Peter und Paul (fol. 1b 16-28 und fol. 2).
Eine kurze Beschreibung des Fragments und eine Abbildung von fol. 1b
und 2a liegt im Katalog der Sinai-Funde vor (Tarnanidis 1988: 100-102,
196-197).

Bisher wurde nur der Text des Kanons in kyrillischer Umschrift herausgegeben, und zwar von Tarnanidis selbst (1990; dort wieder mit einer Tafel von fol. 1b und 2a, jetzt aber irrtümlicherweise umgekehrt
abgedruckt). Leider ist die Edition nicht diplomgetreu und ist außerdem
der Anfang von fol. 2b (und zwar ganz oben auf S. 96: пΑΒΕΛ҄Ъ СЪ
Β҄ΡЪΝ҄ЪИ...) nicht angedeutet. Die einleitende Bemerkung, daß "[s]quare
brackets containing three dots indicate that part of a word is illegible
or ruined; square brackets containing four dots mean that part of a
phrase is illegible or ruined" (1990: 94), erübrigt sich, da die unleserli-
chen Stellen überall mit nur drei Punkten (irrtümlicherweise?) verzeichnet sind. In der Ausgabe finden sich schließlich manche falsche Trans-
kribierungen und Worttrennungen (etwa vom Typ "ИСТЪИ" 2b statt И
С(ΒѦ)ТЪИ oder "ΑΝҔ(Ε)ΛЪСКΑ ΕΓΟ" 2b statt ΑΝҔ(Ε)ΛЪСКΑΕΓΟ; vgl. dazu
Mareš 1993: 130) sowie ganz unwahrscheinliche Rekonstruktionen (z. B.
"Ц(Α)Ρ(ЬС)КѪЖ" 2b statt Ц(҄ΤСΑ)Ρ(ЬС)КѪЖ oder "П[ОС]Β҄ΚΤИСΤΑ" 2b statt
П[РОС]Β҄ΚΤИСΤΑ; vgl. Birnbaum und Schaeken 1997: 149 – dort auch weitere Bemerkungen zum Wortschatz von MenSin.).

Wegen der mangelhaften Angaben lassen sich bisher nur ganz vorläufige Bemerkungen über die Sprache von MenSin. machen. Das Fragment weist anscheinend nur éin Jerzeichen auf, und zwar ъ, das in
schwacher Position mehrmals ausfällt, in starker dagegen hier und da
zu e, o vollvokalisiert wird. Letzteres gilt nicht nur für etymologisches
ь (ДЪΝΕСЪ 1b 24, Д[Ъ]ΝΕСЪ 2b), sondern auch für ъ (СΟЗДΑ 1b 28, ПΛΟ-
ΤЪСКЪИ 2b, ΒΟСΝ҄ΚΒΟИ 2b, ΒΟПИЖЦ҄Ю 2b, ΒΟПИΕΤЪ 2b), was auf die ma-
kedonische Herkunft des Denkmals hindeutet (ΟΥΠΟΥΒΑΝИΕ 2a 7 statt
ΟΥΠЪΒΑΝИΕ ist wohl am ehesten als Schreibfehler aufzufassen). Weiter
kommen vier Nasalvokale vor (ѫ, ІѪ, ѧ = ε, ІѦ = ЗЕ), die etymologisch
folgerichtig verwendet zu sein scheinen, obzwar auch einmal ο - ѫ

Verwechslung vorliegt: крдиогъⰾъна 2a 12 (im St. Petersburger Oktoich – siehe unten, 3.1 – ist крдижголенъ belegt; vgl. Lunt 1958: 203 sowie Birnbaum und Schaeken 1997: 142). Im Bereich der Orthographie sei der exklusive Gebrauch von и (ȣ) für *i* (auch ъи für *y*) erwähnt. Was die Morphologie betrifft, so soll außer der oben bereits angeführten unkontrahierten Adjektivendung in дин(е)лъскдего 2b noch die altertümliche Nominativ Singularform кдмъи 2a 11 (sonst nur im Codex Suprasliensis belegt) hervorgehoben werden.

2.8 1975: Missale Sinaiticum (MisSin.)

Aufbewahrungsort: Katharinenkloster, Sinai – MS 5/N.
Schriftart und Umfang: glagolitisch, etwa 80 fol.
Zur Entdeckungsgeschichte siehe oben, 2.4.
Die Handschrift ist leider schwer beschädigt und nur z.T. lesbar. Eine vorläufige Beschreibung bietet Tarnanidis (1988: 103-108), während eine vollständige Edition inzwischen in Wien von H. Miklas u.a. in Angriff genommen zu sein scheint. Es handelt sich um ein Bruchstück eines Meßbuches, dessen Inhalt aufgrund der von Tarnanidis identifizierten Textstellen mit der byzantinisch-römischen Petrusliturgie zusammenhängt (vgl. dazu Schaeken 1989, Tkadlčík 1989: 167-168, Mareš 1989-90: 205, 1990: 134, 1991: 230 und Parenti 1994; siehe auch weiter unten).

In seinem Katalog unterscheidet Tarnanidis (1988: 103) bei MisSin. zumindest drei Hände; die erste schrieb vom Anfang bis fol. 30a und dann von fol. 47a bis 58a "in a tall calligraphic script similar to that of the Sinai Euchologion", die zweite schrieb von fol. 30b bis 42a und hat "a larger and less elegant style resembling that of the Kiev Missal", und die dritte Hand schrieb auf jeden Fall von fol. 42b bis 46b, "his writing being more square, larger, and spread out". (Die ersten 12 und letzten 10 Blätter von MisSin. sind übrigens völlig zerstört, "having rotted and stuck together in a mass".)

Was die erste Hand von MisSin. (siehe die freilich kaum brauchbaren Farbabbildungen von fol. 13b und 20b bei Tarnanidis 1988: 194-195) und ihre Ähnlichkeit zur Schrift von Euch. betrifft (vgl. die Abbildungen unten), so meint Momina (1991: 145), daß beide Sprachdenkmäler auch aufgrund einiger lexikalischer Sonderübereinstimmungen (vgl. Birnbaum und Schaeken 1997: 150) aus derselben Schreibstube herrühren. Nach Mathiesen deuten die zwei bei Tarnanidis abgedruckten Fotos und die kurze Beschreibung der Handschrift sogar darauf hin, daß

"MS 5/N is not a separate manuscript at all, but a further part of the Euchologium Sinaiticum, MS 37/O + 1/N. The present separate binding of MS 5/N, of which only a small fragment is left, need not be original; the hand and orthography of its first scribe, as well as its layout and its size, all appear to be the same as those of the Euchologium" (1991: 194; vgl. ähnlich auch Dobrev 1989-90: 174, 176). Mathiesen geht noch einen Schritt weiter (1991: 194, Fn. 10) und meint, daß vielleicht auch die Kiever Blätter (KBl.) einst zusammen mit Euch. und MisSin. zum selben Kodex gehört haben. Dabei verweist er auf die bereits von Hamm (1979: 94, 118) angedeutete und später von Pantelić (1985: 25-41) ausführlich erörterte paläographische Übereinstimmung zwischen der ersten, jüngeren Rekto-Seite der Kiever Blätter und den jüngeren paschalienartigen Aufzeichnungen auf fol. 2a des zu Euch. gehörenden Sinaitischen Služebniks (SinSluž., Uspenskij-Bifolium, St. Petersburg – RNB Glag. 2; vgl. die Abbildungen unten). Schon früher, und zwar in einem Aufsatz von 1985, hat Mathiesen die Meinung geäußert, daß Euch. ursprünglich auch den Text der Petrusliturgie sowie den der Chrysostomosliturgie enthalten hat und daß im genannten Uspenskij-Fragment das Ende des letztgenannten und der Anfang des erstgenannten Textes überliefert worden ist.[2] In seiner Rezension des Katalogs der Sinai-Funde ist Mathiesen (1991: 195) "now confident that a much larger fragment of this same text of the liturgy of St. Peter is still extant in MS 5/N [= MisSin. – JS] and that Uspenskij's Bifolium belongs to this part of the Euchologium Sinaiticum".

Rekonstruierend hätte es also nach der Meinung Mathiesens einen ehemaligen sinaitischen Kodex gegeben, in dem liturgische Texte verschiedenen Ursprungs und Alters zusammengefügt waren: KBl. (einschließlich fol. 1a), Euch. (einschließlich SinSluž.) und MisSin. Die Maße der betreffenden Handschriften (KBl. etwa 140 x 105 mm., Euch. und SinSluž. etwa 140 x 110 mm., und MisSin. etwa 140 x 100 mm.) lassen eine solche Vermutung übrigens ganz gut zu.

Weiter sei laut brieflicher Mitteilung (30.12.1997) von R. Marti (Saarbrücken) der Schreiber von KBl. fol. 1a nicht nur identisch mit dem der Paschalien in SinSluž. (Uspenskij-Fragment), sondern "mit an Sicherheit grenzender Wahrscheinlichkeit" auch mit dem Schreiber des glagolitischen Abecedariums in PsDim. (siehe oben, 2.6), von dem Marti Fotos von fol. 1 und 2 untersuchen konnte. Schließlich soll dieser Schreiber laut H. Miklas (Wien) auch noch mit der zweiten Hand von MisSin. identisch sein.[3] Letztere Behauptung scheint aber in chronologischer Hinsicht im Widerspruch mit der von Mathiesen (und auch Do-

brev) vertretenen Hypothese über die Identifizierung der ersten Hand
von MisSin. mit derjenigen von Euch. zu stehen, jedenfalls wenn man
die neuentdeckte Handschrift zeitlich gesehen als eine Einheit betrachtet; entweder wäre MisSin. mit dem älteren Euch. gleichzeitaltrig, oder
mit der jüngeren Rekto-Seite der KBl. sowie mit den Paschalien in
SinSluž. und dem Abecedarium in PsDim.

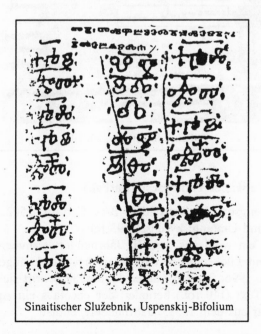

Kiever Blätter, fol. 1a

Sinaitischer Služebnik, Uspenskij-Bifolium

366

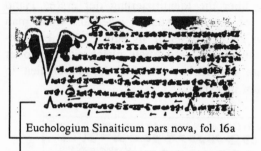

Euchologium Sinaiticum pars nova, fol. 16a

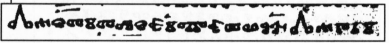

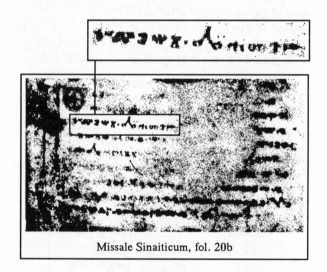

Missale Sinaiticum, fol. 20b

2.9   1982: Vatikaner Palimpsest (VatPal.)

Aufbewahrungsort: Vatikanstadt – BAV Cod. gr. 2502.

Schriftart und Umfang: kyrillisch, 93 fol.

VatPal. ist ein wohl aus dem 11. Jahrhundert stammendes Aprakosevangelium (mit Lücken; siehe das Verzeichnis der Evangelienstellen bei
Krǎstanov u.a. 1996: 211-215), deren kyrillische Schrift sich unter einem
griechischen Text (140 fol.) befindet, der ebenfalls ein Aprakosevangelium, und zwar aus dem 12.-13. Jahrhundert, enthält.

Der Palimpsesttext wurde 1982 von Krăstanov anhand einer Inventarliste von griechischen Handschriften der BAV für die Wissenschaft entdeckt. Vor zwei Jahren erschien der bloße Text im Druck (Krăstanov u.a. 1996), leider mit nur einer ganz kurzen, allgemeinen Einleitung und ohne (para)kritischen Apparat, ohne Faksimile und ohne Glossar. Ausführlichere Beschreibungen (einschließlich einiger Abbildungen) liegeń bei Džurova u.a. (1985: 196-201 und Abbildung CCXI) und Krăstanov (1988a; vgl. auch den kurzen Forschungsbericht 1988b) vor. Obwohl in diesen beiden Beschreibungen von 99 Palimpsestblättern die Rede ist, bietet die Ausgabe nur 93 Blätter (mit übrigens hier und da offenbar falschen Angaben: fol. 156 statt richtigem 56, fol. 121 statt 21, fol. 178 statt 78). Schließlich sei noch die Einzelstudie Musakovas (1994) über die Schmuckelemente in VatPal. erwähnt.

3. Die neu entschlüsselten Sprachdenkmäler

3.1 1958: St. Petersburger Oktoich (SPbOkt.)

Aufbewahrungsort: St. Petersburg – RNB Q.p.I.64.
Schriftart und Umfang: glagolitisch, 8 fol. (einseitig)
SPbOkt. ist ein Palimpsesttext auf fol. 1b, 2a, 3b, 4a, 5b, 6a, 7b und 8a, der später, im 13. Jahrhundert, mit einem Fragment eines mittelbulgarischen kyrillischen Florilegiums überschrieben wurde (zur Handschrift Q.p.I.64 siehe die Bemerkungen bei Lunt 1965: 310, Fn. 5, und Zagrebin 1979: 62-64; vgl. auch die Abbildung bei Velčeva 1995: 520). Der glagolitische Grundtext aus dem Ende des 11. Jahrhunderts enthält einzelne Troparien der Kanons des Oktoichs.

Die acht Blätter wurden 1859 von Konstantin Tischendorf aus dem Katharinenkloster am Sinai nach Rußland gebracht. Daß es sich um ein Palimpsest handelt, wußte bereits Miklosich (vgl. Jagić 1911: 72, 230). Einen kleinen Teil (21 Zeilen) des nur z.T. lesbaren Textes wurde erst 1958, und zwar von Lunt, in lateinischer Transkription herausgegeben (1958: 206-207). Aufgrund einer paläographischen und sprachlichen Analyse des Bruckstücks gelangt Lunt in dieser Ausgabe zum Schluß, SPbOkt. sei "an Old Church Slavonic text of the Macedonian type" und "was written in the latter part of the eleventh century, very likely in Raška or Zahumje" (1958: 204 bzw. 205). In einem späteren Aufsatz formuliert er die Herkunft von SPbOkt. ein wenig anders: "a text that I believe to have been written [...] by a scribe from Zeta or Zahumje, and would call late OCS or earliest Serbo-Croatian Slavonic" (1965: 309-310). Sonstige Bemerkungen über die Sprache von SPbOkt. finden

368

sich bei Schaeken (1994: 383, Fn. 6), Velčeva (1995) sowie Birnbaum
und Schaeken (1997: 141-142).

3.2 1971: Codex Zographensis² Palimpsest (Zogr²Pal.)

Aufbewahrungsort: St. Petersburg – RNB Glag. 1.
Schriftart und Umfang: glagolitisch, 16 fol.
Bekanntlich stellen 17 Blätter des Codex Zographensis eine jüngere
glagolitische Ergänzung aus dem 12. Jahrhundert dar, die gewöhnlich
als Codex Zographensis² (auch Zographensis^b) bezeichnet wird (fol.
41-57 = Mt 16: 20 bis 24: 20). Von diesen 17 Blättern sind 16 ein Palimpsest, dessen ebenfalls glagolitisch abgefaßter Grundtext ein aus dem
Ende des 11. Jahrhunderts stammendes Fragment eines Tetraevangeli-
ums beinhaltet.

Obwohl der Codex Zographensis bereits 1843 entdeckt und 1879
erstmals vollständig von Jagić herausgegeben wurde, liegt eine Edition
von Zogr²Pal. erst seit 1971 vor. Der Herausgeber, Dobrev, konnte leider nur fünf Seiten entziffern (1971: 160-163, kyrillische Umschrift), und
zwar einige Abschnitte aus dem Matthäusevangelium (Mt 18: 3-9, 20:
27-34, 21: 1-2, 11-25, 24: 6-13). Kurze Bemerkungen zur Sprache von
Zogr²Pal. finden sich auch noch bei Tóth (1978: 245-246), Dobrev
(1985a: 738-739), Cejtlin u.a. (1994: 33-34) sowie Birnbaum und Schaeken (1997: 142).

3.3 1972: Palimpsest von Bojana (BojPal.)

Aufbewahrungsort: Moskau – RGB Grig. 8 (M. 1690).
Schriftart und Umfang: glagolitisch, 42 fol.
Das aus dem Ende des 11. Jahrhunderts stammende Palimpsestfrag-
ment eines Aprakosevangeliums befindet sich unter einem mittelbulgarischen kyrillischen Text des 12.-13. Jahrhunderts (109 fol.), der ebenfalls
ein (unvollständiges) Aprakosevangelium enthält.

Die Handschrift wurde 1845 von Grigorovič im Dorf Bojana (in der
Nähe von Sofia) gefunden und nach Rußland gebracht. Obwohl zwei
Seiten bereits von Jagić im Jahre 1911 in glagolitischer Schrift veröffentlicht wurden (1911: 129, 233-234 und Abbildungen IV/8, V/9), kam
eine Edition des Textes erst 1972 heraus. In dieser von Dobrev besorg-
ten Ausgabe sind 26 der insgesamt 84 Palimpsestseiten entziffert und in
kyrillischer Transkription veröffentlicht (samt Glossar, aber ohne Faksimile; vgl. die Rezensionen von Štefanić 1972 und L'vov 1975). Eine ge-
naue Inhaltsangabe der identifizierten Evangelienstellen findet sich bei

Dobrev (1972: 123-124). Moszyński (1979) bietet eine textkritische Würdigung, während kurze sprachliche Analysen weiter noch bei Tóth (1978: 246-247), Dobrev (1985b), Cejtlin u.a. (1994: 33) sowie Hauptová und Večerka (1997: 24-25, samt Textprobe) vorliegen.

4. Schlußbemerkungen

Die seit dem Ende der fünfziger Jahre neuentdeckten und neu entschlüsselten Sprachdenkmäler bilden etwa ein Viertel des jetzigen Umfangs des Korpus altkirchenslavischer Handschriften. Dabei ist jedoch zu beachten, daß es unter den neuen Denkmälern mehrere gibt, die relativ jüngeren Alters sind und die auf jeden Fall aus dem Ende des 11., wenn nicht bereits aus dem Anfang des 12. Jahrhunderts stammen: ApEn., Triod., SPbOkt., Zogr^{2}Pal., BojPal., und anscheinend auch PsDim. und MenSin. Hauptmerkmal dieser späteren Handschriften ist die sog. "éin-Jer"-Orthographie (vgl. dazu grundsätzlich Tóth 1978), sei es nur ь (so Triod.) oder nur ъ (ApEn., MenSin., BojPal. sowie mit nur wenigen Ausnahmen auch Zogr^{2}Pal. und SPbOkt.; vielleicht auch PsDim.). Weitere Besonderheiten sind der relativ begrenzte Gebrauch von jotierten Buchstaben und mehrere Fälle von Verwechslung der ursprünglichen Nasalvokale. Die einschlägigen Sprachmerkmale kommen auch in einigen altbekannten und oft zum klassischen Kanon des Altkirchenslavischen gerechneten Denkmälern vor, die aber wenig umfangreich sind: die Blätter Undol'skijs (2 fol.; nur ъ), das Blatt Hilferdings (auch Makedonisches kyrillisches Blatt genannt; nur ь) und die jüngere Rekto-Seite der Kiever Blätter (nur ъ). Die soeben genannten Neufunde bilden zusammen mit diesen drei Bruchstücken eine umfangsmäßig beträchtliche Handschriftengruppe und geben den Anlaß, um von einer speziellen "spätaltkirchenslavischen" Sprachperiode zu reden, welche den Übergang zwischen der klassischen altkirchenslavischen und mittelbulgarischen Epoche bildet.[4]

Universität Groningen

ANMERKUNGEN

[1]   Daß es noch eine sechste glagolitische Handschrift gegeben habe, und zwar "a big Glagolitic codex, containing a complete homiliary" (so Altbauer 1987: 39 in einem früheren, vorläufigen Bericht; vgl. Veder 1981: 31), welche dann später bei der

370

Katalogisierung übersehen worden wäre (vgl. die Mutmaßungen bei Mathiesen 1991: 196; dazu auch Trunte 1997[4]: 22), ist wohl unwahrscheinlich.

[2] Zum Inhalt von SinSluž. siehe neuerdings ausführlich auch Parenti (1991).

[3] Im Vorwort zur Edition von Ps. 2/N (Mareš u.a. 1997: VIII) schreibt Miklas über MisSin. und Euch., daß sie sich paläographisch und kodikologisch so nahe stehen, daß "ihre Abstammung aus ein und derselben Schule bzw. demselben Skriptorium kaum von der Hand zu weisen ist". Siehe auch den Bericht Bärlievas (1997: 110-111).

[4] Zu bemerken ist, daß weitere Untersuchungen herausstellen sollen, ob nicht einige Sinai-Neufunde (darunter besonders PsDim.) doch besser als (früh)mittelbulgarische Denkmäler zu werten sind. Dasselbe gilt übrigens auch für Triod.

LITERATURVERZEICHNIS

Aitzetmüller, R.
1978-79   "Zur Einstufung des Apostolusfragments von Enina", Anzeiger für slavische Philologie 10-11, 19-24.
Alekseev, A.
1988   Rez. von Tarnanidis (1988), International Journal of Slavic Linguistics and Poetics 37, 190-197.
Altbauer, M.
1987   "Identification of newly discovered Slavic manuscripts in St. Catherine's Monastery in Sinai", Slovo 37, 35-40.
Altbauer, M. und F.V. Mareš
1980   "Fragmentum glagoliticum Evangeliarii palaeoslovenici in codice Sinaitico 39 (palimpsestum)", Anzeiger der Österreichischen Akademie der Wissenschaften. Phil.-hist. Klasse 117/6, 139-152.
1981   "Das Palimpsest-Fragment eines glagolitischen Evangeliars im Codex Sinaiticus 39 − Ein neues altkirchenslavisches kanonisches Denkmal", Wiener Slawistischer Almanach 7, 253-258.
Arranz, M.
1988   "La liturgie de l'eucologe slave du Sinai", Christianity among the Slavs. The heritage of Saints Cyril and Methodius (Hg. E.G. Farrugia u.a.), 15-74. Roma.
Atanasov, A.
1980   "Eninskijat apostol − novootkrit starobălgarski pismen pametnik ot sredata na XI v.", Vekovni bălgarski ezikovi tradicii (Hg. E. Georgieva und N. Todorova), 75-78. Sofija.
Bakker, H.P.S. (= M.)
1994   "The New Testament lections in the Euchologium Sinaiticum", Polata knigopisnaja 25-26, 155-212.
1996   Towards a critical edition of the Old Slavic New Testament. A transparent and heuristic approach. Amsterdam.

371

Bărlieva, S.
1997   "Glagolitica – simpozium, posveten na načaloto na slavjanskata pis-
        mena kultura", *Palaeobulgarica/Starobălgaristika* 21/2, 107-112.
Bernštejn, S.B.
1966   Rez. von Mirčev und Kodov (1965), *Sovetskoe slavjanovedenie*
        1966/1, 102-103.
Birnbaum, H.
1989   Rez. von Tarnanidis (1988), *Die Welt der Slaven* 34, 173-181.
1998   Rez, von Mareš u.a. (1997), *International Journal of Slavic Lin-
        guistics and Poetics* 42. (im Druck)
Birnbaum, H. und J. Schaeken
1997   *Das altkirchenslavische Wort: Bildung – Bedeutung – Herleitung* (=
        Altkirchenslavische Studien I). München.
Bláhová, E.
1966   Rez. von Mirčev und Kodov (1965), *Slavia* 35, 496-498.
1989   Rez. von Tarnanidis (1988), *Byzantinoslavica* 50, 64-68.
Cejtlin, R.M., R. Večerka und E. Bláhová (Blagova) (Hg.)
1994   *Staroslavjanskij slovar' (po rukopisjam X-XI vekov)*. Moskva.
Demirčeva-Chafuzova, N.
1964   "Beležki po otkrivaneto na starobălgarskija pismen pametnik 'Eninski
        apostol' ot XI vek", *Bălgarski ezik* 14, 527-533.
Dobrev, I.
1971   "Palimpsestovite časti na Zografskoto evangelie", *Konstantin-Kiril
        Filosof. Dokladi ot simpoziuma, posveten na 1100-godišninata ot
        smărtta mu* (Hg. P. Dinekov u.a.), 157-164. Sofija.
1972   *Glagoličeskijat tekst na Bojanskija palimpsest. Starobălgarski pamet-
        nik ot kraja na XI vek.* Sofija.
1985a   "Zografsko evangelie", *Kirilo-Metodievska enciklopedija* I (Hg. P.
        Dinekov), 734-740. Sofija.
1985b   "Bojanski palimpsest", *Kirilo-Metodievska enciklopedija* I (Hg. P.
        Dinekov), 236. Sofija.
1989-90 "A new collection of Slavonic manuscripts from the Sinai peninsula",
        Cyrillomethodianum 13-14, 159-177.
1990   "Bălgarska narodna leksika v edin răkopis ot XII vek", *Christomatija
        po săvremenen bălgarski ezik* (Hg. L. Ilieva), 10-28. Blagoevgrad.
Dobrev, I. und T. Slavova
1995   *Starobălgarski tekstove. Christomatija za universitetite.* Sofija.
Dogramadžieva, E.
1985   "Eninski apostol", *Kirilo-Metodievska enciklopedija* I (Hg. P. Dine-
        kov), 652-655. Sofija.
1994   "Učastie na evangelieto v izgraždaneto na Sinajskija evchologij", *Sta-
        robălgarska literatura* 28-29, 62-65.
Dostál, A.
1966   Rez. von Mirčev und Kodov (1965), *Byzantinoslavica* 27, 433-434.
Drobena, T.J.
1990   Rez. von Tarnanidis (1988), *The Slavic Review* 49, 684-685.

372

Duridanov, I. u.a.
1991   *Gramatika na starobălgarskija ezik. Fonetika, morfologija, sintaksis.*
        Sofija.
Džurova, A., K. Stančev und M. Japundžić
1985   *Opis na slavjanskite răkopisi văv Vatikanskata biblioteka.* Sofija.
Fetková, P.
1997   Rez. von Bakker (1996), *Slavia* 66, 350-353.
Hamm, J.
1979   *Das Glagolitische Missale von Kiew.* Wien.
Hannick, Chr.
1985   "Der liturgische Standort der Prager glagolitischen Fragmente", *Litterae slavicae medii aevi* (= Fs. F.V. Mareš, Hg. J.M. Reinhart),
        107-117. München.
Hauptová, Z.
1971   "Lexikální rozbor apoštola Eninského. Příspěvek k analýze nejstaršího textu staroslověnského apoštoláře", *Studia palaeoslovenica* (= Fs.
        J. Kurz, Hg. B. Havránek), 105-121. Praha.
1993   "*Slovník jazyka staroslověnského* a nově nalezené rukopisy na Sinaji",
        Die slawischen Sprachen 32, 43-53.
Hauptová, Z. und R. Večerka
1997   *Staroslověnská čítanka.* Praha.
Jagić, V.
1879   *Quattuor evangeliorum codex glagoliticus olim Zographensis nunc
        Petropolitanus.* Berolini.
1890   *Glagolitica. Würdigung neuentdeckter Fragmente.* Wien.
1911   "Glagoličeskoe pis'mo", *Ènciklopedija slavjanskoj filologii.* 3: *Grafika u Slavjan* (Hg. V. Jagić), 51-262. Sanktpeterburg.
Koceva, E.
1985   "Osobenosti v kalendara na Eninskija apostol", *Palaeobulgarica/Starobălgaristika* 9/1, 104-110.
Koch, Chr.
1983   "Anmerkungen zum Fragmentum sinaiticum", *Zeitschrift für slavische Philologie* 43, 6-27.
Kodov, Chr.
1966   "Fragment ot starobălgarski răkopis s glagoličeska pripiska", *Kliment
        Ochridski. Sbornik ot statii po slučaj 1050 godini ot smărtta mu,*
        121-131. Sofija.
1969   *Opis na slavjanskite răkopisi v bibliotekata na Bălgarskata Akademija
        na Naukite.* Sofija.
1983   *Eninski apostol.* Sofija.
Kopylenko, M.M.
1966   Rez. von Mirčev und Kodov (1965), *Voprosy jazykoznanija* 1966/4,
        158-160.
Krăstanov, T.
1988a   "Bălgarski Vatikanski palimpsest (Kirilsko kratko izbᴏrno evangelie
        ot X v. v Cod. Vat. gr. 2502)", *Palaeobulgarica/Starobălgaristika*
        12/1, 38-66.

1988b   "Apografo di evangeliario cirillico dei secoli X-XI nel 'palinsesto bulgaro' (Vat. gr. 2502)", *Christianity among the Slavs. The heritage of Saints Cyril and Methodius* (Hg. E.G. Farrugia u.a.), 261-265.

Krăstanov, T., A.-M.Totomanova und I. Dobrev
1996   *Vatikansko evangelie. Starobălgarski kirilski aprakos ot X v. v palimpsesten kodeks Vat. Gr. 2502.* Sofija.

Lunt, H.G.
1958   "On Slavonic palimpsests", *American contributions to the Fourth International Congress of Slavicists. Moscow, September 1958*, 191-209. 's-Gravenhage.
1959   "Contributions to the study of Old Church Slavonic", *International Journal of Slavic Linguistics and Poetics* 1-2, 9-37.
1965   "On the loss of declension in Bulgarian and Macedonian", *Die Welt der Slaven* 10, 305-312.

L'vov, A.S.
1975   Rez. von Dobrev (1972), *Sovetskoe slavjanovedenie* 1975/1, 90-93.

Mareš, F.V.
1989-90   Rez. von Tarnanidis (1988), *Slovo* 39-40, 204-205.
1990   "Himan *Slava va višnjih Bogu* (velika doksologija) u Sinajskom psaltiru i u hrvatskoglagoljskim misalima", *Croatica-Slavica-Indoeuropaea* (= Fs. R. Katičić, Hg. G. Holzer), 131-135. Wien.
1991   "Význam staroslověnských rukopisů nově objevených na hoře Sinaj", *Slavia* 60, 225-231.
1993   "Význam staroslověnských rukopisů nově objevených na hoře Sinaj. K hlaholským rukopisům 3/N a 4/N", *Slavia* 62, 125-130.
1994   "Spicilegium etymologicum", *Slavia* 63, 129-133.
1995   "Očenaš u Sinajskom psaltiru", *Proučavanje srednjovekovnih južnoslovenskih rukopisa* (Hg. P. Ivić), 245-249. Beograd.

Mareš, F.V. u.a.
1997   *Psalterii Sinaitici pars nova (monasterii s. Catharinae codex slav. 2/N).* Wien.

Mathiesen, R.
1985   "Uspenskij's Bifolium and the chronology of some early Church Slavonic translations", *Slavica Hierosolymitana* 7, 77-86.
1991   "New Old Church Slavonic manuscripts on Mount Sinai", *Harvard Ukrainian Studies* 15, 192-199.

Minčev, G.
1993   "Mjastoto na novootkritite listove ot Sinajskija evchologij sred drugite tekstove ot răkopisa. Filologičeski i liturgičeski analiz na molitvite ot denonoštnija bogoslužeben cikăl (ΑΙΣΜΑΤΙΚΗ ΑΚΟΛΟΥΘΙΑ)", *Palaeobulgarica/Starobălgaristika* 17/1, 21-36.

Minčeva, A.
1966   Rez. von Mirčev und Kodov (1965), *Bălgarski ezik* 16, 520-522.

Mirčev, K.
1963   "Za ezikovite osobenosti na novootkriti fragmenti ot naj-star slavjanski apostolski tekst – Eninski apostol ot XI v.", *Slavjanska filologija. 3: Dokladi, săobštenija i statii po ezikoznanie*, 81-103. Sofija.

374

Mirčev, K. und Chr. Kodov
1965   Eninski apostol. Starobălgarski pametnik ot XI v. Sofija.
Momina, M.A.
1988   "Ob odnom fragmente iz bolgarskoj rukopisi XI-XII v.", Kirilo-Me-
            todievski studii 5, 109-130.
1991   Rez. von Tarnanidis (1988), Voprosy jazykoznanija 1991/6, 141-148.
Moszyński, L.
1971   "Fragmenty psałterzowe Apostoła Enińskiego wobec tzw. Psałterza
            Synajskiego", Konstantin-Kiril Filosof. Dokladi ot simpoziuma, po-
            sveten na 1100-godišninata ot smărtta mu (Hg. P. Dinekov u.a.),
            143-156. Sofija.
1979   "Głagolski tekst Bojańskiego Palimpsestu wobec innych cyrylometo-
            dejskich ewangeliarzy", Izsledvanija vărchu istorijata i dialektite na
            bălgarskija ezik (= Gs. K. Mirčev, Hg. V.I. Georgiev u.a.), 271-275.
            Sofija.
Musakova, E. (Mussakova)
1994   "Der kyrillische Palimpsest in Cod. Vat. gr. 2502 und sein
            Schmuck", Palaeobulgarica/Starobălgaristika 18/1, 37-57.
Nedeljković, O.
1967   Rez. von Mirčev und Kodov (1965), Slovo 17, 191-195.
Pantelić, M.
1985   "O Kijevskim i Sinajskim listićima", Slovo 35, 5-56.
Parenti, S.
1989   Rez. von Tarnanidis (1988), L'Altra Europa 6, 150-152.
1991   "Influssi italo-greci nei testi eucaristici bizantini dei 'Fogli Slavi' del
            Sinai (XI sec.)", Orientalia Christiana Periodica 57, 145-177.
1994   "Glagoličeskij spisok rimsko-vizantijskoj liturgii sv. Petra (Sin. glag.
            5/N)", Palaeobulgarica/Starobălgaristika 18/4, 3-14.
Popov, G.
1985   Triodni proizvedenija na Konstantin Preslavski (= Kirilo-Metodievski
            studii 2). Sofija.
Rosenschon, U.
1991   "Ein glagolitisches Fragment medizinischen Inhalts", Südost-For-
            schungen 50, 251-257.
1993   "Sechs Seiten medizinischer Rezepte im glagolitischen Psalter 3/N
            des Sinaiklosters", Sudhoffs Archiv. Zeitschrift für Wissenschaftsge-
            schichte 77, 129-159.
1994   "Sechs Seiten medizinischer Rezepte im glagolitischen Psalter 3/N
            des Sinaiklosters", Byzantinoslavica 55, 304-335.
Schaeken, J.
1989   "Vorläufige Bemerkungen zum neuentdeckten glagolitischen Missale
            Sinaiticum", Die Welt der Slaven 34, 32-40.
1994   "Altkirchenslavische Silbentrennung und reduzierte Vokale am Zei-
            lenschluß", Dutch contributions to the Eleventh International Con-
            gress of Slavists, Bratislava: Linguistics, 369-387. Amsterdam-At-
            lanta.
1996   "Anmerkungen zum neuen Handwörterbuch der altkirchenslavischen
            Sprache", Byzantinoslavica 57, 182-187.

Schnitter, M. und H. Miklas
1993 "Kyrillomethodianische Miszellen", *Anzeiger für slavische Philologie* 22/1 (= Fs. R. Aitzetmüller 1), 141-220.
Schütz, J.
1967 Rez. von Mirčev und Kodov (1965), *Die Welt der Slaven* 12, 110-111.
Ševčenko, I.
1982 "Report on the Glagolitic fragments (of the *Euchologium Sinaiticum?*) discovered on Sinai in 1975 and some thoughts on the models for the make-up of the earliest Glagolitic manuscripts", *Harvard Ukrainian Studies* 6, 119-151. (Nachdruck in: I. Ševčenko, 1991, *Byzantium and the Slavs in letters and culture*, 617-650. Cambridge-Napoli.)
1991 "Addenda", *Byzantium and the Slavs in letters and culture*, 725-740. Cambridge-Napoli.
Šima, P.
1971 "Archaický protograf kódexu 7784", *Slavica Slovaca* 6, 264-266.
Simonov, R.A.
1967 "Primenjalsja li znak Ч v zapisi čisla v Eninskom apostole XI veka?", *Sovetskoe slavjanovedenie* 1967/3, 75-76.
Šiškova, L.
1992 "Fitonimi v glagoličeskija lekarstvenik ot manastira 'Sv. Ekaterina' v Sinaj", *Slavia* 61, 177-186.
Slavova, T. und I. Dobrev
1996 *Starobǎlgarski tekstove*. Sofija.
Slovník jazyka staroslověnského
1958ff. *Slovník jazyka staroslověnského* (Hg. J. Kurz, ab 1982 Z. Hauptová). Praha.
Smjadovski, S.
1987 "Eninskijat apostol ot XI v. – Problemi sled faksimilnoto mu izdanie", *Bǎlgarski ezik* 37, 366-374.
Špadijer, I.
1990 Rez. von Tarnanidis (1988), *Arheografski prilozi* 12, 341-347.
Stanislav, J.
1966 Rez. von Mirčev und Kodov (1965), *Slavica Slovaca* 1, 102-103.
Štefanić, Vj.
1972 Rez. von Dobrev (1972), *Slovo* 22, 173-177.
Tarnanidis, I.C.
1988 *The Slavonic manuscripts discovered in 1975 at St Catherine's Monastery on Mount Sinai*. Thessaloniki.
1990 "Glagolitic Canon to Saints Peter and Paul (Sin. Slav. 4/N)", *Filologia e letteratura nei paesi slavi* (= Fs. S. Graciotti), 91-97. Roma.
Tkadlčík, V.
1989 Rez. von Tarnanidis (1988), *Slavia* 58, 165-170.
Tóth, I.H. (Tot)
1978 "K izučeniju odnoerovych pamjatnikov XI v.", *Studia Slavica Hungarica* 24, 229-258.

376

Trunte, H.
1997[4]   Слов'кньскъи ꙗзъікъ. *Ein praktisches Lehrbuch des Kirchensla-*
               vischen in 35 Lektionen. I: *Altkirchenslavisch.* München.
Ugrinova-Skalovska, R.
1970   "Eninskiot apostol vo sporedba so nekoi drugi apostoli", *Kiril So-*
               lunski. Simpozium: 1100-godišnina od smrtta na Kiril Solunski 2
               (Hg. V. Iljoski u.a.), 405-417. Skopje.
Večerka, R.
ˊ1966   Rez. von Mirčev und Kodov (1965), *Sborník prací filozofické fakulty*
               brněnské univerzity A 14, 187-188.
Veder, W.R.
1981   "The Second Summer Colloquium on Old Bulgarian studies", *Polata*
               knigopisnaja 5, 29-41.
Velčeva, B.
1988   "Novootkriti räkopisi v Sinajskija manastir 'Sveta Ekaterina'", *Pa-*
               laeobulgarica/Starobälgaristika 12/3, 126-129.
1991   "Novootkrit lekarstvenik, napisan s glagolica", *Starobälgarska litera-*
               tura 25-26, 95-97.
1995   "Leningradski palimpsest", *Kirilo-Metodievska enciklopedija* II (Hg.
               P. Dinekov), 519-521. Sofija.
Velkovska, E.
1996   *Nuovi paralleli greci dell'Eucologio slavo del Sinai,* Roma.
Zagrebin, V.M.
1979   "O proischoždenii i sud'be nekotorych slavjanskich palimpsestov Si-
               naja", *Iz istorii rukopisnych i staropečatnych sobranij (issledovanija,*
               obzory, publikacii) (Hg. L.L. Al'bina u.a.), 61-80. Leningrad.

Dutch Contributions to the Twelfth International Congress of Slavists, Cracow, Linguistics (= *Studies in Slavic and General Linguistics* Vol 24), 377–390. RODOPI, Amsterdam – Atlanta, GA 1998.

SOME MORPHOLOGICAL CHARACTERISTICS OF RESIAN SUBSTANTIVES CONTAINING THE SUFFIX -(J)UST

HAN STEENWIJK

1. Introduction

Resian complex substantives derived by means of the suffix -(j)ust[1] show some characteristics that seem to be peculiar to this Slovene dialect. In the following I propose to give a short outline of these special features and will vent on a diachronic explanation for at least some of them. The questions that will be addressed are:
- the domains on which the formation rule draws;
- the semantics of the formations;
- the distribution of the allomorphs -ust and -just;
- the gender and paradigm class assignment of the formations.

As will be shown, a historical explanation of the Resian patterning can be made when the informations obtained in these fields are interconnected.

The formations to be analysed are taken from sources containing Resian lexical material: word-lists, texts collected for dialectological purposes and texts written by native speakers. This excludes two substantial corpora that are not purely Resian, the *Christjanske uzhilo od teh Sedan SS. Sacramintu* dating from the middle of the 19th century and *To kristjanske učilo po rozoanskeh* published in 1927. The former was probably written by Francesco Galizia from the nearby Friulian village of Moggio/Mužac, the latter is the work of Jozef Kramaro, a native of the Natisone Valleys. Both works contain demonstrably non-Resian elements and for this reason one cannot exclude that lexemes attested here are in fact ad hoc loans or formations introduced by non-natives. Only when such lexemes are also being used by native authors and thus become engaged in relations with formally similar derivates of Resian origin have they been incorporated into the data.

Within the general framework of dialectology the study of lexical morphology is hampered in several ways. Firstly, although the body of

378

Resian material that stands at disposal is huge with respect to most other Slovene dialects, it is still extremely small if compared to established literary languages. This restricted size is almost sure to cause the information on the paradigmatic relations that formations partake in to be incomplete. Secondly, variation seems to be the rule rather than the exception in a speech community in which the written use of the language is no everyday phenomenon. The usage of individual authors can differ notably, making it particularly difficult to distinguish the *langue* from the *parole*. However, for a diachronical approach this variation can prove to be helpful as it may hint at some of the successive stages of a language change.

As concerns the collected data, the following points should be borne in mind:

a) For some formations no base is identifiable in the language as an independent lexeme (*jarust, manjust, žalust*). Such cases are also encountered with in established literary languages, but for Resian it cannot be ruled out that the respective base lexemes are actually there, only waiting to be attested.

b) For one formation no meaning can be given (*žalust*). It only occurs in the Resian version of the *Dies irae*, a religious text that is part of the oral tradition, and has no exact equivalent in the Latin original.

c) Quite a few of these formations were attested only once (*bilust, bratrust, fwalust, maluwridnust, manjust, pamotjust, skröwnust, svetust, zbüdjust, žalust*). For the moment it cannot be decided whether these are established lexemes or nonces.

d) Some formations are only encountered repeatedly in texts by one and the same author (*jarust* (R. Quaglia); *lonust, salvanust* (M. Di Lenardo); *rawnust, risnust, wežjust* (S. Paletti); *vïdust* (L. Di Floriano)). Also for these lexemes doubts can be raised as to their establishedness.

e) For several formations meanings were attested that clearly represent semantic derivations from their primary meanings.

The analysis will in the first place concentrate on those derivates that were attested repeatedly in different sources.[2] The lexemes cited above will only be drawn upon to supply secondary evidence for the formal aspects of the derivation. The majority of the substantives enumerated under c) and d) are likely to have come into existence recently, coined by the authors who use them. Their semantics, as well as the semantic derivations from meanings of a longer standing, are more properly discussed in a separate study on neologisms. In this study I propose to concentrate on the patterning that provides the background for such deliberate innovations.

2. Domain and meaning

The derivation rule encompasses at least two and maybe three domains.

Firstly, there is a sizable group of deadjectival formations A → A + (j)ust:

lip	'beautiful'	*lip(j)ust*
mlad	'young'	*mladjust*
möćan	'strong'	*möćn(j)ust*
punïžan	'humble'	*punïžnust*
smïlan	'compassionate'	*smïl(n)ust*
tožan	'sorrowful'	*tožnust*

Most of these have the semantics 'being of the quality A', like *lip(j)ust, punïžnust, tožnust*. This is a pattern encountered in every member of the Slavonic branch, to which Resian makes no exception. Lexicalised meanings have to be construed for *mladjust* 'period of being of the quality A' and *möćn(j)ust* 'being of the quality A and excerting this over others'.

Secondly, a small group consists of deverbals V → V + *just*:

branit	'to protect'	*branjust*
trüdit	'to tire'	*trüdjust*

They display the semantics 'being in a state resulting from having been V-ed'. This part of the rule represents a Resian innovation and needs some discussion. It is quite conceivable that in previous language stages a deadjectival **trüdnust* (cf. *trüdan* 'tired') lost its *n* and yielded *trüdust*, a form actually attested in the spoken language: *trụdust* O. A similar development is observable in the pair *smïlnust/smïlust* that was analysed as deadjectival. The reason for classifying the latter lexeme as deadjectival is the presence of a variant form containing the *n*. For *trüdjust*, however, no variant form with *n* is part of the actual language stage while the verb is. Therefore on the synchronic plane *trüdjust* can be analysed as deverbal.

For *branjust* the analysis can raise no doubts whatsoever. There is no adjective that could be posited as its base and the only non-verbal lexeme that could possibly furnish one is the substantive *bran* that because of its meaning 'gate (in a fence)' can at best be regarded an improbable candidate.

For the remaining derivates the domain they originate from cannot be readily made out. A third group contains formations that synchronically speaking could as well be deadjectival as deverbal:

stär	'old'	star(j)ust[3]
starët	'to grow old'	
vësël	'joyful, blissful'	vësalust
se vasalët	'to be merry'	
zdräw	'healthy'	zdrawjust
zdravët	'to heal'	
žïw	'alive'	žïwjust
žïvit	'to live'	

Although both derivations are formally possible, a semantic description that encompasses all four lexemes is not within reach, irrespective of the choice of an adjective or a verb as the base. In fact, vësalust is analysed as deadjectival by native speakers and star(j)ust is likely to be judged on a par with mladjust. This leaves zdrawjust and žïwjust as two formations with an ambiguous domain status, both of which have lexicalised meanings, as they cannot be construed with the semantics given for the deadjectivals or deverbals discussed earlier.

In a fourth group there is the sole derivate skärbjust for which only can be ascertained that on the synchronical plane it is not deadjectival.[4] A base for this formation can be equally furnished by the verb skarbët 'to worry' as by the substantive skärb 'worry'. If deverbal the formation is a nominalisation of the action expressed by the verb, if desubstantival it represents a synonym, possibly belonging to a different register.

The formations classified as secondary evidence support the identification of three domains. Most derivates are deadjectival (bilust, rawnust, risnust, skröwnust, svetust). Here also belong salvanust with the participle salvän 'saved' as adjectival base and maluwridnust with a phrase malu wridan '??' headed by an adjective as the base. Some formations are again deverbal (fwalust, vïdust, wežjust, zbüdjust), but also two clearly desubstantival formations can be discerned: bratrust and pamotjust (cf. bratar 'brother', pamot 'wisdom'). However, it should be noted that more than 160 years separate the sources containing these attestations: bratrost is from a source dating from 1818 and pamotjust is found in a text written around 1985. Notwithstanding the facts that such a desubstantival derivation is possible and that this possibility seems to be around in Resia for quite some time, it has spawned only few formations. Thus the substantive as a domain remains poorly documented. The lexeme *lonust* presents a problem similar to that of *skärbjust*, because both the verb *lonat* 'to reward' and the substantive *lon* 'reward' can be posited as its base. As semantically it is a derivation of the phrase *Bug an lonaj!* 'thank you!' the verb is the more likely candidate here.

The bases the rule for *-(j)ust* draws upon thus encompass, besides the inherited domain of the adjectives, also verbs and possibly substantives. It seems as if the suffix is becoming the formative *par excellence* to derive abstracts, irrespective of the particular part of speech the base belongs to. Bearing in mind what has been said initially on lexical morphology as applied to dialects I propose the following hypothesis to account for this situation.

Judging by the data known, present-day Resian does not have other suffixes to derive abstracts at its disposal that could block the spreading of *-(j)ust* apart from the productive deverbal suffix *-një*. But with the latter suffix mainly action nouns are derived, being mere transpositions or having the meaning 'manner of performing the action expressed by the verb', e.g. from *pravit* 'to talk' *prawjanjë* '(manner of) talking'. These semantics differ from the one construed for formations in *-(j)ust*, that refer to states rather than actions.[5] For other suffixes deriving abstracts examples are very rare, so rare that one doubts whether the native speaker would synthesise new formations with them. Attested are the suffixes *-'ë*, *-ïja*, *-uta* for deadjectivals (*vasajë* 'bliss', *zdrawjë* 'health'; *bogatïja* 'riches'; *dubruta* 'goodness', *gurkuta* 'heat', *lakuta* 'thirst') and *-a*, *-ba* for deverbals (*mëra* 'measure', *nawada* 'habit'; *posodba* 'loan'). The abstracts occurring in the spoken language are overwhelmingly of Romance, mainly Friulian origin. It is well conceivable that the borrowed abstracts have caused lexemes, containing various inherited suffixes that were used to derive abstracts, to disappear or to become marginalised. Only derivates in *-(j)ust* managed to survive in sufficient number: the attested formations in the spoken language are *mlad(j)ust*, *star(j)ust*, *trüd(j)ust*, *zdrawjust* and *žïwjust*, while several more are known passively (*smïl(n)ust*, *tožnust*).

This may explain why the suffix under discussion could be used to coin new formations, but still begs the question of the, from a Slavonic point of view, unusual array of domains the derivation rule draws upon. I think at least a partial explanation is possible. The reinterpretation of *-(j)ust* as deverbal as well as deadjectival may well be due to the pre-

382

sence of the formations *zdrawjust* and *žïwjust.* These are by far the most frequent ones and cannot be unequivocally identified as either deadjectival or deverbal. Clearly deverbal formations like *branjust* then came into existence on the basis of analogy to this pair. For the reinterpretation of *-(j)ust* as a desubstantive formative I am at a loss to find a plausible clarification.

3. Distribution of the allomorphs

The suffix has, besides the inherited form *-ust,* a variant form *-just.* To get a better insight into the distribution of the allomorphs, the attestations from the spoken language are considered together with the ones found in the texts. Three groups can be distinguished:

a) the formative appears only as *-ust: bilust, bratrust, fwalust, lonust, maluwridnust, punïžnust, rawnust, risnust, salvanust, skröwnust, smïl-(n)ust, svetust, tožnust, vёsalust, vïdust;*

b) the formative appears in both forms: *lipust/lipjust, mladust/mladjust, möćnust/möćnjust, starust/starjust, trüdust/trüdjust;*

c) the formative appears only as *-just: branjust, pamotjust, skärbjust, wežjust, zbüdjust, zdrawjust, žïwjust.*

A phonological motivation for this distribution cannot be found, cf. especially stems ending in *n-,* that appear in all three groups. A division made on the parts of speech the bases belong to, does not show a clear regulation either, but at least a tendency appears. For deadjectivals the form *-ust,* in 10 formations attested without variation, is the more usual one while exclusively *-just* does not occur. Within the group of deverbals, however, there are 2 instances of only *-ust* against 3 of *-just* without variation. Doublet forms occur mainly with deadjectivals and rarely with deverbals. The desubstantival formations are too small in number to be taken into account. From a synchronical point of view the distribution of the allomorphs can only be stated to be lexically motivated. The allomorph *-ust* is used with a wide array of different stems, but the doublet forms show that the epenthetic *j* is gaining further ground among deadjectivals. This *j* is inserted at the morpheme boundary and gives the suffix more phonological weight.

The following table, containing the lexemes current in the spoken language as attested in the four main dialectal varieties, gives some further information on the distribution of the allomorphs:

SG	G	O	S
zdráwjust	zdráwjust	zdráwjust	zdráwjọst
žíwjust	žíwjust	žíwjust	žíwjọst
mládjust	mlédjust	mládust/-just	mlõdọst/-jọst
trúdjust	trúdjust	trúdust/-just	
stárust	stárust/-just	stárust	stárọst

In the lexeme star(j)ust -just is relatively rare, and only occurs as an alternative form. For mlad(j)ust and trüd(j)ust both possibilities are attested. In the conservative dialects of Oseacco and Stolvizza -just appears as an alternative, but in the innovating dialects of San Giorgio and Gniva this is already the only form of the suffix attested with these lexemes. This confirms the observation about the gradual expansion of -just at the cost of -ust.

In order to hypothesise on a historical explanation for the origin of this epenthetic j and its present distribution I return to the pair zdrawjust and žïwjust. As can be seen from the distribution of the dialect forms, they are the only formations in the spoken language for which the innovative variant -just is stable. The absence of doublet forms, as opposed to other formations, is an indication that within this group these were the first to develop the j. Also within the inherited group of deadjectivals, to which zdrawjust and žïwjust because of their ambiguous domain status can be reckoned, -just is without an alternative form in only these two formations. As was argued above, the rise of the deverbal status of -(j)ust can possibly be ascribed to the existence in the system of zdrawjust and žïwjust. This could also explain the more frequent use of the innovative allomorph -just for deverbals: these started to be coined only after the variant form -just had come into existence.

The rise of an epenthetic j in exactly zdrawjust and žïwjust can be made plausible if their semantics are taken into account. In Standard Slovene their closest counterparts are zdravlje and življenje. Of these the former actually occurs in Resian in the lesser used form zdrawjë, showing the regular sound change *lj → j. A Resian form corresponding to življenje has never been attested, but if such a form once existed, it also will have undergone the change *lj → j. That such a Resian form may already have had the second meaning 'livelihood', a meaning foreign to Standard Slovene, is not unlikely on the basis of the obirsko (Schaida/Šajda) attestation žəwléːje that also conveys this meaning (Karničar 1990: 271) The allomorph -just came into existence by isolating the stems zdrawj- and *žïwj- and adding the formative -ust.[6]

384

The lexemes thus coined were then again reanalysed as *zdraw* + *just*, *žïw* + *just*. From that point on the innovative form variant started to spread to the already existing deadjectivals. The reason for the deadjectivals to be analogically remodeled on the innovative *zdrawjust* and *žïwjust* must again be sought in the relatively high frequency of these two lexemes in respect to the other formations used in the spoken language.

This also means that the omnipresence of abstracts from Romance origin was not the only driving force behind the marginalisation of inherited abstracts containing other suffixes than *-(j)ŭst*. The suffix under discussion itself is partly responsible for the extinction of semantically equivalent abstracts. This is presently observable with the pairs *skärbjust-skärb* (if *skärbjust* is desubstantival), *vësalust-vasajë* and *zdrawjust-zdrawjë*.[7]

A line of reasoning that takes the innovative deverbals as a point of origin and spreading of *-just* cannot be developed here because the stem the formation is built upon is as yet unclear. If it is the present stem of the verb, as in *wežjust*, it is difficult to find a reason for introducing an epenthetic *j*, cf. *wežën* 'I tie up'. If the form of the past passive participle plays a role, the rise of a *j* can already be more easily accounted for, cf. *wbranjën* 'protected'. More importantly, I can see no reason why such deverbals, rare in the spoken language, would have exerted analogical influence first on relatively frequent forms like **zdrawust* and **žïwust* and only then on other deadjectivals.

4. **Gender and paradigm**

As was first noted by Matičetov (1993: 71), apart from the inherited assignment to the Slavonic i-declination that in Resian only contains feminines, substantives in *-(j)ust* tend to vary as to their gender and paradigm class assignment. On the basis of the Gsg case forms *jarosta* and *mladosta* he concludes that the formations can also be masculines and take endings of the Slavonic o-declination.

These statements can be modified as follows. The Resian paradigm corresponding to the o-declination contains both masculines and neuters, the gender of which is only distinguished in the NA cases. Judging by their agreement with inclinable modifiers, attestations of such case forms from the four main dialectal varieties of Resian show that, apart from being treated as feminines, in the spoken language these substantives are treated as neuters far more frequently than as masculines. As to their paradigm class assignment, apart from taking endings in the oblique cases these substantives also, be it sporadically, tend to be indeclinable.

This makes Matičetov's hypothesis (ibid.), based on analogy to the masculine substantives *must, post* [or rather, *pöst*] and *pust* [or rather, *püst*], offered as an explanation for the variation in paradigm class assignment rather difficult to accept. Consider the following proportions that are taken from the dialect of Oseacco:

masculine/neuter			masculine	
accent class (a)			accent class (b)	
Nsg *stárust*	*pųst*		*múst*	*pọ́st*
Gsg *stárustạ*	*pųstạ*		*mostạ́*	*postạ́*

Because they are accent class (b) substantives *must* and *pöst* can be ruled out as sources of analogical influence. But also the accent class (a) substantive *püst* is an unlikely candidate, as accentuation and vowel quality differ. Also, a clear motivation for an analogical influence exerted by any of these substantives is lacking. It is true that some lexemes originally belonging to the i-declination are changing over or have changed over to the feminine a-declination, but on the whole the Resian correspondent to the i-declination cannot be said to be marginal as it is replenished by Romance loans (Steenwijk 1990: 25-26). So neither a drag exerted by the masculine substantives cited nor a push because of marginalisation of the inherited paradigm class can be identified to account for the change. The differing gender assignment is now added to these problems, as no explanation is offered for the neuter gender of substantives in *-(j)ust*.

In my opinion the lexemes *zdrawjust* and *žïwjust* are again the key to a solution. Their etymological antecedents *zdrawjë* and **življenje* were both neuters and as an alternative this property was passed on to the lexemes derived from them by means of the formative *-ust*. This eventually caused a competition between feminine and neuter in all substantives showing this formative. The analogical influence *zdrawjust* and *žïwjust* exerted on the other lexemes has already been demonstrated and explained above. As neuters appear only in the o-declination, the change in gender automatically entails a switch to this paradigm class.

Further developments are posterior to this change and are a reaction to the conflict that arose from the new paradigm class assignment. Within the Resian correspondent of the o-declination all substantives having a NAsg case form ending in a consonant other than those containing the suffix *-(j)ust* are masculine. Neuters other than those in *-(j)ust*, on the other hand, never have a NAsg case form that ends in a consonant. One way to neutralise this conflict is to assign the substantives in *-(j)ust* the property masculine. Another way is to drop inclinability altogether. This development is paralleled by some neuters belonging to the accent classes (b) and (c). From the substantives belonging to these marginal classes some two-syllable roots tend to become indeclinable in the innovating dialects of San Giorgio and Gniva, eg. Dsg *rašató/rašatṷ* SG, *rušutǫ́* G 'riddle', but not so elsewhere: Dsg *rašató* O, S.

5. Recapitulation

Although the paper started out with a survey of formations attested in written Resian, it may have become clear that I regard the situation in the spoken language, where within a small group two frequent lexemes exhibit special characteristics, as the main driving force behind the changes that affected several morphological features of substantives in *-(j)ust*. Also for written Resian the two lexemes are the most frequent ones, but within that context newly coined formations cause shifts in the network of paradigmatic relations.

Assuming the lexemes *zdrawjust* and *žïwjust* came into existence as is hypothesised above, problems regarding allomorph distribution, gender and paradigm class assignment can neatly be accounted for. As to a reason for the domain extension no exhaustive explanation could be offered, but at least part of this development might be due to the same factors. As to the semantics of the non-inherited domains, this remains unsatisfyingly elucidated.

Sorbisches Institut/Serbski institut, Cottbus/Chośebuz

ABBREVIATIONS

Dialects:		Grammatical terms:	
G	Gniva/Njïwa	A	accusative
O	Oseacco/Osoanë	G	genitive
S	Stolvizza/Solbica	D	dative
SG	San Giorgio/Bila	N	nominative
		sg	singular

NOTES

[1] The notation of the suffix and the lexemes cited is an abstraction of the actual dialectal realisations and is used as a convention for the purposes of this paper. Only occasionally cited forms provided with accent signs represent such actual realisations.

[2] A complete listing of lexemes in -(j)ust together with sources and meanings is given in the appendix.

[3] As the vowel alternations occurring in the derivational process do not deviate from those found elsewhere in the morphological system they are not discussed here.

[4] Also diachronically it is probably not deadjectival. The lexeme skärbnust, that is contained in the Christjanske uzhilo (2, 14), has the meanings 'effort, consent'. This semantical distance to skärbjust makes it likely that the latter lexeme is no innovative form of the former as the result of a development similar to the one mentioned for trüdjust.

[5] But not exclusively so, cf. skärbjust. However, a possibly competing lexeme skarbinjë 'worry' (a nonce proposed as a modern alternative for the archaic skärb) is derived as expected by means of deverbal -një.

[6] Note that this is another indication that substantives do consitute a domain of the derivation rule.

[7] See for a discussion of the former pairs Steenwijk 1998.

REFERENCES

Baudouin de Courtenay, Jan (ed.)
1913   Materialien zur südslavischen Dialektologie und Ethnographie III: Resianisches Sprachdenkmal "Christjanske uzhilo", Sanktpeterburg: Tipografija Imperatorskoj Akademii nauk.
Karničar, Ludwig
1990   Der Obir-Dialekt in Kärnten: Phonologie, Morphologie, Mikrotoponymie, Vulgonamen, Lexik, Texte (= Österreichische Akademie der Wissenschaften, Philosophisch-historische Klasse, Sitzungsberichte Bd. 551), Wien: Verlag der Österreichischen Akademie der Wissenschaften.
Kramaro, Jozef
1927   To kristjanske učilo po rozoanskeh, Gorica: Katoliška tiskarna.
Matičetov, Milko
1993   "Per un resiano grammaticalmente corretto", in: H. Steenwijk (ed.), Fondamenti per una grammatica pratica resiana: atti della conferenza internazionale tenutasi a Prato di Resia (UD) 11-12-13 dicembre 1991, Padova: CLEUP, pp. 67-84.

Steenwijk, Han
  1990   "The nominal declension of Friulian loans in the Slovene dialect of
            Val Resia", in: *Slovene Studies* 12/1, pp. 23-31.
(Steenwijk, Han)
  1998   "Einige Neologismen im Resianischen", to appear in: G. Spieß (ed.),
            *The Modernization of the Vocabulary of European Regional and Mi-
            nority Languages*, Tübingen: Gunter Narr Verlag.

APPENDIX: DATA

For all lexemes containing the suffix -*(j)ust* that were attested, up to three tokens from different text sources are cited in chronological order. A text source is any stretch of text that contains a lexeme under survey in a new context. These sources are indicated by abbreviations a list of which is added. Following the primary meanings and separated from them by a semicolon relatively recent semantic derivations are given. The tokens are preceded by a conventional form that is used for reference in the main text.

Formations only to be found in *Christjanske uzhilo* or *Kristjanske učilo* or that have been copied from them together with their context are not included here.

[*bilust*]: Gsg *biluste* Mat Can 455 'whiteness'
[*branjust*]: *bragniost* Lib can 3, *brenjost* Kon SFl 7, *braniust* AOC 68/2 (1995): 3 'salvation, security'
[*bratrust*]: *bràtrost* But-Mat 84 'brotherhood'
[*fwalust*]: *fualos* Flo-Mat 2 'praise'
[*jarust*]: *jaröst* Pet 95, Gsg *jarosta* Pet 115 'anger; hate'
[*lipust/lipjust*]: Gsg *lipuste* Mat Can 455, *lipjost* AOC 64/4 (1991): 7 'beauty'
[*lonust*]: *lonist* AOC 68/2 (1995): 3, *lonust* AOC 68/2 (1995): 11 'gratitude'
[*maluwridnust*]: *màluuridnost* But-Mat 85 'cowardice'
[*manjust*]: Gsg *megnuste* Mat Can 455 'courage' (The written form leaves room for the alternative interpretation *mо̄ćnust*, as *ọ́*, *ọ* are sometimes rendered by the grapheme *e*, cf. *žyviest* [*žị́wjọst* S], and non-prevocal *ć* is often represented by *g*, cf. *mognost*, by Resian authors. If 'courage' can be rephrased as 'confidence in one's strength', semantics do not preclude this interpretation.)

[*mladjust*]: Gsg *mlàdiustë* AOC 17/1 (1983): 4, Gsg *mladjoste* Roz kol 1991: 5, *mladjöst* AOC 69/2 (1996): 9 'youth'

[*móćnust/móćnjust*]: *mognost* But-Mat 85, *móćnost* BdC Tex 653, *móč'niust* AOC 16/3 (1982): 1 'power; security'

[*pamotjust*]: *pamotjost* Bog uča 3 'prudence'

[*punižnust*]: *bonižnost* AOC 23/4 (1984): 7, *punižnost* AOC 66/3 (1993): 7 'humility; humiliation'

[*rawnust*]: *raunost* Bog uča 2 (twice) 'justice'

[*risnust*]: *risnost* AOC 24/4 (1985): 1, *risnost* Roz kol 1990: 4, Lsg *risnostje* AOC 64/4 (1991): 7 'truth, reality'

[*salvanust*]: *salvànust* AOC 66/3 (1993): 7, *salvanust* AOC 68/2 (1995): 3 'salvation'

[*skärbjust*]: *skerbjosti* AOC 16/2 (1982): 1, *skrbjost* AOC 23/4 (1984): 7 'worry; exile'

[*skröwnust*]: Apl *scrounuste* Flo-Mat 1 'mystery'

[*smïlnust/smïlust*]: Apl *smilnoste* Flo-Mat 1, *zmylost* Mer Lju 388, *smilnost* AOC 15/3 (1981): 1 'compassion; benevolence'

[*starust/starjust*]: *stárust* BdC Opy 44, Isg *starustio* Mat Can 455, *starijöst* AOC 69/2 (1996): 9 'old age; antiques'

[*svetust*]: *svẹtost* BdC Tex 656 'holiness'

[*tožnust*]: *toshnost* But-Mat 86, *tožnost* Nov Sta 197, *tọ̈žnost* Caf-Ple II: 680 'sorrow; melancholy'

[*trüdjust*]: *trudjost* Roz kol 1989: 10, *trüdyjöst* AOC 69/2 (1996): 9, Isg *trüdjustjo* Pra lis 8 'tiredness; effort'

[*vësalust*]: *veselost* But-Mat 86, *vesilos* Flo-Mat 1, Lsg *veselosti* Roz uiž 116 'joy, bliss'

[*vïdust*]: Apl *viduste* Flo-Mat 1, Gsg *viduste* Flo-Mat 2 'face, sight'

[*wežjust*]: *uežost* Lib can 6, *uežjost* AOC 64/4 (1991): 7 'harmony'

[*zbüdjust*]: *zbudjost* AOC 64/4 (1991): 7 'awakening'

[*zdrawjust*]: *sdràujost* But-Mat 86, Gsg *strauiuste* Flo-Mat 2, *sdràuiust* AOC 16/3 (1982): 1 'health'

[*žalust*]: *salos* Flo-Mat 3, *žalust* Mer Lju 386 '??' (Corresponding to the Latin phrase *Quantus tremor est futurus* the Resian version of *Dies irae* has *Stra valek valika žalust.*)

[*žïwjust*]: *shiujost* Rez kat 4, *žíwjust* BdC Opy 97, *žyviest* Vas Ned 13 'life, livelihood'

390

SOURCES

AOC	*All'Ombra del Canin/Ta pod Ćanynowo sinco: bollettino parrocchiale di Resia.*
BdC Opy	Jan Baudouin de Courtenay: *Opyt fonetiki rez'janskich govorov*, Varšava-Peterburg: È. Vende i Ko. & D.E. Kožančikov, 1875.
BdC Tex	Jan Baudouin de Courtenay: *Materialien zur südslavischen Dialektologie und Ethnographie I: Resianische Texte*, St. Petersburg: Tipografija Imperatorskoj Akademii nauk, 1895.
Bog uča	*Bogave učanje zdrave tuo dušo*, Parrocchia di S. Maria Assunta, Rezija, Udine: Arti Grafiche Friulane.
But-Mat	Milko Matičetov & Gaetano Perusini: "Un dizionaretto e due Paternoster resiani inediti", in: *Ricerche Slavistiche* 4, 1955-56, pp. 76-87.
Caf-Ple	Maks Pleteršnik: *Slovensko-nemški slovar I-II*, Ljubljana 1894-95.
Flo-Mat	Luigia Di Floriano: *Prosegne roseansche*, dal suo quaderno trascritto da Milko Matičetov 16.6.1962.
Kon SFl	*Konsakraciun ut te nove carkvè ut svetaha Sin Florjene, Gniva/Dedicazione della nuova chiesa di S. Floriano, Gniva*, Parokia od svete Marije Asunte, Rezija/Parrocchia di S. Maria Assunta, Resia, 1991.
Lib can	*Libro dei canti*, Parrocchia di S. Maria Assunta, Resia, 1990.
Mat Can	Milko Matičetov: "Canzoni resiane: un foglio volante stampato a Gemona nel 1930", in: *Ce fastu?* 41-43 (1965-67), pp. 453-459.
Mer Lju	Pavle Merkù: *Ljudsko izročilo Slovencev v Italiji/Le tradizioni popolari degli sloveni in Italia*, Trst/Trieste: Založništvo tržaškega tiska/Editoriale Stampa Triestina, 1976.
Nov Sta	"Stabat mater", in: *Novice* 20/24, 1862, p. 197.
Pet	B. Petris (ed.): *Autori resiani*, Editrice Grillo, 1984.
Pra lis	*Ta prawä pravicä od lisïcä od Rezija/La vera storia della volpe di Resia*, a cura del Circolo Culturale Resiano "Rozajanski Dum", Tolmezzo: Treu Arti Grafiche, 1997.
Rez kat	Jan Baudouin de Courtenay (ed.): *Rez'janskij katichizis, kak priloženie k "Opytu fonetiki rez'janskich govorov"*, Varšava-Peterburg: È. Vende i Ko. & D.E. Kožančikov, 1875.
Roz kol	Silvana Paletti: *Rozajanske Kolindren*, 1989.
Roz uiž	*Te Rozajanske uiže/I Canti resiani*, a cura del Coro "Rože Majave", Tolmezzo: Treu Arti Grafiche, 1995.
Vas Ned	*Sred vasi*, aprile 1980, numero unico (progetto di rivista del Centro Studi Nediža).

Dutch Contributions to the Twelfth International Congress of Slavists,
Cracow, Linguistics (= Studies in Slavic and General Linguistics Vol 24),
391-428. RODOPI, Amsterdam - Atlanta, GA 1998.

O ŹRÓDŁACH TRADYCJI CERKIEWNOSŁOWIAŃSKIEJ
W POLSCE

HANNA TOBY

1. Wstęp

Jednym ze spornych zagadnień dotyczących spuścizny cyrylometodejskiej w Słowiańszczyźnie zachodniej jest tradycja cerkiewnosłowiańska w Polsce i jej udział w rozwoju kultury staropolskiej. Za-
sadniczą kwestią nurtującą badaczy jest znalezienie źródeł tej tradycji:
czy była ona bezpośrednią kontynuacją misji cyrylometodejskiej, czy też
może jedynie zjawiskiem późniejszym, odzwierciedlającym procesy
wtórne, które związane były z wpływami cerkiewnosłowiańskimi pro-
mieniującymi z sąsiadujących Czech i Rusi.

Szukanie pierwotnych źródeł tradycji cerkiewnosłowiańskiej sprowadza się przede wszystkim do zagadnienia istnienia w Polsce liturgii
słowiańskiej. W literaturze przedmiotu ścierają się głównie dwa stanowiska. Według pierwszego liturgia słowiańska dotarła do Polski już w
IX wieku w wyniku bezpośredniego działania misji morawskiej, czyli
stanowi ona bezpośrednią spuściznę Cyryla i Metodego. Zwolennicy
drugiego stanowiska wykluczają zaszczepienie liturgii słowiańskiej i
związanego z nią piśmiennictwa cerkiewnosłowiańskiego przez Metodego lub jego uczniów. Kwestionują oni wszelkie ewentualne ślady tradycji cerkiewnosłowiańskiej w Polsce przed w. XIV, kiedy to za pośrednictwem czeskim ufundowane zostały w Krakowie i Oleśnicy klasztory benedyktynów słowiańskich, lub też tłumaczą ślady tej tradycji
wcześniejszym pośrednictwem czeskim.

W niniejszym artykule podjęłam próbę podsumowania dotychczaso-
wego stanu wiedzy o źródłach tradycji cerkiewnosłowiańskiej w Polsce.
Zasadniczym celem tej pracy jest znalezienie odpowiedzi na pytanie, czy
polska tradycja cerkiewnosłowiańska jest, chociażby częściowo, tradycją
cyrylometodejską. Odpowiedzi tej będę szukać na polu historyczno-
archeologicznym i językowym. Artykuł ten nie porusza wpływów cer-

kiewnosłowiańskich, które przenikały z Rusi – badanie tych wpływów nie przyczynia się bowiem do poszukiwań pierwotnej genezy tradycji cerkiewnosłowiańskiej w Polsce. Są one stosunkowo późne i mają niewątpliwie wtórny charakter.[1] Termin "tradycja cerkiewnosłowiańska" rozumiany jest tutaj w szerokim ujęciu. Dotyczy on kontaktów Polski z liturgią słowiańską i piśmiennictwem cerkiewnosłowiańskim oraz śladów języka scs. w słownictwie polskim.

Biorąc pod uwagę uwarunkowanie geograficzne Polski, za teoretycznie możliwe możemy przyjąć przenikanie tradycji cerkiewnosłowiańskiej z sąsiadujących ziem czeskich i ruskich, oraz wcześniejsze, bezpośrednie przejęcie tradycji scs. przez południową Małopolskę z państwa wielkomorawskiego. Związki kulturowe łączące Polskę z Czechami i Rusią potwierdzają wpływy wtórne. Czy dysponujemy dzisiaj dostatecznymi podstawami, aby twierdzić, że pierwotnym źródłem tradycji cerkiewnosłowiańskiej w Polsce była misja morawska, innymi słowy – czy polska tradycja cerkiewnosłowiańska jest tradycją cyrylometodejską?

2. Pośrednictwo czeskie

2.1 Hipotetyczne pośrednictwo czeskie w IX-X w.

W literaturze przedmiotu, szczególnie polskiej i czeskiej, powszechnie podkreśla się rolę Czech w przekazywaniu Polsce tradycji cerkiewnosłowiańskiej już w IX-X wieku. Losy Czech Przemyślidów łączone są z historią Wielkich Moraw[2] – po ich upadku w Czechach kontynuowana byłaby tradycja cyrylometodejska i stamtąd przenikałaby do południowej Polski, która przed 945 r. znajdowała się częściowo pod panowaniem czeskim.

Badania historiograficzne i filologiczne hipotezy tej nie potwierdzają. Na podstawie tekstów średniowiecznych[3] większość badaczy czeskich, a za nimi polskich zakłada, że początki chrześcijaństwa w Czechach związane są z morawską działalnością Metodego. Liturgia słowiańska i piśmiennictwo scs. istniałyby w Czechach przed działalnością klasztoru sazawskiego (klasztor ten działał w okresie 1032-1096/97, z przerwą w latach 1055-1061). Fakt, że źródła te mają charakter literacki i nie są współczesne opisywanym w nich wydarzeniom historycznym, kwestionuje w dużym stopniu ich obiektywność. Nie możemy wykluczyć, że część zawartej w nich informacji jest interpolacją. Słuszne wydają się uwagi de Vincenza (1988), który podkreśla, że śladów misji morawskiej w Czechach należy szukać jedynie w tych źródłach pisanych, o których istnieje absolutna pewność, że powstały w okresie działalności misji morawskiej. Warunki te spełnia bawarska kronika łacińska Annales Fuldenses, która nie zawiera jednak jakichkolwiek wzmianek o przejęciu chrześcijaństwa w wyniku misji metodejskiej, lecz w wyniku misji bawarskiej (845 r.). Wzmianek o chrystianizacji Czech w duchu cyrylometodejskim nie ma także w Żywocie Konstantyna i, jak można by oczekiwać, w Żywocie Metodego (Graus 1971: 168).

Biliturgiczności Czech w okresie przedsazawskim nie poświadczają też badania filologiczne. Przedmiotem analizy językowej są głównie teksty zachowane w redakcjach ruskich i chorwackich, w mniejszym stopniu serbskich i bułgarskich (część z nich jest późna, pochodząca nawet z XII-XVI w.).[4] Trudno jest ustalić, które z nich rzeczywiście są proweniencji czeskiej, i jeżeli tak, czy pochodzą one (lub ich ewentualny pierwowzór) z okresu przedsazawskiego. Jednakże nawet Mszał kijowski i Fragmenty praskie bywają niesłusznie przyjmowane za pewny dowód istnienia bezpośredniej kontynuacji tradycji cyrylometodejskiej w Czechach, gdyż ich czas i miejsce powstania są sporne (por. Birnbaum 1985: 59, Tóth 1993: 199, Eggers 1996: 114-118).

Bezpośredniej kontynuacji morawskiej tradycji scs. w Czechach nie potwierdza też kult świętych – Cyryla i Metodego. Jest on jest zjawiskiem późnym (zostali oni uznani patronami Czech w 1347 r.) i związany jest z wtórnymi wpływami cerkiewnosłowiańskimi z Chorwacji. Brak jest jakichkolwiek dowodów kultu Cyryla i Metodego w Czechach w okresie wcześniejszym (Graus 1971: 183, Eggers 1996: 119-120).

Ze względu na brak jednoznacznych dowodów potwierdzających istnienie liturgii słowiańskiej (i piśmiennictwa scs.) w Czechach Przemyślidów w IX i X wieku, założenie, że liturgia słowiańska przeniknęła w tym okresie do Polski z biliturgicznych Czech pozostaje jedynie hipotezą nie popartą materiałem dowodowym. Dostępne nam dzisiaj materiały źródłowe potwierdzają słowa Jagicia, który scharakteryzował pozycję liturgii słowiańskiej w Czechach tymi słowy: "Da war sie immer nur eine zarte Zimmerpflanze, die bei jedem rauheren Windhauch Schaden leiden mußte" (Jagić 1913[2]: 108).

2.2 Polsko-czeskie kontakty kulturalne

Intensywne związki kulturowe między Polską i Czechami, zapoczątkowane pośrednictwem czeskim w procesie chrystianizacji ziem polskich w obrządku łacińskim, stanowiły podatny grunt do przenikania do

Polski niektórych elementów tradycji cerkiewnosłowiańskiej. Mam tu na myśli słownictwo pochodzenia scs., które obecne było w zasobie języka staroczeskiego oraz pośrednictwo czeskie w założeniu klasztorów benedyktynów słowiańskich w południowej Polsce w XIV wieku. Sprowadzane do Polski czeskie duchowieństwo łatwo mogło wypełniać· obowiązki katechizacyjne, gdyż różnice między językami staropolskim i staroczeskim były wtedy niewielkie i nowa terminologia chrześcijańska przynoszona przez misjonarzy czeskich była w Polsce stosunkowo łatwo przyswajalna. O tym, jak silny był wpływ kleru czeskiego w procesie chrystianizacji kraju, świadczy ilość czeskich zapożyczeń wyrazowych. Według Klicha (1927: 147) około 77% polskiej zapożyczonej terminologii chrześcijańskiej ma formę zgodną z językiem czeskim, co wskazywałoby na jej czeską proweniencję. Są to przede wszystkim terminy religijne pochodzenia łacińsko-greckiego, zapożyczone przez język czeski bezpośrednio lub częściej za pośrednictwem średnio-wysoko-niemieckiego (np. łac. *pater noster* > stczes. *páteř* > stpol. *pacierz*, łac. *episcopus* > śrwniem. *biscof* > stczes. *biskup* > stpol. *biskup*). Małą grupę zapożyczeń, które przeniknęły do polszczyzny za pośrednictwem czeskim stanowią wyrazy o etymologii scs., np. scs. *bogorodica* > stczes. *bohorodičě* > stpol. *bogurodica*. Zapożyczenia te udokumentowane są w staropolszczyźnie poczynając od wieku XIV, lecz najprawdopodobniej przyjęte zostały wcześniej — w opinii Milewskiego w wieku X (1965: 19), według Havránka przed połową XI wieku (1956: 304). Zakłada się więc, że słownictwo to przeniknęło do polszczyzny w wyniku czeskiego pośrednictwa w okresie chrystianizacji Polski, czyli zasadniczo w okresie, w którym istnienie tradycji cyrylometodejskiej w Czechach nie jest udowodnione. Jednakże nawet brak tej tradycji w Czechach przed 1032 r. i czeska rola pośrednika w pożyczkach z języka scs. nie wykluczają się wzajemnie. Język czeski mógł mieć wtedy w swoim zasobie słownikowym wyrazy pochodzenia scs., gdyż występowanie ich w czeszczyźnie nie musi być związane z kontynuacją morawskiej tradycji cyrylometodejskiej.[5] Czeskie wyrazy pochodzenia scs. mogły z kolei zostać przejęte przez język polski wraz z inną terminologią religijną w okresie przyjmowania chrześcijaństwa i utrwalić się później (od ca. drugiej połowy XIV w.) w wyniku oddziaływania czeskiej literatury religijnej na polską. Wiele zapożyczeń przeniknęło najprawdopodobniej do polszczyzny drogą tłumaczeń, które bardzo często wykazują silne czeskie zależności tekstowe (np. Psałterz floriański, Biblia królowej Zofii). Słownictwo pochodzenia scs. przejęte za pośrednictwem czeskim nie dowodzi istnienia w Polsce liturgii słowiańskiej, lecz odzwierciedla czeskie wpływy językowe. Wszelkie próby rekonstrukcji procesu chrystianizacji Polski, w której dużą rolę odgrywałby wprowadzony przez Czechów język scs., będący nawet według Havránka oficjalnym językiem Kościoła w Gnieźnie (Havránek 1956: 304), są czysto spekulatywne i opierają się głównie na hipotezie bilíturgiczności Czech przed okresem sazawskim.

Nie pozostało bez echa w Polsce także czeskie odrodzenie liturgii słowiańskiej. W latach 1380 i 1390 ufundowano klasztory benedyktynów słowiańskich (głagolaszy) w Oleśnicy i w Krakowie na Kleparzu na wzór praskiego Emaus. Sprowadzeni z Pragi chorwaccy głagolasze przynieśli ze sobą piśmiennictwo głagolickie i cerkiewnosłowiański język liturgiczny chorwackiej redakcji. Obydwie fundacje okazały się krótkotrwałe: klasztor krakowski przetrwał do lat 1470-1480, oleśnicki – do 1505 roku.

3. Hipoteza o bezpośrednim kontakcie Polski z piśmiennictwem scs. Kwestia istnienia liturgii słowiańskiej w Polsce

Po raz pierwszy hipoteza zakładająca istnienie w Polsce liturgii słowiańskiej została wysunięta i naukowo opracowana w 1786 r. przez Ch. G. von Friese. W wieku XIX podtrzymywana była m.in. przez historyków: J. Bandtkiego, A. Bielowskiego, J. Lelewela i M. Gumplowicza. Zainteresowanie zagadnieniem liturgii słowiańskiej w Polsce wzrosło po II wojnie światowej, kiedy to za jej istnieniem opowiadało się wielu badaczy, jak np. Widajewicz (1947, 1948), Dvorník (1949, 1962, 1970), Umiński (1953), Paszkiewicz (1954), Havránek (1956), Lanckorońska (1954, 1961), Milewski (1965), Łowmiański (1970). Negatywnie ustosunkowali się przede wszystkim: Szcześniak (1904), Lehr-Spławiński (1932, 1961a, 1961b, 1961c, 1961d, 1961e, 1968), Szymański (1963), de Vincenz (1982 [1984], 1983), Urbańczyk (1988) i Eggers (1996).

W wielu pracach uderza błędne użycie terminów "liturgia słowiańska" i "obrządek słowiański", gdzie obydwa pojęcia przyjmowane są za synonimy. Termin "obrządek słowiański" implikuje w ujęciu Szymańskiego (1963: 41) istnienie odrębnej od łacińskiej, zhierarchizowanej słowiańskiej organizacji kościelnej oraz odrębnego rytuału. "Liturgia słowiańska" oznacza jedynie użycie cerkiewnosłowiańskiego języka liturgicznego,[6] jednakże w wielu przypadkach nazywana jest obrządkiem słowiańskim. Opierając się na definicji Szymańskiego, pojęcie "obrządek" uzasadnione jest jedynie w tych hipotezach, które zakładają istnienie w Polsce odrębnej metropolii słowiańskiej, niezależnej od metropolii

396

łacińskiej (np. Umiński 1953, Lanckorońska 1954, 1961, Paszkiewicz 1954). Koncepcje takie są bardzo śmiałe, gdyż współistnienie słowiańskiej i łacińskiej hierarchii episkopalnej nie jest poświadczone ani na Morawach, ani w Czechach.

Hipotezy o istnieniu w Polsce liturgii słowiańskiej różnią się w szczegółach, lecz wszystkie przyjmują jej oddziaływanie w średniowiecznej Polsce przed końcem XIV wieku (kiedy to ufundowano klasztory benedyktynów słowiańskich w, Krakowie i Oleśnicy).

Zakłada się, że liturgia słowiańska mogła zostać wprowadzona do Polski (przed 1380 r.) w następujących okresach:

1. Już w wieku IX, w wyniku bezpośredniej działalności misji morawskiej na terenie Małopolski.
2. W wieku X, w rezultacie panowania czeskiego w Małopolsce i na Śląsku (zakładając, że biliturgiczni Czesi założyli na tych terenach słowiańskie ośrodki liturgiczne).
3. Poczynając od 966 roku, w wyniku chrystianizacji Polski za pośrednictwem biliturgicznych Czech.

Jak starałam się wykazać wcześniej, pośrednictwo Kościoła czeskiego w zaszczepieniu w Polsce liturgii słowiańskiej w X wieku nie jest uzasadnione źródłowo. Jednocześnie bezsprzeczna jest czeska działalność misyjna, wprowadzająca do Polski chrześcijaństwo z liturgią łacińską.

Zdecydowana większość badaczy przyjmuje jednak za pierwotne źródło liturgii słowiańskiej misję metodejską w Małopolsce (m.in. Umiński, Widajewicz, Lanckorońska, Dvorník, Milewski, Rospond). W ich przekonaniu kontakty Polski z Czechami (co jest dla nich jednoznaczne z przenikaniem stamtąd wpływów piśmiennictwa cerkiewnosłowiańskiego) utwierdziły i podtrzymały zaszczepioną przez misję morawską tradycję cyrylometodejską.

Ze względu na dużą rozbieżność zdań dotyczących kwestii istnienia liturgii słowiańskiej w Polsce, przedstawione tu zostaną najważniejsze i najczęściej przytaczane argumenty mające dowodzić słuszności tej tezy. Podstawy te mają charakter historyczny, archeologiczny i językowy.

3.1 Argumenty historyczne

Ponieważ zagadnienie liturgii słowiańskiej w średniowiecznej Polsce zajmowało głównie historyków, najbardziej rozbudowaną i do tej pory najobszerniej opracowaną podbudową tej hipotezy jest analiza historyczna. W swojej argumentacji zwolennicy hipotezy opierają się na ciągle tych samych przekazach źródłowych, mających służyć za dowód historyczny istnienia w Polsce liturgii słowiańskiej. Do najważniejszych należą:

1. Fragment z rozdziału XI Żywotu Metodego.
2. Ustęp w liście biskupów bawarskich do papieża Jana IX z 900 r.
3. Lista z katalogu biskupów krakowskich, według której najstarszymi biskupami w Krakowie byli *Prochorus* i *Proculphus*.
4. Denary króla polskiego Bolesława Chrobrego (992-1025) z napisanym cyrylicą imieniem *Boleslavъ*.
5. Fragment pieśni żałobnej autorstwa kronikarza Galla Anonima na śmierć Bolesława Chrobrego (1025).
6. Wzmianka w kronice tegoż Galla o dwóch metropolitach.
7. List księżnej szwabskiej Matyldy do Mieszka II.
8. Wzmianka Rocznika kapituły krakowskiej o śmierci dwóch arcybiskupów polskich w latach 1027-1028.
9. Pochodzący z XIV w. kalendarz wiślicki, w którym wymienione jest imię św. Gorazda.
10. Kult św. Cyryla i Metodego w Polsce, poświadczony w późnośredniowiecznych mszałach i brewiarzach.

W kolejnych punktach omówię pokrótce wymienione powyżej podstawy źródłowe. Główna uwaga zostanie skoncentrowana na możliwości ich różnorodnej interpretacji.

(1) Fragment z Żywotu Metodego:

"Poganьskъ kъnęzь silьnъ velьmi, sědę vъ Vislě [w niektórych odpisach "vъ Vislěxъ"– H.T.] rọgaaše sę xristьjanomъ i pakosti dějaaše. Posъlavъ że kъ njemu reče: dobro ti sę krъstiti, synu, voljejọ svojejọ na svojeji zemli, da ne plěnjenъ nọdьmi krъštenъ bọdeši na štuždei zemli, i pomęneši mę; ježe i bystъ" (por. Lehr-Spławiński 1959: 115).

Ta wzmianka hagiograficzna, dopuszczająca różne warianty interpretacyjne, stanowi dla większości badaczy kluczowy dowód wczesnej chrystianizacji Polski w duchu cyrylometodejskim. Na podstawie tego fragmentu kreślony bywa najczęściej następujący przebieg wydarzeń: Do silnego pogańskiego księcia państwa plemiennego Wiślan (z centrum w Wiślicy, ewentualnie w leżącym nad Wisłą Krakowie), który prześladował chrześcijan, przybyło poselstwo Metodego wzywające go do przyjęcia chrześcijaństwa. Ponieważ książę Wiślan tego dobrowolnie nie uczynił, proroctwo Metodego spełniło się. Wzięty do niewoli książę przyjął pod przymusem chrzest na obcej ziemi (czyli z rąk Metodego w państwie wielkomorawskim), a w podbitym przez Świętopełka kraju Wiślan, które przyłączone zostało do Moraw, wprowadzono chrześcijaństwo z liturgią słowiańską.

Zdarzenia te miały według Milewskiego (1965: 9-10) miejsce mniej więcej między rokiem 875 (w którym Milewski zakłada przybycie do państwa Wiślan poselstwa Metodego) a rokiem 885 (śmierć Metodego), zaś do podbicia państwa Wiślan i jego chrystianizacji doszłoby najprawdopodobniej około 880 roku (ibidem: 10), czy też w latach 877-878 (Vlasto 1970: 136). Taka rekonstrukcja wydarzeń stanowi punkt wyjścia w argumentacji u zdecydowanej większości zwolenników tej hipotezy. Lanckorońska (1961: 11), a za nią Milewski (1965: 9-10) i Rospond (1968: 132) posuwają się w swojej interpretacji jeszcze dalej, gdyż nie wykluczają oni zakorzenienia się chrześcijaństwa wśród Wiślan jeszcze przed przymusowym chrztem księcia. Do takich swobodnych interpretacji fragmentu Żywotu Metodego najbardziej krytycznie ustosunkowują się Lehr-Spławiński (1932, 1961a, 1961b, 1961c, 1961d, 1961e, 1968), de Vincenz (1982 [1984], 1983), Leśny (1982 [1984]) i Urbańczyk (1988). Chociaż Lehr-Spławiński, w przeciwieństwie do de Vincenza, nie kwestionuje faktu nawrócenia podbitego państwa Wiślan, przeciwny jest jednoznacznej interpretacji zakładającej, że zaszczepiona tam liturgia była liturgią słowiańską. Według niego z Moraw mogło dotrzeć chrześcijaństwo z liturgią łacińską, gdyż: "[...] na Morawach działało także duchowieństwo z sufraganem Wichingiem na czele – mogło więc ono rozciągnąć swoje wpływy na kraj podbity" (1954: 158). De Vincenz (1983: 646) wskazuje też na możliwość interwencji innego sąsiadującego państwa chrześcijańskiego, np. Czech czy Niemiec. Według niego analiza tekstu pozwala jedynie na wysuwanie wniosku o konflikcie, prawdopodobnie małopolskiego księcia z chrześcijanami, a nie o podboju i chrzcie jego kraju.

(2) Ustęp w liście biskupów bawarskich do papieża Jana IX z 900 r. zawiera informację o wysłaniu sufragana niemieckiego Wichinga z misją do nowo nawróconego ludu:

"Anteccesor vester Zuentibaldo duce imperante, Wichingum consecravit episcopum et nequaquam in illum antiquum Pataviensem episcopatum eum transmisit, sed in quandam neophitam gentem, quam ipse dux bello domuit et ex paganis christianos esse paravit" (por. Widajewicz 1947: 72).

Dla zwolenników hipotezy o istnieniu liturgii słowiańskiej w Polsce przekaz ten stanowi znakomite uzupełnienie wiadomości zawartych w Żywocie Metodego. Jako pierwszy Widajewicz (1947: 72-74) identyfikuje Wiślan, podbitych przez Świętopełka z "neophita gens", do którego wysłano sufragana bawarskiego Wichinga. Rospond posuwa się w swoich rozważaniach jeszcze dalej. Chociaż wszelkie informacje źródłowe przekazują, że Wiching był przeciwnikiem liturgii słowiańskiej, Rospond (1968b: 134), interpretując jego imię jako słowiańskie Vich, Vichinus (z łacińskim przyrostkiem -inus), które byłoby skrótem morawskiego imienia Witosław, kwestionuje tym samym jego pochodzenie niemieckie oraz związek z liturgią łacińską.

Lehr-Spławiński (1961c) odrzuca interpretację Dąbrowskiego (1958) opartą na informacji zawartej w bulli papieskiej z 880 roku, zakładającą wysłanie Wichinga do Nitry. Ze wzmianki tej wynikałoby, że nowo nawróconym ludem byli Słowacy. Silnym argumentem Lehra-Spławińskiego przeciwko teorii Dąbrowskiego jest fakt, że w 900 r. mieszkańcy ziemi nitrzańskiej nie mogli być neofitami w świeżo pokonanym kraju, gdyż Nitra została przyłączona do państwa morawskiego już w 833 roku, zaś chrześcijaństwo w Nitrze poświadczone jest w drugiej ćwierci IX w. De Vincenz (1982 [1984]: 73) zgadza się z poglądem Dąbrowskiego, zaś sprzeczności faktograficzne tłumaczy niedokładnością zawartą w liście biskupów. Wskazuje on także na błąd metodyczny interpretacji Widajewicza: hipoteza o wysłaniu Wichinga do Małopolski jest bowiem oparta na hipotezie, że Małopolska jest chrześcijańska. Eggers (1996: 59) zwraca uwagę na przypuszczenie Dąbrowskiej (1970), która zauważa, że nowo nawróconym ludem nitrzańskim nie musieli być wcale Słowacy, lecz pozostałości plemienia awarsko-bułgarskiego mieszkającego w regionie Nitry.

(3) Lista z katalogu biskupów krakowskich (pochodząca z XIII w., prawdopodobnie odpis wcześniejszego oryginału) wymienia imiona dwóch biskupów: Prochor i Prokulf (Prochorus i Proculpus). Obaj biskupi umieszczeni są na liście przed arcybiskupem Popponem, o którym poświadczają inne źródła historyczne, że był w 1000 roku pierwszym biskupem krakowskim. Widajewicz (1948) wskazał na fakt, że imię Prohor (właściwie Prochor) jest pochodzenia greckiego (por. grec. Πρόχορος), zaś Prokulf – niemieckiego. W osobie Prochora widzi on więc powiązania bizantyjsko-słowiańskie, zaś Kraków łączy z siedzibą metropolii słowiańskiej, założoną w Krakowie jeszcze przed metropolią "łacińską". Metropolia ta istniałaby jedynie kilka lat; utrzymałaby się naj-

wyżej do śmierci Metodego w 885 roku, gdyż: "[...] za życia jego ten tylko obrządek przenikać mógł do Wiślan" (Widajewicz 1947: 114). Rządy obu biskupów przypadałyby więc według Widajewicza na koniec w. IX. Prochor byłby tam pierwszym biskupem ordynariuszem podległym metropolii morawskiej, a po upadku liturgii słowiańskiej na Morawach Prokulf usunąłby ze swojej diecezji krakowskiej liturgię słowiańską, zastępując ją łacińską (por. Lehr-Spławiński 1961c: 72). Łowmiański wskazuje na błędność wysuwania wniosków opierających się na etymologii, gdyż obydwa te imiona znane są nie tylko w Bizancjum, lecz także we Włoszech. Przypuszcza on, że Prochor i Prokulf oznaczają jedną i tę samą osobę (1970: 500-501).

De Vincenz (1982 [1984]: 73) zakłada, że w katalogu tym doszło do kompilacji, gdzie imiona biskupów zaczerpnięte zostały z tekstu nie mającego nic wspólnego z Krakowem, lub też, że chodzi tam o dwa warianty tego samego imienia. Labuda (1984), opierając się na silnej podstawie źródłowej, tzw. Roczniku Traskim, poświadczającym okres funkcjonowania Prochora na lata 970-986, a Prokulfa na lata 986-995, wyklucza możliwość ich działalności w IX w. i wszelkie związki z misją morawską. Według Labudy, którego stanowisko podziela Urbańczyk (1988: 342-344), byli oni najprawdopodobniej biskupami ołomunieckimi, gdyż Kraków, wchodzący w tym okresie w skład państwa czeskiego, podlegał jurysdykcyjnie diecezji w Ołomuńcu.

(4) Na podstawie znalezionych 10 monet Bolesława Chrobrego z inskrypcją cyrylicką wysuwa się przypuszczenia, że język scs. równolegle z łaciną, pełnił w Polsce w czasie panowania Chrobrego (992-1025) funkcję oficjalną. Ponieważ w Polsce średniowiecznej monety były wybijane przez mennice biskupie, denary te mogłyby służyć za poszlakę dla hipotezy o istnieniu w Krakowie słowiańskiej hierarchii kościelnej (Milewski 1965: 15). Milewski odrzuca krytykę Lehra-Spławińskiego, wskazującą na fakt, że inskrypcje są cyrylickie, zaś (hipotetyczne) cerkiewnosłowiańskie piśmiennictwo w Polsce posługiwałoby się głagolicą (Lehr-Spławiński 1932: 6). Według Milewskiego to właśnie cyrylica była pismem inskrypcyjnym, a znajomość jej mogła już na początku X w. dotrzeć do Polski. Możliwe jest jednak wybicie tych monet w Kijowie (opanowanym czasowo przez Chrobrego) lub w rejonie tzw. Grodów Czerwieńskich, terenów ruskich włączonych do ziem polskich na początku XI wieku.

(5) Fragment Carmen lugubre Galla Anonima na śmierć Bolesława Chrobrego:

"Tanti viri funus mecum omnis homo recole
Dives, pauper, miles, clerus, insuper agricole,
Latinorum et Slauorum quotquot estis incole"
(por. Michałowska 1996²: 125).

Najbardziej powszechna interpretacja tego fragmentu zakłada, że zmarłego króla opłakiwali wszyscy mieszkańcy kraju, niezależnie od ich bogactwa, stanu i języka liturgicznego. "Latinorum et Slauorum" nie musi jednak, według opinii Lehra-Spławińskiego (1961b: 59) oznaczać przedstawicieli obrządku łacińskiego i słowiańskiego, lecz cudzoziemców posługujących się łaciną oraz Polaków mówiących językiem słowiańskim (czyli polskim). Boba nie wyklucza, że opłakującymi byli katoliccy Polacy i ortodoksyjni Rosjanie zamieszkujący zdobyte przez Chrobrego ziemie wschodnie (Boba 1973: 970, Eggers 1996: 133).

(6)   W Kronice Galla Anonima zawarta jest także wzmianka o dwóch metropolitach: "[...] suo tempore Polonia duos metropolitanos cum suis suffraganeis continebat" (por. Lehr-Spławiński 1961b: 59).

Kronika Galla jest jedynym źródłem historycznym, polskim i obcym (oprócz wzmianki w kronice Kadłubka, opierającej się na tekście Anonima), zawierającym informację o istnieniu dwóch metropolitów w Polsce. Według hipotezy o liturgii słowiańskiej, a w tym wypadku nawet o obrządku, jednym z arcybiskupów byłby metropolita słowiański zasiadający w Małopolsce. Lehr-Spławiński, kwestionujący w swoich artykułach większość argumentów przytaczanych jako dowody istnienia liturgii słowiańskiej w Polsce, także w tej kwestii ustosunkowany jest negatywnie. Widzi on (1961b: 60) duże prawdopodobieństwo, że drugim metropolitą był przebywający w Polsce w czasie panowania Bolesława Chrobrego arcybiskup misyjny św. Bruno z Kwefurtu, lub też arcybiskup krakowski Aron z okresu późniejszego (1046-1059). Dziewulski (1965: 43) tłumaczy wzmiankę Galla tym, że: "[...] terytorium podległe Chrobremu należało pod względem kościelnym do dwóch metropolii: gnieźnieńskiej (macierzyste ziemie polskie) i moguckiej (Morawy oraz – przez bardzo krótki zresztą czas należące do państwa Chrobrego – Czechy)". Według Łowmiańskiego (1970: 496, 1971: 8) drugą metropolią była metropolia kijowska.

(7)   W liście księżnej szwabskiej Matyldy do Mieszka II, pochodzącym z okresu 1025-1034, podkreślona jest jego znajomość trzech języków:

"Quis in laudem Dei totidem coadunavit linguas? Cum in propria et in latina Deum digne venerari posses, in hoc tibi non satis graecum superaddere maluisti" (por. Milewski 1965: 17).

Umiejętności Mieszka II do modlitwy w językach "własnym", łacińskim i greckim mają być świadectwem ścisłych związków Polski z kulturą bizantyjsko-słowiańską. Dvorník (1949: 253) interpretuje *in propria* jako staro-cerkiewno-słowiański: "Since the lady was referring to divine worship, "your own tongue" could only mean the Old Slavonic". Za argument uzupełniający uważa się ofiarowany Mieszkowi przez Matyldę Ordus Romanus, co przekonuje wielu badaczy, że chodzi tu nie tylko o języki, lecz o obrządki. Umiński (1953: 16) wnioskuje nawet, że w liście Matyldy mowa jest nie tylko o obrządku słowiańskim i łacińskim, lecz także o bizantyjskim. Lehr-Spławiński (1932: 7) podkreśla, że w liście wyliczone są jedynie języki, którymi władał Mieszko, zaś język *in propria* to jego własny język, czyli polski. Interpretacja taka budzi sprzeciwy innych badaczy, gdyż w liście będącym pochwałą wysokiego wykształcenia króla, nie chwalono by jego znajomości języka ojczystego (de Vincenz 1982 [1984]: 74). Według de Vincenza, który kategorycznie odrzuca hipotezę o istnieniu liturgii słowiańskiej w Polsce, list ten mógłby być jedynym, chociaż wątpliwym dowodem na jej istnienie, lecz nie w rezultacie misji morawskiej w Małopolsce, a w rezultacie misji czeskiej (1982 [1984]: 76).

(8) W Roczniku kapituły krakowskiej zawarta jest następująca informacja:

"1027 Ipolitus archiepiscopus obiit, Bossuta successit.
1028 Stephanus archiepiscopus obiit" (por. Umiński 1953: 18).

Podobnie jak fragment Galla Anonima o dwóch metropolitach, wzmianka o prawie równoczesnej śmierci dwóch arcybiskupów, i to w okresie panowania wspomnianego wyżej Mieszka II, stanowi przesłankę do hipotezy o istnieniu na ziemiach polskich dwóch metropolii. Zwraca się tu uwagę na małe prawdopodobieństwo, aby w ciągu dwu lat kalendarzowych aż trzy osoby sprawowały funkcję arcybiskupa. Dla zwolenników hipotezy o liturgii słowiańskiej w Polsce bardziej logicznym wydaje się uzasadnienie tego faktu istnieniem słowiańskiej hierarchii kościelnej w Polsce. Wzmianka w roczniku dotyczyłaby więc śmierci przedstawicieli dwóch odrębnych stolców arcybiskupich – obrządku łacińskiego i słowiańskiego. Dvorník (1970: 200) dodaje jeszcze jeden argument: imię jednego z metopolitów – *Hipolit* – nawiązywałoby do wpływów bizantyjskich. Vlasto (1970: 137) kwestionuje słuszność takiej interpretacji. Zwraca on uwagę na fakt, że imię to znane jest także w Bawarii oraz podkreśla chaos w dokumentach rocznika, które w innym miejscu przypisują dwóch biskupów arcydiecezji gnieźnieńskiej.

(9) Podczas okupacji hitlerowskiej Zathey znalazł w zbiorach Biblioteki Narodowej w Warszawie fragmenty kalendarza polskiego pochodzącego z biblioteki Wikariuszy w Wiślicy. Kalendarz ten, powstały według Zatheya (1949) w wieku XIV i stanowiący najprawdopodobniej odpis wcześniejszego oryginału, był jedynym zabytkiem polskim, w którym dzień 17 lipca zaznaczony został jako dzień liturgiczny św. Gorazda. Na podstawie tego zapamiętanego szczegółu z kalendarza (który spłonął w czasie powstania warszawskiego w 1944 r.) Zathey wskazał na możliwość istnienia w Małopolsce kultu św. Gorazda, oficjalnego następcy Metodego na Morawach. Święto liturgiczne Gorazda byłoby według Zatheya (1949: 77) pozostałością tradycji z okresu wcześniejszego. Fakt, że kalendarz ten pochodzi z tej samej Wiślicy, z którą łączony jest fragment o chrzcie księcia z Żywotu Metodego (vъ Vislě/ Vislěxъ jest najczęściej identyfikowane z Wiślicą), daje przesłanki do jeszcze śmielszych hipotez. Lanckorońska (1961: 19) i Dvorník (1970: 198) zakładają, że Gorazd po wygnaniu z Wielkich Moraw przybył do państwa Wiślan, gdzie pełnił funkcję pierwszego metropolity morawskiego na ziemiach polskich. Dittrich (1962: 307) nie wyklucza działalności Gorazda w Małopolsce między rokiem 886 a 898.

Imię św. Gorazda w kalendarzu wiślickim tłumaczone być może jednak wpływami z Czech. Lehr-Spławiński wiąże je z benedyktyńskim klasztorem na Kleparzu (1961b: 63), Szymański (1963: 46-47) – z udokumentowaną działalnością czeskiego kanonika w Wiślicy w latach 1352-1368. Eggers (1996: 135), który sceptycznie ustosunkowuje się do wartości tego dowodu historycznego, opartego jedynie na zapamiętanym (czyli niesprawdzalnym) szczególe, wskazuje na interpretację Boby (1973: 971), zakładającą pomyłkę Zatheya. Boba przyjmuje możliwość, że w rzeczywistości imię wspomniane w kalendarzu brzmiało Zvorad (łaciński wariant imienia Świ(e)rard). Święty ten był znany powszechnie w południowej Polsce, Słowacji i północnych Węgrzech.

(10) Także fakt, że Cyryl i Metody uznani zostali w XVI w. za patronów diecezji gnieźnieńskiej oraz modlitwa w późnośredniowiecznym brewiarzu nostrosque apostolos et patronos[7] bywają przyjmowane za dowód istnienia w IX wieku w Polsce misji morawskiej. Na podstawie opracowanej przez Schenka (1982 [1984]) historii kultu braci sołuńskich

w Polsce wnioskować można, że kult ten przeniknął do Polski z terenów czesko-morawskich. Pierwsze polskie teksty liturgiczne o Cyrylu i Metodym zawarte są w Mszale krakowskim z lat 1410-20, zaś statuty synodalne zawierają wzmianki o liturgicznym obchodzie ich święta (9 marca) od roku 1436. Na Morawach kult ten poświadczony jest już od początku wieku XIV, a w Czechach od założenia klasztoru Emaus. W wyniku bliskich kontaktów kulturalnych polsko-czeskich kult Cyryla i Metodego przedostał się najprawdopodobniej (drogą tłumaczeń kazań i brewiarzy czeskich) do Polski. Schenk (ibidem: 60) zauważa także, że pierwsze i jedyne trzy kościoły polskie pod wezwaniem tych świętych powstały dopiero w 1873 (prawosławny) oraz w latach 1926 i 1936 (rzymskokatolickie).

Omówione powyżej, najczęściej przytaczane w dyskusji argumenty historyczne istnienia liturgii słowiańskiej w Polsce nie potwierdzają. Broniąc słuszności hipotezy, jej zwolennicy wskazują również na wiele innych przesłanek pośrednich (np. wezwania niektórych kościołów polskich, legendy, teksty ruskie). Najbardziej rozbudowaną argumentację opartą na takich przesłankach podjęła Lanckorońska (1954, 1961), wywody której zostały poddane ostrej krytyce przez Lehra-Spławińskiego (1961b), Szymańskiego (1963) i Dziewulskiego (1965). Na przesłankach pośrednich oparte są też hipotezy Paszkiewicza (1954) i Łowmiańskiego (1970, 1971).

3.2 Argumenty archeologiczne

W 1949 roku podjęto w Wiślicy badania archeologiczne, wyniki których dowodzą istnienia tam w średniowieczu dużego ośrodka kościelnego. Przez wiele lat większość archeologów datowała część znalezisk na wiek IX. Interpretacja taka, wiązana z poszlakami zawartymi w Żywocie Metodego oraz imieniem Gorazda w kalendarzu wiślickim, sprzyjała hipotezie o istnieniu w Polsce chrześcijaństwa wcześniejszego od oficjalnie przyjętego w 966 roku. Za najstarszy zabytek o charakterze religijnym uznawano obiekt gipsowy w kształcie niecki, określony jako "misa chrzcielna". Chrzcielnica ta służyłaby do masowych chrztów i tym samym świadczyłaby o fazie panowania morawskiego w Wiślicy (Antoniewicz 1968: 114). Wysuwano także przypuszczenia, że najstarszy napis (łaciński, datowany na ca. 1170 rok) na posadzce krypty kościoła romańskiego został wyryty w celu usunięcia innej, wcześniejszej (tj. głagolickiej) inskrypcji. "Napis ten [łaciński] mógłby więc powstać po

405

roku 1170 i stanowi chyba terminus ad quem ewentualnej liturgii słowiańskiej w Wiślicy" (por. Moszyński 1971: 259).

Rezultaty badań archeologicznych, które początkowo podpierały hipotezę o istnieniu w Wiślicy ośrodka liturgii słowiańskiej, później ją
podważyły. W ostatnich latach zweryfikowano wcześniejsze interpretacje
dotyczące datowania i funkcji tzw. misy chrzcielnej. Według Kalagi i
Górnej (1982 [1984]: 20) obiekt ten nie mógł powstać wcześniej niż w
drugiej połowie XI wieku, i ze względu na układ stratygraficzny innych
znalezisk, nie może być jednoznacznie interpretowany jako baptyste-
rium. Ustalono też (ibidem: 21), że pozostałości po najstarszym wiślickim zabytku sakralnym, kościele św. Mikołaja, pochodzą z okresu:
koniec X w. - XIII w.

Śladów archeologicznych dowodzących istnienia liturgii słowiańskiej
szuka się także w Krakowie, leżącym w średniowieczu na szlaku mię-
dzynarodowym łączącym Pragę z Kijowem i wiązanym z siedzibą metropolii słowiańskiej. W świetle ostatnich badań wiadomo, że funda-
menty najstarszych kościołów krakowskich nie pochodzą, jak przy-
puszczano wcześniej, z IX wieku, lecz z okresu: druga połowa X wieku
- początek XI wieku (Labuda 1984: 400-401). Ponieważ w okresie ca.
945-988/989 Kraków wchodził w skład państwa Przemyślidów, jest wysoce prawdopodobne, że część tych budowli została wzniesiona przez
Czechów. Według Labudy (ibidem: 410) z rządami czeskimi należy
wiązać kościół św. Michała, najstarszy kościół w Krakowie. Nie' ma
jednak żadnych podstaw archeologicznych do twierdzenia, że kościoły
te były związane z liturgią słowiańską, a nie łacińską. Bezpośrednim
dowodem na związek tych obiektów z liturgią słowiańską byłyby zabytki piśmiennictwa cerkiewnosłowiańskiego (np. inskrypcje głagolickie). Zabytków takich nie znaleziono. Trudno się zgodzić z Rospon-
dem (1968b: 133-34), który sugeruje przeoczenie przez archeologów inskrypcji głagolickich, wynikające z faktu, że ze względu na swoją
formę, mogły one być przyjmowane za znaki ornamentacyjne, a nie pi-
sarskie.

W badaniach archeologicznych Małopolski i Śląska (czyli terenów do
których dotarłaby misja Metodego) nie natrafiono na żadne ślady
chrześcijaństwa z wieku IX i początku wieku X (Labuda 1984: 286,
1988: 50). Wyniki wykopalisk wskazują na utrzymanie się tam wyraź-
nych śladów kultu pogańskiego do końca wieku X (Lehr-Spławiński
1961c: 74, Labuda 1988: 51).

3.3 Argumenty językowe. Wpływ języka scs. na język polski

Czy występujące w polszczyźnie wyrazy pochodzenia scs. zapożyczone zostały bezpośrednio z języka scs., czy też za pośrednictwem czeskim i/lub wschodniosłowiańskim? Udowodnienie bezpośredniego wpływu języka scs. na język polski uzupełniałoby poszlaki historyczne, które wskazywałyby na istnienie liturgii słowiańskiej w Polsce. Słownictwo zapożyczone pośrednio potwierdzałoby założenie, że tradycja cerkiewnosłowiańska w Polsce jest zjawiskiem wtórnym i odzwierciedla wpływy językowe z Czech i Rusi.

3.3.1 Ogólny przegląd literatury

Hipoteza o istnieniu liturgii słowiańskiej w Polsce wysuwana jest przede wszystkim przez historyków, a nie językoznawców, co tłumaczy fakt powstania rozległych opracowań historycznych, lecz do tej pory dość skąpych badań na polu językowym. Poparcie językowe hipotezy sprowadza się najczęściej do powoływania się na krótki artykuł Havránka "Otázka existence církevní slovanštíny v Polsku" (1956), w którym autor przyznaje, że część polskich terminów religijnych (także słownictwo w Bogurodzicy) ma wyraźne źródła cerkiewnosłowiańskie. Havránek, przekonany o biliturgiczności Czech przed okresem sazawskim, zauważa, że część terminologii chrześcijańskiej nie została zapożyczona ze staroczeskiego, gdyż: "[...] neexistovala tehdy vlastně ještě terminologie česká, ale pouze česko-staroslověnska", lecz z cerkiewnosłowiańskiego czeskiej redakcji: "[...] staropolská terminologie náboženská vznikla na podkladě české redakce staroslověnského jazyka – mohli bychom konečně i říci západní redakce – před polovinou XI. století" (Havránek 1956: 304).

Na metodyczną niepoprawność konkluzji, że terminologia chrześcijańska o etymologii scs. miałaby dowodzić istnienia w Polsce liturgii słowiańskiej zwracał uwagę Lehr-Spławiński (1932: 11, 1961b: 53). Polskie terminy chrześcijańskie, które mają swoje ścisłe odpowiedniki w języku scs., znane są także w słownictwie staroczeskim. Lehr-Spławiński wskazał, że znalezienie odpowiedzi na pytanie, czy doszło do bezpośredniego kontaktu językowego między polszczyzną a językiem scs. uwarunkowane jest znalezieniem w zasobie słownikowym tych obydwu języków wyrazów, które nie są znane językowi staroczeskiemu (1961b: 53). Tezę tę zmodyfikował później de Vincenz, podkreślając słusznie, że językowym potwierdzeniem wpływu misji morawskiej w południowej Polsce byłoby wskazanie tych wyrazów pochodzenia scs. w języku polskim, które nie występowały i *nie mogły* występować w staroczeskim (1983: 651). Ponieważ spełnienie tego drugiego warunku jest niemożliwe, niemożliwe jest też udowodnienie oddziaływania misji morawskiej w południowej Polsce na polu językowym. Biorąc pod uwagę fakt, że polska terminologia chrześcijańska odpowiada na ogół terminologii czeskiej, logicznym wydaje się, że: "[...] cała staropolska terminologia chrześcijańska została przeważnie zapożyczona z czeskiego bez względu na różnice pierwotnego pochodzenia odnośnych terminów" (Lehr-Spławiński 1961a: 49). Podobnego zdania są Grivec (1960: 140-141), Vlasto (1970: 140), de Vincenz (1982 [1984], 1983) i Urbańczyk (1988).

Zagadnienie wpływu języka scs. na słownictwo polskie nie zostało jeszcze kompleksowo opracowane. W pracach ogólnych, dotyczących wpływów obcych (np. Brückner 1915, Klemensiewicz 1974) nie poświęcono uwagi roli języka scs. w rozwoju słownictwa polskiego. Jedynie Klich w swojej monografii "Polska terminologia chrześcijańska" (1927) wskazał na szereg terminów religijnych wspólnych polszczyźnie i językowi scs. W pracy tej nie wysuwa on jednak daleko idących wniosków, że terminy wspólne językowi polskiemu i scs. przeniknęły do polszczyzny bezpośrednio z języka scs. Przeciwnie – wskazuje on na pośrednictwo czeskie. Jednakże zasygnalizowane przez Klicha wyrazy wspólne polszczyźnie i językowi scs. (np. *anioł, apostoł, cerkiew, chrześcijanin, krzyż, kmotr, kościół, msza, papież, żyd*), często przytaczane przez badaczy jako dowód wpływu języka scs. na polszczyznę, nie są istotne w dyskusji. Funkcjonowały one bowiem w językach słowiańskich jako pożyczki z innych języków w dobie szerzenia się tam chrześcijaństwa już w okresie przedcyrylometodejskim i nie ma żadnych podstaw ku temu, aby przyjąć, że weszły do języka polskiego za pośrednictwem scs. Mylne są więc uwagi Karpluk (1978: 494, 1981: 595), która wnioskuje, że wskazane przez Klicha słownictwo polskie wspólne z językiem scs. stanowi jedynie część rzeczywistej terminologii chrześcijańskiej zapożyczonej przez polszczyznę za pośrednictwem czeskim z języka scs.

Problematyka pożyczek scs. w języku polskim znalazła najszersze opracowanie w pracach Karpluk i Siatkowskiego, którzy szukali w polskiej terminologii chrześcijańskiej argumentów językowych popierających hipotezę o istnieniu na ziemiach polskich liturgii słowiańskiej. Starali się oni dowieść, że w zasobie słownictwa staropolskiego istnieją wyrazy przejęte bezpośrednio z języka scs. W ich opinii przeniknęłyby one do polszczyzny nie w wyniku misji morawskiej, lecz w wyniku oddziaływania liturgii słowiańskiej wprowadzonej do Małopolski przez Czechy.

3.3.2 Badania onomastyczne

W serii artykułów (1972, 1973, 1977, 1978, 1981) Karpluk stara się udowodnić, że część staropolskich imion chrześcijańskich wykazuje ślady wpływów liturgii słowiańskiej w Polsce. Na podstawie analizy materiału onomastyczego zauważa autorka, że szereg tych imion występuje w opozycyjnych formach, które można wyprowadzić zarówno od podstawy greckiej, jak i łacińskiej. Warianty bazujące na formie greckiej przyjmuje ona za ślady językowe liturgii słowiańskiej w Polsce. Porównując odpowiedniki tych imion w językach stpol., stczes. i scs., Karpluk wychodzi z założenia, że: "Jeżeli będzie tu występować całkowita zgodność i z polskiej strony odpowiednio archaiczne cechy fonetyczne, można sądzić, że imię należy do najstarszej warstwy terminów religijno-kościelnych, które dadzą się związać z obrządkiem cyrylo-metodejskim w Czechach i takąż liturgią w Polsce" (1977: 84-85).

Wnioski wysuwane przez Karpluk, nie poparte żadnymi argumentami historycznymi, mogą być łatwo obalone twierdzeniem, że wczesna onomastyka staropolska odzwierciedla wpływy językowe czeskie (i pośrednie scs.) oraz łacińskie – wszystkie staropolskie imiona wskazane przez Karpluk posiadają bowiem swoje odpowiedniki w stczes. Chociaż autorka nie twierdzi explicite, że wyniki jej badań dowodzą jednoznacznie istnienia liturgii słowiańskiej w Polsce, konkluduje: "Since the Christian names belong to the oldest group of Polish Christian terminology, connected through Bohemian with the Old Church Slavonic forms, and became subject to Latin influence only at a later period (e.g. Klimont-Klemens), I link them with the Cyrillo-Methodian mission and the Slavonic rite penetrating into South Poland from Moravia and Bohemia" (1981: 583). Taka interpretacja budzi wiele wątpliwości, gdyż w rzeczywistości wyniki badań Karpluk w pełni potwierdzają pośrednictwo czeskie w procesie zapożyczenia.

3.3.3 Słownictwo pochodzenia scs. w języku polskim

Śladów liturgii słowiańskiej w słownictwie polskim szukał także Siatkowski (1981a, 1981b, 1982 [1984], 1984, 1985). Według Siatkowskiego słownictwo pochodzenia scs. zostało przejęte do języka polskiego trzema drogami. Wyróżnia on tutaj trzy warstwy (1981a: 13, 1984: 108, 1985: 159):

1. Warstwa najstarsza obejmuje wyrazy zapożyczone bezpośrednio z języka scs. w X wieku w wyniku oddziaływania liturgii słowiańskiej w południowej Małopolsce. Do wyrazów tych zalicza on: *miłosirdy, sumnienie/sąmnienie, sąmnieć się, zbawić* oraz *zbawiciel.*
2. Warstwa młodsza obejmuje pożyczki scs. za pośrednictwem czeskim, które związane są z procesem chrystianizacji Polski. Do słownictwa tego typu należą według Siatkowskiego: *błogosławić, bogurodzica, dziesięcina, gospodzin, kamienować, kwietna niedziela, licemiernik, męczennik, miłosierdzie, miłosierny, prorok, rozgrzeszyć, uczennik, wskrzesić, wszechmogący, zakonnik, zwolennik* (Siatkowski 1981a: 15, 1984: 110, 1985: 164) oraz przypuszczalnie: *mięsopust, młodzieniec* (w znaczeniu 'infans') i *trójca.* Autor argumentuje etymologię scs. jedynie dla: *błogosławić, bogurodzica, licemiernik* i *rozgrzeszyć.*
3. Warstwa najmłodsza obejmuje wyrazy zapożyczone za pośrednictwem języków wschodniosłowiańskich.

Dokonana przez Siatkowskiego klasyfikacja pożyczek scs. w polszczyźnie jest umotywowana jedynie dla dwóch ostatnich warstw, gdyż pośrednictwo czeskie i wschodniosłowiańskie udowodnione jest na polu historycznym i językowym.

3.3.3.1 Hipotetyczny bezpośredni wpływ języka scs. na polszczyznę

Spełnienie postulowanego przez Lehra-Spławińskiego warunku świadczącego o bezpośrednim wpływie scs. na język polski – braku poświadczeń odpowiedników stczes. – daje Siatkowskiemu podstawę do przypuszczenia, że stpol. *miłosirdy, sumnienie/sąmnienie, sąmnieć się, zbawić* oraz *zbawiciel* przeniknęły do polszczyzny w wieku X bezpośrednio z języka scs. W opinii Siatkowskiego piśmiennictwo scs. wprowadzone zostało wraz z liturgią słowiańską do Polski południowej przez Czechy. Hipotezę tę popierałyby dowody pośrednie, za które autor uznaje biliturgiczność Czech w X w., imię Gorazda w znalezionym przez Zatheya kalendarzu wiślickim, równoczesne funkcjonowanie dwóch biskupów Prochora i Prokulfa oraz wyniki badań onomastycznych Karpluk (Siatkowski 1981: 14, 1984: 109, 1985: 163).

Hipotezy Siatkowskiego nie potwierdzają nie tylko dowody historyczne, lecz też przekonywujące argumenty językowe. Fakt, że stczes. odpowiedniki stpol. *miłosirdy, sumnienie/sąmnienie, sąmnieć się, zbawić* i *zbawiciel* nie są poświadczone w źródłach pisanych, lub są poświadczone sporadycznie lub w innym znaczeniu, przyjmuje Siatkowski za podstawę do przypuszczenia, że przeniknęły one do polszczyzny w wyniku bezpośredniego kontaktu z językiem scs. Chociaż, jak sam przyznaje Siatkowski, brak poświadczeń stczes. nie jest jednoznaczny z brakiem występowania tych wyrazów w języku czeskim, wychodzi on z założenia, że wyrazy te, będąc specyficznymi formami literackimi, nie weszły do czeszczyzny mówionej i w związku z tym język czeski nie mógł pośredniczyć w przejęciu ich do polszczyzny (1981a: 13, 1981b: 409, 1985: 162). Uważa on, że uznawane dotychczas w literaturze pośrednictwo czesko(morawskie) w zapożyczeniu tego słownictwa może być, ze względu na możliwe bezpośrednie oddziaływanie języka scs. w Małopolsce, kwestionowane (1982 [1984]: 99).

Należy tu zauważyć, że większość wskazanych przez Siatkowskiego leksemów to kalki niemieckie/łacińskie. Chociaż autor sam podkreśla, że ustalenie, czy wyrazy tego typu powstały w dobie przedcyrylometodejskiej, czy też w okresie działalności Cyryla i Metodego lub jego uczniów, jest zadaniem bardzo trudnym, wychodzi z założenia, że pochodzą one z okresu cyrylometodejskiego. Już Lehr-Spławiński (1932: 11) zwrócił uwagę, że wyrazy scs. będące pochodzenia niemiecko-słowiańskiego lub grecko-łacińskiego nie powinny być w dyskusji brane pod uwagę, gdyż: "Dostały się one niewątpliwie w większości właśnie od Słowian zachodnich z zachodu Europy (Morawian) do języka Cyryla i Metodego, a nie odwrotnie, są to bowiem terminy które przeniknęły do Słowian zachodnich z zachodu Europy".[8] Tak więc analizując zapożyczenia scs. w języku polskim należy pominąć słownictwo przejęte do Słowiańszczyzny panońsko-morawskiej i bałkańskiej w wyniku rozpoczętej już w VIII w. chrystianizacji Słowian ze strony Kościoła zachodniego. Wyrazy tego typu uznawane są powszechnie w literaturze za morawizmy. Ze względu na uwarunkowania geograficzne i historyczno-kulturowe najbardziej logiczne jest, że obecność ich odpowiedników w staropolszczyźnie nie jest związana z hipotetycznymi wpływami scs., lecz odzwierciedla wpływy językowe wynikające z chrystianizacji zachodniej Słowiańszczyzny przez misje zachodnie.

Przyjrzyjmy się bliżej wyrazom, które w opinii Siatkowskiego przeniknęły do języka polskiego w wyniku bezpośredniego kontaktu z językiem scs.:

miłosirdy – 'czyniący miłosierdzie'.

scs. *milosrьdъ*, *milosrьdьnъ* (Stsl. 326), kalka z goc. *armahaírts*, łac. *misericors* (por. Humbach 1969).

Forma stpol. *miłosirdy* stanowi hapax legomenon (Kazania świętokrzyskie), częste są stpol. postacie: *miłosierny*, *miłosierdny* (Słstp. IV

257-258). Wśród slawistów brak jest zgodności, czy odczytanie zapisu w Kazaniach świętokrzyskich: *milosirdī skuthkem* jako *milosirdym skutkiem* jest słuszne (Taszycki 1950a, 1950b). Havránek zwrócił uwagę na możliwość istnienia staroczeskiego odpowiednika tej formy (*milosrdý*) w okresie wcześniejszym i jej późniejszego zaniku (por. Siatkowski 1981b: 409, 1982 [1984]: 100, 1985: 160). Biorąc jednak pod uwagę fakt, że scs. *milosrьdъ* jest kalką gocką/łacińską, która w tekstach scs. bywała wcześnie zastępowana przez *milostivъ*, zaś czasownik scs. *milosrьdovati* – przez *milъ byti* (por. Basaj 1966: 51), należy wnioskować, że wyraz ten jest morawizmem.[9] Jako morawizm wyraz ten nie udowadnia bezpośredniego kontaktu piśmiennictwa scs. z językiem polskim.

sąmnienie/sumnienie – 'świadomość odpowiedzialności za swoje czyny'.

scs. *sǫmьněnie, sumьněnie* (Stsl. 683), kalka z łac. *con-scientia* (por. Siatkowski 1982 [1984]: 102-103, 1985: 16-161).

sąmnieć się – (1) 'mieć wątpliwości'; (2) 'bać się, lękać się'; (3) 'wstydzić się czegoś, żałować czegoś'.

scs. *sǫmьněti sę, sumьněti sę* (Stsl. 683).

Mimo braku poświadczeń staroczeskich (stczes. zna *svědomí*), udokumentowane są zachodniosłowiańskie: *sumení* (z pogranicza morawsko-słowackiego), starosłowackie *sumenie* (notowane w XVI-XVII w.) oraz *soumene, souměnÍ, soumnění* z obszarów słowackich (Siatkowski 1982 [1984]: 102, 1985: 160-161). Nie można wykluczyć, że *sumnienie/sąmnienie, sąmnieć się* weszły do polszczyzny we wczesnym średniowieczu bezpośrednio z dialektów morawskich, gdyż Kraków podlegał w końcu X w. jurysdykcyjnie najprawdopodobniej diecezji morawskiej w Ołomuńcu (Urbańczyk 1988: 344). Występowanie tej kalki łacińskiej w zachodniej Słowiańszczyźnie (na obszarze morawsko-słowackim) oraz poświadczenie jej, m.in. w Mszale kijowskim, Homiliach Grzegorza Wielkiego i Żywocie św. Wacława (SJS z. 42, 405-407) wskazywałoby na morawizm.

Nieprzekonywujące jest też przypuszczenie, że stpol. *zbawić* i *zbawiciel* świadczą o bezpośrednim kontakcie języka polskiego z piśmiennictwem scs.

zbawiciel – 'redemptor'; *zbawić* – 'salutare'.

scs. *izbaviteľь* (Stsl. 248) w znaczeniu 'redemptor, liberator, ereptor'.

scs. *izbaviti* (Stsl. 249) w znaczeniu 'salutare'.

412

Jeszcze w 1979 r. przyjmuje Siatkowski wraz z Basajem (Basaj i Siatkowski 1979: 33), że wyrazy te, ze względu na występowanie w zabytkach wykazujących wyraźne wpływy czeskie, są niewątpliwie zapożyczone ze scs. za pośrednictwem czeskim. Później uznane są (Siatkowski 1981b: 411-412, 1982 [1984]: 101-102, 1985: 161) za bezpośrednie zapożyczenia semantyczne ze scs. *izbaviteľь, izbaviti*, a nie za bezpośrednie pożyczki z czes. *zbavitel, zbaviti.* Autor argumentuje to faktem, że formy czeskie różniły się semantycznie od polskich i scs., gdyż sporadycznie poświadczony stczes. *zbavitel* i powszechnie występujący *zbaviti* miały znaczenie bardziej ogólne, odbiegające od 'redemptor' i 'salutare'.

3.3.3.2 Zapożyczenia scs. za pośrednictwem czeskim

Trudności w uchwyceniu w polszczyźnie słownictwa pochodzenia scs. zapożyczonego poprzez medium czeskie związane są głównie z pokrewieństwem języków słowiańskich, które szczególnie we wczesnych etapach swojego rozwoju, wykazywały dużo cech wspólnych. W wielu przypadkach trudno jest stwierdzić, czy dany polski wyraz o podstawie słowiańskiej jest formą rodzimą (będący kontynuacją języka prasłowiańskiego, lub nową rodzimą formacją), czy też wynikiem kontaktu językowego. Zadanie jest szczególnie utrudnione, gdy funkcjonująca w języku polskim pożyczka (której poświadczona forma jest w wielu przypadkach dużo późniejsza od faktycznego momentu zapożyczenia), nie wykazuje na płaszczyźnie językowej znamion obcości.

Sporną bywa też kwestia pochodzenia niektórych wyrazów obecnych w zasobie słownictwa scs. i stczes, szczególnie w przypadku replik u-tworzonych na bazie łacińsko-niemieckiej. Logiczne jest rozumowanie, że leksemy te przejęte zostały przez język scs. z zachodniej słowiańszczyzny (a nie odwrotnie – przez zachodnią słowiańszczyznę z języka scs.). Tak więc nie należy tłumaczyć obecności ich odpowiedników w staroczeskim wpływem języka scs., i tym samym nie należy uznawać ich odpowiedników w języku polskim za pożyczki scs., które przeniknęły za pośrednictwem czeskim, lecz za bohemizmy.

Uważam, że nie wszystkie wyrazy wskazane przez Siatkowskiego jako zapożyczenia scs. za pośrednictwem czeskim wskazują na pośredni wpływ scs. na język polski. Za elementy czeskie uznałabym: *kamienować, zwolennik, miłosier(d)ny, męczennik, trójca, wszechmogący, zakonnik.* Dwa pierwsze nie są poświadczone w zabytkach scs., lecz cerkiewnosłowiańskich[10] – nie mogą więc udowadniać wpływu scs. na polszczyznę. Pozostałe wyrazy uznawane są w literaturze za elementy zachodniosłowiańskie w scs.

Czasownik *kamenovati* udokumentowany jest źródłowo jedynie trzy-krotnie w Homiliach Grzegorza Wielkiego, zabytku scs. redakcji czes-kiej (SJS II 9) i uznawany jest za bohemizm (Mareš 1963: 438, Reinhart 1980: 81). Scs. odpowiednikiem stpol. *(u)kamienować, (u)kamionować* i stczes. *(u)kamenovati* jest zwrot *kamenijem bijeti.* Także strus. zna je-dynie *pobiti kameniemь* (Srez. I 1184; por. też *kamenobienie,* Srez. I 1185). Na bohemizm w polszczyźnie wskazują także filiacje tekstowe.

Stpol. *zwolennik* i stczes. *zvoleník* nie posiadają poświadczonego od-powiednika w scs. Forma *izvoljenikъ* 'electus' występuje jedynie w Praskich fragmentach, Homiliach Grzegorza Wielkiego i Fragmentach fryzyńskich (SJS I 727), czyli w zabytkach powstałych na obszarze mo-rawsko-panońskim, zaś jego odpowiednikiem w tekstach cerkiewno-ruskich jest *izvoliteľь* (Srez. I 1041). Daje to uzasadnioną podstawę do przypuszczenia, że *izvoljenikъ* jest morawizmem. Por. też Mareš 1963: 436, L'vov 1968: 316, Wiehl 1974: 43.

Za wyrazy pochodzenia scs. w polszczyźnie nie należy uznawać sta-ropolskich: *kwietna niedziela, miłosierny, męczennik, wszechmogący* i *zakonnik.* Ich odpowiedniki scs. uznawane są w literaturze za mora-wizmy. Argumentuję to następująco:

Chociaż formacja scs. *nedělja cvětьnaja* jest w opinii Jagicia (1913[2]: 300) i Sławskiego (SE III 489) oparta na grec. κυριακὴ τῶν βαίων, Ma-reš (1956) uznaje ją za kalkę łac. *dominica florum,* i tym samym za morawizm. Potwierdzałoby to też występowanie w stczes. zarówno *květná neděle,* jak i *kvietna dominica* (Gebauer II 190).

Jak zwróciłam już uwagę wcześniej, za morawizm należy uznać scs. *milosrьdъ, milosrьdьnъ.*

Forma scs. *mǫčenikъ* uznawana jest w literaturze za formację po-wstałą na gruncie morawsko-panońskim. Stanowi ona odpowiednik stwniem. *martirunga* (Frinta 1918: 46), czy też stwniem. *martyr* (Wiehl 1974: 25-26).

Chociaż występowanie stpol. *trójca* (pierwotna forma *troica*) tłuma-czone jest pośrednim wpływem scs., (Urbańczyk 1965: 122, Basaj i Siatkowski 1977: 33, Siatkowski 1982 [1984]: 99), wyraz ten, jako kalka łac. *trinitas,* uznawany jest za morawizm (de Vincenz 1995).

414

Za morawizm przyjmuje się też scs. *vъsemogy*, fem. *vъsemogǫšti*. Jest to kalka z łac. *omnipotens*, której odpowiednikiem bazującym na wzorcu greckim (z grec. παντοκράτωρ) jest scs. *vъsedrъžiteľъ* (por. Mareš 1963: 436, Wiehl 1974: 31, Siatkowski 1985: 197, Schaeken 1987: 134-135).

Kalką niemiecką jest także scs. *zakonьnikъ* (ze stwniem. *êwarto* (*êwart*) 'ksiądz, duchowny', gdzie do pierwszego członu złożenia *êwa*, przetłumaczonego jako *zakonъ*, dodano sufiks -*nikъ* (por. Wiehl 1974: 41, Schaeken 1987: 135). Staropolski *zakonnik* występuje w znaczeniach: 'mnich' i 'faryzeusz żydowski'. W scs. tłumaczeniach ewangelii *zakonьnikъ* udokumentowany jest wyłącznie w znaczeniu 'znający prawo'. Jedynie Mszał kijowski oraz zabytek piśmiennictwa cerkiewnosłowiańskiego redakcji czeskiej – Homilie Grzegorza Wielkiego – dokumentują znaczenie 'duchowny'. W tym znaczeniu uznany jest już przez Sobolewskiego za morawizm (por. Horálek 1948: 117, Mareš 1963: 439, Wiehl 1974: 42, Cejtlin 1977: 73). Fakt, że w stczes. doszło do zmiany semantycznej na 'mnich' (Frinta: 1918: 73, Basaj i Siatkowski 1979: 25, Rusek 1988: 33) i 'faryzeusz żydowski' (Basaj i Siatkowski ibidem), i to właśnie w tych znaczeniach wyraz ten przeszedł do polszczyzny, potwierdzałby bezpośrednią pożyczkę czeską.

Za prawdopodobne morawizmy można uznać wyrazy, które mogą stanowić kalkę łacińską czy niemiecką. Do wyrazów dla których etymologię scs. w czeskim uznałabym za sporną należą: *dziesięcina*, *mięsopust* oraz *pirzwieniec*.

dziesięcina – 'dziesiąta część zbiorów składana jako danina'. Scs. *desętina* (Stsl. 186) występuje w zwrocie: *desętinǫ dajati*, który Molnár (1985: 143) uznaje za kalkę z łac. *decimare* i *decimas (partes) dare* oraz z grec. ἀποδεκατεύειν. Według Molnára kalki te mogły powstać niezależnie od siebie: wśród Słowian z liturgią łacińską – na wzorcu łacińskim, zaś wśród Słowian z liturgią słowiańską – na wzorcu greckim. Stpol. *dziesięcina* przyjmowana jest za pożyczkę ze stczes. *desětina* sprzed w. XIV (Reczek 1968: 115). Obecność tego leksemu w stczes. związana jest najprawdopodobniej z oddziaływaniem misji zachodnich.

mięsopust – 'zapusty, ostatki'. scs. *męsopustъ* (Stsl. 341) w znaczeniu 'okres postu'. Scs. *męsopustъ* jest najprawdopodobniej kalką z łac. *carnisprivium* (Jagić 1899: 29, Moszyński 1989: 164) i nie posiada odpowiednika

greckiego (StSl 341). Moszyński przypuszcza, że jest to morawizm.
(Moszyński ibidem). Wyraz ten występuje w większości języków słowiańskich w znaczeniu 'dzień postny' albo 'pierwszy (lub ostatni) dzień
postu'. Fakt, że jedynie w polskim i czeskim doszło do zmiany semantycznej — znaczenie zostało przeniesione na 'ostatni dzień przed
postem' (Machek 353, Basaj i Siatkowski 1970: 33) — wskazuje na bohemizm w polszczyźnie.

pirzwieniec — 'syn pierworodny'.
scs. *prьvěnьcь* (Stsl. 532), kalka z łac. *primogenitus*, odpowiednik
grec. πρωτότοχος.
Oparta na rdzeniu psł. forma *pirzwieniec*, pochodząca z Psałterza
floriańskiego jest jedynym przykładem staropolskim (Słstp. VI 106).
Obecność tego wyrazu w zabytku wykazującym czeskie zależności tekstowe wskazuje na wpływ czeski. Podobne filiacje tekstowe stczes. *prvěnec* ze scs. *prьvěnьcь* (forma występuje w tekstach nawiązujących do
Ewangelii Łukasza 7.2. i w psałterzach, m.in. w Psałterzu wittenber-
skim, wskazują w przekonaniu Siatkowskiego na scs. pochodzenie czeskiego wyrazu (Siatkowski 1981a: 16, 1984: 110, 1985: 165). Ponieważ
jest to kalka łacińska, jest wysoce prawdopodobne, że scs. *prьvěnьcь*
pochodzi z okresu przedcyrylometodejskiego. Możliwe jest też, że
stczes. *prvěnec* jest kalką łacińską, która powstała niezależnie od formy
scs.

Za pożyczki najprawdopodobniej pochodzenia scs. uznałabym wskazane przez Siatkowskiego: *gospodzin, młodzieniec* (w znaczeniu
'dziecko płci męskiej'), *prorok, smiłować się, ucze(n)nik* oraz *wskrzesić*. Niewykluczone jest jednak, że leksemy te są formacjami rodzimymi
lub bezpośrednimi pożyczkami czeskimi.

gospodzin — 'Bóg'; zapożyczenie semantyczne ze stczes. *hospodin*, w
którym pierwotne znaczenie 'pan' ograniczyło się pod wpływem scs.
gospodinъ do 'Bóg'. Por. Frinta 1918: 24-25, Havránek 1963: 292, Basaj
i Siatkowski 1967: 10, Machek 177-178.

młodzieniec — 'dziecko płci męskiej'; zapożyczenie semantyczne
poprzez stczes. *mládenec* w tym znaczeniu ze scs. *mladьnьcь, mlade-
nьcь, mladěnьcь*. Por. Urbańczyk 1946: 30, Basaj i Siatkowski 1971:
6-7.

prorok — za pośrednictwem stczes. *prorok* ze scs. *prorokъ* (kalka z
grec. προφήτης). Forma ta rozpowszechniona jest na terenie całej Sło-

wiańszczyzny, oprócz języków łużyckich i połabskiego, które posiadają
odpowiedniki pochodzenia niemieckiego (Basaj 1966: 67-68). Por. też
Frinta 1918: 52, Basaj i Siatkowski 1974: 11-12, Vasmer III 337.

ucze(n)nik — za pośrednictwem stczes. *učen(n)ík* ze scs. *učenikъ*.
Por. Čech 1948, Basaj 1966: 50, Reczek 1968: 49, Basaj i Siatkowski
1978: 7-8.

wskrzesić — za pośrednictwem stczes. *vzkřesiti* ze scs. *vъskrěsiti*.
Por. Reczek 1968: 86, Basaj i Siatkowski 1979: 5-6.

Spośród słownictwa uznanego przez Siatkowskiego za zapożyczenia
scs. za pośrednictwem czeskim za pożyczki pewne można przyjąć jedynie: *błogosławić, bogurodzica, licemiernik,* oraz *rozgrzeszyć.*

błogosławić — ze stczes. *blahoslaviti,* które stanowi przekształcenie
scs. *blagosloviti* (kalka z grec. εὐλογεῖν), gdzie w drugiej części złożenia, pod wpływem rzecz. *sláva,* wprowadzone zostało wtórne -*a.* Por.
Frinta 1918: 5, Havránek 1956: 304, Basaj 1966: 31-32, Siatkowski
1981a: 15, 1982 [1984]: 99-100, 1984: 109, 1985: 164.

bogurodzica — pierwotnie *bogorodica* za pośrednictwem stczes. *bo-
horodicě* ze scs. *bogorodica* (kalka z grec. θεοτόκος). Por. Havránek
1956: 304, Basaj i Siatkowski 1964: 69.

licemiernik — za pośrednictwem stczes. *liceměrník,* który stanowi
przekształcenie scs. *liceměrьnъ,* od rzecz. *liceměrъ.* Por. Basaj 1966:
48-49, Siatkowski 1981a: 15, 1985: 164-165.

rozgrzeszyć — za pośrednictwem stczes. *rozhřešiti* będącego
przekształceniem scs. *razdrěšiti.* Por. Havránek 1956: 304, 1963: 292,
Basaj 1966: 69, Siatkowski 1981a: 15, 1982 [1984]: 100, 1985: 165.

smiłować się — za pośrednictwem stczes. lokalnej innowacji *smilovati
sě* ze scs. *milovati, pomilovati.* O pośrednictwie świadczą też zależności tekstowe oraz względy semantyczne. Por. Basaj i Siatkowski 1974:
31-32, Siatkowski 1981a: 15, 1982 [1984]: 100, 1984: 109, 1985: 165.

3.3.4 Uwagi końcowe

Na podstawie wyników badań onomastycznych Karpluk oraz analizy
wyrazów przyjętych w literaturze za zapożyczenia scs. w języku polskim
nie można udowodnić istnienia bezpośredniego wpływu języka scs. na
język polski. Szereg polskich wczesnośredniowiecznych imion chrześcijańskich zgodnych z formami scs. nie dowodzi oddziaływania misji

metodejskiej w południowej Polsce, lecz odzwierciedla czeskie wpływy
językowe. Za pośrednictwem czeskim przeniknęło do polszczyzny także
omówione słownictwo pochodzenia scs. Większość leksemów uznawa-
nych za wyrazy pochodzenia scs., które zapożyczone zostały przez język polski za pośrednictwem czeskim, jest w rzeczywistości, jak starałam się dowieść, bohemizmami.

4. Podsumowanie i konkluzje

W świetle przedstawionych w tym artykule argumentów nie ma do-
statecznych podstaw do uznania tradycji cerkiewnosłowiańskiej w
Polsce za tradycję cyrylometodejską. Znane nam przekazy źródłowe nie
potwierdzają wprowadzenia liturgii słowiańskiej w Polsce południowej u
schyłku IX w. przez misję morawską i utrwalenia się jej na ziemiach
polskich. Także ewentualne pośrednictwo Czech w zakładaniu, początkowo w Małopolsce, a po 966 roku w pozostałych częściach kraju
ośrodków liturgii słowiańskiej, nie jest zweryfikowane źródłowo, gdyż
opiera się na hipotetycznej kontynuacji tradycji cyrylometodejskiej w
Czechach. Tak więc argumenty zwolenników hipotezy o istnieniu liturgii, a nawet metropolii słowiańskiej zainicjowanej w Polsce przez samego Metodego lub Czechy Przemyślidów nie są przekonywujące, gdyż
nie opierają się na niezaprzeczalnych faktach historycznych, lecz na hipotezach i dowolnej interpretacji świadectw pośrednich.

Tradycji cyrylometodejskiej w Polsce nie potwierdza też archeologia.
Wykopaliska z obszarów południowej Polski nie wskazują na jakiekol-
wiek ślady chrześcijaństwa w ciągu wieku IX i początku X wieku. Zna-
leziska archeologiczne w Wiślicy, wiązanej na podstawie poszlak zawartych w Żywocie Metodego z działalnością misji morawskiej, są
datowane przez archeologów na okres późniejszy. Podobnie z okresu
późniejszego pochodzą najstarsze kościoły Krakowa, uznawanego przez
wielu badaczy za centrum metropolii słowiańskiej.

Jednocześnie udokumentowane historycznie są (późne) wpływy cerkiewnosłowiańskie z Czech oraz z Rusi, które nie stanowią bezpośredniej kontynuacji spuścizny Cyryla i Metodego. Krótkotrwała działalność
klasztorów benedyktynów słowiańskich w Krakowie na Kleparzu i w
Oleśnicy, stanowiąca jedyny poświadczony historycznie ślad istnienia
polskich ośrodków liturgii słowiańskiej, związana jest z wpływami czeskimi i pośrednio – chorwackimi.

Staropolska terminologia chrześcijańska pochodzenia scs. poświadcza
czeskie pośrednictwo w procesie zapożyczenia. Wyrazy wskazywane w

418

literaturze przedmiotu za pożyczki scs. występują także w słowiańszczyźnie zachodniej. Daje to podstawy do twierdzenia, że przeniknęły one do polszczyzny za pośrednictwem zachodniosłowiańskim. Mimo faktu, że przeanalizowane tutaj pożyczki uznawane za scs. stanowią zapewne tylko część terminów religijno-kościelnych pochodzenia scs., słuszną wydaje się konkluzja, że wszystkie starocerkiewizmy w języku polskim są pochodzenia zachodnio- i wschodniosłowiańskiego. Bezpośredni wpływ języka scs. na polszczyznę wymagałby intensywnego i w miarę długiego kontaktu językowego między biorcą i dawcą, czego nie potwierdzają dane historyczne.

Podsumowując, stan wiedzy na dzień dzisiejszy pozwala przyjąć, że polska tradycja cerkiewnosłowiańska nie ma swoich korzeni w misji cyrylometodejskiej w Polsce, lecz jest odzwierciedleniem tradycji cerkiewnosłowiańskiej w Czechach i Rusi. Nie mamy też bezsprzecznych dowodów na nieistnienie tradycji cyrylometodejskiej, lecz jak słusznie podkreślił Lehr-Spławiński (1961e: 81):

"[...] aby uznać jej realność, trzeba by znaleźć jakieś nowe, poważne, nie budzące krytycznych zastrzeżeń dane, które by mogły tezę tę sprowadzić ze sfery patriotycznej fantazji na grunt rzeczywistości historycznej".

Uniwersytet Groningen

PRZYPISY

[1] Problematyka ta poruszana była marginesowo przez m.in. Ogijenko (1929), Lehra-Spławińskiego (1961a), Moszyńskiego (1971), częściowo też w materiałach z sesji naukowej poświęconej polskim kontaktom z piśmiennictwem cerkiewnosłowiańskim (Moszyński, L. i H. Wątróbska (ed.) 1982 [1984]). Część zapożyczeń scs., które weszły do polszczyzny za pośrednictwem wschodniosłowiańskim omawiała Minikowska (1980) oraz Karpluk (1988a, 1989, 1996).

[2] Streszczenie dyskusji w: Ludvikovský (1965), Kantor (1990: 30-46).

[3] Do najważniejszych należą: Chronica Boemorum Kosmasa († 1125), Legenda Christiani oraz Diffundente sole.

[4] Maksymalistą jest Mareš, zwolennik teorii istnienia w Czechach w X i XI w. języka cerkiewnosłowiańskiego czeskiej redakcji, stanowiącego bezpośrednią kontynuacją morawskiego piśmiennictwa scs. W swojej antologii (1979) uznaje on 27 zabytków literackich (głagolickich i cyrylickich) za teksty cerkiewnosłowiańskie, wyka-

zujące w jego opinii ewidentne wpływy języka czeskiego (ale ze skalą malejącego prawdopodobieństwa).

⁵ Por. de Vincenz (1988: 597-598).

⁶ Abstrahuję tutaj od niepotwierdzonej teorii Vašicy, według której liturgia słowiańska była tzw. *Liturgią św. Piotra*, zawierającą elementy rzymskie i bizantyjskie (por. Umiński 1953: 5-6, Grivec 1960: 179-184, Schaeken 1987: 8-9, Eggers 1996: 76-77).

⁷ Modlitwa "Omnipotens sempiterne Deus, qui nos per beatos Pontifices et confessores tuos, nostrosque patronos, Cyrillum et Methodium ad unitatem fidei Christianae vocare dignatus es, praesta quaesumus, ut [...]" stanowiła podstawę dla przypuszczenia, że Cyryl i Metody byli misjonarzami, którzy jako pierwsi wprowadzili chrześcijaństwo w Polsce (por. Moszyński 1971: 262).

⁸ Por. Urbańczyk (1988: 344), który podkreśla: "Wenn irgendwelche Wörter der polnischen, tschechischen und kirchenslavischen Sprache gemeinsam und zugleich fremder Herkunft sind (das heißt etymologisch nicht slavisch sind), darf man sie der mährischen Epoche zurechnen".

⁹ Uznany też za morawizm przez de Vicenza (1995: 38).

¹⁰ Ponieważ w literaturze spotyka się czasami błędne, synonimiczne użycie terminów "staro-cerkiewno-słowiański" i "cerkiewnosłowiański", zwracam uwagę, że za pożyczki scs. uznaję jedynie scs. elementy leksykalne, które udokumentowane są w zabytkach piśmienniczych do końca XI w. (słownictwo tego okresu zebrali Cejtlin, Večerka i Bláhová 1994). Stanowią one, w przeciwieństwie do wyrazów poświadczonych w odpisach późniejszych, "pewny" językowy element scs. Zwracam tu uwagę, że część słownictwa poświadczonego w SJS pochodzi z zabytków późniejszych, związanych z lokalnymi redakcjami cerkiewnosłowiańskimi, a nie z zabytków piśmiennictwa scs.

SKRÓTY

Gebauer	Gebauer 1970²
Machek	Machek 1962²
RKJL	*Rozprawy Komisji Językowej*, Łódzkie Towarzystwo Naukowe, Łódź.
SE	Sławski 1952-1977
SFPS	*Studia z Filologii Polskiej i Słowiańskiej*
SJS	Kurz (ed.) 1958ff.
Słstp.	Urbańczyk et al. (ed.) 1953ff.
Srez.	Sreznevskij 1893-1903
Stsl.	Cejtlin, Večerka, Bláhová 1994
Vasmer	Vasmer 1964-1973

420

BIBLIOGRAFIA

Antoniewicz, W.
1968   "Znaczenie odkryć w Wiślicy", *Silesia Antiqua* 10, 105-115.
Auty, R.
1969   "The Western lexical Elements in the Kiev Missal", *Slawisch-deutsche Wechselbeziehungen in Sprache, Literatur und Kultur* (ed. W. Krauss et al.), 3-6. Berlin.
1976   "Lateinisches und Althochdeutsches im altkirchenslavischen Wortschatz", *Slovo* 25-26, 164-179.
Basaj, M.
1966   *Bohemizmy w języku pism Marcina Krowickiego* (= *Komitet Słowianoznawstwa Polskiej Akademii Nauk. Monografie Slawistyczne* 9). Wrocław.
Basaj, M. i J. Siatkowski
1964-1979   "Przegląd wyrazów uważanych w literaturze naukowej za bohemizmy", 1, *RKJŁ* 10, 1964, 60-75; 4, *SFPS* 6, 1967, 7-24; 5, *SFPS* 7, 1967, 5-31; 6, *SFPS* 8, 1969, 5-33; 7, *SFPS* 9, 1970, 5-35; 8, *SFPS* 10, 1971, 5-34; 9, *SFPS* 11, 1972, 5-46; 11, *SFPS* 13, 1974, 5-36; 12, *SFPS* 14, 1974, 5-41; 15, *SFPS* 17, 1978, 5-50; 16, *SFPS* 18, 1979, 5-50.
Birnbaum, H.
1985   "Zur Problematik des Westkirchenslavischen", *Litterae slavicae medii aevi. Francisco Venceslao Mareš sexagenario oblatae* (= *Sagners Slavistische Samlung* 8, ed. J. M. Reinhart), 53-65. München.
1987   "On the Genealogical and Typological Classification of Old Church Slavonic and its Textual Evidence", *Die Welt der Slaven* 32, 362-407.
1991   *Aspects of the Slavic Middle Ages and Slavic Renaissance Culture.* New York.
Boba, I.
1973   "Methodian and Moravian Continuity and Tradition in Poland", *VII Międzynarodowy kongres slawistów,* 969-971. Warszawa.
Bosl, K.
1964   "Probleme der Missionierung des böhmisch-mährischen Herrschaftsraumes", *Cyrillo-Methodiana. Zur Frühgeschichte des Christentums bei den Slaven 863-1963* (ed. M. Hellman et al.), 1-38. Köln-Graz.
Brückner, A.
1915   "Wpływy języków obcych na język polski", *Język polski i jego historia z uwzględnieniem innych języków na ziemiach polskich* (= *Encyklopedia polska* 2, III/I), 100-153. Kraków.
Budzyk, K.
1955   *Szkice i materiały do dziejów literatury staropolskiej.* Warszawa.
Čech, E.
1948   "*Učeník-mučeník-zvoleník,* Studie ke vzniku staročeské terminologie", *Slovanské studie. Sbírka statí, věnovaných prelátu univ. prof.*

dr. Josefu Vajsovi k učtění jeho životního díla (ed. J. Kurz et al.), 174-181. Praha.

Cejtlin, R.M.
1977   *Leksika staroslavjanskogo jazyka.* Moskva.

Cejtlin, R.M., R. Večerka i E. Bláhová (ed.)
1994   *Staroslavjanskij slovar' (po rukopisjam X-XI vekov).* Moskva.

Čiževskij, D. (Tschiževskij)
1968   "Kirchenslavische Literatur bei den Westslaven", *Cyrillo-Methodianische Fragen. Slavische Philologie und Altertumskunde* (= *Acta Congressus historiae Slavicae Salisburgensis in memoriam SS. Cyrilli et Methodii anno 1963 celebrati*), 13-28. Wiesbaden.

Dąbrowska, E.
1970   "La Pologne du Sud et l'État de Grande Moravie au 9. siècle", *I Międzynarodowy kongres archeologii słowiańskiej* 3, 180-184. Wrocław.

Dąbrowski, J.
1958   "Studia nad początkami państwa polskiego", *Rocznik Krakowski* 34/1.

Dittrich, Z.R.
1962   *Christianity in Great Moravia.* Groningen.

Dvorník, F.
1949   *The making of Central and Eastern Europe.* London.
1962   *The Slavs in the European History and Civilization.* New Jersey.
1970   *Byzantine Missions among the Slavs. SS. Constantine-Cyril and Methodius.* New Brunswick.

Dziewulski, W.
1965   "Próba regeneracji teorii o obrządku słowiańskim w Polsce", *Kwartalnik Historyczny* 72/1, 39-46.

Eggers, M.
1996   *Das Erzbistum des Method. Lage, Wirkung und Nachleben der kyrillomethodianischen Mission* (= *Slavische Beiträge* 339). München.

Frinta, A.
1918   *Náboženské názvosloví československé.* Praha.

Gebauer, J.
1970²   *Slovník staročeský* 1-2. Praha.

Graus, F.
1971   "Die Entwicklung der Legenden der sogenannten Slavenapostel Konstantin und Method in Böhmen und Mähren", *Jahrbücher für Geschichte Osteuropas* 19, 161-211.

Grivec, F.
1960   *Konstantin und Method. Lehrer der Slaven.* Wiesbaden.

Havránek, B.
1956   "Otázka existence církevní slovanštiny v Polsku", *Slavia* 25, 300-305.
1963   "Vlivy spisovné češtiny na jiné jazyky slovanské v době feudalismu", *Studie o spisovném jazyce*, 291-304. Praha.
1975   "Vztahy kláštera na Slovanech k jazyku a literatuře charvátskohlahólské", *Z tradic slovanské kultury v Čechách*, 145-148. Praha.

422

Havránek, B. et al. (ed.)
1968ff.   *Staročeský slovník.* Praha.
Horálek, K.
1948   "K otázce leksikálních bohemismů v staroslověnských památkách",
             *Slovanské studie. Sbírka statí, věnovaných prelátu univ. prof. dr. Jo-
             sefu Vajsovi, k učtění jeho životního díla* (ed. J. Kurz et al.), 115-119.
             Praha.
Humbach, H.
1969   "Aksl. *milosrъdъ*, got. *armhaírts* und lat. *misericors*", *Die Welt der
             Slaven* 14, 351-353.
Jagić, V.
1899   "Die slavischen Composita in ihrem sprachgeschichtlichen Auftre-
             ten", *Archiv für slavische Philolologie* 21, 28-40.
1913²   *Entstehungsgeschichte der kirchenslavischen Sprache.* Berlin.
Kalaga, J. i D. Górna
1982 [1984] "Wczesnośredniowieczny kompleks osadniczy przy ul. Batalionów
             chłopskich w Wiślicy w świetle najnowszych badań", *Polskie kon-
             takty z piśmiennictwem cerkiewnosłowiańskim do końca wieku XIV
             (= Zeszyty Naukowe Humanistycznego Uniwersytetu Gdańskiego,
             Slawistyka* 3), 17-24. Gdańsk.
Kantor, M.
1990   *The Origins of Christianity in Bohemia. Sources and Commentary.*
             Evanston.
1993   "A Question of Language. Church Slavonic and the West Slavs", *XI.
             medzinárodný zjazd slavistov. Zborník resumé*, 320-329. Bratislava.
Karpluk, M.
1972   "Ślady liturgii słowiańskiej w staropolskich imionach chrześcijań-
             skich (typ Koźma, Łuka)", *Z polskich studiów slawistycznych* 4, *Ję-
             zykoznawstwo*, 155-161.
1973   "O staropolskim przejmowaniu imion wczesnochrześcijańskich (typ
             Bartłomiej, Maciej)", *Onomastica* 18, 152-172.
1977   "Argumenty onomastyczne w dyskusji nad liturgią słowiańską w
             Polsce", *Onomastica* 22, 79-92.
1978   "Dalszy ślad liturgii słowiańskiej w staropolskiej antroponimii: Pa-
             weł", *Z polskich studiów slawistycznych* 5, *Językoznawstwo*,
             493-499.
1980   "Staropolskie warianty imienia Mikołaj (na tle słowiańskim)", *Ono-
             mastica* 5, 103-114.
1981   "Traces of the Slavonic Rite in Poland", *Proceedings of the Thir-
             teenth International Congress of Onomastic Sciences, Cracow, August
             21-25, 1978* (ed. K. Rymut), vol. 1, 593-598. Wrocław.
1982 [1984] "Imiona apostołów i ewangelistów jako świadectwo oddziaływania li-
             turgii słowiańskiej w Polsce", *Polskie kontakty z piśmiennictwem
             cerkiewnosłowiańskim do końca wieku XIV (= Zeszyty Naukowe Hu-
             manistycznego Uniwersytetu Gdańskiego, Slawistyka* 3), 63-68.
             Gdańsk.

423

1988a   "Elementy starobułgarskie i cerkiewnosłowiańskie w polszczyźnie XVI w.", *Z polskich studiów slawistycznych* 7, *Językoznawstwo*, 179-187.
1988b   "O najwcześniejszym polskim słownictwie chrześcijańskim", *O języku religijnym* (= *KUL. Zakład badań nad literaturą religijną* 13, ed. M. Karpluk, J. Sambor), 89-102. Lublin.
1989   "Słownictwo cerkiewne w polszczyźnie XVI wieku. Wybór przykładów", *Chrześcijański Wschód a kultura polska* (ed. R. Łużny), 127-147. Lublin.
1996   *Z polsko-ruskich związków językowych. Słownictwo cerkiewne w polszczyźnie XVI wieku*. Warszawa.
Klemensiewicz, Z.
1974   *Historia języka polskiego* 1-3, Warszawa.
Klich, E.
1927   *Polska terminologia chrześcijańska*. Poznań.
Kurkiewicz, A. et al.
1974   *Tysiąc lat dziejów Polski. Kalendarium*. Warszawa.
Kurz, J., od 1982 Z. Hauptová (ed.)
1958ff. *Slovník jazyka staroslověnského – Lexicon Linguae Palaeoslovenicae*. Praha.
Labuda, G.
1984   "Kraków biskupi przed rokiem 1000. Przyczynek do dyskusji nad dziejami misji metodiańskiej w Polsce", *Studia Historyczne* 27/3 (106), 371-411.
1988   "Jakimi drogami przyszło do Polski chrześcijaństwo?", *Nasza Przeszłość* 69, 39-82.
Lanckorońska, K.
1954   "Le vestigia del rito Cirillo-Metodiano in Polonia", *Antemurale* 1, 13-28.
1961   *Studies on the Roman-Slavonic Rite in Poland*. Roma.
Lehr-Spławiński, T.
1932   "Misja słowiańska św. Metodego a Polska", *Collectanea Theologica* 13, 3-12.
1954   "Konstantyn i Metodiusz w walce o liturgię słowiańską", *Rozprawy i szkice z dziejów kultury Słowian*, 149-162. Warszawa. Przedruk z: *Przegląd Zachodni* 12, 626-638.
1959   *Żywoty Konstantyna i Metodego (obszerne)*. Poznań.
1961a   "Czy są ślady istnienia liturgii cyrylo-metodejskiej w dawnej Polsce?", *Od piętnastu wieków. Szkice z dziejów i pradziejów kultury polskiej*, 42-50. Warszawa. Przedruk z: *Slavia* 25, 1956, 291 i ns. (n.v.).
1961b   "Nowa faza dyskusji o zagadnieniu liturgii słowiańskiej w dawnej Polsce", *Od piętnastu wieków. Szkice z dziejów i pradziejów kultury polskiej*, 51-67. Warszawa. Przedruk z: *Nasza Przeszłość* 7, 1958, 235 i ns. (n.v.).
1961c   "Pierwszy chrzest Polski", *Od piętnastu wieków. Szkice z dziejów i pradziejów kultury polskiej*, 68-75. Warszawa. Przedruk z: *Slavia* 29, 1960, 341-349.

1961d   "Przyczynki krytyczne do dziejów dawnych Wiślan", *Od piętnastu wieków. Szkice z dziejów i pradziejów kultury polskiej*, 35-41. Warszawa. Przedruk z: *Prace z dziejów Polski feudalnej ofiarowane Romanowi Grodeckiemu*, 35 i ns. Warszawa, 1960 (n.v.).

1961e   "Dookoła obrządku słowiańskiego w dawnej Polsce", *Od piętnastu wieków. Szkice z dziejów i pradziejów kultury polskiej*, 76-81. Warszawa. Przedruk z: *Księga pamiątkowa ku czci Stanisława Pigonia* (ed. Z. Czerny et al.), 127-132. Kraków, 1961.

1968   "Reichte die slavische Liturgie-Praxis einmal bis nach Polen?", *Cyrillo-Methodianische Fragen. Slavische Philologie und Altertumskunde* (= *Acta Congressus historiae Slavicae Salisburgensis in memoriam SS. Cyrilli et Methodii anno 1963 celebrati*), 89-94. Wiesbaden.

Leśny, J.

1982 [1984]   "Sprawa tzw. państwa Wiślan. Z przeszłości politycznej obszaru dorzecza górnej Wisły w IX-X wieku", *Polskie kontakty z piśmiennictwem cerkiewnosłowiańskim do końca wieku XIV* (= *Zeszyty Naukowe Humanistycznego Uniwersytetu Gdańskiego, Slawistyka* 3), 35-46. Gdańsk.

Ludvíkovský , J.

1965   "Great Moravia Tradition in the 10th Cent. Bohemia and Legenda Christiani", *Magna Moravia. Sborník k 1100. výročí příchodu bizantské mise na Moravu* (ed. J. Macůrek), 525-556. Praha.

L'vov, A.S.

1968   "Češsko-moravskaja leksika v pamjatnikax drevnerusskoj pis'mennosti", *Slavjanskoje jazykoznanije. VI. Meždunarodnyj s"ezd slavistov (Praga, avgust 1968 g.). Doklady sovetskoj delegacii* (ed. V.V. Vinogradov et al.), 316-338. Moskva.

Łesiów, M.

1958   "Czy staropolskie imię Klimont i jego postaci pochodne mogą być świadectwem istnienia liturgii słowiańskiej w Polsce?", *Onomastica* 4, 131-138.

Łowmiański, H.

1970   "Zagadnienie liturgii słowiańskiej w Polsce", *Początki Polski. Z dziejów Słowian w I tysiącleciu naszej ery* 4, 493-515. Warszawa.

1971   "The Slavic Rite in Poland and St. Adalbert", *Acta Poloniae Historica* 29, 5-21.

Machek, V.

1962²   *Etymologický slovník jazyka českého*. Praha.

Mareš, F.V.

1956   "Nedělja cvětnaja. *Květná neděle*, dominica in Palmis", *Slavia* 25/2, 258-259.

1961   "Drevneslavjanskij literaturnyj jazyk v velikomoravskom gosudarstve", *Voprosy jazykoznanija* 10/2, 12-23.

1963   "Česká redakce cirkevní slovanštiny v světle Besěd Řehoře Velikého (Dvojeslova)", *Slavia* 32, 417-451.

1979   *An anthology of Church Slavonic texts of Western (Czech) origin, with an outline of Czech-Church Slavonic language and literature and with a selected bibliography*. München.

Michałowska, T.
1996²   *Średniowiecze*. Warszawa.
Milewski, T.
1965   "Język staro-cerkiewno-słowiański w średniowiecznej Polsce", *Zeszyty Naukowe Uniwersytetu Jagiellońskiego. Prace Językoznawcze* 15, 7-21. Kraków.
Minikowska, T.
1980   *Wyrazy ukraińskie w polszczyźnie literackiej XVI w.* (= *Towarzystwo Naukowe w Toruniu. Prace Wydziału Filologiczno-Filozoficznego* 27/3). Toruń.
Molnár, N.
1985   *The Calques of Greek Origin in the Most Ancient Old Slavic Gospel Texts*. Budapest i Köln-Wien.
Moszyński, L.
1969   "Kryteria stosowane przez Konstantego-Cyryla przy wprowadzaniu wyrazów obcego pochodzenia do tekstów słowiańskich", *Slavia* 38, 552-564.
1971   "Liturgia słowiańska i głagolskie zabytki w Polsce", *Slovo* 21, 255-273.
1985   "Kto i kiedy ustalił słowiańskie dni tygodnia", *Litterae slavicae medii aevi. Francisco Venceslao Mareš sexagenario oblatae* (= *Sagners Slavistische Samlung* 8, ed. J. M. Reinhart), 223-230. München.
1989   "Polskie określenia trzech niedziel poprzedzających Wielki Post. Dominica septuagesima, sexagesima i quinquagesima", *Chrześcijański Wschód a kultura polska* (ed. R. Łużny), 163-177. Lublin.
Moszyński, L. i H. Wątróbska (ed.)
1982 [1984] *Polskie kontakty z piśmiennictwem cerkiewnosłowiańskim do końca wieku XIV* (= *Zeszyty Naukowe Humanistycznego Uniwersytetu Gdańskiego, Slawistyka* 3). Gdańsk.
Ogijenko, I.
1929   "Język cerkiewno-słowiański na Litwie i w Polsce w w. XV-XVIII", *Prace Filologiczne* 14, 525-543.
Paszkiewicz, H.
1954   *The Origin of Russia*. London.
Reczek, J.
1968   *Bohemizmy leksykalne w języku polskim do końca XV wieku. Wybrane zagadnienia* (= *PAN Oddział w Krakowie. Prace Komisji Słowianoznawstwa* 17), Wrocław.
Reinhart, J.M.
1980   "Methodisches zu den lexikalischen Bohemismen im Tschechisch-Kirchenslavischen am Beispiel der Homilien Gregors des Großen", *Wiener Slavistisches Jahrbuch* 26, 46-102.
Rospond, S.
1966   "Chrystianizacja Polski a badania językoznawcze", *Nasza Przeszłość* 25, 7-32.
1968a   "Badania milenijne językoznawcy", *Biuletyn Polskiego Towarzystwa Językowego* 26, 11-31.

426

1968b   "Problem liturgii słowiańskiej w południowej Polsce", *Silesia Antiqua* 9, 128-142.

Rusek, J.
1988   "Z dziedzictwa cyrylo-metodyjskiego w językach bułgarskim i polskim na przykładzie wybranych grup semantycznych terminologii chrześcijańskiej", *Tradycje Cyryla i Metodego w językach i literaturach słowiańskich* (ed. A. Bartoszewicz et al.), 23-36. Warszawa.

Schaeken, J.
1987   *Die Kiever Blätter* (= *Studies in Slavic and General Linguistics* 9). Amsterdam.

Schenk, W.
1982 [1984] "Kult liturgiczny świętych Cyryla i Metodego w Polsce", *Polskie kontakty z piśmiennictwem cerkiewnosłowiańskim do końca wieku XIV* (= *Zeszyty Naukowe Wydziału Humanistycznego Uniwersytetu Gdańskiego, Slawistyka* 3), 57-62. Gdańsk.

Siatkowski, J.
1981a   "Wpływy staro-cerkiewno-słowiańskie w języku polskim", *Trzynaście wieków Bułgarii. Materiały polsko-bułgarskiej sesji naukowej, Warszawa 28-30 X 1981* (ed. J. Siatkowski), 13-18. Wrocław.

1981b   "Po văprosa za neposredstvenoto vlijanije na starobălgarskija ezik vărxu staropolskija", *Bălgarski ezik* 31/5, 407-412.

1982 [1984] "O cerkiewizmach w najstarszej polskiej terminologii chrześcijańskiej", *Polskie kontakty z piśmiennictwem cerkiewnosłowiańskim do końca wieku XIV* (= *Zeszyty Naukowe Wydziału Humanistycznego Uniwersytetu Gdańskiego, Slawistyka* 3), 97-105. Gdańsk.

1984   "Za vlijanieto na starobălgarskija ezik vărxu polski posredstvom češki ezik", *Palaeobulgarica/Starobălgaristika* 18/2, 108-110.

1985   "Przedcyrylometodejska i starobułgarska terminologia chrześcijańska w języku polskim", *Od Wisły do Maricy*, 154-167. Kraków.

Sławski, F.
1952-1977 *Słownik etymologiczny języka polskiego* 1-5. Kraków.

Sławski, F. (ed.)
1974ff.   *Słownik prasłowiański*. Wrocław.

Sreznevskij I.I.
1893-1903 *Materialy dlja slovarja drevnerusskogo jazyka* 1-3. Sanktpeterburg.

Szcześniak, W.
1904   *Obrządek słowiański w Polsce pierwotnej rozważony w świetle dziejopisarstwa polskiego*. Warszawa.

Szymański, J.
1963   "Czy w Polsce istniał obrządek rzymsko-słowiański? Uwagi na marginesie książki K. Lanckorońskiej, Studies on the Roman-Slavonic Rite in Poland", *Zeszyty Naukowe KUL* 6/2 (22), 41-56.

Taszycki, W.
1950a   "Staropolskie miłosirdy", *Poradnik językowy* 5, 18-20.
1950b   "Na marginesie ostatniego wydania 'Kazań świętokrzyskich'", *Poradnik językowy* 2, 1-5.

Tóth, I.H. (Tot)
1993   "Vyšegrad na Dunae i Sazava", *Studia Slavica Hungarica* 38, 191-202.
Umiński, J.
1953 [1957] "Obrządek słowiański w Polsce IX-XI wieku i zagadnienia drugiej metropolii polskiej w czasach Bolesława Chrobrego", *Roczniki Humanistyczne Katolickiego Uniwersytetu Lubelskiego* 4, 1-44.
Urbańczyk, S.
1946   *Z dawnych stosunków językowych polsko-czeskich.* 1: *Biblia królowej Zofii a staroczeskie przekłady Pisma św.* (= *Rozprawy Wydziału Filologicznego Akademii Umiejętności* 67), 88-171. Kraków.
1965   "Polskie trójca i słowiańskie rzeczowniki odliczebnikowe", *SFPS* 5, 119-122.
1988   "Wirkte die methodianische Mission in Polen?", *Symposium Methodianum: Beiträge der Internationalen Tagung in Regensburg (17. bis 24. April 1985) zum Gedenken an den 1100. Todestag des hl. Method* (ed. K. Trost et al.), 341-346. Neuried.
Urbańczyk, S. et al. (ed.)
1953ff.   *Słownik staropolski.* Warszawa.
Vasmer, M. (Fasmer)
1964-1973 *Ètimologičeskij slovar' russkogo jazyka* (perevod s nem. i dopolnenija O. N. Trubačeva, pod red. B. A. Larina). Moskva.
Večerka, R.
1963   "Velkomoravská literatura v přemyslovských Čechách", *Slavia* 32, 398-416.
1965   "Velikomoravskie istoki cerkovnoslavjanskoj pis'mennosti v češskom knjažestve", *Magna Moravia. Sborník k 1100. výročí příchodu bizantské mise na Moravu* (ed. J. Macůrek), 493-524. Praha.
1990   "Mysli i predpoloženija o vozniknovenii Kijevskix glagoličeskix listkov", *Dissertationes Slavicae. Slavistische Mitteilungen. Materialy i soobščenija po slavjanovedeniju. Sectio Linguistica* 21, 297-312. Szeged.
Vincenz, A. de
1982 [1984] "Krytyczna analiza dokumentów dotyczących kontaktow Polski z misją cyrylometodejską", *Polskie kontakty z piśmiennictwem cerkiewnosłowiańskim do końca wieku XIV* (= *Zeszyty Naukowe Humanistycznego Uniwersytetu Gdańskiego, Slawistyka* 3, 68-78. Gdańsk.
1983   "The Moravian mission in Poland revisited", *Okeanos* (= Fs. I. Ševčenko, ed. C. Mango, O. Pritsak), 639-654. Cambridge.
1988   "Die altkirchenslavischen Elemente des westslavischen Wortschatzes und das sog. cyrillo-methodianische Erbe in Böhmen", *Symposium Methodianum: Beiträge der Internationalen Tagung in Regensburg (17. bis 24. April 1985) zum Gedenken an den 1100. Todestag des hl. Method* (ed. K. Trost et al.), 593-598. Neuried.
1995   "Zur Herkunft von aksl. троица", *'Ite meis manibus gestati saepe libelli'. Studia Slavica Ioanni Schultze* (ed. W. Lehfeldt), 37-40. Göttingen.

428

Vlasto, A.P.
1970   *The Entry of the Slavs into Christendom. An Introduction to the Medieval History of the Slavs*. Cambridge.
Widajewicz, J.
1947   *Państwo Wiślan* (= *Biblioteka Studium Słowiańskiego Uniwersytetu Jagiellońskiego A/2*). Kraków.
1948   "Prohor i Prokulf, najdawniejsi biskupi krakowscy", *Nasza Przeszłość* 1, s. 17 i ns. (n. v.)
Wiehl, I.
1974   *Untersuchungen zum Wortschatz der Freisinger Denkmäler. Christliche Terminologie* (= *Slavische Beiträge* 78). München.
Zathey, J.
1949   "O kilku przepadłych zabytkach rękopiśmiennych Biblioteki Narodowej w Warszawie", *Studia z dziejów kultury polskiej*, 73-95. Warszawa.

Dutch Contributions to the Twelfth International Congress of Slavists,
Cracow, Linguistics (= Studies in Slavic and General Linguistics Vol 24),
429–463. RODOPI, Amsterdam – Atlanta, GA 1998.

ЧТО ТАКОЕ *РУССКАЯ РЕДАКЦИЯ* ЦЕРКОВНО-СЛАВЯНСКОГО ТЕКСТА?

УИЛЬЯМ ФЕДЕР

Антону Ван ден Баару к 75-летию

В статье рассматривается значение термина *русская редакция* на примере данных по трансмиссии текста *О Писменехъ* и типологических их параллелях. Доказывается, что термин основан на смешении понятий *рукопись* и *текст*, которое неизбежно ведет до неточных сравнений списков, а также до заслонения самых существенных проблем в истории церковнославянского языка. Предлагается определить церковнославянский язык в дальнейшем не как язык *рукописей* (Р.М. Цейтлин вслед за традицией науки), а как язык *текстов* (С. Темчин).

Все понятия церковнославянской[1] филологии основаны на сравнении списков текстов[2] и тем самым относительны.[3] Относительны таким образом и понятия, предназначенные отграничить этапы развития, как *старославянский язык*: по определию Ван-Вейка (1957) оно охватывает *памятники, написанные в старославянский период* (с. 42) и отражающие *правильное употребление носовых гласных* (с. 36). Спорны тут, ибо относительны, термины *памятник, старославянский период* и *правильное употребление*: первый двузначен, обозначая и рукопись, и текст (которое значение актуализируется, зависит от типа сравнения); второй неопределен, имея лишь верхнюю границу, 863 г., но нет нижней,[4] а равно и нет определенной территории распространения; третий лишен значения, потому что он исключает добрую половину покрываемых вторым термином источников, несмотря на то, что вообще нет источников без неправильных употреблений.[5] Одним словом, концептуальное построение *старославянского языка* валидно лишь до тех пор, пока не нарушается консенсус о ее приемлемости.

Так же относительно и понятие *русская редакция*, основывающееся на двух отличительных по отношению к церковнославянскому тексту признаках, качествах *русскости* и *редакции*, которые устанавливаются путем сравнения текста предполагаемой русской редакции с церковнославянским текстом.

430

1.　Проведем сначала, вслед за Трембовольским (1989), сравнение одного из текстов русского *Рогожского сборника* XV в. (= *Р*) с тем же текстом по древнейшему списку, болгарскому *Иван-Александровскому сборнику* 1348 г. (= *Л*):[6]

(1:1-9:6 <u>пропущено</u> *Р*)

   Гл. 9:7 (9:8-10 <u>пропущено</u> *Р*)

Л　дондеже бꙁ̄ раꙁдѣли ꙗꙁыкы при стльпотвореньи такоже пишеть.

Р　По стлꙁпотвореньи же бы̄ еꙋ̈а раꙁдѣлиша ꙿ таꙁьlци.

   9:11-12

Л　тако и нрави и обычае и оустави. ꙁакони. и хытрости. на ꙗꙁыкы.

Р　тако ⸗ раꙁдѣлиша ꙿ и нрави. и обычаи. и оуставь. и ꙁаконы. и хитро̄ на таꙁыкы.

   9:13-14

Л　египтѣнѡм же ꙁемемѣрение. а персѡмꙁ и халдѣѡмꙁ и асиреѡмꙁ.

Р　тако̄ се гл̄ю. ё таꙁыкꙁ егѵпескыи. емꙋ̄ достало са ꙁемлевѣрїе. а персо̄. и халдеꙋ̄. и асоурїемꙁ.

   9:15-16

Л　ꙁвѣꙁдочьтение. вльшвение. врачевание. чарованиа. и всѣ хытрость чл̄ча.

Р　астрономїе. ꙁьꙁдотеченїе. влꙁшвенїе. _ и чарованїе.

   9:17, 23 (9:18-22 <u>пропущено</u> *Р*)

Л　жидовом же стꙑꙗ книгы. еллинѡмꙁ граматикиа. риторикиа. философиꙗ.

Р　жидовомь ⸗ стыа книгы. еллиномꙁ ⸗ доста са. граматикїа и риторикїа. и философїа.

   Гл. 10:1

Л　нꙗ прѣже сего еллини не имѣхꙗ своимꙁ аꙁыкомь писмен꙼.

Р　нь испрьва еллини не имѣахꙋ̈ оу себе грамоты.

   10:2-3

Л　нꙗ финичьскыми писмены писахꙗ своꙗ си рѣчь. И тако бѣшꙗ многа лѣта.

Р　нꙁ афинеискою грамотою ноужахоӱ са писати свою рѣ̄. и тако бѣша по многа лѣта.

   10:4

Л　панамидь же послѣжде пришедꙁ.

Р　бы̄ нѣкто в ньй философꙁ. именѣ̈ панамидь. й̈ послѣди прише̄.

   10:5-6

Л　начензꙁ ѿ алфы и виты. ѕ҃і писменꙁ тꙁкмо еллинѡмꙁ ѡбрѣте.

Р　сꙁтвори елли̇нӧ абоукоӱ. наченꙁ сице. алфа. вита. и положи словꙁ числѡ̄. ѕ҃і тꙁкмо елли̇но̄ иꙁꙁꙑбрѣте.

   10:7

Л　прѣложи же имꙁ кадьмꙁ милисꙗ̈ писмена. г҃.

Р　по том же по нѣколицѣ лѣтѣ инꙁ книжникꙁ. именѣ̈ кадомꙁ. и сꙗ̈ приложи й̈ три слова писменаа.

   10:8-9

Л　тѣмже многа лѣта. ѳ҃і писмены писаахꙗ.

Р　тѣ̄м и по многа лѣта. девꙗ̈ на десатꙗ̈ю словꙁ свою аꙁбꙋ̈кꙋ̈ своими писмены нꙋ̈жахꙋ̈ са писати.

   10:10

Л　и по томꙁ симонидꙁ ѡбрѣтꙁ приложи двѣ писмени.

Р　по томꙁ ⸗ инꙁ граматикꙁ. именѣ̈ симонидꙁ. обрѣтꙁ еще приложи й̈ два слова писменнаа. и оуже сꙁлагает са число словꙁ й̈. к҃а.

10:11-12

Л епихарїи же сказатель. г҃. писмена ѡбрѣте. и събра са ихъ. к҃д҃.

Р епихарїи же нѣкто сказатель книгꙋ҇ сїи иꙁꙁобрѣте и приложи й три слова писменнаа. и тако събра са аꙁбꙋка гр҆чьскаа. словꙁ число҇. к҃д҃.

10:13-14

Л по мноꙁѣх же лѣтѣхъ дионисꙁ граматикꙁ. ѕ҃. двогласныхъ ѡбрѣте.

Р по томꙁ҇ по мноsѣ лѣтѣ. дїонисꙁ нѣкто ѕѣло граматикꙁ. ѕ҃. двогласны҇ словꙁ иꙁꙁѡбрѣте.

10:15-16

Л по томь же дроугыи. е҃. и дроугыи г҃. чисменитаа.

Р по сй же дроугыи философꙁ. е҃. словꙁ приложи. а инꙁ книжникꙁ. г҃. слова имй числа пишꙋ҇т са. шестое ꙁаве и дева҇ десатое. и дева҇ сотное.

10:17-18

Л и тако мноsи многыми лѣты едва събрашꙗ. ли҃. писменꙁ.

Р и тако по многа лѣта мноꙁи философи едва събрали со҇ аꙁбꙋкꙋ гр҆чьскꙋю. словꙁ число҇ ли҃.

Гл. 11:1-2

Л по том же многомꙁ лѣтѡмꙁ минꙗвшемꙁ. бж҃иемꙁ повелѣниемь ѡбрѣте са. о҃. мꙗжь.

Р по томь҇ многы҇ лѣто҇ миношѣши҇. бж҃ий промыслѡ҇ ѡбрѣтоша҇. о҃. мꙋ҇ мꙋдрецꙁ.

11:3-4

Л иже прѣложишꙗ ѿ жидовꙁскаа на грꙁчьскыи ꙗꙁыкꙁ.

Р й преложили книгы ѿ жидовьска ꙗꙁыка на гр҆чьскыи.

Гл. 12:1-2 (12:3-14:10 пропущено Р), [*14:11-12*]

Л а словѣньскꙁı единꙁ сватꙁи конꙁстантинꙁ. нарицаіемꙁıи кирилꙁ.

[ст҃ыи Кѡнстантинꙁ философꙁ нарицаемыи кирꙁлꙁ.]

Р по то҇ тако҇ лѣто҇ многы҇ миношѣшимꙁ. констатинꙁ. нарицаемыи к҃урилꙁ.

Гл. 14:15-16 (14:17-20 пропущено Р)

Л и меѳодие братꙁ его.

Р и меѳодїи бра҇ его. състависта аꙁбꙋкꙋ грамоты роускыꙗ.

14:21-22

Л вꙁ врѣмена михаила цр҃е гр҆чьскаго.

Р при цр҃и михаилѣ гр҆чьстѣ҇. при патрїарсѣ ѳотїи.

14:24-26 (14:27-15:7 пропущено Р)

Л и бориса кнаꙁа блꙁгар҆скаго. и растица кнаꙁа мор҆ска. и коцелѣ кнаꙁа блатен҆ска.

Р в лѣта бориса кнаsа болгарскꙗ. и растица кнаsа моравскаго. и костелѣ кнаsа блатенскаго. вꙁ кнаженїе кнаsа великаго всеꙗ роуси рюрика. погана соущи и не кр҃щена. ꙁа. ре҃. лѣ до крещенїꙗ роускыꙗ ꙁемлꙗ.

Казалось бы, все ясно: то, что подчеркнуто — редакция, а то, что напечатано жирным шрифтом — русское, и это *дает основания считать этот отрывок русской переработкой «О Писменехъ» XV века* (Трембовольский 1989: 85).

Однако ясно лишь то, что данное заключение валидно только пока мы допускаем, что сравнимость *памятников* не подвержена ограничениям. На самом же деле, если между рукописями нет прямой генетической связи *родитель → потомок* (в текстологических терминах: *антиграф → апограф*), сравнение их дает не больше, чем сравнение

432

собаки с носорогом или, оставаясь на почве филологии, соспоставление русского слова *чаша* с фламандским *tasje*, которое, как предупреждают учебники по сравнительно-историческому языкознанию, неизбежно ведет к *народной этимологии*. Об этом, к сожалению, молчат учебники по текстологии. Вот *P* никак не восходит к *Л*: *9:13* ʒємлєвѣрїє не из ʒємємѣрєниє с͏̈-єн-, *10:1* имѣахȣ с -ъа- не из имѣхѫ, *10:7* приложи не из прѣложи и *14:25* моравскаго не из мор᾽ска. Кроме того *Л* передает не церковнославянский текст как таковой, а является так же, как и *P*, списком с какого-то антиграфа, отношение которого к антиграфу *P* пока остается неразъясненным. И, наконец, *P* содержит немало нерусских признаков: в *редакции* наблюдается 2 употребления имперфекта и 6 аориста (1 в двойственном числе) на не более 3 перфекта; 3 раза употребляется нерусское определение по многа лѣта, а не менее 10 раз – слово в значении *буква*; кроме того вызывает сомнение русское происхождение интерполяций *14:16* състависта аʒбȣкȣ грамоты (с двойственным числом аориста) и *14:22* при патрїарсѣ фотїи (со второй палатализацией).

2. Посмотрим, каково положение с перспективы серьезного изучения родословия рукописей, и сопоставим рукопись с наиболее родственными[7] ей списками: *P* передает ту же версию текста, как и рукопись *Пс*,[8] происшедшая вместе с *П2 Кт* (гипархетип[9] μ') от старшего гипархетипа μ, а также рукописи *Пл Ш* (гип-архетип λ'), произошедшие вместе с *T* от старшего гипархетипа λ; старшие гипархетипы в свою очередь восходят к еще старшему гипархетипу *x*, противопоставленному по ряду чтений гипархетипу δ с рукописями *Мол Вр* (младший гипархетип ζ), *Ч У1 П1* (младший гипархетип θ), *Вл1 Вл2* (младший гипархетип η); тем самым устанавливается группа в 14 списков, которые передают версию общего источника γ, противопоставленного по своим чтениям всем другим версиям данного текста.[10] С версией, с которой произошла рукопись *Л*, она имеет, кроме своей зависимости от общего всем версиям источника (*архетипа*), не более, чем одну точку соприкосновения в рукописи *Мол*, заимствовавшей из нее шесть чтений.[11]

Если – условно – определить текстологическое поколение сроком в 50 лет, то возникновение гипархетипа μ нужно отнести ко времени не позднее 1350 г.,[12] и, соответственно, *x* – ко времени не позднее 1300 г., а γ – не позднее 1250 г. Схематически отношения можно представить в виде следующей стеммы, где затенены отрезки родословия без сохранившихся списков:[13]

1200	1250	1300	1350	1400	1450	1500	1550	1600	1650	1700	1750

Гл. 9:7-8

γ   ДОNДЕЖЕ БГЪ РАЗДѢЛИ АЗЫКЫ. ПРИ СТЛЪПОТВОРЕNИИ. ꙗКОЖЕ ПИШЕТЬ.

δ   ДОNДЕЖЕ БГЪ РАЗДѢЛИ ꙗЗЫКЫ. ПРИ СТОЛПОТВОРЕNİИ. ꙗКОЖЕ ПИШЕТЬ.

к   ДОNДЕЖЕ БГЪ РАЗДѢЛИ АЗЫКЫ. ПРИ СТЛЪПОТВОРЕNИИ. ꙗКОЖЕ ПИШЕТЪ.

λ   ДОNДЕЖЕ БГЪ РАЗДѢЛИ АЗЫКИ. ПРИ СТОЛПОТВОРЕNИ. ꙗКОЖЕ ПИШЕТЪ.

μ   ДОNДЕЖЕ БГЪ РАЗДѢЛИ ꙗЗЫКЫ. ПРИ СТОЛПОТВОРЕNИИ. ТАКО ПИШЕТЪ.

Р   ПО СТЛЪПОТВОРЕNİИ ЖЕ БЫ ЕГА РАЗДѢЛИША ꙗЗЫЦИ.

Пс ДОДЕЖЕ РАДѢЛИ БГЪ АЗЫКИ ПРИ ТОПОТВОРЕNИИ ТАКО ПИШЕ

μ' ДОNДЕЖЕ БГЪ РАДѢЛИ ꙗЗЫКЫ. ПРИ СТОЛПОТВОРЕNИИ. ТАКО ПИШЕТЪ.

9:11-12

γ   ТАКО И NРАВИ. И ОБЫЧАИ. И ОУСТАВИ. И ЗАКОNИ. И ХЫТРОСТИ NА АЗЫКЫ

δ   ТАКО И NРАВИ. И ОБЫЧАИ. И ОУСТАВИ. И ЗАКОNИ. И ХЫТРОСТИ NА АЗЫКЫ

к   ТАКО РАЗДѢЛИША СА И NРАВИ. И ОБЫЧАИ. И ОУСТАВИ. И ЗАКОNИ. И ХИТРОСТИ NА АЗЫКЫ

λ   ТАКО РАЗДѢЛИША СА И NРАВИ. И ОБЫЧАИ. И ОУСТАВИ. И ЗАКОNИ. И ХИТРОСТИ NА АЗЫКИ.

μ   ТАКО РАЗДѢЛИША СА И NРАВИ. И ОБЫЧАИ. И ОУСТАВИ. И ЗАКОNИ. И ХИТРОСТИ NА ꙗЗЫКЫ

Р   ТАКО РАЗДѢЛИША И NРАВИ. И ОБЫЧАИ. И ОУСТАВЫ. И ЗАКОNЫ. И ХИТРО NА ꙗЗЫКЫ

Пс ТАКО РАДѢЛИША И NРАВИ И ОБЗНЧА. И УСТАВИ. И ЗАКОNИ И ХИТРОСТИ NА ꙗЗЗКИ.

μ' ТАКО РАЗДѢЛИША СА И NРАВИ. И ОБЫЧАИ. И ОУСТАВИ. И ЗАКОNИ. И ХИТРОСТИ NА ꙗЗЫКЫ

9:13

γ   ЕГѴПТОМЪ ОУБО ЗЕМЛЕМѢРИЕ.

δ   ЕГѴПТѠ ОУБО ЗЕМЛЕМѢРИЕ.

к   ꙗКО СЕ ГЛЮ ЕСТЬ ꙗЗЫКЪ ЕГѴПЕТЬСКЫИ. ЕМѸЖЕ СА ѸБО ДОСТАЛО ЗЕМЛЕМѢРИЕ.

λ   ꙗКОЖЕ СЕ ГЛЮ ЕСТЬ ꙗЗЫКЪ ЕГИПЕТЬСКИИ. ЕМѸЖЕ СА ѸБО ДОСТАЛО ЗЕМЛЕМѢРИЕ.

μ   ꙗКО СЕ ГЛЮ ЕСТЬ ꙗЗЫКЪ ЕГѴПЕТЬСКЫИ. ЕМѸ ѸБО ДОСТАЛО СА ЗЕМЛЕМѢРИЕ.

Р   ꙗКО СЕ ГЛЮ. Е ꙗЗЫКЪ ЕГѴПЕСКЫИ. ЕМѸ ДОСТАЛО СА ЗЕМЛЕВѢРИЕ.

Пс ꙗКО СЕ ГЛЮ ЕСТЬ АЗЫКЪ ЕГИПЕСКИИ ЕМѸ ѸБО ДОТАЛО СА ЗЕМЛЕМѢРИЕ.

μ' ꙗКО СЕ ГЛЮ ЕСТЬ ꙗЗЫКЪ ЕГѴПЕТЬСКЫИ. ЕМѸЖЕ ѸБО ДОСТАЛО СА ЗЕМЛЕМѢРИЕ.

9:14-15

γ   А ПЕРЬСОМЪ. И ХАЛДЕОМЪ. И АСѴРИОМЪ. ЗВѢЗДОЧЬТИЕ. ВЛЪШВЕNИЕ. ВРАЧЕВАNИЕ. ЧАРОВЕ.

δ   А ПЕРЬСѠ. И ХАЛДѢѠ. И АСѴРИѠ. ЗВѢЗДОЧЬТИЕ. ВЛЪШВЕNИЕ. ВРАЧЕВАNИЕ. ЧАРОВЕ.

к   А ПЕРСОМЪ. И ХАЛДЕОМЪ. И АСѴРИОМЪ. ЅВѢЗДОЧЕТИЕ [на поле АСТРОNОМИЕ]. ВЛЪШВЕNИЕ. ВРАЧЕВАNИЕ. ЧАРОВЕ.

λ   А ПЕРСОМЪ. И ХАЛДЕОМЪ. И АСИРИОМЪ ЅВѢЗДОЧЕТИЕ. ВРАЧЕВАNИЕ.

μ   А ПЕРСОМЪ. И ХАЛДЕОМЪ. И АСѸРИОМЪ. АСТРОNОМИЕ. ЅВѢЗДОЧЕТИЕ. ВЛЪШВЕNИЕ. ВРАЧЕВАNИЕ. ЧАРО.

434

Р а персо̃. и халдеш̃. и асоуріемъ астрономїе. ѕѣздотеченїе. влъшвенїе. и чарованїе.
Пс а персо̃ и ха̃де̃ и асирїо̃ астрономіе. астрономіе. свѣ̃дочетие во̂швение. врачеваⷩие чаро̊̃
μ' а персомъ. и халдѣомъ. и асириомъ. астрономие. астрономие. ѕвѣ̃здочетие. волшвение.
врачеваⷩие. чаро̊̃.

9:16-17

γ и въсака хытрость чл҃ча. жидовомь [на поле егреⷲмь] же ст҃ыа книгы.
δ и въсака хытрость чл҃ча. егреⷲмь же ст҃ыа книгы.
к и всака хитрость чл҃ча. жидовомь [на поле евреомъ] же ст҃ыа книгы.
λ і ина хитрость чл҃ча. жидомъ же и евреомъ ст҃ыа книги.
μ и всака хитрость чл҃ча. жидовомь [на поле евреомъ'] же ст҃ыа книгы
Р жидовомь ⸗ ст҃ыа книгы
Пс и встⷮа͠а хиⷬрость чл҃ча евре̃о̃ же свⷮзⷮга кни̃ги.
μ' и всака хитрость чл҃ча. евреомъ' же ст҃ыа книгы

9:23

γ еллиномъ же граматикиа. риторикиа. философиа.
δ а еллиномъ граматикиꙗ. риторикиꙗ. философиꙗ.
к ел'лином же граматикиа. и риторикиа. и философиа.
λ ел'линомъ же изобрѣтоша са граматикиа і риториа. и философиа.
μ еллином же **дасть са** гра̃̂матикиа. и риторикиа. и философиа.
Р еллиномъ ⸗ доста са. граматикїа и риторикїа. и философїа.
Пс е̃ли̃но̃ же да̃тъ стⷶ гра̃̂матикига и риторикига и ꙫилософиа.
μ' еллином же дасть са грамотикиа. и риторикиа. и ꙫилософиа.

Гл. 10:1

γ Nъ прѣжде сего ел'лини не имѣахꙗ своимь аꙁыкомь писменъ.
δ Nъ прѣжде сего ел'лини не имахꙗ своимь аꙁыкомь писменъ.
к Nо прежде сего ел'лини не имѣахꙋ своимъ аꙁыкомъ писменъ.
λ Nо преже сего ел'лини не имѣахꙋ своимъ аꙁыкомъ писменъ.
μ Nь прѣ̃де сего еллини не имѣахъ своимъ аꙁыкомъ писменъ.
Р Nь **испрьва** еллини не имѣахъ **оу себе грамоты**
Пс Nо прѣ̃де сего е̃лини не имⷷꙗхⷹ своимъ аⷥзкⷪ̃ пи́мⷷ̃
μ' Nо прѣ̃де сего еллини не имѣахꙋ своимъ гаꙁыкомъ писменъ.

10:2-3

γ но финичьскыми писмены писахꙗ своꙗ си рѣчь. и тако быша многа лѣта.
δ но финичьскыми писмены писахꙗ своꙗ си рѣчь. и тако быша многа лѣта.
к нꙗ финичьскыми писмены писахꙋ своꙋ рѣчь. и тако бѣша многа лѣта.
λ но финическыми писмены писахꙋ свою рѣчь. и тако бѣша многа лѣта.
μ нꙁ финическыми писмены писахъ свою рѣчь. и тако бѣша **по** многа лѣта.
Р нꙁ **афинеискою грамотою** ноуⷤꙗхоу са писати свою рѣ̃ и тако бѣша по многа лѣта.
Пс но ꙫиническими пи́менꙁ писахꙋ свою рѣчь и тако бѣша во̃̃нога лѣта.
μ' но финийскыми писмены писахꙋ свою рѣчь. и тако бѣша по многа лѣта.

10:4

γ панамидъ же послѣди пришедъ.
δ панамидъ же послѣди пришедъ.
к **быⷭ нⷷкто въ' нихъ философъ** имеⷩ̃ панамидъ. **иⷤ** послѣди пришедъ.
λ Быⷭ нⷷкто въ' нихъ философ имеⷩ̃ панамидъ. аⷤ послѣди пришедъ.
μ быⷭ нⷷкто въ' нихъ философъ имеⷩ̃ панамидь. иже послѣди пришⷷ̃.
Р бы́ нⷷкто в ни философъ. имеⷩ̃ панамидь. и́ послѣди пришⷷ̃
Пс бꙁⷮкть нⷷкто в ни ꙫилосо̃ имеⷩ̃ понимꙗ иже по̃леди пришⷷ̃
μ' быⷭ нⷷкто въ' нихъ ꙫилософъ имеⷩ̃ понамꙗ. иже послѣди пришⷷ̃.

10:5-6

γ НАЧЕНЗ. ѿ АЛФЫ ВИТЫ Ѕ҃ι ПИСМЕНЗ ТѯКМО. ЕЛЬЛИНОМЗ ѠБРѢТЕ.

δ НАЧЕНЗ. ѿ АЛФЫ ВИТЫ Ѕ҃ι ПИСМЕНЗ ТѯКМО. ЕЛ'ЛИНОМЗ ѠБРѢТЕ.

к СЗТВОРИ ЕЛЬЛИНОМЗ АЗБꙊКꙊ. НАЧЕНЗ ѿ АЛФЫ ВИТЫ И ПОЛОЖИ ИМЗ. Ѕ҃ι ПИСМЕНЗ. ТѯКМО ЕЛЬЛИНОМЗ ОБРѢТЕ.

λ СОТВОРИ ЕЛЛИНОМЗ АЗБꙊКꙊ. НАЧЕНЗ ѿ АЛФЫ ВИТЫ. И ПОЛОЖИ ИМЗ. Ѕ҃ι ПИСМЕНЗ. ТОКМО ЕЛЛИНОМЗ ОБРѢТЕ.

μ СЗТВОРИ ЕЛЬЛИНОМЗ АЗБꙊКꙊ. НАЧЕНЗ ѿ АЛФЫ ВИТЗΙ И ПОЛОЖИ ИМЗ ШЕСТЬ НА ДЕСѦТ ПИСМЕНЗ. ТѯКМО ЕЛЬЛИНОМЗ ОБРѢТЕ.

Р СЗТВОРИ ЕЛЛΙНѲ҃ АБОУКОУ. НАЧЕНЗ СИЦЕ. АЛФА ВИТА. И ПОЛОЖИ СЛОВΖ ЧИСЛѲ҃. Ѕ҃ι ТѯКМО ЕЛЛΙНѲ҃ ИЗЗѠБРѢТЕ

Пс СѠВОРИ ЕЛ҃ΙНѲ҃ АБУКУ. НАЧѢ ѿ АѲΖΙ ВИТЗΙ И ПОЛОЖИ Й ШЕ꙯ТЬ НА ДЕСАТ ПΙ҃МѢ ТОКМО ЕЛ҃ΙНѲ҃ ѻ҅БРѢТЕ.

μ' СОТВОРИ ЕЛЬЛИНОМЗ АЗБꙊКꙊ. НАЧѢ ѿ АЛФЫ ВИТЗ. И ПОЛОЖИ ИМЗ ШЕСТЬ НА ДЕСА҃ ПИСМЕНЗ. ТОКМО ЕЛЬЛИНОМЗ ОБРѢТЕ.

10:7

γ ПРИЛОЖИ ИМЗ КАДЗМЬ МИЛИСИИ. ПИСМЕНА ТРИ.

δ ПРИЛОЖИ ИМЗ. КАДЗМЬ МИЛИСΙИ. ПИСМЕНА ТРИ.

к По ТОМЗ ЖЕ ПО НѢКОЛИЦѢ ЛѢТЕХЗ. ИНЗ КНИЖНИКЗ ИМЕНЕМЗ КАДОМЗ МИЛИСΙИ. И СΙИ ПРИЛОЖИ ИМЗ ТРИ СЛОВА ПИСМЕН'НА.

λ По ТОМЗ ЖЕ ПО НѢКОЛИЦѢ ЛѢТЕХ. ИНЗ КНИЖНИКЗ ИМЕНЕМЗ КАДОМ МИЛИСΙИ. И СЕЙ ПРИЛОЖИ ИМЗ. Г. СЛОВА ПИСМЕН'НА

μ По ТОМЗ ЖЕ ПО НѢКОЛИЦѢ ЛѢТЕХЗ. ИНЗ КНИЖНИКЗ ИМЕНЕМЗ КАДОМЗ МИЛИСЕИ. И СΙИ ПРИЛОЖИ ИМЗ ТРИ СЛОВА ПИСМЕННАА.

Р ПО ТОМ ЖЕ ПО НѢКОЛИЦѢ ЛѢТѢ ИНЗ КНИЖНИКЗ. ИМЕНѢ҃ КАДОМЗ. И СΙИ ПРИЛОЖИ Й ТРИ СЛОВА ПИСМЕНАА.

Пс По Тѻ҃ ЖЕ ПО НѢКОЛИЦѢ ЛѢТѢ ИНЗ КН҃ЖΙКЗ ИМЕНѢ҃ КАДѻ҃ МИЛИСЕ. И СΙИ ПРИЛОЖИ Й ТРИ СЛОВА ПΙМЕННАꙖ

μ' По ТОМЗ ЖЕ ПО НѢКОЛИЦѢ ЛѢТЕХЗ. ИНЗ КНИЖНИКЗ ИМЕНЕМЗ КАДОМЗ МИЛИСЕИ. И СΙИ ПРИЛОЖИ ИМЗ ТРИ СЛОВА ПИСМЕННАА.

10:8-9

γ ТѢМЗЖЕ МНОГА ЛѢТА. ДЕВАТИЮ НА ДЕСАТЕ ПИСМЕНЫ ПИСАХꙊ҄.

δ ТѢМЗЖЕ МНОГА ЛѢТА. ДЕВАТИЮ НА ДЕСАТЕ ПИСМЕНЫ ПИСАХꙊ҄.

к ТѢМЗЖЕ МНОГА ЛѢТА. Ѳ҃Ι СЛОВЗМИ СВОЮ АЗБꙊКꙊ СВОИМИ ПИСМЕНЫ НꙊЖДАХꙊ СА ПИСАТИ.

λ ТѢМЗЖЕ МНОГА ЛѢТА. Ѳ҃Ι СЛОВЗМИ СВОЮ АЗБꙊКꙊ СВОИМИ ПИСМЕНЫ НꙊЖДАХꙊ СА ПИСАТИ.

μ ТѢМЖЕ МНОГА ЛѢТА ДЕВАЮ НА ДЕСАТЬ СЛОВЗ СВОЮ АЗБꙊКꙊ СВОИМИ ПИСМЕНЫ НꙊЖДАХꙊ СА ПИСАТИ.

Р ТѢМ҃ И ПО МНОГА ЛѢТА. ДЕВА҃ НА ДЕСАТΙ҄Ю СЛОВЗ СВОЮ АЗБꙊКꙊ СВОИМИ ПИСМЕНЫ НꙊЖꙖХꙊ СА ПИСАТИ.

Пс ТѢ҃ЖЕ МНОГА ЛѢТА ДЕВА҃Ζ НА ДЕСΙ҄А СЛѻ҃ СВОЮ АБУКУ СВОИМИ ПΙМЕНЗ НꙊ҃ДАХУ СΙА ПИСАТИ.

μ' ТѢМЖЕ МНОГА ЛѢТА ДЕВАЮ НА ДЕСАТЬ СЛОВЗ СВОЮ АБꙊКꙊ. СВОИМИ ПИСМЕНЫ НꙊЖДАХꙊ СА ПИСАТИ.

10:10

γ И ПО ТОМЗ СИМОНИДЗ ОБРѢТЗ ПРИЛОЖИ. В҃. ПИСМЕНЕ.

δ И ПО Тѻ҃. СИМОНИДЗ ОБРѢТЗ ПРИЛОЖИ. В҃. ПИСМЕНЕ.

к По ТОМ ЖЕ ИНЗ ГРАМА҃ТИКЗ ИМЕНЕМЗ СИМОНИДЗ ОБРѢТЗ ЕЩЕ ПРИЛОЖИ ИМЗ ДВА СЛОВА ПИСМЕНАꙖ. И ꙊЖЕ СЛАГАЕТ СА ЧИСЛОМЗ СЛОВЗ ИХЗ. К҃А.

λ По ТОМ ЖЕ ИНЗ ГРАМА҃ТИКЗ ИМЕНЕМЗ СИМОНИДЗ. ОБРѢТЕ И ЕЩЕ ПРИЛОЖИ ИМЗ. ДВА СЛОВА ПИСМЕННАꙖ. И ꙊЖЕ СЛАГАЕТ СА ЧИСЛО ИХЗ. К҃А.

μ По том же инъ граматикъ именемъ симонꙗ обрѣ еще приложи имъ два слова писменаꙗ. и ꙋже слагает са числомъ словъ ихъ. к҃д.

Р по томъ ᵐ инъ граматикъ. именѣ симонидъ. обрѣтъ еще приложи й два слова писменнаа. и оуже съдагает са число словъ й. к҃д.

Пс По то҃ же й грамо́никъ именѣ симонꙗ обрѣ еще приложи й два слова писменаꙗ и ꙋже слагаѐ ста чиломъ сло҃ й к҃д.

μ' По том же инъ грамотикъ именемъ симонꙗ обрѣ еще приложи имъ два слова писменаꙗ. и ꙋже слагаѐ са числомъ словъ ихъ. к҃д.

10:11

γ епихарии же сказатель. три писмена обрѣте.

δ епихарии же сказатель. три писмена ѡбрѣте.

κ Епихарии же нѣкто сказатель книгамъ. сꙋ изобрѣтъ и приложи имъ три слова писменнаꙗ.

λ Епихарии же нѣкто сказател книгамъ. сеи изѡбрѣтъ и приложи имъ три слова писменнаꙗ.

μ Епихарии же нѣкто сказатель книгамъ. сꙋ изобрѣте и приложи имъ три слова писменнаꙗ.

Р епихарꙗ же нѣкто сказатель книг҃. сꙋ изобрѣте и приложи й три слова писменнаа.

Пс Епихарии же нѣкто сказатѐ кнг҃ꙋ се. йобрѣте и приложи й три слова писмейаꙗ.

μ' Епихарии же нѣкто сказатель книгамъ. сеи изобрѣте и приложи имъ три слова писменнаꙗ.

10:12

γ и събра са ихъ. к҃д.

δ и събра са й. к҃д.

κ И тако събра са азбꙋка грьчьскаа. словъ числомъ. к҃д.

λ и тако собра са азбꙋка греческаа. словъ числомъ. к҃д.

μ И тако събра са азбꙋка грьчьскаа. словъ числомъ два десать и четыри.

Р и тако събра са азбꙋка грьчьскаа. словъ число́. к҃д.

Пс И тако собра ста ꙁбꙋка греческаꙗ сло҃ число́ два десꙗ и четꙁре.

μ' И тако събра са азбꙋка греческаа. словъ числомъ два десать и четыри.

10:13-14

γ по мноsѣ же лѣтѣхъ. дионисъ граматикъ. ѕ. двогласныхъ ѡбрѣте.

δ по мноsѣ же лѣтѐ. диѡнисъ граматикъ. шесть двогласнꙑ ѡбрѣте

κ По том же по мноsѣ лѣтехъ дионисъ нѣкто sѣло грамматикъ. ѕ. двогласныхъ словъ изобрѣте.

λ По том же по мноꙁѣ лѣтехъ дионисъ нѣкто sѣло грамматикъ. и тои. ѕ. двоегласных словъ изобрѣте.

μ По том же по мноsѣ лѣтѐ дионисъ нѣкто sѣло грамматикъ шесть двогласныхъ словъ йобрѣте.

Р по томъ ᵐ по мноsѣ лѣтѐ. дїонисъ нѣкто sѣло граматикъ. ѕ. двогласнꙑ словъ изꙁѡбрѣте.

Пс По то҃ же по мноsѣ лѣтѐ диониꙗ нѣкто sѣло грамо́никъ шѐть двоюгласнꙗ сло҃ йобрѣте.

μ' По том же по мноꙁѣ лѣтѐ дионисъ нѣкто sѣло грамотикъ шесть двоюгласныхъ словъ йобрѣте.

10:15

γ по том же дрꙋгꙑи. е҃.

δ по то҃ же дрꙋгꙑи. е҃.

κ По том же дрꙋгꙑи философъ. е҃. словъ приложи.

λ по том же другꙑи философ. е҃. словъ приложи.

μ По том же дроугыи философъ пать словъ приложи.

Р по сй же дроугыи философъ е̄. словъ приложи.

Пс По то̄ же другии филосо̄ пта̄ сло̄ приложи.

μ' По том же дроугыи философъ пать сло̄ приложи.

10:16

γ инъ же. г̄. чисменитаа.

δ инъ же. г̄. чисменитаа.

к И инъ книжникъ три слова. имиже числа пишꙋ̄т са. ѕ̄. е. ч. е. ц̄. е.

λ и инъ книжникъ. г̄. слова. имиже пишꙋ̄т са. ѕ̄. е. ч. е. ц. е.

μ и инъ книжникъ три слова. имиже числа пишꙋ̄т са шестое. и дева̄ десатное. дева̄ сотное.

Р д инъ книжникъ. г̄. слова. имй числа пишꙋ̄т са. шестое та̄въ и дева̄ деса̄тое. и дева̄ сотное.

Пс И инъ книжникъ три слова имиже числа пишӯ са ше̄тое и дева̄ деста̄ное дева̄ со̄ное.

μ' и инъ книйникъ три слова. имиже числа пишꙋ̄т са шестое. и дева̄ десатное. дева̄ сотное.

10:17-18

γ и тако мноѕи многыми лѣты едва събраша. ли. писменъ.

δ и тако мноѕи многыми лѣты едва събраша. ли. писменъ.

к и тако мноѕи философи многыми лѣты едва събраша азбꙋкꙋ грьчьскꙋю. ли. писменъ.

λ и тако мноѕи философи многими лѣты едва собраша азбꙋкꙋ греческꙋю. ли. писмен.

μ и тако мноѕи философи многыми лѣты едва събраша азбꙋкꙋ грьчьскꙋю. три деса̄ и осми писманъ.

Р и тако по многа лѣта мнози философи едва събрали сꙋ̄ азбꙋкꙋ грьчьскꙋю. словъ число̄. ли.

Пс И тако мноѕи философи многими лѣтъı едва собраша а̄букꙋ греческꙋю три деста̄ и ѻми пӣма̄.

μ' и тако мноѕи философи многыми лѣты едва собраша азбꙋкꙋ греческꙋю. три деса̄ и осми писманъ.

Гл. 11:1-3

γ по томъ же многыимъ лѣтомъ минꙋ̄вшемъ. бж҃имъ повелѣниемъ. обрѣте са. о̄. мꙋжь.

δ по томъ же многыимъ лѣтомъ минꙋ̄вшемъ. бж҃имъ повелѣниемъ. ѡбрѣте са. о̄. мꙋжии.

к По томъ же многыимъ лѣтомъ минꙋ̄вшимъ. бж҃иимъ повелѣниемъ. обрѣте са. о̄. мꙋ̄жь мꙋ̄дрь.

λ По томъ же многыимъ лѣтомъ минꙋвшимъ. и бж҃иимъ повелѣниемъ обрѣте са. о̄. мꙋ̄жь мꙋ̄дрыхъ.

μ По томъ же многыимъ лѣтомъ минꙋ̄вшимъ. бж҃иимъ промыслꙋмъ обрѣте са. о̄. мꙋ̄жь мꙋ̄дрець.

Р по томь ̄ многꙑ̄ лѣто̄ миноше̄ши. бж҃ий промыслꙋ̄ обрѣтоша ‘. о̄. мꙋ̄ моудрецъ

Пс По то̄ же многимъ лѣто̄ минꙋвшӣ. бж҃имъ промꙁӣ лꙋ̄ обрѣте са. о̄. муже мꙋ̄рецъ

μ' По том же многꙑ̄ лѣтомъ минꙋ̄вшимъ. бж҃иимъ промыслꙋмъ обрѣте са сѣмь десать мꙋ̄жеи мꙋ̄дрець.

11:4-5

γ иже прѣложиша ѿ жидовьска на грьчьскыи азыкъ.

δ иже прѣложиша ѿ жидовьска на грьчьскыи азыкъ.

к иже прѣложиша книгы ѿ жидовьска азыка на грьчьскыи азыкъ.

λ иже преложиша книги ѿ жидовьска азыка на греческии газыкъ.

μ иже прѣложиша книгы ѿ жидов'ска газыка на грьчьскыи газыкъ.

Р й преложили книгы ѿ жидовьска газыка на грьчьскыи.

Пс иже преложиша книги ѻ жидо̄ска азꙁка на греческии газꙁкъ.

μ' иже преложиша книгы. ѿ жидов'ска газыка на греческыи газꙋ̄.

438

Гл. 12:1-2 [Гл. 14:11-12]

γ а словеньскыи единъ с͂тыи коньстантинь. нарицаемыи кѵриль.

[с͂тыи константинь философь. нарицаемыи кѵриль.]

δ а словеньскыи единъ с͂тыи константинь нарицаемыи кѵриль.

[с͂тыи константинь философь. нарицаемыи кѵриль.]

к а словеньскыи единъ с͂тыи коньстантинъ. нарицаемыи кѵрилъ.

[с͂тыи коньстантинъ философъ. нарицаемыи кѵрилъ.]

λ а словеньскии единъ с͂тыи коньстантинъ. нарицаемыи кирилъ.

[с͂тыи коньстантин философ. нарицаемыи кирил.]

μ а словеньскыи единъ с͂тыи кон꙼стантинъ нарицаемыи кѵрилъ.

[с͂тыи ко͂стантй философъ. нарицаемыи кирй]

Р по то͡ тако͡ лѣто͡ многӹ миноше͡шимъ. константинъ. нарицаемыи кѵрилъ.

Пс словенскиι еди͂ с͡тзι ко͂ста͂тй нарицаемзι кирилъ

[свѣ͂зι ко͂стантй философъ нарицаемзι кирй]

μ' а словеньскыи единъ с͂тыи кон꙼стантинъ нарицаемыи кирилъ.

[с͂тыи ко͂стантй философъ. нарицаемыи кирй.]

Гл. 14:15-16

γ и меѳодии братъ его. слꙗть бо еще живи. иже слꙗть видѣли.

δ и меѳд̄ брӓ его.

к и меѳодй̈ братъ его. състависта азьбѹкѹ грамоты словеньскиꙗ.

λ и меѳод братъ его состависта азбѹкѹ грамоты словеньскиꙗ.

μ и меѳодй̈ братъ его. състависта азьбѹкѹ грамоты рѹ͂скыа.

Р и меѳодй̈ брӓ его. състависта азбѹкѹ грамоты роускыа.

Пс и меѳд̄ брӓ его. со͂тавита а͂бѹкѹ грамотзι грчскиа.

μ' и меѳд̄ братъ его. состависта азьбѹкѹ грамоты рѹ͂скыа.

14:21-22

γ въ врѣмена михаила ц͡ра грьчьска.

δ въ врѣмена михаила ц͡ра грьчьска.

к во времена михаила ц͡ра грьчьска. при патриарсѣ фотии.

λ во времена михаила ц͡ра греческа. и при патриарсѣ фотѣи.

μ во времена михаила ц͡ра грьчьска. при патриарсѣ фотии.

Р при ц͡ри михаилѣ грьчьстѣ. при патрı͡арсѣ фотй̈.

Пс во времена михаила ц͡рıа греческа при па͂рıарсе ѳотеι

μ' во времена михаила ц͡ра греческа. при патриарсѣ фотии.

14:24-26а

γ в꙼ лѣта бориса кнꙗѕа блъгарьска. и растица кнꙗѕа моравьска. и костела кнꙗѕа блатеньска.

δ и бориса кнꙗѕа блъгарьска. и растица моравьска. и костела кнꙗѕа блатеньска.

к в꙼ лѣта бориса кнꙗѕа болгарьска. и растица кнꙗѕа морав꙼ска. и костела кнꙗѕа блатенска.

λ в꙼ лѣта бориса кн͂ѕа болгарьска. и растица кн͂ѕа морав꙼ска. и костела кнꙗѕа блатенска.

μ в꙼ лѣта кнꙗѕа бориса болгарска. и растица кнꙗѕа морав꙼ска. и костела кнꙗѕа блатенска.

Р в лѣта бориса кнꙗѕа болгарскӓ. и растица кнꙗѕа моравскаго. и костелѣ кнꙗѕа блатенскаго.

Пс в лѣта кн͂ѕıа бориса бо͂гарска. и растица кн͂ѕıа моравска и ко͂телıа кн͂ѕа блатѣ͂ска

μ' в꙼ лѣта кнꙗѕа бориса болгарска. и растица кнꙗѕа морав꙼ска. и костела кнꙗѕа блатенска.

14:26б

к <u>въ кнѧжение кнѧsа великаго всеа рȣси рюрика. погана сȣща не крщена. za. рк̃. лѣтz до крщениѧ рȣскыѧ zемлѧ.</u>

λ. въ кнѧжение кнѧsа великаго всеа рȣси рюрика. погана сȣща не крщена. za. рк̃. лѣтz до крещениѧ рȣскиа zемлѧ.

μ въ кнѧжение кнѧsа великаго всеа рȣси рюрика. погана сȣща не крщена. za. рк̃. лѣтz до крщениѧ рȣскыѧ zемлѧ.

Р въ кнѧженїе кнѧsа великаго всега роуси рюрика. погана соущи и не крщена. za. рк̃. лѣ до крещенїа роускыга zемлѧ.

Пс в кнѧжение кнѕа великаго всега росии рюрика погана суща не крщена. sa. рк̃. лѣ до крщенига рȗкиа·zемли.

μ' в кнѧжёе кнѧsа великаго всеа рȣси рюрика. погана сȣща не крщена. za. рк̃. лѣтz до крщениѧ рȣскыѧ zемлѧ.

Подчеркнуты изменения текста, не принадлежащие *Р*. Оказывается, большинство из них принадлежит **х** и возникло не позже 1300 г., а пять принадлежит **μ** (перестановка возвратной частицы *9:13*, вставка глагола *9:23*, предлога *10:3*, окказиональная лексическая замена *11:2*, вставка номинального суффикса *11:3*) и возникло не позже 1350 г. *Р* принадлежат два приспособления текста на местах купюр (*9:7*, взятое из *Хронографа, гл. 121*, ст. Скаzание о словенскомz ѩzыцѣ, нач.: По стопотворении же егда раzдели бг̃ чл̃овѣкы, и *12:1*, повторяющее *11:1*) и одно во избежание склонения греческих имен (*10:5*), одна поправка ошибки в падежной форме (*10:10*), четыре окказиональные лексические замены (*10:1-2 и 15*) и семь по заданным текстом моделям (*9:23* по *9:13*, *10:2* по *10:9*, *10:6 и 18* по *10:10 и 12*, *10:6* по *10:11 и 14*, *10:8 и 17* по *10:3 и 12*, *14:21* по *14:22*), десять замен грамматических форм (*9:14-15, 18, 11:3-4 и 14:24-26*) и десять ошибок (*9:11-13, 15, 10:2, 16, 11:1, 4, 14:26*). Одна лексическая замена (писма → грамота, *10:1-2*) выдает, что извлечение данного пассажа из полного текста была проведена не самостоятельно, а по образцу текста *О Грамоте*, или статьи О сложении еллинскиа грамоты из *гл. 12 Хронорафа* (см. дальше внизу).

Из изменений, внесенных в текст писцом *Р* (отмеченных жирным шрифтом) редакционными можно признавать только приспособления текста, поправку и замены по заданным самим текстом моделям (гармонизацию); остальные не поддаются однозначному определению. Редакция в *Р* таким образом сводится до неполной гармонизации и адаптации на швах купюр извлеченного по готовому образцу данного пассажа из полного текста **х**. Тем самым она далека от словарного определения редактирования (*устранение недочетов в содержании произведения, его построения, стиля и т.д.*) и от само себя разумеющегося требования, чтобы она была *целенаправленной, сознатель-ной*.[14] *Русского*, наконец, в ней не более десяти морфологических замен, вряд ли целенаправленных или даже сознательных. Фактически она представляет собой не более, чем *контаминацию* двух сочинений[15] и их текстов.

3. При более подробном рассмотрении изменений, внесенных писцом **х** в текст версии **γ**, бросается в глаза то, что они не распространяются ни на гл. *1:1 - 9:6*, ни на гл. *12:2 - 14:14*, ни на гл. *14:27 - 15:7* (где для обозначения письменных знаков и их совокупности, помимо единичного бȣква *5:6*, встречается только писма), а ограничиваются приведенным пассажем. Только здесь встречаются азбȣка - *система письменных знаков*[16] и слово - *буква*. Последнее обстоятельство вызывает необходимость в привлечении еще одного текста, *О Грамоте*, установленного по 28 спискам Федером (1998).[17] Приведем версию **n** его, на которое обращал внимание уже Ягич (1895: 347 сл.) и которую Трембовольский (1998: 87-88) по случайному списку сопоставлял с *Р*, а также версию **х**[18] по трем спискам *Хронографа 1620 г.*:[19]

Гл. 9:7-8

к ДОНДЕЖЕ БГЪ РАЗДѢЛИ АZЫКЫ. ПРИ СТАZПОТВОРЕНИИ. ГАКОЖЕ ПИШЕТЪ.
9:11-12

к ТАКО РАZДѢЛИША СА И НРАВИ. И ОБЫЧАИ. И ȣСТАВИ. И ZАКОНИ. И ХИТРОСТИ. НА АZЫКЫ.
9:13-14

к ГАКОЖЕ СЕ ГЛЮ ЕСТЬ ГАЗЫКЪ ЕГИПЕТЬСКЫИ. ЕМȣЖЕ СА ȣБО ДОСТАЛО ZЕМЛЕМѢРИЕ. А ПЕРСОМЪ. И ХАЛДѢОМЪ. И АСȣРИОМЪ.
9:15-16

к ЅВѢZДОЧЕТИЕ [*на поле* АСТРОНОМИЕ]. ВЛЪШВЕНИЕ. ВРАЧЕВАНИЕ. ЧАРОВЕ. И ВСАКА ХИТРОСТЬ ЧЛЧА.
9:17, 23

к ЖИДОВОМЬ [*на поле* ЕВРЕОМЪ] ЖЕ СТЫА КНИГЫ. ЕЛ'ЛИНОМ ЖЕ ГРАМАТИКИА. И РИТОРИКИА. И ФИЛОСОФИА.
Гл. 10:1

n О ГРАМОТѢ. ГРЕЧЕСКȣЮ ГРАМОТȣ.

к NO ПРЕЖДЕ СЕГО ЕЛ'ЛИНИ НЕ ИМѢАХȣ СВОИМЪ АZЫКОМЪ ПИСМЕNЪ.
10:2-3

к NO ФИНИЧЕСКЫМИ ПИСМЕНЫ ПИСАХȣ СВОЮ РѢЧЬ. И ТАКО БѢША МНОГА ЛѢТА.
10:4-5

n д҃.Е ПОЧАЛЪ ТВОРИТИ ПАЛАМИДЪ.

х СЕЙ ЖЕ ПАЛАМИДЙ ФИЛОСОФЪ ВО ЕЛЬЛИНЫ ПРИШЕ И СОТВОРИ ИМЪ ȣБȣКȣ

к БЫСТЬ NѢКТО В' НИХЪ ФИЛОСОФЪ ИМЕNЕ̃ ПАЛАМИДЬ. ИЖЕ ПОСЛѢДИ ПРИШЕДЪ. СЪТВОРИ ЕЛЬЛИНОМЪ АZБȣКȣ NАЧЕNЪ ѿ АЛФЫ ВИТЫ.
10:6-7

n ѕ. СЛОВЪ А Б В Г Д Е. КАДЬМЬ И МИЛИСИИ Г. СЛОВА. Ж Ѕ Z.

х СЛОВЪ ЧИСЛОМЬ. ѕ҃і. ПО ТОМЬ ЖЕ КАДȢ̃Ъ МИЛИСИNЪ ПРИЛОЖЙ ТРИ СЛОВА.

к И ПОЛОЖИ ИМЪ. Ѕ҃І ПИСМЕНЪ ТЪКМО ЕЛЬЛИНОМЪ ОБРѣТЕ. По ТОМЪ ПО НѢСКОЛИЦѢ ЛѣТЕХЪ ИНЪ
КНИЖНИКЪ ИМЕНЕМЪ КАДОМЪ МИЛИСИИ. И СИ ПРИЛОЖИ ИМЪ ТРИ СЛОВА ПИСМЕН҃НА.
10:8-9

п ТЪ ЖЕ СѪТЬ ДРЪЖАЛИ. д҃. СЛОВЪ

к ТѣМЪЖЕ МНОГА ЛѣТА. д҃і СЛОВЪМИ СВОЮ АЗБѸКѸ СВОИМИ ПИСМЕНЫ НѸЖДАХѸ СА ПИСАТИ.
10:10

п И ПО ТОМЪ СИМОНИДЪ ПРИЛОЖИ ДВА СЛОВА. И І

х ПО ТОМЬ ЖЕ СИМОНЬ ПРИЛОЖИ ДВА СЛОВА.

к По ТОМЪ ЖЕ ИНЪ ГРАМ҃АТИКЪ ИМЕНЕМЪ СИМОНИДЪ. ОБРѣТЪ ЕЩЕ ПРИЛОЖИ ИМЪ ДВА СЛОВА
ПИСМЕНАА. И Ѹ҃ЖЕ СЛАГАЕТ СА ЧИСЛО СЛОВЪ ИХЪ. К҃А
10:11-12

п ЕПИХАРИИ.҃ і СЛОВЪ К Л М Н О П Р С Т Ѵ. И СОБРА СА. К҃А СЛОВЪ

х ПО ТОМЪ ЖЕ ЕПИХАРИИ ПРИЛОЖИЛЪ ТРИ СЛОВА. И ТАКО СОБРАША СІА ДВА ДЕСАТЬ ЧЕТЫРЕ СЛОВА.

к ЕПИХАРИИ ЖЕ НѢКТО СКАЗАТЕЛЬ КНИГАМЪ. СИ ИЗОБРѣТЪ И ПРИЛОЖИ ИМЪ ТРИ СЛОВА
ПИСМЕННАА. И ТАКО СЪБРА СА АЗБѸКА ГРЬЧЬСКАА. СЛОВЪ ЧИСЛОМЪ. К҃Д
10:13-14

п ПО МНОЅѣХЪ ЖЕ ЛѣТѣХЪ. ДИОНИСИИ. ГРАМОТ҃НИКЪ ПРИЛОЖИ. Ѕ҃. СЛОВЪ Ф Х Ѿ Ц Ч Ш.

х ПО ТОМЪ ЖЕ ДИОНИСЪ НѢКТО ГРАМОТИКЪ ШЕСТЬ ДВОЕСЛО҃НЫХЪ СЛОВЪ ОБРѣТЕ.

к По ТОМЪ ЖЕ ПО МНОЅѣ ЛѣТЕХЬ ДИОНИСЪ НѢКТО ЅѢЛО ГРАМ҃АТИКЪ. ШЕСТЬ ДВОГЛАСНЫХЪ СЛОВЪ
ИЗОБРѣТЕ.
10:15-16

п А ДРѸГѸЮ. Е҃. СЛОВЪ. ПО ТОМЪ ПРИЛОЖИ. Ш З Ы Ь Ѣ. А ИНЪ Г҃. СЛОВА Ю Ѡе А.

х ПО СИ ЖЕ ИНЪ ФИЛЛОСОФ ДЕСАТЬ СЛОВЪ. ИН҃ ТРИ СЛОВА. ИМИЖЕ ЧИСЛА ПИШѸТЪ

к По ТОМ ЖЕ ДРѸГИИ ФИЛОСОФЪ ПАТЬ СЛОВЪ ПРИЛОЖИ. И ИНЪ КНИЖНИКЪ ТРИ СЛОВА. ИМИЖЕ
ЧИСЛА ПИШѸТ СА. Ѕ҃ Е҃ Ч҃ Е҃ Ц҃ Е҃.
10:17-18

п ТЪ ЖЕ ЗА МНОГА ЛѣТА ЕДВА СЪВЪКѸПИША.

х И ТАКО ЕДВА СОВѢШИ СІА ГРАМОТА ЕЛЬЛИНСКАІА ЕЖЕ ЕСТЬ ГРЕЧЕСКАІА.

к И ТАКО МНОЅИ ФИЛОСОФИ МНОГЫМИ ЛѣТЫ ЕДВА СЪБРАША АЗБѸКѸ ГРЬЧЬСКѸЮ. Л҃И. ПИСМЕНЪ.
Гл. 11:1-3а

п ПО ТОМ҃ ЖЕ ПАКЫ ПОСЛѣДИ МНОГИМЬ ЛѣТОМЪ МИНѸВШИМЬ. БОЖИИМЬ ПОВЕЛѣНИЕМЪ ОБРѣТЕ
СА.

к По ТОМ ЖЕ МНОГЫМЪ ЛѣТОМЪ МИНѸШИМЪ. Б҃ЖИИМЪ ПОВЕЛѣНИЕМЪ. ОБРѣТЕ СА.
11:3б-4

п о҃. МѸЖЬ. ИЖЕ ПРЕЛОЖИША Ѿ ЖИДОВЪСКА ІАЗЫКА НА ГРЕЧЕСКЫИ ІАЗЫКЪ.

к о҃. МѸЖЬ МѸДРЬ. ИЖЕ ПРЕЛОЖИША КНИГЫ Ѿ ЖИДОВЬСКА АЗЫКА НА ГРЬЧЬСКЫИ ІАЗЫКЪ.
Гл. 12:1-2 [Гл. 14:11-12]

п И ПРЕЛОЖИ КНИГЫ НА СЛОВЕНСКИИ ІАЗЪКЪ КИРИЛ ФИЛОСОФЪ.

к А СЛОВЕНЬСКЫИ ЕДИНЪ С҃ТЫИ КОНЬСТАНТИНЪ. НАРИЦАЕМЫИ КУРИЛЪ
[С҃ТЫИ КОНЬСТАНТИНЪ ФИЛОСОФЪ. НАРИЦАЕМЫИ КУРИЛЪ.]
Гл. 14:15-16

к И МЕФОДИИ БРАТЪ ЕГО. СЪСТАВИСТА АЗЬБѸКѸ ГРАМОТЫ СЛОВЕНЬСКЫА.
14:21-22

к ВО ВРЕМЕНА МИХАИЛА Ц҃РА ГРѣЧЬСКА. ПРИ ПАТРИАРСѣ ФОТИИ.
14:24-25

к В҃ ЛѣТА БОРИСА КНАЅА БОЛГАРЬСКА. И РАСТИЦА КНАЅА МОРАВ҃СКА.
14:26

к И КОСТЕЛА КНАЅА БЛАТЕНСКА ВЪ КНАЖЕНИЕ ВЕЛИКАГО КНАЅА ВСЕА РѸСИ РЮРИКА ПОГАНА СѸЩА
НЕ КРЕЩЕНА. ЗА. Р҃К. ЛѣТЪ ДО КР҃ЩЕНИІА РѸСКЫІА ЗЕМЛА.

В х отразились и лексика, и фразеология, и фактическое содержание х, т.е. текста *Хронографа* (подчеркнуты в тексте; текст n, хотя и близкий, нельзя считать источником видоизменений ввиду интерполяций из *Хронографа*, приведенных внизу). Вкрапление их в рядовой текст версии γ становится заметным с *10:4* и продолжается до *12:1*. При этом самостоятельный вклад х в развитие текста скромен: помимо двух вставок глаголов в номинальные предложения (*9:11* и *13*), он состоит главным образом в ограниченной данным пассажем эксплицитации текста шестью лексическими распространениями (*9:13*, *10:1* с неправильным употреблением аориста, *10:4, 6, 10, 11*), двумя перестановками текста (*10:16* уточнение из *гл. 7:11 О Писменехъ*, *11:4* кнꙇгы из *12:1*), заменой анахронизма сꙗть бо еще живи. иже сꙗть видѣли (γ) на нейтральное състависта аꙁьбѹкѹ грамоты словеньскꙇа (*14:16*) и распространениями исторической датировки (*14:21* и *26*). Последние, вероятно, также заимствованы из *Хронографа*: на это указывают глосса *9:15*, которая восходит к сообщению Атласъ же астрономию скаꙁа. сего ради глю. ꙗко атласъ вь нбо бьетъ. рекъше нбсное иматъ в срци своемъ, непосредственно предшествующей заглавии версии х, и летописная запись *14:26*, которую можно связать со статьей *гл. 121 О проꙗвлении крещениꙗ рѹскиꙗ ꙁемли*, следующей за статьей Скаꙁание о словенскомъ ꙗꙁыцѣ; где-то между этими статьями и статьей Ѡ прѣложении книгъ (*гл. 123*) *Хронграфа*, наверно, можно будет и найти источник уточнения датировки по правлению патриарха Фотия (*14:26*).[20] Тем самым и работу писца х нельзя принимать за *редакцию*, тем более не за *русскую*, а лишь за *контаминацию*, как и работу писца *Р*.

4.   При контаминации х наблюдается осложнение обозначений, как глагольных положи ... обрѣте (*10:5* с совмещением двух аористов), обрѣтъ ... приложи (*10:10*) и иꙁобрѣтъ и приложи (*10:11* с лишним союзом), так и именных аꙁбѹкѹ ... писменъ (*10:18*) и аꙁбѹка ... словъ (*10:12*), аꙁьбѹкѹ грамоты (*14:16*), словъми ... аꙁбѹкѹ ... писмены (*10:9*), слова писмен'на[а] (*10:7, 10, 11*) и двогласныхъ словъ (*10:14*). Такое совмещение чтений самый верный признак контаминации. Однако, помимо того, оно указывает на самую существенную проблему за всю историю церковнославянского языка: проблему значения как отдельных слов и словосочетаний, так и текста в целом.[21] Что по существу значили для писца х (или μ, или *Р*) текст в целом и составляющие его слова и словосочетания в частности? Осознал ли он

различия в значении двух или трех его источников, а тем более произведенного им самим текста?

Вот писец **х** переписал текст своего антиграфа **γ** с такой же верностью, как переписали свои антиграфы и писцы других гипархетипов и рукописей. Только в объеме *9:7 - 14:26* решил он кое-где нарушать эту верность. Почему? Очевидно, потому что там появился конфликт между текстом **γ** и параллельным текстом **х**, который он опознал как относящийся к тому же предмету и к которому он оказался обязанным таким же долгом верности. Решение вплести **х** в **γ**, таким образом, свидетельствует о сознании значимости обоих текстов в целом. Однако решение при одновременной их передаче совмещать чтения свидетельствует скорее всего о лингвистической неуверенности: писец оказался не в состоянии выбирать между конкурирующими обозначениями. Такое заключение подтверждается и бескритичным восприятием сербизма слово - *буква* и, тем более, отсутствием распространения — употребительного[22] — термина боукꙑ с изолированного положения *(5:6)* на другие места в тексте, и, наконец, полным отсутствием даже попыток глоссировать, комментировать или эксплицитировать темные места в тексте,[23] устранить из него анаколуфы,[24] осмыслить пунктуацию.[25] Равным образом это относится и к писцу **μ**, так же бескритично воспринявшему текст **х**, но при этом осложнившему его совмещением астрономїе. sвѣꙁдочетие, и к писцу *Р*, воспринявшему текст **μ** и осложнившему гамму конкурирующих понятий еще и понятием грамота (по-видимому, по вторичному обращению к параллельному тексту **n**). Таким образом, хотя и развивается текст, язык его лишь осложняется проблемами.

5.   Лингвистической неуверенностью, казалось бы, характеризуется лишь работа писца **х**. Однако и писец **δ**, помимо двух ошибок (*14:24-25*), дает свидетельство о том, что ему были ясны не все отношения в тексте: в *9:23* он заменил *именительный* на *винительный* падеж, выдавая тем самым, что и сходные формы в *9:13, 15* и *17* читал как формы *винительного*; кроме того он заменил в имени *Мефодия (14:15)* суффикс *-ij-* на нулевой, подобный суффиксу имени *Дионисия (10:13)*, что повторили независимо от него и писцы зависимых от старшего гипархетипа **х** младших **λ** и **μ'**, а также рукописи *Пс*. Для того, чтобы установить, в какой мере эти и другие колебания индивидуальны, рассмотрим еще раз данный пассаж, но с самой верхней точки зрения реконструкции *древнейшего достижимого текста*[26] и всех его версий,[27]

тем более, что одна из них, ε, также была удостоена званием *русская редакция*.[28]

Гл. 9:7-8

ω ⰗⰑⰓⰀⰈⰄⰡⰎⰊ ⰛⰔ ⰉⰕⰀⰈⰄⰀⰎⰊ ⰈⰋⰍⰑⰂⰕⰐⰡⰕ. ⰃⰡⰈ ⰑⰕⰀⰈⰂⰃⰑⰕⰂⰑⰓⰡⰐⰡⰓⰌⰆ. ⰀⰡⰆⰍⰆ ⰃⰡⰛⰟⰕⰌⰆ.

α ДОНʼДЕЖЕ Б҃Ъ РАЗ̄ДѢЛИ АZЫКЫ ПРИ СТЬЛПОТВОРЕН҃Ӥ ӺКОЖЕ ПИШЕТЬ.

β ДОНДЕЖЕ РАZМѢСИ Б҃Z АZЫКЬІ ПРИ СТЛZПОТВОРЕН҃ІИ. ӺКОЖЕ ПИШЕТЬ.

γ ДОНДЕЖЕ Б҃ГZ РАZ̄ДѢЛИ АZЫКЬІ ПРИ СТОЛПОТВОРЕНИИ. ӺКОЖЕ ПИШЕТЬ.

ε РАZ̄ДѢЛИ Б҃ГЬ АZЫКЬІ ПРИ СТЬЛПОТВОРЕНИИ. ӺКОЖЕ ПИШЕТЬ.

s ДОНЬДЕЖЕ Б҃Z РАZ̄ДѢЛИ ҤAZЫКЫ ПРИ СТЛZПОТВОРЕН҃ІИ. ӺКОЖЕ ПИШЕТЬ.

b ДОНЬДЕЖЕ РАZ̄ДѢЛИ Б҃Ь АZЫКЬІ ӺКОЖЕ ПИШЕТЬ.

9:11-12

ω ⰕⰀⰍⰑ Ⱁ ⰓⰐⰀⰂⰋ. Ⱁ ⰑⰁⰟⰝⰀⰌ. Ⱁ ⰑⰆⰔⰕⰀⰂⰋ. Ⱁ ⰈⰀⰍⰑⰐⰋ. Ⱁ ⰘⰟⰕⰓⰑⰔⰕⰋ. ⰐⰀ ⰈⰋⰍⰑⰂⰕⰐⰡⰕ.

α ТАКО И НРАВИ И ОБЬНАѦ И ОУСТАВИ. И ZАКОНИ. И ХЫТРОСТИ. НА АZЫКЫ

β ТАКО И НРАВИ. И ОБЬЧАИ. И Ȣ̈СТАВИ. И ZАКОНИ. И ХЫТРОСТИ НА АZЫКЫ

γ ТАКО И НРАВИ. И ОБЬЧАИ. И ОУСТАВИ. И ZАКОНИ. И ХЫТРОСТИ НА АZЫКЫ

ε ТАКО И НРАВИ. И ОБЬЧАИ. И Ȣ̈СТАВИ. И ZАКОНИ. И ХИТРОСТИ НА КОАӜДО АZЫКЫ

s ТАКО И НРАВИ. И ОБЬЧАИ. И ОУСТАВИ. И ZАКОНИ. И ХЫТʼРОСТИ НА ҤAZЫКЫ

b ТАКО И НРАВИ. И ОБЬЧАѦ. И Ȣ̈СТАВИ. И ZАКОНИ. НА КЬІΑ АZЫКЫ

9:13-15а

ω ⰅⰃⰟⰒⰕⰀⰐⰑⰍⰟ Ⱄ̈Ⰵ ⰈⰄⰌⰎⰅⰍⰌⰓⰅⰐⰊⰅ. Ⱚ ⰓⰟⰔⰑⰍⰟ. Ⱁ ⰘⰀⰎⰄⰡⰑⰍⰟ. Ⱁ ⰀⰔⰋⰓⰅⰑⰍⰟ. ⰈⰂⰡⰈⰄⰑⰝⰟⰕⰅⰐⰊⰅ.

α ЕГѶПТАНОМʼ ЖЕ ZЕМЛЕМѢРЕНИЕ А ПЕРʼСОМЬ И ХАЛʼДѢОМЬ И АСИРЕОМЬ. ZВѢZДОЧЬТЕНИЕ.

β ЕГѶПТ̈Ȣ̈ Ȣ̈БО. ZЕМЛА МѢРЕН҃ІЕ. А ПРZСОМЬ. И ХАЛДѢ̈О. И АСⸯГРИῼ̈. SВѢZДОЧЬТῙ̈Е.

γ ЕГѶПТОМZ ОӰБО ZЕМЛЕМѢРИЕ. А ПЕРЬСОМZ. И ХАЛДѢОМZ. И АСⸯРИОМZ. SВѢZДОЧЬТИЕ.

ε ЕГѶПʼТАНОМZ Ȣ̈БО ZЕМЛЕМѢРІЕ. ПЕРʼСОМЬ ЖЕ И ХАЛZДѢОМZ И АССИРЮМZ. SВѢZДОЧЕТІЕ.

s ЕГѶПʼТⰤНОМZ ОӰБО ZЕМЛЕМѢРЕНИⰤ. А ПЕРСОМZ И ХАЛZДѢОМZ И АСⸯРЕОМZ ZВѢZДОЧЬТИѤ.

b ЕГѶПʼТѢНОМЬ ДАСТЬ ZЕМЛА МѢРЕНИЕ. ПЕРЬСОМЬ. И ХАЛЬДѢѠМЬ. И РОУСОМЬ. ДАСТЬ ZВѢZДОЧЬТЕНИЕ.

9:15б-17

ω ⰂⰎⰟⰸⰛⰂⰅⰐⰊⰅ. ⰂⰓⰀⰝⰅⰂⰀⰐⰊⰅ. ⰝⰀⰓⰑⰂⰋ. Ⱁ ⰂⰔⰀ ⰘⰟⰕⰓⰑⰔⰕⰟ ⰂⰎⰝⰀⰂⰟ. ⰆⰋⰄⰑⰂⰑⰍⰟ

   [на поле ⰅⰂⰓⰅⰌⰏⰟ] ⰍⰅ ⰔⰕⰟⰋⰅ ⰉⰐⰋⰃⰟ.

α ВЛЬШЕВЕНИЕ. ВРАЧЕВАНИЕ. ЧАРОВАНИΑ. И ВЬСА ХЫТРОСТЬ Ч҃ЛЧА. ЖИДОВОМʼ ЖЕ СТ҃ЫΑ КНИГЫ.

β ВЛАШВЕН҃ІЕ. ВРАЧЕВАН҃ІЕ. ЧАРОВЕ. И ВСА ХЫТРОСТЬ ЧЛЧА. ЖИДОМZ ЖЕ. СТ҃ЫΑ КНИГЫ.

γ ВЛАШЕВЕНИЕ. ВРАЧЕВАНИЕ. ЧАРОВЕ. И ВЬСАКА ХЫТРОСТЬ ЧЛЧА. ЖИДОВОМЬ [на поле ЕⸯРЕѠМЬ] ЖЕ СТ҃ЫΑ КНИГЫ

ε ВЛАШВЕН҃ІЕ. И ЧАРОТВОРЕНІЕ. И ВʼСА ХИТРОСТЬ Ч҃ЛВЕЧА. ЕВРЕОМЬ ЖЕ СТ҃ЫΑ КʼНИГЫ

s ВЛАШʼВЕНИЕ. ВРАЧЕВАНИЕ. ЧАРОВАНИΑ. И ВЬСΑ ХЫТʼРОСТЬ Ч҃ЛОВѢЧА. ЖИДОВОМZ ЖЕ СВАТЫΗΑ КZНИГЫ.

b И ВЛЬ̈ХВОВАНИЕ. И ЧАРОВАНИЕ. И ВЬСА ХЫТРОСТИ ЧЛОВѢЧА. ЖИДОВОМЬ ЖЕ ДӒ КНИГЫ.

9:23

ω Ⱚ ⰅⰎⰎⰋⰐⰑⰍⰟ ⰃⰓⰀⰍⰀⰕⰊⰍⰋⰀ. ⰓⰋⰕⰑⰓⰋⰍⰋΑ. Ⱁ ⰚⰋⰎⰑⰔⰑⰚⰋΑ.

α ЕЛʼЛИНОМЬ ГРΑМΑТИКИΑ. РИТОРИКИΑ. ФИЛОСОФИΑ.

β А ЕЛЛИНОМЬ ГРАМОТИК҃ІΑ. РИТОРИК҃ΙΑ. ФИЛОСОФΙΑ.

γ ЕЛʼЛИНОМZ ЖЕ ГРΑМΑТИКИΑ. РИТОРИКИΑ. И ФИЛОСОФИΑ.

ε ЕЛʼЛИНОМЬ ЖЕ ГРΑМʼМАТИКІΑ. РИТОРИКІΑ. И ФИЛОСОФІΑ.

s ЕЛЛИНОМZ ЖЕ ГРΑММАТИКИΑ. РИТОРИКИΑ И ВЬСΑ ФИЛОСОФИΑ.

b ЕЛИНОМЬ ДӒ ГРΑМАТИКИΑ И РИТОРИΑ.

Гл. 10:1

ω ⰓⰂ ⰃⰎⰀⰃⰑⰎⰅ ⰔⰅⰃⰑ ⰵⰎⰠⰂⰅⰎⰀⰐⰅ ⰓⰅ ⰴⰓⰀⰕⰠⰏⰅ ⰔⰂⰑⰅⰏⰠ ⰈⰅⰜⰠⰂⰀⰕⰠⰈⰅⰏⰅ ⰃⰑⰈⰀⰅⰓⰅ.

α Нь прѣжде **сего** ел҃лини не имахѫ своимь азыкомь писмень.

β Nꙁ прѣже **сего** ел҃лини не имѣахѫ писменꙁ.

γ Nꙁ прѣжде **сего** ел҃лини не имѣахѫ своимь азыкомь писменꙁ.

ε Но прежде **сего** ел҃лини не имѣахꙋ своимь азыкомь писмень.

s Nѫ прѣжде еллини не имѣхѫ своимꙁ ꙗзыкꙁмь писменꙁ.

b nѫ прѣжде елини и роумене не имѣхѫ своимь азыкомь писмень.

10:2-3

ω ⰓⰂ ⱇⰻⰐⰻⱍⰠⰔⰠⰍⰠⰏⰻ ⰃⰑⰈⰀⰅⰓⰀⱅ ⰃⰑⰔⰀⱅⰠⰎⰅ ⰑⰓⰂⰅⰜ ⰠⰴⰀⰂ. ⰘⰑ ⱅⱅⰑⰠⰅ Ⱋ⸱ⰅⱅⱌⰅ ⰎⰅⰓⰅⰴⰀⱅ ⰆⰀⱅⱅ.

α Нь финичьскыми писмены писахѫ своꙗ си рѣчь. и тако бѣша многа лѣта.

β Nꙁ финич҃скыми писмены писахѫ своꙗ рѣчь. и тако бѣша многа лѣта.

γ Nо финичьскыми писмены писахѫ своꙗ **си** рѣчь. и тако бышла многа лѣта.

ε Нь финичьскыми писмены писахꙋ свою рѣчь. и тако быша м҃нога лѣта.

s Nѫ финичьскыми писмены писахѫ своꙗ ' рѣчь. и тако бѣше м҃нога лѣта.

b nѫ питьч҃скыми писмени писахѫ своꙗ рѣчи. и быша много лѣтꙁ.

10:4-5

ω ⰃⱅⰀⱅⰆⰑⰎⰅ ⰍⰅ ⰃⰑⰈⰀⰴⰀⰍⰋⰅ ⰎⰠⰡⰎⰅⰎⰅ. ⰓⱅⰅⰂⰓⰅ ⱑⰕⰕ ⱅⰀⰆⰅⰕⰠⰕ Ⰷ ⰂⰀⱅⱅⰠⰕ.

α Панамидь же послѣжде пришьдꙁ. начень ѿ ал҃фы и виты.

β Палгмидꙁ же послѣжде пришедꙁ. начень ѿ алфы виты.

γ Панамидꙁ же послѣди пришедь. наченꙁ ѿ алфы виты.

ε Паламидь послѣди пришедь. и начьнь от альфы.

s Паламидꙁ же послѣжде пришьдꙁ. начынꙁ отꙁ альфы и виты.

b Тогда же гаманаиль дидаскаль послѣди пришьдь. и сьтвори имь начьнь ѿ лѣпа.

10:6-7

ω ⰵⱅ. ⰃⰑⰈⰀⰅⰓⰅ ⱅⱅⰂⱅⰅⱅⰅ ⰵⰎⰠⰂⰅⰓⰅⰍⰅ ⰵⰜⰠⰴⱅⱅⱅ. ⰃⱅⰆⰀⱅⰍⰅ ⰍⰅ ⰔⰍⰅ ⱅⰴⰑⰍⰅⰅ ⰍⰅⰈⰀⰅⱅⰴ ⰃⰑⰈⰀⰅⰓⱅ. Ⰲ.

α ЅІ писмень тьк҃мо ел҃линомь обрѣте. приложи же имь кадьмь милисіи писмена. Г̄.

β ЅІ писменꙁ токмо ел҃линомꙁ ꙍбрѣте. приложи же имꙁ кадьмꙁ милисии. писмена три.

γ ЅІ писменꙁ тꙁкмо. еьллиномꙁ обрѣте. приложи имꙁ. кадꙁмꙁ милисии. писмена три.

ε ЅІ писмень ток҃мо ел҃линомꙁ обрѣте. приложи же имь кад҃мось и милисии писмена. Г̄.

s ЅІ писменꙁ тꙁкꙁмо еллиномꙁ обрѣте. приложи же имꙁ Кадꙁмꙁ Милисіи писмена. Г̄.

b ЅІ словь. иꙁь жидовьскыхь книгь.

10:8-9

ω ⱅⰀⰍⰅⰂⰍⰅ ⰍⰅⰓⰈⰀⱅ ⰆⰀⱅⱅ. Ⰵⱅ. ⰃⰑⰈⰀⰅⰓⰅⱅ ⰃⰑⰈⰀⱅⱅⰍⰅ.

α Тѣмꙁже многа лѣта. ѲІ писмены писахѫ.

β Тѣмже многа лѣта. ѲІ те писмены писахѫ.

γ Тѣмꙁже многа лѣта. деватию на десате писмены писахѫ.

ε и сꙁставиша сꙗ. ѲІ писмень. и писахѫ тѣми писмены лѣта многа.

s Тѣмьже м҃нога лѣтꙁ. ѲІ писмены писахѫ.

b тѣми же словесы писахѫ своꙗ рѣчи. ѲІ лѣтꙁ.

10:10

ω ⰃⰅ ⱅⱅⰍⰅⰂⰅ ⰑⰈⰍⰅⰓⰅⰴⰀⰅ ⰵⰜⰠⰴⱅⱅ ⰃⰠⰴⰀⰴⰍⰅ. Ⱋ. ⰃⰑⰈⰀⰅⰓⰅ.

α и по томь симонидь обрѣть приложи двѣ писмени.

β по томꙁ симонинꙁ ꙍбрѣте и приложи два писменѣ.

γ и по томꙁ симонидꙁ обрѣтꙁ приложи. В̄. писмене.

ε по томь симонидь обрѣть приложи. В̄. писмена.

s по томь Симонидꙁ приложи д҃вѣ пис҃мени.

b симонидъ же обрѣте сапи копа словесъ. и приложи имъ д҃вѣ словѣ.

10:11-12

ω ⰵⱂⰻⱈⰰⱃⰻⰻ ⰶⰵ ⱄⰽⰰⰸⰰⱅⰵⰾⱐ. ⰲ҃. ⱂⰻⱄⰿⰵⱀⰰ ⱁⰱⱃⱑⱅⰵ. ⰻ ⱄⱏⰱⱃⰰ ⱄⱔ ⰻⱈⱏ. ⰻ҃ⰴ.

α епихаріи же сказатель. г҃. писмена обрѣте. и събра сѧ ихъ. кд҃.

β епихаріи же сказатель. три писмена ѡбрѣте. и събра сѧ и҃х. кд҃.

γ епихарии же сказатель. три писмена ѡбрѣте. и събра сѧ ихъ. кд҃.

ε епихарии же сказатель. г҃. писмена обрѣте. и сьбра сѧ ихъ. кд҃.

s Епихарии же сказатель г҃ письмена обрѣте. и събра сѧ симь. к҃. и. д҃.

b епихаритъ же ѡбрѣте сапи копа словь. и приложи имъ. г҃. слова. и сьбра сѧ имъ. ѕ҃і словъ.

10:13-14

ω ⱂⱁ ⰿⱀⱁⰸⱑⱈⱏ ⰶⰵ ⰾⱑⱅⱑⱈⱏ. ⰴⰻⱁⱀⰻⱄⱏ ⰳⱃⰰⰿⰰⱅⰻⰽⱏ. ⰵ҃. ⰴⰲⱁⰳⰾⰰⱄⱀⱏⰹⰻⱈⱏ
ⱁⰱⱃⱑⱅⰵ.

α по мнозѣхъ же лѣтѣхъ. діонисъ граматикъ. ѕ҃. двѡгласныхъ обрѣте.

β по мнозѣ҃х же лѣтѣ҃х. диѡнисъ граматикъ. ѕ҃. двогласны҃х ѡбрѣте.

γ по мнозѣ҃х же лѣтѣхъ. диѡнисъ грамматикъ. шесть двогласныхъ ѡбрѣте.

ε по мнозѣхъ же лѣтѣхъ. диѡнисъ грамматикъ. ѕ҃. дѕвогласныхъ обрѣте.

s По м҆нозѣхъ же лѣтѣхъ Дионисии грамматикъ. ѕ҃. д҆вогласьныхъ обрѣте.

b по мнозѣхъ же лѣтѣхъ. диѡнисъ философъ. приложи имъ. д҃. слова.

10:15-16

ω ⱂⱁ ⱅⱁⰿⱏ ⰶⰵ ⰴⱃⱆⰳⱏⰹ. ⰴ҃. ⰻ ⰴⱃⱆⰳⱏⰹ. ⰲ҃. ⱍⰻⱄⰿⰵⱀⰻⱅⰰⰰ.

α по томъ же дроугы. є҃. и дроугы. г҃. чисменитаа.

β по том же дрꙋгы. є҃. и дрꙋгы. три чисменитаа.

γ по том же дрꙋгы. є҃. инъ же. г҃. чисменитаа.

ε по томъ же дрꙋги. є҃. и инь. г҃. чисменитаа.

s по томь дроугы. є҃. и дроугыи. г҃. чисьменитаꙗ.

b дрꙋгыи приложи имъ. г҃. слова и сьбра сѧ имъ. кд҃. слова.

10:17-18

ω ⰻ ⱅⰰⰽⱁ ⰿⱀⱁⰸⰻ ⰿⱀⱁⰳⱏⰹⰿⰻ ⰾⱑⱅⱏⰹ. ⰵⰴⰲⰰ ⱄⱏⰱⱃⰰⱎⱔ. ⰾ҃ⰷ. ⱂⰻⱄⰿⰵⱀⰵ.

α и тако мнози многыми лѣты едва събраша. ли҃. писмень.

β и тако мнози многыми лѣты едва събраша. л҃. и ѡсмь писменъ.

γ и тако мнози многыми лѣты едва събраша. л҃. и. и҃. писменъ.

ε и тако мнози м҆нозѣми лѣты едва сьбраша. ли҃. писмень.

s И тако м҆нози м҆ногыми лѣты ѥд҆ва събраша. л҃. писменъ и. и҃.

b тако и мнозѣмь сѫщемь вь мнозѣхь лѣтехь. едва сьставише граматꙋ.

Гл. 11:1-2 [пропущено **b**]

ω ⱂⱁ ⱅⱁⰿⱏ ⰶⰵ ⰿⱀⱁⰳⱁⰿⱏ ⰾⱑⱅⱁⰿⱏ ⰿⰻⱀⱘⰲⱎⰵⰿⱏ. ⰱⱁⰶⰻⰵⰿⱏ ⱂⱁⰲⰵⰾⱑⱀⰻⰵⰿⱏ.

α по том҆ же многомь лѣтомь минѫв҆шемь. б҃жиемь повелѣниемь

β по том же многомъ лѣто҃ минѫвшемъ. б҃жиимъ повелѣниемь.

γ по томъ же многымъ лѣтомъ минꙋвшемъ. б҃жиимъ повелѣниемъ.

ε по томъ же мнозѣмь лѣтомь минꙋв҆шемъ. б҃жимь повелѣніемь

s По томь же. м҆ногомъ лѣтомъ минѫвъшемъ. б҃жиемь повелѣниемь

11:3-5 [пропущено **b**]

ω ⱁⰱⱃⱑⱅⰵ ⱄⱔ. ⱁ҃. ⰿⱘⰶⱏ. ⰻⰶⰵ ⱂⱃⱑⰾⱁⰶⰻⱎⱔ ⱁⱅⱏ ⰶⰻⰴⱁⰲⱐⱄⰽⰰ ⱑⰸⱏⰹⰽⰰ. ⱀⰰ
ⰳⱃⱏⰽⱐⱄⰽⱏⰹⰻ ⱑⰸⱏⰹⰽⱏ.

α ѡбрѣте сѧ. о҃. мѫжь. иже прѣложиша ѿ жидовъска на грьчьскыи ꙗзыкь.

β обрѣте сѧ. о҃. ть. мѫжь. иже прѣложиша ѿ жидовска ꙗзыка. на греческыи ꙗзыкь.

γ обрѣте сѧ. о҃. мѫжь. иже прѣложиша книгы ѿ жидовьска на грьчьскыи ꙗзыкъ

ε обрѣте сѧ. о҃. мꙋжеи. иже прѣложиша оть жидовьска ꙗзыка к҆нигы на гречьскии ꙗзыкь.
повелѣніемь егѵпьтьскаго ц҃ра п҆толомеа.

s обрѣте сѧ. о҃. мѫжь. иже прѣложиша отъ жидовьска ѩзыка кънигы на грьчьскыи.

Гл. 12:1-2 [*Гл. 14:11-12*]

ω   Ⱅ ⰑⰎⰑⰂⰡⰐⰌⰔⰍⰟⰠⰠ ⰐⰓⰌⰃⰟⰞⰟ. Ⰳ̄. ⰟⰂⰓⰟⰁⰑⰔⰕⰀⰐⰟⰕⰟⰐⰠ ⰐⰀⰓⰠⰘⰀⰅⰏⰟⰌ ⰍⰠⰓⰌⰎⰠ. *(глаголица)*
     [ⰟⰓⰟⰁⰑⰔⰕⰀⰐⰟⰕⰟ ⰘⰑⰎⰑⰔⰑⰜⰟ. ⰐⰀⰓⰠⰘⰀⰅⰏⰟⰌ ⰍⰠⰓⰌⰎⰠ.]

α   а словеньскыа **КНИГЫ**. единь стыи кон'стан'тинь нарицаемыи криль.
     [стыи константинь философь нарицаемыи криль.]

β   а словеньскыа **КНИГЫ** единъ константинъ. нарицаемыи крилъ.
     [стыи константинъ философь. нарицаемыи крилъ.]

γ   а словеньскы единъ стыи коньстантинь. нарицаемыи криль.
     [стыи константинь философь. нарицаемыи криль.]

ε   а словеньскаа **ПИСМЕНА** единь стыи коньстан'тинь. нарицаемыи въ м'нишескомъ чинѹ
     криль философь. [стыи коньстан'тинь философь. нарицаемыи криль.]

s   Словеномъ единъ святыи Костан'тинъ. нарицаемыи Криллъ.
     [святыи Костан'тинъ философь. нарицаемыи Крилъ.]

b   а словеньскыа **КНИГЫ** единь костаньтинь нарицаемыи криль
     [коньстаньтинь солоунскыи. философь. нарицаемыи криль.]

Гл. 14:15-17

ω   *(глаголица)*

α   и меѳодие брать его.

β   и меѳодїи братъ его. сѫть бо еще живи. иже сѫть видѣли й.

γ   и меѳодии братъ его. сѫть бо еще живи. иже сѫть видѣли.

ε   и меѳодии брать его. епкпь моравьски.

s   и Мефодие братъ его.

b   и меѳодие брать его.

14:21-23

ω   *(глаголица)*

α   въ времена михаила цра грьчьскаго.

β   въ времена михаила цра греческа.

γ   въ времена михаила цра грьчьска.

ε   вь времена михаила цра греческаго. и мтре его ѳеодѡры, иже правовѣрнѹю вѣрѫ ѹтвердиста.

s   въ врѣмена Михаила царга грьчьскаго.

b   вь врѣма михаила цр҃е грьчьскаго.

14:24-25

ω   *(глаголица)*

α   и бориса кнаѕа бльгарьскаго. и растица кнаѕа морьваска.

β   и бориса кнаѕа болгарска. и растица кнѕа моравска.

γ   и бориса кнѕа блъгарьска. и растица кнѕа моравска.

ε   и бориса кнѕа бльгарьска. и растица кнѕа моравьска.

s   и Бориса   кнаѕга моравьска.

b   и бориса кнаѕа бльгарьскааго. и растица кнаѕа моравьскааго.

14:26

ω   *(глаголица)*

α   и коцела кнаѕа блатеньска.

β   и коцьла кнаѕа блатеньска.

γ   и костела кнаѕа блатьньска.

ε   и костела кнѕа блатиньска.

s   и Коцелга кзнаѕга блатьньска.

b   и коцьла кнаѕа блатьньскаго.

Все версии обнаруживают индивидуальные отклонения от реконструкции оригинала ω, от единичных (αγ) и немногих (βs) до частых, эксплицитирующих (ε)[29] и массивных, редакционных (b).[30] Ни одна из них не сводима к другой: они независимы одна от другой, а зависимы лишь самостоятельно от глаголического оригинала ω, о чем и свидетельствуют их индивидуальные глаголитизмы.[31] Тем самым они оказываются не просто версиями текста, а его *кирилловскими архетипами*. Они намного древнее сохранившихся рукописей: их необходимо отнести к той поре, когда существовала пергаменная тетрадь с глаголическим оригиналом, т.е. между 935 г.[32] и 1050 г.,[33] а, вероятно, не позже 971 г.[34]

Помимо индивидуальных отклонений – частных осмыслений оригинала (αβγεs) или наложения на него новых замыслов (b) – шесть архетипов дают ценные свидетельства о ранних проблемах более общего характера на всех уровнях текста (отмеченных выше жирным шрифтом), для которых транскрипторы находили неодинаковые решения: [1] для анахронизма *14:16-17* сѫть бо еще живи. иже сѫть видѣли и – замену нейтральной информацией (ε, как позже в гипархетипе x) или пропуск (αsb, как позже в гипархетипах и рукописях от β и γ); [2] для авторского анаколуфа *2:1(-3)* а словѣньскꙑ кнꙑгꙑ. (а̃. коньстантинь. нарицаемꙑи курилъ. и писмена сътвори. и кнꙑгꙑ прѣложи) – перевод кнꙑгꙑ из *12:1* в *11:4* (γ) при одновременной замене прилагательного словѣньскꙑ существительным (s) или замене всего сочетания выражением словеньскаа писмена (ε); [3] для дублетности ꙗзꙑкь – в *11:4* иже прѣложиша отъ жидовьска ꙗзꙑка. на грьчьскꙑи ꙗзꙑкь – пропуск либо первого (αγ), либо второго (s); [4] для авторских сочетаний дательного с именительным падежом – замену именительного винительным в *9:11* (αb) и *23* (βb) или вставку глагола в *9:13, 15, 17* (b, как позже в гипархетипе x). Уточнение значения [5] времени *10:2* бꙑша достигалась заменой на бѣша (αβs), [6] поссессивности (балканским) сдвоением местоимения *10:2* свои → свои си (αγs), [7] дистрибутивности – добавкой *9:12* коѧждо (ε) и кꙑꙗ (b). На проблемы в понимании [8] авторского употребления союзов указывают замены *9:13* оубо → же (α), а → же (γεs) и пропуск его (αa), а также добавка *10:10* и (αγ); [9] причастных форм – *10:4-5* и *10* добавка к причастию лишнего союза (εb) и *10:10* подгонка причастия под аорист (βb) или пропуск его (s); [10] *10:1* прѣжде в качестве предлога – пропуск сего (sb). На проблемы в словообразовании указывают [11] колебания *9:15* между основами влъшьв- и влъхв- (b), [12] переоформление сложения *9:13* земле- + мѣр- → земла + мѣр- (βb)

и [13] добавка суффиксов -ѣн- к *9:13* егѵпьт- (αεsb) и -ен- к *9:13* -мѣр-
(αβsb), *15* -чьт- (αb), чаров- (αsb, ε с распространением -творен-) или
замене их *10:4* послѣжде → послѣди (γεb), *14* дионисии → дионисъ
(αβγεb, как позже *14:15* меѳодии → меѳодъ в гипархетипах и рукописях от γ и ε). На проблемы [14] склоняемости мъногъ указывает
замена следующего за ним винительного падежа лѣта родительным
лѣтъ *10:3* (b) и *8* (s); [15] различения типов склонения — *9:17* замена
основы на -*и* основой на -*о* жид- (βb); [16] окончаний двойственного
числа — *10:10* писменѣ (β), писмене (γ) и замена его множественным
писмена (ε); [17] различения двух типов окончаний прилагательного —
замены неопределенных определенными *11:1* (γ), *14:21* (αεsb), *24* (αb)
и *25-26* (b). Последняя проблема, а также и [8] выше, осложняется
проблемой написания двойных гласных, как [18] в кажущихся определенных окончаниях *10:15-16* дроѵгъ и → дроѵгъіи (α, см. и замены
второго употребления на инъ же в γ и и инь в ε), и, наоборот, в про-
пуске союза *10:4* алъфъі и витъі → алъфъі витъі (βγ), а также в замене
суффикса имперфекта *10:1* -ѣа- → -а- (α) или -ѣ- (sb), *10:2* и *9* -аа- →
-а- (γsb). Наконец, [19] проблемы различения глаголических букв Ꙛ и
Ᵽ[35] довели до раздвоения традиции по чтению имени *Паламид* на
пал- (αγb) и пан- (βεs, так и в тексте *О Грамоте*).[36]

Об общих для всех транскрипторов проблемах свидетельствуют и
данные правописания текста. Из них рассмотрим вкратце, кроме
ван-вейковской *правильности употребления носовых гласных*, употребление ѣ, ъ и ь. Из преполагаемых в ω 19 носовых (6 Ꙗ и 13 ꙗ) восстанавливаются во всех архетипах 6, а невозможна реконструкция 9 ε,
2 γ, 2 b (смешение носовых), 1 β; кроме того наблюдается употребление ꙗ вместо ѣ или ꙗ 10 ε, 9 γ, 7 αβ и 1 b. Из предполагаемых в ω
26 ѣ восстанавливаются во всех архетипах 19, а невозможна реконструкция 3 β, 2 ε, 1 γb, где он передается через є. Из предполагаемых
в ω 106 еров (62 ъ, 31 ь и 13 неопределенных в корнях алʼф-, грамʼм-,
егѵпʼт-, елʼа-, кадʼм-, конʼстанʼт-, перʼс- и халʼд-) во всех архетипах
восстанавливается 9 ь, а вообще не восстанавливается ъ в 1 (сказ-),
ь в 2 (-бр-) и неопределенный в 1 (грамм-) случаях; кроме того ер или
паерок сохранился в одних в εs в 13 (дзв-, къниг-, кънаѕ-, мъног-, чʼл-)
случаях. Сохранность еров и замещающих их паерка или выноса выше
всего в s (84%) и αεb (78-74%), и ниже всего в γ (67%) и β (55%), а
ошибочность их употребления ниже всего в s (1) и выше всего в полностью одноерьевом b. Ни один из архетипов не свободен от ошибок
и не последователен в правописании. Из наблюдаемого можно за-
ключить, что в глаголическом архетипе ω носовые употреблялись

450

этимологически правильно, а уже при транскрипции на кириллицу отражалась деназализация ѫ (ε 4, γ 1 + 1 в индивидуально раскрытом числительном) и ѧ (γ 1, s 1); о том, что от деназализации не свободны и αβb свидетельствует то, что при разделении глаголического ѧ на ъ/ѩ последнее передавалось через ѧ (за исключением согласно написанного ꙗкоже, ꙗ встречается только в s[37]). Ввиду того, что [1] нет согласия архетипов хотя бы в одном написании ꙁ при наличии такого в ь, [2] количество ь везде превышает ожидаемые 33% минимально на 6-9% (βγs), а максимально на 50-67% (αεb), и [3] ь преобладает (85%) в случаях с неопределенным ером, можно с уверенностью предположить, что в глаголическом архетипе ω употреблялся только ь, а разделение ь/ꙁ было наложено при транскрипции с глаголицы на кириллицу.[38]

Итак и кирилловский архетип ε, несмотря на то, что он представлен рукописями исключительно белорусского, русского и украинского происхождения,[39] как, впрочем, и архетип β,[40] не содержит ничего собственно *русского*, ни тем более *редакции*. Несмотря на проявляющуюся на местах тенденцию к *эксплицитации*, основную установку писца к задаче передачи текста можно охарактеризовать как *верность антиграфу*, такую же, какую проявляли в своих транскрипциях αβγ и s.

6. Известных списков *О Писменехъ* — 125 (из них обследовано мной 82), гипархетипов — 30, кирилловских архетипов — 7, глаголического архетипа — 1, то есть свидетелей текста — минимум 163 за почти 9 столетий с 935 до 1830 г. и по всей территории от юго-западных Балканов до северовосточной Руси. Один из них знал, почему и как пишет, 7 видели его текст (1, b, подверг его редакции), а 155 лишь имели известия о тексте из вторых до энных рук и просто переписывали его по одному своему антиграфу (5 из них, x и рукописи Кв, Мол, Сол1,[41] Р, контаминировали его с другой версией текста). Правда, и в них текст развивается, но прежде всего за счет дефектов рукописей-антиграфов и порчи их текстов, а лишь в незначительном объеме за счет мелких контаминации с пометами на полях[42] или заученными текстами.[43] Язык текста после кирилловских архетипов, однако, никак не развивается, а лишь осложняется и портится, значение убывает.[44] Без преувеличения можно сказать, что ни один из списков *О Писменехъ*, какого бы ни было времени или происхождения, не передает полностью связный текст сочинения, ни позволяет реконструкцию оригинала без помощи всех других.

Трансмиссия *О Писменехъ* повторяет модель трансмиссии других церковнославянских текстов, которые исследователями были удостоены *русскими редакциями*, как *Пандекты Антиоха*[45] и *Патерик Скитский*,[46] но которые скорее всего принадлежат к начальному комплекту перевезенных из Преслава на Русь книг, как *Изборник грешного Иоанна*,[47] *Протопатерик Скалигера*,[48] и *Учительное евангелие* Константина Преславского:[49]

и текст, и язык приобрели свою индивидуальность по *пониманию* глаголического протографа через *идиолект* анонимных транскрипторов, создавших ряд кирилловских архетипов авторского текста, не то с эксплицитациями, не то с контаминациями, по которым сначала замещались одни чтения другими, а со временем все больше совмещались.[50] *Редакция*, т.е. сознательная и целенаправленная переделка текста под новый замысел — явление редкое,[51] а удачное — и с языковой, и с художественной точки зрения — редчайшее.[52] Распространеннее всего — простое копирование антиграфа со всеми его особенностями, дефектами и ошибками. Первооснова трансмиссии текстов в средневековом православном славянстве — *верность антиграфам.*[53]

Ввиду очерченных, правда, на ограниченном материале, обстоятельств трансмиссии текстов в средневековом православном славянстве, понятие *русская редакция* имеет право на существование только, если будет доказано, во-первых, что она *редакция*,[54] и во-вторых, что создание или усиление *русского* начала в тексте — составная часть ее замысла.[55] Также не имеет права на существование понятие *памятник* как обозначение единства текста и языка:[56] язык задан раз и навсегда *автором текста*, а последующие его свидетели, от кирилловских архетипов до младших рукописей, в этот язык вносят только свои с ним проблемы; в них нет своего языка.[57] Из этого следует, что значение рукописи по принципу может быть лишь опосредованным: оно всегда составляет лишь одну долю общего количества сохранившихся свидетелей, рукописей и реконструируемых звеньев трансмиссии, от архетипа до младших гипархетипов.[58] Из этого следует также, что неправомерно проводить в корпусе источников церковнославянского языка отграничения по иному критерию, чем *время и место возникновения текста*, и что тем самым понятие *старославянский*[59] по отношению к рукописям,[60] а не к *текстам*,[61] лишено значения.

Тексты составляют ядро всякой христианской культуры. Изучение их трансмиссии больше, чем одно изучение их восприятия, осмысления, распространения и сохранения в отдельности, это — изучение действия и типа культуры. Церковнославянская филология XXI века призвана заниматься именно этой задачей, начав с того, чтобы установить, как пользовались церковнославянским языком те, кто вложил в тексты замысел и смысл — авторы, и тем самым раскрыть всю полноту проблем значения и текстов, и составляющих их единиц языка при последующей трансмиссии. Если рукописи превращаются в фетиш, если порча текста принимается за язык и за редакцию,[63] она не будет в состоянии справляться с такой задачей и не будет в мере ни постигать сущности отличий в трансмиссии текстов средневекового православного славянства от трансмиссии вернакулярных текстов западной и средней Европы,[64] ни установить какие бы то ни было абсолютные параметры шире всех распространенного, но менее всех известного из славянских языков.

Амстердамский университет

ПРИМЕЧАНИЯ

[1] Пользуюсь термином *церковнославянский* для обозначения всего континуума текстов на данном языке, безразлично от временного или пространственного приурочения.

[2] К наиболее спорным в церковнославянском языкознании относятся сравнения данных списков с данными живых диалектов, напр. Заимов 1983. Ведь сравнение текстов с каким бы то ни было из живых славянских языков по принципу неправомерно, пока не будет (1) доказано, что церковнославянский был языком не только текстов, но и людей, и (2) уточнено соотношение церковнославянского с древними формами местных диалектов (а исследование их до сих пор водится в *порочном* круге стихийного обращения к спискам церковнославянских текстов, см. собранные Жуковской (1987) статьи, за ярким исключением древненовгородского диалекта, см. Зализняк 1996).

[3] Относительны прежде всего датировка и локализация преобладающего большинства дошедших до нас списков текстов (см. Лант 1982, Федер 1988), но и в точно датированных и локализированных списках остается относительным происхождение текста, пока не будет точно установлено родословие его по примеру *Пандектов Антиоха* (см. Поповский 1989), *Изборника 1076 г.* (см. Турилов 1994), *Откровения* (см. Грюнберг 1996), *Пролога к Учительному евангелию* и *О Писменехъ* (см. Федер 1998).

[4] Хотя Ван-Вейк определяет нижнюю границу *1100 годом*, но он допускает, что *некоторые памятники, может быть, восходят к более поздней эпохе* (с. 36).

[5] См. предложение по предварительной (без новонайденных в 1975 г. синайских славянских рукописей) классификации рукописей и надписей до 1200 г. у Федера 1988.

[6] Список *Л* опубликован Куевым 1967: 187 слл., 1981: 182 слл.

[7] Определение степени родства списков — кропотливейшая работа, приемы которой, вплоть до деталей орфографии и приемов реконструкции *гипархетипов* (см. сн. 9), изложены Федером 1998.

[8] Сиглы рукописям и гипархетипам даны Коссовой 1980: 72-75, за исключением *Р* и ς ϑ η λ' μ', введенных Федером 1997б.

[9] *Гипархетип*, т.е. родитель по отношению к потомкам-апографам, может представлять накопление отличительных признаков более, чем одной рукописью.

[10] Термин *версия* здесь обозначает текст, который восходит к тому же прародителю (*архетипу*), как и другие версии, но не может быть возведен ни к одной из них, т.е. является *несовместимым* с ними.

[11] См. Федер 1997б, 1998.

[12] Таким образом гипархетип μ оказывается практически ровесником рукописи *Л*.

[13] В стемме точно определяются нижние пределы (*termini ante quem*) γ δ ϰ ϑ и μ; отнесение возникновения остальных гипархетипов к старшему поколению условно.

[14] Эти критерии выдвигает Лихачев 1983: 132-133, вслед за Истриным. Тов 1992: 160-161 и Федер 1994в обращают внимание на то, что признание видоизменения текста *редакцией* требует ответа не столько на вопрос *Как?*, сколько на вопрос *Зачем?*

[15] *Сочинение*, т.е. систему замыслов автора, следует отделить от *текста*, т.е. материального его воплощения, потому что первое уникально, между тем как последнее может быть представлено более, чем одной *версией*; кроме того есть случаи, когда близкие тексты могут оказаться разными сочинениями (см. сн. 17).

[16] Здесь целесообразно напомнить, что ϰ распространяет и заглавие, добавляя аꙁбꙋка: О аꙁ'бꙋкъ словен'скꙋ и о елиньскои сиръчь греческꙋ скаꙁанїе. Распространение идет от заглавия n (см. гл. *10:1*, распространенное в свою очередь в гипархетипах q: Начало грамотъ греческои и рꙋскои и о: Скаꙁание ѡ греческꙋи грамотъ) с характерной для ϰ заменой грамота → аꙁбꙋка.

[17] Федер 1997в еще исходил из мысли, что данный текст представляет собой сокращение полного текста; Федер 1998 доказывает, однако, что она на самом деле — написанный глаголическим письмом самостоятельный перевод с той же греческой рукописи, которая послужила источником и при составлении трактата *О Писменехъ*; более того, она, вероятно, послужила и основным стимулом и образцом в составлении его.

[18] Версия ϰ не была учтена Федером 1997в, и вопрос о соотношении ее с другими версиями текста *О Грамоте* пока еще остается открытым.

[19] Рукописи Саратов, НБСУ, 175, 177 и 178 (XVII-XVIII вв.) исползованы по микрофильмам в Research Center for Medieval Slavic Studies (Columbus, OH), а рукопись Columbus, OSUL, Aronov 3 (XVII в.) — в оригинале. В составе *Хронографа* данная версия входит в *гл. 12 О еверѣ и о евреискихъ писменахъ* под подзаглавием *О сложении еллинскиѧ грамоты*. О *Хронографе* в общем см. Творогов 1975.

[20] Сходные с **х** летописные записи встречаются в новой текстовой рамке первой из двух транскрипций обослобленной *Азбучной молитвы* (см. сн. 49), а именно в начале: и въ дни кнѧѕа рюрика новъгородскаго. егоже сномъ рꙋсскаѧ ѕемлѧ преиде; и в конце: крꙋщена бысть ѕемлѧ рꙋсскаѧ. въ дни блговѣр-наго кнѧѕа владимера. сна стославла. внꙋка же игорева и ольжина. положьшиѧ првое начало крꙋщениѧ въ ѕемли рꙋстѣи. а правнꙋка рюри-кова. в лѣто. „ѕучѕ.

[21] Проблему значения исследователи до сих пор, как правило, миновали, относя к одной греческой самые различные славянские лексемы, как будто бы все без исключения славянские списки текстов являются самостоятельными переводами с греческого, притом последовательными и точными (см. бескритичное пред-ложение Жуковской 1976 (1976: 88-110) построить на основе взаимоисключа-ющихся лексем словарь синонимов). На уровне текста проблему с надлежащим весом поставил пока лишь Томсон 1978: 115-117. Выявление проблем значения слов, сочетаний их и текстов должно стать первоочередной задачей церковно-славянской филологии XXI века.

[22] Термин боукꙁı или боуква был употребительным уже тогда, когда тран-скрибировали данный текст с глаголицы на кириллицу (между 935 и 971 гг., возможно и до 1050 г.), так как семь транскрипторов передали им оригинальное боукꙁстава, а лишь один из них оставил от этого след в псевдо-глоссе боуквамъ. то есть статикꙁвамъ.

[23] Почему, например, нет следов объяснения жджж (*1:21*), ѿ аѕа начатъ обое (т.е. греческую и славянскую азбуку, *3:3*), ал'фа бо. ищи. глет сѧ грьчьскымь аѕыкомь (*4:9*), четыре междꙋ десатьма (*6:4*), иждоконь (*8:5*), свож си рѣчь (*10:2*), да тѣм сѧ постраѧеть. и еще (по отношению к св. Кириллу, *13:3*), грьчⷭкь такожде многажды сѧть постраѧли (какой греческий? *13:4*), оудобѣе бо есть послѣди потворити. неже правое сътворити (*13:9*), книг'чиа (*14:1*), ини ѡвѣти. аже ин'де речемь (*15:2*), или имен собственных акула, симьмахъ, моравьскъ, блатьньскꙁ?

[24] Почему, например, остались в тексте или внесены в него явно не связные гѧше. ꙗко трьми ли аѕыкы бъ есть повелѧлъ книгамъ быти (*8:10-11*), такоже наꙋчихом' сѧ. и ꙗко взса по радꙋ бываѧть ѿ бꙗ (*8:20-21*), раѕмѣшеномъ же бывꙁшемъ аѕыкомъ. и такоже аѕыци раѕмѣсиша сѧ (*9:9-10*), и полꙃжи имъ. ѕı. писменъ. тꙁкмо еллиномъ обрѣте (*10:6*), обрѣтъ и еще приложи (*10:10*), иꙁобрѣтъ и приложи (*10:11*)?

[25] Из несуразностей пунктуации, встречающихся во всех списках, обращаю внимание лишь на стыи курилъ. сътвори. прьвое писма. аꙁъ (*5:1-2*), тѣм сѧ постраѧеть. и еще. ѿвѣтъ речемъ (*13:3-4*).

[26] Реконструкция глаголического оригинала подробно обоснована Федером 1998.

27 Реконструкция версий обосновывается с подробным разбором и оценкой чтений в работах Федер 1996а (b, до 1225 г.), 1996б (α, до 1350 г.), 1997а (ε, до 1400 г.), 1997б (γ, до 1350 г.), 1998 (свод всех версий); значение вариации анализируется в работе Федер 1997г.

28 Так версию ε отождествила Языкова 1979. Тут, к сожалению, недостает текст еще одной *русской редакции* (= г, см. Коссова 1980: 78-89, 1981), по простой причине, что антиграф его оборвался после *9:6*, а дефект восполнился текстом *О Грамоте*. Тот факт, что с последним совмещен отрывок из *Жития св. Стефана Пермского*, никак не значит, что предшествующий им текст трактата *О Писменехъ* подвергался обработке писцами, совместившими эти три текста. В самом деле в обработке первых двух текстов нет никаких совпадений (см. Федер 1998).

29 К приемам *эксплицитации* относятся *интерполяции 10:8* с переоформлением *9, 11:5, 12:2, 14:15* и *23*, и добавка дистрибутивного местоимения в *9:12*.

30 К приемам редакции в b относится прежде всего наложение новых замыслов параллелями понеже глѫть грьци. ѿ нашихь сѫть книгь извели словѣньскы книгы (*8:2*) = чьто глѫть грьци безоумнии. ѣко ѿ нашихь книгь извѣдоша словѣньскыѧ книгы (*во второй части компиляции*) и книга словѣньска стѫ есть. свѧть бо мѫжь створи ѭ (*12:10*) = стѫ есть бльгарьска литоургиѫ. стꙁ бо мѫжь стави ѭ (*во второй части компиляции*), сокращение текста на почти 60% оригинала и добавление второй части с акростихом *Азъ есмь Богъ* (см. Федер 1996а). Кроме того, в b, как и в гипархетипе х и рукописи Р (см. выше), но уже до 1225 г., сказывается контаминация с текстом *О Грамоте* по свидетельству вкрапления именно в данном пассаже слова *слово* в значении *буква* (см. Федер 1997г).

31 За исключением *10:4* в данном пассаже не представлено глаголитизмов; о них см. Федер 1997г, 1998.

32 После 935 г. из тех, кто еще видел св. Мефодия (*14:16-17*), мало кто остался в живых.

33 С серединой XI в. связаны последние, вероятно, уже не системно организованные транскрипции глаголических рукописей на кириллицу, напр. в Македонии *Битольской (Кичевской) Триоди* (см. Заимов 1984), в Новгороде (1047 г.) *Толковых пророков* Упырем Лихим и в Киеве *Пандектов* Антиоха (см. Поповский 1989).

34 В 971 г. (вопреки настоянию Литаврина 1987 на *неофициальных путях* перемещения) из библиотек Великого Преслава было вывезено в Киев значительное количество глаголических и кирилловских рукописей (см. далее сн. 45-49), среди которых и кирилловский архетип ε, который на новом месте уже до 1100 года был использован при составлении новой текстовой рамки для извлеченной из глаголического автографа *Учительного евангелия* Константина Преславского *Азбучной молитвы* (см. сн. 20, 49 и Федер 1998).

35 О графической близости глаголических букв ꙋ и ꙗ см. в *Преславском глаголическом абецедарии* у Медынцевой 1984: 49-54 и табл. VII.

36 Такое же раздвоение традиции на основе разночтения глаголических букв наблюдается, как сообщила 5 ноября 1997 г. в Columbus, OH, Емилия Гергова,

456

и в *Минее*: напр. *Песнь 1, Тропарь 1* канона в честь св. Якова брата Господня (23 октября) в греческом начинается со слова ἔργα, а в славянском или со слова чаюнию (напр. ркп. Афон, Великая Лавра, 55), или со слова даюнию (напр. ркп. Саратов, НБСУ, 109), которые оба восходят к глаголическому ⰿⰰⰀⰑⰅⰀ.

[37] Относительную правильность орфографии s, в том числе и в йотации гласных, возможно, следует приписать на счет издателя ныне утраченной рукописи, Срезневского (1848).

[38] Наложение при транскрипции на кириллицу двуерового правописания на одноерьевое глаголического антиграфа имеет прочно установленные типологические параллели (см. сн. 45-46 и Федер 1994б).

[39] Среди свидетелей ε есть и одна, поздняя, сербская рукопись, *Бе*, но она, вероятнее всего, списана с восточнославянского антиграфа.

[40] Об архетипе β не утверждалось, что он представляет *русскую редакцию*.

[41] Рукопись *Кв* представляет *глубокую* (распространенную на весь текст с замещением чтений) контаминацию со списком от архетипа ε, а рукопись *Мол* — *мелкую* (нераспространенную с совмещением чтений) со списком от архетипа α; рукопись *Сол1* от архетипа β контаминировала пассаж нашего примера с текстом *О Грамоте*, как и **bⰊ***P* (см. и сн. 28 и Федер 1998).

[42] См. различные решения по замещению или совмещению в связи с пометами *9:15* астрономие (х) и *9:17* эⰏьⰀⰅⰂⰂ-Ⱃ (ω), а также совмещение в **b** *10:10* и *11* дважды пометы переводчика или читателя сапи копа слⷪ.

[43] Напр. к цитату из *Бытия 20:11* Бⷸ сътвори нбⷪ и ꙃемлѭ. и вьса ꙗже на нею **b** *9:19* добавляет из *Бытия 1:1* искони, а в заключительной формуле вз бесконьчьнꙀⷨⰊꙗ вⷵкꙀⷬ. аминь β совмещает по богослужебным молитвам вⷵковⷸ, ⰏⰓ - вⷵкоⷭ, а ε замещает вз вⷵкы вⷵкомь. аминь.

[44] Порча текста заметнее всего в **b**, где 31% из оставшихся после сокращения синтагм стал бессмысленым; в рукописи *Бп* порча наросла до 38%, а в *Мв* до 51% (см. Федер 1996а).

[45] В *Пандектах Антиоха* отождествлял *русскую редакцию* Копко 1915-16. Поповский 1989: 131-135 установил, что все русские списки восходят к одной — сохранившейся — рукописи середины XI века (Москва, ГИМ, Воскр. 30п), которая представляет собой прямую транскрипцию автографа переводчика пятью, вероятнее всего киевскими (Поповский 1989: 109-113), писцами, каждый из которых, помимо своих недопониманий и ошибок, внес в текст по различным правилам и с различным успехом не только все пометы переводчика на полях, но и разделение еров на Ⰸ и ь (Поповский 1989: 31-35, 99-108); кроме этого главный редактор добавил по завершении книги на свободных страницах из других книг апофтегму *О чтении книг* Иоанна Златоуста и *Алфавитарь* Григория Богослова (см. Поповский 1989: 60-61, 65-66). Наряду с ней сохранились в южнославянских и одном украинском списке и две старшие, повидимому еще преславские, транскрипции того же глаголического автографа (Поповский 1989: 123-132).

46 В *Патерике Скитском* отождествлял *русскую редакцию* Ван-Вейк 1975. Федер 1994аб установил, что с одноерьевого глаголического протографа, повидимому в Преславе, было изготовлено не менее семи кирилловских архетипов, из которых не менее пяти были перевезены на Русь и бесследно исчезли из южнославянской традиции. *Патерик Скитский*, кроме того, интересен и тем, что изменеия в последовательности и комплектованности тетрадей книжного тела — расплетенного для удобства организированной многократной транскрипции на кириллицу — его глаголического оригинала прямо отразились в макроструктуре кирилловских его архетипов и дают достоверные сведения об относительной хронологии транскрипций.

47 *Изборник грешного Иоанна* (прямой список с которого является *Изборник 1076 года*) — компиляция из компиляций, т.е. контаминация не менее трех и не более пяти предварительно контаминированных книг (см. Федер 1983, Турилов 1994).

48 В *Протопатерике Скалигера* по механической схеме одновременного использования по направлению с начала на конец и обратно были переплетены *Патерик Скитский*, *Патерик Египетский Краткий*, *Лествица* и еще один неизвестный источник (см. Федер 1981).

49 Как ни странно, *Учительное евангелие* Константина Преславского до сих пор не было удостоено *русской редакцией*. Федер 1997д установил, что с авторского его автографа было изготовлено на Руси, вероятнее всего в Киеве до 1100 г., четыре независимые транскрипции на кириллицу. Транскрипции производились попарно, полным текстом с последующим извлечением из него *Азбучной молитвы*. Второй транскриптор полного текста в *Пролог* внес авторские маргиналии, предназначенные для устного выступления до конца 893 г. в присутствии самого св. Наума Охридского, заместив ими четий текст. Это обстоятельство позволяет и датировать произведение, и доказать перевозку на Русь именно автографа сочинения.

50 Контаминация (на уровне текстов и книг: *компиляция*) и последующая за ней потребность в гармонизации расходящихся обозначений — вероятно самый мощный фактор видоизменения текстов, в частности их лексики, и книг. *Четьи сборники* (*сборники неустойчивого состава*) фактически представляют собой контаминации *книг* (см. Федер 1990): весьма возможно, что основа их состава, *хаотизация* (у Федера 1990 менее точно *randomisation*), входит в тенденцию, общую с совмещением чтений (*juxtaposition*, Федер 1981, одной из разновидностей которого впоследствии стало пресловутое *плетение словес*), в которой проявляется один из *канонов* поэтики средневекового православного славянства.

51 Чаще всего *редакция* встречается в виде *сокращения* текста. От нее следует отделить *извлечение* предложений, пассажей и т.д. из текстов, потому что новый в них замысел относится не столько к отдельному извлечению, сколько к построению новой макроструктуры, в которую они входят (см. Федер 1981).

52 Самые удачные известные мне примеры контаминации с редакцией — слово *Некоего калугера о чтении книг*, служащее прологом *Изборника грешного Иоанна* (см. сн. 46), составленное из апофтегмы Иоанна Златоуста и слова Григория *О чтении книг* (см. Федер 1986), и сказание *О милостивом Созомене*, служащее

458

его эпилогом, основанное на гл. 69 *Жития св. Нифонта*: его редакция производилась в два приема — извлечением и сокращением для *Княжьего Изборника* до 950 г. и последующей контаминацией с *Патериком Скитским*, гл. В:22, и еще одним источником с гармонизацией лексики в *Изборнике грешного Иоанна* до 971 г. (см. Федер 1992).

[53] Верность антиграфам (ей же славистика обязана за бережное сохранение всех перипетий церковнославянских текстов от зарождения их до захоронения в печатных изданиях), очевидно, допускает развитие текста эксплицитациями и контаминациями. Она наблюдается и при трансмиссии библейских текстов (см. Баккер 1996, Ван дер Так 1998), и ее не отменяют более частые, чем при передаче других типов текстов (но во всех случаях ограниченные по последовательности и глубине проникновения) обращения к параллельным, нередко греческим спискам. Последние можно рассматривать, на равных с указанными контаминациями и эксплицитациями началах, как воплощения обычного призыва к читателю-передатчику блдгословите. не кльнѣте (*Рим. 12:14*). д испрдвивꙁше чьтѣте.

[54] *Редакция* — отступление от первоосновы и поэтому она должна в каждом отдельном случае быть тщательно установлена и обоснована путем предельно точных сравнений, способных пролить свет на всю родословную текста.

[55] Если снять конкретный графический облик, транскрибируя список по правилам *Полаты книгописной* 17-18 (1987): 28, отпадает значительное количество локализирующих примет, а если нормализировать его написания по правилам Ван-Вейка, Лескина, Селищева или другого пособия по старославянскому языку, как правило, их не остается вообще. Нет ни одной *русской редакции*, которая бы выдержала это испытание и которая оказалась бы сознательным и целесообразным наложением на грамматику церковнославянского текста грамматики русского языка (и не может быть, потому что такая обработка была бы равна переводу на русский язык). Это перекликается с выводом Тота (1985: 334) о том, что *нет таких комплексных примет, по которым можно было бы объединить эти рукописи* (т.е. корпус 10 рукописей XI-XII в., приуроченных к Руси, см. Тот 1985: 12-66.

[56] Идея о единстве языка и текста в рукописях порождена массивной вариативностью церковнославянских библейских текстов, возведенной на уровень парадигмы. Однако эта вариативность одновременно оказывается и бессистемной, в особенности в новозаветных текстах, а поэтому ее следует толковать скорее как проявление индивидуальной заботы об исправности текста, чем как свободное наложение диалектных черт (см. сн. 53).

[57] Если со временем развивается текст без того, чтобы развивался и язык, то даже в реконструируемых кирилловских архетипах, а тем более и в списках их *нет языка людей*, а есть только свидетельства об их индивидуальных проблемах с *языком текста*. Данное наблюдение перекликается с выводами массового лингво-статистического обследования церковнославянских рукописей, проводимого за последние 25 лет кафедрой математической лингвистики С.-Петербургского университета: вариация в глагольной и именной морфологии оказывается не соотносимой с факторами географического или хронологического порядка, а только с типологией текстов (см. Герд 1974-1986).

[58] В нашем примере сохранились три пары *антиграф* → *апограф*, следовательно значение каждого списка равно 1/160 или 0,6%. См. об ограниченности значения отдельного списка Кронштайнер 1993.

[59] Неправомерно не только привилегированние одной группы рукописей по ван-вейковским критериям, но и полное исключение из рассмотрения текстов, заведомо написанных в Первом болгарском царстве до 1018 г., но сохранившиеся в рукописях или позднейшего, или же русского происхождения, тем более, что работа по изготовлению кирилловских архетипов глаголических текстов, начатая еще в Преславе, очевидно просто продолжалась на Руси.

[60] Хотя Жуковская (1976: 9-11) и Цейтлин (1986: 10-11) отделяют рукопись от текста (его же они обозначают термином *памятник*), они вслед за традицией науки принимают за реальность только рукопись. Такое решение связано с парадигмой западно- и среднеевропейских вернакулярных текстов (см. сн. 64) в изучении средневековой православной славянской книжности. Наложение этой парадигмы, конечно, стало возможным благодаря преимущественной сохранности с древнейшей поры библейских текстов, которые характеризуются существенными отличиями в трансмиссии от других, прежде всего своей большей вариативностью (см. сн. 53, 56). Такое решение, помимо неверного толкования этой вариативности, представляет и удобный выход из положения, так как избавляет от трудоемкой задачи реконструкции исходных текстов (см. сн. 7).

[61] В своей диссертации Темчин 1989 показал, как частичное и непоследовательное наложение видовой характеристики глагольной основы уже в дервнейших *рукописях* не успела заслонить сохранившееся в евангельском *тексте* более древнее состояние без взаимосвязи времени и вида, и аргументировал определение старославянского языка как *языка несохранившихся первоначальных славянских переводов* с греческого.

[62] См. красноречивое, но солидно обоснованное предостержение об зтом Кронштайнера 1993 и сн. 58.

[63] Тут напрашиваются критические по качеству списков текстов отзывы митрополита Григория Цамблака (1414-1420) «кни́гы несло́жни въ рѣчехъ ꙗви́ша са и раꙁоꙋмѣнїи гръчьскыихъ писанїи несъгла́сны. деба́вствѡм же сваꙁаны и не гла́дкы къ течен́їꙋ гла́номоꙋ» и справщика типографии Киево-Печерской Лавры Тарасия Земки (1629) «вса кни́ги славенскїа ѿ колико сѡ лѣтъ преписꙋю са невѣжами, токмо черни́лѡ мажꙋ́щими, ꙋма не имꙋ́щими, ꙗꙁыка не оꙋмѣющими и силы словесъ не вѣдꙋ́щими» и «въ славенскїа же вникъ, бесчисленаа и множайшаа погрѣшенїа ѡбрѣтохъ».

[64] Помимо проблем значения, церковнославянская филология XXI века призвана заниматься вопросом отличий в функциях текстов и трансмиссии их в средневековом православном славянстве от тех в западной и средней Европе. Вот некоторые, стало быть, ключевые вопросы в этой задаче: Почему в наших текстах наблюдается тенденция к нарастанию архаизмов (см. напр. отмеченную Федером 1997б постепенную замену *о*-основы *слав- s*-основой *словес*-), которая в западной и средней Европе встречается практически только в подделках? Почему в наших текстах не осовременивается язык и стиль? Почему в наших текстах до появления справщиков в XVI-XVII вв. неизвестны редакции в смысле *устранения недочетов в содержании произведения, его построения, стиля и т.д.,*

460

ни аннотации, глоссирования или комментирования? Почему в наших текстах продолжается на равных началах трансмиссия всех версий текстов, каковы бы искаженные они ни были, и почему со временем появляется их все больше, с бо́льшими недостатками?

УКАЗАННАЯ ЛИТЕРАТУРА

Баккер (Bakker, H.P.S.)

1996   *Towards a Critical Edition of the Old Slavic New Testament. A Transparent and Heuristic Approach.* Amsterdam (диссертация).

Ван-Вейк, Н.

1957   *История старослвянского языка.* Москва (перевод В.В. Бородича; оригинал: N. van Wijk: *Geschichte der altkirchenslavischen Sprache, Bd. 1.* Berlin).

1975   *The Old Church Slavonic Translation of the* 'Ανδρῶν ἁγίων βίβλος *in the Edition of Nicolaas van Wijk,* edited by D. Armstrong, R. Pope, C.H. van Schoonveveld. The Hague-Paris.

Ван дер Так (van der Tak, J.G.)

1998   *The Old Slavic Apostolos. The Pentecost Lessons and Their Abstracts.* (диссертатция) Amsterdam.

Герд, А.С.

1974   (соавт. Л.В. Капорулина, Е.В. Колесов, О.А. Черепано́ва, М.П. Рускова) *Именное склонение в славянских языках XI-XIV вв.: Лингвостатистический анализ.* Ленинград.

1977   (соавт. Н.И. Мещерский, Л.В. Капорулина, Е.В. Колесов, О.А. Черепанова, М.П. Рускова) *Именное склонение в славянских языках XV-XVI вв.: Лингвостатистический анализ.* Ленинград.

1982   "Ареальная типология славянских текстов XIV-XVI вв.", *Советское славяноведение* 5, 74-82.

1986   "К морфологической типологии древнеславянских текстов", *Совет-ское славяноведение* 2, 97-101.

Грюнберг (Grünberg, K.)

1996   *Die kirchenslavische Überlieferung der Johannes-Apokalypse.* (= *Heidelberger Publikationen zur Slavistik, Linguistische Reihe, Bd. 9*). Frankfurt am Main.

Жуковская, Л.П.

1976   *Текстология и язык древнейших славянских памятников.* Москва.

1987   (ред.) *Древнерусский язык в его соотношении к старославянскому.* Москва.

Заимов, Й. (Zaimov, J.)

1983   "За смекчаването на съгласните и за замяната на носовките в Асеманиевото евангелие", *Старобългаристика* 7, 3: 43-57

1984   The Kičevo Triodium", *Polata knigopisnaja* 10-11.

Зализняк, А.А.

1996   *Древненовгородский диалект.* С.-Петербург.

461

Копко, П.М.
1915-16   "Исследование о языке Пандектов Антиоха", *Известия Отделения русского языка и словесности Императорской Академии наук* 20, 3: 139-216; 20,4: 1-92.
Коссова (А. Джамбелука-Коссова)
1980   *О Писменехъ Черноризца Храбра*. София.
1981   "La rielaborazione russa del Trattato Sulle lettere di Černorizec Chrabär", *Константин-Кирил Философ. Материали от научните конференции по случай 1150-годишнината от рождението му.* 204-222. София. (по-болгарски: "Руската преработка на «За буквите» от Черноризец Храбър", *Литернатурна мисъл* 22, 4: 107-122).
Кронштайнер (Kronsteiner, O.)
1993   "Handschriften-Fetischismus oder kritische Ausgaben? Lebt die Slawistik noch im Mittelalter?", *Die slavischen Sprachen* 34: 47-65.
Куев, К.М.
1967   *Черноризец Храбър.* София.
1974   *Азбучната молитва в славянските литератури.* София.
1981   *Иван Александровият сборник от 1348 г.* София.
Лант (Lunt, H.G.)
1982   "On Dating Old Church Slavonic Gospel Manuscripts", *South Slavic and Balkan Linguistics* (= *Studies in Slavic and General Linguistics* 2), 215-231.
Лихачев, Д.С.
1983   *Текстология. На материале русской литературы XI-XI веков.* Ленинград (1. издание 1962).
Литаврин, Г.
1987   "Культурный переворот в Болгарии и Древняя Русь", *Кирило-Методиевски студии* 4, 393-400.
Медынцева, А.А., К. Попконстанинов
1984   *Надписи из Круглой церкви в Преславе.* София.
Поповский (Popovski, J.)
1989   *Die Pandekten des Antiochus Monachus. Slavische Übersetzung und Überlieferung.* Amsterdam (диссертация).
Сампимон, Я. (J. Sampimon)
1998   *The Declension of Consonant Stems in the Homily against the Bogomils by Cosmas Presbyter.* Amsterdam (дипломная работа).
Срезневский, И.И.
1848   "Древние писмена славянские", *Журнал Министерства народного просвещения*, ч. 59, отд. II: 18-49.
Творогов, О.В.
1975   *Древнерусские хронографы.* Ленинград
Темчин, С.Ю.
1989   *Реконструкция видо-временной системы языка первых славянских переводов с греческого.* Москва (автореферат диссертации).
Тов (Tov, E.)
1992   *Textual Criticism of the Hebrew Bible.* Minneapolis-Assen.

462

Томсон (Thomson, F.J.)
1978   "The Nature of the Reception of Christian Byzantine Culture in
              Russia in the Tenth to Thirteenth Centuries and its Implications for
              Russian Culture", *Slavica Gandensia* 5, 107-138.
Тот, И.
1985   *Русская редакция древнеболгарского языка в конце XI - начале
              XII вв.* София.
Трембовольский, Я.Л.
1989   "Древнеболгарский памятник 'О Писменехъ' Чрьноризца Храбра
              на Руси", *Старобългаристика* 13, 4: 68-90.
Турилов (A.A. Turilov, W.R. Veder)
1994   *The Edificatory Prose of Kievan Rus'.* (= *Harvard Library of Early
              Ukrainian Literature. English Translations, Vol. 6.*) Cambridge, MA.
Федер (Veder, W.R.)
1981   "Elementary Compilation in Slavic", *Cyrillomethodianum* 5, 49-66.
1983   "The Izbornik of John the Sinner: a Compilation from Compilations",
              Polata knigopisnaja 8, 15-37.
1986   "Three Early Slavic Treatises on Reading", *Studia Slavica Medi-
              aevalia et Humanistica Riccardo Picchio dicata, Vol. II*, 717-730.
1988   "Археография и 'канон' старославянских памятников", (K. Trost
              и др. (ред.)) *Symposium Methodianum. Beiträge der Internationalen
              Tagung in Regensburg (17. bis 24. April 1985) zum Gedenken an
              den 1100. Todestag des Hl. Method*, 693-670. Neuried.
1990   "Literature as a Kaleidoscope: The Structure of Chet'i Sborniki",
              (E. de Haard и др. (ред.)) *Semantic Analysis of Literary Texts*,
              599-613. Amsterdam.
1992   "The Merciful Nestor and Sozomen: Early Rusian Text Transmission
              in a Stratigraphic Perspective", *Studies in Russian Linguistics* (=
              Studies in Slavic and General Linguistics 17), 321-382.
1994a   "Die Collatio XII Anachoretarum: Zur Rekonstruktion einer metho-
              dianischen Übersetzung und ihrer Überlieferung ca. 884-1050",
              Anzeiger für slavische Philologie 22, 2, 177-197.
1994б   "One Translation — Many Transcriptions", *Dutch Contributions to the
              Eleventh International Congress of Slavists. Linguistics* (= *Studies in
              Slavic and General Linguistics* 22), 433-465.
1994в   "Славянска текстология", *Проглас* 3, 3, 15-31; "Текстология
              в действие: примерът на О Писменехъ", *Проглас* 6, 1-2, 32-47.
1996a   "The Earliest Attested Text of the Treatise *O Pismenexъ* (The Para-
              dosis of Text Family b before ca. 1225)", *Studies in South Slavic and
              Balkan Linguistics* (= *Studies in Slavic and General Linguistics* 23),
              221-254.
1996б   "Linguistic Problems in the Transmission of *O Pismenexъ*. The Para-
              dosis of Text Family α", *Slavica Gandensia* 23, 7-29.
1997a   "La «redaction russe» d'O Pismenexъ. La paradosis de la famille de
              texte ε", *Ricerche Slavistiche* (в печати).
1997б   "Redaction in Old Slavic Texts. The Paradosis of O Pismenexъ Text
              Family γ before ca. 1300", *Festschrift Moszyński*. Gdańsk (в печати).

1997в   "Кратките версии на О Писменех. Парадозата на разклонението m (до 1050 год.)", *Сборник Иван Гълъбов*, 2. Велико Търново (в печати).

1997г   "Вариация в кругу семьи О Писменех", *Variation in the Witnesses of Medieval Texts*. София (в печати).

1997д   "Защо и как да се реконструира църковнославянски текст. Парадозата на Учителното евангелие на Константин Преславски", *Международна конференция посветена на 1090 години от смъртта на св. княз Борис I*. Шумен (в печати)

1998   *Utrum in alterum abiturum erat? A Study of the Beginnings of Text Transmission in Church Slavic*. Bloomington (в печати).

Цейтлин, Р.М.

1986   *Лексика древнеболгарских рукописей X-XI вв.* София.

Ягич, И.В.

1895   "Рассуждения южнославянской и русской старины о церковно-славянском языке", *Исследования по русскому языку*, т. I. С.-Пб. 1885-1895; отд. изд. Berlin 1896 (под загл. *Codex slovenicus rerum grammaticarum*), München 1968.

Языкова, А.Ю.

1979   *Русские редакции Сказания О писменех Черноризца Храбра.* Новосибирск (дипломная работа).

Dutch Contributions to the Twelfth International Congress of Slavists, Cracow, Linguistics (= Studies in Slavic and General Linguistics Vol 24), 465-526. RODOPI, Amsterdam – Atlanta, GA 1998.

ON THE RENDITION OF VOWEL LENGTH IN PETRE HEKTOROVIĆ'S *RIBANJE* (1568)

1.1 The purpose of this contribution[1]

In 1568 the Venetian printer Giovanni Francesco Camocio (or Camozio) published a modest-looking book entitled RIBANYE I RIBARSCHO PRIGOVARANYE I RAZLICHE STVARI INE SLOXENE PO PETRETV HECTOROVICHIV HVARANINV. In the original edition, "Ribanje" opens as follows:

> VItéxe nárední = Bartuceuichiu moy,
> Sfím gliubchí i mední = chí znayú razúm tuóy:
> Choyinas sfih brání = u potribe naſce,
> I brez çquárni hrání = chacho zláte caſce:
> Choyínas sfih chruní = po mnoga zlamenyá,
> Choyímſmo pripuni = sfachóga poctényá:
> Naydoh çtéch lípu ſtuar = gdi múdrí gouoré,
> Brez izminé niſctár = dugo ſtát ne more.[2]

Most of the vowels that carry an acute accent in this fragment are long in most SCr systems that happen to have retained the inherited system of vowel quantities without fundamental changes.

The realization that the accents in the Hektorović's 1568 book render vowel length is quite old, see already Maretić (1889: 23), cf. also Mladenović (1968: 22-23) and Wagner (1970: 25-29). Unfortunately the material has never been evaluated and it is the purpose of this contribution to make a beginning with that task by examining some of the principal features of Hektorović's use of accent marks. Due to limitations of space and the complexity of the issues involved, discussion of many important problems will have to be deferred to another occasion.

The article is intended as a tribute to Milan Rešetar, whose epoch-making description of the language of the lectionaries appeared exactly

466

a century ago and whose investigation of vowel quantity as marked in the texts of the sixteenth-century Dubrovnik playwright Marin Držić (Rešetar 1927) is so far the only detailed treatment of vowel length in a pre-modern Croatian text corpus written in the Latin alphabet. In my view the factual mistakes and incorrect readings Rešetar's investigation contains (van den Berk 1969) do not detract from the value of his conclusions or the solidity of his method.[3]

1.2 The text

Although the 1568 edition may conceivably not have been the first, it is the earliest to have survived. A second edition appeared in 1638, again in Venice, with three of the "stvari ine" omitted and a large number of typographical errors added, a fact about which the critical notes accompanying Vončina's edition (1986) leave no doubt. Since Hektorović's manuscripts are lost and the second edition is entirely based on the first, the 1568 book is the closest we can get to Hektorović's intentions.

All modern editions produced so far have suppressed all information about vowel length. This holds even for the critical editions published in the series *Stari pisci hrvatski* (1874 and 1986).[4] Hence as a measure preliminary to making the present contribution possible at all it has proved necessary to establish a new text reproducing as closely as possible the 1568 edition, on the basis of the photographic reprint that appeared in Zagreb in 1953 and the textual remarks in the critical editions, in particular Vončina's (1986). The problems raised by the text (most of which are anyhow marginal from the point of view of accentuation) will be discussed elsewhere.

In connection with the fourth centennial of the 1568 book quite a few publications were devoted to Hektorović's language, notably Klaić (1968), Mladenović (1968), and Wagner (1970). There are few if any pre-modern Croatian authors about whose language so much has been written. Hektorović's language is a representative of the great tradition of producing texts in the Latin alphabet on a coastal or insular Čakavian basis. The tradition appears to have arisen at some stage before the middle of the fourteenth century in North Dalmatia (Rab, Zadar, Šibenik) and subsequently spread to Central Dalmatia (Split, Hvar). In the hands of Marulić, Hektorović, Zoranić, Baraković and others it became the vehicle of a remarkable secular literature. For a discussion of the origin of the tradition see Vermeer (1996; on Hektorović's position in it see Table J, p. 305).[5]

1.3 Accent symbols in Hektorović: generalities

The fragment quoted in the introduction, brief though it is, strongly suggests that the acute accent does not indicate the place of the stress. If it did, the frequent presence of two acute accents on the same word form (as in *nárední, brání, hrání, poctényá, múdrí*) would be difficult to understand. Moreover, it is only in very few attested systems that we find the stress on the syllables that carry an accent mark in such examples as *VItéxe, sfachóga* or *izminé*. Such systems exist in two areas where the place of the stress is determined by a general rule that operates starting from the end of the word, as in classical Latin:

(1) Central Čakavian Oštarije and surroundings, on which see Ivić (1961: 200-202) with references to earlier literature.

(2) The northeastern part of the Kajkavian dialect area, e.g. Virje, on which see Fancev (1907) and Lončarić (1977: 228), cf. also the discussion in Vermeer (1979: 373-374).

Both areas are quite far away from Dalmatia. All Dalmatian prosodic systems we know anything about (from Rab in the north to Dubrovnik in the south) are much more conservative. Indeed, most of them have retained the Proto-Slavic place of the stress without significant modifications. This holds in particular for the systems that can be assumed to continue Hektorović's linguistic background (Hvar and surrounding islands). Hence it would not be realistic to expect that the accentual system reflected in Hektorović's language displays the effects of far-reaching innovations of the kind found in Oštarije and Virje.

It is also likely on the basis of the quoted fragment already that accent marks are not obligatory in the sense that they are printed on each and every vowel that happens to be long. The pronoun 'koji' is used twice in what would seem to be exactly parallel fashion (lines 3 and 5). Yet it carries no accent mark the first time (*Choyinas*) and an acute accent the next (*Choyínas*). Similarly if the acute accent in *tuóy* was intended, it is reasonable to expect one in *moy*, too.

The optional character of Hektorović's accent marks is in line with practices of indicating prosodic features as current in pre-modern times. It gives rise to the problem of determining how often length is actually indicated and how often it is left unmarked. Borrowing Zaliznjak's convenient term (1990: 18), we have to determine the "koëffi-cient vyražennosti" of vowel length in Hektorović's book. This is the principal issue addressed in this contribution. It can only be approached on the basis of large quantities of factual material.

1.4 On presenting the material

The principles adhered to in listing examples are the following:

(1) Unless otherwise indicated, lists of examples are exhaustive. However, examples that are somehow problematic and could not have been incorporated without detailed discussion have been tacitly omitted.

(2) All examples are cited in the original orthography. Hektorović's orthography is by a long stretch the best system for writing the language in the Latin alphabet to have been devised before the Counter-Reformation (e.g. Faust Vrančić and Bartol Kašić). Nothing is gained by transcribing examples in modernized orthography.[6]

(3) Contrary to Hektorović's practice, who often incorporates clitics into his word forms, modern word boundaries will be observed. If, for instance, it would be necessary to adduce the forms of the pronoun "koji" attested in the fragment given in the beginning of this article, they would be cited as follows: Nsm *Choyi* (3), *Choyí* (5), Ism/n *Choyím* (6), rather than *Choyinas*, *Choyínas*, *Choyímſmo*.

(4) Only a single type of capital letters is used. Examples which in the original text begin with large initials followed by ordinary capitals (e.g. Ⅴ*Itéxe*) will be quoted with ordinary capitals (e.g. *VItéxe*).

References to the original text are provided according to the following system, which incorporates the traditional numbering of the verses of the various pieces; in addition to that, minor prose sections such as headings are explicitly included and the seven different pieces involved are identified by the use of letters (with absence of an identifying letter indicating "Ribanje"):

0a	Title page of the book (prose).
0b	Heading of "Ribanje" (prose).
0c	Heading of the First Day of "Ribanje" (prose).
1-508	The First Day of "Ribanje" (verse).
508a	Heading of the Second Day of "Ribanje" (prose).
509-1078	The Second Day of "Ribanje" (verse).
1078a	Heading of the Third Day of "Ribanje" (prose).
1079-1684	The Third Day of "Ribanje" (verse).

a0	Heading of the first letter to Mikša Pelegrinović (prose).
a1-a60	Main text of the first letter to M.P. (prose).
a61	Concluding remark about the first letter to M.P. (prose).
b0	Heading of the second letter to M.P. (prose).
b1-b15	Main text of the second letter to M.P. (the nature of the material is heterogeneous: b1-b4 and b12 are prose, whereas b5-b11 and b13-b15 are verse reproducing lines 595-601 and 698-700 of "Ribanje" respectively).
c0	Heading of the letter to Gracioza Lovrinčeva (prose).
c1-c202	Text of the letter to G.L. (verse).
d0	Heading of the epitaph to Frane Hektorović (prose).
d1-d46	Text of the epitaph to F.H. (verse).
e0	Heading of the letter to Hjeronim Bartučević (prose).
e1-e60	Main text of the letter to H.B. (verse).
e60a-e60b	Concluding remarks about the letter to H.B. (prose).
f0	Heading of the letter to "Mavro kalujer" alias Mavro Vetranović (prose).
f1-f160	Main text of the letter to M.k. (verse).
f160a-f160b	Concluding remarks about the letter to M.k. (prose).

Unfortunately a traditional internal numbering is absent in the case of the two letters to Mikša Pelegrinović (the two major prose pieces) and I have been forced to adopt a system of my own devising, for which I refer to the Appendix.

A small proportion of the text (mainly headings of various kinds) is printed entirely in capitals. Since in such fragments no accent symbols are used they will not be taken into account here. They are: 0a, 0b, 0c, 508a, 1078a, a0, b0, b4, b12, c0, d0, e0, e60b, f0, f160b.

2.1 Some statistics

The text contains approximately 28581 vowel letters, of which some 3389 (12%) carry an accent symbol. These figures should be understood as approximations, despite their apparent exactness. The photographic reproduction does not allow one to tell in all cases whether or not a vowel carries an accent symbol and, if so, which. Moreover, the decision whether or not a given letter is a vowel letter is to some degree arbitrary, notably in the case of u, which corresponds to both u and v in modern orthography.

There are some differences between the five different types of vowel letters (see Table A).

Table A: proportion of accented vowels				
basic colour	*attested possibilities*	*number of attestations*	*of which accented*	*percentage accented*
a	a, A, á, à	6937	1289	19%
e	e, E, é, è	5330	678	13%
i	i, y, I, í, ì	7773	522	7%
o	o, O, ó, Ó, ò	5524	433	8%
u	u, U, ú, ù	3017	467	15%

2.2   The problem of *i*

The low frequency of *í* is caused by a curious property of the printed text. Table B shows what is going on. It turns out that the number of occurrences of *í* fluctuates much more strongly than that of the other vowels. From the beginning of "Ribanje" up to verse 800 the proportion of accented *í* is similar to that of *é*. Then it drops to about half of its earlier frequency. After verse 1411 of "Ribanje" there are only 24 attestations.

Table B: the case of *i*				
stretch	*total*	*i*	*í*	*ì*	*perc. í*
1-800	2576	2230	343	3	13%
801-1411	2195	2043	150	2	7%
801-1200	1415	1334	80	1	6%
1201-1411	780	709	70	1	9%
1412-f160a	3002	2978	24	0	0.8%

In view of this it will be necessary in the sequel to differentiate between the three sections of the book, as follows:

– A (1-800): use of *í* comparable to that of other vowels.
– B (801-1411): *í* used considerably less than other accented vowels.
– C (1412-f160a): *í* virtually absent.

This is not the only problem involving the letter *i*. Wagner (1970: 27) has drawn attention to several instances of what would seem to look like the printed sequence *íi* in positions in which length is surprising in the light of what is otherwise known about the average SCr accentual system, e.g. *poſídé* (32), *ſí* (no reference, but many attestations, cf. 366, 371, 372, 373 etc.). Wagner regards these examples as "wypadki mylnego użycia znaku ´ na oznaczenie samogłosek krótkich".

As a matter of fact it is unlikely that in such examples an acute was actually intended. The sequence *ſi* is usually printed as a single typographical unit and if it is, the dot on the *i* may resemble an acute accent and often does. There are several reasons for not actually reading acute accents in such cases.

Most importantly, the sequence *ſi* is frequently printed in this way in the Latin and Italian passages in the book in positions where an acute accent would be totally out of place, e.g. *ſitim, promdſit, riſit, ſigna* in the Latin poem on p. 49r. Unless we are prepared to read these words as **ſítim, prompſít, riſít, ſígna*, we are not entitled either to read an acute accent in words that are printed in exactly similar fashion in the Croatian text.

Moreover, a genuine sequence *ſí*, with the *í* making up a distinct typographical element, is also used from time to time: Ns *ſín* 'son' (486), prls *proſím* (332), Is *ſínçom* (746). This shows that there was a perfectly satisfactory way of printing the sequence *ſí* if it was really considered necessary.

Finally, as seen by Wagner, if an acute accent is read in such instances of *ſi* with an acute-like dot on the *i*, we are stuck with quite a few examples of length that do not tally at all with the remainder of the evidence offered by Hektorović's text, e.g. in Gs *ſilé* (22), imp2s *beſidi* (130), NAp *beſide* (543), NAp *ſidine* (477), du *ſiromaha* (528), imperf2/3s *beſiyáſce* (598), inf *ſiſti* (728), etc. It goes without saying, however, that this point will acquire force only after the principal characteristics of the accentual system reflected in Hektorović's text will have been established, which is not yet the case.

2.3 Other irregular distributions

The only capital letter to appear with an accent symbol is *Ó*. It is attested only five times, always in the pronominal Ns *Ón* and in a limited stretch of the book (1207, 1317, 1386, 1402, 1462). Inside this stretch there are three attestations of *On* without an accent mark (1240, 1354, 1414), outside it another eleven (128, 389, 464, 538, 737, 757, 966, 1107, 1604, 1617, c51). When not printed with a capital letter, accented *ón* (365, 742, 777, 938, 1043, 1167, 1191, 1198, 1243, 1360, 1383, 1399, 1441, 1466, 1543, 1626) outnumbers unaccented *on* (29,

472

474, 489, 557, 606, 744, 1012, 1363, e59) by more than three to two (16/9).

Less spectacular fluctuations that appear to involve all vowels are presented in table C. It turns out that in the beginning of "Ribanje" the proportion of vowel letters provided with an acute accent is far above average. From then on to the end of "Ribanje" the proportion of vowels provided with an acute hovers around 13%, with the following exceptions: the two *bugarštice* (523-591, 595-685) are much more sparingly accented than the main text, a fact that becomes evident as soon as one separates the *bugarštice* from the *dvanaesterci*; the stretch consisting of the verses 701-800 is more consistently accented than average, whereas the stretch consisting of the verses 1401-1500 is sparingly accented. Note also that the "Stvari ine" are significantly less abundantly accented than "Ribanje".

Table C: accented vowels in different stretches of text							
stretch	vowels[7]	acute	á	é	í	ó, Ó	ú
1-100	1205	220 (18%)	66	41	61	23	29
101-200	1215	158 (13%)	59	18	42	22	17
201-300	1241	164 (13%)	58	26	44	14	22
301-400	1208	160 (13%)	44	27	43	26	20
401-500	1202	166 (14%)	59	29	36	16	26
501-600	1311	126 (10%)	52	20	30	10	14
601-700	1331	100 (8%)	44	15	22	9	10
501-700 bug.	2150	162 (8%)	76	25	34	15	12
501-700 dvan.	504	65 (13%)	20	11	18	4	12
701-800	1252	206 (16%)	59	36	65	23	23
801-900	1221	143 (12%)	58	37	16	17	15
901-1000	1247	149 (12%)	52	34	23	18	22
1001-1100	1224	156 (13%)	50	35	23	21	27
1101-1200	1205	163 (14%)	80	33	18	17	15
1201-1300	1229	161 (13%)	64	26	36	16	19
1301-1400	1231	159 (13%)	60	25	30	19	25
1401-1500	1219	125 (10%)	45	24	9	17	30
1501-1600	1207	145 (12%)	61	44	3	16	21
1601-1684	1013	126 (12%)	58	27	4	16	21
a1-a61	1889	170 (9%)	75	34	7	38	16
b1-b15	227	8 (4%)	5	1	0	2	0

c1-c100	1204	114	(9%)	52	23	0	20	19
c101-c202	1225	133	(11%)	49	40	3	17	24
d1-d46	554	35	(6%)	16	9	0	7	3
e1-e60a	763	73	(10%)	32	18	1	10	12
f1-f100	1201	110	(9%)	44	30	1	14	21
f101-f160a	757	70	(9%)	29	13	0	18	10

3.1 The grave accent: the material

Maretić describes Hektorović's use of accent marks in the following words: "Hektorović upotrebljava znakove ´ i ` i ńima obično bilježi duge slogove; znak ˙ mnogo je rjeđi od znaka ´" (1889: 23). Mladenović (1968: 22-23) and Wagner (1970: 27) agree. However nice this consensus may be, so far it rests on nothing more than the personal authority of three individuals who have not publicly evaluated the evidence. The first problem we are going to tackle is the question as to whether or not systematic differences between the use of the two accent symbols can be observed.

The grave accent is found in 49 examples, amounting to a mere 1.5% of the total number of vowels that carry an accent symbol. In the case of each example all attestations of the same or basically the same form marked with the acute accent are given. In most cases attestations that are not provided with any accent symbol are also given, to provide material for the preliminary discussion of the relationship between accented and unaccented forms in section 3.3.

(1) Adv zdòla (103). Although this form is not attested elsewhere, in comparable formations the element -dol- often carries an acute accent, cf. zlólu (b1, read: *zdólu), nizdóla (454), nizdólu (875), zdól (514), cf. also the acute accent on -gor- in zgóra (170, 343, 354, 384, 1165, c9), zgóri (454, 1620), uzgóra (387), uzgóru (838), zgór (1089, 1096), and absence of an accent symbol in zgora (d21), Zdol (f155).

(2) Aor3p odlùcilce (202). The same form is also attested with an acute: odlúcilce (839), cf. the acute accents in 1p odlúcilmo (735) and 1s odluícih (43, read: *odlúcih) and the absence of any accent symbol in 1s Odlucih (17), and gpt odlucif (f53).

(3) Gpt dàfsci (320). Although this particular form is not attested elsewhere, there are quite a few attestations of forms in -avši with an acute on the -a-: mucáffci (207, 865), pogledáffci (1190), uxgáffci (417), fpulcchiáffci (430), popegliáffci (1098), poznáffci (768), polpáffci (751),

obráſſci (767, d17), *ueceráſſci* (507), *stáſſci* (723), *ſtáſſci* (866), *stáſſci* (1131), *Stáſſci* (c12), *poſtáſſci* (429, 1097), *uſtáſſci* (752), *priuézáſſci* (724), *Puſcchiáfsci* (18), cf. also the acute in *potocíſſci* (516), *Sſíſſci* (66), *píſſci* (756), *popíſſci* (240), *bugaríſſci* (688), *Cúſſci* (365).

Absence of an accent symbol in the syllable preceding *-vši* is significantly less frequent in the case of *-avši* and much more frequent in that of *-ivši* and *-uvši*: *sliſcauſci* (c115), *zadaſſci* (d18), *ſurgaſſci* (1081), *naſpaſſci* (508), *Staſſci* (652), *staſſci* (603), *ſtaſſci* (558), *stauſci* (e29), *uſtaſſci* (208, 1082), *zazuauſci* (c139), *pricházaſſci* (1189); *priprauifsci* (20), *oſtauifsci* (19), *Zábiſſci* (833), *izgubiſſci* (f10), *razbiſſci* (f9), *sfarſciſſci* (1619), *ſuarſciſſci* (689), *ſcchiédiſſci* (732), *narédiſſci* (731), *pouidiſſci* (463, 1138), *Zacudiſſci* (154), *ſcáliſſci* (968), *naciniſſci* (1216), *pochloſniſſci* (757, read: **pochloniſſci*), *napiſſci* (967), *pochripiſſci* (293), *potarpiſſci* (1620), *prichriſſci* (c197), *gouoriſſci* (1215), *odgouoriſſci* (464), *otuoriſſci* (c198), *ochuſiſſci* (239), *obrátiſſci* (294), *urátiſſci* (a16), *uputiſſci* (758), *Louiſſci* (1129), *Poloxiſſci* (647), *douoziſſci* (1137), *pouoziſſci* (515); *cuſſci* (156), *Vzmachnufsci* (12), *potégnuſſci* (1234), *oddahnuſſci* (1025), *chlichnuſſci* (c190), *primuchnuſſci* (1233).

(4) Npm *Razúmnì* (377). Although this particular form is not otherwise attested, the same ending is better attested with an acute, cf. *druzí* (484), *múdrí* (7), *mudrí* (845, 971).

(5) Inf *uzàyti* (394). There are no other attestations of this form, cf. however the acute in *náyti* (393), *dóyti* (955), *úyti* (128), and in the following examples: pr3s *náyde* (1005), *záyde* (1006), *dóyde* (c84, f112), *póyde* (c198); imp1p *náydimo* (113); aor1s *náydoh* (267), *ſáydoh* (268), 2/3s *záyde* (463), *Izáyde* (1135), *úyde* (127).

Absence of an accent mark is amply attested in the same forms (inf, pr3s, imp, aor1s and 2/3s), cf. inf *Nayti* (259), *poyt* (258, 387, c116), *poyti* (18, a1), pr3s *doyde* (c197), *doyde* (f70, possibly aorist), *proyde* (c106, c160, f111), *proyde* (f69, possibly aorist), imp2s *doydi* (685), aor1s *doydoh* (157, c142), *naydoh* (45, a12), *Naydoh* (7), *Naydóh* (212), *poydoh* (1475, 1652, c141), 2/3s *doyde* (a31, c108), *proyde* (c107).

In other forms absence of an accent mark is the only attested possibility, cf. pr1s *naydem* (c121), *naydu* (c106), 2s *doydeſc* (544), 1p *poydemo* (617), 3p *doydú* (e12, f101), *obaydú* (c105), *poydú* (e11), *poydu* (c137); aor1p *doydoſmo* (867, 1467, 1641), *naydoſmo* (868), *obaydoſmo* (1097), *otaydoſmo* (1098), *poydoſmo* (499, 1194), *Poydoſmo* (109, 763, 1082), *proydoſmo* (1468), aor3p *doydoſce* (866, 1072, 1102, 1524), *naydoſce* (1134), *oydoſce* (98), *poydoſce* (1101, 1133, 1523), *Poydoſce* (87).[8]

A curious regularity crops up in this material: accent marks are never used in the plural aorist forms, common as they are (22 attestations). The point will be taken up briefly below (section 5.3).

(6) Ns *pùt* (416) 'flesh'. The only other attestations of this form carry an acute: *pút* (413, f85).

(7) Inf *razyagmìti* (619). This form is also attested with an acute: *razyagmíti* (617). The material contains two further examples of an acute accent on the *-i-* preceding the *-ti* or *-t* of the infinitive: *oſtauít* (34), *prauít* (33). These examples are dwarfed by more than 300 infinitives in *-iti* or *-it* in which no accent symbol is present.

At this point a brief excursus is necessary to discuss Wagner's assumption that the accent marks in *prauít* and *oſtauít* are mistakes (1970: 27). I think this idea (which Wagner merely states without trying to substantiate it) cannot be upheld.

To begin with, although the number of examples is small (4+1), it is large enough to make the idea that mistakes are involved unattractive in itself.

Furthermore, the acute in these examples is supported by the *l*-pns *razxalílo* (674) and by similar forms attested among polysyllabic verbs with infinitives in *-ati* and *-nuti*: *pogledáti* (235), *trúyáti* (f90), *Obrochouát* (1026), *nádiyát* (1252), *dragouála* (524), *ſapſouála* (531), *pohitáli* (629), *razbignúti* (585).

As a matter of fact, the evidence of living dialects suggests the possibility that length in this position was a feature of Hektorović's language. As noted by Rešetar (1900: 33) already, in the dialect of Stari Grad on Hvar **a* has a long reflex (*o*, written as *ǒ* by Rešetar) in the infinitive and *l*-participle of (a)-stressed verbs, e.g. *plȉvǒt*, *plȉvǒla*, *kȕcǒt*, *kȕcǒli*. Later investigators have shown that this feature is widespread in the Čakavian dialects of Hvar and Brač, e.g. Brusje (Hvar) *grȉjot*, *grȉjo(l)*, *grȉjola*, *grȉjolo* (Hraste 1926-27: 206), Brač *glȅdo(t)*, *glȅdola*, *glȅdolo* (Hraste 1940: 59). Since the difference between long and short *i* and *u* has been obliterated in posttonic position in the dialects of Hvar and Brač, the evidence of the living dialects that continue Hektorović's immediate linguistic background is inconclusive.

However, as was first noted, I think, by Rešetar (1900: 33, 159-160), length in (a)-stressed verbs in *-iti*, *-ati* and *-nuti* is widespread in the dialects of what is nowadays known as the "Zeta-Lovćen" group, e.g. Prčanj/Ozrinići *pâmtīt*, *gȁzīt*, *kȕpīt*, *gȉnūt*, *umȕknūt*. Later investigators have amply confirmed the correctness of Rešetar's findings, cf., e.g.,

476

"tematski vokal u infinitivu uvek je dug ako je nenaglašen", and examples like *pâmtīt, pâmtīla, găzīt, găzīla, plăkāt, kăjāt, svĕtkovāt, komândovāt* reported by Pešikan (1965: 72-76), cf. also *udărīt, udărīli, pozdrăvīćeš* (Ćupić 1977: 163, 165), and, in particular, Dragoljub Petrović's explicit confirmation of the correctness of Rešetar's observations about the dialects of the southern part of the Boka Kotorska, illustrated by examples like *izrĕzāti, glĕdāla, rĕzāli, zadïmīti, stăvīli, pogïnūti, prekïnūla* (Petrović 1974: 122).

As for areas closer to Hektorović's home (in particular the coastal stretch and the islands between the southern part of the Boka Kotorska and Hvar), we are hampered by the fact that the dialects of South Dalmatia have been covered much less thoroughly than those of Montenegro. However, Pavle Ivić (1957: 406) has found length in Goveđari on Mljet (*-ati* and *-nuti*), and Orebić and surroundings on Pelješac (apparently only *-ati*). In the dialects of neighbouring Korčula all three types of infinitives have length, at least if Kušar's (1895: 333), Rešetar's (1900: 33) and Moskovljević's (1950: 185) observations are correct in principle, which is for the time being somewhat uncertain in view of the persistent unclarity about the synchronic phonology of the dialect. In (a)-stressed verbs in *-nuti*, length is also attested in Northwest Čakavian (Novi, Omišalj, Kastav) and Kajkavian (Bednja), see further Vermeer (1994: 481, with examples and references).[9]

(8) *Zatìm* (686). This form is much better attested with an acute: *zatím* (1473), *Zatím* (73, 83, 163, 243, 497, 755, 1081), cf. also the acute in Is *tím* (415, e52) and numerous other attestations of the pronominal Is in *-ím*, cf. *chím* (134, 346, 784, 1228, 1406), *Chím* (783), *Choyím* (6, 85), *cím* (895, a21), *Cím* (114, 1274), *gním* (62, 135, 223, 232, 753, 773, 1147, 1606), *oním* (726), *ouím* (745), *sfím* (727). Absence of any accent symbol is even more frequent: *zatim* (912, 1621, c19, e29, f37), *Zatim* (289, 723, 848, 866, 1065, 1157, 1218, a47, c65, f12), *chachouim* (f142), *chim* (60, 958, f146), *Chim* (27), *choyim* (a1, e18), *Choyim* (b2), *cim* (943, 1296, c11, f131), *Cim* (1298, c34, f110), *gnim* (633, 643, 1211, 1605, c62), *onim* (a58), *Onim* (e16, possibly Dpl), *ouim* (a58, f141), *sfim* (a18, c173), *sfim* (1667, possibly Dpl), *fasfim* (e20), *sfoyim* (639), *tachouim* (c15), *taohouim* (f142, read: *tachouim*), *Yednim* (1166).

(9) Gs *buchliè* (813). The same ending carries a grave accent in two other examples: *Dobrotè* (1407), *ftránè* (c45). Whereas *buchliè* happens to be attested only once, the catchword corresponding to *Dobrotè* has

an acute (*Dobroté*) and the Gs of *strana* is attested twice with an acute: *stráné* (825, e33). In other nouns the same ending is attested abundantly with an acute, cf. *barziné* (1230), *buché* (c32), *chgnigé* (1372), *choxé* (1671), *chriuiné* (589), *chuchié* (750, 1094), *diché* (e23), *druxiné* (1660), *drúxbé* (c192), *Galiyé* (1195), *Goſpodé* (a6), *gniué* (c132), *goré* (610, 731, 1649, f13), *goſpodé* (c150), *grihoté* (33), *hiné* (c134), *hixé* (1096, f96), *huálé* (1545), *iſtiné* (567, c133), *izminé* (8), *lipoté* (34), *louiné* (1659, 1673), *lúché* (1072, 1134), *mayché* (714), *miloſcchié* (c182), *miré* (870, 1062, c24, e42), *mochriné* (437, 456), *neueré* (932), *nezgodé* (c201), *paſcé* (57), *práfdé* (1568), *pripraué* (754), *priſcé* (181), *protiué* (389), *Ribé* (1647), *rapé* (1636), *razpraué* (1362), *ribé* (90), *riché* (277), *ríché* (854), *roté* (d13), *ſabgliçé* (541), *Sabgliçé* (716), *Silé* (1266), *sfarhé* (f100, f114), *ſárxbé* (1429), *ſcchodé* (858, 1309), *ſilé* (22, d5), *ſitoſcchié* (1258), *ſrichié* (867), *ſridé* (c179), *ſtatiré* (1061), *ſtrilé* (d6), *ſúmgnié* (a52), *tminé* (f61), *tuardiné* (1175), *uiré* (1571, e41), *uodé* (185, 350), *Vodé* (303), *uoglié* (949, 970), *yié* (814), *zemglié* (1531, 1585). Attestations without an accent symbol are significantly less frequent: *beſide* (1589), *Beſide* (d12), *ciſtochie* (1435), *dobrote* (d14), *dúſce* (f65), *mire* (f66), *priliche* (e24), *Sabgliçe* (716, 717), *ſúmgnie* (961, 1394), *ſumgnie* (286), *taſcchine* (1574), *uode* (425), *uoglie* (521, 1028, c69, c88, c162), *uruchine* (420).

(10) Gs comp *ſtàróga* (820). In the only other attestation of this form the stem syllable happens not to carry an accent: *staróga* (1219). Cf. however the acute in Nsm *ſtári* (1140), Dsm/n *Stárómu* (1656), Lsm/n *ſtáróm* (a61, e60a), Npm *ſtári* (1298, 1366), Dp *ſtárim* (1246), Apm *ſtáré* (a4), Asf *stárú* (72).

(11) NAsn *Chò* (893). This form is much better attested with an acute, cf. *chó* (211, 212, 893, 916, 921, 1034, 1156, 1269, 1482, 1636, f44), *Chó* (431, 1033). Absence of an accent mark is less frequent: *cho* (126, 141, 260, c141, f142), *Cho* (f46).

(12) Inf *razdìliti* (916). This form is attested once without an accent mark: *razdiliti* (561). Compare also the acute in *oddíliti* (569), *l*-pfs *razdílila* (529), aorlp *razdíliſmo* (1193), *nadíliſmo* (173). Absence of any accent mark is more frequent, cf. inf *diliti* (1310), *Diliti* (c118), pr3s *dili* (a27, d40), aor2/3s *nadili* (c9, e18), *udili* (c166), aorlp *diliſmo* (1666), aor3p *diliſce* (77, 172), *nadiliſce* (a21), *l*-pms *razdilio* (574), *nadilil* (e48), *l*-pfs *dilila* (525), gpt *razdiliſ* (526).

(13) Pr3s *tirà* (1024). This same form is twice attested with an acute: *tirá* (809, 1391). The pr3s ending *-a* quite often has an acute, cf. *oblahcá* (900), *odnáſcá* (1527), *búçá* (62), *napadá* (f77), *obádá* (1156), *obládá* (1611), *odchládá* (1155), *gledá* (863), *pogledá* (c111), *Vgledá* (452), *uſpredá* (c112), *dogodá* (1030), *bigá* (1391), *ſcmigá* (1392), *chuhá* (445, 449, 1241), *dúhá* (446), *odurachiá* (1353), *stráchiá* (1354), *pripráfgliá* (f121), *oſtáugliá* (f122), *priçigniá* (1399, read: *pricigniá*), *razcigniá* (1400), *imá* (337, 396, 401, 421, 919, 1004, 1012, 1410, f129), *nimá* (846, 1023), *otimá* (927), *poyimá* (402), *uyimá* (205), *uazimá* (206, 1409), *nímá* (375, 377, 1049), *zná* (68, 486, 788, a47, c78, e54, f111), *zná* (d.) (475), *Zná* (1522), *stará* (814, 987, 1532), *igrá* (1036), *proſtirá* (e49), *izuirá* (e50), *pohuatá* (1059), *hitá* (e3), *prolitá* (902), *ſplitá* (f30), *poſartá* (1228), *biuá* (959, 1420), *pribiuá* (1481), *dobiuá* (960), *odiuá* (1419), *pochriuá* (1482), *prizriuá* (f108), *proſiuá* (436), *bíuá* (50, 340, 435), *zachríuá* (339), *nazíuá* (49), *mnoxá* (1048, f76), *prigáyá* (c158), *sláyá* (35), *poráyá* (36), *sfiyá* (1136), *syá* (803). Absence of an accent symbol is less frequent, cf. *upráſca* (876), *protiça* (804), *pala* (384, read: *pada*), *zapada* (1066), *ſpouida* (c54), *uyida* (1039), *docecha* (547), *pourachia* (903), *ſtráchia* (904), *ſtauglia* (1323), *oſtáuglia* (1324), *ima* (308, 802, 928, 1006, 1257, 1372, c18, f125), *nima* (d46), *uazima* (376, a27), *zna* (a25, f17, f69), *ſtupa* (1374), *priſtupa* (1373), *zamira* (321), *ozira* (1392), *proſttira* (322, read: *proſtira*), *zabiua* (f62), *zahuagliua* (1499), *pochriua* (1500), *obſiua* (f61), *razbiya* (1081), *ſya* (1664), *podbúya* (1432), *trúya* (1431).[10]

(14) Pr3s *dà* (1029). The same form is much better attested with an acute accent, cf. *dá* (286, c112, c146, c200, f128); absence of an accent symbol occurs twice: *da* (1293, f159).

(15) The superlative formans in *nàypriya* (1082). The same morpheme is once attested with an acute: *náyboglie* (1021). In the overwhelming majority of cases, however, no accent mark is present, cf. *naybogli* (1440), *nayboglia* (46), *naybogliá* (961), *nayboglie* (522, 950, 1027, 1187, 1471, a54), *naybogliu* (e10), *Naybogliega* (1381), and also *naybarxé* (891, 902), *naychoriſtniyu* (1356), *naygore* (1039), *naylipglié* (887), *naylipgliú* (164), *nayliſce* (441, 503, 1267, 1451), *Nayliſce* (1291), *naymagni* (331, e40), *naymagniu* (1181, a43), *nayobicniyu* (1355), *nayparui* (a35), *nayparuo* (a6), *nayslaye* (432, f46), *nayſtariye* (883), *nayuechi* (a51), *nayuechie* (1031, f120), *nayuechié* (889), *Nayuechie* (1399), *Nayuechiu* (802), *nayuiſce* (442, 1153), *nayurucbié* (749, read: *nayuruchié*), *nayyacé* (895).

(16) *Goſpodàr* (1139). This form is better attested with an acute: *Goſpodár* (856, 1205), *Coſpodár* (291, read: *Goſpodár), cf. also the other case forms Gs *Goſpodára* (114, 246), DLs *Goſpodáru* (222, 590, 591, 684). Absence of an accent mark is attested once: *Goſpodaróm* (1325).

(17) *pàs* 'belt' (1203). There are no other attestations of this word.

(18) *nàc* (1331). In the same form, the acute accent is attested three times: *nác* (175, 1007, 1577), cf. also the acute in *zác* (721, 735, a30, a49), *Zác* (995, 1494, 1533, d6). Absence of an accent symbol is not attested in these words.

(19) Gpr *budùch* (1347). This form is twice attested with an acute: *budúch* (27, f67). With other verbs, the same ending is abundantly attested with an acute, cf. *izticúch* (342), *techúch* (330), *iſcchiúch* (f54), *Laxúch* (1461), *maxúch* (1043), *gledayúch* (f73), *cechayúch* (c122), *Nuchayúch* (c135), *znayúch* (904, c121), *poſtayúch* (965), *odpiuayúch* (966), *poyúch* (1222), *minuyúch* (1070), *obsluxuyúch* (1360). Absence of an accent symbol is however more frequent: *placuch* (d44), *bgliuduch* (f132), *moguch* (24), *techuch* (1167), *chaxuch* (1044), *Cháxuch* (1400), *pritéxuch* (402), *podnáſcayuch* (1592), *sliſcayuch* (1232, f74), *buçayuch* (88), *gledayuch* (502), *hayuch* (c60), *práſcchiayuch* (446), *ſpuſcchiayuch* (87), *práſchiayuch* (1591), *upráfgliayuch* (1587), *poſtupayuch* (1231), *dáyuch* (1588), *Pitayuch* 'feed' (1581), *Pitáyuch* 'ask' (f51), *ſtayuch* (903), *poſtayuch* (501), *poyuch* (697), *poduichuyuch* (1069), *obuchuyuch* (1582), *odchupuyuch* (1581). The closely related ending *-úći* offers a similar picture: presence of an acute, though well attested, is less frequent than absence of an accent symbol, whereas in this case the grave accent is not attested at all, cf. *pridiſcúchi* (447), *budúchi* (347, a44), *pechúchi* (1074), *techúchi* (70), *iſcchiúchi* (c42), *mechiúchi* (1123), *napirúchi* (694, 1067), *sliſcayúchi* (a58), *gledayúchi* (233), *ſpráugliayúchi* (c39), *pyúchi* (1238), *chlichuyúchi* (583) vs. *ſchácuchi* (1639), *primicuchi* (448), *poticuchi* (188, 234, 633), *máſcuchi* (1640), *buduchi* (123), *xeliuchi* (a18), *zacigniuchi* (695), *chunuchi* (f18), *Proſtiruchi* (1071), *dayuchi* (c171), *ufayuchi* (a36), *nuchayuchi* (c40), *urachiayuchi* (332), *primayuchi* (1583), *ſtayuchi* (331), *poháyayuchi* (1584), *dáyuchi* (242), *xeliyuchi* (c41), *poyuchi* (241), *chlichuyuchi* (678), *ctuyuchi* (c172).

(20) Pr3s *nì* (1372). In this form the acute accent is much more common: *ní* (33, 44, 389, 424, 460, 864, 1243, 1321, 1325, f43), *Ní*

480

(1339). Absence of any accent symbol is even more frequent: *ni* (358, 797, 991, 1150, 1276, 1455, 1521, 1549, c5, c49, c94, c134, e24, f55, f102, f143), *Ni* (393, 1342, 1435, c158, e40). In the other negated forms of the present tense of 'be' containing the morpheme *ni*- the facts are comparable, cf. 1s *níſam* (23, 92), 2s *nís* (739), 3p *níſu* (707) vs. *niſam* (c89), *niſám* (a29), *Niſam* (218), *niſi* (1253, a40), *niſu* (786, f55, f59), *Niſu* (707, 708, c179).

(21) Gs *Dobrotè* (1407). See (9).

(22) Nsm comp *pràui* (1420). This case is related to that of *ſtàróga* (see (10)). The same form has four times an acute: *práui* (255, 1667, c20, f1), cf. also the acute of Nsn *práuó* (1286), Gsm/n *práuóga* (366), Ism/n *práuim* (c32), Gs fem *práué* (a6), DLs fem *práuóy* (c54), Is fem *práuóm* (a43).

(23) Imp2s *zagrùbi* (1449). There are no other attestations of this form. In the only other attestation of the same verb the stem vowel carries an acute: pr3s *zagrúbi* (1544).

(24) Gerpr *cinèch* (1451). There is one other attestation of the same ending with a grave accent *zelèch* (f92, read: **xelèch*). The former example is also attested with an acute: *cinéch* (1417). In the ending the acute is frequent: *sliſcéch* (1414), *ſidéch* (1509), *beſidéch* (1510), *Vidéch* (f45), *Hodéch* (1016), *zahodéch* (506), *dohodéch* (f149), *prohodéch* (505, 1629), *Yizdéch* (c193), *Misléch* (c11), *miſléch* (203), *Mnéch* (f40), *tarpéch* (1014), *ſpéch* (c135), *gouoréch* (352, 361), *Gouoréch* (226, 1281), *noſéch* (492), *Noséch* (71), *Noſéch* (754), *zanoſéch* (f98), *ctéch* (f43), *çtéch* (7, read: **ctéch*), *htéch* (41, 692, 860, 1055, 1239), *ſtéch* (c136), *darxéch* (511), *boyéch* (1108), *uozéch* (60, 1134), *uozéchi* (78, read: **uozéch*), *barzéch* (696). Absence of an accent symbol is much less frequent: *gliúbech* (1593), *yácech* (f95), *ſcchiédech* (f51), *Videch* (21, 201), *uuhlech* (1043), *stech* (252), *prauech* (1109), *téxech* (850), *darxech* (697), *táyech* (1632).

(25) *Cèſto* (1454). The same form is better attested with an acute accent: *céſto* (1392), *Céſto* (446, f92), cf. also the acute in NApn *céſta* (990). Absence of an accent mark is also common, cf. *ceſto* (1239, 1684), *Ceſto* (597, b7), cf. also the absence of an accent mark in the collocation *ceſtochrát* (865, c177).

(26) Ns *mnòx* (1573). There are no other attestations of this form.

481

(27) Ns *Yà* (1600). There is one other attestation of a grave accent in the same form: *yà* (c153), which however does not diminish the fact that the acute accent is much better attested *yá* (91, 131, 161, 175, 188, 201, 239, 467, 484, 545, 557, 686, 743, 1090, 1103, 1185, 1209, 1211, 1513, 1601, 1663, c96, c97, e21, f36, f137), *Yá* (115, 137, 360, 1013, 1683). Absence of an accent mark is significantly less common: *ya* (76, 139, 143, 153, 223, 255, 263, 560, 821, 1375, 1651, a42, c83, f7, f25, f42, f144, f155), *Ya* (785, 1619, c7).

(28) Imp2p *náʃtòyte* (1656). This form is not otherwise attested. Imperatives ending in a vowel plus -*j* occasionally carry an acute, cf. 2s *Puʃcchiáy* (714), *htíy* (120), *stóy* (155), *Cúy* (1405), *Verúy* (c155), 2p *znáyte* (353), *póyte* 'sing' (1655). In an overwhelming majority of cases, however, such forms carry no accent symbol at all, cf. *chuʃcay* (412, 423), *sluʃcay* (412), *day* (15, 75, 213, 889, 1160, 1246, 1264, 1317, a25, c123), *Day* (d19), *priday* (1615), *chay* (1547), *Puʃcchiay* (713 twice), *ʃpraugliay* (c118), *imay* (d19), *znay* (133, 290, 456, 859, 1213, 1643), *Znay* (348), *Saznay* (1269), *cháray* (1443), *zamiray* (c147), *razbíray* (702, 703), *poʃtay* (76), *cuuay* (1245), *Cúuay* (1020), *poháyay* (1263), *Proliy* (425), *uoliy* (1457), *htiy* (398, d21), *Htiy* (949), *uiy* (c121), *pouiy* (119), *yiy* (1670), *poy* 'go' (75, 1052), *Poy* 'go' (405), *zbroy* (144), *ʃtoy* (1051, c163), *naʃtoy* (1289, 1327, 1337), *náʃtoy* (1247, d41), *duoy* (c81), *cuy* (256, 1271), *Cuy* (1265), *izchuʃcuy* (1335), *nasliduy* (1269), *napriduy* (c174), *iziʃchuy* (455, 1336), *uʃiluy* (c173), *daruy* (137), *ueruy* (418), *Veruy* (1034), *uiruy* (1390), *miruy* (1270), *opʃuy* (1272), *poctuy* (194), *Pametuy* (852), *chazuy* (264, 897), 1p *daymo* (1574), *Htiymo* (1577), *Naʃtoymo* (1433), *Miluymo* (1260), 2p *posluʃcayte* (324), *dayte* (809), *znayte* (323), *cuyte* (1654).

(29) NAp *ʃtuàri* (a12). This form is much better attested with an acute: NAp *stuári* (21, 1578, f99), NAp *ʃtuári* (196, 826, 1176, 1323, 1382, a55, f115), NAp *Stuári* (956), cf. also the acute in other forms of the same word: Ns *stuár* (a14, c95), Ns *ʃtuár* (295, 915, 928, 1568, 1682, a6, a37, c67, f34), Gs *ʃtuári* (944), Gs or NAp *ʃtuári* (1297), Gp *ʃtuári* (f127), Gp *ʃtuárí* (729), Ip *ʃtuári* (1184). Attestations without an accent symbol are somewhat less numerous, cf. Ns *stuar* (449, 1301, a18, a27), *ʃtuar* (7, 11, 292, 399, 412, c161, f7, f63), Gs or NAp *stuari* (a49), NAp *stuari* (153, 808, e25), NAp *ʃtuari* (a41, a52, f154), Gp *ʃtuari* (a22).

(30) L-pms *poznàl* (a45). This form is not otherwise attested. Roughly similar forms provided with an acute are not unknown, e.g. *poslál* (1667), *uſtál* (514).

(31) Is *laxòm* (a46). This form is not otherwise attested. Other feminine nouns with an endingless Ns have a different ending (*-yu*). However, in nouns with a Ns in *-a* the ending *-om* usually has an acute accent, cf. *ribóm* (196), *ſabgliçóm* (641, 651), *ſinçóm* (187), *beſidóm* (1500), *Voyeuodóm* (657), *praudóm* (a7), *chgnigóm* (f153), *dichóm* (781), *Vladichóm* (a17), *richóm* (303, 395), *rúchóm* (1282), *xeglióm* (e45), *uoglióm* (135), *pomgnióm* (a58), *pómgnióm* (f126), *nepómgnióm* (858), *huálóm* (782, 1180, c22, c88), *sſilóm* (1204), *argutlóm* (163), *ranóm* (d16), *Licminóm* (58), *iſtinóm* (266, a43), *druxinóm* (520, 611, 657), *ueróm* (715), *goróm* (1223), *zoróm* (1224), *lipotóm* (513), *rotóm* (f18), *dobrotóm* (779), *gláuóm* (845), *molituóm* (c157), *Mrixóm* (90), *Goſpoyóm* (a17). Absence of an accent symbol is less frequent, cf. *druxbom* (e21), *dúſcom* (1611), *ſcibiçom* (c193), *duſciçom* (561), *Chupiçom* (818), *mrixariçom* (a2), *ſínçom* (746), *beſidom* (c44), *chgnigom* (a19), *odichiom* (f154), *pomgniom* (c163), *pómgniom* (206), *Liuiom* (a17), *gorcinom* (c103), *druxinom* (640), *gorom* (609).

(32) Nsn *tò* (a49). This form is much better attested with an acute accent: *tó* (57, 284, 733, 861, 1020, 1057, a17, a38, a58, c121, f47). It is even more frequent without an accent mark: *to* (15, 36, 256, 369, 473, 487, 532, 541, 545, 551, 553, 580, 598, 609, 612, 617, 633, 650, 652, 658, 667, 671, 675, 681, 1481, 1491, 1550, 1535, 1607, 1651, 1668, 1569, a42, a53, b8, c13, c83, f74, f125, f145, f152), *To* (885).

(33) PPP Nsf comp *poctouánà* (c1). Whereas this form is not otherwise attested, the ending is much more frequent with an acute, cf. *drugá* (344, a33), *huyá* (f64), *iná* (416), *naybogliá* (961), *ſuncená* (436), *tretá* (a34), *uelá* (1613, e2), *yacá* (896).

(34) PPP Nsn sim *huàglieno* (c13). The past passive participle of *hvaliti* is better attested with an acute accent, cf. NApn *huágliena* (1085, probably comp), Np masc sim *huáglieni* (42, 800), cf. also the verbal noun Gs *huáglienyá* (1413), and the past pass part of *pohvaliti*: Nsf sim *pohuágliena* (a14), Npm sim *pohuáglieni* (934), Nsn sim *pohuáglieno* (478), Nsn *P[o]huáglieno* (e2, probably comp); absence of an accent mark is found in Isf comp *pohuaglienom* (a17).

(35) Pr3p *chiè* (c33). This form is much better attested with an acute, cf. *chié* (39, 60, 585, 973, 977, 978, 985, 1282, 1345, 1497, c41, c113, c138, d30). Absence of an accent symbol is less frequent, cf. *chie* (302, 1528, c115). The only two attestations of the negated form lack an accent symbol: *néchie* (845), *Nechie* (1348).

(36) Gsm/n *tuòga* (c38). This and similar forms are better attested with an acute, cf. *móga* (1604, a20, e14), *tuóga* (589, 1397), *sfóga* (631). Absence of an accent mark is attested in *moga* (e45), *tuoga* (a40, e7, f152), *sfoga* (1640, f2).

(37) Gs *ſtránè* (c45). See (9).

(38) Gerpr *molèchi* (c59). The same form is better attested with an acute, cf. *moléchi* (1590, f49), and occurs once without an accent mark: *molechi* (c99). In the ending the acute is very frequent, cf. *zarcéchi* (307), *tiſcéchi* (1589), *ucéchi* (1056, 1587), *gladéchi* (1389, 1404), *ſidéchi* (188), *uidéchi* (1642, c7), *hodéchi* (1555), *ohodéchi* (510), *dohodéchi* (771), *prohodéchi* (339, 499), *brodéchi* (77), *cudéchi* (1135), *ueſeléchi* (187, 298), *xeléchi* (d20), *boléchi* (841), *misléchi* (211, 1299), *Misléchi* (c113), *cinéchi* (1015, 1069, 1460, 1556, 1585, f50), *pinéchi* (1070), *ſpéchi* (1077), *chupéchi* (431), *yidréchi* (109, 212), *xuberéchi* (1078), *gouoréchi* (297, 379, 500, 835, 876), *Gouoréchi* (843), *zoréchi* (324), *noſéchi* (842), *podnoſéchi* (1459), *ctéchi* (a45), *letéchi* (1099), *htéchi* (858, 873, 1102, 1193, d19, f89), *hotéchi* (a22, f94), *caſtéchi* (1554), *slauéchi* (1390), *louéchi* (772, 1101, 1641), *lexéchi* (1016, c109), *Poyéchi* (1582), *naſtoyéchi* (f47), *uozéchi* (509, 836, 875, 969, 1136, 1624). Absence of an accent mark is less common, cf. *múcechi* (833), *bdechi* (23), *çídechi* (380), *çídechi* (340), *prohodechi* (1100), *brodechi* (a58), *cudechi* (c48), *trúdechi* (24), *xalechi* (f11), *huálechi* (1403), *mislechi* (c47), *sfitlechi* (1665), *cinechi* (c110, f12), *linechi* (1079), *morechi* (c60), *gouorechi* (f93), *chrátechi* (1588), *Ctechi* (f158), *htechi* (c160), *xiuechi* (1311), *naſtoyechi* (1586), *slúſechi* (816, read: *slúxechi*), *uozechi* (1080), *puzechi* (110), *púzechi* (1623).

(39) Ip *uràti* (c120). There are no other attestations of this form.

(40) Ns *yà* (c153). See (27).

(41) Pr3p *ozdrauè* (c183). Although there are no other attestations of this particular form, the ending is abundantly attested with an acute, cf. *gliúbé* (1542), *pogriſcé* (f104), *uzuiſcé* (f103), *oducé* (f90), *mucé* (a34, f89), *nasfadé* (1010), *ſádé* (165, c73), *sfidé* (f105), *poſidé* (32),

uidé (31, 305, 1485, 1572, f106), *nenauidé* (1590), *zapouidé* (306), *hodé* (c32, f117), *nahodé* (c31), *shodé* (857, c202), *brodé* (616), *nauodé* (f118), *udé* (c187), *cudé* (789, 1227), *zacudé* (1308), *prudé* (c188), *xúdé* (958), *neuoglié* (a34), *hualé* (e26), *hráné* (202), *ciné* (374, 1341, 1577), *hiné* (1298), *progoné* (1434), *zuoné* (1496), *uáré* (1566), *miré* (1572), *zamiré* (1306), *gouoré* (7, 356, 377, 985, c117), *razgouoré* (319), *chosé* (14), *noſé* (c187), *donosé* (13), *traté* (74), *praué* (1361), *opraué* (1506), *ſpraué* (53), *izpraué* (c184), *staué* (54, 753), *ſtaué* (300), *oſtaué* (1505), *loué* (741), *darxé* (a47), *sluxé* (311), *slúxé* (811), *druxé* (312), *broyé* (1381, 1595), *naſtoyé* (975), *stoyé* (1596). Absence of an accent symbol is much less common, cf. *zgarbe* (f81), *oſcchiarbe* (f82), *ſtraſce* (58), *blide* (f75), *uide* (1002), *dohode* (186, 426), *uzprohode* (f29), *cude* (32), *trúde* (1299), *ſçine* (a52), *chupe* 'collect' (f88), *choſe* (c188), *noſe* (d27), *chiúte* (f83), *ſmúte* (f84), *protiue* (f120), *darſe* (a52, read: *darxe*), *goye* (f88), *naſtoye* (c149).

(42) Adv *barxè* (c198). This form is also attested with an acute accent: *barxé* (227) and without an accent mark: *barxe* (195, 310), *Barxe* (1067), cf. also the acute in *naybarxé* (902), *yacé* (1067), *ceſchié* (1498) *Vridniyé* (1247); note that absence of an accent mark is much more frequent, cf. *uiſce* (697, 1180), *Viſce* (1096, 1180), *nayuiſce* (1153), *ceſc-chie* (1128), *nayuechie* (f120), *Nayuechie* (1399), *daglie* (1125), *boglie* (161, 766, 969, 1071, 1474, 1633, c87, c190, c194), *nayboglie* (522, a54), *lipiglie* (162, read: *lipglie*), *ſarcenie* (c123), *magnie* (24), *Snaxnie* (c191), *gore* (f74), *naygore* (1039), *blixe* (409), *nixe* (697), *nayslaye* (f46).[11]

(43) Aor2s *zadà* (d6). This form is not otherwise attested, but cf. the acute accent in aor2/3s *podá* (1577, c65), *dá* (294, 787, e53). Cf. also the absence of an accent symbol in *da* (491, e51).

(44) PPP NAp fem *nareſcene* (d38). Exactly the same form is also attested with an acute accent: *nareſcene* (776), cf. also the acute in Nsm *nareſcen* (c52), *ureſcen* (783), *l*-pms *nareſcio* (a7).

(45) Asf *tachù* (f34). Exactly the same form is also attested with an acute: *tachú* (292).

(46) Pr3p *ſtèpgliayú* (f91). This is the only attestation of this verb.

(47) Pr3p *ſtinù* (f91). Although this form is not otherwise attested, two similar ones are attested with an acute: *uenú* (d20), *poſarnú* (c176), as is the case with virtually all types of 3p in -*u*: *zamicú* (444),

485

oticú (f87), *doticú* (354), *iſticú* (353, 443), *pridiſcú* (1073), *píſcú* (15), *dádú* (811), *napádú* (579), *grédú* (984), *pridú* (c179), *yidú* (1241), *yídú* (1262), *budú* (10, 33, 917, 1479, 1486, 1574, a23, f73), *dobudú* (f38), *obaydú* (c105), *doydú* (e12, f101), *poydú* (e11), *mogú* (287, 374), *pechú* (192), *techú* (462), *chogliú* (1369, c104), *zouú* (336, 411), *uzmaxú* (1389), *potéxú* (772), *uéxú* (771), *doſtixú* (299), *poduixú* (300), *slácayú* (943), *dayú* (e37), *uládayú* (1614), *padayú* (55), *pouidayú* (1447), *pomágayú* (346), *hayú* (196), *ſtèpgliayú* (f91), *naslagniayú* (f92), *imayú* (955, 990, 1224), *uxinayú* (1475), *znayú* (2, 956, 1599), *poznayú* (370, 984), *potipayú* (f97), *ſtarayú* (989, f116), *priſtayú* (345), *uſtayú* (d33), *pliuayú* (56), *umiyú* (981, 1483), *riyú* (165, 982), *proſiyú* (1484), *poyú* (d23), *cuyú* (1365), *zacuyú* (583), *izblaguyú* (282), *uzmiluyú* (f106), *zlamenuyú* (281), *sſituyú* (c183), *putuyú* (1223, c176). Absence of an accent symbol is attested in the following examples: *locu* (426), *pridadu* (e12), *idu* (c180), *budu* (974), *poydu* (c137), *diu* (476, c73), *uapiu* (d5), *riu* (c74), *iztégnu* (152), *pocinu* (f92), *uarnu* (c175), *cháxu* (1390), *duixu* (1153), *uznaſcayu* (c22), *padayu* (439, f82), *ugágniayu* (1056), *uogniayu* (f81), *imayu* (1478, f115), *nimayu* (1002), *znayu* (1055, 1223, f152), *poznayu* (1448, d34, e38), *obſtupayu* (147), *hitayu* (148), *pitayu* (1001), *motayu* (f98), *dariuayu* (a22), *dobíuayu* (983), *diyu* (e33), *umiyu* (a41), *dariyu* (e34), *ſiyu* (c74), *potribuyu* (c184), *cuyu* (e16, e25, f152), *zaduſcuyu* (f86), *uzpriporucuyu* (c151), *napriduyu* (c175), *luduyu* (f105), *Schrachiuyu* (c92), *zaslipgliuyu* (1366), *minuyu* (144), *ctuyu* (e26), *poctuyu* (d36), *chazuyu* (e15), *prichazuyu* (d35), *opuzuyu* (f85).

(48) Gerpr *zelèch* (f92). See (24).

(49) Negated pr3s *nèchie* (f133). The same form is much more frequent with an acute accent: *néchie* (16, 105, 189, 203, 457, 1019, 1171, 1360, 1439, 1562, 1566, c174, f98), *Néchie* (254, 307, 415), cf. also the acute accent in 1s *néchiu* (201, 473, 882, 1008), *Néchiu* (a29), 2s *néch* (422, 1673), 3p *néchie* (845). Absence of an accent mark is less frequent: 1s *nechiu* (c155, c199), 2s *nechieſc* (429, 1460), 3s *nechie* (f131), 3p *Nechie* (1348).

3.2 The grave accent: discussion of the evidence

In the previous section all 49 attestations of the grave accent have been examined. The results can be summarized as follows:

– The pronoun *ja* (27, 40) provides the only instance of a form that is attested more than once with a grave accent. In that very form the acute accent is attested more than thirty times.

– Three endings are attested more than once with a grave accent: Gs *-e* (three times), pr3s *-a* (twice), gpr *-eć* (twice). In all three cases attestations carrying an acute are much more abundant.

– In 28 cases at least one attestation of the same word form carries an acute accent: 2, 6, 7, 8, 11, 13, 14, 15, 16, 18, 19, 20, 21, 22, 24, 25, 27, 29, 32, 35, 36, 37, 38, 40, 42, 44, 45, 49. With very few exceptions there are more attestations of the acute than of the grave, whereas the reverse possibility never occurs at all.

– In 17 cases the form itself is not attested elsewhere, but attestations of closely related forms carry an acute accent: 1, 3, 4, 5, 9, 10, 12, 23, 28, 30, 31, 33, 34, 41, 34, 47, 48.

– In four cases neither the form itself nor closely related forms are attested elsewhere: 17, 26, 39, 46.

These facts substantiate the correctness of the traditional assumption that the grave accent does not have an independent function, but is to be regarded merely as an infrequent optional variant of the acute.

3.3 A tentative regularity

The material that was presented to examine the function of the grave accent can also serve to enhance our understanding of the way accent symbols are used in Hektorović's text, cf. Tables D-F.

Table D: accent symbols on *a*									
	tira	*da*	*nač*	*ja*	*stvari*	*stvar*	*hvaljen*	*-avši*	*najti*	*naj-*
grave	1	1	1	2	1	0	1	1	1	1
acute	83	5	11	31	16	11	8	20	8	1
bare	33	2	0	21	8	12	1	12	12	42

Table E: accent symbols on e							
	Gs -e	-eć	-eći	3p -e	3p će	neć-	često	-reš-
grave	3	2	1	1	1	1	1	1
acute	83	38	71	70	14	24	4	4
bare	20	11	27	20	3 (+2)	6	4	0

Table F: accent symbols on o and u									
	zdola	ko	Is -om	to	tvoga	dojde	stoj(te)	-uć	-ući	3p -u
grave	1	1	1	1	1	0	1	1	0	1
acute	13	13	41	11	6	3	2	17	14	79
bare	1	6	16	42	6	44	12	27	23	54

The case of *i* differs from that of the other vowels in that, as we have seen, the frequency of accented *í* is different in different sections of the original text (see Table G).

Table G: accent symbols on i							
	zatim	Is -im	3s ni	ni-	-ivši	dili-	-iti
grave	1	0	1	0	0	1	1
acute	6/1/2	16/5/2	5/5/1	4/0/0	5/0/0	3/1/0	3
bare	2/6/7	5/7/20	3/4/14	4/1/6	17/11/8	6/2/9	>300

The figures displayed in the Tables D through G bring to light the following tentative regularity:

• If a form carries an accent symbol once on one of the vowel letters *a*, *e* or *o*, the chances are that it does so in a majority of cases. The same holds for *i* in section A of the book.

This regularity represents a first move towards establishing the "koéfficient vyražennosti" of vowel length in Hektorović's book. Deviations from the regularity should be regarded as potential sources of information, unless the number of examples is so small that any regularity can be expected to break down. As a matter of fact the material we have looked at so far contains several obvious deviations:

— If the vowel concerned is followed by *-j-* (printed as *-y-*), as it is in the examples of the type *najti*, *naj-*, *dojde*, *stoj(te)*, an accent symbol tends to be much less frequent. This point will be returned to in section 5.3.

– In the endings of the present gerund, *u* carries an accent mark in only two fifths of the cases (18/27 and 14/23). The difference with the gerund endings containing an *e* is striking. We shall be returning to this point below (5.1, 5.2).

– The form *to* constitutes the subject of the next section.

3.4 The case of *to*

As soon as one separates different types of context it becomes clear that the deviation is caused by the fact that there are several different kinds of *to*. For reasons that will become clear, in this case the word boundaries of the original will be respected:

(1) No acute is present whenever *to* is preceded by *za* (16x). In these cases, *to* is always printed together with the preceding word: *záto* (15, 1481), *zátoſe* (1550), *Záto* (256, 473, 487, 1535, 1569), *Zátoga* (1607), *Zátoſe* (1651, f125), *Zato* (369, 1491, a53, c83), *zatoti* (a42).[12]

(2) No acute is present in seventeen other examples in which *to* is printed together with the preceding word, which in all cases is obviously orthotonic: *Onotomi* (532), *Nemoytomi* (541), *Nemoytoſe* (580), *Nemoytoyoy* (545, 551), *Da reçito* (553), *Teretomi* (598 = b8, 609, 667), *Teretomu* (650, 675), *Nechatoyih* (617), *Zagnimtomi* (633), *Staſſcitomi* (652), *Odmetnito* (658), *Vechtomiye* (671), *Choyimtoye* (681). Note that these examples, though quite numerous, are limited to the *bugarštice* and may be foreign to Hektorović's language.

(3) Of the eleven instances of *to* printed as a separate word, it carries an acute accent in six cases, cf. *Tomu chi tó haye* (284), *yermiſe ciní tó* (733), *A tó (ca mogu znat) = yoſc uechie cigniáſce* (861), *nemoy tó dati* (1057), *uiy uchóm stányu = naydemſe tó znayúch* (c121), *A tó naſtoyéchi* (f47) vs. *Dami ſarçu pochoy = to uechi poráyá* (36), *Da paruo to biſce ſtraxiçe razredio* (612), *Daltiye to ime* (c13), *sfi chi to cuyu* (f152), *A uſci ſcuſcgniati = to gore sliſcayuch* (f74).

(4) In three cases *to* is printed together with following clitics and in most or all such cases it is probably to be regarded as orthotonic. In one of them it carries an acute accent: *Toye yediní Bóg* (885), *Na tome douede* (f145), *nemoy = u tóſe zaplesti* (1020).

(5) In four cases, *to* is printed together with preceding *a*. In all four cases it carries an accent mark: *Ató* (a38), *ató* (a17, a58), *atò* (a49). Here it is likely that *a* is to be regarded as proclitic and *to* as ortho-

tonic, cf. the fact that in the same collocation it is also printed separately (e.g. 861). A related type of example is *I nató* (57), contrast *Na tome* (f145); if these two examples are representative, the case of *na to* is different from that of *za to*. It is also likely that the following case is similar: *Neto çichia potrib = neg zarad gliúbaui* (1668). Unfortunately here are no parallel examples with which it can be compared.

Table H: accent symbols on *to*

	zato	*teretomi*	*#to#*	*toje*	*ato, nato*	enclitic	orthotonic
accented	0	0	6	1	4	0	11
bare	16	17	5	2	1	33	8

It follows that there are at least two kinds of *to*. On the one hand a *to* which never carries an accent symbol in two types of cases in which it can plausibly be regarded as enclitic, on the other a *to* which is found in the remaining types of cases, in most if not all of which it must have been orthotonic and in which just over half of the attestations are provided with an acute. This analysis shows that the attestations of orthotonic *to* turn out to be well in accordance with the tentative regularity formulated in section 3.3.

4.1 More evidence

In the sections that follow we are going to investigate more thoroughly the validity of the tentative regularity proposed in section 3.3, by looking at a number of forms that have multiple attestations, at least one of which carries an acute accent.

4.2 Examples of *á*

(1) The inserted *-a-* in the Ns and Gp of *dan* (18/3): Ns *dán* (138, 253, 435, 906, 1186, c156, c159, d20), *dan* (1078, c169, f160a), Ns (uncertain) *dán* (e60a), Gp *dán* (17, 860, 1534, a16, a35, a61, e18, f23), cf. *fyutradán* (a31).

(2) The stem vowel of the noun *dar* (13/4): Ns *dár* (296, 1264, 1334, 1364, 1490, 1609), *dar* (d25), Gs *dára* (171, c185), DLs *darú* (c164), *dárom* (1264), Is *darom* (e48), Np *dári* (1365), Gp *darof* (a23), *dári* (1314), Ap *dáre* (1361, c7). In Gp *darof* the stem vowel may actually have been short (cf. the discussion of such cases in Vermeer 1994: 473, with references).

(3) The stem vowel of the noun *grad* (20/3): Ns *grád* (28, 258, c3), Gs *gráda* (172, 596), *Gráda* (473, al, f6), *grada* (b6), DLs *grádu* (598, 605, 1200, 1656, e11), *Grádu* (a9, al2, a21), *gradu* (b8), Vs *gráde* (599, b10), *Gráde* (600), *gradu* (b9, read: *grade), Np *grádi* (1614).

(4) The root *hval-* in several types of cases, in particular:
– The stem vowel of the noun *hvala* (17/1): Ns *huála* (240, 593, 1501, e43), Gs *huálé* (1545), Gs *huáli* (sic, 1518), As *huálu* (1317, 1615, a25, c12, e37), Is *huálóm* (782, 1180, c22, c88), NAp *huále* (294, 476), *Huale* (c171).
– The stem vowel of the verb *hvaliti* (9/4): inf *huáliti* (846), inf *huálit* (1313), aor1p *huáliſmo* (759), gpr *huálechi* (1403), aor2/3s *Pohuáli* (1149), aor1p *prihuáliſmo* (844), aor1s *zahuálih* (686), aor3p *zahuáliſce* (171, 316), vs. *l*-pmp *hualili* (c64), pr1s *hualím* (1375), pr3s *Huali* (e30), pr3p *hualé* (e26). To this the examples adduced in section 4.1 (34) have to be added (9/1).

In other derivations no length is attested, cf. pr1s *zahuagliuyu* (f151), pr3s *zahuagliua* (1499), Np *pohuale* (c92).

(5) The stem vowel of the fem noun *plav* (17/4): Ns *pláſ* (63, 168, 200, 225, 724, 753, 961, 1073, 1081, 1195, c195), *plaſ* (50, 53, f8), Gs *pláui* (1106, 1185), DLs *pláui* (745, 1123), Is *pláſyu* (1098), Is *Plauyu* (837), NAp *pláui* (771).

(6) The stem vowel of the pronoun *sam* (34/12): Nsm *Sám* (522, 856, 890), *sám* (392, a40), *ſám* (188, 225, 886, 951, 1308, 1385, 1400, 1635, a25, c11, f28), *ſam* (207, 283, 664, d43, e21), Nsn/Adv *ſámo* (257 420, 464, 1131, 1342), *Sámo* (c183), *Sá[m]o* (a9), *Samo* (1653), Gsm/n *ſamoga* (94, 1465, 1552, 1594), GAsm *ſáma* (911), Nsf *Sáma* (385), *ſáma* (c93), Gsf *ſamé* (277), Asf *ſamu* (1641), Npm *ſámi* (164, 180, 312, 509, 800, 993, 1104, e27), *ſami* (f82).

(7) The prefix *za-* in *zabiti* and *zaviditi* (12/2): inf *zábiti* (d19), *zabiti* (f64), *l*-pmp *zábili* (816), *pozábili* (176), gpt *Zábiſ* (1279), gpt *Zábiſſci* (833), pr2s *zabudeſc* (c163), pr3s *zábude* (1244, 1402), aor2/3s *zábi* (209), aor3p *pozábiſce* (872), Verbal Noun Gs *zábitya* (576), inf *záuidit* (c41), imperf3s *záuiyaſce* (1489).[13]

(8) The *-a-* in the endings of the present tense of *ā*-verbs:
– 1s (19/7): *dám* (453, a42, c12), *Vſám* (c33), *napráſgliám* (27), *oſtaugliám* (28, 599), *imám* (a37), *Imám* (1654), *znám* (159, 601, 601,

806, 944, c162, f38, f42), *prictiuám* (e21), *prixiuám* (e22); *narúcam* (543), *Plachiam* (c159), *oſtaugliam* (b9), *znam* (263, b11, b11, c106).

– 2s (21/5): *dáſc* (120, c59), *imáſc* (487, 1285, 1343, a28, c71), *nimáſc* (1053), *znáſc* (119, 403, 462, 890, 941, 1670, 1672, c66, c67), *Znáſc* (141, 411, 420), *izaznáſc* (a36), *pitáſc* (c68); *chuſcaſc* (418), *zádaſc* (1294), *imaſc* (1344), *znaſc* (c87), *poznaſc* (a37).

– 3s (90/35), see section 4.1 (13-14) and Table D.

– 1p (2/0): *nímámo* (747), *známo* (364).

– 2p (1/0): *znáte* (217).

– 3pl: none of the more than twenty attestations adduced in section, 4.1 (47) carries an accent mark on the *-a-*.

(9) The *-a-* in past gerunds in *-av* (16/4): *dáf* (755, c140), *prigledáf* (409), *Dáf* (d4), *izabráf* (1187), *Veceráf* (1076, 1510), *poſtáf* (365, 497, 686, 1188, 1196), *uſtáf* (293), *Vſtáf* (316, 469), *putouáf* (962); *ſtaf* (305, f41), *Oſtaf* (1001), *Scházaf* (1359).

4.3 Examples of é

(1) The stem of the noun *teg* (7/0): Ns *tég* (1627, c61, e7), Gs *téga* (55), Is *Tégom* (820), Is *tégom* (c60), Ap *tége* (1556).

(2) The second stem syllable of the noun *vitez* (12/4): Ns *Vitéz* (476, 644), *Vitez* (533, 534, 652, 678), DLs *uitézu* (184), *Vitézu* (a42), Vs *Vitéxe* (549, 677, 1667), *VItéxe* (1), *Vitéſe* (e6, read: *Vitéxe*), Np *Vitézi* (535, 1519), Gp *Vitézí* (166).

(3) Verbs of the types *pisati, ležati, hvaliti* and *dignuti* with a long é in the stem in at least one attestation (41/3): inf *potézat* (82), imperf2/3s *iztézáſce* (1110), pr3s *potéxe* (422), pr3p *potéxú* (772), gpr *pritéxuch* (402); inf *uézati* (662), pr3p *uéxú* (771), gpt *priuézáfſci* (724), pass part *uézánu* (58), *ſauézán* (27, 128), *obézan* (156), *obézani* (a11); inf *téxati* (c137), pr3s *téxi* (1093), gpr *téxech* (850); inf *ſcchiéditi* (189), gpr *ſcchiédech* (f51), gpt *ſcchiédiſſci* (732); aor1s *narédih* (1506), gpt *narédiſſci* (731); pr3s *hlépi* (1024), imp2s *hlépi* (1297); *l*-pms *naréſcio* (a7), pass part *naréſcen* (c52), *naréſcene* (776), *narèſcene* (d38), *uréſcen* (783); inf *ſpoménuti* (c161), aor3p *ſpoménuſce* (1066), pr3s *ſpoméne* (c101), imp2s *ſpoméni* (1244), imp1p *ſpoménimo* (1416); aor3p *chrénuſce* (869), pr3s *chréne* (307, 1599), imp2s *chréni* (224); aor3p *natégnuſce* (870), gpt *potégnuſſci* (1234), *l*-pfs *uztégnula* (602) pr3p *iztégnu* (152), vs. pr3s *ſtexe* (e5), *obezán* (e17), inf *texati* (1627).

(4) The adverb *opet* (8/0): *opét* (87, 354, 493, 526, 926, 970, a27, f39).

(5) The adverb *prem* (9/5): *prém* (494, 728, 745, 919, 1065, 1619, 1647, c86), *Prém* (720), *prem* (172, 424, a6), *Prem* (43, 1345).

4.4 Examples of *í*

(1) The stem syllable of the noun *svit* 'world' (3/4, 0/6, 0/11): Ns *sfít* (42, 161), *sfit* (157, 788, 887, 895, 1521, 1529, c72, c178, f63, f102), Gs *sfíta* (347), *sfita* (775, 901, c118), DLs *sfitu* (478, 929, 950, 1315, 1539, a51, c55), Ls *sfiti* (c156).

(2) The stem syllable of the noun *rika* (9/6, 1/1, 0/0): Ns *rícha* (318, 348), Gs *riché* (854), *riché* (277), DLs *ríçi* (315), *riçi* (267), As *ríchu* (273), *Ríchu* (325), Is *richóm* (303, 395), NAp *ríche* (345, 353, 400), *riche* (462), *Riche* (1230), Ip *ríchami* (342), *richami* (444).

(3) The Ns of the noun *vrime* (7/1, 3/3, 0/8): *uríme* (106, 465, 469, 517, 523, 719, 773, 1026, 1029), *Vríme* (1027), *urime* (899, 1269, c59, c107, c141, c169, f129, f131), *Vrime* (177, 916, 1527, 1659).

(4) The stem vowel of the adjective *lip* (14/1, 7/4, 1/4): *líp* (1646), *lípa* (235, 244, 502, 1086), *lípo* (233, 524, 529, 623, 992, 1248, 1508), *Lípo* (235, 524, 525, 622, 623, 1105, 1375), *lípu* (7), *lípi* (245, 996); *lip* (c44), *Lipa* (c55), *lipo* (525, 1204, 1625, c140), *lipu* (1007, 1093), *Lipu* (1004).

(5) The NAp of the numeral *tri* (5/1, 0/2, 0/0): *trí* (43, 213, 283, 527, 543), *tri* (218, 1073, 1174).

(6) The Gp ending *-i* (4/1, 1/3, 0/7): *pifní* (1232), *dinárí* (730), *ftuárí* (729), *prozorí* (151), *Vitézí* (166); *rici* (214), *gliúdi* (1522, 1612), *dni* (1658), *limúni* (1192), *dári* (1314), *ftuári* (f127), *ftuari* (a22), *zuiri* (1041), *ufti* (c49, e50).

(7) The *-i-* in the adjectival Ip ending *-imi* (0/2, 2/6, 0/7): *ifchargnímí* (1270), *dobrímí* (1256) vs. *drágimi* (1202), *mnogimi* (c1), *Morifc-chimi* (831), *uifcchimi* (1152), *nebefchimi* (978), *oftalimi* (a51, c131), *zlimi* (1254), *obránimi* (c129), *guozdenimi* (a11), *uernimi* (c132), *dobrimi* (c2), *múdrimi* (804), *biftrimi* (443), *barzimi* (444). In the pronouns there is a single example of an acute accent: *tachími* (1017), which is opposed to the following attestations without an accent mark: *sfimi* (803, 1116, 1184, a51, e38, e40), *chimi* (268, 1118), *Chimi* (c9,

c10), *tachimi* (1479), *nichimi* (a2), *gnimi* (30, 174, 269, 580, 997, 1113, 1154, 1164, 1366, 1481, 1576, a34), *onimi* (a3), *timi* (341, 977, 1115, 1575), *ouimi* (461), *choyimi* (a22, f149), *moyimi* (92, a2, e39), *tuoyimi* (e40).

(8) The *-i-* in the adjectival Is and Dp endings *-im* (3/5, 2/5, 1/18): *Sarbſchím* (519), *ueſelím* (a18), *oholím* (1310), *perením* (639), *sfétím* (780), *druzím* (1409) vs. *Mládim* (f111), *pridragim* (c154), *sfachim* (1450), *ſuachim* (c97), *gliubchim* (f141), *teſcchim* (c98), *neumichim* (1588), *tihim* (606), *priſtalim* (1376), *ſarcenim* (f141), *umiglienim* (1309), *uichoſgnim* (a11), *iſchargnim* (c25), *inim* (a53, e16), *iſtinim* (e15), *razúmnim* (794), *doſtoynim* (f139), *ſtárim* (1246), *dobrim* (d40), *uítim* (641), *práuim* (c32), *ſtariyim* (314), *túyim* (1328), *Boxyim* (c154), *Mnozim* (669), *druzim* (1168, f27).

(9) In this connection it is interesting to notice that there is no single attestation of an acute in the adjectival GALp ending *-ih* (0/4, 0/12, 0/15): *mládih* (1320), *sfachih* (168), *golih* (1582), *oholih* (947), *pitomih* (1043), *bludnih* (1587), *Vmiglienih* (948), *iſchargnih* (1350), *inih* (1381), *uſilnih* (1592), *Xaloſnih* (1589), *dobrih* (1042), *múdrih* (41), *priyátih* (c152), *Priproſtih* (1587), *mínútih* (17), *Minútih* (e18), *Martuih* (1585), *ſtariyih* (272), *diuyih* (1041), *drázih* (d42), *mnozih* (1654, a8), *druzih* (912, 1275, 1385, a38, a55, a57, c101), *Druzih* (976). Among the pronouns there are no attestations of length either (0/15, 0/28, 0/49): *sfih* (3, 5, 485, 1033, 1212, 1222, 1265, 1330, 1410, 1522, 1536, 1591, a22, d23), *Sfih* (1612, c140, d20, d42), *chih* (1448, 1519, 1546, 1573, 1578, a26, c136, c152), *Chih* (23, 1116), *gnih* (271, 276, 818, 994, 1091, 1150, 1155, 1202, 1304, 1380, 1480, 1521, 1525, 1599, 1624, a55, a57, c36, f40, f112, f127), *onih* (1590, a23, d20), *ouih* (17, e18), *Chachouih* (994), *yih* (147, 148, 219, 617, 619, 815, 984, 1105, 1108, 1111, 1172, 1214, 1242, 1324, 1521, 1527, 1577, 1586, 1599, a49, c116, c182, e25, f106), *gih* (1107, f106, read: **yih*), *sfoyih* (40), *choyih* (797, 1520, c31), *Choyih* (1220, e36), *moyih* (39), *tuoyih* (1252, c49, c61, d42).

(10) The *-i-* in the endings of the present tense of *ī*-verbs:
– 1s (9/6, 5/1, 3/22): *dím* (135, 385, 1103, c159, c167), *Dím* (249, 373), *uidím* (a4), *hualím* (1375), *Molím* (1008), *ſmislím* (1213), *mním* (774, 785), *proſím* (332), *uím* (136, 1013), *prauím* (26); *dim* (250, a57, f119), *xelim* (a60, c97), *molim* (545, c95), *molin* (sic, a25), *uolim* (1309, c96), *ſmislim* (f41), *umim* (360, a5, a32), *mnim* (254), *ozrim*

494

(c105), *chiutim* (c103), *uim* (721, a47, c117, e3, f7, f38), *Vim* (c186), *pouim* (a56), *zbroyim* (c117, f41), *ſtoyim* (253, f42).

- 2s (1/4, 2/11, 0/10): *dobauiſc* (1250), *ſtauiſc* (417), *oſtauiſc* (1247); *uidiſc* (601, b11, c85, f142), *prohodiſc* (f4), *prouodiſc* (f3), *pocudiſc* (a29), *ueliſc* (266), *xeliſc* (265), *moliſc* (c126), *Vmiſc* (945), *mniſc* (1292), *gouoriſc* (1053), *progouoriſc* (c45), *zatuoriſc* (c46), *otuoriſc* (1054), *noſiſc* (f3), *uiſc* (909, 1291), *proslauiſc* (1249), *naprauiſc* (1248), *pouiſc* (910).

- 3s (32/20, 27/66, 1/96): *izgubí* (987), *naucí* (1384), *dí* (1383), *uu-ridí* (1463), *ſidí* (1178), *slobodí* (342), *hodí* (335), *nahodí* (939), *obhodí* (336), *dohodí* (343), *uzhodí* (341, 344, 457), *plodí* (895), *potuardí* (490), *pogárdí* (489), *udí* (1399), *prudí* (940), *trúdí* (744), *yizdí* (229), *xelí* (204, 1319), *gúlí* (1411), *brání* (3), *hrání* (4), *ciní* (37, 357, 400, 733, 1038, 1315, 1382), *mní* (357, 908, 1210), *zuoní* (1374), *Zuoní* (1044), *sní* (992), *Napuní* (419), *ſpuní* (224), *chruní* (5), *chupí* 'collect, gather' (73), *ſchupí* (437), *uarí* (1183), *nosí* (310), *prosí* (302), *raztratí* (1240), *plátí* (228), *ctí* (1220), *uartí* (1128), *slauí* (766, 788, 1204), *ſtauí* (1048), *dáuí* (1124), *louí* (72), *bixí* (152), *uzdarxí* (890), *boyí* (285), *priſtoyí* (1388) vs. *gliubi* (1600), *gliúbi* (1543), *zagrúbi* (1544), *dici* (e52), *izſchoci* (f9), *toci* (f10), *plaſci* (1128), *uci* (1441), *muci* (1383, 1442), *di* (1597, 1603), *blidi* (1023), *slidi* (c144, c178, f136), *ſidi* (962, 1384), *uidi* (129, 588, 961, 1177, 1429, 1464, c136, c143, c177), *nenauidi* (1364, 1430), *slídi* (1024, 1363), *zgodi* (1292, 1421), *hodi* (1258, 1377, 1394, 1531, d10, f69), *nahodi* (432, 458, 953, 1257, 1378, 1393, 1427, 1438, a51, f43), *iznahodi* (899), *ſcchodi* (940, 1428), *nadhodi* (896), *do-hodi* (954, 1264), *pohodi* (1263), *prohodi* (893), *Prohodi* (903), *uzhodi* (c194), *porodi* (1532), *uodi* (f44, f70), *douodi* (1437), *prouodi* (1354), *prudi* (849, 1400), *trúdi* (850, 1036), *optichi* (1342), *Huali* (e30), *Veli* (1551), *xeli* (c144), *dili* (a27, d40), *misli* (1456), *umi* (1385), *rani* (1039), *obráni* (928, 1040, c201), *hráni* (1162), *dohráni* (c100, c202), *ſhráni* (927, c130), *uhráni* (f24), *cini* (434, 923, 1442, 1550, c145), *ucini* (f15), *razcini* (f31), *lini* (c135), *promini* (1037), *mni* (1316, 1441, a28, a39, a56, c50), *Mni* (1200), *uchloni* (924, c128), *zuoni* (790), *uz-biſni* (1268), *napuni* (c186), *ſpuni* (c100), *chruni* (c185), *hlépi* (1024), *zaſtúpi* (438), *priuari* (302, f128), *uári* (1324), *zamiri* (c142), *razmiri* (c141), *tiri* (1042), *obori* (1619), *domori* (f157), *gouori* (864, 942), *raz-gouori* (f158), *stuori* (453), *oſctri* (1406), *pochoſi* (c120), *noſi* (301, 1191, 1198, 1407), *zanoſi* (1530), *odnoſi* (a55), *proſi* (1529), *iſproſi* (1408), *plati* (e44), *potrati* (200), *priurati* (f20), *pouráti* (199, f19), *cti* (f4), *ociti* (f124), *Hiti* (f123), *poſchiti* (1334, 1376), *ceſtiti* (1333), *otústi*

(1340), *grufti* (251), *zapúfti* (1339), *grúfti* (1658), *dobaui* (f13), *slaui* (c53), *proslaui* (c88), *praui* (482, 746, c87), *pripraui* (1541, f123), *ftaui* (f14), *poftaui* (d25), *obyaui* (f124), *poui* (257), *gotoui* (450), *lexi* (1094), *téxi* (1093), *priloxi* (c102), *darxi* (1237), *tuxi* (f79), *dotúxi* (f80), *boyi* (1330), *posfoyi* (c129), *goyi* (1387), *broyi* (a51), *odbroyi* (c130), *stoyi* (183, 286), *ftoyi* (1170, 1329, c120, f129), *priftoyi* (184, f130), *izgazi* (f24), *uzuozi* (c196).[14]

– 1p (2/2, 1/3, 0/5): *uidímo* (936), *fchrátímo* (111), *pozdrauímo* (659); *dicimo* (a1), *uidimo* (296, 1262, 1415, 1570), *nahodimo* (1536), *xelimo* (994), *obesélimo* (114)[15], *Mnimo* (1483), *uzpómnimo* (935).

– 2p (3/2, 0/0, 0/4): *fidíte* (326), *uefelíte* (241), *ciníte* (242); *gliúbite* (1597), *natocite* (219), *uidite* (325), *umite* (1494), *uite* (1493), *obslúxite* (1598).

(11) The -*i*- in past gerunds in -*iv* (2/4, 0/9, 0/4): *obazríf* (243), *fpuftíf* (84); *Zábif* (1279), *naucif* (1359), *odlucif* (f53), *Vzbúdif* (1224), *razdilif* (526), *Pochlonif* (1499), *urátif* (880, 1195), *puftif* (1229, c189), *fprauif* (1133), *uprauif* (408), *stauif* (1261), *poftauif* (407), *Stauif* (450), *priloxif* (a43), *Priloxif* (1379).

4.5 Examples of ó

(1) The stem syllable of the neuter noun *more* (26/6): Ns *móre* (145, 152, 336, 339, 343, 354, 374, 380, 393, 1070, 1468, 1650), *more* (330, c197, f14), Gs *móra* (344, 346, 353, 1166), *mora* (1670, a58), DLs *móru* (110, 444, 748, 837, 1190, 1476, 1515, 1639, 1646, 1665), *moru* (376).

(2) The (only or final) stem syllable of other nouns, notably in the Ns. This requires some comment. In stem syllables, ó is rare, due not so much to some irregularity in Hektorović's use of accent marks as to the fact that long *ō is infrequent in the Common Slavic dialect that underlies SCr and is often secondary and/or mysterious in attested varieties of the language. In Hektorović, several types of cases must be distinguished. To begin with, there are *dvor* and *nož*, which in most varieties of SCr are (b)-stressed and retain length in all forms: Ns *duór* (1095, f124), Ns *nóx* (1406). In the case of both words, the characteristic retention of length is also attested in Hektorović: DLs *duóru* (747, c146), Gs *nóxa* (1047), cf. also the absence of an accent mark in Ap *duoroue* (664). Then there are several distinct types of nouns in which

length in the Ns is opposed to absence of evidence for length in other forms:

(2a) Monosyllabic (c)-stressed masculine nouns, where length is Common Slavic. It seems likely that most or all of the following cases of ó can be explained along these lines (14/4, not counting *bog*): *bóch* (1129), *dóm* (145), *lóf* (50, 79, 1643, 1676), *plód* (a24), *ród* (e57), *rod* (d7), *róch* (c122, f111), *ſchóch* (f112), *ſmóch* (1130), *znóy* (51), *znoy* (1472, c60, f59), *zuón* (1044). The Ns of *bog* does not usually carry an acute accent (1/13), cf. *Bóg* (885), *Bog* (1160, 1333, 1338, 1541, 1577, a7, c9, c50, c116, c127, c200, e44, f160). There are no instances of ó in other attestations of these words, which are unfortunately too few to be very informative (0/4, again excluding *Bog*): DLs *domu* (259), Gs *loua* (173, 1511), Gs *ſchocha* (235), cf. also Gs *Boga* (1408, 1551, 1593, c125, f1, f48), DLs *Bogu* (294, 316, 888, 1540, 1580, 1615, a25, c58, c80, e60), DLs *Bugu* (1396, read: *Bogu).

(2b) Feminine (c)-stressed nouns, where length is Common Slavic at least in monosyllabic forms and where attested SCr tend to have length in polysyllabic forms as well (28/15): *móch* (401, 403, 421, 436, f127), *nemóch* (a31), *nóch* (435, 906, 908, 1620), *pomóch* (38, 1416, c123, c153), *chripóſt* (975, 1224, 1355), *Chripóſt* (1361), *milóſt* (1334, a47, c57), *ſchupóſt* (1363), *ſtaróſt* (159, f70, f113, f136), *uridnóſt* (a17, c78) vs. *chripoſt* (d24), *Chripoſt* (1481), *miloſt* (1144, 1613, c100), *mladoſt* (f69), *mudroſt* (e53), *sfitloſt* (f61), *slaboſt* (f76), *sladchoſt* (1232), *stároſt* (c108), *ſtaroſt* (f80), *Tihoſt* (c23), *uridnoſt* (f157), *xaloſt* (d18).[16] Other forms of these and similar nouns never carry an acute, despite being quite frequent, e.g. Gs *choſti* (1107), *nochi* (253, f58), *ſoli* (73), DLs *nochi* (934), Is *mochyu* (433, a54, f49), *nochyu* (434, f50), NAp *mochi* (c91), *nemochi* (f88); Gs *chripoſti* (799, 1378, 1419, 1490), *miloſti* (1312, c14), *Miloſti* (f48), *mladoſti* (c26, d46), *sladchoſti* (375), *ſtaroſti* (1320), *Staroſti* (932), *xaloſti* (d45), DLs *miloſti* (592, 1502, c166), *mladoſti* (f103), *radoſti* (e52), *sfitloſti* (1420), *ſtaroſti* (f104), *uridnoſti* (1501), Vs *Chripoſti* (f5), *mladoſti* (d1), *Tihoſti* (d15), Is *chripoſtyu* (937, a7), *hárnoſtyu* (f140), *miloſtyu* (c15, e48), *sfitloſtyu* (e47), *uridnoſtyu* (c16), NAp *chripoſti* (14, 483, 1412, 1433, 1518, a26, c165, c188, e36), *dragoſti* (c25), *hrabroſti* (1525), *miloſti* (a27, c80), *pſoſti* (1258), *radoſti* (1526, f56), *slaboſti* (c91), *tamnoſti* (1411), *xaloſti* (f55), Ip *chripoſti* (c1).[17]

(2c) Other cases of ó in the Ns: *chógn* (632), *chogn* (c189), *pochóy* (e58), *pochoy* (15, 36, 52, 1440, c59, f40, f60, f144), *nepochoy* (1462, d8), *ſtól* (1063), *zachón* (1373), *záchón* (1359, 1544), *záslóu* (747, read:

497

*záslón). In attestations of other case forms of the same words the acute accent does not occur (0/25), cf. Gs *chognia* (608, 631), DLs *chogniu* (644, 647), Vs *chogniu* (634, 634, 635, 636, 636), Np *chogni* (981), Ap *chognie* (527, 602, 629, 630), Gs *pochoya* (c112, d46), Vs *pochoyu* (d12), Ls *ſtoli* (74), Is *ſtolóm* (1267), Gs *zachona* (1570), Np *záchoni* (1545), *Záchoni* (1595), Ap *zachone* (1598), *Zachone* (c172). In such cases length is not Common Slavic or Common SCr, but due to a dialectal lengthening of originally short vowels followed by word-final resonants under certain conditions. Note that in many cases no length is marked, cf. (alongside the examples already given) Ns *arbor* (53), *blagoslof* (283), *broy* (826, 1116, 1150, 1504, c89, c102, c181, d42, e36, f43, f62), *Izgouor* (c44), *odgouor* (120, 889, a53), *periuoy* (1149, 1162), *pochlon* (e12), *razgouor* (30, e17, f40), *Razgouor* (242). Indeed, the only examples that do carry an acute are ones in which it is reasonable to assume that the vowel concerned was originally stressed.

(3) The adverb *totu* (8/3): *tótu* (174, 252, 317, 363, 1102, 1469, 1651), *Tótu* (1513), *totu* (507, 905), *Totu* (1073).

(4) As we saw in section 3.1 (31), in feminine nouns the Is ending -*om* is provided with an accent mark in nearly three fourth of the attestations (42/16). The masculine/neuter Is ending -*om* also sometimes carries an accent mark, but only in a quarter of the cases (17/48): *trúdóm* (211), *ſmíhóm* (1406), *ſtolóm* (1267), *úmóm* (485, 1284, f103), *chipóm* (f98), *Goſpodaróm* (1325), *miróm* (960, 1377), *Sulétóm* (722), *xiuotóm* (780); *zlóm* (1353, f81), *putóm* (56), *Goſpodſtuóm* (a7), *umiglienſtuóm* (a7), *blagodárſtuóm* (a7) vs. *xdribom* (1166), *miſeçom* (828), *obidom* (1132), *stidom* (c43), *trudom* (15), *trúdom* (f94), *tégom* (c60), *Tégom* (820), *ſtráhom* (1108), *yunachom* (606), *ribgniáchom* (1179), *Obláchom* (438), *tíchom* (1225), *ſcchitchom* (639), *pobuchom* (88), *múchom* 'moan' (606), *chruhom* (494), *razúmom* (1333, 1374, 1613), *ſtánom* (1387), *nacinom* (e15), *nácinom* (519, a11), *Pelinom* (d37), *pochlonom* (f139), *répom* (1127), *chipom* (f143), *darom* (e48), *peharom* (868), *dárom* (1264), *glaſom* (e26), *gláſom* (d5), *dneuom* (434, f50), *pochrouom* (170, 745, 1183); *blágom* (1419), *dilom* (1450), *tilom* (1610), *imenom* (c15), *brimenom* (c98), *urimenom* (c97), *zlátom* (234, 832), *Zlátom* (1203, d38).

For the correlating soft ending -*em* the evidence is comparable (2/13): *Líçém* (920), *listyém* (1156) vs. *putem* 'road' (c32), *uinçem* (1474), *ſarçem* (a18), *pogliem* (229), *oblicyem* (1376), *Vlyem* (1063),

Ichladanyem (f142), *pil'ányem* (f141), *uminyem* (a7), *Vminyem* (118), *chopyem* (641), *ol'ctaryem* (1047), *Oruxyem* (126).

There cannot be much doubt about the underlying cause of the difference between the two endings: the *-o-* in the feminine ending is long wherever it is attested in SCr (of course provided that contrastive length is possible in the relevant position), whereas in the masculine/ neuter ending it is short unless the system involved has lengthened short vowels before the reflex of syllable-final *-m*. The facts suggest that the prosodic system reflected by Hektorović's use of accent marks had carried through lengthening of short *o* before word-final *m* (otherwise we would not find so many accent marks), but only in part of the cases (otherwise the proportion of accented and unaccented *o* would be quite different), cf. the case of *to* analyzed in section 3.4. As we shall see, the difference is connected with the place of the stress.

Before turning to the effect of stress we have to remove from the sample two types of examples where length is probably underlying, i.e. not due to the influence of the syllable-final resonant.

(a) The case of *listyém* has to be interpreted against the background of the fact that neuter nouns with a stem in a consonant plus *-j-* often have length in endings that are ordinarily short, cf. NAs *ribanyé* (a43), *znanyé* (a43), *radouanyé* (a30), *bityé* (1279), *xityé* (f72), *Ipoménutyé* (1454), *sdrauyé* (f57), Gs *Milol'ardyá* (1579), *Schoncányá* (1678), *poctényá* (6), *uminyá* (777), DLs *ufányú* (c122), *mogliényú* (c147), *xiuinyú* (13, 1485, c27), *l'atyú* (492), *bityú* (f134), NAp *Ichládanyá* (f53), *Chiuchienyá* (f84), *zlamenyá* (5), *pityá* (943).[18] Nouns of this type have long endings in much of Dalmatian Čakavian, e.g. Vrgada (Jurišić 1966: 76). In the dialects that continue Hektorović's immediate linguistic background, which have lost distinctive length in posttonic position, the relevant nouns have length only in case of end stress, and in the case of stem stress the tell-tale *-o* (< *ā*) in the Gs and NAp betrays the original presence of length (cf., e.g., Hraste 1935: 23-24, 1940: 40, Šimunović 1977: 11, 35-36).

(b) The nouns in *-stvo* (*gospodstvo, umiljenstvo, blagodarstvo*) may also have had long endings, as they often do in Dalmatian Čakavian, both in some of the systems that continue Hektorović's immediate linguistic background (Hraste 1935: 24, Šimunović 1977: 11, 35) and in Vrgada (Jurišić 1966: 76). If this is correct, it follows that the absence of accent marks in the other attestations of nouns in *-stvo* is due to chance, which is awkward but conceivable because of their small number: Ns *difſtuo* (1435), *mnoſctuo* (1031), *uboſctuo* (1032), Gs *Bogogliubſtua* (c20), *umiglienſtua* (d15).

The elimination of two types of neuter derivations (those in *-stvo* and those with stems ending in consonant plus *-j-*) leaves 63 attestations of the Isg in *-om* (15/48) and 6 of that in *-em* (1/5).

Most nouns that are attested with an acute in the ending belong to Stang's accent type (b) and accordingly have end stress (or the reflex of end stress) in the Is, cf. Brusje *trȗd trūdä̀, žìvȍt -votä̀, putȍ -ä̀* (Dulčić/Dulčić 1985), Brač/Hvar/Vis *trȗd trūdä̀, smȋh smȋhä̀, stǫ̑l stolä̀, gospodȏr gospodōrä̀, žìvȍt životä̀, zlȍ, putȍ* (Hraste/Šimunović/Olesch 1979), Vrgada *trȗd trūdä̀, smȋh smȋhä̀, stȏ stolä̀, gospod°ȃr gospod°ārä̀, žìvȍt životä̀, zlȍ, lȋcë̀* (Jurišić 1973).[19] And although *mir* is (c)-stressed in Brač/Hvar/Vis (*mȋr mȋra*) and Vrgada (*mȋr -a*), it is (b)-stressed in the system described by Daničić (1925: 22).[20]

Turning now to the nouns that are not attested with an accent mark on the ending *-om*, most of them belong to accent type (a) or (c) in most SCr systems and as such can be expected to have stem stress in the Isg, cf. Brusje *mȉsec -a, obȋd obȉda, tȇg -a, strȏh* (given s.v. *strȍšäc*; the falling tone implies (c)-stress), *pȍbuk -a, krȕh -a, stȏn -a, pelȋn -lȉna, glȏs -a*, Gs *dnèva* (implying a stem-stressed Is), *pokrȏv -krȍva, blȏgo -a, tȋlo -a, brȉme brȉmena*, Brač/Hvar/Vis *mȉsec –, obȋd obȉda, stȋd –, tȇg –, strȏh –, ȍblok –, pȍbuk –*[21]*, krȕh –, rȃzum –, stȏn –, pelȋn pelȉna, dȏr –, glȏs –*, Gs *dnèva* (implying stem stress in the Is), *pokrȍv pokᵣȍva, blȏgo, dȉlo, tȋlo, ȉme ȉmena, brȉme brȉmena, vrȋme vrȉmena, zlȍto*, Vrgada *mȉsēc mȉsēca, obȉd -a, stȋd -a, str°ȃh -a, ȍbl°āk -a, pȍbūk -a, krȕh krȕva, räzūm -a, st°ȃn -a, n°ȃčȉn* or *n°āčȋn*, Gs *n°āčȉna, pelȋn pelȉna, d°ȃr -a, gl°ȃs -a*, Is *dnèvon* (s.v. *d°ȃn*), *pōkrȍv pōkrȍva, bl°ȃgo -a, dȉlo -a, tȋlo tȋla, ȉme -ena, brȉme -ena, vrȋme vrȉmena, zl°ȃto zl°ȃta*. The noun *junak* always has (b)-stress: Brusje *junȏk -nōkä̀*, Brač/Hvar/Vis *junȏk junōkä̀*, Vrgada *jun°ȃk -°ākä̀*.

The evidence is contradictory in the case of four nouns: Brusje *ždrȋb -a, pehȏr -hōrä̀, rȇp rēpä̀*, Brač/Hvar/Vis *kȋp kīpä̀, ždrȋb ždrībä̀* (explicitly limited to Brač), *pehȏr pehȃra, rȇp rȇpä̀*, Vrgada *kȋp -a, ždrȋb -a, peh°ȃr -°ārä̀, rȇp -a*.

Seven nouns are not attested in any of the three Dalmatian dialect dictionaries: *um, Sulet, ribnjak, tik, šćitak, muk, poklon*, so we have to look further afield. For the purposes of this article attention wil be limited to the Vuk/Daničić system, where the noun *um* is (b)-stressed (*ȗm úma*), whereas *ribnjak, tik* and *poklon* are not: *rȉbnjāk, tȉjek –*,

500

pȍklōn. This leaves three unattested nouns. The noun *šćitak* is a diminutive of a (b)-stressed noun (*štȋt štíta*) and accordingly must have been (b)-stressed. The accentuation of *muk* (which is a very rare word) is not reliably attested, nor is that of the toponym *Sulet*, which appears to have died out in the living language (it has yielded to *Šolta*), cf. on both words the Zagreb Academy Dictionary.

In cases of vacillation among sources I shall assume that the type of accentuation attested geographically closest to Hektorović stands the best chance of being the same as the one found in the system he was rendering (e.g. Brusje prevails over Brač/Hvar/Vis, Vrgada over Vuk/Daničić, etc.). It follows that we expect stress on the ending in *trud, smih, stol, um, kip, gospodar, život, zlo, puto, ždrib, junak, šćitak, rep* (19 attestations: 12/7), and on the stem in *mir, misec, obid, stid, teg, strah, ribnjak, oblak, tik, pobuk, muk, kruh, razum, stan, način, pelin, poklon, dar, pehar, glas, dnev-, pokrov, blago, dilo, tilo, ime, brime, vrime, zlato* (45 attestations: 2/43).

This shows pretty conclusively that the appearance of an accent symbol on the masculine/neuter Isg ending -*om* depends on the accentual type of the noun involved. Note that *mir*, which is the only noun that is attested with an accent mark on the ending in Hektorović without being (b)-stressed in the best available evidence, is (b)-stressed in Vuk/Daničić (*mȋr míra*).

(5) The adjectival ending -*oga* (30/14): *drugóga* (48), *yáchóga* (c136), *yunacchóga* (235), *Brácchóga* (720), *tanchóga* (55), *gliudſchóga* (1413), *nebeſchóga* (c125), *Nebeſchóga* (f1), *morſchóga* (56, 1511), *zalóga* (1260), *uelóga* (1110), *umárlóga* (1454), *lacnóga* (1581), *xédnóga* (1582), *perenóga* (238), *Difnóga* (596), *duhofnóga* (1580), *teleſnóga* (1579), *izuarſnóga* (819), *ſmartnóga* (924), *Slaunóga* (a1), *lounóga* (171), *staróga* (1219), *ſtàróga* (820), *múdróga* (1322), *sfétóga* (786), *ſcéſtóga* (e4), *práuóga* (366), *nouóga* (172); *sfemogoga* (e46), *drugoga* (110), *yunacchoga* (608), *Nebeſchoga* (f54), *ribarſchoga* (a20), *tihoga* (559), *Tihoga* (563), *ſedmoga* (a61), *perenoga* (237), *difnoga* (b6), *ſmartnoga* (a33), *dobroga* (848, 1259), *zíuoga* (980, read: **xíuoga*). The acute accent on -*ga* in *ſceſtogá* (f160a) is best regarded as a displaced accent mark instead of **ſceſtóga* (see note 15). An acute accent in the ending -*oga* is also attested in several pronouns, in particular:
— *ki* (12/8): *chóga* (149, 321, 439, a16, c71, f35, f35), *Chóga* (97, 774, 790, 1110, e41), *choga* (476, 1009, 1272, 1415, c94, c126), *Choga* (1358, 1418);

- *svaki* (1/6): *sfachóga* (6), *sfachoga* (504, 1453, 1638, c37, c135, c186);
- *taki* (2/1): *tachóga* (479, 923), *tachoga* (c185);
- *moj/tvoj/svoj* (7/6), see for the examples section 4.1(36);
- *ovi* (1/6): *ouóga* (e13) vs. *ouoga* (135, 365, 1109, 1220, a58, f36).

In other pronouns the acute is not attested at all, cf.:
- *niki* (0/3): *nichoga* (1272, 1398), *Nichoga* (1333);
- *sam* (0/4): *ſamoga* (94, 1465, 1552, 1594);
- *jedan* (0/3): *yednoga* (47, 979, 1551);
- *oni* (0/14): *onoga* (109, 245, 346, 410, 490, 503, 560, 576, 1512, a1, a20, a31, a58), *Onoga* (1263);
- *taj* (0/20): *toga* (17, 93, 136, 246, 285, 309, 345, 409, 466, 475, 480, 489, 785, 841, 847, 1209, 1253, 1375, 1603, a19), *Toga* (1473).

The corresponding soft ending -*ega*, which is much less frequent than -*oga*, is attested as follows in the adjectives (3/5): *uicgniéga* (f110), *mlayéga* (250), *ſtariyéga* (249) vs. *Naybogliega* (1381), *magniega* (215), *iſchargniega* (1594), *tretyega* (530), *Boxyega* (c18). There is a single case of an acute accent in a pronoun: *naſcéga* (1680), cf. absence of an accent symbol in the following attestations: *naſcega* (a50, f160a), *sfega* (452, 1147, 1541, 1593, c69, f109, f118), *Sfega* (f71, uncertain), *gniega* (27, 115, 679, 774, 1180, 1207, 1359, 1430, 1542, 1552, 1602, 1606), *Gniega* (c170, f49), *tega* (451), *sfoyega* (596), *moyega* (562, 1148), *suoyega* (b6), *tuoyega* (c17).

(6) The adjectival DLs ending -*omu* (8/4): *drugómu* (1557), *yunácchómu* (644), *ribaſchómu* (a37, read: *ribarſchómu), *tihómu* (837), *uelómu* (1038), *recenómu* (a21), *yedínómu* (1318), *Stárómu* (1656); *drugomu* (979, 1326), *cudnomu* (1486), *Izuarſnomu* (a42). In the pronouns the facts are the following:
- *ki* (5/4): *chómu* (142, 789, 1570, d7), *Chómu* (355) vs. *chomu* (1130, a35, a44), *Chomu* (1019);
- *svaki* (1/11): *sfachómu* (f107), *sfachomu* (26, 219, 260, 1037, 1050, 1246, 1316, 1380, 1540, f80), *Sfachomu* (911);
- *taki*: no examples;
- *moj/tvoj/svoj* (7/4): *mómu* (25, 197), *tuómu* (367, c47, c48), *sfómu* (1012, 1558), *sfomu* (385, 756, f147), *tuomu* (f148);
- *ovi* (0/6): *ouomu* (198, 929, 1315, 1539, a1, f108);
- *niki* (0/3): *nichomu* (1325, f37), *Nichomu* (1334);
- *sam*: no examples;

– *jedan* (0/2): *Yednomu* (1557), *yednomu* (96);
– *oni* (0/4): *onomu* (1264, a37, a42, a44);
– *taj* (0/15): *tomu* (32, 198, 368, 386, 389, 901, 930, 1011, 1095, 1289, 1317, 1329, 1379, 1595), *Tomu* (284).

The corresponding soft ending -*emu* happens not to be attested in adjectives. In the pronouns there are attestations of length in *ki* and *moj/tvoj/svoj*, but not in other types of cases, cf. *choyému* (1488, f29), *moyému* (c147) vs. *cemu* (472, 936, 954, 991), *naſcemu* (1516, a21), *sſemu* (368, 687, 768, 844, 1317, 1602, a44, a59, c56), *gniemu* (116, 255, 484, 487, 557, 661, 665, 686, 767, 843, 1601, 1605, 1608, a27, a27, c168), *Gniemu* (731), *ſemu* (c55), *temu* (f30), *sſoyemu* (644).

4.6 Examples of *ú*

(1) The stem syllable of the noun *ljudi* (14/7): Np *gliúdi* (74, 1227, 1477, c22), *Gliúdi* (797, 1308), *gliudi* (190, 996, a58, c115), Gp *gliúdi* (1522, 1612), Dp *gliúdem* (957, 1021, 1447, f120), *gliudem* (10, 794), Ip *gliúdi* (1479, 1504), *gliudi* (e38).

(2) The stem syllable of the noun *put* (11/5): Ns *pút* (688, 842, 865, 1676, a4, a43, c20), *put* (111, f110), Gs *púta* (366, 1512), *puta* (a31), *putá* (a16), DLs *pútu* (c144), Is *putem* (c32), Ap *púte* (a26), cf. the use of the Ns of *put* as a preposition: *pút* (78, 172, 1136), *put* (110).

(3) The second stem syllable of the noun *razum* (16/4): Ns *razúm* (2, 787, 1500, 1611, c99, e35, e53), *Razúm* (1480), *razum* (255, c17, e19, f146), Gs *razúma* (479, 1321), *Razúma* (792), DLs *razúmu* (367, 1303), Is *razúmom* (1333, 1374, 1613). Note the parallellism with *vitez*.

(4) The stem syllable of the noun *duša* (11/3): Ns *dúſca* (1610), Gs *dúſce* (f65), NAp *dúſce* (1566), *Dúſce* (1540), As *dúſcu* (927, 1344, 1368, c124, e20), As *Dúſcu* (f128), Is *dúſcom* (1611); DLs *duſci* (1578), As *duſcu* (a33, c104).

(5) The root *drug-/druž-* in several types of cases, in particular:
– The noun *drug* (5/1): Gs *drúga* (c17, c68), Vs *drúxe* (519), Np *drúzi* (175, 1099) vs. Vs *druxe* (132).
– The noun *družba* (5/3): Ns *drúxba* (231), Gs *drúxbé* (c192), DLs *drúxbi* (267), As *drúxbu* (690), *Drúxbu* (c40) vs. Ns *druxba* (798), As *druxbu* (1088), Is *druxbom* (e21).
– The verb *družiti* (4/1): inf *zdrúxiti* (f160), aor1p *ſdrúxiſmo* (1132), *l*-pfs *sdrúxila* (a17), ppp *ſdrúxeni* (a5), vs. pr3p *druxé* (312).

Other derivations from the same root never carry an acute, e.g. the frequent noun *družina* (0/16) and the adjective *družben* (with its derivative noun *družbenik*), Ns *druxina* (275, 588, 590, 602, 603, e29), Gs *druxiné* (1660), DLs *druxini* (856), As *druxinu* (830), Is *druxinóm* (520, 611, 657), *druxinom* (640), Vs *druxino* (532, 619, 666); *druxbene* (691), Np *druxbeniçi* (d27).

(6) The root *ljub-* in several types of cases:
- The stem syllable of the feminine noun *ljubav* (9/8): Ns *gliúbáf* (1143, 1323), *Gliúbaf* (e5), Gs *gliúbaui* (264, 766, 1668, c19, c125), Is *gliúbafyu* (a5) vs. Ns *gliubaf* (a6, d31, f60), *Gliubaf* (f150), Gs *gliubaui* (d26, f153), DLs *gliubaui* (c54, e43).
- The stem syllable of the verb *ljubiti* (14/5): inf *gliúbiti* (1418, 1444, 1606), *gliúbit* (1603), aor2/3s *Pogliúbi* (1145), pr3s *gliúbi* (1543), pr2p *gliúbite* (1597), pr3p *gliúbé* (1542), imp2s *gliúbi* (1450), imp1p *gliúbimo* (1261), imp1p *Gliúbimo* (1259), gpr *gliúbech* (1593), ppp *gliúbglien* (1604), *gliúbglieni* (a10); inf *gliubit* (40), *l*-pms *obgliubio* (571, 572), pr3s *gliubi* (1600), imp1p *gliubimo* (1607).

Several other derivations from the same root never carry an acute, in particular the adjective *ljubak* (0/7): *gliubach* (1327), *gliubcha* (1538), *gliubchí* (2), *gliubchim* (f141), *gliubcho* (958, e24), *Gliubcho* (f58).

(7) The root *slug-/služ-* in several types of cases, in particular:
- The stem vowel of the noun *sluga* (4/1): Ns *slúga* (232, 1420), NAp *slúge* (680), Dp *slúgam* (c151) vs. Dp *slugam* (c154).
- The stem vowel of the noun *služba* (2/1): As *slúxbu* (691, f50), As *sluxbu* (242).
- The stem vowel of the verb *služiti* (13/2): inf *slúxiti* (134, 767, 1326), aor3p *slúxiſce* (817), pr1s *slúxu* (718), pr2p *obslúxite* (1598), pr3p *slúxé* (811), imp2s *obslúxi* (1548), imp1p *slúximo* (1608), gpr *slúſechi* (816, read: **slúxechi*), imperf3p *slúxáhu* (a3), *slúxahú* (271), ppp *slúxeni* (a3) vs. inf *ſluxiti* (116), pr3p *sluxé* (311).

(8) The root *trud-* in several types of cases, in particular:
- The stem vowel of the noun *trud* (9/3): Ns *trúd* (35, 518, e44), Gs *trúda* (f51, f60, f86), DLs *trúdu* (446), Is *trúdóm* (211), *trúdom* (f94) vs. Ns *trud* (a35), Gs *truda* (86), Is *trudom* (15).
- The stem vowel of the verb *truditi* (9/1): aor3p *trúdiſce* (1186), *l*-pms *utrúdio* (1120), pr3s *trúdí* (744), *trúdi* (850, 1036), pr3p *trúde*

(1299), imp2s *trúdi* (1304, c168), gpr *trúdechi* (24) vs. aor3p *utrudiſce* (82).

(9) The stem vowel of the neuter noun *sunce* (4/9): Ns *ſúnçe* (506, 749), *Súnçe* (498), Gs *ſúnça* (233) vs. Ns *ſunçe* (427, 1066, 1619, 1664), *Sunçe* (430), Gs *ſunça* (400, 1002), *ſunza* (f32, read: *ſunça*), DLs *ſunçu* (1053).

5.1 Accent marks on vowels not followed by a syllable-final resonant

For a discussion of the material presented in the preceding sections to make sense, we have to distinguish between vowels followed by syllable-final resonants on the one hand and all other positions on the other. For the present section it is only the latter that are at issue. Table I summarizes the facts as found in stem syllables.[22]

Table I: accent symbols expressing long vowels in stem syllables				
vowel	*references*	*attestations*	*accented*	*percentage*
a	3.1 (16, 29), 4.2 (2-6)	148	118	80%
e	3.1 (25), 4.3 (1-4)	86	73	85%
i (A)	3.1 (12), 4.4 (1-4)	59	41	69%
i (B)	idem	28	13	46%
i (C)	idem	32	1	3%
o	3.1 (1), 4.5 (1-3)	123	84	68%
	id., excluding *bog*	109	83	76%
u	3.1 (2, 5), 4.6 (1-8)	168	125	74%

Taken as a whole this confirms the tentative regularity formulated in section 3.3 on the basis of a limited sample: if a stem vowel is long, the odds that its length will be expressed are at least two to one. Generally speaking this regularity holds for all individual cases as well, with allowance being made for the statistical distortions that gain the upper hand as the number of relevant examples becomes smaller.

One individual case deviates strikingly from the general tendency: in the noun *bog* Hektorović prefers not to write an accent symbol.

Endings present a partly different picture, see Table J. Here again, word forms ending in a syllable-final resonant have not been taken into account (pr1s -*am* and -*im*, Is/Dp -*im*, Is -*om*), nor have endings that are poorly attested. In the case of -*i*-, attention is limited to the state of affairs to be found in section A of the text.

	pr3s -*a*	pr2s -*aš*	Gs -*e*	pr3p -*e*	gps -*eć*	gps -*eći*	adj -*oga*	pr3p -*u*	gps -*uć*	gps -*ući*	pr3s -*i*-
acc.	90	21	86	86	40	72	30	80	18	14	32
unm.	35	5	20	25	11	27	14	54	27	23	20
att.	125	26	106	111	51	99	44	134	45	37	52
perc.	72%	81%	81%	77%	78%	73%	68%	60%	40%	38%	61%

Table J: endings containing long vowels not followed by a syllable-final resonant

Generally speaking, here too the tentative regularity formulated in section 3.3 is corroborated. Note that as in the case of stems the proportion of marked vowels is highest in the case of *a* and *e*.

The only important departure from the regularity is provided by the low proportion of marked vowels in the case of the gerund endings -*uć* and -*ući*. This is a point we shall be returning to.

5.2 Accent marks on originally long vowels followed by a syllable-final resonant

In investigating vowels followed by a syllable-final resonant one has to take into account an additional complication arising from the fact that in this position length can have broadly speaking two types of origin: it can be either original or the outcome of a relatively recent lengthening process of short vowels followed by tautosyllabic resonants. Although for reasons of space an exhaustive discussion of this complex subject will have to await a later occasion, there is no harm in summarizing the tendencies that come to light in the material surveyed so far.

In stems, vowels with original or underlying length followed by a tautosyllabic resonant appear to behave no differently from long vowels in other positions, as shown in Table K.

Note however the limitations of the evidence. In view of the small number of relevant examples attention is limited to word forms containing word-final resonants. The only vowel to be abundantly attested in different types of cases is *a*; the vowels *e*, *o*, and *u* are each attested only in a single type of cases; *i* is not attested at all.

506

Table K: stems containing original (underlying) long vowels followed by tautosyllabic resonants				
vowel	references	attestations	accented	percentage
a	3.1 (16, 29), 4.2 (1-2, 5-6)	90	66	73%
e	4.3 (5)	14	9	64%
o	3.1 (1)	4	3	75%
u	4.6 (3)	12	8	67%

As they are, the figures conform closely to the regularity formulated in sections 3.3 and 5.1. The same holds for all individual instances apart from that of the Ns of *stvar*, where accented and unaccented attestations are more or less equally frequent (11/12, see 3.1 (29)).

Endings are displayed in Table L.

Table L: endings containing or presumably containing underlying long vowels followed by tautosyllabic resonants							
	prls -*am*	adj Is/Dp -*im*			prls -*im*		Is -*om*
ref.	4.2 (8)	4.4 (8)			4.4 (10)		3.1 (31)
acc.	19	3	2	1	9	5	3	42
unm.	7	5	5	18	6	1	22	16
att.	26	8	7	19	15	6	25	58
perc.	73%	(37%)	(28%)	(5%)	(60%)	(83%)	(12%)	72%

Again the limitations of the available facts have to be kept in mind. In all cases the resonant involved is word-final -*m*. For the vowels *e* and *u* there is no evidence. Within these limitations, we find that the facts concerning the vowels *a* and *o* are in conformity with the regularity proposed in sections 3.3 and 5.1. In the case of *i*, it turns out that we have to distinguish between adjectival endings and the prls of the verb. This point requires some discussion.

One might be inclined to attribute the difference between the adjectival endings and the verbal prls to a statistical fluctuation caused by the small numbers involved. That it is not is shown by the fact that it recurs in all three sections of the book.

Moreover, a quite similar difference crops up among some closely related forms. Though here, too, the numbers are small, they consistently point in the same direction: in the present tense of the verb length is reasonably common, cf. 2s -*iš* (1/4, 2/11, 0/10), 1p -*imo* (2/2,

1/3, 0/5), 2p *-ite* (3/2, 0/0, 0/4), whereas in the oblique plural cases of the adjective length is positively exotic, cf. Ip *-imi* (0/2, 2/6, 0/7), GALp *-ih* (0/4, 0/12, 0/15). Note however that even in section A of the book, the proportion of accented *í* in the pr1-2s and pr1-2p taken together is lower than the regularity formulated in sections 3.3 and 5.1 would lead one to expect: 15/23, or 39% of the total number of attestations. The pr3s, by contrast, is quite normal, with 61% (Table J).

This is reminiscent (almost down to the exact percentages) of the relatively low proportion of accented vowels in the case of the gerund endings *-uć* and *-ući* as compared with the pr3pl ending *-u*. It turns out that at least in endings, Hektorović was less inclined to indicate length on the high vowels in non-final position than he was to do on the same vowels in final position and on all other vowels in all positions. We shall come across some more examples of this in section 5.3.

The case of the adjectives is clearly very different. There, length is downright exceptional and the chances are that in Hektorović's prosodic system the *-i-* was or could be short in adjectival endings. Note however that the *-o-* was very obviously long, at least in *-oga* and *-omu*.

5.3 Accent marks on originally short vowels followed by a syllable-final resonant

We can now turn to cases of length that are due to lengthening of an originally short vowel followed by a syllable-final resonant. Such instances of length are quite frequent in Hektorović's language, but the details are intricate and not always straightforward, even apart from the obvious fact that we cannot in the case of every single vowel determine in advance whether it has to count as underlyingly long or short.

We have examined in detail the case of the masculine/neuter Is ending *-om* (section 4.5 (4)). If the ending can be assumed to have been stressed, an accent mark is present by and large according to the regularity formulated in sections 3.3 and 5.1, quite as if we are dealing with original length. If, on the other hand, it was not stressed, accent marks appear exceptionally, if ever.

This is not the only type of cases where lengthening of short vowels followed by syllable-final resonants appears to depend on the presence of stress. Although in most cases the evidence is less abundant, we find it also in the endingless Ns of nouns and adjectives with a stem in *-l*, cf. *Chabál* (1467), *Ítól* (1063), *mál* (513, 1339, c157), *zál* (932) vs.

uartal (1087), *poſal* (c151, f31), *izgibil* (1422), *miſal* (1383, f30, f123), *mal* (1631, c89, f43), *mil* (780, 1337, c52, e7), *priſtal* (c43), *ueſel* (136, 687, 696, 959, 1139, 1207, a12), *Veſel* (590), *Neueſel* (1011).

Monosyllabic forms (*stol, mal, zal, mil*) will be assumed to have been stressed. As for the other examples, cf. Brusje *Kabôl, vãrtal, posôl, věselo,* Brač/Hvar/Vis *Kabôl, vãrtal, posôl, mîsal, věsel,* Vrgada *Kabᵒã, vȑtᵒã, posᵒã, mîsᵒã, věsē.* The noun *izgibil* and the adjective *pristal* are not attested in any of the three Dalmatian dialect dictionaries; for *izgibil* cf. however Brač/Hvar/Vis *pogȉbil,* which has the same morphological structure; for *pristal* cf. Vuk/Daničić *prìstao,* pointing to stress on the final syllable.

In examples in which end stress is certain or plausible (*Kabal, posal, stol, mal, zal, pristal*), length is indicated in half of the cases (6/6), whereas among those words that are likely to have had non-final stress (*vartal, misal, vesel/nevesel*) there are no examples of length (0/13); *mil* and *izgibil* have not been counted here because only a single one of the relevant attestations is found in section A of the book, so that the evidence is without value.

Cases of lengthening of vowels in arguably unstressed syllables are so rare that they have probably to be explained as underlyingly long. Although limitations of space preclude a complete discussion of the material, it is interesting as an illustration to take a look at the masculine singular of the *l*-participle, where forms with underlying and secondary length are inextricably intertwined. Several types of cases have to be distinguished:

(1) If the vowel preceding the -*l* is an -*a*- reflecting **a,* presence of an acute is frequent (9/9): *dál* (739), *Nahitál* (741), *pál* (c158), *poslál* (1667), *poznàl* (a45), *sliſcál* (a38), *uſtál* (514), *uzbúyál* (1340), *ſpiuál* (a54), vs. *Dal* (c13, c17, c43), *imal* (c90), *iſpiſal* (a54), *piſal* (a44), *radoual* (a29), *ſiloual* (386), *Tiral* (f26). In *dal* it is reasonable to expect underlying length; in *pal, poslal, poznal, ustal, uzbujal, imal, ispisal,* and *pisal* one expects final stress and hence lengthening; in *nahital, slišal, spival, radoval, siloval,* and *tiral* one expects non-final stress and hence no accent marks, unless the vowel is underlyingly long. Since *Nahitál* and *sliſcál* display an acute accent, we have to conclude that these forms had underlying length, which strikes one as surprising at first sight, but is actually quite in line with the evidence provided by the accent marks in *pohitáli* (629) and infinitives like *pogledáti* (235), which also point to underlying length (see section 3.1 (6)). We have to con-

clude that any -a- reflecting *a preceding the final -l of the masculine singular of the l-participle is long. This is exactly what we find in the dialects that continue Hektorović's immediate linguistic background, where -a- < *a is always reflected as -o- in the masculine singular of the l-participle, cf. prô(l), grȉjo(l) (both with underlying length, cf. próla, prôlo, grȉjola, grȉjolo), čuvô(l) (with underlying brevity, cf. čū- vāla, čūvālo), examples given by Hraste (1926-27: 205-206).

(2) If the vowel preceding the -l is an -a- reflecting a secondary jer, an acute is exceptional (1/17): muchál (797), dotechal (1355), mogal (a6, a46), odrechal (250), Pomarchal (d45), pofcal (573, a41), potechal (225), Rechal (1547), rechal (226, 390, 1356, c90, c133, f17), stechal (249), zatechal (f18). Except in pošal one expects non-final stress in all these cases. The Hvar dialects have unstressed -a- (i.e. the reflex of short *a) in such examples, cf. Brusje trésa(l), strȉga(l) (Hraste 1926-27: 202).[23]

(3) If the vowel preceding the -l is an -i- (reflecting *i or *ě), an acute is less frequent than in the case of -a- reflecting *a even in the case of section A of the book (8/13, 1/8, 0/18): bíl (773, 783, 1140), chúpíl (760), çtíl (774: read: *ctíl), hodíl (759, 779), htíl (760), imíl (740) vs. bil (460, 764, 780, 794, 906, 1682, e8, e13), Bil (1667), bu- garil (a54), chiutil (f144), dícil (784), gouoril (459, 1046, f27), htil (373, 739, 1045, 1055, c51), imil (793), mnil (f28), nadilil (e48), ochri- lil (e47), ostauil (e8), oftauil (1254), otuoril (460), Plátil (247), poftauil (1253), pozlouoglil (a24), priprauil (c119), sloxil (f156), fril (1139), fta- uil (a42), uidil (401, e39), umil (480, a54), zapouidil (1338). The low proportion of accented vowels probably reflects Hektorović's disinclina- tion to provide high vowels with an accent mark in non-final position in endings.

(4) Other vowels are too rare to offer suitable material for a discus- sion (2/4): cúl (774), pocél (a35) vs. Cul (283, 1487), cul (467), fel (960).[24]

The connection between stress and lengthening of short vowels has a counterpart in the dialects that continue Hektorović's immediate lin- guistic background. As usual we have to be content with the fact that information about posttonic length has been retained only in the case of *a. In the following examples from Hvar we find ô < stressed *a and a < posttonic *a: dlôn, krôj, rōžôń, pakôl, badôń, kabôl, jūbôv, nōrôv, jedôn, vs. Pëtar, vârtal, čâval, jâval, Pâval. In the case of underlying length we find o even in posttonic position, e.g. ôblok Gs ôbloka, rȉbor

Gs *rȉbora*, Gp *móčok, prósoc, dȍloc* (examples from Hraste 1935: 17-35).

It by no means follows from this that the state of affairs reflected by the accent marks in Hektorović's book is identical to the one attested in the modern dialects of Hvar and Brač. The most striking difference consists in that in Hektorović's book, length is much less consistently indicated than one would expect on the basis of the regularity formulated in sections 3.3 and 5.1.

This appears to hold already to some extent for forms ending in *-l*. It holds much more strongly for forms in *-j*, of which we examined an example above (section 3.1 (28)). Substantially the same pattern recurs in all types of material. The Nsm of the possessive pronouns *moj, tvoj* and *svoj*, to give another example, occasionally carries an acute accent, but usually does not (4/43): *móy* (a32), *tuóy* (2, c51, e57) vs. *moy* (1, 35, 132, 223, 263, 279, 519, 546, 825, 1612, 1676, a43, a53, e3, e20, e40, e44, f39, f145), *Moy* (600, b10), *tuoy* (566, 592, 859, 914, 1248, 1251, 1290, 1338, 1359, 1398, 1501, a60, c82, c99, d7, e13, e19, e35, f146), *sfoy* (16, 122, 481, 754, 942, 1084, 1363, 1461, 1500, c5, c151, c200, e55). Or compare the Ns of *kraj* (3/9): *chráy* (277, 1090, 1629), vs. *chray* (60, 720, 788, 1616, c18, c77, f9, f22), *Chray* (1070).

The challenge posed by this material can be formulated as follows: the examples carry an accent mark in too many cases to make the assumption of mistakes plausible, but the proportion of accented and unaccented forms does not conform to the regularity formulated in sections 3.3 and 5.1. This clashes with everything we have seen so far of Hektorović's use of accent marks.

I think an explanation has to be found along the following lines. Lengthening of originally short vowels followed by syllable-final resonants is the consequence of an earlier neutralization of the contrastive difference between long and short vowels in the relevant position. This stage is still found as such (usually in part of the cases) in quite a few living dialects, e.g. that of Novi Vinodolski, where a distinction between short and long vowels followed by syllable-final resonants exists only in pretonic position. Otherwise speakers of the dialect tend to lengthen non-contrastively any vowel that is followed by a tautosyllabic resonant. They are actually unable to pronounce a convincing short vowel even in non-dialectal words like *hotel* (realized as *hotȇl*) even when speaking the standard language. In rapid speech the impression that all vowels followed by syllable-final resonants are long tends however to disappear.[25]

I assume that Hektorović's book expresses a stage at which vowel length was optional or perhaps even neutralized in vowels followed by syllable-final *-j* and probably *-l*. Hektorović used accent marks in those cases that for whatever reason he found sufficiently salient. This practice may also account for the curious rule we came across in section 3.1 (5) while examining the compounds of **iti* (i.e. examples like *najti*): accent marks are attested in the following forms: inf, pr3s, imp1p, aor1 s, and aor2/3s; on the other hand accent marks never appear in the plural forms of the aorist.

6. Vowel length in the stem of the verb *činiti*

To wind up the discussion we shall take a brief look at the kind of patterns that become noticeable as one gains some insight into the workings of Hektorović's way of using accent marks. As an example I shall choose the frequent verb *činiti*. In attested accentual systems, the verb *činiti* ordinarily has a short stem vowel in all forms. There are however several types of exceptions to this:

– If the imperative is formed without an ending, the stem vowel is occasionally lengthened in those systems that lengthen short vowels followed by syllable-final resonants, e.g. Vrgada *čȋn* (Jurišić 1973: 37). As a matter of fact this is rare both in Vrgada and in related dialects, to the extent that they have been described in sufficient detail.

– In some dialects some compounds have a long stem vowel throughout and are, accordingly, (b)-stressed, e.g. Omišalj pr3s *činȋ*, *l*-pns *činêlo*, inf *učinȉt*, pr3s *učinȋ*, imp2s *učinȉ*, *l*-pms *učinê*, *l*-pfs *učinêla*, PPP *učińenȍ* vs. *načinȉt*, pr3s *načīnȋ*, imp2s *načīnȉ/nǎčīni*, *l*-pfs *načīnȉla*, PPP *načȋńen* (Vermeer 1980: 461).[26]

In Hektorović, the stem vowel of *činiti* ordinarily does not carry an acute accent, cf. inf *ciniti* (946, 950, 1305, 1434), *cinit* (834, 1384), *razciniti* (859), *uciniti* (545, 1458, a22), *ucinit* (1343), *l*-pms *cinio* (880), *l*-pmp *cinili* (520), gpt *naciniʃci* (1216), aor1s *Cinih* (53, 1185), *ucinih* (c83), aor2/3s *cini* (1159), *ucini* (d3), *Vciní* (292), aor1p *uciniʃmo* (749), aor3p *ciniʃce* (1644), *uciniʃce* (1188, 1663), imperf2/3s *cigniáʃce* (861), imperf3p *cigniahu* (1212), pr3s *ciní* (37, 357, 400, 733, 1038, 1315, 1382), *cini* (434, 923, 1442, 1550, c145), *cin[í]* (1209), *razcini* (f31), *ucini* (f15), pr2p *ciníte* (242), pr3p *ciné* (374, 1341, 1577), gpr *cinéchi* (1015, 1069, 1460, 1556, 1585, f50), *cinechi* (c110, f12), *cinéch* (1417), *cinèch* (1451).

Nevertheless an acute accent is printed on the stem vowel in a small number of forms:

– To begin with, there are several attestations of length in the imperative in zero: 2s *cín* (1254), *Cín* (1245), *cin* (1265, 1281), *Cin* (1059), *Vcin* (1286), 1p *cinmo* (1579), *Vcínmo* (221), 2p *Cínte* (1598).

– More surprisingly, there is also an attestation of length in an imperative in -*i*: 2s *cíni* (279), cf. *cini* (488, 1297), *Cini* (1332), *ucini* (404, 1266), 1p *cinimo* (295, 1569).

– Finally, we find an acute accent in the only attestation of the pr1s in -*u*: *cígniu* (690).

Although it is always possible to regard these forms as errors, examples of vowels that are incorrectly indicated as long are exceedingly rare in Hektorović's text.[27] Moreover, most of them involve acute accents that belong on an adjacent syllable, e.g. Gs *putá* (a16) instead of **púta* (see note 15) and since neither the imperative ending -*i* nor the pr1sg ending -*u* are ordinarily long, *cíni* and *cígniu* cannot plausibly be regarded as mistakes of this kind.

In this context it is interesting to see that the imperative has a long stem vowel in Bartol Kašić's printed *Piesni duhovnae* of 1617, an interesting text in which a complex system of accent symbols, double vowels, and double consonants is employed to indicate vowel length and the place of the stress.

In Kašić, as in Hektorović, most attestations of *činiti* have no indication of length in the stem vowel, cf. inf *cinìtti* (10, 105), *cinitti* (47, 89), *Cinitti* (2, 133), *cinìt'* (111, 112), *cinit'* (149), *Cinit'* (92), aor3p *cinìſce* (35, 100), *ciniſce* (116, 148, 155), *cíniſce* (sic) (67), *l*-pms *cinìl* (sic) (59), *cinnío* (162), (42, 162), *l*-pfs *cinilla* (13, 143), *l*-pmp *cinilli* (17), *Cinilli* (78), pr1s *cinijm* (74, 133), pr3s *cinij* (94, 104, 126), *cinij* (2, 14, 30, 41, 44, 94, 117, 118, 136), *Cinij* (62), pr3p *ciné* (51, 61, 128), gpr *cinécch'* (162), *cinécchi* (44, 124), imperf3p *cignáhu* (127); inf *ucinìtti* (93), *ucinìt'* (59, 67, 93, 114), *Vcinít'* (5), *Vcinit'* (149), aor1s *ucinih* (69, 127), *ucinih* (165), aor2/3s *ùccini* (89), *uccini* (12, 57, 160), *Vccini* (57, 158), *l*-pms *ucinil* (130), *ucinío* (18, 29, 59, 130, 142, 159), *Vcinío* (26, 144), gpt *ucinivſci* (59), *Vcinivſci* (151).

Length is also absent (in contradistinction to what we find in Hektorović's system) in all attestations of the imperative if it is endingless, cf. imp2s *cin'* (70), *cin'* (16), *Cin'* (50, 116, 129), *ucin'* (31), *Vcin'* (135). Like Hektorović, however, Kašić has length as soon as the imperative takes the ending *-i*, cf. imp2s *cijni* (20, 166), *Cijni* (113), 2p *cijnite* (13), 2p *cinítte* (7).[28]

In addition Kašić has length in the aor2/3s of the simple verb: *cijni* (56, 104, 164), aor2/3s *Cijni* (104). In the case of this form Hektorović's evidence (consisting as it does of a single attestation that is not provided with an accent mark) is inconclusive.

As for the pr1s in *-u*, which unfortunately is not attested in Kašić, it is important to realize that familiar accentological rules force one to expect length. In SCr, the simple verb *činiti* usually belongs to Stang's accent type (c). Now if the stem contains a heavy syllabic nucleus, as it does in the case of *čin-*, one expects to find length in disyllabic stem-stressed forms, e.g. pr1s *čȋńu, aor2/3s *čȋni.[29]

End-stressed forms, on the other hand, must have had a short vowel in the stem, e.g. aor1s *činìxъ, in the same way that the Vuk/Daničić system opposes As *rûku* to DILp *rùkama*. In the noun, where stem-stressed forms are both basic and numerous, analogical reintroduction of length in end-stressed forms has been common, beginning with a very early generalization of length in disyllabic forms, see Kortlandt (1975: 33); in other types of cases traces of brevity abound, cf. in addition to Daničić's *rùkama* such examples as Omišalj Lp *stupîh* (opposed to NAp *stûpi*, my material; the dialect lacks a tonal contrast), Vrgada Gp *sinôv*, DILp *sinîn* opposed to Ns *sîn*, Gs *sîna* (Jurišić 1966: 74-75).

It follows that Hektorović's *cígniu* can be regarded as a genuine attestation of a long vowel which has to be reconstructed on the basis of well-established accentological laws, but has so far failed to turn up in real life, on the one hand because the pr1s in *-u* is poorly attested in material that has preserved evidence of vowel length, and on the other because length has tended to be analogically replaced with the short vowel that is regular in the overwhelming majority of forms (which are end-stressed) and in the corresponding forms of compounds (which are not disyllabic), cf. Vuk/Daničić aor2/3s *ùčî*.

7. Conclusions

(1) In the 1568 edition of Hektorović's selected works a comfortable majority of long vowels (between three and four fifths) are provided with accent marks. There are two major exceptions to this:

(1a) For *i* the regularity holds only in the first 800 verses of "Ribanje", after which accented *í* becomes much less frequent.

514

(1b) In endings, the vowels *i* and *u* conform to the regularity only in absolute final position, whereas in non-final position only about two fifths of arguably long vowels are indicated as such.

(2) An examination of all relevant examples confirms the traditional view (Maretić, Mladenović, Wagner) that the grave accent is not functionally distinct from the acute.

(3) Lengthening of short vowels followed by syllable-final resonants is never indicated in arguably unstressed syllables.

(4) In stressed syllables length is indicated regularly before word-final *-m*, in half of the cases before word-final *-l* and only rarely before word-final *-j*.

(5) Although this contribution has been devoted not so much to Hektorović's language as to his use of accent marks, we have had occasion to notice several features of his language that remain hidden if one does not consider the prosodic facts, e.g.:

(5a) The evidence shows that Hektorović distinguished clitic *to* containing a short *-o* from orthotonic *to* containing a long *-ō*.

(5b) Hektorović has evidence of length in the infinitive and the *l*-participle of polysyllabic (a)-stressed verbs not only in *-ati* (where the modern dialects that continue Hektorović's immediate linguistic background have the regular reflex of length), but also in verbs in *-iti* and *-nuti*, where the evidence of the modern dialects of Hvar and Brač is inconclusive.

(5c) It appears that in the adjectival inflection the *-i-* in the Is ending *-im* and the oblique endings of the plural was short.

(5d) Hektorović's accent marks show the presence in the (c)-stressed verb *činiti* of length alternations that have not so far been observed in living material.

(5e) If Hektorović's text is reliable, the old name of the island nowadays called Šolta was (b)-stressed: *Sul̃êt*, Gs *Sulētà*.

University of Leiden

APPENDIX

This Appendix contains the text of Hektorović's two prose letters to Mikša Pelegrinović, in order to enable the reader to follow the system of references (for which see further section 1.4).

515

[a0] OVO PISCE PETRE HECTOROVICH HVARANIN,
POCTOVANOMV GOSPODINV MICHSCI
PELEGRINOVICHIV, VLASTELINV HVARSCHOMV,
CHANCILIRV ZADARSCHOMV.

[a1] PRigodámiſe po ouomu napochongniem uſcharſenyu
Pelegrínouichiu mili poyti do onoga Slaunóga Gráda (choyimſe
sfi dicimo) Dubrounicha,

[a2] ſnichimi rodyáçi i ſpriategli moyimi, u ormánu brigentinu,
ſyednóm mrixariçom pod zapouid naſcu,

[a3] gdi nas biſce duádeſét po broyu, meu onimi choyi slúxáhu i chí
slúxeni bihu, liſce priſidáç, namirnichóf i priatégl,

[a4] Na chí pút ueleme podtachnú xeglia da uidím i ſtáré priateglie i
noue, naulaſtito niché nigdar paruo neuidine,

[a5] I doſcadſci tamo priyati biſmo i ſdrúxeni ſuelichom gliúbafyu
choyuti neumim iſpiſati ni mogu,

[a6] i prem dabih mogal bilabi ſtuár uele duga pobráyati gliubaf
imiloſcchiu choyu priyáſmo nayparuo od oné prisfitlé i práué
Goſpodé

[a7] (Choyu chachoye Bog miloſtiui Goſpodſtuóm darouao, tachoyuye
pamétyu i uminyem i umiglienſtuóm i blagodárſtuóm i praudóm i
chripoſtyu naréſcio)

[a8] i potóm choyuſmo imali od priatégl mnozih,

[a9] Sámo ti[30] nayedno gouoru, ne liſto u Grádu da uaſdi u darxaui i
chotáru gniegouu gdigodiſmo doſcli (a proſcligaſmo i uidili doſti)

[a10] uaſdiſmo bili po cudnouati nácin uidíni gliúbglieni i obilno
obdarouáni,

[a11] tacho dagimſmo[31] oſtali sfim uechie nego guozdenimi uerugami
uichofgnim nácinom obézani,

[a12] Vchóm Grádu meu ſtuàri iné naydohſe ueſel nemalo,

[a13] chada uidih daye i ondi poznáno ime tuoye yere iſpitouán bih
doſti za tebe,

[a14] I uelemi pohuágliena bi Iyubcha tuoya, chachono stuár zamirita i
izuarſna,

[a15] choyúno ti nichad u pridgniá urimena sloxi náredno i upiſa,

[a16] Schóga putá nachon duádeſet i pét dán urátiſſciſe domóm,
pouidán mi bi yedan glas uele drág i ugodan,

[a17] ató daſeye tuoya uridnóſt sdrúxila ſ Goſpoyóm Liuiom Vladichóm
narednóm plemenitóm i pohuaglienom,

[a18] Zachu stuar tiſe raduyu ſa sfim ſarçem i ueſelím, xeliuchiuam
dug xiuot, ſchladan, miran, ceſtit i dobar,

516

[a19] I za Zlamenye od toga ſcagliuti ſouóm chgnigom pripiſano
[a20] (izuan onoga ribanya móga i ribarſchoga prigouaranya)
[a21] ono cím mene u recenómu Grádu Dubrounichu i potom u
naſcemu, na zaurachienyu nadiliſce,
[a22] hotéchi tebe od sfih ſtuari choyimi mene dariuayu dilnicha
uciniti,
[a23] Toytichie biti na miſto onih darof choyiſe budú priategliem na pir
poſilati,
[a24] I pouidaſcemi do nicholicho urimena potóm, daſiſe pozlouoglil
yeretiye parui plód pomagnchao,
[a25] Nemoy molinte, da na sfém day huálu Bogu, Choyi ſám i yedini,
zna canamye za boglie,
[a26] i chinam dáye mnoge púte po chih moremo chripoſti od
uſtarpinyá pochazati,
[a27] Choyi nam dili miloſti i dáye ono caye drago gniemu, i uazima
opét (chachono stuar sfoyu) chadaye gniemu ugodno,
[a28] Buditi doſti poznati da imáſc uireniçu plodnu, caſi (tachoſe meni
mni) uele xelio,
[a29] Néchiu daſe pocudiſc datiſe niſám pria radoual nego ſada,
[a30] yedno zác i pozdno radouanyé nie nigdár pohuyeno,
[a31] drugo zaſcto i nemogoh, yere ſyutradán chachoſe uárnuh ſputa
onoga doydemi yedna cudnouata nemóch
[a32] choyuti neumim izrechi, i choyami omrazi xiuot móy,
[a33] Zatóm drugá choyáme douede do ſmartnoga meyaſca, tacho dami
yedua u ſtaru chipu neuoglnu duſcu oſtaui,
[a34] za gnimi tretá i cetuárta (choyemi ne tribuye pobrayati) tacho da
ouo ſcéſti miſéc[32] tece da me mucé i neuoglié
[a35] i maloye dán da ſamſe pocél duizati ſodra i pomalo poſtupati, u
chomu stányu nay parui trud priyáh tebi ouo piſati,
[a36] ufayuchi chada izaznáſc iſtinu od mene, da michieſc sfe priyáti za
dobro,
[a37] Azaſcto imám ſúmgniu nemalu datichie u onomu ribaſchómu[33]
prigouaranyu yedna ſtuár biti neugodna dochleyoy uzroch
nepoznaſc,
[a38] Ató yereſi (moxebiti) i od druzih sliſcál bugarſchiçe one choyéſu
moyi ribári bugarili, i onu iſtu piſan choyu obadua zayedno
pripiuaſce,
[a39] imnimiſe damichieſc rechi uſebi,
[a40] Zaſcto niſi sám od tuoga uma choyegodi bugarſcchine i piſan
izmislio i sloxio,

[a41] negoſi poſcal one ſtuari che i druzi umiyu pouidati?

[a42] zatoti dám znati, Daſam ya uelichu pómgniu ſtauil iſpiſati
Izuarſnomu Vitézu onomu

[a43] i dati na znanyé sfe ribanyé moye i uas pút moy práuóm iſtinóm
onacho chachofye bio, ne priloxif yednu ric naymagniu,

[a44] Yerſe inácho nie priſtoyalo ni onomu chomu piſah, ni meni
choyiſam piſal, budúchimi drága bilá uaſda iſtina usſemu,

[a45] I tolicho uechie, Zaſcto tchogodibi ctéchi poznàl daſu rici nouo
sloxene i izmiſcgliene

[a46] mogalbi potóm uerouati i darxati daye i sfe oſtáló ono slaxòm
sloxeno i izmiſcglieno,

[a47] Zatim yoſcchie uim da zná tuoya milóſt, Chachono Latini darxé
(prauo i doſtoyno) Hiſtoriu za ric iſtinnu,

[a48] yereyoy ſtauglieno yeſt ime od one rici choyáſe zoue Hiſter, ca
zlamenuye uidinye ali poznanye,

[a49] atò zác nitchor ini nepiſce tey stuari nego tchoyihye uidio i
poznao,

[a50] Tachoti i mi i sfe ſtrane naſcega yezicha

[a51] (choyiſe meu sfimi oſtalimi na sfitu nayuechi broyi i nahodi)

[a52] darſe³⁴ i ſçine bugarſcchiçe za ſtuari iſtinne, brez ſúmgnié sfache,
a ne za laxne chachoſu pripouiſti niche i piſni mnoge,

[a53] Zato ouo budi odgouor moy i tebi i sfim inim,

[a54] choyiſam ſa sfóm mochyu (chachoſam umil nayboglie) iſpiſal sfe
ono caye Paſchoy i Nichola bugaril i ſpiuál,

[a55] Choye ſtuári aliſuſe oni od druzih naucili ali druzi od gnih, toy
meni niſctore ni daye ni odnoſi,

[a56] I achochieſc dati pouim ono caſe meni mni

[a57] dimti daye uechie prilicno ch iſtini daſuſe oni od druzih naucili
nego druzi od gnih,

[a58] atò yereſu oni ribari i gliudi od mora, choyi brodechiſe nigda
ſouim anigda ſonim, niſctoſu od ouoga a niſcto od onoga sliſcali,
i ſpomgnióm sliſcayúchi naucili,

[a59] I nómi³⁵ neoſtaye da rechu za ſada, nego datiſe u sfemu
priporucuyem,

[a60] i da xelim sfachi tuoy napridach i poctenye i caſt chachoſam
xelio uaſda chrát,

[a61] Vſtáróm Huáru na duádeſét dán miſeça octobra ſedmoga
godiſcchia od ſpaſenya, uarhu tiſuchia pét ſát i petdeſét.

518

[b0] PETRE HECTOROVICH ISTOMV GOSPODINV MICHSCI
PELEGRINOVICHIV.[36]
[b1] EVoti fcagliu Chripoftni i náredni Gofpodine Michfca, oni
Sarbfchi nácin[37] (oudi zlólu[38] upifán)
[b2] Choyimye Pafchoy i Nichola sfachi po febi bugarfcchiçu bugario,
[b3] I tochóye nácin od oné pifni I chlice Deuoycha: Choyufu obadua
zayeduo[39] pripiuali.
[b4] BVGARSCCHIÇA.
[b5] Chadamife radofaue uoyeuoda od digliafce,
[b6] Od fuoyega grada difnoga fiuerina
[b7] Ceftomife radofaf na fiuerin obzirafce,
[b8] Teretomi ouacho bellu gradu befiyafce
[b9] Ouomite oftaugliam belli gradu[40] fiue rine
[b10] Moy difni gráde
[b11] Neznam uechie uiyulite, neznam uechie, uidifc lime
[b12] PISAN.
[b13] Ichlice deuoy cha, Pochlice deuoy cha
[b14] Yofc clice[41] deuoy cha mladami tere giz daua,
[b15] Mlada te re giz daua, fabrig bel la deuoycha dunaya.

NOTES

[1] I am indebted to Adriaan Barentsen for his moral support at a critical stage of the preparation of the typescript.

[2] Quoted on the basis of the photographic reproduction (1953).

[3] Another important investigation into vowel quantity in a sixteenth-century text is Stjepan Ivšić's well-known analysis of the language of Pergošić (1937), which however is much less detailed than Rešetar's work on Marin Držić.

[4] Several editions have limited themselves to "Ribanje", omitting the "stvari ine" altogether; the most important of these are Ramiro Bujas's 1951 edition, with its indispensable commentary, and Marko Grčić's parallel translation published in 1988. For a list of editions up to the mid eighties see Vončina (1986: 33-34).

[5] In this connection I would like to make my position clear on an issue that is often regarded as unproblematical. The undeniable fact that Classical Čakavian is close to the language actually spoken in North and Central Dalmatia has tempted scholars to jump to the conclusion that pre-modern Čakavian authors wrote in their local dialects, at least in principle, so that, say, Zoranić, Marulić and Hektorović are presented as using the spoken dialects of Zadar, Split and the western part of Hvar respectively. This picture is not only unlikely on general grounds (dialect poetry is by and large a product of Romanticism), but impossible to reconcile with the evidence of the texts themselves, which invariably combine features that can never have figured simultaneously in a sin-

gle local dialect. An example: from the Split Lectionary of 1495 onwards the masculine singular *l*-participle in *-o* (like modern standard *bio*) is quite common in Classical Čakavian. Yet with very few and marginal exceptions all Čakavian dialects have either retained the original ending *-l* or carried through innovations that are incompatible with the previous presence of *-o* (e.g. complete loss of final *-l* or the rise of forms like *bija*), all of which are also attested in Classical Čakavian.

6 For Hektorović's orthography see Mladenović (1968: 7-22) and Wagner (1970: 20-25). The principal differences with respect to the modern system are the following:
— *s* is printed as *ſ* and *s*, e.g. *stado, paſtir*;
— *y* corresponds to modern *j*, e.g. *moy*;
— Hektorović's *u* stands for modern *v* and *u*, e.g. *nouu* 'novu'; capital *V* is the equivalent of *u*, e.g. *Vuídro* 'u vidro'; In certain clusters and in syllable-final position *-v* usually appears as *f*, e.g. *sfe* 'sve', *sfoy* 'svoj', *plaf* 'plav', *ſpuſtíf* 'spustiv', *nepráſdu* 'nepravdu';
— modern *š*, *ž*, and *č* appear as *ſc/sc*, *x*, and *c* respectively, whereas Hektorović's *ç* is the counterpart of modern *c*, e.g. *sluſcay* 'slušaj', *Znáſc* 'znaš', *potéxe* 'poteže', *caſce* 'čaše', *mrixiçu* 'mrižicu';
— modern *lj* /ĺ/ and *nj* /ń/ appear as *gl* and *gn* (in syllable-final position or before *i*) or *gli* and *gni* (before other vowels than *i*), *priategl* 'prijatelj', *Zadouoglni* 'zadovoljni', *zlouogliti* 'zlovoljiti', *gliudem* 'ljudem', *gnimi* 'njimi', *gniega* 'njega';
— modern *k* appears as *ch*, e.g. *chacho* 'kako', *ſcchodu* 'škodu', *sfachomu* 'svakomu', *chgnixniçi* 'knjižnici';
— modern *ć* appears as *ch* (in syllable-final position or before *i*) or *chi* (before other vowels than *i*), e.g. *pomóch* 'pomoć', *uechi* 'veći', *xeſcchí* 'žešći', *urachiaſce* 'vraćaše', *ſrichiu* 'sriću';
— it follows that the only significant ambiguity is provided by the letter *u* and by the sequences *gn*, *gl* and *ch* in syllable-final position and before *i*.

7 Given the fact that a dodecasyllabic line basically contains twelve syllables, one would expect any stretch of a hundred lines to contain exactly 1200 vowels. In reality, however, the number of vowels is always higher. There are four different reasons for this:
— quite a few dodecasyllabic lines contain more than twelve vowels because the poet expected adjacent vowels to be realized as a single syllable;
— in *Ribanje*, quite a few lines are prefaced by indications of the speaker, in particular "Pasc(h)." or "Nich.";
— also in *Ribanje*, several poems containing longer lines have been incorporated;
— there are some minor sources of contamination, in particular typographical errors.

8 In view of the limited occurrence of capital *Ó*, the value of the absence of an accent symbol in the first syllable of *POydoſce* (509) is doubtful.

9 The form ****iſduihnuuch* 'i (v)zdvignuh', which Dragica Malić (1989: 151) reads in the early Classical Čakavian text known as *Žića svetih otaca* (f. 19r), and which with its double vowel appears to point to a posttonic long vowel of the type intended here (Vermeer 1994: 481), has turned out to rest on an incorrect reading. The original text, which can now be consulted on the basis of the photographic reproduction published by Dragica Malić, has *iſduihuuch* (Malić 1997: 223). This makes no sense and has proba-

520

bly to be read as *iſduihnuch, which is actually the reading adopted by Vinko Premuda in his pioneering edition of the text (1939: 127).

[10] The semantics of tense and aspect in Classical Čakavian has not been the subject of research worth speaking of and is at present very poorly understood. Hence it should be realized that for the time being it is impossible to separate reliably the pr3s from the aor2/3s, particularly in those cases that could be interpreted as historical presents. The list of examples should therefore be regarded as preliminary and suggestive rather than definitive and clinching. Forms in -á that I consider aorists are the following: pricá (1657), Pocá (1649), PRigodá (a1), pochimá (845), uxiná (496), odpaſá (660), poctouá (1145), zuá (1141), yá (738); absence of an accent mark is attested in pouida (1147), posla (1161), Pozna (1139), upiſa (a15), poſchita (1192), zamota (392), umota (102), ſta (203), oſta (128, 1620), daroua (824, c11), zaya (c157), priya (650, 651). Note that in this case absence of an accent mark is more frequent than presence of an acute. The chances are that in Hektorović's language such forms as sta and posla had a short vowel, as they have in Vuk/Daničić. For the aorist forms of dati see under (43).

[11] These lists are not exhaustive.

[12] Wagner (1970: 27) regards the acute in záto (256) as a mistake. This is completely arbitrary. Length in this form is not only amply confirmed in Hektorović's text, but also well attested in living dialects.

[13] Wagner (1970: 27) regards the attestations of the acute accent in zábi (209) and pozábili (176) as mistakes. In view of the large number of supporting examples this is out of the question. Note that length is confirmed by Bartol Kašić (1617/1978), who has aor1p zábismo (144), l-part mp Zábili (144), and by the testimony of quite a few living varieties of Čakavian, not only such dialects as Omišalj (inf pozābȉt, l-part pozābȉla, pr1s pozābīm, my material), Orbanići in Istria (Kalsbeek 1998, section V.1.1), and Susak (Hamm, Hraste and Guberina 1956: 183), but also systems that continue Hektorović's immediate linguistic background, cf. Brusje inf zōbȉt, pr1s zōbin (Dulčić/Dulčić 1985: 738).

[14] Here again the figures should not be regarded as exact because as in the case of the pr3s in -a it is not always possible to separate presents from aorists.

[15] Wagner (1970: 27) regards this example as a mistake instead of *obeselímo. Although no argumentation is provided, I am inclined to agree with this. On the one hand the -i- in the present tense often carries an acute accent; on the other the syllable -sel- in the adjective vesel and its derivations never carries an accent symbol (0/27), cf. ueſel (136, 687, 696, 959, 1139, 1207, a12), Veſel (590), ueſela (590), ueſelo (63, 70, 259, 685, 1468), Veſelo (693, 1656), ueſelím (a18), ueſeli (830, 984), Neueſel (1011), Neueſelo (f72), inf ueſeliti (115), pr2p ueſelíte (241), imp2s ueſeli (d11), imp2p ueſelite (194), gps ueſeléchi (187, 298). Elsewhere in Hektorović's text there are several convincing examples of accent marks that appear to belong to an adjacent syllable, e.g. Ns xitách (1278, read: *xítach), Gs ſiná (166, read: *ſína), mirá (1023, read: *míra), putá (a16, read: *púta), DLs darú (c164, read: *dáru), As guſtirnú (1087, read: *guſtírnu), Ns stároſt (c108, read: *staróſt), Gs ſceſtogá (f160a, read: *ſceſtóga), pr1s niſám (a29, read: *níſam), pr2s zádaſc (1294, read: *zadáſc), pr3s pridé (c139, read: *príde), gps Pitáyuch 'ask' (f51, read: *Pítayuch or *Pitayúch), aor1s Naydóh (212, read: *Náydoh),

l-part fs *bilá* (a44, read: *bíla), *l*-part ns *zbiló* 'turn into reality' (1514, read: *zbílo), *chité* 'ki te' (c185, read: *chíte), imperf3p *slúxahú* (271, read: *slúxáhu, also Wagner).

[16] Cf. also the length in *mnòx* (1573).

[17] This list is not exhaustive.

[18] The lists of examples are not exhaustive. In all types of cases absence of an accent mark is more frequent.

[19] The three important Dalmatian dialect dictionaries are the following: (a) Dulčić and Dulčić (1985), devoted to Brusje on Hvar; (b) Hraste/Šimunović/Olesch (1979), which incorporates lexical material from the Čakavian dialects of Brač, Hvar and Vis. (c) Jurišić (1973), devoted to the dialect of the small island of Vrgada opposite Biograd na Moru in North Dalmatia.

Although all three dictionaries are extremely informative, each of them has its own drawbacks from the point of view of the problem that is being investigated in the present contribution.

(a) The Dulčić/Dulčić dictionary does not incorporate many words the dialect shares with the standard language and by that token omits quite a bit of information that is vital from an accentological point of view.

(b) The Hraste e.a. dictionary combines information from different dialects, which forces the authors to adopt a certain amount of normalization, particularly in phonological matters. This is unfortunate, because the synchronic phonology of the dialects of the Brač/Hvar/Vis area has been shown to display quite a few local differences, in particular with respect to the continuation of vowel quantity, in other words: with respect to the very feature that is the subject of the present article. Matters are made worse by the contradictions present in the literature, which point to unresolved phonological problems. As an example I would like to mention the question whether or not the dialect of Komiža on the island of Vis (one of the major sources of the dictionary) has contrastive vowel quantity at all and if so, in which positions. Whereas several investigators report quantity distinctions, Pavle Ivić states (on the basis of unpublished investigations by Robert Earl Whyte, whose work is explicitly discounted by Hraste/Šimunović/Olesch 1979: XIV) "da je došlo do prefonologizacije kvantiteta u vokalski kvalitet" (1972: 264), in other words: that contrastive vowel quantity has been eliminated. Šimunović (1981a: 259-260) has it both ways: after giving distinct systems consisting of long and short vowels he states that the difference sometimes disappears, leaving the reader with the problem of conjecturing what on earth is going on.

(c) Jurišić's dictionary, which lacks the serious dialectological and lexicographic drawbacks of the other two dictionaries, describes a North Dalmatian dialect that cannot be regarded as an immediate continuation of Hektorović's linguistic background; nevertheless I have decided to adduce material from it because it is the most closely related system to have retained posttonic vowel length as such and to have been thoroughly decribed.

[20] In the chapter of the *Fonološki opisi* that is devoted to Vrbanj on Hvar, Šimunović quotes the Ns of the word with a long rising tone: *mȋr*, opposed to *mì:r* (i.e., in conventional notation, *mȋr*) 'wall' (1981b: 273). If correct, this would imply that *mir* 'peace' is (b)-stressed in a dialect that is among those that immediately continue Hektorović's linguistic background. However, it is possible that something has gone wrong here:

522

elsewhere, 'wall' is given with a rising and 'peace' with a falling tone, see, e.g., Hraste e.a. (1979: XXIV, 547).

[21] The posttonic length indicated in the Ns and implied for the Gs (because no separate Gs is given) clashes with the short vowel indicated in Is *pöbukon* given in the example (from Brusje) and with the statement that "Nach dem Akzent sind alle Längen gekürzt worden" (o.c.: XXIV). It is probably a mistake of some kind.

[22] Note that Ns of *gospodar, stvar, dar, plav, sam, razum* have not been counted because in them the vowel involved is followed by a syllable-final resonant.

[23] I wonder if the acute accent in *muchál* is not due to analogical introduction of the length found in the inf *müknūti*, cf. *razbignúti* (585) and the discussion in section 3.1 (7).

[24] Note that there is not a single case of length if -*o* appears instead of -*l*, cf. *pricao* (662), *otaſcao* (640), *chuſcao* (653), *pridao* (681), *pomagnchao* (a24), *poslao* (682), *poznao* (a49), *razigrao* (632), *Oſtao* (568), *razggniuao* (679), *darouao* (a7), *dozuao* (680); *bio* (610, 1645, a43), *zagubio* (564, 589), *obgliubio* (571, 572), *dicio* (c62), *naréſcio* (a7), *griſcio* (1630), *razredio* (612), *uidio* (92, 604, 929, 1200, 1629, 1646, a49), *odio* (1199), *pogardio* (1308), *utrúdio* (1120), *xelio* (a28, a60), *razdilio* (574), *izmislio* (a40), *imio* (122, c61), *umio* (654, f156), *cinio* (880), *proçinio* (930), *mnio* (91), *Pochlopio* (639), *popio* (626), *priſtupio* (661), *bugario* (b2), *priuario* (672), *Vdrio* (608), *Smirio* (646), *gouorio* (371, 1307), *htio* (879), *hotio* (372), *upuſtio* (643), *ſprauio* (627), *poſtauio* (669), *sloxio* (a40), *tuxio* (121), *broyio* (f155), *zbroyio* (1119); *odueo* (664); *zacuo* (678), *Padnuo* (611), *zaginuo* (636), *izuarnuo* (648).

[25] These observations are based on my own lengthy exposure to the dialect in 1973 and 1974. Contrary to what is the case in most SCr systems, *v* does not count as a resonant. The fact that in pretonic position the distinction is not neutralized is clear from Steinhauer's analysis (1973: 169-170) of the data in Belić (1909). The fact that the impression of length tends to disappear in rapid speech (which is not the case with ordinary length) has a counterpart in Belić's practice of not indicating length in clitics like *san, joj* etc. (Steinhauer 1973: 170).

[26] The initial stress of *näčīni* is the consequence of an optional rule according to which additional urgency is imparted to an imperative by stressing the initial syllable (for further examples and a brief description of the semantics of this phenomenon see Vermeer 1980: 449-450).

[27] A thirty-page discussion of this point which was part of an early version of this contribution had to be left out for reasons of space.

[28] Cf. also the examples from Ivan Bandulavić's edition of the Lectionary (1613) quoted by Daničić (1925: 282, originally 1872).

[29] On the accentuation of the (c)-stressed pr1s see Stang (1957: 108-111); for other evidence of stem stress in the (c)-stressed pr1s in SCr see also Vermeer (1984: 347n).

[30] At first sight the source appears to give *Sánoti*, but closer examination shows that the third letter is really an *m*, the left-most section of which is no longer visible.

[31] Read: *dayimſmo*.

523

32 Read: *miſéç.

33 Read: *ribarſchómu.

34 Read: *darxe.

35 Read: *Inómi.

36 This brief letter is in several ways atypical:
(1) Much of it (more specifically: b5-11, 13-15) consists of text the printers have done their best to align with the notes of the melody under which it is printed. As a consequence the text contains some unusual cases of word spacing within words: *od digliaſce* (b5, this could also be a normal instance of a word space after a verbal prefix), *ſiue rine* (b9), *uidiſc lime* (b11), *deuoy cha* (b13, twice, b14), *giz daua* (b14, b15), *te re* (b15), *bel la* (b15).
(2) In other respects, too, these lines are very unusual, note in particular:
– the uniquely low proportion of vowels provided with an accent symbol (see section 2.3, Table C);
– the use of double *ll* in the adjective meaning 'white': *bellu* (b8), *belli*, (b9), *bel la* (b15); these are the only double consonants in the entire book (Mladenović 1968: 12);
– the consistent absence of capitals as the initial letter of names: *radoſaue* (b5), *radoſaf* (b7), *ſiuerina* (b6), *ſiuerin* (b7), *ſiuerine* (b9), *dunaya* (b15);
– the unique spelling *suoyega* (b6), with *u*, as opposed to the normal spelling with *-ſ-*, (e.g. *sſoyega* in the parallel passage, 596), which is attested 46 times.

37 It looks as if there are two acute accents on the á.

38 Read: *zdólu.

39 Read: *zayedno.

40 Read: *grade. The printed form *gradu* looks like a mistake under the influence of the previous line, which contains the Ds *gradu*. The parallel passage in 599 has *gráde* and so has the Vs in the next line (b10).

41 Read: *chlice.

REFERENCES

Belić, A.
1909   "Zamětki po čakavskim govoram", *IORJaS* 14/2, 181-266.
Berk, Ch. A. van den
1969   "Nekoliko opaski o kvantitetu i akcentu u starom Dubrovniku", in: Ravlić (1969), 299-310.
Bujas, R. (ed.)
1951   *Ribanje i ribarsko prigovaranje, Petar Hektorović*. Zagreb.
Ćupić, Dr.
1977   *Govor Bjelopavlića*. Beograd (= *Srpski dijalektološki zbornik* 23).
Daničić, Đ.
1925   *Srpski akcenti*. Beograd-Zemun (= *Posebna izdanja SKA* 58, *Filosofski i filološki spisi* 16).

524

Dulčić, J. and P. Dulčić
1985   Rječnik bruškoga govora. Zagreb (= Hrvatski dijalektološki zbornik
            7/2).
Fancev, Fr.
1907   "Beiträge zur serbokroatischen Dialektologie: Der kaj-Dialekt von
            Virje, mit Berücksichtigung der Dialekte Podravina's (Koprivnica-
            Pitomača)", Archiv für slavische Philologie 29, 305-389.
Fancev, Fr.
1907   "Beiträge zur serbokroatischen Dialektologie: Der kaj-Dialekt von
            Virje, mit Berücksichtigung der Dialekte Podravina's (Koprivnica-
            Pitomača)", Archiv für slavische Philologie 29, 305-389.
Franičević, M. (ed.)
1968   Hanibal Lucić. Petar Hektorović. Zagreb (= Pet stoljeća hrvatske
            književnosti 7).
Grčić, M.
1988   Petar Hektorović: Ribanje i ribarsko prigovaranje. Hanibal Lucić: Ro-
            binja. Izvornik i prijevod. Zagreb.
Hamm, J., M. Hraste and P. Guberina
1956   "Govor otoka Suska", Hrvatski dijalektološki zbornik 1, 7-213.
Hektorović, P.
1568   Ribanye i ribarscho prigouaranye i razliche stuari ine sloxene po Pet-
            retu Hectorouichiu huaraninu. Venetia.
1953   Photographic reprint of Hektorović (1568). Zagreb.
Hraste, M.
1926-27   "Crtice o bruškom dialektu", Južnoslovenski filolog 6, 180-214.
1935   "Čakavski dijalekat ostrva Hvara", Južnoslovenski filolog 14, 1-55.
1940   "Čakavski dijalekat ostrva Brača", Srpski dijalektološki zbornik 10,
            1-65.
Hraste, M., P. Šimunović and R. Olesch
1979   Čakavisch-deutsches Lexikon 1. Köln/Wien (= Slavistische Forschun-
            gen 25/1).
Ivić, P.
1957   "Izveštaj o terenskom dijalektološkom radu u severnoj Hrvatskoj i juž-
            noj Dalmaciji u leto 1957 godine", Godišnjak Filozofskog fakulteta u
            Novom Sadu 2, 401-407.
1961   "Prilozi poznavanju dijalekatske slike zapadne Hrvatske", Godišnjak
            Filozofskog fakulteta u Novom Sadu 6, 191-211.
Ivić, P. et al. (eds.)
1981   Fonološki opisi srpskohrvatskih/hrvatskosrpskih, slovenačkih i make-
            donskih govora obuhvaćenih Opšteslovenskim lingvističkim atlasom.
            Sarajevo (= Posebna izdanja ANUBiH 55).
Ivšić, Stj.
1937   "Osnovna hrvatska kajkavska akcentuacija u Pergošića (1574)", in:
            Zbornik lingvističkih i filoloških rasprava A. Beliću o 40-godišnjici
            njegova naučnog rada, 183-195. Beograd.
Jurišić, Bl.
1966   Rječnik govora otoka Vrgade I. Uvod. Zagreb.
1973   Rječnik govora otoka Vrgade II. Rječnik. Zagreb.

Kalsbeek, J.
1998   (forthc.) *The Čakavian dialect of Orbanići near Žminj in Istria*, Amsterdam/Atlanta.
Kašić, B.
1617   *Piesni duhovnae od pohvalaa boxyieh*. U Rimu.
1978   Photographic reprint of Kašić (1617). München.
Klaić, Br.
1968   "Jezik Hanibala Lucića i Petra Hektorovića. Prilog historijskoj gramatici hrvatskog jezika", in: Franičević (1968), 267-324.
Kortlandt, F.H.H.
1975   *Slavic Accentuation*. Lisse.
Kušar, M.
1895   "Lumbaradsko narječje", *Nastavni vjesnik* 3, 323-338.
Lončarić, M.
1977   "Jagnjedovački govor (s osvrtom na pitanje kajkavskoga podravskog dijalekta", *Hrvatski dijalektološki zbornik* 4, 179-262.
Malić, Dr.
1989   "Grafija i pravopis hrvatskog latiničkog rukopisa 14. stoljeća 'Žića sv. otaca' ", *Rasprave ZJ* 15, 129-177.
1997   *Žića svetih otaca. Hrvatska srednjovjekovna proza*. Zagreb.
Maretić, T.
1889   *Istorija hrvatskoga pravopisa latinskijem slovima*. Zagreb (= *Djela JAZU* 9).
Mladenović, A.
1968   *Jezik Petra Hektorovića*. Novi Sad.
Moskovljević, M.
1950   "Govor ostrva Korčule", *Srpski dijalektološki zbornik* 11, 153-222.
Pešikan, M.
1965   *Starocrnogorski srednjokatunski i lješanski govori*, Beograd (= *Srpski dijalektološki zbornik* 15).
Petrović, Dr.
1974   "O nekim osobinama akcenatskog sistema u govorima Luštice i Krtola", *Zbornik za filologiju i lingvistiku* 17/2, 119-124.
Premuda, V.
1939   "Starohrvatski latinički rukopis 'Žića sv. otaca'", *Starine JAZU* 40, 103-220.
Ravlić, J. (ed.)
1969   *Marin Držić. Zbornik radova* (= *Zbornik radova o Marinu Držiću*), Zagreb.
Rešetar, M.
1898a   "Primorski lekcionari XV. vijeka", *Rad JAZU* 134, 80-160.
1898b   "Primorski lekcionari XV. vijeka (Konac)", *Rad JAZU* 136, 97-199.
1900   *Die serbokroatische Betonung südwestlicher Mundarten*. Wien (= *Schriften der Balkancommission* 1).
1927   "Kvantitet u djelima Marina Držića", *Rad JAZU* 233, 145-196.
Šimunović, P.
1977   "Čakavština srednjodalmatinskih otoka", *Čakavska rič* 7/1, 5-63.
1981a   "Komiža (OLA 42)", in: P. Ivić et al. (eds.), 259-265.

526

1981b   "Vrbanj (OLA 44)", in: P. Ivić et al. (eds.), 272-274.
Stang, Chr. S.
1957   Slavonic Accentuation. Oslo.
Steinhauer, H.
1973   Čakavian studies. The Hague/Paris.
Vermeer, W.
1979   "Innovations in the kajkavian dialect of Bednja", in: Jan M. Meijer
            (ed.), Dutch Contributions to the Eighth International Congress of
            Slavists. Lisse, 347-381.
1980   "Die Konjugation in der nordwestčakavischen Mundart Omišaljs",
            Studies in Slavic and General Linguistics 1, 439-472.
1984   "On clarifying some points of Slavonic accentology: the quantity of the
            thematic vowel in the present tense and related issues", Folia Linguis-
            tica Historica 5/2, 331-395.
1994   "Vowel length in Čakavian texts from the fourteenth century", Studies
            in Slavic and General Linguistics 22, 467-491.
1996   "The twofold origin of Classical Čakavian", Studies in Slavic and Gen-
            eral Linguistics 23, 255-318.
Vončina, J. (ed.)
1986   Djela Petra Hektorovića. Zagreb (= Stari pisci hrvatski 39).
Wagner, Zd.
1970   Ze studiów nad językiem Petra Hektorovicia. Wrocław/Warszawa/
            Kraków.
Zaliznjak, A.A.
1990   'Merilo pravednoe' XIV veka kak akcentologičeskij istočnik. Mün-
            chen (= Slavistische Beiträge 266).